EMPIRES IN THE MOUNTAINS

ALSO BY RUSSELL P. BELLICO

Sails and Steam in the Mountains:
A Maritime and Military History of Lake George and Lake Champlain

Chronicles of Lake George:
Journeys in War and Peace

Chronicles of Lake Champlain:
Journeys in War and Peace

AS EDITOR

Life on a Canal Boat:
The Journals of Theodore D. Bartley, 1861-1889

EMPIRES IN THE MOUNTAINS

*French and Indian War Campaigns and Forts in the
Lake Champlain, Lake George, and Hudson River Corridor*

Russell P. Bellico

PURPLE MOUNTAIN PRESS

Fleishmanns, New York

To Jane

EMPIRES IN THE MOUNTAINS:
French and Indian War Campaigns and Forts
in the Lake Champlain, Lake George, and Hudson River Corridor

First edition 2010

Published by Purple Mountain Press, Ltd.
1060 Main Street, P.O. Box 309
Fleischmanns, New York 12430-0309
845-254-4062, 845-254-4476 (fax), purple@catskill.net
http://www.catskill.net/purple

ISBN-13 978-0-916346-83-6
ISBN 0-916346-83-8
Library of Congress Control Number: 2010925746

All illustrations printed with the permissions of those credited.

Cover:
A South View of the New Fortress at Crown Point, watercolor by Thomas Davies.
(Winterthur Museum)

Back cover:
Detail of *A Plan of the Town and Fort of Carillon at Ticonderoga* by Thomas Jefferys
(Fort Ticonderoga Museum)

Attaques Du Fort William-Henri, August 7, 1757, by Lieutenant Cöntgen Therbu.
(Fort William Henry Museum)

5 4 3 2 1
Manufactured in the United States of America.
Printed on acid-free paper.

Contents

Acknowledgments   7

Introduction   9

1. Contest for a Continent 1609-1713   11

2. Fort St. Frédéric   23

3. Expedition Against Fort St. Frédéric   41

4. Battle of Lake George 1755   53

5. Stalemate and New Forts   71

6. Fort William Henry Under Siege 1757   97

7. Battle of Carillon 1758   131

8. British Advance to Lake Champlain 1759   181

9. Expedition to Canada 1760   215

10. Epilogue: Forts Revisited   255

Appendix: French and Indian War Forts and Exhibits in the Lake Champlain, Lake George, and Hudson River Corridor   301

Notes   303

Index   359

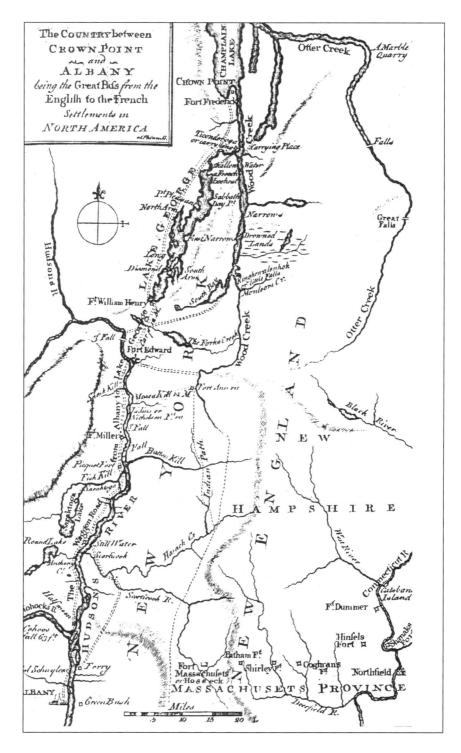

"The Country between Crown Point and Albany" from *The Scots Magazine*, **August 1758.**

Acknowledgments

I AM GRATEFUL TO MANY INDIVIDUALS AND INSTITUTIONS for their assistance with my research and their help in the production of this book. I am also indebted to the authors of earlier works on the French and Indian War, who have laid the foundation for the continuing analysis of this era. I am very appreciative of the assistance that the dedicated staffs of libraries and archives have afforded me during my research: the New York State Library and Archives in Albany, the Fort Ticonderoga Thompson-Pell Research Center, the National Archives of Canada in Ottawa, the Library of Congress, the Huntington Library in San Marino (CA), the Connecticut State Library in Hartford, the Massachusetts Historical Society in Boston, the American Antiquarian Society in Worcester, the Boston Public Library, the Ticonderoga Historical Society, the Houghton Library of Harvard University, the New York State Historical Association, the State University of New York at Albany, the William L. Clements Library at the University of Michigan (Ann Arbor), the University of Massachusetts Library at Amherst, the Amherst College Library, the Mount Holyoke College Library, the Smith College Library, the Crandall Library in Glens Falls, and the Sherman Library in Port Henry.

I also received important historical information from a number of individuals, including Lieutenant Colonel Herman C. Brown (ret.), Gary S. Zaboly, Peter Barranco, Nicholas Westbrook, and Joseph W. Zarzynski. I wish to thank Maryann Nesto, reference librarian at Westfield State College, for her prompt attention to my requests for interlibrary loans and to Christopher D. Fox, Curator of Collections at the Fort Ticonderoga Thompson-Pell Research Center, for his expert assistance in locating a number of important documents in the fort's collection. I greatly appreciate the use of the superb artwork of Ernest Haas, L. F. Tantillo, and Gary S. Zaboly.

I owe a debt of gratitude to Rebecca Miller and Danielle Bramucci, who carefully transcribed my hand-written drafts onto a computer. I am especially appreciative of the help from Dr. Frank Salvidio, a retired professor of English with a keen knowledge of history, for his diligent proofreading and valuable recommendations, which greatly improved the readability of the book. Most of all, I am deeply grateful to my wife, Jane, for her patience, support, careful proofreading, and thoughtful suggestions. I wish to recognize the continuing support of my books by Wray and Loni Rominger of Purple Mountain Press. Their 36-year-old company currently has more than 100 books in print, including 26 titles dealing with colonial history. The reading public has been rewarded with a remarkable number of exceptional books from their press.

Finally, I would also like to commend the work of my colleagues at Bateaux Below, Inc., for their extraordinary efforts to preserve the only remaining intact warship of the French and Indian War, the radeau *Land Tortoise*, as well as the wrecks of bateaux lying on the bottom of Lake George. My work with this organization has inspired me to continue researching the French and Indian War period.

Joseph W. Zarzynski, executive director of Bateaux Below, Inc., alongside the upper-bow section of the 1758 radeau *Land Tortoise*, the oldest intact warship in North America and a National Historic Landmark (Lake George). Photo by author.

Introduction

THE FRENCH AND INDIAN WAR (1754-1763), the North American theater of the Seven Years' War, would change the map of the continent and set the stage for the American Revolution. The conflict, which pitted the French and their Indian allies against the English, has often been misunderstood and largely received minor treatment in most general histories of America. To some, the name of the war itself has been puzzling and somewhat misleading because Britain also had Indian allies during the war. The war represented a culmination of a century-old struggle for control of North America. The clash was inevitable. English settlers increasingly pushed westward and northward from their original settlements on the east coast, displacing the French and Native Americans. The French population in North America, approximately 55,000 by the middle of the eighteenth century, lived principally along the St. Lawrence River; but New France claimed a vast amount of territory to the west, linked by a string of isolated trading posts and forts. In contrast, the population of the English colonies had expanded from a quarter million inhabitants in 1700 to 1.2 million by 1750. English land companies soon began to encroach on territories claimed by the French. To defend their land holdings, the French built a series of substantial fortifications on the strategic water routes of their empire, including along the Richelieu River-Lake Champlain corridor.

The French and Indian War, blundered into at Jumonville Glen (Pennsylvania) in 1754, cascaded into a world war by 1756, engulfing all of the great powers of Europe in the Seven Years' War. In this first global war, hostilities occurred in North America, Europe, the Caribbean, India, West Africa, the East Indies, as well as on the high seas. By any standards, the conflict was an enormous, highly-complex logistical undertaking, setting two of the world's dominant powers, Britain and France, in a monumental contest for hegemony over far-flung possessions. The North American phase of the war involved the most decisive battles, hastening the end of the Seven Years' War. Great Britain's success in the war created the basis for her subsequent global empire.

The defeat of New France made the independence of the English colonies in North America possible. For Great Britain, victory had unintended consequences. The economic and political conditions created by the war led directly to the subsequent challenges by colonial assemblies to British rule. The British Proclamation of 1763, limiting western land grants by colonial governors, caused a backlash in the English colonies that fostered resistance to British policy (see "Consequences of Peace" in chapter 9). During the war, provincial assemblies and officers in the field exhibited a certain degree of resistance to British authority. Latent hostility toward British officers had grown during wartime as a result of their arrogant and often contemptuous treatment of provincial officers and troops. However, the French and Indian War provided a training ground for future American officers, building confidence in their ability to later challenge the most formidable army in the world. The war also furnished Americans with valuable experience in mobilizing large numbers of men and supplies.

The French and Indian War should not be romanticized; troops endured horrific conditions, including exposure to disease (especially smallpox), terrible injuries, and brutal punishments. As in modern wars, men were subjected to the randomness of being killed or wounded by pieces of flying metal. Despite the frightful circumstances of the war, provincial soldiers were driven by a strong emotional reaction to French and Indian attacks on English villages, as well as the memory of the 1757 "massacre" at Fort William Henry. In reality, both sides employed the instrument of intentional terror, often resulting in unimaginable atrocities. In addition to the fighting, the men, particularly provincial troops, were constantly engaged in the arduous task of building breastworks, forts, and vessels.

I have used the words of participants as much as possible in the book. Although the journals of soldiers were usually written using phonetic spelling and simple grammar and punctuation, they provide a firsthand human dimension in recounting the extraordinary events of the war. The men recognized that their participation in these military expeditions would be the greatest adventure of their lives, and so they recorded their experiences in minute detail. The large number of provincial diaries was also related to the high degree of literacy, particularly in New England, where the prevalence of fervent Protestantism led directly to the establishment of a system of public schools.

There are probably more written documents dealing with eighteenth-century military campaigns than twentieth-century wars. The absence of modern technology meant that military communications were written down and carried by messengers. Original firsthand accounts, however, often vary in their description of places, conditions, and events. (Additional eyewitness accounts are provided in the endnotes.) Despite some limitations, primary documents are still the best method of revealing the factual story behind the military campaigns of the French and Indian War. On July 4, 1963, President John F. Kennedy wrote that "primary sources constitute the backbone of written history" and stressed the need "to publish as completely as possible the original papers essential to a full understanding of our nation's birth."[1] The narrative of the war will never be final because new original documents will undoubtedly be discovered and circumstances and events reinterpreted.

Until the 250th anniversary of the French and Indian War, many Americans had only a vague understanding of the war, despite the crucial role that it played in creating the conditions that led to American independence. It is important to remember the history that unites Americans as a nation. Unless we recognize and understand our common roots, we will be unable to sustain our ideas, beliefs, values, and institutions.

Today tourists can visit Rogers Island, Fort William Henry, Fort George, Fort Ticonderoga, and Crown Point. These sites are hallowed ground, where soldiers made the ultimate sacrifice at a time when the political destiny of North America hung in balance.

1. Contest for a Continent 1609-1713

Detail of the 1609 battle between Samuel de Champlain and the Mohawk warriors from his 1613 edition of *Voyages*, showing the only contemporary image of Champlain.

THE PRESENCE OF FORTS AT LAKE GEORGE AND LAKE CHAMPLAIN was the result of a prolonged struggle between the rival colonial empires of France and England. French presence in the Champlain Valley began with the 1609 voyage of Samuel de Champlain. His encounter with a body of Mohawks of the Iroquois Nation while accompanying a war party of Algonquins, Hurons, and Montagnais resulted in the first battle at Lake Champlain involving Europeans. On the night of July 29, 1609, Champlain reached a cape on the western shore and encountered a war party of Mohawks, who "began to fell trees with poor axes. . .and they barricaded themselves well."[1] This is undoubtedly the first written account of a defensive work in the Champlain Valley. The following day, as the Mohawks raised their bows and arrows at Champlain and his Indian allies, he took aim with his "arquebus" and fired, killing two Mohawk leaders and wounding a third.[2] During the ensuing battle, Champlain's allies "killed several [Mohawks] and took ten or twelve prisoners."[3]

Recognizing the important role that Hurons and Algonquins played in the fur trade with New France, the French government supported their Native American allies in Canada in their fight with the Iroquois. French authorities were convinced that peace with the Iroquois and their integration into the Huron fur trading network would divert trade to the rising Dutch economic base at Fort Orange (present-day Albany). Following Henry Hudson's epic 1609 voyage of exploration aboard the *Half Moon* on the present-day Hudson River, a Dutch merchant company established a fur trading post in 1614 on the north end of Castle Island (south of the present site of Albany) called Fort Nassau. The post was evacuated in 1617 due to spring flooding, but in 1624 the Dutch West India Company constructed Fort Orange on a flat plain on the west side of the Hudson River. The number of furs traded at the new post doubled from 5,000 pelts in 1624 to 10,000 eight years later. Inasmuch as Native American culture did not embrace the accumulation of wealth, why were they willing to engage in trade with the Europeans?

The Trading House, **known as Fort Nassau, 1614. Painting by Len Tantillo.**

The preeminence of European technology in iron tools, metal pots, cloth, firearms, and other goods persuaded Native Americans that trade was indeed necessary.[4]

The road to peaceful trade, however, was marred by bitter rivalries. Eventually, the Mohawks displaced the Mahicans for control of trade with Fort Orange, and the Dutch concluded a peace treaty with them in May 1643.* The Mohawks, on the other hand, engaged in prolonged hostilities with the French in Canada. Although Samuel de Champlain's engagement with the Mohawks in 1609 might be considered the source of a deep-seated antagonism by the Iroquois for the French and their Native American allies, a myriad of reasons were involved in the conflict. Ironically, early Iroquois raids against New France's Native American allies may, in part, have been an attempt to win a favorable place for themselves as a French ally. Attempts at peace by the Iroquois were often rejected by French authorities, who felt that any reconciliation between the Iroquois and their Huron allies could divert the fur trade to Fort Orange. The object of Iroquois forays into Canada was often to replenish their numbers by substituting captives for those who were

*During this period a Dutch observer wrote the following description of Native Americans: "The Indians are of ordinary stature, strong and broad shouldered; olive color, light and nimble of foot, subtle in disposition, of few words, which they previously well consider; hypocritical, treacherous, vindictive, brave and pertinacious in self defence; in time of need, resolute to die. They seem to despise all the torments that can be inflicted on them, and do not utter a single moan, they go almost naked, except a flap which hangs before their nakedness, and on their shoulders a deer skin, or a mantle, a fathom square, of woven turkey feathers, or of peltries sewed together; they make use now generally of blue or red (duffels), in consequence of the frequent visits of the Christians. In winter they make shoes of deer skin, manufactured after their fashion."[5]

lost during waves of epidemics beginning in 1634 that wiped out more than half of their population. With no immunity to common European diseases, the Native American population was drastically reduced in both North and South America. Large numbers of young Hurons and Algonquins were assimilated into the Iroquois "melting pot," replacing those lost to disease and war. In addition to captives, Iroquois men sought respect, power, and honor through warfare, making war a permanent way of life.[6]

To protect their settlements along the St. Lawrence River from Mohawk attacks, the French began construction of a palisaded fort at the mouth of the Richelieu River (Fort Richelieu) on August 13, 1642. Seven days later "a band of three hundred Iroquois" attacked the fort, but were repulsed.[7] Several peace treaties between the Mohawks and the French and their Algonquin allies punctuated the long hostilities, including a treaty settled at a peace conference in July 1645 at the French fortified post at Three Rivers. On July 14 Father Barthélémy Vimont, a Jesuit missionary, noted that the Mohawks concluded a peace and agreed to "commit no act of hostility against the Hurons" or other French allies.[8]

The following May, Father Isaac Jogues, a French Jesuit missionary, wrote a letter to the head of the Jesuits in Canada, Father Jerome Lalemant, offering his services as a peace missionary to the Mohawks. Shortly thereafter, the governor of New France, Charles-Jacques Hault Montmagny, met with Lalemant, along with Mohawk ambassadors, at Three Rivers for a final council of peace. Montmagny accepted Lalemant's choice of Jogues as a peace ambassador, as did the Mohawk representatives, and Jogues departed on an ill-fated journey on May 16, 1646.*

The 1645 peace treaty was only a temporary interruption of hostilities. The Mohawks were able to acquire an increasing number of firearms from English and Dutch traders, and in 1648 the Dutch government initiated an official policy of selling firearms to the Mohawks: 400 muskets were sold immediately. In 1648 and 1649 the Mohawks and Senecas attacked Huron villages. By late autumn of 1649 the Huron confederation and trading system had been devastated. Four years later four Iroquois league members (the Cayugas, Oneidas, Onondagas, and Senecas) inaugurated peace talks with the French, and in late 1653 the Mohawks concluded a peace treaty with the French at Three Rivers. However, Iroquois attacks against Hurons and other tribes in the Great Lakes region continued and the Mohawks were again at war with the Mahicans.

In 1664 England under Charles II was ready to finally displace the Dutch presence in North America. By September, four English ships "with six hundred soldiers" that had

---

*Father Isaac Jogues and two lay brothers were later captured in their canoes on the St. Lawrence River by a Mohawk war party on August 2, 1642.[9] Jogues was taken to the Iroquois villages on the Mohawk River where he suffered beatings and mutilation of his fingers.[10] The following year, Arendt Van Corlaer, a Dutch Reformed minister, aided Jogues in an escape from his Mohawk captors. In 1646 Jogues traveled through present-day Lake George, arriving on the eve of the Blessed Sacrement, whereupon he changed the Iroquois name Lake "Andiatarocté…there where the lake is shut in" to "Lac du St. Sacrement."[11] Although his visit to the Iroquois villages was overtly amicable, Jogues alienated some of the Mohawks, who were suspicious of sorcery and spells. On June 16, 1646, he departed from the Mohawk village, but "some distrustful minds did not look with favor on a little chest, which the Father had left as an assurance of his return; they imagined that some misfortune disastrous to the whole county was shut up in that little box," despite the fact that Jogues had opened the chest, revealing only "small necessaries."[12] After returning to the Mohawk village in the fall, Father Jogues was blamed for the destruction of their corn by caterpillars and slain on October 18, 1646. Although unintended, the "black robes" and other Europeans had been responsible for decimating the Native American population in the New World by bringing disease and creating dissension within their traditional culture.

Fort Orange and the Patroon's House, circa 1650. **Painting by Len Tantillo.**

been commissioned by the king's brother James, the Duke of York, anchored off New Amsterdam (Manhattan).[13] Sixty-eight prominent citizens of the community petitioned Director-General Peter Stuyvesant to accept "an honorable and reasonable capitulation" based on letters from the English besiegers "promising, in case we voluntarily submit, that we shall not experience the least loss or damage."[14] New Amsterdam capitulated on September 5 (August 27 on the old Julian calendar). Fort Orange was subsequently renamed Albany and the Mohawks made peace with their new neighbors. But nine years later a squadron of armed Dutch ships anchored in the Hudson River, and the commanders of the vessels issued a proclamation on September 20, 1673, for the restitution of New Netherlands. However, less than a year later (February 1674), the Treaty of Westminster restored New Netherlands to English rule for good.

The challenge of New France in the north would dominate the affairs of North America for much of the next century. The escalation of French military power in reaction to Iroquois attacks on New France began in 1663 with a report by the governor, Baron Dubois d'Avaugour, outlining plans for new forts to protect settlers from the Iroquois and appointing Alexandre de Prouville de Tracy as lieutenant general/viceroy.[16] However, action was not forthcoming until 1665 when Louis XIV, the king of France, ordered Tracy to sail from the West Indies to Quebec. The king's instructions included building forts and dealing with the Iroquois as "irreconcilable enemies of the Colony," who had massacred French inhabitants and prevented the cultivation of land with their continued "ambuscades."[17] Fort Richelieu (burned earlier by the Iroquois) was rebuilt and Fort St. Louis (later Fort Chambly), a 144-foot square stockaded fort, was constructed in 1665 at the Richelieu River rapids.

Apprehensive over the change in French policy and the arrival of Carignan-Salières regulars in Canada, the Iroquois concluded a peace treaty with officials of New France in

Fort St. Anne, 1666 on Isle La Motte. Painting by Ernest Haas.

December 1665, but the Mohawks failed to participate in the proceedings. As a consequence, Daniel de Courcelles, the new governor-general of New France, led a daring winter raid to destroy the Iroquois villages along the Mohawk River. Departing on January 9, 1666, with a total of 500-600 troops from the Carignan-Salières Regiment and Canadian volunteers, Courcelles and his army traveled south on Lake Champlain and the Hudson River, but were hindered by dreadful winter conditions. Despite the employment of Algonquin guides, the expeditionary force lost its way and on February 14 the troops found themselves near the Dutch settlement of Schenectady, rather than at the Mohawk villages. Following a minor skirmish with the Mohawks, Courcelles was convinced that most of the Mohawks were away hunting. On February 21 the army began an arduous 15-day journey back to Canada but suffered losses as a result of an ambush of the rear-guard by Mohawk warriors. The French army was also plagued by starvation and exposure to the elements.

French authorities were determined to end the Mohawk menace and during the summer dispatched Captain de la Motte (Pierre de Saint-Paul, Sieur de la Motte-Lussière) and the Carignan-Salières Regiment to build a fort on an island on Lake Champlain (present-day Isle La Motte). The outpost, called Fort St. Anne, was completed by July 26, 1666, on the northwest end of the island and represented the first real fort built in the Champlain Valley. It was 144 feet in length and 96 feet wide, surrounded by a double log wall with four bastions.

A peace initiative by the Iroquois Nation in early July of 1666 had seemed to offer the possibility of a lasting truce, but the death of a captain in the Carignan-Salières Regiment, who was Viceroy Tracy's nephew, at the hands of the Mohawks led to a new expedition against the Mohawk villages. Assembling at Fort St. Anne on September 28, 1666, both Governor Courcelles and Viceroy Tracy led the expedition—the former departing with

400 troops a few days before Tracy embarked with the main body of the army. The total force consisted of approximately 1,300 regulars, Canadian volunteers, and Huron and Algonquin warriors. The invaders traveled south on Lake Champlain in 300 bateaux and canoes, stopping at present-day Ticonderoga, where a small stockade was constructed.[18] The army then traversed Lake St. Sacrement (Lake George), hiding its vessels on the southern shore. The French army marched the rest of the distance overland, dragging two small cannons to the Iroquois villages along the Mohawk River. The Mohawks, learning of the French advance, disappeared into the forest. According to the contemporary journal of Benjamin Sulte, "The Mohawks having fled at the sound of the drums, he [Tracy] burned their four villages with all their grain; there were in all 100 great cabins."[19] The French found the Iroquois villages more substantial than they had anticipated. On the return trip, blustery fall weather and rain scattered the French armada on Lake Champlain, causing two canoes to sink with the loss of eight men. The exhausted army limped back to Canada on November 5, leaving only 60 troops at Fort St. Anne.

By relying on a diet of bread and bacon, 40 of the 60 regulars at Fort St. Anne came down with scurvy the following winter. Eventually the garrison received food supplies, which saved the lives of the dying men. In time, sleighs were provided to transport the sick to Montreal. While the decimated garrison recovered at Fort St. Anne during the spring of 1667, a small group of Iroquois ambassadors, repatriating several French prisoners, made their way to the island outpost. The French expedition of the previous fall had the desired effect: the Iroquois sought peace and subsequently requested missionaries. A permanent mission was later established with the Iroquois, and relative peace was maintained in the region for 20 years.

Increasing friction over the extension of English land patents and influence over trade with Native Americans by English authorities led to renewed tensions with New France during the 1680s. In 1684 Thomas Dongan, the English governor of New York, began awarding land grants that pushed into territories claimed by the French, including the Champlain Valley. In addition, French officials were convinced that the English were arming the Iroquois and inciting them to break the peace. Dongan had declared sovereignty over the Iroquois confederacy and licensed fur expeditions as far as present-day Michigan. Joseph-Antoine Le Febvre de La Barre, the governor of New France, failed to intimidate the Iroquois during a futile expedition to La Famine (on the eastern shore of Lake Ontario in present-day Oswego County) in 1684. The following year the king appointed Jacques de Brisay Denonville the next governor of New France with instructions that Canada's Native American allies in the Great Lakes region "must be sustained" while the "pride of the Iroquois must be humbled."[20] In June 1687 Denonville assembled a new expedition, consisting of 832 regulars, 930 militia, and 300 Indians, at Isle St. Hélène near Montreal for a campaign against the Senecas in New York. On July 13 the French force was "vigorously attacked by 800 Senecas," but the Senecas quickly fled after assailing the rear elements of Denonville's army.[21] Denonville's Indians "cut the dead [Senecas] in quarters...in order to put them into the kettle."[22] The French invaders remained in the area of four abandoned Seneca villages until July 24, "laying waste [to] the Indian corn" and killing "a vast quantity of hogs."[23] Denonville's army then proceeded to the mouth of the Niagara River (Lake Ontario) to establish a fort.

KING WILLIAM'S WAR

By late August 1687, Iroquois war parties retaliated for Denonville's raid against the Senecas by assaulting settlements near Montreal, destroying farms and killing French colonists. By the next spring, conditions had only worsened. Both the English and French formulated plans to secure their frontiers. Governor Dongan of New York dispatched an envoy to England to advance a plan to build forts at Niagara, La Famine, and at Lake Champlain. In 1688 Denonville proposed a strategy to extend French influence by deploying "a strong detachment of fifty to sixty men…to be stationed [at] Pointe au Chevelure [Crown Point]."[24] The governor of Montreal, Louis-Hector Callières, advanced a plan to move a 2,000-man army through Lake Champlain, Lake St. Sacrement, and the Hudson River to "seize Man[h]at[tan]," thus dividing the English colonies.[25] Louis IV finally consented to the plan and enumerated reasons, including the English "exciting the Iroquois nation…to make war on the French" and interrupting trade in territories claimed by New France.[26] The French king was also responding to the fact that the new English monarch, William III, who replaced the deposed James II, had entered into the War of the League of Augsburg, known in North America as King William's War (1689-1697). On August 5, 1689, before the French could implement any plan, 1,300-1,500 Iroquois warriors surprised and destroyed the village of La Chine near Montreal. French authorities reported that the Iroquois captured "more than 120 persons after a massacre of 200 [who were] burned, toasted alive, [and] devoured."[27] The Iroquois struck the region again on November 13.

Leadership in New France changed hands once more with the replacement of Denonville by the 69-year-old former governor, Louis de Buade de Frontenac. In Decem-

Schenectady Town **before the French and Indian raid of 1690. Painting by Len Tantillo.**

ber 1689 Frontenac invited the Iroquois to a peace conference, but the Iroquois spurned the offer and exhorted English officials to cooperate in an attack on French Canada. Early the following year, Frontenac ordered multiple raids into New York, New Hampshire, and present-day Maine, rather than implementing Callières' grand plan for the conquest of New York City. A 210-man French army, including 96 Native Americans, departed from Montreal at the beginning of February 1690 for a planned assault on Albany, but the expedition diverted to Schenectady eight days later after the Indians objected to an attack on Fort Orange (Albany). About 11 or 12 o'clock at night, the village gate was burst open; Schenectady was torched and sixty men, women, and children were massacred over a two-hour period.[28] Some six or seven of the 80 dwellings were saved through the influence of Captain Sander Glen, who had befriended the French during an earlier period. The raiders, with 27-30 prisoners, began their journey back to Montreal at once. On February 10 a militia and Mohawk party under Captain Jonathan Bull was sent in pursuit of the French. However, only the Mohawks were able to engage some of the French stragglers in a brief skirmish just before they reached Montreal. To prevent another surprise attack, Captain Jacobus de Warm from Albany, along with 12 militiamen and 20 Mohawks, was dispatched by New York's lieutenant governor/acting governor, Jacob Leisler, in late March to observe any new French movements. At Chimney Point, de Warm and his men built "a little stone fort."[29] Another small English scouting party under Captain Abram Schuyler was later sent to Otter Creek and ventured as far north as Fort Chambly on the Richelieu River.

A plan spearheaded by Jacob Leisler to invade Canada via Lake Champlain was accepted by Massachusetts and Connecticut officials. After a prolonged debate, Connecticut's Fitz-John Winthrop, son of a former governor of Connecticut, was selected to lead an 800-man colonial army and a contingent of Mohawk warriors on the expedition. At the same time, an English naval fleet would attack Quebec. Upon arriving in Albany on July 21, 1690, Major General Winthrop complained that the "design against Canada [was] poorly contrived" and the lack of preparations resulted in only 150 of the 400 troops promised by New York.[30] Despite an outbreak of smallpox and other problems, Winthrop's army reached Lake Champlain's Wood Creek (in the vicinity of present-day Whitehall) on August 6. Nine days later a council of war decided that it was "advisable to return" because it was too late in the season to peel bark to construct canoes and there was "no possibility of getting provi[s]ion[s] to support the forces here any longer."[31] The army returned to Albany on August 18. Before Winthrop's army retreated however, Captain John Schuyler (grandfather of Major General Philip Schuyler of Revolutionary War fame) volunteered to head a raiding party into Canada, departing from Wood Creek on August 13 with 29 militiamen and 120 Native Americans. On the southern section of Lake Champlain Schuyler met Captain Sander Glen from Schenectady with "28 whites and 5 savages" on their way back to Albany after manning an advance post for eight days at present-day Ticonderoga.[32] Schuyler recruited 13 militiamen and the 5 Mohawks from Glen's party to join the expedition to Canada. On August 23 Schuyler's men attacked the outpost of Fort La Prairie (near Montreal), burning houses outside the fort, killing 150 head of cattle and oxen, and taking "19 prisoners and 6 scalps."[33] Schuyler arrived back in Albany on August 30. In the meantime, New York officials had thrown Major General Winthrop and several of his officers in jail, holding them responsible for the failure of the main expedition. They were released in September after a plea from Connecticut's governor to Acting Governor Jacob Leisler.*

The second component of the 1690 campaign also failed. On October 6, after sailing his armada through the tricky sections of the St. Lawrence River to reach Quebec City, Sir William Phips dispatched a message demanding the surrender of the city from Count de Frontenac, governor of New France. Frontenac replied that his answer would come "from the mouths of my cannon and musketry."[35] Two days later about "1,400" soldiers from the English fleet landed, fewer than planned due to an outbreak of smallpox.[36] Although low on ammunition, the English fleet engaged Quebec's shore batteries for several days without success. After days ashore, the land forces were unable to storm the city and hurriedly reboarded their vessels at night, leaving five cannons behind. Another attack was planned for the following day, "but then a storm arose w[hi]ch separated o[u]r fleet and a great snow fell and ye cold was so extreme…we could not w[i]th safety continue longer in ye river."[37] Having departed from Boston on August 9, the fleet finally returned on November 19, except for six vessels that had lost their way. After one of these vessels wrecked on Anticosti Island, five survivors constructed a cabin on a small open boat and sailed nearly 1,000 miles in 40 days to Boston.

The next year, 33-year-old Peter (Pieter) Schuyler, mayor of Albany and a major in the militia, repeated the raid that his brother, Captain John Schuyler, had undertaken against La Prairie in 1690. Schuyler departed from Albany on June 21, 1691, with a force of 120 militia, about 60 "River Indians" (mostly Mahicans) and Schaghticokes, and 15 Mohawks.[38] On June 30 at "the last carrying place" (some distance before reaching Wood Creek), the raiding party paused to build canoes.[39] Eighty Mohawks subsequently com-

**Nineteenth-century print of the "Defense of Quebec"
during the attack by English forces in 1690. (National Archives of Canada)**

*Acting Governor Jacob Leisler had gained power in New York in 1689 during the political upheaval following the ouster of King James II. Arriving in March 1691, the newly-appointed English royal governor, Henry Sloughter, had Leisler tried for treason and executed on May 16, 1691. Ironically, Sloughter himself died suddenly barely a month later on June 23, 1691.[34]

pleted canoes at Lake St. Sacrement and met Schuyler's party at Ticonderoga on July 17, bringing the total number of men in the expedition to "260 Christians and Indians."[40] The army advanced to Crown Point and then to "Otter Kill" where "a small Stone fort breast high" was constructed.[41] On August 1 Schuyler's force engaged French troops and Indians near Fort La Prairie and subsequently burned hay and corn in the vicinity of the fort. Later that same day the English invaders fought a second successful battle against 340 French and Indians between La Prairie and Fort Chambly. Schuyler and his men departed shortly thereafter, returning to Albany on August 9, 1691.

A year and a half later Governor Frontenac organized a new expedition to "destroy the Mohawks, and afterward to commit as great ravages as possible around Orange [Albany]."[42] On January 27, 1693, French troops and militia departed from Fort Chambly. Three days later their Indian allies joined the expedition, bringing the total number of men to 625. The French army surprised the Mohawks during the second week of February when most of their warriors were away hunting. After burning three Mohawk villages, the troops decided against menacing Albany and began their retreat northward with 280 prisoners. Leading a contingent of militia and Iroquois, Major Peter Schuyler pursued the French raiders. Schuyler's mixed force of 250 troops and 290 Indians encountered the French and their Indian allies north of present-day Saratoga, where the retreating column had built a fort or log breastwork. Schulyer's men also constructed a simple log barricade. Unable to dislodge their English and Iroquois adversaries from behind their barricade in three attacks, the French abandoned some of their captives and set out for Lake St. Sacrement, but an early thaw forced them to march along the densely-forested shoreline of the lake. More of the Mohawk captives were released at Lake St. Sacrement with a promise that they would voluntarily come to Canada in the spring! The French army finally reached Chimney Point on Lake Champlain by early March, only to discover that their stashed food supply had spoiled. The half-starved legion resorted to eating boiled moccasins and the Indians devoured some of the prisoners who had died. The emaciated army finally arrived in Canada in mid-March. Schuyler later reported that "between 40 and 50 prisoners" were rescued by his army.[43] The French expedition had the desired effect: the Mohawks ended their raids on Montreal and met with Governor Frontenac in 1694 for peace negotiations.

There were additional raids for several more years, but the 1693 French incursion was the last major expedition into the Lake St. Sacrement and Lake Champlain region during King William's War. However, 76-year-old Governor Frontenac personally led one more French offensive into Iroquois territory—a foray against the Onondaga village in western New York. As his army of 2,200 trudged through the forest, the French governor was carried in an armchair fastened to two long poles. Just before Frontenac reached the Iroquois capital on August 2, 1696, the Onondagas burned their village and fled, leaving their food supply to be destroyed by the French invaders, who later burned an Oneida village before returning to Canada.

The War of the League of Augsburg ended with the Peace of Ryswick in September 1697, but news of the peace, which ended King William's War, did not reach North America until the next year. Unfortunately, the accord left most of the issues unsettled in both Europe and North America.

QUEEN ANNE'S WAR

In 1701 a peace treaty between New France and the Iroquois Five Nations resulted in a buffer of neutrality in New York State, but it did not prevent raids into New England from Canada by Native Americans allied with the French. Peace between the Iroquois and Great Lakes Indians at the same time led to a redirection of the fur trade from Montreal to Albany. French expansion into the Midwest and Great Lakes regions, however, raised the concern of British officials and ultimately contributed to the rationale for another period of warfare.

The War of Spanish Succession in Europe, known as Queen Anne's War (1702-1713) in North America, renewed hostilities. Plans were developed by French officials in Canada to raid and destroy English settlements on the borders of New England. Probably the most deadly incursion occurred at Deerfield, Massachusetts, in February 1704. In response to the continuing attacks on New England villages, British authorities devised an ambitious plan to conquer the French colonies in North America. The plan of the 1709 campaign, similar to the 1690 English plan, envisioned an invading force traveling north on Lake Champlain at the same time that a naval armada attacked Quebec on the St. Lawrence River. Colonel Francis Nicholson, who had served as an officer in Europe and as a lieutenant governor of New York (1688-1689), was chosen to lead the army against Canada. Nicholson's orders included cutting a road to Wood Creek, where bateaux and canoes would be constructed for the expedition. Colonel Peter Schuyler departed from Albany on June 1, 1709, with the first troops of Nicholson's 1,600-man army. At the southern end of the "Great Carrying Place" (present-day Fort Edward), Schuyler's men constructed the first of three forts built for the expedition. Named Fort Nicholson, the stockaded fort was commanded for a time by John Schuyler, brother of Colonel Peter Schuyler. A second fort, called Fort Schuyler for Peter Schuyler, was located on Wood Creek near present-day Fort Ann and was to be used as the final staging area for the expedition. A third, smaller fortified outpost lay to the south of Fort Nicholson. A large number of birch canoes and 110 bateaux were built at Wood Creek and the "Great Carrying Place" in preparation for the journey to Canada.[44]

Philippe de Rigaud de Vaudreuil, governor of New France, dispatched 1,500 troops under Sieur Claude de Ramezay to intercept the English army's invasion of Canada. Ramezay advanced southward with some of his men with a plan "for seizing Crown Point," but 228 English troops and Indians under John Schuyler discovered the French detachment and a fierce skirmish ensued. According to Governor Vaudreuil, "this mishap" interfered with French plans to take Crown Point and "prevented M. de Ramezay pushing on f[a]rther" to Wood Creek.[45]

As the season dragged on, most of Vaudreuil's 1,500 troops never moved from Fort Chambly, and many English soldiers at Wood Creek succumbed to smallpox and other camp diseases as they awaited news of the English fleet's planned attack on Quebec City. By October Nicholson learned that the English fleet had been diverted to Lisbon, Portugal. With that news, the army retreated to Albany, after destroying its boats and forts.

During the winter of 1710, Francis Nicholson and Peter Schuyler, along with four Mohawk leaders, sailed to London to convince English authorities to renew the expedition to conquer French Canada. Although the primary campaign was not resumed during that year, Nicholson led an expedition that succeeded in capturing Port Royal, Acadia (Nova Scotia), on October 13, 1710. However, the following year a land and naval campaign to capture Canada, similar in strategy to the 1690 and 1709 expeditions, received full English support.

Francis Nicholson, a lieutenant general in 1711, again commanded the land expedition consisting of 2,310 men — British regulars, militia from several colonies (New York, New Jersey, and Connecticut), and Native Americans.[46] Using 600 bateaux built at Albany, Nicholson's troops advanced to the ruins of Fort Nicholson and Fort Schuyler, the latter rebuilt and renamed Fort Anne. The 1711 expedition benefited from better preparation, more adequate supplies, sufficient bateaux, and a cleared road to Wood Creek that had been completed two years earlier. On September 10 Thomas Buckingham, a chaplain from Connecticut on the expedition, observed "between 30 and 40 wagons, some carrying battoes…the rest laden with stores" depart from Fort Nicholson for Wood Creek.[47] As supplies and boats were moved to Wood Creek, scouting parties were sent as far as Lake St. Sacrement and Crown Point. However, on September 19 "melancholy news" reached Nicholson's camp of the loss of eight transports and a provision vessel during the naval campaign against Quebec.[48] Sir Hovendon Walker, who had only limited naval experience, led an armada of 15 British men-of-war, each carrying 36-80 cannons, and 40 or more transport vessels loaded with 6,400 British regulars and 1,500 provincial troops under Brigadier General Jack Hill into the channel of the St. Lawrence River.[49]

Writing to the governor of New York, Hill recounted that the vessels had accidentally crashed on "the north shore" of the St. Lawrence River at night during "a great fog," resulting in the loss of "one thousand soldiers."[50] Apparently, Walker misinterpreted the landmarks and ordered a tack in the wrong direction before retiring for the night. A council of war was held among Walker's officers, who "were unanimously of [the] opinion that the river is wholly impracticable by reason of the ignorance of the p[i]lots which were given us at New England," and voted to cancel the expedition.[51] Two days after receiving the news at Wood Creek, Nicholson ordered the army to return to Albany. On October 1 and 2 the men "carr[ied] up our battoes into the pastures" at a stockaded fort on the east side of the Hudson River opposite the mouth of the Fishkill.[52] On October 11 contracts were signed by Nicholson and the governor to build a fort, chapel, and house for missionaries in Mohawk country, fulfilling a promise made by the Queen during the London visit of the four Mohawk sachems in 1710. Fort Hunter, located at the confluence of the Mohawk River and Schoharie Creek, was designed to be "150 feet square, ye curtains [walls] made with logs…[to a] height of twelve f[ee]t," with two-story blockhouses at each corner.[53]

Queen Anne's War finally ended with the signing of the Treaty of Utrecht on April 11, 1713. France relinquished control of Acadia, Newfoundland, and Hudson Bay; the Iroquois Five Nations were recognized as British subjects; Native American allies of the British were allowed to trade in New France; and the boundary line between New France and New York was set at Split Rock on Lake Champlain, although French officials in Canada never accepted the new border. Other basic issues that had contributed to war in North America, however, were left unsettled by the treaty.

2. Fort St. Frédéric

RELATIVE PEACE BETWEEN NEW FRANCE AND THE ENGLISH COLONIES endured for several decades after the end of Queen Anne's War. However, the expansion of English farms and forts on the frontier provoked Chief Grey Lock of the Abenakis and his followers to threaten settlements in western Massachusetts from their camp in Canada on Missisquoi Bay (Lake Champlain). By 1730 the old rivalry and suspicions between New France and the English colonies resurfaced. In 1730 the governor of New France, Charles de Beauharnois de la Boische, observed that "the English of Orange [Albany] were going to Lake Champlain and its vicinity to trade with the Indians...The English, bent on augmenting their possessions in America, profit by the peace to advance into the country of Canada."[1] As a result, Beauharnois sent an officer, Michel Dagneaux, and 30 soldiers to Lake Champlain to drive the English traders away, but none were discovered. The governor of New France also suggested that the "King of England has granted Lake Champlain to the children of...Peter Sc[h]u[y]l[er]...therefore, we must anticipate the establishment they may form at Crown Point."[2] Beauharnois reasoned that erecting a French fort at Crown Point would forestall English control of the region, as had French forts at Niagara and Detroit. Beauharnois's letter to the king of France noted that "when [we are in] possession of Crown Point, the road will be blocked on the English should they wish to pass over our territory, and we will be in a position to fall on them when they least expect it."[3] The French monarch, Louis XV, approved the plan: "his Majesty desires that a stockaded fort be erected at that place [Crown Point], until a stronger one can be constructed."[4]

By September 22, 1731, a 100-foot-square stockaded fort with four bastions was completed at present-day Chimney Point on the east side of the lake by workers and soldiers under Zacharie-François Hertel de la Fresnière. "Pointe a la Chevelure" at Chimney Point was also the site of an early French settlement. By tradition, the name Chimney Point resulted from the blackened chimneys left standing after French settlers burned their houses before evacuating in 1759.[5] In October 1731 *The American Weekly Mercury* reported "an account from Albany, dated the 25th of last month [September], that the French of Canada with about eighty men, have built a fort, and enclosed it with stockades, at Crown Point...and have also built a house of forty feet, and are bus[y]...[e]rect[ing] two more there."[6] The following June (1732) the British ambassador complained that the French

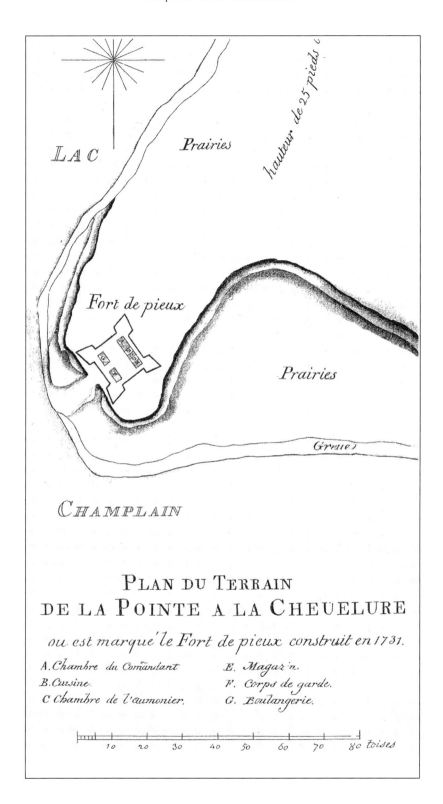

PLAN DU TERRAIN
DE LA POINTE A LA CHEUELURE

ou est marqué le Fort de pieux construit en 1731.

A. *Chambre du Comandant*   E. *Magazin.*
B. *Cuisine.*   F. *Corps de garde.*
C *Chambre de l'aumonier.*   G. *Boulangerie.*

"encroach on the territory of their neighbors…seizing on certain territory" and building a fort at "Pointe de la C[hevelu]re…within the country of the Iroquois…in absolute opposition to Article 15 of the Treaty of Utrecht."[7] Officials of the colony of Massachusetts also objected to the fort and recommended the enlistment of the Six Nations to oppose it.[8] French authorities, however, were unfazed by British objections and Louis XV instructed the governor of New France to oppose "any attempts" by the British "to construct one [fort] on the opposite side of the same lake…incontestably which belongs to France."[9] In addition, a succession of French land grants at Lake Champlain was initiated in 1733.

On October 10, 1734, Governor Beauharnois wrote to France's chief minister that "all necessary measures for the construction" of a new fort at Crown Point, "the Redoubt à Machicoulis," had been made, including workmen to prepare materials "this autumn" to begin building the fort during the early spring of 1735.[10] Beauharnois also instructed the commander at the stockaded fort to place his 30-man garrison on guard, adding that it was "impossible to station. . .any more on account of the smallness of the fort."[11] When the new fort was completed, Beauharnois planned to assign 120 men there and suggested that more troops would be needed. (At the time New France had only a total of 750 soldiers.)

The plan for the new fort at Crown Point was assigned to 52-year-old Gaspard Chaussegros de Léry, the chief engineer in New France who had designed the fortifications at Quebec City and Montreal, as well as at Fort Chambly on the Richelieu River. De Léry had been a student of Sebastien Le Prestre de Vauban, one of the most renowned military engineers of the late seventeenth century. Given the shortage of labor to construct immense bastions and a glacis (adjacent earth slopes), de Léry's plan for Crown Point departed somewhat from Vauban's classic star-shaped fortress and more closely resembled that of a small medieval castle. The actual construction was under the supervision of Dominique-Jason Lapalme (Lapoline), who would later be criticized for the poor workmanship on the fort. The fort was located on the western shore of the lake about a half mile from a limestone quarry. The main feature of the new fort was a four-story stone citadel or tower, having walls six to ten feet thick. The citadel and adjacent curtain walls, with sentry boxes at each of the four corners, were not fully completed until 1737.

Initially, conditions at the fort were far from ideal. Father Emmanuel Crespel, who had served as a chaplain at Fort Frontenac (present-day Kingston, Ontario), was "sent to Point La Chev[e]lure or Scalping Point…[where] in a battle at the point many Indians were scalped."[13] Arriving at Crown Point in November 1735, Crespel discovered "most of our soldiers were afflicted with the scurvy…we found little to eat near the post but a few partridges, and to procure venison we were obliged to go as far as Lake [St.] Sacrement."[14] He lived in a house with walls of "enormous-thickness" but without a roof, which "added greatly to the inconvenience" during periods of rain and snow.[15] The house was completed during the following spring and Crespel departed for Canada on September 21, 1736.

Originally called Fort Beauharnois, in 1737 the Crown Point fortress was officially named for Jean-Frédéric Phélypeau, Comte de Maurepas, the chief minister of France. Because most French forts used the saint designation, the fort was labeled Fort St.

Facing page: **Plan of the fort at "Pointe a la Chevelure" 1731 (Chimney Point, Vermont). (National Archives of Canada)**

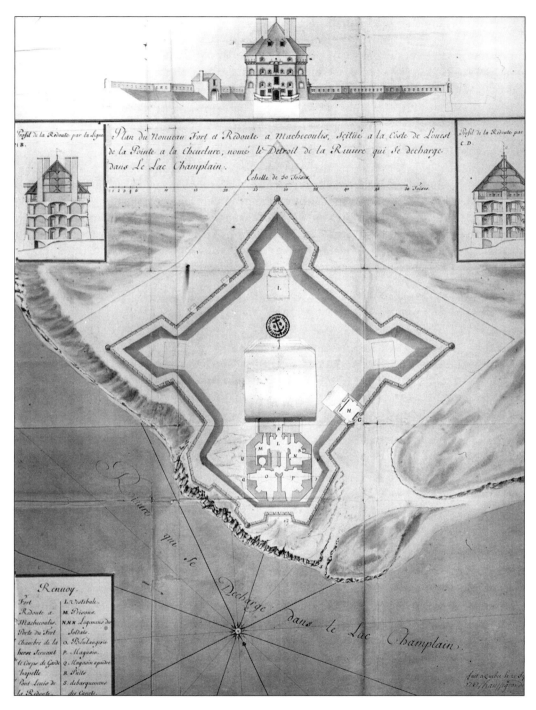

Plan of Fort St. Frédéric by Gaspard Chaussegros de Léry 1737.
(National Archives of Canada)

Frédéric. De Lery also designed a large stone windmill on a small cape of land south of Fort St. Frédéric. Constructed between 1739 and 1740, the windmill not only ground grain for French settlers, but also served as a vital defensive work, having several small cannons mounted on the top floor. (The Champlain Memorial Lighthouse, dedicated in 1912, now occupies the site of the fortified windmill.)

In 1740 Fort St. Frédéric was far from the secure fortress envisioned by its creators. François Beauharnois, the nephew of the governor of Canada, visited the fort in September 1740 and reported "but four guns in shape to be used…fortifications without ditches and without ramparts…no barracks, guard-rooms on the third floor, no cells…embrasures [openings in a wall for guns] without platform[s] for the recoil of the cannon."[16] (Two years earlier Gaspard Chaussegros de Léry had noted "6 four-pounders…and 6 swivels," but the cannons had been mounted on carriages either too low or too high to be usable.)[17] Improvements were later made to the defensive capability of the fort: a report dated July 10, 1742, noted 12 four pounders, 13 swivel cannons, two small mortars, and one two-pound cannon, all properly mounted with ample ammunition.[18] In early October 1740, the governor of New France recommended several additions to the fort, including "a covered way [a path dug into the earth], interior walls in the fort, and two buildings beside the entrance gate." [19] Two years later the improvements to Fort St. Frédéric were complete. A drawbridge over a dry moat and an iron grate (portcullis) that could be raised or lowered provided access through the main entrance of the fort on the north side. A guard house, hospital, barracks, chapel, and ovens were completed in the interior. The earliest detailed description of Fort St. Frédéric by an English visitor was written by Reverend John Norton on August 28, 1746, while in captivity following the surrender of Fort Massachusetts:

> It is something [of] an irregular form, having five sides to it; the ramparts twenty feet thick, the breastwork two feet and a half, the whole about twenty feet high. There were twenty-one or twenty-two guns upon the wall, some four and six pounders, and there may be some as large as nine pounders. The citadel, an octagon, built [four] stories high, fifty or sixty feet diameter, built with a stone laid in lime, the wall six or seven feet thick, arched over the second and third stories for bomb-proof. In the chambers nine or ten guns. Some of them may be nine pounders, and I believe none less than six, and near twenty patararoes [probably swivel guns]. . . . They have stores of small arms, as blunderbusses, pistols, and muskets.[20]

From the beginning of the construction of the fort, an effort was made by the intendant of New France, Gilles Hocquart, to encourage settlers to locate in the southern section of Lake Champlain. Inducements included two or three years without taxation, lower prices with the "king's storekeeper," and free supplies to the first six settlers. Discharged soldiers were central to the settlement of the lands at Crown Point. In 1749 Swedish professor Peter Kalm, a young naturalist and economist visiting the region, noted that French authorities "present each discharged soldier with a piece of land. . . . As soon as a soldier settles to cultivate each piece of land, he is first assisted by the king, who supplies him, his wife and children with provisions during the first three or four years. The king likewise gives him a cow and the most necessary instruments for agriculture. Some soldiers are sent to assist him in building a house."[22] However, Kalm also suggested that the houses "were no more than wretched cottages…The huts…consisted of boards, standing perpendicularly close to each other. The roofs were wood too. The crevices were stopped up with clay to keep the room warm. The floor was usually clay."[23] While the number of soldiers varied yearly from 50 to 120 from 1737 to 1744, during the summer months the total population at Crown Point swelled to an average of 400. A large number of mission Indians, especially Abenakis, also lived near Fort St. Frédéric, peaking during the late winter — 46 baptisms of Indians occurred between 1733 and 1747.[24]

As early as October 1736, plans for a transport sloop were formulated by the governor of New France, who proposed building a sloop "for the conveyance of the supplies for Crown Point," if the lake proved "navigable for sloops," given the lack of "knowledge respecting its rocks and sand bars."[25] Six years later a 45-ton vessel, perhaps named the *St. Frédéric*, was built at Crown Point by the Corbin brothers of Quebec. Joseph Payant St. Onge, the designated captain of the vessel, supervised its construction. During the late 1740s and 1750s, the vessel transported supplies from Fort St. Jean on the Richelieu River to Fort St. Frédéric. In 1750 the fort at St. Jean was described as "picketed in, has two block houses, but no cannon, being designed chiefly as a magazine for the provisions and other stores, to supply the garrison at Crown Point…by a small brig."[26] (Four years earlier, Governor Beauharnois had reported that Fort Chambly "serves as a store or entrepôt for all the munitions destined for Fort St. Frédéric.")[27]

KING GEORGE'S WAR

During King George's War (1744-1748), the defensive status of Fort St. Frédéric changed, and it became an offensive base for raids on the English frontier. Although negotiations between officials of Louis XV and George II offered some hope that another war could be averted, France formally declared war on Great Britain on March 15, 1744. The War of the Austrian Succession in Europe was called King George's War in North America. The war in Europe involved alliances in a struggle for political hegemony, while the issues in North America included dominion over Newfoundland fisheries, control of land, and tension over trade with Indians. In May 1744 the French struck the first blow at Canso, an English-held fishing port on the eastern point of Nova Scotia that was used seasonally as a port for hundreds of fishing schooners and 2,000-3,000 New England fishermen. The French destroyed the fortifications at Canso, taking prisoners to Louisbourg, their fortified seaport on Cape Breton Island. Several months later the French laid siege to the British fort at Annapolis Royal on Nova Scotia but withdrew without achieving victory. Threatened by the presence of Louisbourg, Governor William Shirley of Massachusetts organized a multi-colony expedition against the stronghold. On April 30, 1745, a force of 4,300 New England volunteers led by Lieutenant General William Pepperrell landed at Louisbourg.* Three days later an artillery siege began. The fighting also involved intense musketry: "firing gr[e]at numbers of small arms…not above 3 or 4 rods apart…many kill-'d & many drown[e]d," Major Seth Pomeroy of Massachusetts wrote in his journal.[29] On June 12 Pomeroy recorded that the French "fired a vast many bom[b]s & cannon [and]

*The date from Seth Pomeroy's journal is based on the pre-1752 Julian calendar.[28]

small arms"; but three days later "just before sunset the French sent out a flag of truce," ending the month-and-a-half siege.[30]

Late in 1745 the French and their Native American allies began bolder raids from the Champlain Valley, striking the fort at Great Meadows on the Connecticut River (located at present-day Putney, Vermont) on October 11 and 12. Fifty-three-year-old Paul Marin de La Malgue, who had served earlier at Louisbourg, arrived at Fort St. Frédéric with a French detachment on November 13, followed by his Native American allies four days later. The Indians persuaded Marin to change his planned assault on the villages along the Connecticut River because "the season was too far advanced"; instead, the expeditionary force, consisting of 280 militiamen and 229 Indians, "march[ed] toward Sarat[oga]."[31] One contingent of Marin's men captured the trading house of John Henry Lydius at the Great Carrying Place (present-day Fort Edward) on November 27; the combined force reached the fort at Saratoga early the next day.* The Saratoga fort was described as a "blockhouse and stockade" by an Indian eyewitness allied with the French.[33] Built on the Hudson River flats in 1744, the fort was actually vacant at the time of the French attack. Marin reported burning the fort and all 20 of the buildings in the village, including four mills, and destroying the cattle and provisions. Twelve villagers were killed and 109 taken prisoner, including a number of black slaves.[34] Fifty-year-old Philip Schuyler, son of John Schuyler who had led troops during the expeditions of King William's War and Queen Anne's War, was killed while defending his home. In early December *The Boston Evening-Post* reported that the "barbarous savages…inhumanely rip[p]'d open his body and pull'd out his heart, and cut off his head."[35] On their return to Fort St. Frédéric, Marin's Indian allies burned John Henry Lydius's blockhouse, taking his son and a number of others captive. Lydius, who had been at Albany during the raid, later traveled to Boston several times to urge Governor William Shirley to organize a coalition of colonies to capture Fort St. Frédéric. Ironically, a day before the attack on Saratoga, Governor George Clinton had sent a letter asking British officials to support "a scheme for the reduction of the garrison at Crown Point…which is a very great annoyance to our frontiers."[36] Clinton did gain the financial support of the New York Assembly to rebuild the fort at Saratoga. Completed in March 1746, "Fort Clinton" was constructed adjacent to the site of the last fort.** Luc de La Corne (also known as La Corne Saint-Luc), an officer of the colonial troops, subsequently described the fort as approximately 150 feet long by 100 feet wide "with six wooden redoubts for barracks; four in the angles of the fort and two in the centre of the two main curtains [walls]."[37]

French and Indian raids continued during 1746 from Fort St. Frédéric. Two skirmishes occurred at Fort Number Four, the northernmost English settlement (located near present-day Charlestown, New Hampshire). Built in 1744, the fort consisted of stoutly-constructed log buildings adjoining one another to enclose a parade ground and the whole surrounded by a picketed wood stockade. In June 1746 men under the fort's commander, Captain Phineas Stevens, were ambushed outside the fort. In early August French and

*The date of November 28, 1745, for the attack on Saratoga is based on French records. However, accounts in Boston newspapers recorded the assault on November 16 and Governor George Clinton received the report of the incident on November 19. The difference reflects the English use of the Julian calendar, which was discontinued in 1752 and replaced by the Gregorian calendar.[32]

**According to original documents, the new fort was simply called the fort at Saratoga. The name Fort Clinton was subsequently used by historians.

Indian marauders attacked the fort with small arms over a 24-hour period, departing after torching some outer buildings and killing the cattle. Other French raids included forays to Albany, Saratoga, Deerfield, and the upper Connecticut River settlements. In July 1746 a French detachment was sent to Wood Creek (Lake Champlain) "where they have felled the trees [o]n both sides to render its navigation impractical to our enemies."[38] The tree cutting was subsequently misinterpreted by English authorities as a French effort to construct a fort there. (During the summer of 1777 American soldiers would also cut trees into Wood Creek to block the passage of Lieutenant General John Burgoyne's invading army.)

In June 1746 Governor Clinton wrote to the Duke of Newcastle, the leading member in the House of Commons and Clinton's father-in-law, that he was "taking the necessary & most speedy steps for raising men" for an expedition to capture Canada, but the New York Council and Assembly failed "to provide materials...to transport such troops."[39] Many New York politicians were hesitant to incur the substantial expenditures that a major expedition required. The failure to support Clinton may also have been associated with merchants who were reluctant to further disrupt the illicit commercial trade relationship with Canada. On August 8, 1746, Clinton, along with Lieutenant Governor Cadwallader Colden, presided over a conference with the Six Nations in an effort to enlist the Iroquois in an expedition against Fort St. Frédéric. Seven hundred Iroquois attended the meeting, accompanied by William Johnson, a Mohawk Valley landowner and ally of the Mohawks. The conference was compromised by an outbreak of smallpox and the failure of the Albany Indian Commissioners to participate. (Boston newspapers, however, were overly optimistic about the results of the conference: "800 Indians which go by the name of Warriors, have joined our Indians, and are ready to march.")[40] In the end, the Iroquois nominally maintained their neutrality. However, the Mohawks agreed to assist in the war against the French and their Indian allies, and Clinton appointed Johnson "Colonel of the Warriors of the Six Nations," supplanting the Albany Indian Commissioners following their resignation in November 1746.[41] William Johnson soon dispatched Mohawk parties to Canada. One party attacked villagers near Chambly, killing several men and taking five or six captives. A second party ambushed French carpenters who were gathering wood for ship timbers on Isle La Motte.[42]

In the meanwhile, French officials were concerned about reports of English plans to capture Fort St. Frédéric, which would open the door to an invasion of Canada. In May 1746 French authorities received information that John Henry Lydius had traveled to Boston during the winter "to represent the necessity of taking Fort St. Frédéric."[43] On July 22, 1746, a "Dutchman" captured on Lake St. Sacrement informed the commander at Fort St. Frédéric that 600 English troops had arrived in Saratoga out of "the main body of the army composed of 13,000 men, designed to attack Fort. St. Frédéric."[44] The prisoner also suggested that bateaux constructed in Albany would be used on Lake St. Sacrement and Wood Creek by the invasion force, while "32. . .war [ships] and a quantity of transports [are] destined for the attack on Quebec."[45] In response to the threat, the governor of New France sent François-Pierre Rigaud de Vaudreuil, captain of the marines, with a 400-man detachment to strengthen the garrison at Fort St. Frédéric. In addition, orders were given to raise 1,600 men at Montreal to march to the fort if it should come under attack. Rigaud's orders, however, were "to go in quest of the enemy to their own country, should it be ascertained that the attack on Fort St. Frédéric was abandoned."[46]

Without new evidence of an English expedition, Rigaud planned an offensive operation. Rather than assault Saratoga's new fort, an ambitious campaign was organized to
destroy Fort Massachusetts on the Hoosic River in the northwest corner of the colony near
present-day Williamstown. Joined by Lieutenant Jacques-Pierre Daneau de Muy and several hundred Canadian and western Indians, Rigaud's total force included 440 militiamen
and officers and 300 Indians.[47] According to John Norton, a 30-year-old chaplain, the fort's
commander, Sergeant John Hawks, ordered a defensive fire held until the raiders were
"within twenty rods," whereupon Rigaud's men "fired incessantly" from behind "trees,
stumps, and logs."[48] Norton's journal listed the garrison as 22 men (half had been suffering from dysentery four days earlier), three women, and five children. Captain Ephraim
Williams, who commanded three forts in western Massachusetts, was absent from Fort
Massachusetts at the time of the attack. However, his brother, Dr. Thomas Williams, had
visited the fort on August 15 to remedy an outbreak of dysentery ("bloody flux"). Before
dusk on August 19 the French and Indians were observed "preparing faggots [sticks and
twigs]" to burn the fort, resulting in an order by Hawks "that all the tubs, pails, and vessels…should be filled with water."[49] Between eight and nine o'clock that night the fort was
surrounded and the Indians shouted "the most hideous outcries," but the onslaught was
not renewed until daylight on August 20.[50] Finally at noon, Rigaud offered reasonable surrender terms: all prisoners would remain with the French (not turned over to the Indians)
and exchanged at the first opportunity, children would be allowed to remain with their
parents, and the sick would be carried to French territory. At three o'clock in the afternoon
the garrison surrendered. The only death in the fort was that of Thomas Knowlton, who
had been shot in the head while manning one of the fort's two watch towers. The Indians
carried Knowlton's corpse out of the fort and "scalped it, and cut off the head and arms…a
young Frenchman…dressed the skin of the arm and made a tobacco pouch of it."[51] Two
men in the garrison were wounded, but the French and Indians actually suffered more
casualties: Rigaud was shot in his right arm, four French soldiers and eleven Indians were
wounded, and three of the latter were killed. After the besiegers plundered the contents,
the fort was set ablaze and the prisoners led away. As the raiders departed, they "set fire
to all the houses and grain" within three miles, as well as "barns, mills, churches, tanner-
ies, & c."[52] Most of the women and children were carried on the arduous journey to Wood
Creek and then to East Creek (opposite Ticonderoga), where they boarded canoes for the
final leg to Fort St. Frédéric, arriving on August 27. On September 4 the captives departed
for Canada, reaching Quebec on September 15, 1746.[53]

The attack on Fort Massachusetts was followed by additional raids in rapid succession. On August 25, 1746, a party of 40-60 Abenakis fell upon seven men and a young
woman harvesting hay in Deerfield: "five of the men were killed," two were decapitated
and the woman severely hatcheted on "both sides of the head."[54] In September Ensign
Jean-Baptiste Testard de Montigny and 14 Abenakis from Fort St. Frédéric attacked an
"Independ[e]nt Company" of militia near the fort at Saratoga, killing four and taking four
prisoners. Captain Peter Schuyler (a relative of the New York Schuylers), commanding his
New Jersey militia at the fort, tried to save the men but was nearly captured and "with
great difficulty made his retreat to the fort."[55] In October 1746 a large party of French offi-
cers and Indians attacked two supply wagons between Albany and Saratoga. As late as
December, scouting parties from Fort. St. Frédéric continued their forays to Saratoga.

A continuation of border skirmishes occurred during the following year. On April 10, 1747, Governor William Shirley of Massachusetts ordered the construction of "a good commodious blockhouse at or near the place where the fort called Massachusetts late stood."[56] Under the direction of Lieutenant Colonel William Williams, Fort Massachusetts was rebuilt during the spring of 1747. On June 2 Williams wrote to his second cousin Captain Ephraim Williams that he had left 80 men at the fort to help complete the barracks, "seventy feet in length, thirty in breadth."[57]

Pressure on other frontier forts continued to mount in 1747. In late March Chevalier de Niverville and 60 French troops and Native Americans approached Fort Number Four at Charlestown, New Hampshire, which had recently been reoccupied by Captain Phineas Stevens and 30 militiamen. After being prematurely discovered, the French party attacked the fort "on all sides[and] set fire to the old fences, and also to a log-house… with the most hideous shouting and firing from all quarters," according to Stevens.[58] The siege continued for 37 hours while the French pushed a crude barricade closer to the fort. At 10 o'clock at night the besiegers asked for a cessation of arms until sunrise, when a meeting would be requested. The next morning the French commander proposed surrender terms, which if refused would immediately result in "set[ting] the fort on fire," or alternately 700 French and Indian besiegers would scale the fort's walls.[59] Stevens put the proposal to a vote: "they voted to a man to stand it out, as long as they had life."[60] The fighting was postponed until daylight the next morning when the French again asked for a truce and subsequently proposed that Stevens "sell them provisions [and] they would leave."[61] Stevens replied that he could not legally sell them provisions, but that he would trade five bushels of corn for any captive. The French detachment fired a few muskets toward the fort and departed empty-handed.

During the winter and spring of 1747, attacks also continued on the undermanned garrison at Saratoga, where an outbreak of smallpox compromised its defense. On February 22, thirty Indians ambushed 12 soldiers, who were gathering firewood: "four of whom they kill'd outright, carried off four more prisoners, wounded three more."[62] The captives were taken to Fort St. Frédéric and from there to Montreal. A short time later 60 French and Indians fired a musket volley into an English party near the Saratoga fort, "killing 8 on the spot and wound[ing] several others."[63] Leading 200 men from Fort St. Frédéric in late June, Luc de La Corne was able to draw 102 English militia troops into an ambush outside the walls of the Saratoga fort, resulting in the capture of one officer and "47 of the men. . .and 15 killed."[64] In July François-Pierre de Rigaud de Vaudreuil marched to Saratoga with a large body of French soldiers and Indians to destroy the fort, but his Native American allies withdrew from the expedition and Rigaud returned to Fort St. Frédéric.

In the meanwhile, King Hendrick (Theyanoguin), a Mohawk chief with close ties to William Johnson, led 30 warriors and 10 militiamen from Albany on several raids against French settlements. In response, Lieutenant Jacques Legardeur de St.-Pierre and Luc de La Corne with a combined French and Indian force of 230 men ambushed the raiders in their canoes in Canada, taking "4 Senecas, 4 Oneidas, 1 Mohegan, 1 Mohawk and 4 Dutch-m[e]n."[65] Meeting with Governor Clinton on July 16, "deputies" of the Six Nations promised that "if the English would immediately proceed against the French fort at Crown Point, they would with great alacrity, assist them therein with 1000 of their best warriors," according to newspaper reports.[66] However, a transcript of the conference was less belli-cose in tone. Organizing an expedition against Fort St. Frédéric was hampered by dis-putes between the New York Assembly and Clinton over the failure of the former to pay the troops. Without full multi-colony support, an expedition against Fort St. Frédéric in 1747 was not practical, despite Clinton's efforts. On August 12, 1747, Governor William Shirley addressed the Massachusetts Council and House of Representatives regarding the need to support a plan for the capture of Fort St. Frédéric: "The French fort at Crown Point is doubtless the greatest inlet for the enemy into our western frontiers…[It] affords a most commodius ma[g]azine for their stores, a place of rendezvous from whence to make their incursions, and a safe shelter to them in their retreat."[67] Shirley urged the Massachusetts legislature to "be the leading province" in promoting an expedition against Crown Point, especially if a "Union of Councils in several [colonial] governments" are late in agreeing on quotas and "a general Plan of Operation."[68] On August 14 Shirley received a large packet from the Duke of Newcastle and relayed the decision to Clinton the following day that "the expedition against Canada is laid aside at present."[69]

The only offensive operation during the summer of 1747 involved an expedition to Lake St. Sacrement (Lake George) by William Johnson and his Native American allies. On August 4 Johnson wrote to Governor Clinton that he had dispatched three raiding parties composed of warriors of the Six Nations; two were sent to Canada and one to Crown Point. Two weeks later he informed Clinton that one of the parties had observed 40 Indi-ans at Fort St. Frédéric lodged in "six little houses" constructed of logs, but half of the Iro-quois party at Lake St. Sacrement reported "between five and six hundred men encamped upon an island, from whence they daily send large parties…and if not now prevented, will, I fear ere [before] long kill [an] abundance of our people, burn and destroy all the grain, houses, etc."[70] As a consequence, Johnson was "determined…to march against them."[71] On August 28 Johnson reported to Clinton that "I am just setting off this instant for Lake Sacrement with 400 Christians, mostly volunteers, and about as many Indians."[72] Johnson's army did not find any of the French or Indians at the lake and returned home. However, his actions demonstrated to the Iroquois the willingness of the English to act in the event of a French invasion.

The fort at Saratoga continued to come under attack; in August, newspapers noted that Colonel Peter Schuyler disclosed that he had repulsed an attack "by near 500 French and Indians."[73] The issues of pay and provisions for the New Jersey regiment at the fort came to a head during the fall of 1747 when the troops mutinied over the matter. Clinton had previously used his own credit in England to pay troops and informed the Duke of Newcastle that he had used the "account of Indian presents" to pay the men.[74] On Octo-ber 5, 1747, after failing to resolve financing and staffing problems at the Saratoga fort, Clinton ordered the fort burned after the removal of the artillery and stores.[75] A French and Indian detachment later viewed the ruins of the fort and recorded "twenty chim-neys…standing."[76] French and Indian raiding parties, however, found new targets, attacking "a party of a ser[g]eant and 18 men [who were carrying] provisions" back to their quarters near Albany on October 24 and three weeks later ambushing 12 English sol-diers near Fort Number Four in New Hampshire.[77]

French and Indian attacks on New England and New York settlements and forts per-sisted into 1748. In May Indians attacked militiamen near Fort Dummer on the Connecticut River. (Built in 1724 as protection from the Abenakis, the fort was located at the site of present-day Brattleboro, Vermont.) Departing on a scouting expedition from Fort Dummer on May 13, Captain Eleazer Melven and 18 men reached Otter Creek on May 20. Five days later Melven's party observed two canoes loaded with Indians under sail on Lake Champlain. Running to a point of land a half mile from Fort St. Frédéric, Melven's detachment fired six volleys into the second canoe, which carried 12 Indians; on the fourth volley the French garrison "fired 3 guns [cannons]…[from] Crown Point, which we judged to be 4 pounders"[78] Melven and his men retreated through Otter Creek and camped along the West River on May 31, but the Indians from Fort St. Frédéric pursued them, springing an ambush at the West River campsite, leaving six of Melven's party dead. As Melven ran along the river, "two Indians followed me, and ran almost side by side with me, calling to me 'Come Captain,' 'Now Captain,' but upon my presenting my gun toward them (though not charged) they fell a little back. . . . I looked back and saw nine of the enemy scalping the dead men."[79] Melven and his surviving militiamen ran back piecemeal to Fort Dummer, arriving the next day.

On May 21 another French and Indian attack occurred at Fort Massachusetts, and less than a month later (June 16) 13 militia troops were ambushed by Indians on the road between Fort Hinsdale on the Connecticut River and Fort Dummer. The same road was the scene of a deadly assault on a party of 17 English militiamen on July 14; four were killed and nine taken captive by the Indians. Four days later a bloody skirmish near Schenectady left 19 English inhabitants and militiamen dead and 11 captured or missing. On the second of August, 50 French and Indians were repulsed by Captain Ephraim Williams and his troops during an engagement just outside the walls of Fort Massachusetts.[80]

Meeting with a large party of representatives of the Six Nations and River Indians at Fort Frederick* in Albany from July 25 to 28, 1748, Governors Clinton and Shirley offered presents in an attempt to maintain the support of the Iroquois in the fight against New France. In presenting a large wampum belt, Clinton requested that the Iroquois and River Indians keep the "ax" in their hands "in readiness to use it, jointly with us, whenever you are called upon, as the enemy are committing murders daily upon you."[82] In reply, the Iroquois thanked the English for their support and promised to be ready to face the French. The River Indians remarked that since the beginning of the war "We were ready to join you…and have still our hands on the cocks of our guns to go against our com[m]on enemy whenever we shall be com[m]anded."[83]

Twelve days later, a report reached New York City that the war had been settled in Europe. On August 18, 1748, Clinton and Shirley dispatched a long letter to the Lords of Trade in England concerning problems during the war and making suggestions for the future. The two governors strongly criticized the defunct Albany Commissioners of Indian Affairs, who "had more regard to their private profit than to the public good & their aim & view seems to have been to continue a clandestine trade" with Canada during the war.[84] They suggested that peace would provide an opportunity "to gain sufficient intelligence of the numbers & situation of these distant [Indian] Nations" and to prosper from trade with them.[85] Clinton and Shirley exhorted the Lords to negotiate with the French for the destruction of Fort St. Frédéric, which "is truly an [e]ncroachment of his Majest[y's]

*In 1744 a visitor to Albany described Fort Frederick as two brick buildings (the Royal Governor's House and barracks) enclosed by four bastions mounting eight or ten cannons and garrisoned by 100 soldiers.[81]

territories."[86] Facing reality, however, the governors continued: "But whether this can be obtained or not, it seems necessary to build one or more forts near some of the most considerable passes toward Canada, and as near Crown Point" as possible.[87]

The signing of the Treaty of Aix-la-Chapelle, ending the war, on October 18, 1748, settled very little. All territories conquered were returned, including Louisbourg. New Englanders, who had lost nearly 700 men as the result of fighting and illness during the siege and subsequent occupation of the fortress, were understandably resentful of British officials. The treaty did not end the border problems that led to the war, and the peace only lasted a brief six years. Protests over Crown Point were renewed as early as May 9, 1749, when Governor Shirley of Massachusetts complained to the governor of New France about the presence of French settlers at Fort St. Frédéric as an encroachment on English territory.

DESCRIPTIONS OF FORT ST. FRÉDÉRIC 1749-1750

The most detailed descriptions of Fort St. Frédéric and other French fortifications were written by visitors to the forts during the period following King George's War. Reaching Fort St. Frédéric on July 2, 1749, Peter Kalm recorded that the fort "is nearly square, has high, thick walls made of the same limestone [black], of which there is a quarry about half a mile from the fort. On the eastern part of the fort is a high tower, which is proof against bombshells, provided with very thick and substantial walls, and well stored with cannon from the bottom almost to the very top; and the governor [commandant] lives in the tower."[88] Kalm also described a chapel, stone barracks, and the "windmill built of stone with very thick walls…at the top four or five small pieces of cannon."[89] Kalm remained at the fort until July 19 when he departed for Canada aboard a French packet sloop. Along the way he observed Indians in bark canoes fishing for sturgeon, the remains of Fort St. Anne on Isle La Motte, abandoned French settlements on the western shore, a stone windmill opposite present-day Rouses Point, and Fort St. Jean built in 1748. Kalm noted that Fort St. Jean was about one arpent (175-198 feet) square with four-story wood buildings ("polyangular"), containing openings for cannons and muskets in the two corners that faced the Richelieu River. Two-story wood barracks occupied the other two corners of the fort that faced inland. The walls of the fort (between the corner buildings) were palisades, consisting of double rows of aborvitae logs with loop holes and a firing platform.[90]

In the fall of 1749 Captain Phineas Stevens, the commander of Fort Number Four, was commissioned to deliver a letter from Governor William Shirley to the governor of Canada, Jacques-Pierre Taffanel la Jonquiere, concerning the exchange of prisoners. From October 13th to the 15th, Stevens and ensign John Burk canoed north on Lake St. Sacrement, noting the "wigwams of St. Francois Indians" and French Mohawks.[91] After traveling on Lake Champlain and the Richelieu River, Stevens reached Fort St. Jean on October 26, delivering his letter to the French governor in Montreal three days later. While in Montreal, Stevens made numerous inquiries regarding the English prisoners and also scrutinized the defenses, including an 18-foot wall surrounding the city. On the return trip aboard a large bateau on Lake Champlain, he observed a stone windmill on the east side of the lake (opposite present-day Rouses Point), unoccupied houses on both sides of the lake, and 100 men cutting ship timbers on the west side of the lake. The French officer in

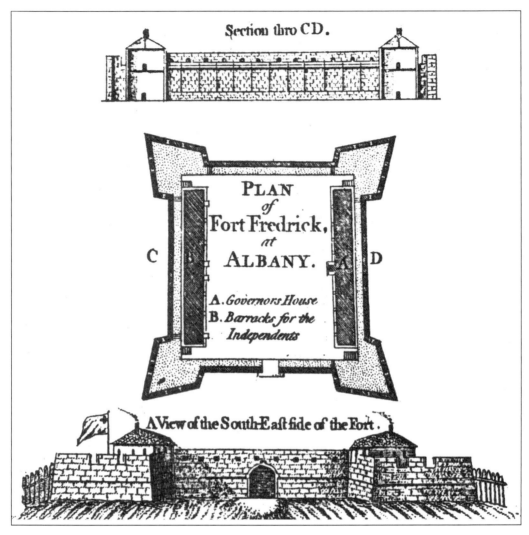

Plan of Fort Frederick, Albany. From *A Set of Plans and Forts in America* **(1763).**

charge "had a comfortable house–the men [had] barracks to live in."[92] Arriving at Crown Point late on November 13, Stevens spent the next day at the fort, recording the following observations:

> It is a large stone fort, I judge about 12 or 14 rods square [198-231 feet]…the citadel …is four stories high, each story contains four convenient rooms; the partitions are walls of stone of great thickness; each story arched over with stone of great thickness, for its twenty-four large stone steps from one story to another; each room has one very large window, three or four feet wide, seven or eight high. The commandant [Captain Paul-Louis Dazemard de Lusignan] lives in the third story, where there are two such windows. In his room, I saw 110 small arms,

50 of them fixed with bayonets, and about 50 pairs of pistols…there are eighteen houses near Crown Point, some on each side of the water, but not all inhabited at present.[93]

Stevens hired two Caughnawaga Indians to guide him through Wood Creek to John Henry Lydius's trading house at the Great Carrying Place. Leaving on November 15 in birchbark canoes, the party was so hampered by ice that it did not reach the Lydius house until November 26. The Caughnawagas expressed "a great desire to live in peace" and Stevens invited their chiefs to Boston.[94]

The following year Governor George Clinton of New York sent Lieutenant Benjamin Stoddert (also spelled Stoddard), a New York infantry officer, to Canada to redeem English prisoners who were to be exchanged for 13 prisoners held by English-allied Indians. On June 27 Stoddert received 24 prisoners in Montreal; 13 other prisoners, however, were not repatriated. Most were living with Indians and chose not to return home. Several, however, were with Indian families who refused to release them. One black slave (Samuel Frement), held by Luc de La Corne, was not released because La Corne insisted that "every negro being a slave wherever he be."[95] After his return, Stoddert wrote a detailed report of all the fortifications in Canada, as well as Fort St. Frédéric. Quebec was characterized as "one of the strongest natural fortifications in America," protected by four batteries, consisting of 43 cannons and two mortars, while Montreal, surrounded by a stone wall, was defended by the "Battery Royal" of 26 cannons.[96]

Stoddert's account of Fort St. Frédéric provided a comprehensive description of the fortress and offered suggestions for an inevitable siege of the fort.

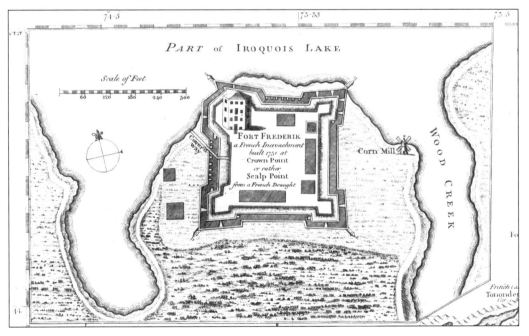

Drawing of Fort St. Frédéric (ca. 1750s). (Library of Congress)

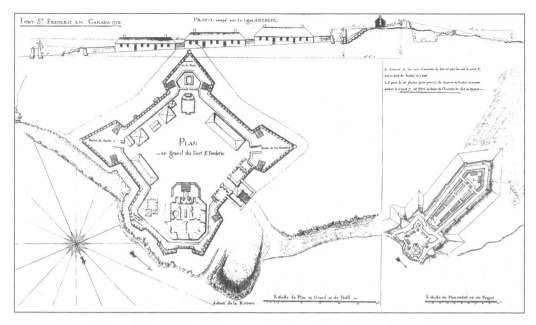

Plan of Fort St. Frédéric 1752. (National Archives of Canada)

Aerial view of the ruins of Fort St. Frédéric. (Photo by the author)

This Fort is built of stone, the walls of considerable height and thickness, and has twenty pieces of cannon and swivels, mounted on the ramparts and bastions, the largest…six pounders, and but a few of them. I observed the wall cracked from top to bottom in several places. At the entrance to the fort is a dry ditch, eighteen or twenty foot square and a draw bridge. There is a subter[r]an[ean] passage under this draw bridge to the lake which I apprehend is to be made use of in time of need to bring water to the fort, as the well they have in it affords them but very little. In the north west corner of the fort stands the citadel: it is a stone building eight square, four story high each turn'd with arches, mounts twenty pieces of cannon & swivels, the largest six pounders, four of which are in the first story, and are useless till the walls of the fort are beat down. The walls of the citadel are about ten foot thick, the roof high and very ta[u]t, covered with shingles.

At the entrance of the citadel is a draw bridge and ditch of the same dimensions of that to the entrance of the fort. To the south south east and south west of the fort the ground is rising and is very advantageous of erecting a battery in case of a siege, as 'tis above three hundred yards distance from the fort. Behind it the land is low, and some thousands of men may lie without receiving any damage from the cannon of the fort, as the ridge is a fine covert and lies circular so far as to flank two of the bastions. They have a chapel and several other wooden houses in the fort which are put to no other use then the storing of their possessions etc. The land near the fort in general is level and good, also on each side of the lake which they are settling, and since the peace there are already fourteen farms on it, a[n]d great encouragement given by the King for that purpose, and I was inform'd that by the next fall, several more families were coming there to settle.[97]

Fort St. Frédéric remained a vital stronghold on the frontier as official land grants continued to solidify French control of the Champlain Valley. Relative peace in the region would last less than six years when renewed raids on the English frontier from Fort St. Frédéric began. The next war would be the culmination of a century of tension and outright warfare and would forever change North America.

Advance units of Major General William Johnson's army departing on August 26, 1755, from Fort Lyman (later Fort Edward) for Lake George. Johnson and Captain Robert Rogers are shown in the foreground. (Drawing by Gary S. Zaboly)

3. Expedition Against Fort St. Frédéric

A TENUOUS PEACE followed King George's War. Although French officials sought promises from their Native American allies to end their raids on English frontier settlements, intermittent assaults continued. The French and their Indian allies became increasingly concerned with the expansion of English settlements. On the eve of the French and Indian War the population of the English colonies had soared to slightly more than one million, whereas the French population, excluding Acadia, had risen to only 55,000.[1] By midcentury, the Ohio Company, organized by Virginia land speculators, had prepared plans to develop the Ohio Valley. To check English expansion into the Ohio territory, François Bigot, intendant of New France, persuaded Governor Ange Duquesne de Menneville to reallocate French military resources to the west. Bigot also favored the move into the Ohio region because he supplied military provisions to the government.[2] The French strategy involved building a series of forts in the western territory, including two completed in 1753: Fort Presque Isle on the southern shore of Lake Erie (near present-day Erie, Pennsylvania) and Fort Le Boeuf on French Creek (south of the first fort). A third outpost, Fort Machault at the Indian village of Venango, was begun in August 1753. However, construction activity slowed as a result of the sheer exhaustion of the troops. A short time later the Native Americans allied with the French army decided to return to Canada.

In early November 1753, after hearing reports of the French forts, Lieutenant Governor Robert Dinwiddie of Virginia dispatched 21-year-old militia major George Washington to Fort Le Boeuf with a letter to the French military commander, demanding that their forts be abandoned. Washington delivered the directive to Captain Jacques Legardeur de Saint-Pierre, who courteously declined. As a consequence and with official British support, Dinwiddie sent a militia company, consisting of 42 militiamen/carpenters, to build a fort at the junction of the Ohio, Allegheny, and Monongahela Rivers (today's Pittsburgh). In early April 1754, newly-commissioned Lieutenant Colonel George Washington was sent with a detachment of 159 Virginia militiamen to reinforce the men at the forks of the Ohio River. In the meantime, 600 French troops under Claude-Pierre Pécaudy de Contrecoeur marched to the Forks, forcing the surrender of the 42 Virginians on April 17, 1754. Contrecoeur's men subsequently constructed Fort Duquesne, making use of the logs that had been cut and squared by the previous builders. After receiving the news, Washington continued northward for the next three weeks, pausing in a valley known as the Great

Meadows, where his men built a storehouse for use as a way station.

With a report on May 27 that the French were nearby, Washington and his men were joined by an Indian ally, Tanaghrisson ("Half-King"), and proceeded to a glen (about 10 miles from the Great Meadows) where a 30-man French detachment, under Ensign Joseph Coulon de Villiers de Jumonville, had camped and had begun to prepare breakfast. Exactly how the ensuing firefight began is still debatable. Washington's men inflicted heavy casualties on the French party and Tanaghrisson's warriors butchered and scalped 13 of the 14 wounded French soldiers, including Jumonville, before Washington intervened. Jumonville's mission had been to deliver a letter to Washington to vacate lands claimed by New France. After receiving reinforcements, Washington advanced toward Fort Duquesne, building a road along the way. However, he was forced to retreat to the Great Meadows at the end of June after learning of the approach of a large French and Indian force. Located in an open field, the Great Meadows camp, named Fort Necessity by Washington, was a simple log storehouse encircled by a rough palisaded wall with trenches along the perimeter. On July 3 Captain Louis Coulon de Villiers (Jumonville's older brother) and 700 French and Indians began an attack on Fort Necessity. Taking French fire from the higher ground, Washington's men defended their position from shallow trenches, but heavy rain compromised their effort. After nine hours and with a good deal of his army's ammunition exhausted, the French commander suspended fire and requested a parley. With 30 men dead and 70 wounded, Washington had little choice but to accept a capitulation. Marching out of the fort with the "honors of war" the next morning, the English troops were stripped of their possessions by the Indians, and several wounded men were killed and scalped. Others fled in panic, pursued by the Indians and taken captive. This scene would portend the turmoil following the capitulation of Fort William Henry three years later. Although some of the captives were released, four were retained by the Indians, despite a French effort to ransom them.[3]

Conditions also deteriorated in the northeast and open warfare seemed inevitable to both sides. Concerned over the loss of Iroquois support, British officials organized a conference in 1754 with the Six Nations and the leaders of seven colonies. A year earlier (June 1753), the Mohawk sachem, King Hendrick (Theyanoguin), and 16 other Mohawks had made a journey to New York City to air their grievances with Governor George Clinton. Hendrick confronted Clinton, suggesting that "the indifference and neglect sh[o]wn toward us makes our hearts a[ch]e, and if you don't alter your Behaviour to us we fear the Covenant Chain will be broken."[4] The Covenant Chain, symbolized by an exchange of elaborately-woven wampum belts, sustained unity and peace, as well as trade relations, between the Iroquois and the British colonies. British failure to uphold the tradition of perpetual presents to the Mohawks, their tolerance of fraudulent sales of Mohawk land, and the destructive rum trade all coalesced to damage relations with the Mohawks. Hendrick also asserted that the French expedition to the Ohio country had caused "a great deal of damage…among our Brethen."[5] On September 18, 1753, after receiving Governor Clinton's letter and minutes of the meeting, the Board of Trade in London sent orders to the new incoming governor of New York, Sir Danvers Osborne, to set a conference date for "renewing the Covenant Chain" and "to examine into the complaints they [the Mohawks] have made of being defrauded of their land."[6] The Board of Trades also dispatched a short letter to another six royal governors with instructions to send commissioners to the meeting as representatives of their colonial assemblies.[7] London officials were distressed over the treatment of the Mohawks by the colony of New York and considered the threat to the Covenant Chain serious, in part because the Chain legitimized British land claims in the Ohio Valley and elsewhere. By the time the letter of instruction had reached New York City, the new royal governor, Sir Danvers Osborne, had committed suicide, leaving the office to Lieutenant Governor James DeLancey, a friend of the Albany merchants who in large part were responsible for the complaints of the Mohawks.

DeLancey set June 14, 1754, for the beginning of the conference to be held in Albany. King Hendrick's address at the meeting involved a long harangue on British policy, criticizing the governors of Virginia and Pennsylvania for allowing their citizens to build houses on Indian land in the Ohio country without asking for Iroquois consent. Hendrick also castigated British military policy: "We would have gone and taken Crown Point, but you hindered us…you burn[ed] your own fort at S[a]ratoga [in 1747]…you have no fortifications about you, no, not even [in] this city, tis but one step from Canada hither, and the French may easily come and turn you out of your doors…Look at the French, they are men, they are fortifying everywhere—but, we are ashamed to say it, you are all like women bare and open without fortifications."[8]

The Albany conference of 1754 was also famous for a proposed colonial union. Following news that the Virginians had surrendered their post at present-day Pittsburgh, Benjamin Franklin's *Pennsylvania Gazette* cautioned readers that the French planned "to establish themselves, settle their Indians, and build Forts" near English counties and warned of the "present disunited state of British Colonies."[10] The disunity was illustrated by a cartoon entitled "Join, or Die," showing a snake sectioned into eight pieces, labeled with the initials of seven colonies and New England.[11] A variation of the cartoon appeared in newspapers throughout the colonies. Franklin traveled to Albany and lobbied persuasively for a union of the colonies. On July 10 Franklin's "Plan of Union" was adopted by the convention. The plan called for a "President General, to be appointed and supported by the Crown; and a Grand Council, to be chosen by the representatives of the people of the several colonies."[12] The powers of the "President General" and the "Grand Council" included the ability to "raise and pay soldiers and build forts…and equip vessels."[13] The plan, however, was rejected by colonial assemblies and London officials.

Although the Albany Plan was not approved, the convention did influence future policies in North America. By 1754 British officials were already planning to coordinate military operations in their American colonies in order to meet the challenge of New France's expansionary strategy. The British government would subsequently appoint a commander in chief of all British and provincial military forces in North America and the Board of Trade would order a conference of colonial commissioners to decide the contribution that each colony would make for the common defense. Meanwhile, Abenaki raiding parties from Crown Point continued to attack frontier settlements, including farms near Fort Number Four (near present-day Charlestown, New Hampshire) in August 1754 and the eastern Hoosic Valley in September. On October 26, 1754, Governor Duquesne of New France apologized to DeLancey for the "ravages" committed by the Abenakis, maintaining that the commandant of Fort St. Frédéric was not aware of their intentions. Duquesne subsequently gave "orders to the commandant of Fort St. Frédéric to withhold all supplies" from the Abenakis.[14]

The die was cast, however, by the autumn of 1754. "Secret instructions" given to Major General Edward Braddock, the newly-appointed British commander in chief for North America, included orders for driving the French from their forts in Ohio, Niagara, Beauséjour (Nova Scotia), and "reducing the fort at Crown Point and erecting another" at Lake Champlain.[15] In a letter to the Board of Trade on December 15, 1754, Lieutenant Governor DeLancey suggested building a number of defensive forts, including one on Wood Creek (southern end of Lake Champlain) and another at the southern end of Lake St. Sacrement.[16] Writing to the British secretary of state on March 24, 1755, Governor William Shirley of Massachusetts, who had sent more than 500 men on an expedition to the Kennebec River (in present-day Maine) a year earlier, proposed that "upwards of 4500 men" would have to be raised in Massachusetts for the Crown Point and Nova Scotia expeditions.[17] Meeting with a council of five governors at Alexandria, Virginia, in April 1755, Major General Edward Braddock proposed the capture of the French forts—Crown Point, Niagara, Beauséjour, and Duquesne. Despite some trepidation expressed by the governors, Braddock's plan called for simultaneous attacks on the French forts, which was beyond the logistical and military capability of the colonies. Braddock, who had limited battlefield experience despite 45 years of service, was essentially fulfilling a plan honed by William Augustus, the Duke of Cumberland (son of King George II). Under the operational plan, Braddock would capture Fort Duquesne; Lieutenant Colonel Robert Monckton, a British regular officer with considerable experience during the War of Austrian Succession and the Jacobite Rebellion, was slated to take Fort Beauséjour. Governor William Shirley, who had planned the successful campaign against Louisbourg in 1745 and was unquestionably the most skilled politician of the colonial governors, was commissioned as Braddock's second in command with the rank of major general. Shirley was given the daunting task of moving a provincial force 300 miles from Albany to Fort Niagara via Oswego. Forty-year-old William Johnson, colonel of the Albany County militia during King George's War and "Colonel of the Warriors of the Six Nations" from 1746 to 1751, was appointed by Braddock to the "sole superintendency and management of the affairs of the Six United Nations."[18] The council of governors and Braddock unanimously selected Johnson to command the expedition to Crown Point. With the approval of Braddock, Johnson was commissioned a major general by Shirley and instructed "to erect a Strong Fortress upon an Eminence near the French Fort at Crown Point"; to this, Lieutenant Governor James DeLancey's directive added "removing the [e]ncroachments of the French on his Majesty's Lands there."[19] Shirley recommended that Johnson's provincial army consist of approximately 4,000 men to be raised in the following manner: 600 from New Hampshire, 1,000 from Connecticut, 400 from Rhode Island, 800 from New York, and 1,200 from Massachusetts.[20] The "beating orders" issued to Massachusetts recruiting officers specified that the men be between 18 and 35, "free from all bodily ails & of perfect limbs," stipulated "no Roman Catholics nor any that are under five feet four inches," and provided an increased scale of bounties for long enlistments.[21]

The first campaign began with Braddock's march toward Fort Duquesne. Leading an army of nearly 2,400 regulars and provincial troops, along with another 400-500 civilians (wagon drivers, sutlers, female camp followers, etc.), Braddock departed on May 29 from the assembly point at the newly-constructed Fort Cumberland (present-day Cumberland, Maryland). Braddock split his force to make time and marched ahead with approximately 1,400 men. On July 9 Braddock's army was only about eight miles from Fort Duquesne when a French force, consisting of about 260 French regulars and militiamen and over 600 Indians, intercepted the British expeditionary army. Lieutenant Colonel Thomas Gage's advance guard spearheaded the column and provided flanking troops for security, but the movement of Braddock's troops was less than stealthy, especially with the noise of felling axes for road clearing and the band blaring the "Grenadiers March."[22] The ensuing battle resulted in the defeat of the British army with about two-thirds killed or wounded. Braddock valiantly directed his men—four horses were shot from under him before he received a mortal wound. George Washington had four musket balls pierce his clothing and two horses shot from under him. William Shirley, Jr., Braddock's secretary and the oldest son of the Massachusetts governor, was killed during the engagement. British neglect of the tactics of irregular warfare ("petite guerre") and the failure to employ more Indians and rangers played a major role in the crushing defeat of Braddock's army.[23]

**"Fall of Braddock," July 9, 1755. Engraving by J. B. Allen
from a painting by C. Schuessele. (National Archives of Canada)**

CROWN POINT EXPEDITION TAKES SHAPE

The northern campaign under William Johnson proceeded at a slow but measured pace. Johnson sought to enlist Iroquois support for the Crown Point expedition or at a minimum make certain that they would remain neutral. He called members of the Six Nations and their allies to a conference on June 21, 1755, at his home, Fort Johnson. Completed in 1749, Fort Johnson was a three-story, Georgian-style stone house protected by several

William Johnson.
Engraving by J. C. Buttre.
(New York State Library)

blockhouses (located one mile west of present-day Amsterdam, New York). Held in high regard by the Mohawks, Johnson had solidified their support by condemning the Kayaderosseras Patent granted to New York land speculators, which he deemed an effort to remove the Mohawks from their traditional hunting grounds in the Saratoga region. The Iroquois considered Johnson to be their chief patron—he often communicated with them in their own language and respected their customs and rituals. At a conference with the Six Nations held in Albany during King George's War, an eyewitness reported that Johnson had arrived at the head of the Mohawks, "dressed…after the Indian Manner."[24] At the June 1755 Iroquois conference, which drew 1,106 men, women, and children, Johnson honored the tradition of giving presents to the Indians by supplying large numbers of cloth items, household articles, and guns and providing wampum belts, as well as abundant food for a feast.[25] Johnson's speeches were translated and written in Iroquois by Daniel Claus, a German immigrant who had mastered the Mohawk language. Before the speech was given, Claus read it to two important sachems of the Onondaga and Oneida Nations. In his first address Johnson urged a rekindling of the friendship between the British and Iroquois, suggesting that their best defense would be to remain together and handed an Iroquoian speaker a bundle of sticks bound together to symbolize strength in unity. In a second speech given on June 24, Johnson entreated the Iroquois not to break the Covenant Chain, not to be deceived by "French boasting or lies," and predicted that upon the commencement of military operations the British would act "like an angry Wolf, and the French will fly before them like Deer."[26] The Iroquois reply was given by Kaghswughtioni, the influencial Onondaga sachem also known as Red Head by the British, who had been singled out by Johnson for special presents. Red Head assured Johnson that the Iroquois would "stand by our Brethren the English & adhere to our Covenant Chain" and agreed to "join and assist you in your undertaking," but "what particular numbers" had not yet been decided.[27] Red Head, however, also criticized British colonists: "Your People are very faulty, they are too thirsty of money and carry on Trade with the French."[28]

On July 1 several sachems privately informed Johnson of their "concern…on account of our Brethren the C[au]ghnawaga [Mohawks of Canada]…[who] are our own flesh and blood."[29] Later another sachem promised that the Iroquois would try to persuade the

Canadian Caughnawagas "to get out of danger and not assist the French against our Brethren the English."[30] King Hendrick (Theyanoguin),* the Mohawk sachem who aided Johnson during the conference, addressed the assembled Iroquois and made an unqualified commitment to join Johnson's Crown Point expedition and also urged the Iroquois representatives to help in Governor William Shirley's Niagara campaign. In the end Johnson wrote to Braddock, who had actually died two days before the letter was written, that he had "found all the Nations except the Mohawks extremely averse to taking any part with us" in the expedition against the French.[32]

During the conference, John Henry Lydius, considered a notorious merchant who had engaged in illicit trade with Canada, arrived at Fort Johnson. Appointed by Governor Shirley to recruit Iroquois for the Niagara expedition, Lydius came under attack by Iroquois leaders for his activities in a fraudulent land deal (Susquehannah Company deed). On July 3 the Onondaga sachem Kaghswughtioni (Red Head) initiated the criticism of the Susquehannah land deal and the Oneida sachem Conochquiesa stood up

Mohawk sachem Theyanoguin, known as Hendrick Peters, was the second King Hendrick. (Library of Congress)

and referred to Lydius as "filth" and a "snake": "That man sitting there (pointing to Col. Lydius) is a Devil and has stole our lands, he takes Indians slyly by the blanket one at a time, and when they are drunk, puts some money in their bosoms, and pers[u]ades them to sign deeds."[33] Johnson, who deemed Lydius "obnoxious," later acknowledged that he had promised the Iroquois that "no snake" would be allowed in the meetings and believed that the allegations of the Iroquois against Lydius were "in a great measure true."[34] The next day (July 4) Johnson admitted to the Iroquois that "many frauds have been made...in the purchasing of your lands which I am very sorry for" and suggested that the governor of New York "will prevent these evil doings in the future."[35]

Johnson had already been troubled by Shirley's attempt to organize the Iroquois into

*Theyanoguin, known as Hendrick Peters, was the second King Hendrick and often confused by historians with the first King Hendrick, Hendrick Peters Tejonihokarawa. The first King Hendrick, a well-known sachem and member of the Mohawk Wolf Clan, was born about 1660 and died sometime after April 1735. Tejonihokarawa was one of the four Mohawk "kings" who had visited Queen Anne in London in 1710. Theyanoguin, the second King Hendrick, was born in Westfield, Massachusetts, in 1692 to a Stockbridge Mohegan father and Mohawk mother. A member of the Bear Clan, Theyanoguin became an important sachem, diplomat, and close friend of William Johnson. He visited King George II in London in 1740 and was killed September 8, 1755, in the first engagement of the Battle of Lake George.[31]

formal militia units and resented Shirley's enlistment of Lydius, who encroached on John-son's role as the "sole" superintendent of the Iroquois Six Nations. Johnson's repudiation of Lydius before the Iroquois and the reversal of Lydius's orders from Shirley to recruit Iroquois for the Niagara campaign led to a contentious exchange with Shirley in Albany on July 15. Shirley pressed Johnson to delete any reference to him in the report of the con-ference to London and ordered Johnson to provide 60-70 Iroquois to accompany him to Oswego. Feeling that an escort was unnecessary through friendly territory, Johnson rejected the request for the Indians. Although Johnson's secretary, Peter Wraxall, dropped the reference to Shirley in the report, he provided the same information in a note. Subse-quently, Shirley sought to discredit Johnson, which resulted in an escalation of the per-sonal conflict between the two leaders. Early in August Johnson complained to Lieutenant Governor James DeLancey that his "character & conduct has been vilified" by Shirley's "falsehoods."[36] DeLancey, whose family had been involved in the illicit trade with Cana-da, resented Shirley for his failure to award supply contracts for the Niagara campaign to his younger brother Oliver, so he endeavored to undermine Shirley's authority.

During June and early July 1755, the provincial troops destined for the Crown Point expedition began to assemble at Albany. On July 9 Lieutenant Colonel Seth Pomeroy from Northampton, Massachusetts, recorded that Johnson viewed a muster of the provincial regiments camped on the "German Flats," about two miles north of Albany, and noted that he "was well pl[e]as'd with the[i]r ap[p]ear[a]nce."[37] Later, however, Johnson wrote that most of his officers were "low lifed ignorant people" and the troops "lazy."[38] Al-though many of the officers, like Pomeroy, had served during the 1745 Louisbourg expe-dition, the troops of the Crown Point army were inexperienced—composed almost entire-ly of New England farmers lacking any formal military training. While the 1755 "beating orders" issued to recruiting officers stated that "his Majesty's cloth[e]s [would be] deliv-

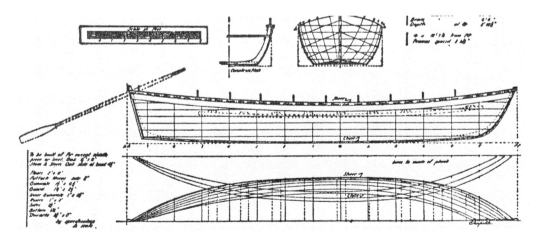

The bateau was the workhorse of eighteenth-century armies in North America. Carrying men and supplies, bateaux ranged from 25 to 38 feet in length and were usually rowed, but sails were often improvised. They were pointed at the bow and stern and construct-ed with flat bottoms of pine planks and oak frames. Line drawing by H. I. Chapelle from an Admiralty drawing. (Author's collection)

ered [to] them before they enter[ed] on actual duty," the men largely wore their own homespun clothes and carried their own personal muskets and hatchets (instead of bayonets).[39] Others purchased muskets with their bounty money and were later reimbursed; only recruits who could not procure a firearm were issued a musket. Even if bayonets were obtainable, the diversity in the size of muskets would have made it impossible to employ them. In late August Colonel Joseph Blanchard complained to the governor of New Hampshire that many soldiers, who had received money for blankets, arrived without them and needed clothes, axes, and hatchets.

William Johnson had only limited military experience in the militia and in organizing Mohawk raids during King George's War. He had no formal military training, as was the case with his second in command, 39-year-old Major General Phineas Lyman, a well-known lawyer and politician from Suffield, Connecticut. Under pressure from the governor of Connecticut, William Shirley had appointed Lyman without consulting Johnson. Captain William Eyre, an engineer of the 44th Regiment of Foot, was the only British regular officer on the expedition. Eyre served not only as the engineer on the Crown Point expedition, but also as the quartermaster general and chief of artillery. Eyre had accompanied Braddock to America and was fortunate to have been assigned to Johnson's campaign, inasmuch as two thirds of Braddock's officers became casualties at the disastrous July 9 battle in Pennsylvania.

On the hot afternoon of July 14, Governor Shirley, who was enroute to Oswego, and William Johnson reviewed a muster of the Crown Point army at two locations—the "German Flats" and Greenbush, on the east side of the Hudson River. By then, preparations for the move north were nearly complete. In early July James Hill, a 20-year-old private from Newbury, Massachusetts, who had been drafted into Colonel Ephraim Williams' regiment to caulk bateaux, noted that he and two others had "finished…one h[u]ndred and 30 boats" and 100 more were completed July 13.[40] On July 17 Johnson issued formal instructions to Major General Lyman to "pr[o]ceed…to the house of Col. [John Henry] Lydius near the Carrying Place [present-day Fort Edward] where you are to erect Log Magazines" and from the "flats" at Albany to the Carrying Place "open the road twenty to thirty feet wide…trees, logs & all obstructions cleared away, the stumps trim[m]ed close."[41]

THE EXPEDITION BEGINS

With 1,200-1,500 troops from Connecticut and Massachusetts, Lyman departed on July 22. The men struggled with the heavily-laden bateaux in passing falls and rapids, often unloading supplies to lighten the weight of the vessels. From July 25th to the 28th, the men were at Stillwater "employed in clearing the road for ye Wagons to come with our stores," according to Captain Elisha Hawley of Northampton, Massachusetts.[42] The task of moving forward was not helped by the news of Braddock's defeat, which filtered through the army in late July. Reaching Saratoga on July 29, Lyman's troops organized their camp, and for the next two days detachments of men were sent forward to clear a road to the north. On July 31 John Burk of Fall Town (near Greenfield), Massachusetts, noted that "our men went out to [the] Saratoga Fort and dug out of the earth 1114 cannon ball[s]."[43] (The fort at Saratoga, only a mile from Lyman's base camp, had been burned in 1747 by order of Governor George Clinton because of staffing problems and repeated

French assaults.) The following day, Lyman's troops moved only about four miles: "We drew the bateaux [180-200 vessels] up the first falls, load and all; it was fatiguing, but the men worked like lions, some [up] to the[ir] neck[s] in water," Burk remarked.[44] With the aid of 30 "Dutch wagons," the first division of the Crown Point army arrived at the Carrying Place (the former site of Fort Nicholson) on August 3. The "Dutch wagons" were large four-wheel Conestoga-type wagons with fabric tops, generally used to carry heavy freight. A newspaper reported that 150 of the "most substantial inhabitants of Albany, with their Slaves and Battoes, and 30 Wagons, voluntarily without Pay or Promise, went to the assistance of their Neighbors of Connecticut, as far as the Carrying-Place."[45]

At the Carrying Place Major General Phineas Lyman's men immediately began construction of a fortified camp. Four days after his arrival, Captain Elisha Hawley recorded "get[t]ing timber & bark for a store & fort"; framing of the structures continued for the next six days.[46] Captain John Burk added that the troops "set up 15 foot stockades" on August 10.[47] Three days later Captain Richard Godfrey from Taunton, Massachusetts, described a "fort house…One Hundred foot one Way, 18 foot the other and near Half an Acre Picketed in And another Guard House 30 foot one way, 14 ye other."[48] On the same day Lieutenant Colonel Seth Pomeroy noted somewhat different dimensions for the store-house: "70 foot one way & 40 ye other," but the same measurement for the two-story guardhouse with "port holes to fire out."[49]

The main mission to proceed north was not neglected—scouting parties were dispatched and Major General Lyman issued orders on August 12 for "a road to be cleared to Wood Cr[ee]k" by 300 men.[50] On August 14 Major General Johnson finally reached the camp at the Carrying Place, accompanied by the rest of the New England troops and 30 Mohawk warriors. Two-thirds of the supplies and "20 cannon" had to be transported by wagon because there was "scarce water to swim a light loaded battoe."[51] The cannons had been borrowed from provincial forts and required the construction of field carriages. Lieutenant Colonel Nathan Whiting from Connecticut noted that the large artillery had to be "drawn all the way by Land on their own Carriages…a very heavy fatiguing piece of Work."[52]

The Mohawks, their "faces painted with all colors" and wearing nose rings, appeared "odious" to many of the young volunteers like James Gilbert.[53] Anticipating the uneasiness of the provincial sol-

"Iroquois Warrior"
by Jacques Grasset de Saint-Sauveur.
(National Archives of Canada)

diers with the Mohawks, Johnson had instructed his officers to use the "utmost Care & Caution" to prevent firing on his Indian allies: "should any of them be killed or wounded the consequences would be most fatal to the Service."[54] Johnson directed the Mohawks to wear red head bands and carry small red flags to distinguish them from the French Indians and to use the password "Warighajage w[h]ich is my Indian Name."[55] Despite Johnson's best efforts, he was able to enlist only about 250 Mohawks for the Crown Point campaign, and his request to the Canadian Caughnawagas via the Six Nations to remain neutral was turned down.

A source of discord in the provincial expeditionary force materialized at the camp at the Carrying Place (named Fort Lyman). On July 25 Phineas Lyman wrote to Johnson bemoaning "a number of women coming up with the [New] York forces and Rhod[e] Island which gives a great uneasiness to ye New England troops."[56] Female camp followers (wives, washerwomen, nurses, and prostitutes) were common to eighteenth-century armies, but the presence of prostitutes bothered Lyman, who felt that it would lead to "sacrificing all our character" and urged Johnson to send them back.[57] Johnson had a more liberal view of the women camp followers, but Lyman's letter compelled him to embrace a high moral stance. Two days later Johnson answered the letter, suggesting that he would discourage any "bad women" in the camps and "suppress" any "immoralities"; "I hope we shall not soil the Justice of our cause with a conduct rebellious against that Almighty Power."[58] However, if the "men's wives...behave decently," Johnson thought that they should be tolerated, for they were "necessary to Wash & mend."[59] Johnson never ordered the women back, and three weeks later on August 18 Lyman won approval of a motion at a council of war "that all the Women in the camp should be removed...& forbid[den] to return."[60] On August 23 Captain John Burk wrote in his diary that "the women were sent to Albany. When they went off there was a great huzza [cheer]."[61]

Progress on the expedition to Crown Point continued slowly during the latter part of August. At a council of war on August 22, nineteen officers voted unanimously to cut a new road to Lake St. Sacrement, despite troops having already "cleared eight miles" on a route to Wood Creek, which connected to Lake Champlain.[62] The change from the original Wood Creek road occurred for a number of reasons: low water in the creek, the insect-infested swampy terrain, and the fact that the creek was still partially choked with trees that the French had felled in 1746 during King George's War. The council had also entertained the possibility of other routes. On August 18 the council had voted to "cut a Road to South Bay," but Captain Nathan Payson of Hartford, Connecticut, scouted the potential route, reporting on August 21 that it was too "mountainous So not...best [for] Cannon or wagons." [63]

On the morning of August 23, the council endorsed Johnson's request for "speedy and sufficient reinforcement," in response to a report that "6000" French troops were being deployed to Crown Point.[64] The next day Johnson wrote to Lieutenant Governor James DeLancey with the news that a new road would be cut to Lake St. Sacrement and of his plans to "build Magazines and raise a defensible Fortification" at the lake.[65] The fort needed to be built, according to Johnson, as a place to await reinforcements before launching the attack on Crown Point or as a safe retreat in the event that the French forces at Crown Point proved too strong. This plan, however, conflicted with Shirley's earlier recommendation. Following the news of Braddock's defeat, on July 26 Shirley had instruct-

The trading house of John Henry Lydius at the Carrying Place. From *The Papers of Sir William Johnson*, Volume 2.

ed Johnson to "Retreat with the Army to the City of Albany" in the event of "Difficulties...from a Superior Force of the Enemy" in the attack on Fort St. Frédéric.[66]

Work on a fort at the Carrying Place continued after Johnson's arrival on August 14. At the council of war on August 18, officers approved plans to erect a fort "near the Spot where Lydius's Trading House now stands," and six days later Johnson informed Thomas Pownall, brother of the Secretary to the Board of Trade in London, that Captain William Eyre had "laid out a. . .fortification here round Lydius's Log House," but that most of the officers felt it was too large and "cannot be finished before we go."[67] On August 24 James Hill reported "cut[t]in[g] timber for the mag[a]z[i]ne and John Burk noted that 120 men had dug trenches for the fort.[68] In early September Eyre described the fort as a "Square with three Bastions, & takes in Col. Lydius's House...palisaded quite round," but he suggested that he did not have enough time to build "the Rampart and Parapet of a sufficient height and thickness, to stand cannon or the Ditch wide and deep enough."[69] The fort retained the name Fort Lyman until William Johnson renamed the outpost Fort Edward on September 21, "in honour to Prince Edward," grandson of King George II.[70]

On August 26 at four o'clock in the afternoon, "6 or Eight Cannon Fired" a salute at Fort Lyman, signaling the departure of Johnson and 1,500 troops on their trek to Lake St. Sacrement.[71] The expeditionary force "had about 150 wagons...and 5 field pieces," according to Captain Elisha Hawley, but due to the late start the troops advanced only four miles on the first day.[72] The pace was rather relaxed the next day: after four or five miles, Johnson and his officers stopped for "ham, bak[ing] bread & cheese, dr[an]k some fresh lemon punch & ye best of wine," Colonel Seth Pomeroy noted.[73] Finally, after 400 troops had cleared the last section of the crude road to the lake, Johnson's army arrived at Lake St. Sacrement at four o'clock in the afternoon on August 28.

4. Battle of Lake George 1755

THE ARRIVAL OF JOHNSON'S TROOPS at Lake St. Sacrement on August 28, 1755, represented the largest English army ever to reach the lake. The view must have been magnificent, with tall pines standing sentinel over the blue water of the unspoiled lake, but apprehension over the impending campaign probably dashed any thoughts of the beauty of the setting. Finding a virgin forest at Lake St. Sacrement, Johnson ordered the men to cut the trees at the southern end of the lake and sent the wagons back to Fort Lyman for additional supplies.

Upon entering the Lake St. Sacrement camp on August 30, King Hendrick and 160 to 170 warriors fired their muskets into the air and were in turn "saluted with a round of guns" by Johnson's troops.[1] Following a cannon salute, Hendrick addressed his Mohawk followers. James Gilbert, with a Massachusetts regiment, observed that "their king is a man of Great el[o]quency," who urged his warriors "to be faithful and true."[2] A few days later Hendrick spoke to Johnson and a number of his officers concerning a "great uneasiness and confusion" caused by Governor William Shirley's comments about Johnson and the governor's attempt to recruit Iroquois for the Oswego campaign. Hendrick assured Johnson that the Mohawks at the lake would "remain steadfast to you," but "had it not been for Governor Shirley's money and speeches, you would have seen all the Six Nations here."[3]

By September 1, after two months of preparation, the provincial troops were disgruntled and restless. In the "morning about 50 men deserted because they were refused their back allowance of rum," Captain Elisha Hawley recorded.[4] Men from Captain John Jones' company of Bellingham, Massachusetts, deserted and walked four or five miles before a 30-man detachment sent after them from Johnson's camp was able to persuade them to return to the lake. Episodes of desertion and mutiny were dealt with more leniently in the provincial army compared to the British army. Before departing from Fort Lyman, Lieutenant Esa Noble, who had been found guilty of "supporting and exciting a Mutinous Disposition," served his sentence by making "a public and audible acknowledgement of his Crime with promises of future good Behavior at the Head of Each Reg[iment] in Camp."[5]

Other problems plagued the camp at the lake. Despite strict orders from Johnson against selling rum to the Mohawks, "Rum was constantly and plentifully sold to the

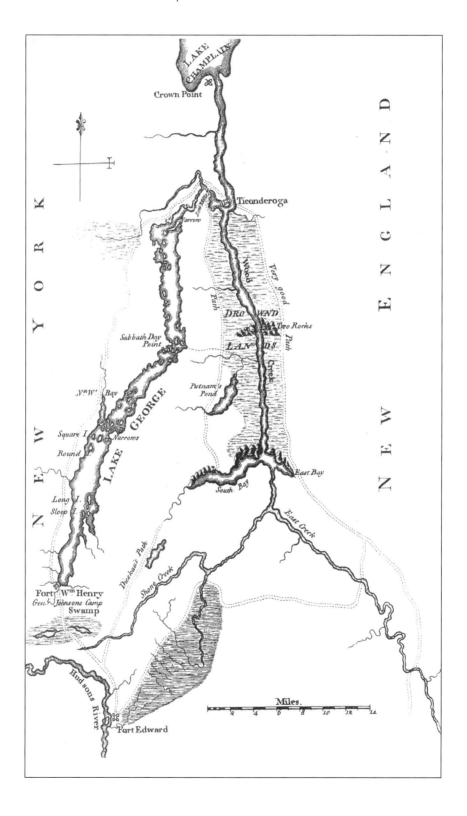

Indians who were in great numbers daily made Drunk."[6] Members of Johnson's council of war agreed to do everything in their power to stop the practice. Johnson also had trouble with the wagon drivers; many had deserted and others "threw the Shot [cannon-balls]…into the Woods, they have plundered the Provisions…in short they are a set of great Rascals."[7] Earlier, Christopher Champline, in charge of a number of wagons, wrote that the drivers were paid "a large sum" and demanded some of the money before starting and cash as soon as they had finished.[8] Johnson also had to contend with troops at the lake who were apprehensive after hearing reports on August 30 that five men had been attacked by Indians while guarding cattle at Fort Lyman—"one man killed, 1 taken, 3 escaped."[9] Two days later, the camp was startled by a nighttime alert, but the warning proved to be a false alarm caused by "a sentry [who] shot at a horse."[10]

On September 3 Johnson described his plans for the campaign in a letter to the Board of Trade in London. He proposed to "go down the Lake with part of the Army and take [a] post…at a pass called Ti[c]onderog[a]…there wait the coming up of the rest of the Army & then attack Crown Point."[11] In the same letter he informed the powerful Board that he had changed the name of Lake St. Sacrement to "Lake George, not only in honor to His Majesty but to ascertain his undoubted Dominion here."[12] To that end, Johnson's provincial soldiers were directed to build a fort and artillery scows. On September 4 James Gilbert noted that troops "Began to Clear the Place to [e]rect a fort," and the next day Private James Hill recorded "Laid out the fort."[13] On September 6 Hill wrote that he had gone to cut timber for "Fla[t]bo[a]ts…about 40 f[ee]t long, and to ro[w] With 20 oars to car[ry] the artiller[y]."[14]

On September 5, as the camp prepared for the expedition north, scouts were dispatched to discover any movement of the French forces. Previously, Johnson and his officers had been informed that the roads to St. Jean were clogged with provision wagons and "the Brig and another Vessel are making [a] constant return to & from Crown Point."[15] French officials had committed a sizable force to North America in 1755. However, on June 18 off Newfoundland, a squadron of British naval vessels, under the command of Admiral Edward Boscawen, nearly destroyed a French convoy carrying troops to Canada. Boscawen captured two French warships, but most of the French vessels disappeared in the North Atlantic fog and delivered six battalions of regulars to New France. The total French force in Canada at this time has been estimated at 20,443 men.[16] The French army consisted of the militia of New France (all males between 16-60 were obligated to serve), regular troops (including the regiments of Languedoc, La Reine, Bern, and Guyenne), Troupes de la Marine or Troops of the Colony (men recruited in France and organized into independent companies in Canada), and New France's Native American allies. The command of the French army in North America was assigned to 54-year-old Major General Jean-Armand Dieskau (Baron de Dieskau), who was born in the German duchy of Saxony and served under the renowned Maréchal de Saxe in Europe. Dieskau's formal instructions from Louis XV, the king of France, stated that his commission was "subordinate" to the governor-general of New France, Pierre de Rigaud de Vaudreuil de Cavagnial, and was "bound to obey the orders and instructions" given by the governor-general. Upon

Facing page: **Map of Lake George and the southern section of Lake Champlain, engraving by John Lodge. From** *The History of the Late War in North-America* **by Thomas Mante (1772).**

arriving in Quebec City in late June 1755, Dieskau met with Vaudreuil and began preparations for a campaign to defend Fort Niagara, but as inflated reports of the size of Johnson's army emerged and news of Shirley's floundering campaign reached Canada, Vaudreuil redirected Dieskau and his army to defend Fort St. Frédéric. Troops from the La Reine and Languedoc regiments were recalled before reaching Fort Frontenac (Kingston, Ontario) and dispatched to Fort St. Frédéric. By the middle of August Dieskau had examined Braddock's papers that had been discovered on the Mononga-hela battlefield, detailing Johnson's plan to capture Fort St. Frédéric. Accompanied by a large contingent of the army, Dieskau arrived at Fort St. Frédéric on August 16.[17] After all the troops arrived at Crown Point, Dieskau's total force numbered more than 3,000 men, including 774 regulars, 1,585 Canadian militia and Troupes de la Marine, 67 artillery-men, and 659 Indians.[18] (Governor Vaudreuil estimated Dieskau's force, including the garrison at Fort St. Frédéric as 3,573 men.[19]) By

Pierre de Rigaud de Vaudreuil de Cavagnial (1698-1778), governor-general of New France from 1755 to 1760. (Library of Congress)

the middle of August French authorities were aware "that three thousand English are coming from Orange [Albany] to besiege Fort St. Frédéric."[20] For two weeks Dieskau languished at Crown Point awaiting clear intelligence on Johnson's army. He later blamed the delay on his Native American allies: "I encountered nothing but difficulties from the Indians…Never was I able to obtain from them a faithful scout."[21] Finally, on August 27, Dieskau received information from a Canadian scout that "3,000 English were encamped at L[y]dius house, where they were constructing a fort."[22] A few days later, Dieskau moved his entire force, except for 400 men left to garrison Fort St. Frédéric, to Ticondero-ga, known to the French as Carillon.* Just before reaching Ticonderoga, an Abenaki returned to Dieskau's army with an English provincial prisoner, who had been captured near Fort Lyman. Whether Dieskau's translator misinterpreted the prisoner's information or the captive deliberately misled the French is the subject of some conjecture.[24] The official French "Journal of the Operations of the Army" recorded that the prisoner was threatened with "the most cruel death" at the hands of the Indians unless he divulged information about the English army.[25] He did so, but "deceived M. de Dieskau and assured him that there remained but 500 men at the fort [Fort Lyman] and that the remainder had

---

* The name Carillon, a French word for chime, was associated with the Ticonderoga peninsula and is believed to be derived from the cascade of water from the La Chute River. The word may also have been derived from the name of a seventeenth-century lieutenant in the French Carignan-Salières Regiment, Philippe de Carrion du Fresnoy, who had passed through Ticonderoga in 1666. He later built a log shed there for use in the illegal fur trade between Albany and New France. In 1756 Major General William Johnson's dispatches to England included an explanation of the Indian word "Ticonderoge signifying ye Confluse of Two Rivers."[23]

returned to Orange [Albany]."[26] In a letter written on September 14, Dieskau verified part of the above version: "only 500 remained there [Fort Lyman] to finish the fort," but he noted that 2,400 men were expected to march to Lake St. Sacrement to build a fort.[27] Dieskau decided on a swift surprise attack on Fort Lyman and selected 220 regulars from the La Reine and Languedoc regiments, 680 Canadians, and 600 Indians for the expedition.[28] He left a large force at Carillon to guard against any English advance and another contingent as a reserve at "Two Rocks."* Dieskau's decision to divide his force violated Vaudreuil's instructions of August 15 to "march against them with the entire...army without dividing his forces."[30] Although Dieskau's plan to use a flying column was based on information from the English prisoner, he may also have been influenced by two Canadian officers, Michel-Jean-Hugues Péan and François-Marc-Antoine Le Mercier, who assured him "of the advantage that the Canadians and Indians had over the English," especially because Johnson's army was entirely composed of militia.[31] Traveling in bateaux and canoes, Dieskau's army reached the "Great Bay [South Bay]" on September 5 and marched overland toward Fort Lyman, leaving 100-120 men to guard the vessels at the bay after listening to concerns from his Indian allies.[32] The French force "encamped beyond the mountains [French Mountain]" on the sixth and, following a mass on Sunday morning (September 7), proceeded closer to Fort Lyman, camping at sunset near "the banks of the Hudson River" several miles north of the fort.[33]

In the meanwhile at the English camp at Lake George on September 7, a council of war, composed of eight officers, approved the construction of a small "picketed Fort [to] be built without delay under the direction of Colonel [Ephraim] Williams, suff[icient] to contain and accommodate 100 men."[34] Johnson was not satisfied with the decision, complaining a week and a half later that the "Obstinacy and Ignorance of those officers...has prevented a Strong Fort being erected here."[35] At four o'clock on the afternoon of September 7, three Mohawk scouts returned to the Lake George camp with a report that a French and Indian party had been near South Bay. The Mohawk scouts had "found three large Roads made by a great Body of Men...marching toward the Carrying Place."[36] After a second council of war, the camp was placed on alert and messengers dispatched to warn Colonel Joseph Blanchard, in command of Fort Lyman with several hundred New Hampshire troops and five companies of New York militiamen. Jacob Adams, a New York wagon driver, volunteered to deliver instructions to Blanchard. Mounting one of Johnson's horses, Adams galloped toward Fort Lyman but within several miles of the fort "found himself in the Midst of the French Army."[37] Adams attempted to force his way through but was "fired at, knocked off the horse & the Dispatches found."[38] A half hour after Adams' departure, two Mohawks and two soldiers were sent on foot to Fort Lyman with a duplicate message. About midnight they returned with a wagon driver who had deserted the Lake George camp earlier in the day along with "80 others [with] their Wagons and horses."[39] The wagoner had "heard a Gun fire, and a man call upon Heaven for Mercy," who he believed was Jacob Adams.[40] The Indians with Dieskau captured 11 wagons on the military road, but all except three of the deserting teamsters escaped, probably by swimming across the Hudson River.[41] Johnson did not dispatch another messenger.

* On October 25, 1755, Governor Vaudreuil wrote that Dieskau had left troops at Carillon and at the "Two Rocks." "Two Rocks" was shown on French and Indian War maps and later identified as the two high cliffs on each side of Lake Champlain at the "Narrows of Dresden [N.Y.]."[29]

Early the next morning Colonel Blanchard sent out several scouting parties; one party of seven men under Lieutenant Jeremiah Gilman returned at about ten o'clock to report that they had discovered "one m[a]n [Adams] killed and scalped, a horse dead and several wagons on fire" and signs of a large army.[42] Another party under Robert Rogers scouted the west bank of the upper Hudson River.

Dieskau continued with his plans to attack Fort Lyman, but when the colonial liaison officer with the Indians, Jacques Legardeur de Saint-Pierre, apprised the Native Americans of Dieskau's intentions, the Caughnawaga Iroquois "refused point blank to march to attack the fort" and purposefully "caused a wrong direction to be taken" in the march toward the fort.[43] Dieskau later told Johnson that the Indians feared "it was defended by Cannon" but were willing to attack the English camp at the lake.[44] The Caughnawagas were the most resolute in their refusal, while the Abenakis, Algonquins, and Nipissings were receptive to Dieskau's plans. The Caughnawaga chiefs "were resolved not to act against the English on territory [Fort Lyman] rightfully belonging to them," but they would participate in an attack at the lake "as the camp of the English was on our territory" and "surrounded with Woods and still exposed and without lines."[45] At daybreak on Monday, September 8, Dieskau's army began marching north on the new English military road in three columns—the Canadian militia on the right, Native Americans on the left, and the French regulars in the middle. After a short time, Dieskau learned from an English prisoner that Johnson had sent 1,000 men from his camp to reinforce Fort Lyman. The French general ordered the Canadians and Indians to "lie flat on the ground [on the sides of the road]…and not make the slightest noise nor discharge a single gun" until the regulars fired.[46] The French regulars were to be stationed at the end of the two lines of Canadians and Indians, forming a "cul de sac" or hook, trapping the English detachment.[47]

FIRST ENGAGEMENT

Earlier, on the same morning of September 8, Johnson had called a council of war and the decision was made to detach 1,000 men and "upwards of 200 Indians" under the command of Colonel Ephraim Williams to prevent an attack on Fort Lyman or "to catch the enemy in their retreat" from the fort.[48] According to Captain Elisha Hawley, the original plan involved sending 500 troops to "Intercept [th]em in their retreat, or find their canoes in the drowned Land."[49] A second "Body of 500 men were to March to the relief" of Fort Lyman, Daniel Claus, Johnson's chief interpreter, later noted.[50] Claus also revealed that King Hendrick objected to this plan. Joseph Burt, an eyewitness, decades later told Timothy Dwight, president of Yale College, that Hendrick, whom he described as "corpulent" and 60 to 65 years old with "white locks," had grasped three sticks—"Put these together," Hendrick argued "and you can't break them. Take them one by one; and you will break them easily."[51] Apparently Hendrick convinced Johnson and his officers; all of the 1,000 troops and Mohawks marched together toward Fort Lyman. Dwight also spoke with Seth Pomeroy, who had witnessed Hendrick's harangue to the Mohawks just before they departed on the fateful march of September 8. Although he didn't understand the

Facing page: **Ambush of provincial troops under Colonel Ephraim Williams and Mohawks led by King Hendrick on September 8, 1755. From "A Prospective-Plan of the Battle near Lake George" by Samuel Blodget. (American Antiquarian Society)**

FIRST ENGAGEMENT
1 The Road, 2 French & Indians,
3 Hendrick on Horseback, 4 Provincials,
5 Mohawks.

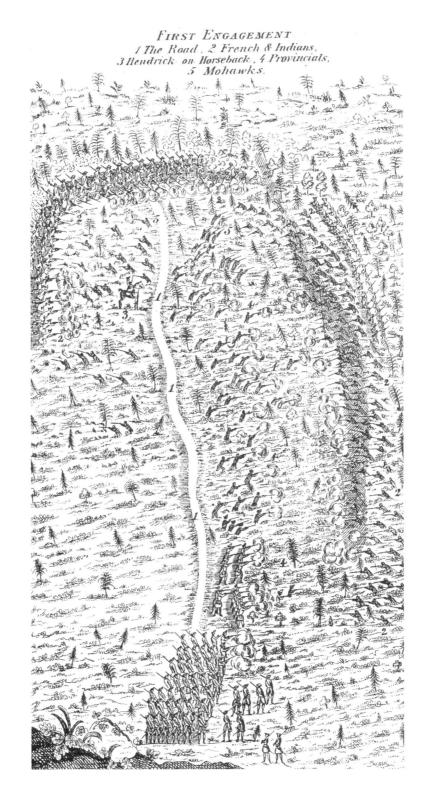

Mohawk language, Pomeroy remarked that he was "more deeply affected with the speech than any other, which he had ever heard…the animation of Hendrick, the fire of his eye, the force of his gesture, the strength of his emphasis."[52]

On September 8 Williams' detachment, consisting of troops from the Third Massachusetts and Second Connecticut regiments, marched "cheerfully" from the Lake George camp between eight and nine o'clock in the morning.[53] King Hendrick, mounted on one of Johnson's horses, led 180-200 of his Mohawk warriors. The detachment traveled two or three miles before sitting down "to Refresh Themselves" and allow time for Lieutenant Colonel Nathan Whiting's Connecticut troops to reach Williams' detachment.[54] The provincial troops then resumed the march in a column "five or Six deep [across]" and the Moh[aw]ks marched in a Single file Before Them."[55] Despite knowledge of Braddock's recent ambush, Williams did not send scouts ahead or deploy flankers, but apparently relied on Hendrick's Mohawks. Although one participant, interviewed years later, mentioned that flankers were "thrown out on the right and left" while the Massachusetts troops waited for Whiting's contingent, there seems to be no corroborating evidence for this.[56] Shortly after the battle, Peter Wraxall, Johnson's secretary, wrote that the Williams' detachment was "surprised, by neglecting to have advance & flank Guards" and surgeon's mate Perez Marsh was confounded that Williams had "no [advance] scouts" because he previously had spoken of "the danger of marching without [them]."[57]

The provincial detachment and Mohawks marched forward along the military road straight into the trap set by Dieskau and his men.* Samuel Blodget, a sutler at the Lake George camp, wrote an account of the first engagement based on information from the surviving participants. "On the Left of the Road [east side]," Blodget noted that the Canadian troops and Indians were "covered with a thick growth of Brush and Trees…on the Right [west] a continu[ous] Eminence filled with Rocks, and Trees, and Shrubs as high as a Man's Breast" helped conceal the assailants.[60] Daniel Claus, who was at the Lake George camp with Johnson, later wrote that the Mohawks in the lead "were challenged in ye Iroquois Tongue [by the Canadian Caughnawagas as to] who they were; upon which Hen[d]r[ick] replied, we are the six confederate Ind[ia]n Nations."[61] The French Indians answered that they were the "7 confederate Ind[ia]n Nations of Canada" and did not intend to "quarrel or trespass against any Ind[ia]n Nation," and urged Hendrick "to keep out of the way" to avert a "War among ourselves."[62] There are several accounts as to who fired the first shot. Claus maintained that it was one of Hendrick's young warriors.[63] Writing a week and a half later, Thomas Pownall, a political ally of James DeLancey and Johnson, stated that "Old Hendrick declared for War and fired the first shot."[64] Dieskau later insisted that the Canadian "Iroquois rose and fired in the air as a warning [to the Mohawks] that there was an ambuscade."[65] Johnson, on the other hand, suggested that "one of the enemy's Muskets by accident went off which alarmed our People."[66] Reports of the time of the first engagement also vary in the original writings of the men at the Lake George camp. Phineas Lyman wrote that the fighting occurred "from before nine o'clock till about half after ten," while Seth Pomeroy mentioned that the engagement occurred

* The exact location of the site is somewhat uncertain. Timothy Dwight, who interviewed some participants and examined the region's historic sites in 1802, suggested that the first engagement was at Rocky Brook.[58] A modern study of the military road concluded that a 20-foot rock cut, made for a nineteenth-century rail line, might be the site of the first battle.[59]

between ten and eleven o'clock.[67] Another participant at the Lake George camp "took out his watch" when the fire began and "penciled the time" as five minutes to eleven and the retreat was not completed until twelve thirty.[68]

At the front of the column the Mohawks and Massachusetts troops experienced the most devastating fire and suffered the most casualties. Ephraim Williams attempted to lead an attack against the enemy position along the hill on the west side, but a thunderous explosion of musket fire from the Canadians and Indians laid great numbers of the English provincials on the ground, including Williams himself.* The troops in the lead, who were nearly all enveloped in the French trap, "fought bravely," but the rearmost troops "fled" and others continued to fight while "retreating a little & then ris[ing] and giv[ing] them a brisk Fire."[71] Hendrick, dressed in a long English coat and a cocked hat, was too old and heavy to dismount and fight. He attempted to retreat back to the Lake George camp, but the "horse was shot [from] under him, and he being unw[i]eldy and not able to disengage himself and get away was stabbed with a Bayonet."[72] Claus noted that Hendrick encountered a group of Canadian Indians, a "Baggage G[u]ard of young Lads and women, who having no fire Arms, sta[bbe]d him in the Back with a Spear or Bayonet" and scalped the old sachem.[73] The French also suffered a loss of one of their leaders during the first engagement of the Battle of Lake George—Jacques Legardeur de Saint-Pierre, the liaison officer to the Canadian Indians who had earlier served on the Ohio expedition.

While the battle raged, the intense firing could be heard at both the Lake George camp and at Fort Lyman. Daniel Emerson, a chaplain at Fort Lyman, "heard great Volleys of small Arms."[74] After listening to "heavy firing" to the south and as the musketry drew closer, Johnson surmised that a retreat was in progress and "detached Colonel [Edward] Cole with 300 men to cover their retreat."[75] With the death of Williams, Lieutenant Colonel Nathan Whiting of New Haven, Connecticut, commanded the retreating troops, many of whom were struck by "Panic…and the whole fled in a disorderly Manner toward the Camp" at Lake George.[76] With the support of Cole's reinforcements, Whiting's survivors made one "Last Fire" about three quarters of a mile from Lake George, "which kill'd gr[e]at numbers of them se[e]n to Drop as Pig[e]ons."[77] One account of the action, published in Boston several weeks later, marveled that the provincial army could "make so good a retreat; annoying the enemy all the while," but surgeon's mate Perez Marsh, who had married the daughter of Colonel Israel Williams, severely criticized Whiting for ordering a retreat "upon the first fire of the enemy," leaving friends to be killed.[78]

* With a feeling of foreboding over the impending campaign, 41-year-old Ephraim Williams had signed his will in Albany on July 22, 1755, bequeathing much of his estate to family members, but specifying that the remaining lands were to be sold and "appropriated toward the support and maintenance of a free school" in a township west of Fort Massachusetts (named Williamstown in 1765).[69] Thirty-six years later the "free-school," opened, and in 1793 the Massachusetts General Court incorporated the institution as Williams College. On the day of the battle, the body of Ephraim Williams was hidden by John Morse and a fellow soldier to prevent scalping by the Indians. On September 9, 1755, Williams was buried by the side of the military road at the foot of a large pine tree. (The site is marked by a large irregular stone on the west side of Route 9N.) During the 1830s Dr. William H. Williams, a grand nephew, removed the skull from the gravesite and brought it to Raleigh, North Carolina. Williams' remains were reinterred at the Williamstown Thompson Memorial Chapel in 1920. In 1854 Williams College alumni erected a marble obelisk on a large boulder to mark the location where Colonel Williams had been killed (east side of Route 9N), and in 2005 a replacement obelisk and new parking area were dedicated on the two-acre memorial plot owned by Williams College.[70]

During the time of the first engagement, Johnson and his men hastily constructed a rudimentary breastwork at the Lake George camp. Claus reported that the breastwork "consisted of some Trees cut down in a hurry at the front of the Camp in some places not above a foot and a half high and which wagons were the principal Shelter."[79] Viewed from a distance, French eyewitnesses described an "entrenchment" comprised "of bateaux turned upside down and of wagons."[80] (Although original sources mention bateaux and wagons as part of the barricade, Samuel Blodget, an eyewitness, did not show either in his drawing of the engagement.) Johnson recounted that his troops "hauled some heavy cannon" to the breastwork and "took possession of some eminences on our left flank, and got one field-piece there in a very advantageous situation."[81] Three large cannons were placed on the southern side of the breastwork facing the military road to Fort Lyman, two mortars faced the swampy area on the west side (today's West Brook), and several cannons were positioned on the lake side—three faced the lake, two faced east, and two pointed west.[82] Captain William Eyre, commander of the artillery, would effectively utilize the cannons to hold back the oncoming French force.

SECOND ENGAGEMENT

Pursued by Dieskau's army, "our people r[a]n into camp with all the Marks of Horror and fear in their Countenances, exag[g]erating the Number of the Enemy," Peter Wraxall recounted, adding that "this infected the Troops in Camp."[83] In a letter to his wife three days after the battle, Major General Phineas Lyman recalled that as the French drew closer, "their arms glistened like the sun, with their bayonets fixed."[84] The survivors of the first engagement "press[ed] right through our men [at the breastwork] and our men began to run after them."[85] The provincial troops were "dejected, tired and choked almost to death with thirst," but Lyman ordered them to the breastwork, warning one soldier that if he did not return to the front he "would kill him in one minute," and repeated the threat to a group of solders a few moments later.[86] According to Lyman, all the soldiers returned to the line. Wraxall noted that Johnson "harangued and did all in his Power to animate our People" and Perez Marsh reported that the men "fough[t] well" after Johnson and other officers "drew their swords and declar'd they would run em thro[ough]."[87] Wraxall rode along the line, promising "a cheap Victory if they behaved with Spirit," and initiated "a huzza which took & they planted themselves at the Breastwork just as the enemy appeared in sight."[88] However, Wraxall also reported that "Great Numbers of our Men hid themselves during the Engagement, and many pretended Sickness."[89] Dieskau planned to rush the Lake George camp on the heels of the retreating English provincials in the midst of the confusion, but upon hearing the "roar of the cannon" at the breastwork his Indian allies "stopped short" until he promised that the regulars would draw the cannon fire.[90] The delay compromised the opportunity to overwhelm Johnson's army before it was fully prepared for the attack. Claus maintained that the delay was due to the reluctance of the Canadian Indians, who "were not for a second attack," because they did not expect to fight the large number of warriors from the Six Nations and wished to return home with the trophies of war from the first engagement.[91]

Marching forward six-abreast on the military road with their bayonets fixed, the reg-

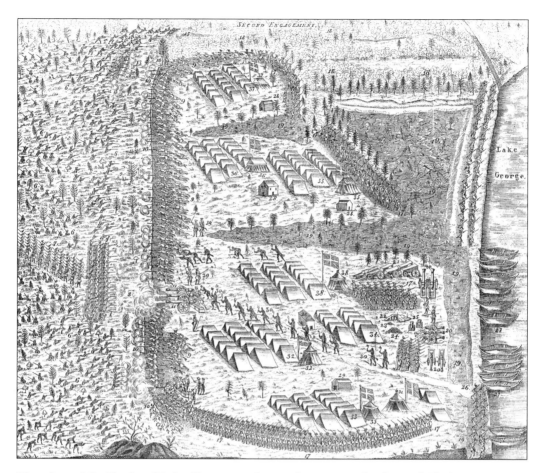

Drawing of the Battle of Lake George on September 8, 1755, by Samuel Blodget. As a sutler with the army, Blodget witnessed the battle and his "Prospective-Plan" was engraved and printed by Thomas Johnston in Boston in 1755. It was republished with slight modifications to the format by Thomas Jeffreys in London in 1756.
(American Antiquarian Society)

ulars under Dieskau stopped 140-150 yards from the breastwork about 11:30 and "made the grand and center attack. The Canadians and Indians squatted and dispersed on our flanks," Johnson wrote in his official report to the colonial governors.[92] The French regulars pressed "forward and made the first and strongest fire in Platoons on the Front, and after they had fired twice. . .took the cover of Trees and Logs."[93] One of Eyre's gunners, Peter Boyle, recalled two days later that the regulars were "much surprised with our Artillery which made Lanes, Streets and Alleys thro[ugh] their army."[94] Although French authorities later reported that the English cannons had little effect, Captain Richard Godfrey from Taunton, Massachusetts, noted that the "artillery played very Smart, and Did Good Execution, so they were immediately Stop[p]ed from Coming in upon our camp."[95] Hearing the cannon firing in the distance, Chaplain Daniel Emerson at Fort Lyman noted in his journal that his "heart trembled" as the men at the fort prepared a defense and prayed "to ye Lord."[96]

As the battle became more heated, the men were astounded by the intense noise of the cannons and muskets. "One continual clangor of cannon and small arms," Lyman remarked, while Seth Pomeroy noted a "most Violent Fire perhaps…Ever was heard of in this Country."[97] Surgeon Thomas Williams recounted the scene of the battle as "nothing but thunder and lightning and perpetual pillars of smoke," which was blown into their faces by a south wind.[98] He described the difficulty of dressing the wounded amid "bullets [that] flew like hail-stones about our ears" while "the bark of the trees and chips fl[ew] in our faces by accidental shots."[99] His tent was shot through in so many places that he retired to the shelter of a small log structure to treat the wounded. However, musket balls passed through the loosely-laid logs. Viewing the troops "shoot so fast, and some of them so carelessly," Major General Lyman worried that the French would "make us shoot till our guns were foul," and so he ran "from one end of the firing to the other," ordering the men "not to shoot unless they had a fair shot."[100]

Battle of Lake George, September 8, 1755. Painting by Frederick Coffay Yohn. From the 1905 Glens Falls Insurance Company calendar. (Author's collection)

To dislodge the Canadian Indians from a position behind a large wind-fallen tree lying a short distance from the southwest end of the breastwork, Colonel Moses Ticomb and Lieutenant Jonathan Barron, both from Chelmsford, Massachusetts, left the protection of the breastwork "to fire at the Enemy with greater Advantage" from behind a large tree.[101] The Indians outflanked the officers and cut them down. Johnson himself was struck in his thigh by a musket ball and retired from the breastwork to have the wound dressed. However, the time at which Johnson received the wound and whether he returned to the battle remain mired in controversy more than 250 years later. Writing to William Shirley two days after the battle, Captain William Eyre disclosed that "General Johnson was wounded soon after the Action began" while "encouraging the Troops" and giving orders to "sustain the Attack."[102] In a letter to his wife on September 11, Phineas Lyman noted that "Gen. Johnson was wounded near the beginning of the battle, and repaired to his tent at the other end of the encampment."[103] Publication of this letter would subsequently lead to an uproar and a rift between factions at the Lake George camp. A month and a half after the engagement, Lieutenant Colonel Edward Cole attacked Lyman's version of the battle, writing that Johnson "did not receive his Wound till about Two o'Clock in the Afternoon: And no sooner was he dressed, th[e]n immediately he again appeared among the Men, and gave the proper Orders in Person."[104] Cole based his account on information from the surgeon who dressed the wound, "Dr. Hunter," and Captain Peter Wraxall, Johnson's aide. At first Wraxall believed that "our Gen[era]ll [was] wounded in the hip, I found he grew stiff and I led him off to get him dressed," and Wraxall was later quoted in a newspaper as saying that Johnson "was wounded in the Hip, Yet kept the field, altho' in great pain."[105] Unfortunately, Wraxall's writings do not specifically corroborate Cole's version, neither regarding the time of the wound nor Johnson's return to the battle. However, Daniel Claus noted that late in the day "Genl. Johnson came in from the lines," but this occurred after Dieskau had been captured at the very end of the battle.[106] Johnson subsequently described his role in the battle to his brother Warren, who suggested that Johnson "did not keep in his Tent, but was very active," despite his wound. The ball was never removed from Johnson's thigh, and the injury plagued him for the rest of his life.[108] The "Constant fire from our Artillery and Troops" took its toll on the French and Indians, and as a result "the Enemy's fire on our Left [east side] grew very faint," and the enemy then moved to the west side of the encampment, Johnson wrote.[109] Captain Peter Boyle, a gunner under Eyre, noted that the "General perceiving danger, ordered me to throw some shells…32 pounders" on the right wing, which soon caused a retreat "in sad disorder."[110] (This report may also provide evidence that Johnson was still giving orders late in the battle.) Several mortar rounds were also fired "into the Swamp [present-day West Brook] on our right Wing, supposed to be full of Indians."[111]

While directing troops from a position between the Canadians and regulars "within 70 paces of [Johnson's] camp," Dieskau was struck in the leg by a musket ball.[112] His second in command, Pierre-André Gohin, Comte de Montreuil, who had received a musket ball in his own arm, washed Dieskau's leg wound with brandy, but the general was hit again by another ball "in the right knee and left hip."[113] Montreuil called two Canadians who were behind nearby trees to move Dieskau out of danger, but one rescuer was killed and collapsed on the general's legs. Dieskau then refused to be removed and instead ordered Montreuil to leave him and take command of the regulars for another assault on the English camp. But Montreuil discovered that a great number of Canadians and Indians had departed and he could not rally the regular troops for another attack, because "the enemy were masters of the field of battle."[114] Dieskau also refused help from his servants and had his vest and coat placed on the ground next to him. Finding Dieskau lying against a tree when the battle ended, an English provincial soldier lifted his musket and aimed at the wounded general, who frantically waved his "hand not to fire," but "the shot traversed both my hips."[115] The soldier, who had emigrated from Canada ten years earlier and spoke perfect French, demanded the surrender of Dieskau. The general vehemently rebuked the soldier for shooting him while he lay wounded and soaked in blood. The provincial soldier replied that he was uncertain whether the general had a pistol. Daniel Claus later suggested that Dieskau had attempted to present "the Hilt of his Sword" to surrender.[116] Before being carried to Johnson, Dieskau reported that English provincials had "stripped me" of possessions.[117] Lieutenant Colonel Seth Pomeroy recorded the capture of Dieskau's official French papers, including maps of Fort Lyman and the camp at Lake George, and noted that Dieskau and his troops "Came with full assurance [of] Lodg[ing] in our Tents that night which to his gr[e]at Surprise [he] Did [as a prisoner]."[118]

Unable to reinvigorate the French regulars for another attack, Montreuil simply tried "to stop the disorder as well as I was able," but "all the troops fell back" for a short time "in spite of all I could do."[119] A piecemeal retreat followed "without any order...Fortunately, the enemy did not follow."[120] Several journals kept by English provincial soldiers indicate that the engagement lasted until "after four o'clock."[121] Johnson's letter to the colonial governors stated that "about four o'clock...our men and Indians jumped over the breast-work, pursued the enemy, slaughtered numbers, and took several prisoners," and Lyman noted that the engagement continued "hot...till past five, when the enemy slackened and retreated; our men sprang over the breastwork, and followed them like lions," returning shortly with "guns, laced hats, cartridge boxes etc."[122] Apparently, the pursuit was limited to the immediate vicinity of the Lake George camp. Johnson's secretary, Captain Peter Wraxall, summarized the aftermath of the second engagement of the Battle of Lake George: "a Trial was made to pursue...However, I don't know but a Pursuit might have been dangerous," because of the lateness of the day, the uncertainty of the whereabouts of the French, the fatigue of the men, the lack of swords and bayonets, and because the troops were "undisciplined & not very high spirited."[123]

THIRD ENGAGEMENT

Following the battle at Lake George, the French and Indians retreated to the site of the first engagement to retrieve their packs and to scalp and plunder the corpses of the Williams detachment. After hearing the distant firing, a relief force from Fort Lyman, consisting of 143 New Hampshire militiamen under Captain Nathaniel Folsom of Exeter and 90 New York troops led by Captain William McGinnis of Schenectady, proceeded north. Nathaniel Folsom's account of the third engagement of the day, written over five months later, is the only detailed report by a participant that has come to light, but unfortunately it is marred by a confusing sequence of events and accusations against the New York troops. As the relief detachment proceeded to Lake George, Folsom determined that the New Yorkers, who were marching ahead, were too slow but decided against marching past them because one of his officers suggested that "he was more afraid of them than of the enemy."[124] The New York militiamen surprised a small number of Indian lookouts who were apparently guarding the French and Indian packs. The New Yorkers halted and Folsom's men finally bypassed them and aggressively pursued the Indians. "We made a loud huzza," Folsom recounted, and "follow[e]d them up a rising ground and then met a large body of French and Indians, on whom we discharg[e]d our guns briskly."[125]

Writing a week and a half after the battle, Thomas Pownall, a political ally of Johnson, noted that the troops from Fort Lyman "Advanced up the Hill and discovered a party of Canadians and Indians to the number of 300 sitting by a run of water in the Valley."[126] Johnson's letter to the governors on September 9 reported that the Canadians and Indians had "gone to scalp our people [who had been] killed in the morning," and Captain John Burk wrote on September 8 that the provincial troops from Fort Lyman had discovered the "enemy stripping our dead."[127] According to Folsom, the fight with the Canadians and Indians lasted three quarters of an hour before his troops retreated a "little way back," but the engagement was soon renewed and "fifteen or twenty of us ran up the hill at all hazard" into the vigorous fire of the enemy.[128] Folsom and his men "made huzzas as loud as we could," but they could not compare to the "yells of our enemies, which seem[e]d to be rather the yelling of devils than of men."[129] Governor Vaudreuil's brief account of the engagement suggested that the Canadians and Indians were ambushed on the military road and retreated. "Toward evening," according to Vaudreuil, "some of the Canadians and Indians had reached the place where they had left their knapsacks" and were ambushed again.[130]

Just before sunset, the New Yorkers decided to return to Fort Lyman and could not be dissuaded until Folsom warned that he "would order our New Hamp[shir]e men to discharge upon them."[131] The New Yorkers remained, and after sunset the detachment tried to frighten the Canadians and Indians by shouting, beating drums, and giving warning of imminent reinforcements, but their enemies were long gone. Among the French packs, Folsom discovered an animal tongue and a loaf of French bread. He raved about the meat and offered a portion to his lieutenant, who informed Folsom that he was eating a horse's tongue. Folsom and his New Hampshire troops joined the New Yorkers in drinking French brandy, "which reviv[e]d us all to th[e] degree that I imagin[e]d we fought better than ever…before."[132]

The time of the engagement and the length of the fight are subject to some variation in the original documents. Folsom stated that the engagement began "about four" in the afternoon and ended with daylight.[133] Other sources agree on the time of the beginning of the battle; Johnson wrote "between four and five o'clock," and James Gilbert observed that "a lit[t]le while" after the French and Indians had retreated from the lake "we heard a consid[er]able…firing which we heard in ye evening."[134] However, Johnson and others recorded that the length of the fight was between two and three hours, and Colonel Blanchard at Fort Lyman indicated that the relief detachment "fought till sun down."[135] Late at night the New York and New Hampshire troops marched to Lake George, using three wagon horses to carry six wounded men and a make-shift stretcher for another; six men were killed or mortally wounded in the engagement and another 14 survived their wounds. When they reached the lake "the whole army shouted for joy."[136] Captain William McGinnis, who had been shot in the head and brought into the camp on one of the horses, later succumbed to his wound. Captain Richard Godfrey noted that the detachment arrived laden "with Packs, as much as they Could Bring in the Evening with Shouting for the Victory and ye Spoil," and James Gilbert observed that "it Began to be Dark so They came up to Ye Camp" after the engagement.[137] Although Folsom had written that his troops began their march to the lake at "daylight," later in the same letter he mentioned that he "was obliged to turn in to Col[one]l Gutridge's tent [at Lake George] for refreshment…it being past midnight."[138]

AFTERMATH

The next day (September 9) Seth Pomeroy wrote in his journal of the "melanc[h]oly work of bur[y]ing our Dead" on a sunny "hot Day."[139] Pomeroy had to bury his younger brother, Lieutenant Daniel Pomeroy, who was among the dead in Ephraim Williams' regiment. On September 10 both Pomeroy and Captain Burk reported burying "136 dead of ours and some French."[140] The following day Wraxall listed casualties on the "Return" from the battle, noting 120 killed, 80 wounded, 62 missing, and 38 Mohawks killed and 12 wounded.[141] A modern detailed accounting of English casualties of the battle recorded 152 deaths and 42 men who died shortly thereafter from wounds or possible camp diseases.[142] Many of those listed as missing in the original accounts were later found dead. Prisoners taken by the French and Indians were slain and scalped: "We found the poor creatures t[i]ed to each other by threes and fours."[143] A large number of the wounded, including Captain Elisha Hawley, died of their injuries during the month after the battle. Devastating injuries were the result of large-diameter balls of soft lead fired at a relatively low velocity from smooth-bore muskets. The ball flattened on contact, severely tearing the flesh, splintering the bone, and drawing pieces of clothing and skin into a large wound. Amputation of limbs was common, especially in cases of compound fractures, damage to joints, abscesses, etc.[144] Some wounds were comparable to those sustained during more recent wars from more destructive weapons; one soldier at Lake George was "bro[ugh]t in alive with the back part of his s[k]ull cut off and his brains naked."[145] Men at the camp linked the high death rate of their wounded comrades to the French and Indians, who supposedly had used poison musket balls. Chaplain Samuel Chandler noted that some of the French musket balls "were cut and a Slip of Leather closed in the cut, Suspected to be a poison" and surgeon Thomas Williams wrote that the enemy balls were "rolled up with a solution of copper and yellow arsenic."[146] However, it is conceivable that pieces of leather were simply placed around the musket balls to create a tighter fit in the barrels of worn muskets.[147] Major General Lyman harassed Dieskau for several days after the battle with charges that his troops had fired poisoned musket balls, and he even "paraded [in front of Dieskau's tent] with two large Mus[ke]teer Cartridge Boxes slung across his Body and a French Musket on his Shoulder."[148] The *New-York Mercury* reported that balls extracted from wounds "appear[e]d surprisingly green," but Dieskau denied giving orders to use poison bullets, and suggested that if any had been fired, "they must have come from the Irregulars of Canada only."[149]

The French losses were considerably fewer than reported by the English provincial sources. In October French authorities reported that 67 regulars and Canadians, as well as 33 Indians had been killed or died of their wounds and that a total of 127 wounded men were still alive.[150] These figures may have counted as dead some of the 24 prisoners held by Johnson's army, "some of them badly wounded."[151] Two of the prisoners included the seriously-injured Dieskau and his aide, Lieutenant Benoit-François Bernier. Johnson showed kindness toward Dieskau and developed a respect for him during the nine days that the French general remained at the Lake George camp. Dieskau later wrote about a perilous first night in Johnson's tent when several Mohawks appeared demanding that Johnson hand him over "in order to burn [me] in revenge for the death of their comrades."[152] Although the Mohawks threatened to abandon Johnson if their wishes were not granted, Johnson assured Dieskau of his safety. Dieskau was moved late that night to another tent, escorted by a captain and 50 men. Nevertheless, one Mohawk attempted to stab him the next morning. On September 16 Johnson issued orders to have Dieskau, who still suffered from a dangerous bladder wound, moved to his home in Albany and arranged for "any Civilities" needed for "a Man of Quality, a Soldier and a Gentleman."[153] At Johnson's Albany house Dieskau was kindly attended to by his sister, Catherine Johnson Farrell, whose husband, Captain Matthew Farrell, had been killed at Lake George. On October 12 Dieskau wrote to William Johnson, expressing his "gratitude" for "all your kind favors" and also to Catherine for "her kind acts, to her care and to her attention."[154] Catherine was taken ill shortly thereafter and died. Dieskau was later transported aboard a sloop to New York City and sent to England on March 13, 1756, where he remained until he was repatriated to France in 1763. He died there four years later.

The collection and distribution of plunder from the dead French soldiers quickly evolved into a controversy. Captain Nathaniel Folsom subsequently complained that the Mohawks had "started very early" on September 9 to gather a "great quantity of packs [and] plunder" left in the vicinity of the first and third engagements.[155] Similarly, Private James Hill noted that the provincial troops and Mohawks "Went out to Pl[u]nder and Got a Great Deal, but the Moha[w]ks Got most of it."[156] However, Captain John Burk and Lieutenant Colonel Seth Pomeroy both reported that great quantities of "plunder and French provisions" were taken by the troops.[157] A September 12 account of the plunder being held by the surviving officers and men of Ephraim Williams' regiment included muskets, blankets, coats, hatchets, gun locks, knapsacks, knives, linen and leather breeches, Indian moccasins, a wampum belt, a cutlass, and a kettle.[158] Although an "equal dividend" of the plunder had been promised, on October 14 Colonel William Cockcraft complained on behalf of his New York regiment that "no Dividend has been Made Either of Plunder or Money."[159] A committee was established by a council of war on October 14, to "take Acc[oun]t of all the Plunder" gathered on September 8, but no further action occurred.[160] The controversy subsided after an auction of many of the articles.

Plundering by the Indians had serious consequences for the burial parties, which had great difficulty distinguishing English provincial troops from French soldiers and militia because both the Canadian Indians and the Mohawks had stripped and scalped many of the corpses. The *New-York Mercury* also reported that "Parties from the Camp were daily sent to discover the Enemy's slain and pick up Arms, &c. and that they had found a great Number of dead Bodies in Swamps and Holes which they had carried off on Biers

[stretchers], 40 of which were found all bloody at the Side of a Pond."[161] According to tradition, Bloody Pond received its name because blood had run into its water.*

On the day after the Battle of Lake George, Johnson's Mohawk allies informed him
"that they proposed to return home as was their Custom after an Engagement wherein
they had met with any considerable Loss."[167] Meeting with Johnson on September 12 at
Lake George, the Mohawks "beg[ged] that the C[au]ghnawagas [from Canada] may
never be again permitted to come and Trade at Albany or Oswego."[168] The Mohawks also
wished to return home to protect their villages in the event of a raid by the Canadian Indians. Some of the troops were happy to see the Mohawks leave Lake George. Seth Pomeroy
wrote that the Mohawks departed with "many of our goods & things left by our People
in ye Battle…if they had n[e]ver C[o]me among us It [would] ha[ve] be[e]n much better
for us."[169] Although the Mohawks promised to return to Lake George, they had achieved
the honor and trophies of victory that they had set out to win. The Mohawks soon arrived
in Albany, bringing "Scalps fixed upon Poles (tis said upwards of 80)."[170] To appease the
Mohawks and to serve as replacements for Hendrick and others who had perished at
Lake George, Johnson delivered "six French prisoners" to a gathering of 600 Mohawks at
Fort Johnson the following February.[171]

Although the Battle of Lake George was the only victory for the British in 1755, the
total casualties were nearly identical on each side and the French attack succeeded in
stopping the Crown Point expedition at Lake George. The English losses were greater as
a result of the lack of reliable intelligence prior to sending Ephraim Williams' detachment
to Fort Lyman and the failure to prepare a stronger entrenchment at Lake George ahead
of time. Nevertheless, untested and essentially untrained provincial volunteers withstood
the attack of a professional army and their Indian allies. Had Dieskau not split his force,
or had he followed his original plan to attack Fort Lyman, the outcome would have been
quite different. It is easy for armchair historians to analyze these events and identify
faulty decisions two and a half centuries later, but those involved in making difficult
choices in the face of uncertainty and raw emotions did the best they could.

---

*Although there is little direct testimony from 1755 that the water turned red with blood, the name Bloody Pond
was in use during the French and Indian War. James Henderson's journal entry of September 9, 1758, described
an ambush "near Bloody Pond."[162] A surveyor's field book in 1764 noted a "small pond call[e]d the bloody one,"
and in 1776 an American officer marching on the military road to Lake George noted that "many Hundred[s]
were killed and thrown into a pond which gave it the name Bloody Pond, many bones are now to be seen in the
Pond and about it."[163] In 1830 Jared Sparks drew a map showing Bloody Pond to the southeast of Fort George,
noting that "the pond is nearly three miles from the Fort. It is a dead pool of water, about 200 feet in diameter."[164] In 1842, 19-year-old Francis Parkman described the pond as "a little dark slimy sheet of stagnant water
covered with weeds and pond-lilies…where hundreds of dead bodies still lie."[165] A 2005 Warren County Historical Society publication on the military road indicated that an 1858 Warren County map placed Bloody Pond
southeast of the present pond identified as Bloody Pond by an historical marker on Route 9N. The publication
suggested that the real Bloody Pond was located 100 feet to the east of the present-day Warren County Bike
Trail, about a mile and a half north of Route 149.[166]

5. Stalemate and New Forts

FOLLOWING THE BATTLE OF LAKE GEORGE, William Johnson's soldiers were too dispirited to renew the campaign and press forward to Fort St. Frédéric. One battle was enough for the citizen soldiers of the English colonies, as it was for the Mohawks. Instead of "being invigorated" by the "repulse we gave the Enemy," Johnson wrote in September, the "resolute & obstinate Attack" made by the French "seems to have given our Troops a dread of the Enemy."[1] Immediately following the battle, Johnson's secretary, Peter Wraxall, wrote to Lieutenant Governor James DeLancey that Johnson's army was "apprehensive…that the French will make a more formidable attack."[2] Papers captured from the French on September 8 included a letter that a total force of 6,000 troops had been "expected at Crown Point," and Robert Rogers later observed several thousand French troops at Ticonderoga.[3] Reports of a "Great army of Fr[e]nch and Indians" ready to attack circulated at the Lake George camp on September 15 and 16, and alarms of an impending French assault occurred as late as mid-November.[4]

The provincials at Lake George were demoralized by the deaths of friends and relatives in the Battle of Lake George on September 8. Thomas Williams, Seth Pomeroy, and others had lost brothers in the fighting. Care of the wounded and the sickness prevalent in the camp also dampened the spirits of the troops. On September 17 Johnson noted that "our Sick daily increase," and a month later surgeon Thomas Williams wrote that the newer "recruits are very sickly & more die" than the provincial soldiers who had arrived earlier.[5] A council of war in October revealed that "near one third of our Army are Sick & Unfit for Duty their Spirits Exhausted & Vigor Enervated" by a "long Dull & Sickly Encampment."[6] The burials continued well into October; on the third of October Seth Pomeroy noted that "9 men Bur[ie]d this day."[7] Still suffering from the wound that he received during the battle, Johnson was confined to his tent during much of October and racked by intense pain on the side of his head and in his ear. Following typical medical practices of the day, he was "bled, blistered and purged," which only served to further weaken him.[8]

Logistical problems plagued the army at Lake George. A big part of the difficulty lay in the attempt to supply two armies through Albany at the same time—Johnson's force at Lake George and Shirley's troops involved in the campaign against Niagara. On September 16 Johnson wrote to Charles Hardy, the governor of New York, that 400-500 wagons

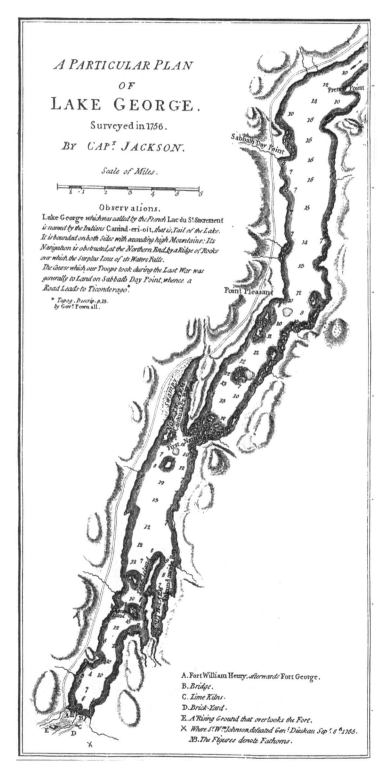

"A Particular Plan of Lake George" from *The American Military Pocket Atlas* by R. Sayer and J. Bennett, London (1776). Sabbath Day Point is mislabeled on the map and should have been located at "Point Pleasant." (Library of Congress)

would be necessary to transport provisions to the Lake George camp in order to press forward. Johnson complained that the inhabitants of Albany "hid their Wagons & dr[o]ve away their Horses" and that a number of horses already in use had been worn out, killed, or "run away."[9] On October 12, officers at a council of war commended Governor Hardy's efforts in contracting for wagons and arranging convoys, but bad weather had made the roads in many areas "almost impassable, [a] number of Wagons broke and destroyed," and horses lost.[10] Others criticized the wagoners; Chaplain Samuel Chandler from Gloucester, Massachusetts, deplored the behavior of some wagon drivers, who were hired to transport the sick back to Albany, but instead "turned them out in the woods & left them, some of whom died."[11] Inadequate supplies resulted in "Short [al]lowances" and exposure to the cold "for want [of] Blank[e]ts and Cloth[e]s."[12] However, some food reached Lake George. On October 4 Captain Nathaniel Dwight mentioned the arrival of "about 50 Oxen from Connecticut and 180 sheep, which w[ere] sent [as] a Present" from the people of Long Island.[13] The next day Johnson received word that a total of "a Thousand Sheep" were being driven to the lake by the "benevolent" people of Long Island.[14] Support for the troops at Lake George also came from the women of Suffolk County (New York), who were "knitting a Number of Stockings and Mittens, to be sent up to the poorer Soldiers of General Johnson's Army."[15]

Controversy in the army at Lake George stymied progress and divided the troops into two factions. Johnson's letter of September 9 to the governors stirred resentment among the New England troops by failing to mention any role for Connecticut's Major General Phineas Lyman, the second in command of the army. Lyman's letter to his wife on September 11, which praised the Connecticut forces for sustaining "the whole of the first onset," but minimized the role of the Rhode Island troops and stated that Johnson had been wounded "near the beginning of the battle and repaired to his tent," intensified the strife following its publication in Connecticut and New York newspapers.[16] The contentiousness was revealed at a September 27 council of war when Johnson addressed the "Groundless False & Malicious Reports" that he had "pulled General Lyman back who was proceeding forward," and that Captain William Eyre was "confined & put into Irons for ordering the Cannon to be fired over the Enemies heads" during the September 8 battle.[17] Reports of the "Differences between Gen. Lyman & Capt[ain] Eyre and the universal dissatisfaction and Quarrels among the officers" reached the office of the New York governor less than a week later.[18] In response to Lyman's published letter and the ongoing criticism of Eyre and Johnson, Lieutenant Colonel Edward Cole of Rhode Island wrote a scathing letter on October 22 (published in the November 17 issue of the *New-York Mercury*), lambasting Lyman's version of events. Cole suggested that Lyman's letter was "a composition of Nonsen[s]e and Falsities," probably written by one "of his mean, ignorant Camp Flatterers," which impugned the Rhode Island regiment by omitting its role in aiding Lieutenant Colonel Nathan Whiting's retreat and by failing to acknowledge that the French attack on September 8 was "first and most formidable" upon the Rhode Island section.[19] Cole also disputed Lyman's comment that Johnson's wound occurred at the beginning of the battle and accused Lyman of "lying on his Belly, with his Face to the Ground" behind a tree during the battle.[20] A letter published in the *Connecticut Gazette* on December 13 castigated Cole's "malicious Aspersions" and slanderous attack on Lyman, suggesting that Lyman had displayed "undaunted Courage" during the battle.[21] A pamphlet written several years later, attributed to William Livingston (a foe of Johnson and later the governor of New Jersey), argued that "a junt[a]" at the Lake George camp had written the October 22 letter and "procured one Cole" to sign it, and insisted that impartial eyewitnesses had observed Lyman "fighting like a lion, and exposing his life in the hottest of the battle."[22]

Although Phineas Lyman and a few officers wished to proceed with the Crown Point expedition, Johnson and the rest of the officers and troops were in no mood to press northward. In addition to problems with supplies, illness, and the insubordination of the troops, Johnson also lacked enough bateaux and vessels to carry the artillery. By the end of October, less than 100 bateaux were fit for service at Lake George, although several hundred were at Fort Edward. After the September 8 battle, in which six carpenters were killed, work on the 40-foot-long artillery scows resumed at a slow pace. Stephen Webster, captain of the carpenters, subsequently reported that as few as 15 men worked on the boats each day. Most of the men refused to work as carpenters because their officers did not excuse them from their military duties. On October 7 Webster finally reported "One Boat fit and 2 partly caulked" and another half built.[23] The boat building had also been hampered by the diversion of men to the construction of the fort and a lack of sufficient tools to complete both projects. Governor Charles Hardy had written to Johnson on October 5, warning him to "have the appearance of doing something" by sending scouting parties out and completing the artillery boats, otherwise he might be perceived as having thrown "Cold Water" on the expedition.[24] However, by early October the prospect of moving against the French was clearly unlikely. In addition to the other problems, Captain William Eyre, commander of the artillery, determined that the number of cannons and mortars was "not sufficient" for proceeding against the French.[25] Eyre and Johnson favored building a strong fort at the lake, which diverted energy and resources away from preparations to advance northward with the army.

Scouting reports of heightened French activity at Ticonderoga also fostered a more cautious approach to the campaign. Captain Robert Rogers of the New Hampshire regiment emerged as Johnson's chief source of intelligence on French defenses. At the end of September Rogers and four rangers viewed a large French army at Ticonderoga "building a fort" and estimated that "about one thousand French and Indians" were at the northern end of Lake George, but "no Fort nor Artillery there."[26] Because of ill health, Johnson instructed Phineas Lyman on October 9 to hold a council of war to answer the question of undertaking "an immediate Attempt upon Ticonderog[a]."[27] The council of officers unanimously voted against an attack, citing insufficient troops and provisions and recommending "that no Tools or Workmen shall be employed on the Flat Bottomed Boats so as to hinder…completing the Fort now building here."[28] Three days later the council judged that "the Season would be so far advanced" to proceed, despite the considerable size of the Crown Point army, then totaling 6,600 men (3,600 at Lake George, 500 at Fort Edward, and 2,500 at Albany or on their way to the lake).[29] On October 20 the council reconsidered the question of proceeding with the expedition and provided additional reasons for not pushing forward, including difficulties transporting supplies on the Hudson River and roads, the possibility of the lake's freezing, the lack of sufficient bateaux, and the illness of nearly a third of the army.[30] On the same day, the *New-York Mercury* reported that wives of Connecticut soldiers were "enraged" after learning of the uncertainty about proceeding with the expedition; many "declare[d] if their Husbands c[a]me back without attacking the French in their Intrenchments, they shall not come near them" and would hurl their pots at their heads.[31] Snow fell four days later at the lake, making life for the men, who were still living in tents, even more miserable. Although meat and other food were in

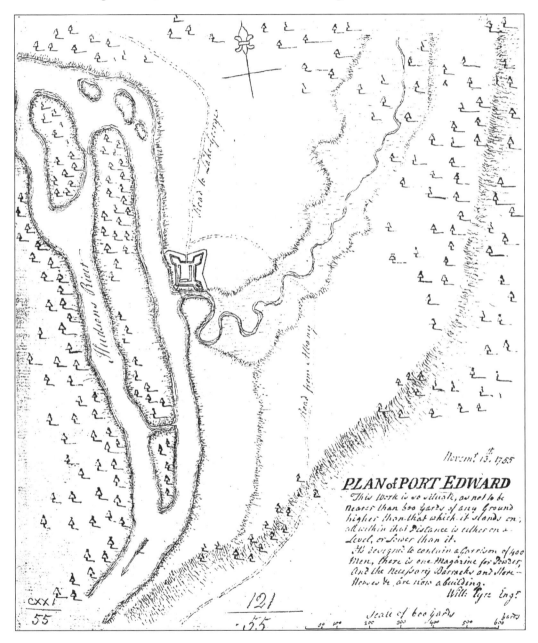

**Plan of Fort Edward by Captain William Eyre, November 13, 1755.
(Crown Collection, New York State Library)**

short supply, some of the troops were able to supplement their rations by fishing and hunting. Samuel Chandler ate venison and lake trout, the latter caught with a hook and line or speared with his sword.[32]

The chief accomplishment of Johnson's army during the fall of 1755 was to construct a substantial fort on the shore of Lake George. The day before the battle of September 8, a council of war had approved building "a Picketed Fort [log stockade]…suffi[cien]t to contain & accommodate 100 men" on land cleared by Ephraim Williams' troops.[33] On September 9, expecting another French attack, Seth Pomeroy recorded "making Some Sort of fortification or Battlement to Stand behind."[34] At a council of war on September 14, Johnson informed the ten officers present that he still favored building a stronger fortification at Lake George "but had yielded to the Opinion of the Council" because the troops "had an Aversion to digging," and the majority preferred a picketed fort.[35] Knowing the likely result, Johnson did not seek a vote on a proposal for a stronger fort. Two days later Johnson reported to Governor Charles Hardy that "Our Breast work is strengthened and carried quite round our camp, a Picketed Fort is building here," noting that the majority of officers were flatly against "a more respectable Fort."[36]

In a September 22 letter to William Shirley, the British commander in chief in North America, Johnson complained about the "Obstinacy" of his officers in preventing the construction of a more substantial fort.[37] While a simple picketed fort was easier to build, it offered little protection from artillery and could not mount cannons on ramparts. Before receiving Johnson's letter, Shirley wrote to Johnson on September 24, informing him that he disagreed with Captain William Eyre's opinion, expressed in his September 10 letter, of the "urgent necessity of immediately erecting a strong regular fort at Lake George," and instead urged strengthening the fort at the "Carrying Place" (Fort Lyman/Edward).[38] However, on September 25 Governor Hardy supported Johnson's position in a letter and recommended a fort "be so constructed for receiving proper Garrisons for their Security this Winter."[39] Four days later at a council of war Johnson complained that "a dozen men" at the site of the picketed fort "were sitting down & no work going forward."[40] Johnson reminded the officers of an earlier agreement to have 500 men working on the fort daily and referred to Hardy's letter endorsing "a more respectable Fort than a picketed One."[41]

After weeks of disagreement over the type of fort, the council of officers finally relented on September 29 and agreed "that a Place of Strength with Magazines & Store houses & Barracks be immediately" built to garrison 500 men and assigned 700 men to work on it.[42] At last Johnson and Eyre were successful in persuading the officers at the Lake George camp to construct a fort "in the manner the French build" with earthen ramparts and firing platforms.[43] On September 30 Private James Hill noted that the men dismantled the picketed fort (located just to the west of the site of the new fort): "we went to Work on [a]nother fort and Left…B[u]ilding the Bo[a]ts in order to Bu[i]ld a fort that Wo[ul]d be Cann[o]n Proof, and to t[e]ar the other down, for it Was not fit for Nothing but Small arms."[44] The new fort (later named Fort William Henry) was built "upon a high sandy Bank twenty F[ee]t above the Lake" near the southwest corner of the lake and faced a "Morass" on the east side (site of West Brook).[45] The fort could serve several purposes, including as a staging area for future expeditions against the French forts at Ticonderoga and Crown Point. The fort would also impede French and Indian raids against New York and Massachusetts settlements by obstructing a traditional route southward. A substan-

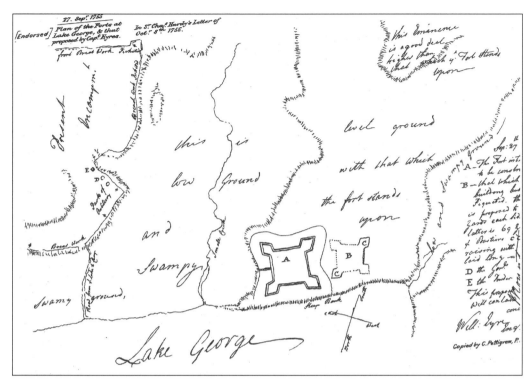

**"Plan of the Forts at Lake George…by Capt. [William] Eyre," September 27, 1755, showing
the location of the picketed fort (B) under construction to the west of the proposed fort (A);
the latter was subsequently named Fort William Henry.
(National Archives of Canada)**

tial fort would enable the British and provincial army to maintain a winter garrison and
store supplies and artillery. Finally, building the fort provided a substitute undertaking
to pressing forward with the expedition to attack the French fortifications.

As work got underway on the fort at Lake George, the troops at Fort Edward labored
to strengthen the fortifications there. On October 2, after scrutinizing Captain William
Eyre's recommendations to deepen the ditch and increase the height and size of the parapets and ramparts at the bastioned fort, Governor Hardy suggested construction of
"proper Barracks."[49] In early October the fort's commander, Colonel Timothy Ruggles
from Hardwick, Massachusetts, employed troops in cutting timber for the barracks and
storehouses. However, the same problems that had plagued the pace of construction at
Lake George were present at Fort Edward—a shortage of tools, sickness in the camp, and
the men's aversion to work. Eyre's instructions of October 17 for work on the fort included barracks 160 feet long on the east side "divided into eight Rooms" and a second barracks 110 feet long with "Chimn[e]ys in the Corners" on the west side.[50] Colonel Richard
Gridley of Massachusetts, the commander at Fort Edward after October 24, wrote to Johnson in November, expressing an urgent need for supplies, "especially Rum, which is quite
necessary for carrying on the Barracks."[51] With only ten to twelve carpenters available, the

east barracks was not completed until late 1755, and the chimneys were not finished until January.[52] The fort would undergo significant improvements over the next three years. The location of Fort Edward aided its defense. The west side of the fort was protected by a bank of the Hudson River, and on the south side a small brook (Fort Edward Creek) shielded the fort.

Meanwhile, work continued on the fort at Lake George. By the beginning of November, four bastions and the ramparts were finished, as well as most of the parapets and magazines, and the barracks were substantially complete. On November 5 James Hill was employed in "Hun[t]i[ng] timber for Platforms [plank floors for mounting cannons]," which were finished six days later.[53] On November 7 Johnson informed William Shirley that he had named the new fort "William Henry after Two of the Royal Family" (William, Duke of Cumberland and Henry, Duke of Gloucester).[54] Work advanced rapidly and "cannon & mortars were ha[u]led over from the camp to the Fort" on November 12.[55] Samuel Blodget, a sutler who had been present at the September 8 battle, later received a sketch and dimensions of the new fort from a friend. Blodget noted that the "foundation" for the walls was 32 feet thick with 16-foot-thick parapets (defensive barrier/wall on the forward edge of the rampart) and "built of Pine Logs…filled with Earth."[56] Captain Nathaniel Dwight, who was present during most of the construction, described a main wall 30 feet thick and parapets 12 feet thick with openings (embrasures) for the cannons. The two-story barracks on the north side was "Divided in [the] middle, a chimney in each half."[57] (However, William Eyre's plan did not show divided barracks.)[58] Dwight noted barracks on the south side, small storehouses, magazines, and a camp to the east of the fort, nearly 700 feet wide from east to west, 297 feet from the lake, almost 1,500 feet deep north to south, and surrounded by a breastwork.[59]

While Johnson's army struggled to finish Fort William Henry, French troops were busy fortifying the Ticonderoga peninsula on Lake Champlain and manning a camp at the northern end of Lake George. Captain Robert Rogers, praised for his "Bravery & Veracity" and as "the most active Man in our Army" by Johnson, made repeated scouting forays to Crown Point and Ticonderoga. On September 27 Rogers and four men departed from the southern end of Lake George in a birchbark canoe; early the next morning Rogers and one ranger observed a large number of French and Indians on both sides of the outlet at the north end of the lake.[60] Later they viewed "a Fort building…[with] a Number of Cannon Mounted" at Ticonderoga and about 3,000 men at a "Grand Encampment" nearby.[61] After watching a large canoe carrying "one Frenchman & Nine Indians" land on an island (perhaps present-day Odell Island), Rogers and his men ambushed them on their return trip.[62] On a subsequent scouting mission, Rogers estimated that there were about "Two Thousand men" at Ticonderoga.[63]

On the cold evening of October 29, Rogers and 30 men were sent to the northern end of Lake George by Johnson "to intercept any Scouting [parti]es" and take prisoners.[64] A brisk northeast wind the next day created "prodigious Great waves and white Caps," slowing Rogers' party aboard four armed bateaux.[65] On October 31, after reaching the northern outlet of the lake, the detachment observed a number of fires on the west shore. Twelve men (six of whom were ill) were sent back in one of the bateaux to inform Johnson of their discovery and request reinforcements. Rogers and five rangers set out in a bateau to scout the French position and "Discovered a Small Fort with Several Small Log

Camps within ye Fort," encompassing a quarter acre and surrounded by a stockaded wall (i.e., "Picketed").[66] Rogers had also sent Captain Israel Putnam and Lieutenant Durkee by land to observe the French camp, but the two rangers were spotted by the French and fired upon; Durkee was wounded in the thigh. By the time Putnam and Durkee returned to the camp, the French had nearly reached Rogers' position on the west shore (near Isle au Mouton/Prisoners Island). Rogers' detachment was nearly caught in a pincer movement formed by two enemy war canoes on the lake and French soldiers on a hill behind Rogers' camp. Rogers ordered "Two Bate[aux] into ye Water [the first with] L[i]eut[enant] [Noah] Grant [the great-grandfather of Ulysses S. Grant] with 6 men" followed by Rogers in the other bateau, also with six men.[67] Another French canoe with 13 men appeared and Rogers hurriedly rowed toward one of the French vessels and "when their Broadside was toward him, fired his Wall-Piece [small swivel cannon]."[68] The French fled but were caught in a crossfire between Putnam's men onshore and Rogers in his bateau. Shortly thereafter, Putnam was barely able to flee with his men in the third bateau. The French raced along the shoreline firing briskly, but Putnam escaped unscathed, despite numerous bullet holes in his blanket. Putnam joined Rogers and his men in the other two bateaux in a pursuit of the French canoes, but Rogers soon discovered French soldiers on both sides of the outlet and "Gave [the]m Each a Broad side which put [the]m to ye Bush, and Gave us a Clear Passage Homewards."[69] Halfway home Rogers encountered the reinforcements that he had requested but decided to return to Johnson's camp, where he reported the engagement of "near 2 Hours."[70]

On November 11, following a scouting report by two Mohawks that "a Large Army of the Enemy [was] on this side [of] the Narrows," Johnson wrote to William Shirley that he had ordered reinforcements from Albany to march to Lake George with all dispatch and requested that Shirley send regular troops.[71] Rogers was positive that the Indian scouts had observed the French at Ticonderoga, but the Mohawks were equally insistent that they had seen them in the Narrows. The report that the enemy was "about 15 miles off" created a "great Stir" in Johnson's camp; the troops "were all called up" and readied their muskets.[72] The day following the report, the cannons and mortars were hauled into the fort. However, after several more scouting expeditions, Johnson informed Shirley that "I grow more & more inclined to believe the Indians were under a mistake."[73] No attack occurred.

Problems with disgruntled troops and desertions occurred during November. Working on short rations and with their enlistments expiring, 500-700 troops from Connecticut marched out of the camp during the second week of November, but they were persuaded to return after receiving an assurance of discharge following 12 additional days of labor on the fort. Complaining about the food, overdue pay, and their officers, about 30 men from the New York regiment took their muskets and packs and marched about a half mile before two officers brought them back. (One of the officers was Captain Philip Schuyler, who later served as a major general during the American Revolution.) Johnson was able to pacify them temporarily. Seven men who had deserted from Fort Edward were also accused of treating officers "with Disrespectful Language"; the men were quickly apprehended and three received "thirty nine Stripes on their naked Backs with a whip of Birch," the fourth man was given 15 "stripes," two had "To Ride the wood[en] horse one hour Each," and the seventh man had to pay a fine.[74] The wooden horse punishment involved straddling two horizontal slabs of wood nailed together to form an inverted V.[75]

On November 18, soldiers at Lake George were awakened a little after four in the morning by an earthquake. Chaplain Samuel Chandler was abruptly roused by "a shock of an earthquake…some of the loose stones fell from the chimney top, [the] House was wrecked, [and] the wheels of the carriages cre[a]ked in the Fort."[76] The 1755 earthquake, centered in Cape Ann, Massachusetts, shook the eastern region of North America from Nova Scotia to South Carolina.[77]

In the evening Nathaniel Dwight recorded that "1000 or 1200" reinforcements arrived from Albany along with 60 oxen sent from Long Island.[78] Dwight estimated that Johnson's army totaled 4,280 men, including the new recruits, but "960 [were]…sick and unfit for Duty" and "Some have died and many Dismissed," reducing the strength of the army.[79] A month earlier Johnson had reported 4,500 men were fit and about 800 sick and unfit.[80] With the Niagara campaign on hiatus, William Shirley met with the governor and lieutenant governor of New York and other officials at Albany on November 17 and recommended that Johnson and his army "advance against the Enemy and attempt to remove them from their encroachments as far as they are able…this Season."[81] After the minutes of the Albany meeting reached Lake George, Johnson placed them before a council of war on November 21 and recommended that "an attempt be made with the utmost Dispatch & Vigour."[82] The provincial officers were not impressed by a recommendation that virtually everyone knew would be impossible to carry out at that late date. The council voted against going forward and adjourned until the next day when its reasons for not advancing against the French would be provided. The following morning the council decided to "avoid Repetition" and referred to the reasons given during the October councils, but added deteriorating weather, lack of clothing, and the availability of only 60 bateaux at the lake.[83]

The hesitancy of Johnson and his officers to move forward was also related to scouting reports, which described French fortifications under construction at Ticonderoga and the presence of thousands of French troops.[84] On September 20, 1755, Pierre de Rigaud de Vaudreuil de Cavagnial, governor-general of French Canada, had instructed 32-year-old Michel Chartier de Lotbinière, a Canadian military engineer, to examine Fort St. Frédéric to decide whether the fort could be enlarged and to "choose the most favourable Site for entrenchments or other fortifications capable of assuring…us the control" of the passage at "Carillon."[85] Vaudreuil's instructions were based on reports that the English "seek to capture Carillon" in their campaign to force the French from Crown Point.[86] Fortifying Ticonderoga and the northern end of Lake George would obstruct the movement of English armies to Fort St. Frédéric and beyond. Lotbinière left promptly for his new assignment, arriving at Crown Point in late September. Subsequently, Lotbinière made his way to Carillon and selected a location for a fort on a ridge approximately a quarter mile from the end of the peninsula, a site that would control the outlet from Lake George, as well as a section of the expanse of Lake Champlain.* Most of the Ticonderoga promontory was still virgin forest except for the rock outcropping at the projected site of the fort and steep cliffs along the channel of the lake. Dieskau's troops had occupied the area a month earli-

---

*Scouting reports and other sources indicate that Lotbinière began the process of selecting a location and building a fort in late September 1755. A year later, however, Lotbinière noted that he had initiated the work at Carillon after October 12.[87]

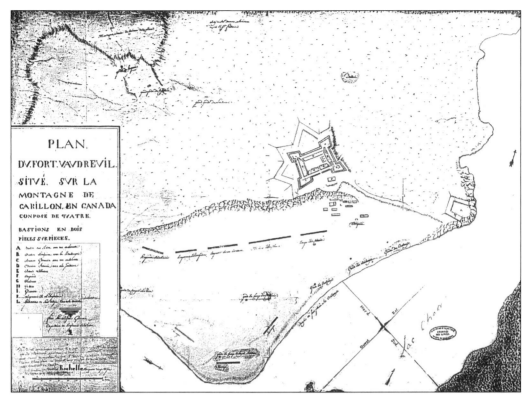

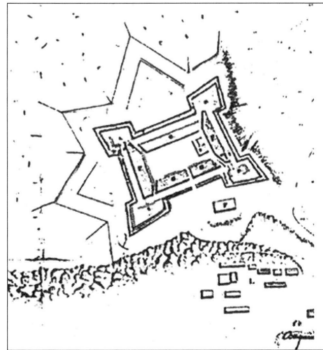

Plan of Fort Vaudreuil/ Carillon 1755 by Captain François-Joseph de Germain. The fort was initially called Vau-dreuil. Detail right. (National Archives of Canada)

er, and by the end of September English scouts reported a large camp there with thousands of French troops. The provincial rangers heard a continuous thud of wood chop-
pers, clearing the forest and shaping logs for the fort. In 1755 Lotbinière "began the parapet…[consisting] of a double row of [oak] timbers [at a] distan[ce] [of] ten feet from one
another and bound together by two cross-pieces dovetailed" at the ends and filled with
earth.[88] By the end of November the wall was seven feet high. The whole peninsula would
be denuded of its trees in the process of building the fort, and French workmen would
subsequently cross the lake for additional timber at present-day Mount Independence.

At the height of the construction activity during the fall of 1755, 2,000-3,000 men
worked on the fort, the majority from the ranks of French regulars and Canadian militia.
Nearly all the men stayed in tents, but huts were constructed, extending from the southern end of the fort site to the water's edge. This area, subsequently known as the "French
Village," would be surrounded by a stockade of logs and contain a blacksmith shop, kilns,
ovens, a canteen, and other structures. On October 24, 1755, Lotbinière wrote that he had
begun the fort at Carillon "too late to expect to finish it this year."[89] Lotbinière remained
at Carillon into February 1756 until "the Barracks had been finished" and then returned
to Montreal to "recuperate from the fatigue of the campaign and the unwholesome food
I had taken."[90] Viewing Carillon from Rattlesnake Hill (present-day Mount Defiance) on
December 21, Rogers observed "two large Barracks in said Fort and some small Houses
and several on the outside of the Fort."[91] Most of the French army had departed on
November 28, leaving a small winter garrison.

Meanwhile, the troops at Fort William Henry were ready to march home. As the campaign drew to a close, a raucous fight in the Lake George camp was indicative of deteriorating discipline. On November 26 Nathaniel Dwight recorded that a Massachusetts
man had sold a New York soldier a mug of beer, but the latter ran away without paying
for it. The Massachusetts militiaman pursued him but was attacked by New York troops,
whereupon men from Lieutenant Colonel Seth Pomeroy's Massachusetts regiment came
to his rescue. A drunken brawl ensued, involving "Clubs and naked Cutlas[s]es and they
Struck one of [the Massachusetts] men and half Scalped him and Drove into our
Reg[imen]t and C[a]me with Swords and Clubs and C[a]m[e] Like Hornets out of their
Nests Swearing and Cursing in the most Hel[l]ish manner."[92] Two Massachusetts men
were wounded by the cutlasses, another by a club, and many others were also cut. Dwight
and another officer were joined by some New York officers in putting down the melee.
Johnson placated the New Yorkers, but Dwight noted that it was "hard pa[ci]fying our
men that rec[eive]d So much Damage."[93]

At ten o'clock on the next day, the Crown Point army finally departed from Lake
George: "ab[ou]t 3000 marched in a Body, the Wagons & Baggage in the center," Chaplain
Samuel Chandler noted.[94] Three days before the army's departure, a council of war held
at Fort William Henry and attended by commissioners from Connecticut, Massachusetts,
and New York, had voted to assign 750 troops as the winter garrisons at the two forts (430
men at Fort William Henry and 320 at Fort Edward).[95] Colonel Jonathan Bagley of Massachusetts was given command of Fort William Henry, while Lieutenant Colonel Nathan
Whiting of Connecticut was assigned to Fort Edward. Before leaving, Captain William
Eyre provided the incoming commander with detailed instructions of what action to take
in the event of an artillery siege. Eyre even delineated the "honours of War" if a "brave

officer" was forced to capitulate after "an obstinate defense."[96] Prophetically, Eyre also furnished advice in defending against an enemy that would "storm the Fort by Escalade [using scaling ladders]."[97] Less than a year and a half later, Eyre would be faced with this exact situation. Johnson left instructions for Bagley to have the "Works completed" and to "clear the Woods" around Fort William Henry as far as a gunshot.[98] The two barracks still needed floors and windows. Captain Jeduthan Baldwin, a 25-year-old officer from Brookfield, Massachusetts, recorded "haul[ing] logs out of the lake for boards" on December 2, working on his "house" five days later, and on a hospital in early February 1756.[99] A shortage of men, illness among the troops, and a lack of supplies handicapped completion of the fort. Whiting faced similar problems at Fort Edward, complaining that he had only "ten or twelve carpenters…What a bad Situation the fort is in."[100]

The conflict between William Shirley and William Johnson continued to fester into the next year. On November 9, 1755, Johnson wrote to Shirley, congratulating him on the recent news that his official commission as commander in chief had arrived in America. (Shirley had a temporary appointment to that position following Braddock's death.) Johnson's main reason for the letter was to give notice of his intention to resign his command of the Crown Point army and devote his "utmost attention" to his appointment as the Sole Superintendent of Indian Affairs.[101] On December 2 Johnson wrote to the colonial governors, surrendering his commission as a major general and commander of the Crown Point army, noting "that if I have fallen short of their [the governors] Expectations & Opinions, it hath been my Misfortune not my Crime, and herein I am very willing to stand the strictest & most impartial Enquiry."[102] Despite Johnson's resignation, Shirley continued in his attempts to undermine Johnson's reputation and revoked Johnson's commission on December 7 as the Sole Superintendent, replacing it with an appointment as Indian Commissioner. However, after meeting with Johnson in New York City three weeks later, Shirley agreed to leave the original commission intact and Johnson used the title at a conference with the Six Nations in February 1756.[103] Shirley's credibility in London was increasingly weakened due to his failure to attack Fort Niagara and because of derogatory letters written about him. A mysterious letter written in early 1756 and signed "Pierre Fidele" raised questions in London about Shirley's intentions and loyalty, and letters by Thomas Pownall, the lieutenant governor of New Jersey, to prominent politicians in England severely criticized Shirley.[104] At the end of March 1756 the British cabinet decided to replace Shirley as governor of Massachusetts. (The decision to replace Shirley as commander in chief with John Campbell, the Earl of Loudoun, had been made earlier.) Pownall was subsequently appointed to the governorship of Massachusetts.

The fortunes of William Johnson, on the other hand, were elevated by the success of the provincial troops at the Battle of Lake George. Johnson became a popular figure who had led an inexperienced provincial force and prevailed while the professional army of Braddock had failed. The victory at Lake George had raised the self-confidence of the English colonists. On December 30, 1755, Johnson arrived in New York City to a hero's welcome; according to the *New-York Mercury*, "Ships in the Harbour saluted him as he passed the Streets, amidst the Acclamations of the People. At Night the City was beautifully illuminated, and the general joy displayed on this Occasion evidenced Gratitude of the People for the singular Services this Gentleman has done his Country."[105] On November 18, 1755, King George II had granted the "dignity of a Baronet of Great Britain" to

**"Sir William Johnson" 1756.
(Library of Congress)**

Johnson, and Parliament awarded him 5,000 pounds.[106] The news of the honor, however, did not reach America until early February.

The accolades for Johnson were not universal, however. A pamphlet written in 1757 by friends of William Shirley criticized Johnson for not pursuing the French at the end of the September 8 battle, for not attacking them at Ticonderoga, and maintained that Johnson admitted that Phineas Lyman "was chiefly to be ascribed the honour of the victory."[107] The October 1759 issue of the *London Magazine* questioned the "victory" at Lake George in 1755, characterizing the campaign as an "expensive expedition without having gained either glory or advantage to the nation; for a little fort which the enemy could so easily reduce, cannot be called an advantage and it cannot surely be said, that it was [in] any way glorious for an army of 4,000 men possessed of a strong camp, and provided with cannon, to repulse an army of 17 or 1800 men. However, so little had we of late been accustomed to hear of victory, that we rejoiced exceedingly at this repulse, which we called a victory."[108]

On the other hand, the first history of the Seven Years' War, *The General History of the Late War* by John Entick, looked favorably upon Johnson's performance. Published in London in 1763, Entick's book defended Johnson against critics who "accuse[d] him of losing the opportunity" to destroy the French army and failing to attack Crown Point.[109] Entick concluded that Johnson's failure to pursue the enemy on September 8 was the result of an expectation that the French would renew their attack. If Johnson had sent out detachments to "scour the country," the reduced strength of the main body of provincial troops would have increased their vulnerability in the event of an attack.[110] The unwillingness to carry the expedition forward was justified by the strength of the French and Indians at the "passes" (Ticonderoga), which if attacked by Johnson's troops would result in "so much fatigue, and perhaps great loss of men" that there would be little hope of carrying the campaign to Crown Point.[11]

1756

The next year witnessed a strengthening of the French position at Ticonderoga and a year of vacillation for the British at Lake George. The transition to a new French military commander to replace Jean-Armand Dieskau proceeded smoothly, but choosing a successor for William Shirley proved to be a cumbersome process for the British and stymied their military efforts in 1756. The appointment of Louis-Joseph de Montcalm as a major general in command of French troops in North America was fairly expeditious, with the new commander reaching Canada on May 11, 1756. On the other hand, John Campbell, the Earl of Loudoun, was selected as the British commander in chief in mid- March, but he did not arrive in New York until late July. In early June Major General Daniel Webb, third in command, arrived in New York harbor to assume the position of temporary commander in chief. However, upon learning that Major General James Abercromby, second in command, would soon reach the city, Webb decided to wait for him. Abercromby landed nine days later and shortly thereafter sailed to Albany with Webb "with 11 transports full of troops."[112] Abercromby assumed temporary command on June 26, only to relinquish it to Lord Loudoun a month later. On July 23, 1756, Loudoun reached New York City with five aides, including Major John Young of the Royal Americans, 17 servants, and his mistress, Jean Masson.

By the time of Loudoun's arrival, most of the provincial army, under Major General John Winslow of Massachusetts, had already been deployed to Fort Edward and Fort William Henry for an offensive against the French forts. In December 1755 William Shirley had begun planning for the campaign, and in 1756 he commissioned Winslow, as did the governors of Connecticut and New York, to command the Crown Point expedition. The Crown Point campaign was once again organized as a provincial operation, while British regulars were to be dispatched to Oswego for an attack on Fort Frontenac (present-day Kingston, Ontario). On July 20, 1756, Winslow arrived at Fort Edward "with a considerable Number of Troops & part of ye Artillery" and "was received by about 2000 men, beautifully drawn up on each side of ye River," and saluted with "a Discharge of ye Cannon," surgeon Ammi Ruhamah Cutter recorded.[113]

Before Lord Loudoun's arrival, Abercromby had to deal with the issue of integrating the provincial army into the British military structure, realizing that any change in the basis upon which the provincial troops had been raised would release them from their enlistment obligations. Shirley had assured the provincial soldiers that they would serve solely under the officers who had enlisted them and he had placed negligible importance on the official British "Rules and Articles of War." Under these rules, provincial officers would be junior to regular officers of the same rank. When combined with regular units, provincial colonels and majors would be demoted to "eldest captains." In response to a query by Abercromby regarding the integration of the provincials with the regulars, Winslow held a council of war with his provincial officers at Fort Edward. Winslow and his officers threatened the dissolution of the provincial army if joining with the regulars resulted in a loss of their rank. Loudoun, who assumed command at the end of July, was determined to place provincial officers in a subordinate position. As a first step, Loudoun met with Shirley, whom he blamed for the defiant behavior of the provincials. Shirley promptly wrote to Winslow, warning of Loudoun's intentions. Before receiving Shirley's dire letter, Winslow, now at Lake George, received a polite request dated July 31 from Loudoun for a meeting in Albany. Believing the letter a mere invitation for a social call and consenting to his officers' advice not to honor the request, Winslow turned down the overture. Convinced that the rejection was proof of insubordination, Loudoun immediately ordered Winslow to Albany. Loudoun and Winslow resolved the issue with a compromise whereby Winslow accepted the authority of the commander in chief but under "the terms and conditions agreed upon" by the colonial governments.[114]

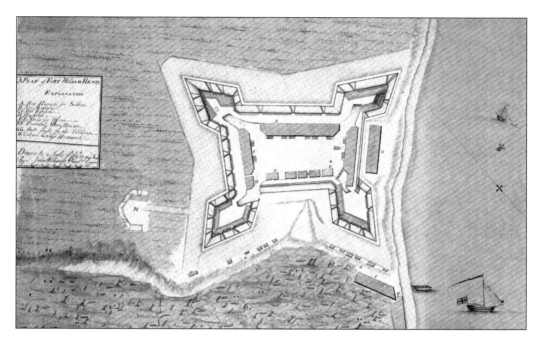

"A Plan of Fort William Henry" 1756 by John Williams, revealing a number of details of the fort and outworks, as well as the sloop *Earl of Loudoun* and two additional vessels. (Collection of J. Robert Maguire)

Facing page: "Plan of Fort Edward" 1756 by engineer Harry Gordon. (Crown Collection, New York State Library)

The 1756 Crown Point army, similar in size and composition to Johnson's force a year earlier, never advanced beyond the southern shore of Lake George. The defenses at Fort William Henry were improved and several sloops and scows were completed at the lake in 1756. In early June, engineer Harry Gordon evaluated Fort William Henry and Fort Edward, providing interesting sketches of both forts. Fort William Henry was described as four bastions connected by curtains (walls) with a ditch (8-foot deep by 30-foot wide) running from the northwest bastion to the southeast bastion. Gordon noted that the "Ramparts and Parapets…[were] faced up with large Logs of Timber bound together with smaller ones. The Rampart is in most Places fifteen Foot broad on the Curtains."[115] The parapets were 15-18 feet thick, curtains 12-15 feet thick, and ramparts 10-11 feet high. Casemates were located beneath the left side of the southeast bastion and east curtain; magazines were built under the northeast and northwest bastions. Gordon recommended raising the walls three feet, where the fort was exposed to higher ground, and building a defensive ravelin (pointed outwork consisting of two ramparts) in front of the southwest curtain. He also recommended building a palisaded covered way to "a detached Redou[b]t, made last Year…to scour the Bank above the Morass [West Brook]."[116] Without these additions, Gordon warned that an enemy could open trenches and a battery within 280 yards of the fort.

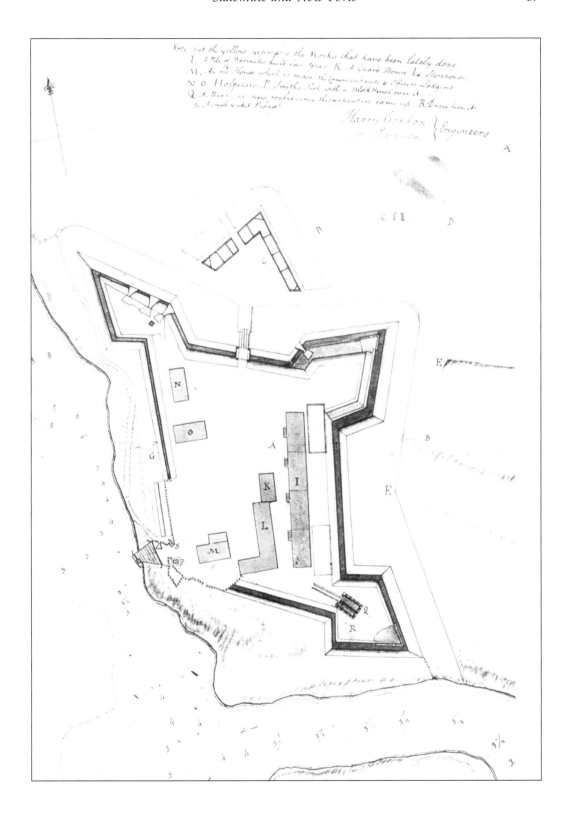

Gordon also described Fort Edward and made similar recommendations to improve its defenses. He delineated three bastions and a half bastion (on the south side adjacent to the Hudson River), two gates, ditches on the north and west sides, and palisades between the ditches and the parapet. Gordon complained that the parapet was only 6-8 feet thick and 8-10 feet high. To strengthen Fort Edward, he suggested that the "Parapets ought to be faced with Logs as at Fort William Henry, and made from 14 to 16 f[ee]t thick," and recommended raising the ramparts on the east and south sides to accommodate casemates "and proper Cover for 2 Magazines under the 2 Bastions."[117] In addition, Gordon proposed construction of a ravelin on the north side, redoubts on the east and south sides, and storehouses on the adjacent island (present-day Rogers Island).

In August 1756 Lord Loudoun sent Lieutenant Colonel Ralph Burton of the 48th Regiment on an inspection tour of Fort William Henry and Fort Edward. His report to Loudoun painted a dismal picture. At Fort William Henry, Burton found the garrison "extremely indolent, and dirty…The Fort stinks enough to cause an infection, they have all their sick in it. Their Camp [is] Nastier than anything I could conceive, their Necessary houses, Kitchens, Graves and places for Slaughtering cattle, all mixed through the encampment."[118] He reported provisions being wasted: "the Men having just what they Please, no great Command kept up" and only one advance guard for the camp.[119] The fort's southeast curtain and east bastion were "so low that the interior [could be] seen" from the higher ground adjacent to the fort, ditches that had been made in the loose sand had crumbled, platforms were deficient, the ravelin on the southeast side was unfinished, the casemates and powder magazine were wet (150 barrels of powder ruined), the barracks were inadequate, the well water was "not fit for Drinking," and some gun carriages had rotted.[120] Burton submitted a laundry list of changes to rectify the inadequacies of Fort William Henry, including raising the southeast curtain and east bastion, constructing new platforms, digging ditches, completing the ravelin, replacing boards and caulking the casemates, adding rain gutters, building a separate hospital, a magazine, ovens, a blacksmith's forge, and a carpenter's shop. He also recommended another "Redoubt or blockhouse" on the high ground southeast of the fort and another redoubt on the "rising Ground to the southwest" about 400 yards from the fort.[121] Burton noted that the road to Fort Edward was "very Stony and broken in many places, extremely dangerous for Convoys" due to "passes" that were vulnerable to an enemy ambush and suggested building a picketed fort at the halfway point.[122]

At Fort Edward, Burton found the garrison, under Major General Phineas Lyman, more disciplined and the men "hard at work Intrenching and Picketing their Encampment" and, unlike the lax security at Fort William Henry, a "Succession of Scouting parties [were sent] out."[123] Nevertheless, he found the fort in "a very weak Condition" and so recommended "that the Fort be entirely rais[e]d…with a Rampart Sufficient to mount cannon."[124] (Only eight cannons were at the fort.) Twenty cannons and 6 mortars were deemed necessary to defend the fort, the ravelin on the north side needed to be completed, and another barracks built. Burton suggested that the "Island opposite the Fort" needed to be fortified because it blocked the view of the west channel of the river from the perspective of the fort.[125] He also proposed huts for the rangers, barracks for 100 men, a hospital, a blacksmith's forge, an apothecary shop, and other facilities on the island. In September Burton was placed in command of Fort Edward by Loudoun.

As Winslow's army vacillated at Lake George during the summer of 1756, events at Oswego would ultimately cancel any possible move northward. To blunt a British campaign against Fort Niagara or Fort Frontenac, the governor-general of New France decided to destroy the British fortifications at Oswego—Forts Ontario, Oswego, and George, located on Lake Ontario at the mouth of the Oswego River. Arriving on August 11 with 3,500 troops and a train of artillery, Major General Louis-Joseph de Montcalm quickly made preparations for a siege of Fort Ontario. Prior to the commencement of the French cannon barrage, the British commander, Lieutenant Colonel James F. Mercer, moved his forces from Fort Ontario to the equally-vulnerable Fort Oswego. Mercer was beheaded by a cannonball during the bombardment on August 14 and the garrison surrendered an hour after his death. Montcalm's army captured 1,700 British and provincial troops and civilians, along with 121 artillery pieces, a vast amount of provisions, and four large sailing vessels. The British forts were razed.

After learning of the disaster, troops of the 44th Regiment, under Major General Daniel Webb, who were on their way to Oswego, hurriedly destroyed the half-completed fort at the "Great Carrying Place" (present-day Rome, New York) and retreated south on the Mohawk River. Montcalm was now ready to reinforce the fort at Carillon. On August 22 the garrison at Fort Edward heard that Oswego had been attacked, but it was not until the beginning of September that "a Confirmation" of the surrender reached Fort Edward, along with reports that English prisoners had been "butchered."[126] The "massacre" of scores of prisoners and the taking of captives by Montcalm's Indians would foretell the tragedy that would occur a year later at Fort William Henry. Because Loudoun believed that additional French attacks were probable, on August 20 he ordered Winslow to cancel the planned assault on Carillon and assume a defensive posture.

Meanwhile, the garrisons at Fort Edward and Fort William Henry battled camp diseases, including "Continual Fevers & D[y]sentery."[127] In spite of numerous problems, troops continued to work on the forts, as well as four sloops and two large sailing scows. Two of the sloops were about 40 tons each, and two 20 tons each. One of the two 40-ton sloops was never finished; the other, the *Earl of Loudoun*, was launched on August 23.[128] Three of the sloops made several forays into the northern section of the lake during the late summer and early fall of 1756. In early August Robert Rogers wrote that he embarked on "a Lighter [sloop] with twenty-four of my Company…& 60 men" from a provincial unit for a scouting expedition to Ticonderoga.[129] On September 2 Major General John Winslow departed on a "Tour round the Lake" with the three sloops : "One sloop with two Six pounders [and] One Seven Inch Mort[a]r and Eight Swivels [with] fifty men, One Sloop four Swivels forty men, One [sloop] two Swivels and thirty five men."[130] Winslow's squadron noticed a French vessel "built after the man[n]er of a Row Galley with about Twenty men" at the northern end of Lake George and fired a six-pound cannon at it.[131] The exact configuration of the British scows on Lake George remains somewhat uncertain. However, in late May 1756 French scouts had observed two sailing scows "shaped like flat barges very wide," being built at Fort William Henry and surmised that the vessels were designed for "the transport of artillery."[132] Other vessels were suggested for the 1756 campaign but never built. In late June William Shirley had written to James Abercromby with a proposal to build a "Floating Battery" on Lake Champlain for the campaign against Carillon and Crown Point.[133]

During the summer and fall of 1756, information from the scouting expeditions of Robert Rogers and others filtered through the British camps. Rogers provided a preponderance of detailed accounts of the French fortifications on Lake Champlain. On June 16 Rogers had observed the burned remnants of the French fortifications at the north end of Lake George and 3,000 men at the French encampment at Carillon. He also had taken depth measurements of Lake George and suggested that "a Ship of 100 Tons may Sail Safely through the Narrows."[134] In late June Rogers embarked with 50 rangers in five whaleboats on his most daring foray to date into French territory. Over a four-day period Rogers and his men "ha[u]led out our Boats…and carried them over a Mountain about six miles" to Lake Champlain.[135] With great exertion and difficulty, the whaleboats, along with swivel guns and other weapons, were drawn over the mountain at present-day Huletts Landing.[136] Rogers had earlier scouted a route to portage the boats between the two lakes "and found a Good Road."[137] On July 7, after scrutinizing a large number of French boats and a schooner proceeding north on Lake Champlain, Rogers and his men landed about one in the morning near Otter Creek.[138] In the pre-dawn hours of July 8 Rogers and his rangers attacked the crews of "Two Lighters" (probably small sailing galleys) about a mile north of Otter Creek, taking eight prisoners and "Destroying & Sinking [the] Ves[s]els and Cargoes—Which was Chiefly Wheat & flour, Rice, Wine & Brandy," except for a few casks that were hidden.[139] After concealing the whaleboats for future expeditions, Rogers' detachment hiked to the northwest shore of Lake George (present-day Hague) where Rogers dispatched his brother, Lieutenant Richard Rogers, to Fort William Henry to bring back bateaux for his rangers and the French prisoners taken on Lake Champlain.

Substantial progress was made on the French fort at Ticonderoga during the 1756 season. Although the fort was briefly called Fort Vaudreuil for the governor-general of New France, the name was changed to Fort Carillon. Chief engineer Michel Chartier de Lotbinière had returned to Carillon at the beginning of May. Although Lotbinière was initially short of skilled workers, the arrival of new troops included carpenters, joiners, masons, and stonecutters in the ranks of the army. A considerable amount of construction in 1756 involved stone work using rocks quarried from a site nearby. On June 1 Captain Gaspard-Joseph Chaussegros de Léry, an engineer and the son of the designer of Fort St. Frédéric, recorded that work had begun on the masonry "foundations of the encircling wall of the Fort" and on the following day wrote that "Two new ovens have been built of brick" for baking bread.[140] Two kilns were used to make a large quantity of bricks and tiles on site. Another construction project involved a large storehouse, "50 feet long…by 24 feet wide" built of oak timbers with a cellar capable of "contain[ing] 150 barrels," completed in June outside the fort on the south side.[141]

Work also continued on the four bastions and casemates. The casemate for the "No.2 Bastion" was enclosed on June 15 and made bombproof by "cover[ing] it with earth"; during a siege it was designed to hold "200 men and 250 quarters of pork," according to Captain de Léry.[142] Supported by a masonry foundation, the casemate was built with "large, square oak timbers" transported to the fort on large two-wheeled "trucks [les diables]."[143]

Facing page: **Map of Lake George, Ticonderoga, and Lake Champlain in 1756, showing the location where "Capt Rogers carried his boats across to Wood Creek" at present-day Huletts Landing. (National Archives of Canada)**

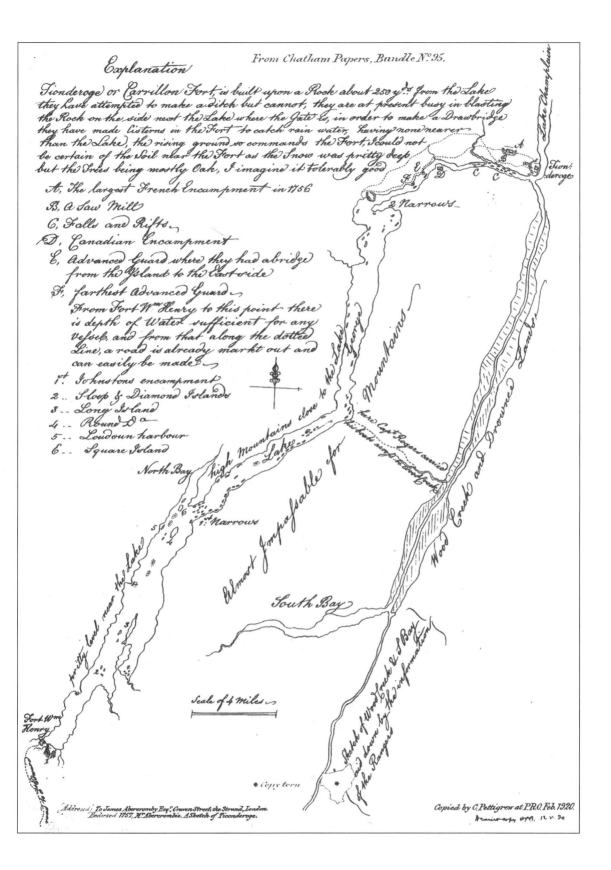

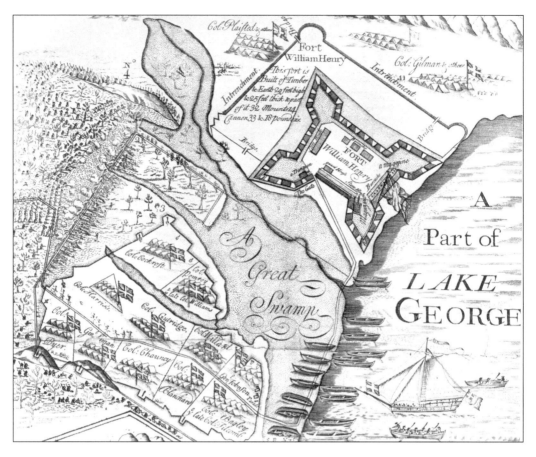

Above: The camp at Fort William Henry in 1756, engraved and printed by Thomas Johnston in Boston. (American Antiquarian Society)

Right: Aerial view of Fort Ticonderoga (Carillon) looking east to present-day Vermon. (Photo by the author)

The four completed bastions were subsequently named La Reine, Languedoc, Germain, and Joannes.[144] The magazine, designed for "35 to 40 thousand pounds of powder," was constructed under the Joannes bastion at the southeast corner of the fort.[145] Facing northeast, the Languedoc bastion contained the main bakery. The northwest bastion, La Reine, would be on the most vulnerable side of the fort during an attack by land and was still under construction in mid-July 1756, although it had already reached a height of 13 feet.[146] The Germain bastion, facing the southwest, was also vulnerable during a land attack and built higher than the two bastions on the east side.

Other structures included stone barracks and the Lotbinière Redoubt (small fort), under construction at the eastern end of the Ticonderoga peninsula, positioned to command the lake channel. A hospital was located near the Lotbinière Redoubt in 1756, but as late as September the hospital at Fort St. Frédéric was still caring for the "sick from the camp at Carillon."[147] In early June the French entrenchment at the northern end of Lake George had been demolished on Lotbinère's orders because it was apparently not located close enough to the lake to fire on English raiding parties. (Rogers had observed the burned remains of the post in mid-June.) To replace the earlier fortification, three defensive outposts or outworks were built on the La Chute River during 1756. An entrenchment was constructed on the west shore of the Lake George outlet (opposite the present site of the Mossy Point boat launch) and two advance posts were built farther north, one on each side of the outlet, connected by a bridge (at the present-day location of the natural stone dam). A sawmill was erected at the lower falls nearest to Carillon.

Life at the French camps at Ticonderoga was not easy. Dysentery and fevers, prevalent during the summer of 1756, were linked to putrid bread made by mixing spoiled and fresh flour together. In early July three of the ovens at Carillon were damaged by a fire and bread had to be temporarily supplied by the ovens at Fort St. Frédéric. The geographic isolation of Fort Carillon was conducive to a high consumption of alcohol—especially for the winter garrison. A monotonous diet of meat, bread, salt, and peas was supplemented by produce from gardens at Carillon during the summer months. Hunting and fishing could be hazardous because of the marauding English rangers and Indians.[148] English scouting reports had made the size of the Carillon camp common knowledge at Forts Edward and William Henry. In August 1756 Chaplain John Graham of Woodbury, Connecticut, noted that scouts from the Massachusetts Stockbridge Indians, led by Jacob Naunauphtaunk, reported that the "Enem[y']s Camp at Ti[c]onderoga looks to be big[g]er than the camps at Fort W[illiam] [Henry] and this place [Fort Edward] both together."[149]

Major General Louis-Joseph de Montcalm spent the first two weeks of July 1756 at Carillon before returning to Montreal to lead the expedition against Oswego. Brigadier General François (François-Gaston) de Lévis, second in command in North America, was left in charge of Carillon with 2,000 troops, including 1,400 regulars. On August 24, as Montcalm and his men made their way back to Montreal from the Oswego campaign, "News [arrived] of English preparations aimed at Lac St. Sacrement…[and] the arrival of Lord Loudoun…oblig[ated] us to speed up our march toward this frontier [Fort Carillon]."[150] On the way to Carillon, Montcalm's aide-de-camp, Captain Louis Antoine de Bougainville, took a critical look at the French forts. On September 5 he noted that Fort St. Jean on the Richelieu River was "badly built…and in bad condition" and four days later remarked that Fort St. Frédéric was "badly located, there being several heights which command it," and other outworks were "badly made and more harmful than useful."[151] Fort Carillon was also criticized by Bougainville the following day. Although he commented that the fort's "position is well chosen on a rugged rock formation," he complained that the "fort [wa]s badly oriented" and too far away from the lake, "which has obliged them to make a redoubt [Lotbinière Redoubt] at the place where the fort should have been."[152] He castigated Lotbinère for "almost never [being] at the works. It is not to his interest that the fort should be completed quickly" because "He has the exclusive privilege of selling wine" to the workmen and soldiers at his canteen.[153] Bougainville also found fault with "buil[ding] this fort of horizontal timbers in a country where stone, limestone, and sand are found in abundance."[154]

Although troop levels at Carillon reached 4,000-5,000 men in 1756, only a small percentage actually worked on the fort. A substantial number of troops and Indians were posted at the outworks at the Lake George outlet, under the command of Captain Claude-Pierre Pécaudy de Contrecoeur and Sieur St. Martin. The ongoing work at Ticonderoga was constantly monitored by the English rangers and Indian scouts. On September 9 and 10, Robert Rogers observed workers at Carillon "height[e]ning ye walls of the Fort…they rais[e]d a large Blockhouse [storehouse] near the Southeast Corn[e]r of the Fort" and mounted a battery of cannons on the east side of the fort.[155] Forty-six pieces of artillery were mounted at Carillon in 1756, which provided a highly visible deterrent to any potential English attack.

Rogers also viewed the French outposts at the north end of Lake George. The Contrecoeur camp at the outlet was used as a staging area for French and Indian raiding and reconnoitering parties dispatched to Fort William Henry and Fort Edward. On September 16, 100 Canadians and 400 Indians departed in 34 canoes, going "ashore beyond Isle La Barque," which lay close to the west shore of Lake George south of Sabbath Day Point.[156] The French and Indian party searched the islands in the Narrows for English troops and climbed a nearby mountain, which provided them a grand view of the lake below and a distant glimpse of Fort William Henry. On September 19 the French and Indians attacked a 50-man provincial detachment along the west shore of present-day Northwest Bay, committing "cruelties even the recital of which is horrible," Bougainville noted.[157] After the garrison at Fort William Henry received the news of the attack from a survivor, 150 men from the fort were sent by land as a relief force, along with the sloop *Earl of Loudoun* and troops in several whaleboats. The next morning a bateau arrived from the original detachment with another survivor and "10 Dead…Some of which had their heads…cut off. Others Scalped & Cut to p[i]eces."[158] The 17 provincial prisoners informed their French captors that only 2,000 men were at Fort William Henry, composed of "all militia, many sick, [and] no plan[s] for an offensive."[159] This, undoubtedly, must have been a surprise because earlier reports had estimated the English army at "20 thousand men."[160]

During the remaining summer and early autumn, the troops at Fort William Henry made improvements to the fort and augmented the nearby entrenchment. Twenty cannons and eight mortars and howitzers were in place to defend the fort. At Fort Edward the integration of regulars with provincial units proceeded uneventfully, although Chaplain John Graham was upset that Phineas Lyman had spent a Sunday afternoon drinking in his tent with regular officers during Sabbath services and never objected to the "Cursing and Swearing in his presence."[161] On September 8, 1756, the garrison at Fort Edward observed "a General Fire of Cannon & small Arms in Commemoration of ye Battle fought at Lake George last year."[162] Desertion, which was prevalent during the fall of 1755, was also a problem in 1756. At daybreak on September 24 a Connecticut regiment at Fort Edward "moved off toward home clandestinely" but was pursued and "fired on."[163] More than 100 men were taken prisoner and confined at Fort Edward.

As was the case in 1755, false alarms were a problem again during the fall of 1756. At Fort William Henry on September 27, Major General Winslow misconstrued the return of a provincial scouting party for a French and Indian detachment and sent urgent messages to Lord Loudoun in Albany for help. Loudoun in turn hurriedly wrote to four New England governors for reinforcements. Substantial preparations were made to send more provincial militia to Lake George before Loudoun wrote to cancel the mobilization.[164] On October 6 Loudoun and some of his staff arrived at Fort Edward for a tour of the northern forts. On the same day a report circulated at Fort Edward that Montcalm was at Carillon "with 12,000 men & [had] designs to pay us a visit."[165] While Loudoun was at Fort Edward, four deserters from the British regulars were hanged; a fifth soldier "broke the Rope twice & was reprieved."[166]

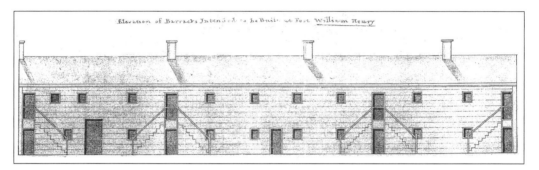

"Elevation of Barracks Intended to be Built at Fort William Henry" 1756. Drawing by Captain James Abercrombie. (Crown Collection, New York State Library)

Loudoun, accompanied by his officers and 500 troops and an entourage from Fort Edward, marched to Lake George on October 14. One provincial soldier at Fort William Henry reported that Loudoun's detachment "Came with Drums beating & Music playing, the Highlanders in the front, then Followed [by] the Gr[e]nad[i]ers" and the baggage wagons in the rear.[167] In the time since Lieutenant Colonel Burton's report, the fort had been cleaned and substantial improvements made. Dr. Ammi Ruhamah Cutter, who was part of the group from Fort Edward, noted that Fort William Henry was "much improved; a fine large Barrack[s] built on ye north side & ye Fort raised."[168] Loudoun had the satisfaction of observing the 40-ton sloop, the *Earl of Loudoun*, named for him. He and his troops left the lake for Fort Edward early on the morning of October 16, remaining there until November 1. Six days earlier Montcalm had departed from Fort Carillon, reaching Montreal on October 31.

On a very cold third day of November, snow fell at Fort William Henry and the provincial troops were ready to go home. In early November a French prisoner from the

Languedoc Regiment, captured at Carillon at the end of October by Robert Rogers, revealed that the French had withdrawn most of their troops at the outlet of Lake George, deciding not to attack Fort William Henry because scouting reports had earlier indicated that the British numbered "8000 & never less th[a]n 5000 strong."[169] The prisoner also divulged that Montcalm had 3,000 regulars and 2,000 Canadians and Indians at Carillon, as well as 36 pieces of artillery there and 18 at Fort St. Frédéric. Furthermore, he disclosed that Montcalm "would take Fort William Henry early in the spring."[170]

On November 10 the troops at Fort William Henry were "Employed in Drawing the Cannon, out of the Camp into the Fort & Leveling the Former," but the men were clearly more interested in "the Prospect of going home soon."[171] Finally on November 11, provincial regiments marched out of Fort William Henry but were hampered by "Snow [that] was 8 inches high w[h]en we Set out, it then snow[ed] & Continued snowing all day."[172] The winter garrison at Fort William Henry consisted of approximately 400 British regulars from the 44th Regiment and 100 rangers, all under the command of Major William Eyre, who had designed the fort in 1755. Major William Sparks of the 48th Regiment commanded a garrison of 500 regulars and four companies of rangers at Fort Edward. The rangers, under Captain Robert Rogers, were lodged in rows of small log huts on the island opposite Fort Edward (present-day Rogers Island).[173] Seventeen fifty-six was a year of fort construction, boat building, scouting forays, deadly ambushes, and vacillation in the Lake George–Lake Champlain Valley. The following year would witness a new military expedition and a deadly turn of events at Fort William Henry.

6. Fort William Henry Under Siege 1757

AT THE CLOSE OF THE 1756 CAMPAIGN, Fort William Henry remained the northernmost outpost of the British and provincial armies. As a staging area for expeditions against the French fortifications on Lake Champlain, Fort William Henry represented a significant threat to the French and thus plans were formulated by French officials to destroy the fort before the fight was carried to Carillon and Crown Point. The question was not "if" the French would attack, but rather, "when." Despite the obvious risk to the fort, resources devoted to its defense proved woefully inadequate in August 1757 when the siege occurred. Once more, blood would be spilled on the southern shore of Lake George.

There was no respite in the perpetual struggle for control of the Champlain Valley during the winter months of 1757. On a bitter January 15, Captain Robert Rogers with 50 rangers and two officers trudged out of Fort Edward with orders to use every opportunity to inflict harm on the French garrisons at Lake Champlain. On January 17, after recruiting more men at Fort William Henry, Rogers and his 85-man detachment departed northward on the frozen lake. As a result of injuries on the ice, Rogers was forced to send a number of men back, reducing his party to 74 men and officers. On January 20 the detachment camped west of Lake Champlain, halfway between Forts Carillon and St. Frédéric. The next morning Rogers observed a horsedrawn sleigh plodding along the icy surface of Lake Champlain on its way to Crown Point. Rogers ordered Lieutenant John Stark and 20 men north to intercept the sleigh, while Rogers would remain at the rear to prevent any escape, and Captain Thomas Speakman with another party would cover the center. To his surprise, Rogers discovered about eight more French sleighs advancing. He immediately dispatched two rangers to tell Stark not to reveal himself until the other sleighs had proceeded farther, but the effort was too late. The ambush was initiated too soon and the rearmost sleighs swiftly reversed course and made a desperate retreat back to Fort Carillon. Rogers captured "three Slays [sleighs], Seven Prisoners & six Horses," but the rest escaped.[1] After questioning the prisoners, Rogers soon recognized the dangerous situation ahead; his position was between two French forts and his presence known to the enemy. The prisoners revealed that 350 regulars were at Carillon, 600 at St. Frédéric, and 250 Canadians and 45 Indians had just arrived at Carillon with an expectation of another 50 Indians. Rogers also learned that the garrison at Carillon was anticipating additional troops, who were slated to "attack our Forts in the Spring."[2] Rogers ordered a retreat following the original route of the ranger expedition, despite the recommendation of his officers to employ a traditional ranger rule and retreat by a different path. But Rogers needed to dry his rangers' wet muskets and relighting the fires from his last campsite would be the easiest solution. The error would soon prove costly, and later that same year Rogers would write his famous "Rules of Ranging," which would include a rule of never returning by the same route.[3]

AMBUSH ON SNOWSHOES

In the meantime, Captain Paul-Louis Dazemard de Lusignan, the commanding officer at Fort Carillon, had dispatched about 115 regulars, Canadians, and Indians to cut off the retreating rangers. As Rogers and his snowshoe-clad rangers made their ascent single-file along a craggy ravine, west of Lake Champlain, "a Volley of 200 Shot" was fired by the French and Indian detachment, "who had formed themselves in a Half-Moon" on the hill above.[4] "At the first Fire," the *New-York Mercury* subsequently reported, "Rogers' Hat was shot off his Head and his Skull grazed."[5] Sixteen-year-old Thomas Brown from Charlestown, Massachusetts, was wounded but followed orders and "knocked [a prisoner] on the Head and killed him, lest he should Escape."[6] Rogers and his men instantly returned fire and then retreated to the other side of the ravine. At the same time, the French pursued the rangers with bayonets drawn, killing several men and taking some prisoners. Rogers and his surviving men joined Lieutenant Stark and 40 rangers on the opposite hillside. The rangers repulsed the onslaught, maintaining a constant fire until sunset. Rogers was subsequently wounded a second time by a musket ball that ripped through his wrist and hand, making it impossible for him to load his musket. In the darkness Rogers met with his remaining officers, "who unanimously were of [the] Opinion that it was most prudent to carry of[f] the wounded of our Party, and take Advantage of the Night to return homeward," before the French "send out a fresh Party upon us."[7] Early the next morning the rangers reached the ice of Lake George and Rogers ordered Stark and two men to forge ahead to Fort William Henry to secure sleighs for the wounded. Finally, on the evening of January 23, Rogers and the surviving members of the detachment, consisting of "forty-five Effective and nine wounded" men, reached Fort William Henry.[8] Fourteen men had been killed, nine wounded, and seven taken prisoner, including young Thomas Brown. According to Captain Lusignan, French losses amounted to 19 killed and 27 wounded; but a French prisoner later revealed that Rogers' detachment had killed 28 during the engagement "and 28 more died afterwards of their Wounds."[9] Three of the prisoners taken by Rogers during the sleigh ambush on Lake Champlain were killed by the rangers, but four others were retrieved alive by the French. Irrespective of the casualties, newspapers praised Rogers' "Courage and Conduct in fighting and opposing 300 [actually 115] of the Enemy."[10]

EXPEDITION ACROSS THE ICE

Two months after Rogers' engagement, the French launched a sizable expedition from Carillon to destroy Fort William Henry. On January 15 Major General Louis-Joseph de Montcalm had submitted a plan to the governor-general of New France, Pierre de Rigaud

Rangers under attack on January 21, 1757, following their ambush of French sleighs on Lake Champlain. (Painting by Gary S. Zaboly)

de Vaudreuil de Cavagnial, to burn, "at least, the outer parts of the fort," using 800 troops under a regular officer, Colonel François-Charles de Bourlamaque—third in command in North America.[11] Governor Vaudreuil, however, decided to employ a larger force commanded by his own brother, François-Pierre de Rigaud de Vaudreuil. The 54-year-old Rigaud had a long military career, as well as political experience as the governor of Trois-Rivières. In 1746 he had led the expedition that ended with the destruction of Fort Massachusetts. The governor-general later maintained that the objective of the winter campaign was only to burn vessels and storehouses at the fort in order "to prevent the enemy [from] making any attempt" on Fort Carillon in the spring.[12] But the strategy and equipment supplied to his brother's army clearly suggested that the aim of the expedition was the capture and destruction of the fort.

The 1,600-man force consisted of approximately 200-250 French regulars, 300 Troupes de la Marine, 650 Canadian militia, and 400 Indians. The accouterments furnished to the men provide an insight into eighteenth-century wilderness warfare. Each man was supplied with two pairs of moccasins, a pair of "Indian Stockings or Leg pieces" and another pair of worsted stockings, a pair of worsted mittens, two cotton shirts, a thick red woolen cap and a hat, a flannel waistcoat, a blue cloth vest and breeches, two coats, a blanket and bearskin, two pocket knives, a large knife worn in a sheath on the chest, a tomahawk, snowshoes, a pair of "Iron Creepers to walk on the ice," a steel and flint, a grenade, needles and thread, and a bag of tobacco.[13] The men were also equipped with scaling ladders over five feet long; three of which could be pieced together to scale the walls of Fort William Henry.

The army left Carillon on March 15 with 12 days of provisions (biscuits, bread, and a half pound of pork per man per day). The men were not issued an allowance of liquor, except rum for the Indians. Each man was provided with a rope-drawn hand sled that was used to haul equipment, provisions, and combustible materials. On March 16 the French detachment "proceeded down the middle of the lake in five columns" and camped in sight of Sugar Loaf Mountain near present-day Huletts Landing.[14] One participant described Rigaud as "a little Man, thin [who] always marched in the Front," and whose only accommodation was a tent, "the only one in the Whole Army."[15] The following night the troops camped north of Northwest Bay, sleeping on the ice without lighting fires.

The army reached Northwest Bay on March 18, remaining there all day as scouts reconnoitered Fort William Henry. Rigaud sent several officers with a spyglass to observe the fort from the vantage point of a hill. The officers reported to Rigaud that the fort "did not appear accessible by ladder."[16] "About 11" at night Rigaud's detachment reached the "Bay of Niacktaron" several miles from the fort.[17] The bay would serve as a depot for supplies, as well as the staging area for the assault on Fort William Henry. After midnight the French army advanced into the black night "determin[e]d to Assault the Fort by Escalade [scaling the walls with ladders] in three different Places at once."[18]

The winter garrison, commanded by Major William Eyre, consisted of 274 British regulars and 72 rangers, the latter under newly-promoted Captain John Stark. (An additional 128 men were unfit for duty due to illness.) In his memoirs, Stark disclosed that the regulars of Irish descent received an extra supply of rum on the night of March 16 "and commenced their carousal which they carried on with unabated vigor through the night and during the ensuing day in honor of St. Patrick."[19] Stark directed the ranger sutler, Samuel

Blodget, not to issue any grog (rum mixed with water) to the rangers without a written order. Consequently, the rangers remained sober and manned the ramparts. Ranger sentries first detected the French movement during the early morning hours of March 19 and alerted the garrison. "About two o'Clock" in the morning, Eyre wrote, "a Noise" was heard at a distance and a "light" observed on the lake; a subsequent French account of the expedition disclosed that "the ice was so smooth that night that the scouts could not walk without making noise [probably from their ice creepers]."[20] Some time after hearing the first noise, the garrison at the fort was confronted with a full-scale assault.

The approach of the intruders was met with a discharge of muskets from the fort and the deafening thunder of its cannons, firing grapeshot (bags of iron balls) and canister shot (tinned containers with musket-size lead balls). The barrage effectively stopped the attack, and the French made several futile attempts to burn one of the sloops and the bateaux. The French reported that troops from the fort "made a sortie to put out the fire in the bateaux," but they were driven back with losses.[21] A French prisoner later suggested that the plan for a surprise attack failed because "the Garrison [was] Alert and so much on their Guard."[22] The raiders withdrew at daybreak and a few men from the fort were sent outside the walls for an inspection, where they discovered several scaling ladders and combustible materials. Later on the morning of March 19, the French renewed their attack on two sides of the fort with "a very heavy & Continual discharge of small Arms" on the right flank "Intended to Cover" men in the rear who "set fire to the Bateau[x] and which burned but Slowly."[23] The French and Indians retired at sunset only to resume the attack after midnight on March 20 and "set on Fire two Sloops and burn[ed] Almost all our Bateau[x]," Eyre wrote.[24]

At dawn the raiders withdrew, only to reappear about midday when the "entire detachment…marched across the lake in full view of the English, parading the ladders ostentatiously."[25] As the men in the fort viewed the display, Captain François Le Mercier and several soldiers approached the fort with a red flag of truce. (A red flag was used because the French flag was white.) Eyre sent an officer and four men to meet the party, who presented a letter from Rigaud. The letter was delivered to Eyre, and Mercier was escorted "into the Commanding Officer's Apartment, where all or most of the officers" were assembled.[26] Rigaud's lengthy message apologized for the "Miseries" of war, but asserted that the English "had made encroachments on His most Christian Majesty's Territories & built Forts," and therefore he requested the surrender of the fort to save an "Effusion of Blood."[27] The garrison was assured "all the Honours of War," but some possessions needed to be "left by the Officers to please & gratify the Indians."[28] If the surrender terms were rejected, then the assault would continue and "the Cruelties of the Savages cou[l]d not altogether be prevented."[29] Eyre replied that he was resolved "to defend His Majesty's Garrison to the last Extremity."[30] This was undoubtedly a wise course of action because a French prisoner later suggested that had the fort been captured, the French "were to give no Quarter" and planned to "put the Garrison to the Sword."[31]

The pause in the fighting allowed time for the troops in the fort to pull the roofs off the adjacent storehouses to prevent the spread of fires from the outbuildings to the fort. The French renewed their musket fire and initiated another full-scale attack that night. Although the general assault failed, French troops and Indians were successful in burning two storehouses and "All the Ranger Huts [17]…inside their Picketed Fort."[32] The

French withdrew at daybreak on March 21; heavy snow fell the rest of the day and into the night, causing a cessation of fighting that extended into the following day. At eleven o'clock on the night of March 22 the raiders finally succeeded in burning a large sloop on the stocks "pierced for sixteen guns," "whose bowsprit touched one of the bastions of the fort."[33]

On Wednesday March 23 Rigaud's weary soldiers began their march back to Carillon, arriving the next day. Eyre noted that the deep snow prevented "any Discoveries of their loss," but a few days later a foray by British troops found "some of the French [dead]…thrust into a Hole, made in the Ice, one Man stuffed into the pile of Chord Wood, which they had set on Fire."[34] Rigaud's men left most of their hand sleds and burned their scaling ladders. On March 29 Lieutenant Colonel George Monro with five companies of the 35th Regiment of Foot relieved Eyre at Fort William Henry. Virtually all of the structures surrounding the fort had been destroyed during the raid. The French reported that "three hundred bateaux" and "four vessels" had been burned during the assault and two "30-oar galleys."[35] In a subsequent letter to the British commander in chief, Lord Loudoun, Eyre disclosed that only the "Whaleboats, Scows or Gondolas & Bayboats h[av]e Escaped the Conflagration."[36] (At the close of 1756, Nathan Whiting had reported that four sloops, four gondolas, and five bayboats were present at Fort William Henry.)[37] Despite Eyre's report, only two sloops were actually destroyed during the March attack. In June 1757 Loudoun noted "one Sloop unhurt, and another that wanted little repair," and on August 1 Major General Webb reported that "two of the Old Sloops" remained at the fort.[38]

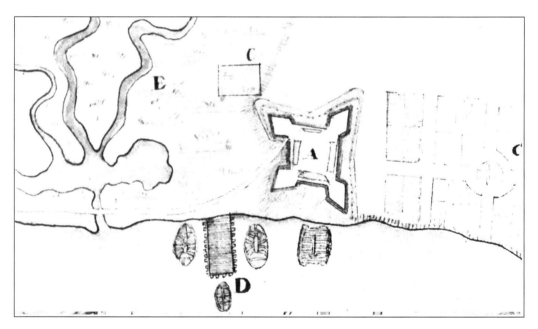

Detail of "A Plan of Fort William Henry and the English Camps & Retr[e]nchment," 1757, showing vessels at the dock. (Crown Collection, New York State Library)

As the days grew longer in April and signs of spring unfolded after a severe winter, the season was marred by preparations for war. The sounds of birds in the wilderness would soon be replaced by the deadly whistle of musket balls and the whack of lethal tomahawks. Because of Robert Rogers' absence from the Lake George-Lake Champlain corridor while recovering from smallpox, and the reassignment of a good portion of his rangers to a campaign in Nova Scotia, the garrisons at Fort Edward and Fort William Henry were left without adequate resources to carry on extensive scouting expeditions. Lord Loudoun had planned to attack Quebec in the spring of 1757, which would have kept Montcalm's army engaged in a defensive action in Canada and would have precluded an assault on Fort William Henry. In anticipation of the 1757 campaign, Loudoun used his time in late 1756 and early 1757 to better organize supply lines and achieve more efficiency in transportation. However, on February 4 William Pitt, the British secretary of state, ordered Loudoun to attack the French stronghold of Louisbourg on Cape Breton Island before making the assault on Quebec.[39] (Loudoun didn't receive the orders for several months.)

On April 22 Rogers received a letter from Loudoun's aide to proceed to Albany with three companies of rangers drawn from Fort Edward and Fort William Henry and after that prepare for embarkation from New York City. Troops boarded transports in New York City "between the 22nd and 25th" of May and sailed a short distance to an anchorage at Sandy Hook, New Jersey.[40] The ships languished there, as Loudoun awaited further intelligence on the French fleet and news of the British fleet slated to rendezvous with him at Halifax, Nova Scotia. Finally, on June 20 the fleet at Sandy Hook, consisting of "97 sail," departed for Halifax with 6,000 troops, including over 500 rangers.[41] Loudoun's fleet reached Halifax on June 30 and over the next week was joined piecemeal by British transports and warships from England under Admiral Francis Holbourne, who arrived with "13 Sail of ye Line" on July 8.[42]

Holbourne's fleet had been hindered by bad weather; this delay in assembling the British invasion force allowed time for three French squadrons, exceeding the firepower of the British fleet, to reach Louisbourg harbor. Lingering fog and adverse winds impeded fresh intelligence on the size of the French fleet. For nine days Loudoun and his senior officers held a council of war at Halifax, hearing testimony from 20 witnesses to decide if an attack on Louisbourg could be successful. On the last day of July the council voted unanimously to proceed against Louisbourg. Four days later, with a long-awaited fair wind, the British fleet prepared for departure, only to be halted as a result of new intelligence on the French fleet at Louisbourg. Learning of the superiority of the French armada, Loudoun gave the orders to abandon the campaign and returned to New York with his troops.

CAMPAIGN AGAINST FORT WILLIAM HENRY

While British and provincial troops prepared for the Louisbourg campaign, French authorities were engaged in a mobilization of forces to destroy Fort William Henry. As early as December 1756, Pierre de Rigaud de Vaudreuil de Cavagnial, the governor-general of New France, began solidifying support from France's Native American allies for a military offensive during the coming year. Holding a conference from December 13th to the 30th in Montreal, Vaudreuil encouraged Nipissings, Algonquins, Caughnawagas, Ottawas from Detroit, Potawatomis from Michilimackinac, and even some Iroquois from New York to resist the English. He urged the Indians to "decide whether the English or the French [were]...more reliable" and suggested that "the English have no other object than to surround you and keep you in irons" and have shown "nothing but deceit and treachery in the[ir] conduct."[43] The meeting was successful: during the last week of June "Canoe loads [of Indians] arrive[d] every day [at Montreal]. The number...from the Far West [primarily the Great Lakes region] now passes a thousand."[44] Some of the Indians were from tribes that were so distant that no Canadian interpreter understood their language.

On May 8 Colonel François-Charles de Bourlamaque left Montreal for Carillon with two regiments of regulars; by May 20 Bourlamaque had 1,400 men at Carillon. According to Montcalm's young aide-de-camp, Captain Louis Antoine de Bougainville, Carillon had been plagued by "disorder, pilferage, and vexations" over the winter under Captain Paul-Louis Dazemard de Lusignan, who personally profited from the sale of wine at four times the price compared to Montreal.[45] By spring, however, the garrison returned to normal military discipline and additional manpower allowed some further work on the fort's defenses. The outposts at the northern end of Lake George and at the sawmill on the La Chute River were restored. Despite preparations for the campaign against Fort William Henry, a number of projects at Fort Carillon were completed, including the north and west demilunes (triangular-shaped outworks or ravelins, consisting of two ramparts separated from the main fort by a ditch and connected by a bridge). Other work involved facing existing surfaces with stone, digging trenches, completing the last curtain wall, and forming covered ways (passageways sheltered by embankments).[46]

By late May British and provincial troops arrived in greater numbers at both Fort Edward and Fort William Henry. On May 28 Colonel John Parker reached Fort Edward with 400 provincial troops from New Jersey ("Jersey Blues," named for the color of their uniform). Marching to a tune on a fife, Parker and his men departed for Fort William Henry the next day, accompanied by 10 wagons and 36 carts. Little new construction occurred at the two forts during the 1757 season, except for projects that were deemed an absolute necessity. On May 26, five days after arriving at Fort Edward with Connecticut troops, Sergeant Jabez Fitch, Jr., was ordered to take "20 Men & Build a Hospital on ye Lo[we]r End of ye Island [present-day Rogers Island] to Put those that Had ye Smallpox."[47] Work parties soon discovered that the "[Black] Flies were V[e]ry Troublesom[e]" on the island and at Fort Edward.[48] Only small improvements were made to Fort Edward, including work on the ditch at the east curtain, which involved placing facines (bundles of sticks) on the sides to retain the earth. Sanitary conditions were clearly specified in the general orders at the fort. (The "Necessary Houses" were "Dug Six Feet Deep & about 100 yards" from the encampments at Fort Edward and every evening the bottom covered with "Fresh Earth."[49]) Likewise, little new construction occurred at Fort William Henry; virtually none of the outbuildings, destroyed during the March raid, were rebuilt. Two row galleys, however, were under construction during the summer of 1757. In late July a hurriedly-built entrenched camp would be erected near the site of William Johnson's 1755 camp.

During the spring and summer of 1757, New France's Native American allies domi-

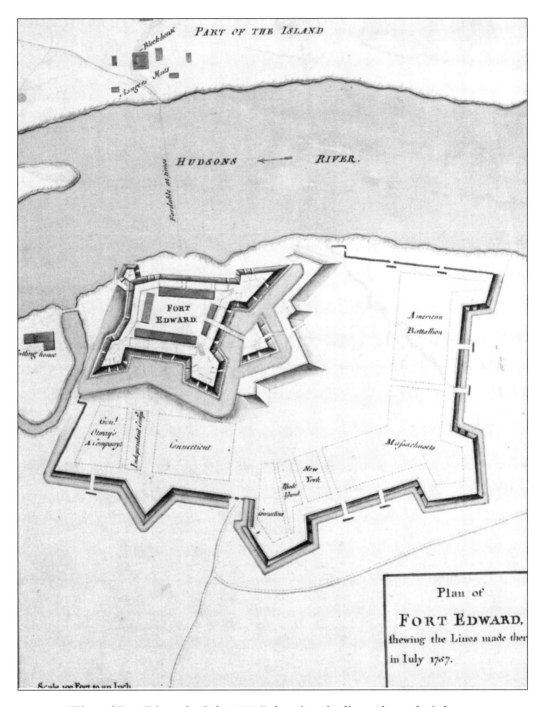

**"Plan of Fort Edward...July 1757," showing the lines, the sutler's house,
and structures on the island. (Collection of J. Robert Maguire)**

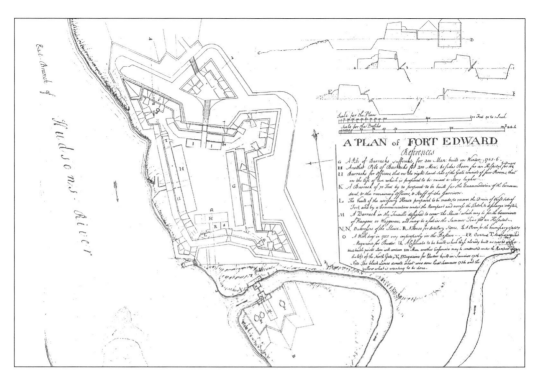

"A Plan of Fort Edward" (ca. 1756/ 1757), delineating the interior structures of the fort. (Crown Collection, New York State Library)

nated the territory between Forts Edward and Carillon. In late April a party of Caughnawagas, Ottawas, and Potawatomis attacked English troops escorting wagons to Fort William Henry, taking "four scalps and three prisoners from the Royal American Regiment."[50] The prisoners informed their French captives that the British were not planning any offensive against Carillon in 1757. Three weeks later, Montcalm's aide-de-camp, Captain Bougainville, mused "that Lord Loudoun is waiting for a squadron in order to attack Louisbourg."[51] A short time later, Bougainville wrote that Governor-General Vaudreuil had decided to attack Fort William Henry "in order to take advantage of the absence of Lord Loudoun, who has led away the best troops."[52]

In early June, Captain Richard Rogers (younger brother of Robert Rogers) led rangers from Fort William Henry and Fort Edward on a mission to destroy the French outpost at the northern end of Lake George. Richard Rogers, accompanied by Captain Jonathan Ogden and his New York provincial rangers, reached the northern end of the lake at dawn on June 7. The detachment of 160 rangers fired on the French stockaded fort, killing one officer, but the English raiders were forced to retreat to their bateaux under a hail of musket balls and mortar rounds. Rogers, who had remained in his boat racked with illness during the skirmish, was rowed back to Fort William Henry, where he died of smallpox two weeks later. The mission had failed to take even one French prisoner.[53] Another engagement occurred three days later near Fort Edward. After receiving reports in early June of the arrival of new troops at the English forts, Colonel Bourlamaque dispatched a scouting party from Carillon to gain fresh intelligence. About 11 o'clock on the morning of June 10 the garrison at Fort Edward was "Alarm[e]d By a Smart Firing...where ye Carpenters w[ere] at work" gathering timber.[54] Troops under Colonel Phineas Lyman of Connecticut pursued the assailants and fired on a party of 100 Indians led by Charles-Michel Mouet de Langlade, a partisan leader of Canadian-Ottawa descent. Five men from the original work detail were missing, four others were killed and scalped, "Some of Them [had] their Brains Run out," and one had his chest "Cut open & His H[e]art Torn out."[55]

Scouting forays and raids continued for the rest of June and throughout July. On June 16 Captain Israel Putnam, commander of the Connecticut provincial rangers at Fort Edward, returned from an 11-day scouting expedition with a French prisoner taken at Carillon, who revealed that the French "Army is Coming Against us Very Soon."[56] Three days later a detachment from Fort Edward on its way to Saratoga was ambushed only a mile from the fort. At 11 o'clock on the moonlit night of June 30, Captain Putnam and his scouting party of 60-80 men observed a large number of bateaux and canoes on Wood Creek. Putnam's men fired on the unsuspecting war party of 226 Indians and nine French officers and cadets. "The Fire continued [for] five Hours, during which Time" the Indians tried to cross the creek twice but "were beat back both times."[57]

In July more reports surfaced of an impending French attack. On July 1 two escapees from Canada informed the garrison at Fort Edward that the French army planned to attack with "8000" men; two days later four deserters from Fort Carillon divulged that the French were "to Attack our Forts."[58] Mohawk scouts returned to Fort Edward on July 10 with a prisoner taken at Crown Point, who again confirmed that Montcalm "with 6000 men had resolved to pay the English a Visit at Fort William Henry."[59] Surprisingly, this additional intelligence of Montcalm's plans did not result in any immediate defensive changes at either of the British forts.

Further evidence of the aggressive tactics of the French and Indians occurred the very next day. A scouting party from Fort William Henry came under attack by 200 Indians on July 11 near South Bay on Lake Champlain and were forced into a hasty retreat back to the fort.[60] On July 23, 80 men from Fort Edward, consisting of carpenters cutting trees and their guards, were attacked less than a half-mile from the fort by 150 Indians, led by Lieutenant Joseph Marin de La Malgue. The *New-York Gazette* reported that "Eleven of the English were kill[e]d, 3 of them regulars, and ten wounded...Four of them kill[e]d...by Bows and Arrows...our Men were scalped and mangled in a most barbarous Manner, some [of] their Throats Cut"[61]

With the increasing level of assaults by Indians, Lieutenant Colonel George Monro, commander of the troops at Fort William Henry, expanded patrols on Lake George to gather the latest intelligence on enemy movements. At the same time, the French dispatched daily reconnaissance parties in bateaux and canoes to observe any English advances, particularly after the raid by the rangers in early June on their stockaded fort at the northern end of Lake George and an attack in July by a Mohawk party on French regulars near their camp on the La Chute River.[62] A clash between the enemy scouting parties on the lake was inevitable. On July 20 Lieutenant François-Xavier de Saint-Ours, commanding a large reconnaissance canoe carrying a crew of nine Canadians and one cadet, encountered a scouting party from Fort William Henry, led by Captain Robert McGinnis of the New York provincials. A skirmish ensued between the parties near "Isle la Barque," identified on a French map as an island near the west shore, south of Sabbath Day Point.[63] Four of the French crew were wounded, two killed, and St. Ours was shot in the hand.[64] Two days after the English attack, Bougainville recorded that "Three hundred men, Indians and Canadians [led by Charles-Michel Mouet de Langlade] are now lying in ambush, part in canoes, part on land, and plan to capture" English patrols on the lake.[65]

PARKER EXPEDITION

On July 23 Colonel John Parker departed from Fort William Henry with 350 men, composed largely of troops from his New Jersey Blues, with the remainder from the New York regiment, aboard "Whale and Bay Boats [small sailing vessels]" to "attack the advance Guard at Ticonderoga."[66] (See endnote 66 for a discussion of the differences in documents regarding the date of Parker's departure.) Some of Parker's men later revealed that the intended attack on the French outposts also included a plan "to burn the [saw]mill at the Falls" on the La Chute River.[67] Earlier, a French prisoner, who had been captured by the Mohawks, disclosed that Montcalm had a large number of bateaux at Ticonderoga with preparations to build rafts by placing "Planks across two of them to transport their Artillery...to attack Fort William Henry."[68] Parker's planned raid was rather ambitious, given the size of his detachment and the large number of French regulars, Canadians, and Indians at Ticonderoga.

On July 23, after learning of English vessels on the lake, "M.de Corbière [lieutenant in Troupes de la Marine] left at once [to reinforce Langlade] with about 450 men, almost all Indians, to lay ambush among the islands."[69] That night Lieutenant Corbière observed "twenty barges [whaleboats] and two skiffs."[70] At daybreak on July 24, after spending the night on an island, three of Parker's whaleboat crews in the lead fell into an ambush laid by the Indians, who had hidden among the trees at Sabbath Day Point. Completely bewildered by the trap, the crews surrendered. Ignorant of the ambush, the men in the next three vessels were captured, and in short order the remaining boat crews found themselves in the midst of a frightening assault.

Some of the original sources, however, offer a slight variation of the narrative of the ambush. A newspaper account based on an "extract of a letter" from Fort William Henry mentioned that the Indians used the first three captured whaleboats as decoys, but Captain Bougainville did not mention this in his account, writing that the next three boats had "followed at a little distance" and were quickly captured.[71] Adam Williamson, a young British engineer at Fort William Henry, wrote that Parker's detachment "Missed three of their boats in the night & hearing some shots [the next day] the whole steered that way & seeing the Enemy on shore they attempted to land"; some of Parker's men, held by the French, seem to corroborate at least a portion of this account, suggesting "that they had separated in the course of the night; that the Indians attacked them at day-break."[72] Nevertheless, reports of the melee that followed were fairly consistent in all accounts. The Indians rushed from a "concealed...point," shrieking blood-curdling yells and firing their muskets as they "jumped into their canoes" and "surrounded" Parker's detachment and began spearing the panic-stricken provincial troops "like fish, and sinking the barges [whaleboats] by seizing them from below and capsizing them...terrified by the shooting, the sight, the cries, and the agility of these monsters, [Parker's men] surrendered almost without firing a shot."[73] Parker and Captain Jonathan Ogden of the New York provincial regiment escaped in four whaleboats with 60-70 men; a few others landed with another boat onshore at Sabbath Day Point "and came over the Mountains" to Fort William Henry.[74]

The prisoners from the Parker detachment were conveyed back to the Indian encampment at Ticonderoga. Father Pierre Roubaud, a Jesuit missionary who had accompanied the St. Francis Abenakis to Carillon, surveyed the forlorn captives, who were paraded around the camp with "ropes around their necks," and had a feeling of compassion for them: "in a very wretched state, their eyes bathed in tears, their faces covered with perspiration and even with blood."[75] Rum taken from the captured whaleboats and ingested by the Indians "caused them to commit great cruelties" and three of the prisoners were "put in the pot" and eaten, according to Bougainville.[76] Witnessing the ritual cannibalism at the camp of the Ottawas, Father Roubaud observed warriors consuming the flesh of a captive "with famished avidity" and drinking "large spoonfuls of this detestable broth" from a cooked Englishman, while ten other prisoners were forced to watch.[77] Roubaud was unable to discourage a young Ottawa warrior from eating the flesh of a roasted Englishman and the Indian responded by offering a piece to the priest. Having taken prisoners, some of the Indians from the Great Lakes region wished to return home and had to be persuaded to remain at Carillon. On July 26 the surviving men from Parker's detachment were taken to Fort St. Frédéric to board a schooner bound for Canada. Considered prisoners of the Indians, the men were ransomed by French authorities in September 1757, taken from Montreal to Quebec, and finally to British-held Halifax, Nova Scotia.

In a letter to Lord Loudoun from his headquarters at Fort Edward, Major General Daniel Webb absolved himself of any blame for the Parker fiasco at "Sabbath Day Point," submitting that the detachment left "without my knowing any thing of the matter till too late to prevent it" and the purpose of the expedition "I real[l]y cannot tell, all the reason they can give for it, was to take some Prisoners."[78] Not only was the loss of men consequential, but the disaster left the vulnerable garrison at Fort William Henry with only five whaleboats for scouting. The men that were slain in the ambush were not easily forgotten. A week later, abandoned whaleboats were observed aground on the beach at Sabbath Day Point and a "large number of English bodies stretched out on the shore or scattered here and there in the woods. Some were cut into pieces, and nearly all were mutilated in the most frightful manner."[79] A year later during the 1758 campaign against Carillon, Sergeant Seth Tinkham from Middleboro, Massachusetts, "landed upon that point" and beheld "several men's bones," as well as a musket and other abandoned accouterments from the Parker ambush.[80]

PREPARATIONS

Despite numerous intelligence reports of an impending attack on Fort William Henry and a letter from Lord Loudoun on June 20 suggesting that probability, Major General Webb failed to initiate needed preparations until the end of July. Webb had suffered from Palsy during the early spring of 1757; his judgment and effectiveness may have been influenced by melancholia brought on by the affliction. However, his performance in 1756, when he hastily retreated before reinforcing the Oswego garrison after hearing reports of Montcalm's advance on the outpost, raised serious questions regarding his competence and fortitude. Although Loudoun had little faith in his third in command, Webb had the support of a well-connected patron—William Augustus, the Duke of Cumberland and son of King George II. Webb had arrived at Fort Edward on June 24 and did not visit the garrison at Lake George until a month later. On July 25 Webb inspected Fort William Henry, accompanied by a large escort of troops, along with Lieutenant Colonel John Young of the 60th Regiment (Royal American Regiment), Captain Thomas Ord of the Royal Artillery, and Major James Montresor, chief engineer. After scrutinizing the fort's defenses, the officers recommended moving troops camped on the northwest side of the fort to "the Rocky Eminence on the S.E. where a redoubt should be raised and some small pieces of Cannon mounted."[81] On July 27 Montresor "traced out the Ground for the new camp" and "Set out the Intrenchments" on the following day on the ground adjacent to William Johnson's 1755 camp.[82]

James Furnis, the British comptroller of ordnance in North America, also arrived with Webb at Fort William Henry. Furnis noted that the 1,000-man encampment, consisting of six companies of the 35th Regiment (under Lieutenant Colonel George Monro) and New Jersey and New Hampshire troops, were relocated to the high ground (southeast of the fort), where "a Breast Work of Logs [was] erected."[83] However, Monro later suggested that "our Breast Work was not near finished" when the French army appeared.[84] On July 27, "a Sort of Council of War," as Montresor characterized the meeting of officers, decided there was "not sufficiency of vessels" to oppose the French on the lake and agreed that "two thousand men" would be adequate to defend Fort William Henry.[85] Monro subsequently complained that Webb insisted that "a thousand men was all he Could possibly spare from Fort Edward."[86] The next day additional defensive steps were ordered, including adding sand to the top of the powder magazine and plugging "the funnels or air holes…with sand & bags," fashioning additional embrasures (openings) for muskets, raising the east bastion by one log, and dismantling storehouses near the fort.[87]

Webb returned to Fort Edward on July 29 and the following day requested reinforcements from the governors of Massachusetts, Connecticut, and Rhode Island. He also asked Sir William Johnson and his Mohawk allies to join him as soon as possible and ordered units of the New York militia to march to Albany. Webb was probably induced into action as a result of a July 28 scouting report by Captain Israel Putnam, disclosing French and Indian canoes on the lake and men on both shores. However, weeks earlier, Webb had abundant intelligence of French preparations for an attack on Fort William Henry. Although Loudoun had recommended that more vessels be built for the defense of Lake George, none were finished and two row galleys remained on the stocks. Only two sloops and two scows, both survivors of the March attack, were still in service. In his August 1 letter to Loudoun, Webb used the excuse of a shortage of carpenters, but still hoped that "we can get them [two row galleys] out in time to recover the command of the Lake"[88] On July 29 "all the Ca[r]pen[t]ers & Bat[eau] men in ye camp [at Fort Edward] set out to work at Lake G[e]orge."[89] The effort, however, was too little, too late.

During July 1757 Major General Webb had between 6,770 and 7,744 troops available in New York. On July 30 the garrison at Fort Edward consisted of 3,432 regulars and provincial troops, but 1,000 men would be ordered to Fort William Henry a few days later, increasing its garrison to 2,372. About 2,500 troops thus remained at other posts in New

York, all of whom were desperately needed at Lake George.[90] Monro begged Webb to send four companies of the 35th Regiment as part of the reinforcements. However, Webb maintained that he "could not spare So Many Regulars," but he did write to Loudoun that he "shall upon any Intelligence of the near approach of the body of the Enemy move up with the remainder of the Army and endeavor to dispute their Landing or make a stand with the whole."[91]

Meanwhile, preparations at Fort Carillon for the conquest of Fort William Henry had been underway for quite some time. As the field commander of the French army in North America, 45-year-old Major General Louis-Joseph de Montcalm had already demonstrated his successful siege tactics during the short bombardment of Fort Oswego in 1756. Montcalm had a long career, having served during the War of Polish Succession (1733-1735) and the War of Austrian Succession (1740-1748), where he exhibited remarkable courage under fire and survived grave wounds. Montcalm's

Louis-Joseph de Montcalm. Engraving by Adolphe Varin from a painting by Antoine Louis-François Sergent. (National Archives of Canada)

second in command, Brigadier General François (François-Gaston) de Lévis began his military career as a second lieutenant in 1735 and had also served in France's earlier European wars. Colonel François-Charles de Bourlamaque, third in command, served as a captain during the War of Austrian Succession and had been placed in charge of the trenches and siege works by Montcalm at Oswego in 1756. Montcalm's aide-de-camp, Captain Louis Antoine de Bougainville, wrote one of the best firsthand accounts of the daily operations of the French army in North America. Bougainville's long career included experience as an army and naval officer, explorer, and scholar. (As a rear admiral at Chesapeake Bay in 1781, he commanded the advance guard of Rear Admiral François Joseph Paul de Grasse's French fleet, which was instrumental in the American victory at Yorktown.)

By the end of July, Montcalm had mobilized a substantial army of 8,021 men—3,081 French regulars, 2,946 Canadian militia, 1,806 Native Americans, and 188 artillerymen.[92] On July 27 Montcalm held a "grand council" of Native Americans at the portage in Ticonderoga in order to solidify support from the 40 Indian nations taking part in the expedition against Fort William Henry. The Indians included Algonquins, Abenakis, Hurons, Iroquois, Micmacs, Nipissings, and tribes from the west (Great Lakes, Mississippi River, and the Ohio Valley), including Ottawas, Chippewas, Missisaugas, Potawatomis, Menominees, Miamis, Winnebagos, Foxes, and Sauks. Addressing the western Indians, Kisensik, a prominent chief of the Nipissings of Kanesetake (northwest of Montreal), thanked his "brothers" from the west for coming "to help us defend our lands against the

François de Lévis, second in command of the French army in North America. Engraving by J. Porreau. (National Archives of Canada)

English who wish to usurp them."[93] Presenting a wampum belt, Montcalm assured the Indians that the king had sent him "to protect and defend you."[94] In addition to removing the English presence on "Lac du Saint Sacrement," the Indians anticipated plunder, prisoners, and scalps. Some officers, such as Captain Bougainville, were wary of the potential cruelties at the hands of New France's Indian allies ("barbarians"). Writing to his brother before the expedition, Bougainville shivered at "the frightful spectacles" of the "Indians, naked, black, red, howling, bellowing, dancing, singing the war song, getting drunk, yelling for 'broth,' that is to say blood."[95] French control over some of their Native American allies could prove difficult because only a handful of interpreters was present, and at times French officers could only communicate indirectly through other Indians.

For weeks French troops had struggled to transport bateaux, artillery, and provisions from Carillon to the northern end of Lake George. Due to a lack of feed for the oxen and horses, most of the work had to be done by hand. Supplies and equipment for the expedition were minimized in order to allow swifter movement; only three tents per company were allowed and a mattress for Montcalm was not taken. Because of a shortfall in the number of bateaux, one division of the army, led by François de Lévis, departed on foot on the morning of July 30, following an old Mohawk trail through the dense forest west of Lake George. Lévis' detachment of 2,488 men, including about 500 Indians, marched in three columns with the Indians forming an advance guard and covering the flanks.[96] On July 29th and 30th, 500 men were ordered to work all night to portage the balance of the boats, cannons, and supplies to Lake George. Bored and impatient at their camp without liquor, the remaining 1,300 Indians left at three on the afternoon of July 31, aboard 150 birchbark canoes, with plans to rendezvous with Montcalm later. Finally, at two o'clock on the afternoon of August 1, Montcalm departed with the largest division of his army aboard nearly 250 bateaux, including "thirty-one pontoons made of two bateaux fastened together with a platform [of planks] on top" to carry the cannons and mortars mounted on their carriages.[97] A violent thunderstorm near Anthony's Nose temporarily interrupted the progress of the bateau flotilla. At five o'clock the fleet stopped to rendezvous with the Indians, who had left the day before and now waited for Montcalm south of "Isle la Barque."[98] With ample daylight left, Montcalm's fleet, now totaling 400 bateaux and canoes, pushed southward, paddling past the soaring mountains bordering the lake and the islands dotting the Narrows. Montcalm and his army rounded the tip of Tongue Mountain at two o'clock in the morning and a short time later observed the three signal fires that Brigadier Lévis had lit. Montcalm continued across "the Bay of Ganaouské" (Northwest Bay), landing on the shoreline of present-day Bolton Landing at daybreak to meet Lévis and his detachment. On the morning of August 2 Lévis resumed his march, stopping at a small bay on the west shore about a mile north of Fort William Henry (later called Artillery Cove) to prepare a base camp and landing site for Montcalm's fleet.[99] After briefly pausing at "Great Sandy bay," Montcalm's main army reached Brigadier Lévis' camp during the evening, but the artillery rafts were kept out of sight in a bay to the north, landing at the main base the next day.

While the French army was organizing its base, two English whaleboats with 13 men on patrol were detected on the lake late that night by the French and Indians. "A sheep belonging to our people began to bleat," Father Roubaud wrote, causing the English crews to turn about and steer for the opposite shore.[100] Hundreds of Indians swiftly pursued their prey, uttering terrifying yells before firing on the outnumbered scouts. "About Eleven o'Clock at night," the men at the fort observed a "flashing & noise of the Guns" on the lake and concluded that "our Guard Boats were attacked" and they were "now convinced of the near Approach of the Enemy."[101] Two Indians were killed during the fight, and three English prisoners were taken and several killed. Before being "massacred" by the Indians in retribution for their losses, the prisoners provided a detailed overview of the size and composition of the garrison at Fort William Henry.[102] A few hours before daybreak, five survivors of the whaleboat scouting party returned to the fort and informed the garrison of the large number of enemy vessels.

The modest garrison at Fort William Henry and the adjacent camp were no match for the French invasion force. Prior to the promised reinforcement, the total troop strength at Lake George was about 1,200 troops, approximately 30 sailors and an equal number of carpenters, a small number of sutlers, and 80 women with perhaps two dozen children. At sunset on August 2 the anticipated reinforcements from Fort Edward reached the entrenched camp at the lake. Colonel Joseph Frye, who had served during the Louisbourg expedition of 1744-1745, led his Massachusetts regiment to the lake. Frye listed a total reinforcement of 1,023 men, consisting of 823 troops from Massachusetts, 100 regulars from the 60th Regiment (Royal Americans) accompanied by Lieutenant Colonel John Young and commanded by Captain Rudolphus Faesch, and 100 men from the New York Independent Companies, under Captain Charles Cruikshanks.[103] The detachment hauled six pieces of artillery from Fort Edward. Having arrived in the early evening, the troops were unable to organize a camp so only pitched a few tents. The garrison at the lake now numbered 2,372 men.[104] The majority of soldiers were located in the entrenched camp, while fewer than 500 troops were actually inside Fort William Henry, under the direction of Captain John Ormsby of the 35th Regiment of Foot. The fort and camp were under the command of Monro, who remained in the entrenched camp during the subsequent siege. Webb had ordered Monro to garrison the fort with "100 Regulars and 300 Provincials," in the event of an attack, but the actual number exceeded Webb's recommendation and included a large contingent of sailors and carpenters.[105]

SIEGE

Montcalm did not waste any time before launching his attack on the fort. In the middle of the night on August 3, he gave orders to advance toward the fort at daybreak and at three in the morning the bateaux fleet began the movement forward. At "about five in the Morning we discovered a considerable Number of Boats, coming down the Lake, on which the Alarm Guns [32 pounders] were immediately fired," James Furnis recounted.[106] The French flotilla first spread "almost across [the lake] to give us an idea of their Strength" and then maneuvered to land but not before gunners "fired at the fort from [three of] their Boats lying at the point [present-day Pine Point]"; their shots fell short and crews "landed their forces and artillery."[107] With Lévis' troops and all the Indians as advance units, Montcalm, along with François-Pierre de Rigaud de Vaudreuil (the governor's brother) and François-Charles de Bourlamaque, began marching with the regulars and militia in three columns through the dense forest on the southwest side of the lake. Lévis's division quickly gained control of the road to Fort Edward and the rest of the army prepared a camp to support the intended batteries.

**"Montcalm Masses His Indians" on a "Rising Ground about 250 yards"
southwest of the fort. (Drawing by Gary S. Zaboly)**

To prevent fires from adjacent structures from spreading to the fort later during the siege, the troops at Fort William Henry burned some huts on the west side of the fort. They also tried to contain the livestock in a picketed "store yard," but the Indians succeeded in "kill[ing] nearly 150 oxen" and delivered 25 live oxen and a number of horses to Montcalm to replace the 18 oxen they had butchered and eaten earlier at Ticonderoga.[108] At nine on the morning of August 3, Monro dispatched three rangers with a letter seeking assistance from Major General Webb at Fort Edward: "I believe you will think it proper to send a Reinforcement as soon as possible."[109] Monro and his troops were busy at the entrenched camp "fortif[ying] in the best manner we Could, with Logs and Stones" and positioning several swivel guns and six cannons: "two brass 6 pounders on a Hill near the Center of the Camp, two brass 12 pound[er]s on the West side of the Encampment, one brass 6 pounder at the Entrance of the Camp from the Lake" and another on the east side facing the swamp.[110] The preparations were not made without losses. Monro acknowledged the loss of some men in "get[ting] Logs to complet[e] Our Breast work."[111]

At the same time, Montcalm's troops began preparing defensive fascines (bundles of sticks tied together) and gablions (bottomless wicker baskets filled with earth, similar in function to sandbags). In the afternoon Montcalm sent an aide under a flag of truce with a letter to Monro requesting surrender, warning of his "Superior artillery" and the certain "Cruelty" of the Indians if the siege continued; but "I have it yet in my power to Restrain the Savages."[112] Monro flatly refused, informing Montcalm that he was "determin[e]d to defend both the Fort and the Camp to the last."[113] At six o'clock that evening Monro again wrote to Webb, reporting Montcalm's surrender request and reiterating that "I make no doubt that you will soon send us a reinforcement."[114] An hour and a half earlier, after receiving Monro's first letter, George Bartman, Webb's aide-de-camp, wrote back that the "General" cannot do anything until "he has more particular intelligence from you…and is determin'd to assist you as soon as possible with the whole army if requir'd."[115] Webb sent several urgent messages to the assistant deputy quartermaster general in Albany, Captain Gabriel Christie, to immediately send the militia to Fort Edward, and he dispatched a letter to William Johnson to march to Fort Edward with his Indians. Late that same evening (August 3), a Canadian lieutenant, while butchering an ox south of Fort William Henry, was captured by two Connecticut rangers from Fort Edward. The prisoner suggested that Montcalm "had 6000 R[e]gulars & 5000 Canadians…But this account was Not all [e]ntirely credited," according to Sergeant Jabez Fitch.[116] Webb, however, chose to believe the prisoner and had his aide dispatch a letter to Monro at noon on August 4 that he "does not think it prudent (as you know his Strength at this place) to attempt a Junction or to assist you till reinforc'd by the Militia of the Colonies…in case he should be so unfortunate from delays of the Militia not to have in his power to give you timely Assistance, you might be able to make the best [surrender] Terms…left in your power."[117] Montcalm's Caughnawaga allies intercepted Webb's party of three messengers with the letter on their way to Fort William Henry, killing one and capturing another (the third outdistanced the Indians). The letter was discovered in the lining of the dead messenger's jacket and Montcalm saved it for the right moment. (Interestingly, the desperate situation at Fort William Henry was not reflected in Phineas Lyman's orderly book at Fort Edward; the entry for August 4 noted "The Men Ordered for Duty are always to Appear With their Hats Co[c]k[e]d & with Shoes & Stockings On Before they March to ye Grand Parade.")[118]

As the French labored at their entrenchments on August 4, the fort's battery of 18-20 cannons (including two 32-pounders), three mortars, one howitzer, and 13 small swivel guns were used effectively against the French position. Under the direction of Lieutenant Thomas Collins of the Royal Artillery, the cannoneers (some of whom were naval gunners) kept a constant fire on the French trench diggers to the northwest of the fort. One of the seven-inch iron mortars burst on August 4 from metal fatigue as the result of repeat-

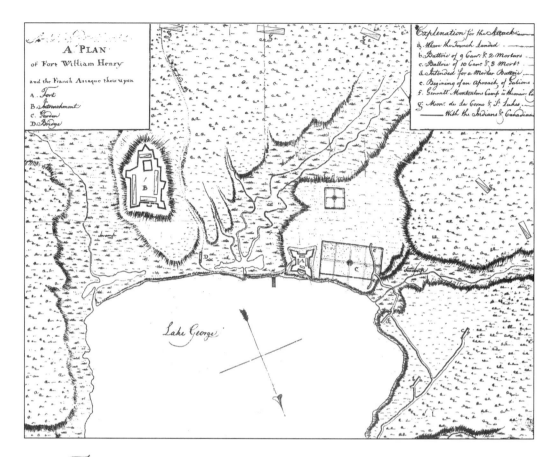

"A Plan of Fort William Henry and the French Atta[ck]," marking Montcalm's siege lines and the English entrenched camp (B) to the east. (National Archives of Canada) *Left:* A detail of the legend.

ed firings, a portent of subsequent problems. The cannons at Monro's entrenched camp held the Indians at bay but losses occurred. When 100 troops from Joseph Frye's Massachusetts regiment were sent out to secure the camp's water supply, several men suffered wounds, and one captain was mortally wounded. Father Roubaud noted that it was impossible for the English to step outside the fort without being killed or captured by the Indians. "An English woman" tried to gather vegetables from the garden on the west side of the fort and was shot by an Indian "concealed in a bed of cabbages," who waited patiently until nightfall to scalp her.[119] To expose any approach of French troops or Indians, Monro ordered "Fires to be made every Evening about a hundred Yards from the Camp [and the fort] all round."[120]

Observing the troops in the fort dismantling and tossing wooden shingles from the roofs of the barracks and storehouses into the lake, the Indians believed that valuable items were being lost and asked Montcalm to put a stop to it. But Montcalm and his troops were busy completing trenches for the first two batteries, along with a connecting road to haul the artillery from the landing site. These two batteries would direct their fire on the "north bastion, and the other to cross its fire onto the same front, both at the same time to deliver ricochet fire on the defenses," Captain Bougainville noted.[121] That night 12 cannons and several mortars that were still aboard the pontoon rafts were unloaded at the landing site in preparation for the siege.

At six o'clock on the evening of August 4, Monro sent another letter to Webb, relating that he was surrounded by Indians and that French troops were "employed in erecting their Batteries" and that he "would therefore be glad (if it meets with Your Approbation) [that] the whole army…[be] march'd" to Lake George.[122] The messenger with Monro's letter, however, was ambushed by the Indians before reaching Fort Edward. The next day (August 5) the gun crews at the fort continued their fire on the French entrenchments, but both 32-pound cannons and one 18-pounder exploded as a result of metal fatigue.[123] A number of French soldiers, who had camped too close to the fort, were pulled back because some of them had been killed in their tents by shells from the fort. A thousand French troops labored all night to complete the left battery (northernmost battery on the west side of the lake) and finished the trench to the right battery. At six o'clock on the morning of August 6, the first French battery, consisting of eight guns (including three 18-pounders and a 9-inch mortar), commenced firing on the northern section of the fort, just missing the two sloops docked there. The solid 18-pound cannonballs that fell inside the entrenched camp were stamped with the British "Broad Arrow" symbol; the garrison believed that the cannonballs had been taken by Montcalm's army at the surrender of Oswego in 1756. (Some of the French artillery at Lake George had been captured after the defeat of Major General Edward Braddock in 1755 and employed by the French army during the 1756 siege of Oswego.) Another 18-pound cannonball "Shot off" the thigh of a sentry at Colonel Joseph Frye's tent.[124] At the fort another French cannonball "carried away the Pull[e]y of our Flag Staff," an eyewitness reported, causing the flag to tumble down to the loud rejoicing of the besiegers, "but it was soon hoisted tho' one of the men [a carpenter] that was doing this had his head Shot off with a Ball."[125] The repeated firings from the fort's cannons resulted in the bursting of another 18-pound cannon and a 12-pounder as well.

Meanwhile, no help was forthcoming from Fort Edward. On August 5 Webb held a council of war with his officers regarding the feasibility of assisting the garrison at Fort William Henry. They decided that it was "Not practicable" to reinforce Monro's army and determined it "proper to retreat" from Fort Edward.[126] At the end of the meeting Webb suggested that the garrison should be "ready to march at a minutes warning," but reserved the decision to retreat on further information.[127] On the same day Webb wrote to Lord Loudoun that he only had 1,600 men fit for duty at Fort Edward and thus "did not think it prudent to pursue my first intentions of Marching to their Assistance."[128] At six in the morning of August 6, Monro sent a letter to Webb, informing him of the bursting of four artillery pieces and the necessity of transferring two 12-pound cannons from the entrenched camp to the fort. About nine o'clock on the morning of August 6, Sir William Johnson arrived at Fort Edward with 1,500 New York militiamen and nearly 200 Indians.[129] Johnson pressed Webb to reinforce Fort William Henry, which resulted in a confrontation that apparently has been embellished in the retelling over time. Timothy

Dwight, president of Yale College at the turn of the nineteenth century, interviewed Captain Eli Noble, who had been present at Fort Edward. According to Noble's testimony, Johnson received permission to march to the relief of Fort William Henry with provincial volunteers. "At the beat of the drum, the provincials turned out nearly to a man," Dwight wrote, but after waiting "almost the whole day," Webb rescinded the permission.[130] However, there is little corroborating evidence to support the incident. Johnson's displeasure with Webb, however, was evident. In a letter to Captain Philip Schuyler following the surrender of Monro's army, Johnson called Webb "a coward" who "was nearly beside himself with physical fear" after the fall of Fort William Henry.[131]

Johnson's intervention may have temporarily influenced Webb, however. Late in the day on August 6 Webb's aide wrote to Monro: "we have now got together by the March of the Militia [to Fort Edward] in the highest spirits three armies of five thousand men…he shall set out in the night with the whole join'd together, and make no doubt of cutting the Enemy entirely off."[132] The letter did not reach Monro until the night of August 9 and Webb obviously did not follow through on his stated intentions. At six on the evening of August 6, Monro had dispatched yet another letter to Webb, giving an account of the deteriorating conditions and acknowledging the receipt of a confusing "Verbal Message by two Rangers mentioning an Expectation You had of being joined by Sir Wm. Johnson & some Indians."[133] He also complained about the failure to receive the promised reinforcements.

During the early morning hours of August 7, 500 French troops completed a second battery, southwest of the first one. At six in the morning two 18-pounders, five 12-pounders, an 8-pounder, two howitzers, and one mortar commenced a barrage on the fort and the entrenched camp. At nine o'clock in the morning, after three hours of bombardment from both French batteries, Montcalm sent Captain Louis Antoine de Bougainville out of the trench with a flag of truce, escorted by 15 French grenadiers and a drummer. Bougainville was ordered to stop at the glacis by the British commander at the fort and was met there by 15 British soldiers and several officers. Adam Williamson, the young engineer who had played the same role in escorting a French officer under a flag of truce to meet William Eyre in March, now blindfolded Bougainville and led him "first to the fort, and then to the entrenched camp" where he handed Monro a note from Montcalm along with the captured, bloodstained letter from Webb.[134] The disclosure of Webb's August 4 letter, relating that no immediate reinforcement would be forthcoming, that a French prisoner had suggested that Montcalm had 11,000 troops, and advising Monro that the "best Terms" of surrender be sought if there was a delay in the advance of the militia, had a disheartening impact on the officers and men.[135] Monro thanked the French for their politeness but refused to surrender, and Bougainville was escorted back. Despite the bad news in Webb's letter, a participant in the event later maintained that "not a single man seem'd daunted," after the contents of the letter were revealed, "nor was there the least mention made of Capitulating" at the time.[136]

Facing page: **"Attack of Fort William Henry…7 August 1757," by Lieutenant Cöntgen Therbu, engineer, showing the line of fire from the French batteries (E, F, G) to the entrenched camp(C), as well as to the fort (A). (National Archives of Canada)**

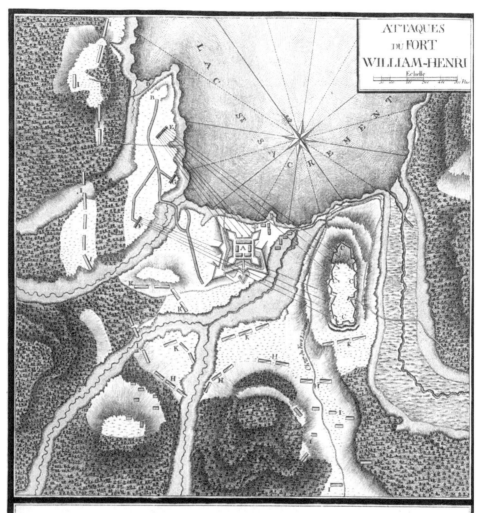

ATTAQUES DU FORT WILLIAM-HENRI
en Amérique
par les troupes françaises aux ordres du Marquis de Montcalm.
Prise de ce fort le 7 Aout 1757.

Renvois

A. Fort William-Henri B. Ouverture des tranchées la nuit du 4 au 5 Aout
C. Camp retranché, que les anglais allèrent occuper lors de l'arrivée des français.
D. Baie où les français débarquèrent leur artillerie. E. Batterie de huit
canons & d'un mortier. F. Batterie de dix canons & d'un mortier. G. Batterie
de six pieces, dont on ne fit aucun usage. H. Position de Mr. de Levi
pendant l'investissement du fort. I. Position des troupes durant le siège.
K. Leur position après la prise pendant la demolition des retranchemens
faits par les anglais. ▬ Troupes sauvages.

C.P.S.C.M.

The French cannonade resumed with firings "every two minutes, to the great diversion of the Indians who uttered cries of joy on seeing the shot and shells falling in the fort."[137] The high trajectory of the mortars and howitzers resulted in "bursting [shells]…filled with deadly missiles [which] caused great destruction of life" inside the fort and the entrenched camp.[138] Adam Williamson wrote that "Most of the Shells fell in the Fort."[139] About noontime on August 7 Captain John Ormsby, in charge of the fort, was wounded when a shell fell into the barracks and burst, leaving the command of the fort in the hands of Captain William Arbuthnot of the Massachusetts regiment. Lieutenant Thomas Collins reported that a ten-inch shell landed on the ammunition box on the north bastion, killing and wounding 16 men, "one of wh[ich] was a Provincial Officer that never was heard of, but part of his Coat was found."[140]

Despite casualties among the provincial troops, Monro maintained a negative opinion of them, a bias also held by other British officers. Monro later suggested "that in general provincials did not behave well."[141] The provincial troops inside the fort, which represented three quarters of the garrison during the siege, "behav'd scandalously," according to Monro, "when they were to fire Over the Parapet, they lay down upon their faces and fir'd str[a]ight up in the Air. I sent Orders to the Cap[tain] who commanded in the Fort [Monro remained in the entrenched camp], to take the first Man, that behav'd in that Manner, And hang him over the Wall to be shot At, by the Enemy."[142] An officer present in the fort during the siege later recounted that Monro had published orders for the gar-

Detail of *Siege of Fort William Henry.* **Painting by Len Tantillo.**

rison in the fort, prescribing the same punishment for "any person proved cowardly or offered to advise giving up the Fort."[143]

After observing a detachment of Indians and Canadians move close to the British entrenched camp "under the Cover of a Small Knol[l]," about three o'clock on the afternoon of August 7, 200 provincial troops were dispatched to reinforce 80 Massachusetts militiamen posted behind some nearby logs.[144] A bloody three-hour skirmish ensued, ending with the retreat of the English provincials. Twenty-one Indians and Canadians were killed or wounded and the French estimated that they had killed 50-60 of the English Troops, but Colonel Frye noted only a loss of "several men besides having several wounded."[145]

During the night French diggers continued work on a trench for a third battery, which would be located close enough to the fort to breach the west wall. However, the men were stymied by a marshy area and a small forked stream (southwest corner of the lake) between their main trench and the proposed site of the third battery, adjacent to the fort's garden. Before noon on August 8 French workers finished a causeway using facines and logs laid across the marsh that would be capable of supporting the artillery. The work was interrupted briefly at four o'clock in the afternoon when Indians reported "a considerable body of the enemy were coming on the road" from Fort Edward.[146] Montcalm mobilized his regulars to meet the English force, but the story proved to be a false alarm. Webb had no intention of reinforcing the fort. At six o'clock on the evening of August 8, his aide,

George Bartman, wrote another letter to Monro, "to acquaint you that it is entirely owing to the delay of the Militia that he has not yet mov'd up to your Assistance…We wish most heartily that you may be able to hold out a little longer, and hope soon to have it in our power to relieve you…tho we are inform'd by a Pris[one]r…that they are eleven Thousand strong."[147] The letter was intercepted by the French. Earlier in the day Monro had dashed off another desperate letter to Webb, assuring him that the Canadian prisoner's story of an 11,000-man French army (mentioned in Webb's August 4 letter) "was greatly Magnified" and that the "Fort & Camp still hold out in hopes of speedy Relief from you"; but the plea was futile.[148]

In spite of the constant fire from the fort, French troops worked on preparations for the third battery all through the night. The garrison at the fort "could hear the Enemy at Work in our Garden on which some Grape Shot was sent."[149] The new battery "parallel to our West Curtain in the Garden, Distance about 150 Yards" with "9 Embrasures [openings for cannon]" was nearly finished at daybreak on August 9.[150] With the route of retreat potentially closed by the battery* and no expectation of assistance from Fort Edward, the British and provincial officers agreed on the evening of August 8 "to hold a Consultation…early the next Morning to propose a Capitulation."[153] An inspection of the fort had revealed timbers from the east bastion "knock'd over two or three Feet," timbers from the northwest curtain "knocked into the Parapet three or four Feet," the "Passage of the Magazine under the North Bastion" had collapsed from a 13-inch shell, the casemate was damaged, and most of the cannons had burst.[154] In addition, the men "were almost Stup[e]fied" from five sleepless nights and traumatized by constant shelling that shook the fort "like an Earthquake."[155]

Early on the morning of August 9 the French shelling resumed "with very great Briskness, and was answered with As much Vigor as our circumstances would admit."[156] While the bombardment continued unmitigated, British and provincial officers met at a council of war and unanimously recommended capitulation. Monro later wrote that the Massachusetts troops had "declar'd to Col. Fry[e], Very Early the Morning of the Capitulation, that they were quite wore out, And would stay No longer, And that they would rather be knock'd in the head by the Enemy As stay to p[e]rish behind the breastwork."[157] The letter to Monro recommending capitulation, signed by Lieutenant Colonel John Young, six additional regular officers, and six provincial officers, cited the new enemy battery "within one hundred Yards of the Fort," and noted that the largest British artillery had "burst" and "there was not the Least Expectation" of reinforcement.[158] Colonel Frye disclosed that only seven pieces of artillery were still usable (the largest being a nine-pounder) at the time of the surrender, but a "Return of Ordnance fit for Service in Fort Wm Henry at the time of Capitulation" listed 16 operable pieces of artillery, including one 12-pounder.[159] In addition, ammunition for the smaller caliber artillery was nearly exhausted, but there was still an abundant supply of shot remaining for the inoperable larger cannons.

*There are some discrepancies in the location of this battery on various maps. Some French and British maps of the siege label the trench parallel to the west side of the fort as "a Work begun but not completed" or simply an "Approach," and identify another battery just north of the southwest corner of the lake as a "Battery Finished but not opened" or an "intended Bat[t]ery."[151] Mary Ann Rocques'1765 Set of Plans and Forts shows "Two intended batteries" on the northern section (both sides) of the trench parallel to the fort's garden and the 1757 GC Wetterstrom map placed the third battery adjacent to the west side of the garden, as well as just north of the southwest corner of the lake.[152]

"At seven in the morning," Bougainville wrote, the garrison at Fort William Henry raised the white flag.[160] Captain Rudolphus Faesch of the 60th Regiment, accompanied by a small escort of soldiers, was initially sent to meet the French, and in a short time Lieutenant Colonel John Young, suffering from a wound, followed on horseback to Montcalm's tent to propose articles of capitulation. Montcalm accepted the surrender with the more lenient terms of the "honors of war," which had not been offered to the Oswego garrison in 1756 because Montcalm considered their defense too brief and inadequate. Under the provisions of the capitulation, the troops at Fort William Henry and the entrenched camp were to "march out with their arms, drums beating, colours flying…with the baggage of the Officers and Soldiers" and be escorted by French troops to Fort Edward; all the artillery and military stores, "Except the effects of the Officers & Soldiers," would be turned over to the French; the English troops could not serve against the French or their Indian allies for 18 months; all captured French, Canadian, and Indians were to be surrendered at Fort Carillon within three months; the English sick and wounded that were unable to travel would remain with the French to be returned "as soon as they are Recover'd"; and as a "mark of Respect…on account of the brave & Hon[ora]ble Defense," Monro and his troops were to be given one cannon.[161]

Montcalm informed Young that he could not sign the articles without first communicating the provisions to his Indian allies, who had not taken part in the negotiations over the articles. Montcalm asked the chiefs to "promise that their young men would not commit any disorder. The "chiefs agreed to everything and promised to restrain" their warriors, according to Bougainville.[162] Actually, the chiefs only acquiesced to the articles of surrender, rather than agreeing to them and subsequently ignored the provisions. Whether the limited number of interpreters could accurately translate the articles in their languages is also questionable. In any case, the "honors of war" meant nothing to the Indians, who had traveled far, fought courageously, and had anticipated trophies of war (including scalps), plunder and captives, either as substitutes for warriors that had been killed or to be held for ransom.[163] While the negotiations over the terms of the capitulation were being settled, "the Savages came into the camp, and began to plunder," but French grenadiers "prevented their carrying off anything considerable," James Furnis recounted.[164]

At noon the fort was turned over to a contingent of French soldiers and the remaining garrison of British regulars and provincial soldiers marched to the entrenched camp with most of their valuables and muskets. During the transfer ceremony, Father Pierre Roubaud noticed that the Indians entered "the fort through the gun-embrasures [openings]" to pillage the contents and promptly butchered many of the sick and wounded men left in the casemate hospital.[165] Roubaud observed one of the Indians emerge from the casemate carrying "a human head, from which trickled streams of blood and which he displayed as the most splendid prize."[166] Captain William Arbuthnot later swore an affidavit in Massachusetts that he "saw the French Indians kill the Sick and Wounded [in the fort] without sparing any one…all which was done in View of the French officers who did not attempt to hinder or prevent it."[167] Many of the sick men in the fort were suffering from smallpox. Scalping these sick individuals had unintended consequences. Infected scalps, sick prisoners, and tainted clothing seized from the English were taken to Indian villages, which subsequently led to an epidemic of smallpox. Robert Rogers later wrote that his brother, Captain Richard Rogers, had "died with the small-pox a few days before this fort was besieged...they dug him up out of his grave, and scalped him."[168] Jonathan Carver, an eyewitness to the Indian atrocities, considered the smallpox scourge that later swept Native American villages "as the immediate judgment of heaven."[169]

Although a detachment of French troops was posted at the entrenched camp, the Indians climbed over the breastwork on the afternoon of August 9 and began to plunder the camp for small possessions. With menacing countenances, the Indians prowled the camp and assailed some of the men in an effort to seize their baggage while women and children watched terror-stricken. Bougainville maintained that "everything was done to stop" the Indians and that he had carried orders from Montcalm "to have the wine, brandy, rum and all the intoxicating liquors spilt" in order to prevent further escalation of the disorder.[170] Colonel Joseph Frye recorded that "the Liquor was all stove by order" to prevent the Indians from "being drunk."[171] In a letter to Lord Loudoun on August 14, Montcalm blamed the disorder on rum given to the Indians, apparently relying on information from Brigadier General Lévis.[172] Two weeks later Monro wrote to Loudoun denying Montcalm's excuse of the liquor, "which is really not fact, as I my Self, Saw every drop of liquor destroyed immediately after the Capitulation."[173]

As the commotion between the Indians and the English captives intensified, Montcalm rushed to the entrenched camp "and did all in his power to restrain and stop these savages," remaining there until nine at night.[174] The expectation of trophies of war by the Indians, however, was still unfulfilled. Earlier in the day an English officer had overheard some Indian chiefs "accuse the French General with having deceived them, in that he had promised them Plunder of the English, which...they were now deprived of by the Capitulation."[175] Late in the day "the Marquis de Montcalm thought it advisable for us to march off by Night," James Furnis recorded, and Joseph Frye noted that Monro ordered "the men paraded and began their march" about midnight.[176] However, "before the Troops were out of the Encampment," Furnis recounted, "this Order was Countermanded. The Marquis de Montcalm signif[y]ing that the Savages [were] not satisfied with the Plunder they had in the Morning, intended to attack us on our March."[177] Others in the entrenched camp similarly reported that Montcalm was apprehensive that the Indians were "too full of Wrath" to have the English prisoners leave at night, "giving Oswego as an instance of the imprudence of Marching Prisoners, before the Passion of the Indians was subsided."[178] Montcalm's decision to cancel the march at night occurred after an "examination of the Indian camp, Two Thirds of them were missing, who, he supposed, had Waylaid the Road."[179] The Indians tried other tactics to gain access to the English prisoners. They told Montcalm that William Johnson was marching "with a large body of Indians" to Lake George, but the story was "invented to excite the General to Sacrifice us," according to one of the English captives.[180]

The march to Fort Edward was postponed until the following morning. The aborted effort to depart only raised the suspicions and ire of the Indians. "All the Remainder of this night," Frye disclosed, "the Indians were in great numbers round our Lines, and seemed to sh[o]w more th[a]n usual malice in their looks which made us Suspect they Intended us mischief."[181] To protect the English encampment, Montcalm ordered several colonial officers, who had been assigned to the Indian auxiliaries during the expedition— Luc de La Corne (La Corne Saint-Luc), Joseph Marin de La Malgue, and Charles-Michel

Mouet de Langlade—to remain in the entrenchment, along with the interpreters. All had been participants in earlier ambushes of British and provincial troops.

The English army spent a fitful night with little sleep during the five hours between midnight and the first rays of dawn. Early on the morning of August 10, as the English parolees prepared to march to Fort Edward, "the Savages surrounded us…got over the Breast Work, and began to plunder," and the "Commanding Officer, very prudently, ordered every man to throw down his Baggage."[182] Colonel Frye "found the Indians in a worse temper (if possible) th[a]n last night, Every one having a Tomahawk, hatchet or some other Instrument of Death, and constantly plundering."[183] Miles Whitworth, a surgeon with the Massachusetts regiment, was tending the wounded at five o'clock in the morning when the French guards were withdrawn and the Indians "dragg[ed] the said seventeen wounded men out of their Huts, Murder[ed] them with their Tom[a]hawks and scalp[ed] them," while some French troops, as well as Luc de La Corne, were only about "forty feet" away.[184] The French officers "were of no Assistance, and advised giving up our Effects…[which] was complied with, as the Officers and Soldiers immediately delivered every Thing up to them, except their Arms and the Cloth[e]s on our Backs."[185] Once the accumulation of the trophies of war had begun, however, the plundering escalated. As the warriors brought the spoils back to their camp, others hurried to the English entrenchment to gain a portion of the plunder, fearful of returning home with less glory than their

Nineteenth-century engraving, depicting the futile French attempt to end the massacre of the English parolees. Provincial soldiers later wrote that the French did not come to their assistance during the initial Indian attacks. (Fort William Henry Museum)

brothers. The Indians "proceeded with out interruption in taking the Officers Swords, Hats, Watches, Fuzees [fusils/muskets], Cloth[e]s and Shirts leaving [them] quite na-ked."[186] After being "disrobcd" and relieved of his money, Private Jonathan Carver rushed to a French guard for protection, who called him "an English dog," and pushed him back to the Indians.[187] The Indians proceeded to "Pic[k] out the negro[e]s, M[u]la-t[t]o[e]s, and Indi[a]ns and Drag[ge]d them Away and we Know not what Became of them."[188] The captives were valuable prizes; most were taken to Canada and later ran-somed to French authorities.

In a state of panic and vulnerability, the first contingent of the 35th Regiment and artillerymen departed from the entrenched camp on the fateful morning of August 10. Earlier, the parolees had been assured that under the "honors of war" they would march out "with their Arms & one charge of powder & ball & one p[iece] of cannon"; newspa-pers later reported that the garrison was to leave with "their Arms charged" or with "some ammunition."[189] However, Private Jonathan Carver recalled that "we were per-mitted to carry off our arms yet were not allowed a single round of ammunition."[190] By the time the men left the entrenchment many of them already had their muskets taken by the Indians; the rest of the troops were ordered to carry their muskets by the barrel with-out bayonets ("clubbed"). At the back of a long column, the Massachusetts regiment emerged from the entrenched camp with "great difficulty" and "were no sooner out then the Savages fell upon the Rear killing & Scalping," Colonel Frye disclosed.[191] With the pandemonium at the rear, orders to halt were given in "great Confusion," but "as soon as those in the front found the Rear was Attack'd, they again press'd forward, and then the Confusion Continued & Increased."[192] The English officers advised their men "to be strip[ped] without Resistance" because opposition might be construed as a breach of the capitulation, resulting in the "unbounded fury" of the Indians.[193] Contrary to the advice of both the English and French officers, those that "made the least Resistance" were more likely scalped, Captain Furnis reported.[194]

The New Hampshire troops were the last to clear the entrenchment. Private John Pol-lard, with the New Hampshire contingent, observed an Indian, covered with warpaint dash from the forest and leap upon a stump and bellow a "terrific War Whoop," which "was immediately answered by hundreds of his companions"; Captain Jean-Nicolas Desandrouins, a young French engineer, also noted that the Indians sounded "the cry of war" during the frenzy of plundering.[195] The ensuing turmoil was described by Frye as a "horrid Scene of Blood & Slaughter," and Carver recounted that "men, women, and chil-dren were dispatched in the most wanton and cruel manner and immediately scalped. Many of these savages [probably Ottawas] drank the blood of their victims." [196] Witness-ing the "Barbarous Treatment," the British troops declared that they should have fought "as long as we could and at last die Like Soldiers; preferable to the Shocking Brutality" at the hands of "Savages."[197] While modern historians have questioned whether the grue-some details were exaggerated or "invented," the vivid descriptions of participants seem to provide compelling evidence of butchery. Indians were observed "tearing the Children from their Mothers Bosoms and their mothers from their Husbands, then Singling out the men and Carrying them in the woods and killing a great many whom we saw lying on the road side."[198] Frye also saw "Women & Children" carried away, "Some of which later they killed & Scalp'd in the Road."[199] Major General Webb informed Lord Loudoun on

August 11 that women and children had been dragged from the men "and most inhuman[e]ly butchered" and in the same letter used the term "Massacred" to describe the killing of soldiers; Captain Desandrouins also used the words "massacred" and "butchery."[200] Writing to the governor of Rhode Island from Fort Edward on August 14, Lieutenant Colonel Samuel Angell also wrote of a "horrible scene of massacre."[201] Twenty-two-year-old Private Seth Metcalf of Rutland, Massachusetts, recorded in his journal at Fort Edward that the Indians "Rav[i]sh[ed] the women and then Put them to the Slaughter, young Children of the Regular forces had their Brains Dash[ed] out Against the Stones and trees," and diarist Jabez Fitch had nearly the identical entry on August 10 of children taken "from their Mothers & Dash[ed] their Brains out against ye Ston[e]s."[202] Newspaper accounts published in August 1757 undoubtedly embellished the details: "The Throats of most if not all the Women were cut, their Bellies rip[ped] open, their Bowels torn out and thrown upon the Faces of their dead and dying Bodies…Children were taken by the Heels, and their Brains beat out against the Trees or Stones."[203] Father Pierre Roubaud, who witnessed "butchery" and children torn from parents, was surrounded by "a crowd of women…with tears," who "threw themselves at my feet" for protection.[204] After learning that a six-month-old English baby was being held by a Huron warrior, Roubaud traded a scalp procured from a friendly Abenaki for the infant.

As the carnage continued, English officers sought help from the "Officers of the French guard," but "they refused, and told them they must take to the woods."[205] Jonathan Carver observed French officers walking nearby "with apparent unconcern," and Major General Webb later wrote that the 300-man French guard were "quietly looking on" during the bloodbath.[206] The French version of events placed the blame on the English parolees, who "wished to march before our escort was collected," had provided the Indians with "some rum to drink," and were "panic-stricken," which "emboldened the Indians."[207] In this French account the English panicked and threw "down arms, baggage, and even their clothes," which, to a large extent, agrees with an original English document that noted that the men "were Scared to such a degree that they threw away Arms, Am[m]unition and everything and each man endeavored to shift for himself."[208]

With no immediate help from the French guards, many of the men fled into the forest and ran breathless and half-naked to Ford Edward, arriving at the fort exhausted, disorientated, and famished on August 10 and over the next few days. On August 10 Sergeant Jabez Fitch noted "all this Day our People Kept Coming in [to Fort Edward] By Small Part[ies] Appearing in ye Most pit[i]ful Manner Som[e] of them Strip[ped] [e]ntirely Naked other[s] Rob[be]d …This & Yesterday are ye Two Most Sorrowful Day[s] that Ever were Known to N England."[209] Following a narrow escape from the clutches of two Indians and after observing an "Indian's tomahawk gash into…[the] back" of an English soldier, Jonathan Carver bolted into the woods and hid, spending three nights in the wilderness before reaching Fort Edward.[210] Similarly, Colonel Frye arrived on the third night of his trek to Fort Edward. The garrison helped guide the escapees to the fort by firing a cannon at two-hour intervals. Samuel Blodget, a sutler with the New Hampshire regiment who had also witnessed the 1755 Battle of Lake George, hid under a bateau for several hours, but upon emerging from his sanctuary was discovered by the Indians and "stripped of every vestige of clothing."[211] He escaped into the woods and, like many others, reached the safety of Fort Edward. John McKeen, also from New Hampshire, was not as lucky. Unable to break away from the Indians, McKeen was stripped of his clothing, tied to a tree, and used as a mark for the knives and tomahawks of the Indians before being set on fire.[212] Another New Hampshire militiaman, Ezekiel Stevens, struggled with the Indians and was knocked to the ground and scalped while still alive. Bleeding profusely, he sat upon a log and was quickly seized as a prisoner by another Indian, but fortunately was rescued by French soldiers. He survived the ordeal and later returned to Derryfield, New Hampshire, and thereafter wore a close-knit cap.[213]

Indians pursued Captain James Furnis for three miles before overtaking him, but he "was luckily retaken by a French Guard" and escorted into Fort William Henry with others who had surrendered to French soldiers for protection from "the Cruelty of the Savages."[214] However, numerous English prisoners were dragged by the Indians to their canoes at the lake and disguised as Indians to avoid retrieval by French troops. Captain Desandrouins wrote that the Indians "killed their prisoners by hitting them on their heads rather than abandoning them," but "a great number" of prisoners were dragged to the canoes and the Indians escaped with them.[215] After hearing the commotion, Montcalm and his officers, "ran the risk of their lives" to save the parolees and "at length" quieted the Indians and released "immediately about 400."[216] Some of the Indian chiefs were said to have persuaded many of the warriors to release their captives and "make a present to Montcalm of 400 of these prisoners."[217] Not all the prisoners were released. Intent on keeping the remaining captives, the majority of Indians hurriedly departed on the afternoon of August 10 with hundreds of prisoners. The French and British officers thereafter parceled out the meager remaining garments to the partially-clad surviving parolees.

Montcalm came under immediate criticism by British officials for violating the capitulation agreement and tolerating the slaughter of parolees. In the first English history of the French and Indian War (*The General History of the Late War* published in 1763), John Entick suggested that Montcalm had "permitted" the Indian attack when "the Indian chief insisted upon a previous agreement," promising "the plunder of the English."[218] On the other hand, Father Roubaud wrote that Montcalm, "who was not apprised of the affair for some time, on account of the distance of his tent—came at the first notice to the place of the uproar…[and] used prayers, menaces, promises; he tried everything, and at last resorted to force" to stop the assault.[219]

On August 14 a French party, under a flag of truce, delivered letters from Montcalm at Fort Edward for Webb and Loudoun, regarding the return of the remaining prisoners. The next day two companies of French grenadiers, commanded by Captain de Poulairès of Royal Roussillon Regiment, and 200 Canadian troops, led by Luc de La Corne, escorted Monro on horseback and 400 forlorn English soldiers and civilians about half way to Fort Edward, where they were met by a detachment from the fort.[220] A horse dragged a small brass cannon that was specified in the "honors of war" capitulation agreement.

The total losses of provincial troops remain uncertain. Monro wrote that it was "not less than 4 officers & about forty men" from the provincial units killed and "very near, as many more men wounded," and he listed about 47 regulars either killed or wounded; however, by the end of 1757 over 300 soldiers who had survived the siege were still missing or listed as dead.[221] This number does not include an unknown number of civilian losses. Many of the English captives were subsequently ransomed from the Indians by the French and eventually repatriated to the colonies. However, black soldiers serving in provincial regiments were considered valuable assets and were not returned until the defeat of New France in 1760. John Bush, a free Black citizen of Shrewsbury, Massachusetts, had reenlisted in 1757 as a company clerk. Bush was a skilled engraver who had carved elaborate designs on powder horns for many officers, including Robert Rogers and Israel Putnam. Bush was taken captive by the Indians on August 10 and transported to Canada, perishing as a prisoner aboard a French ship in 1758.[223]

The demolition and burning of Fort William Henry and the adjacent entrenched camp required three days to complete. During the process, Father Roubaud observed that the casemates were "filled with dead bodies, which for several days furnished fresh fuel for…the flames."[224] A British review of the siege, written in November 1757, concluded that the parolees "were detain'd Five days" at Lake George to avoid "any interruption in Demolishing the Fort."[225] On the night of August 14 the garrison at Fort Edward somberly observed the "Light of ye Fire Most of ye Night," according to Jabez Fitch.[226] Montcalm's men also burned the two row galleys on the stocks but used the two sloops and two scows to transport captured provisions and artillery to Fort Carillon, including 2,974 barrels of flour and salt pork, 23 cannons, 17 swivel guns, a howitzer and 2 mortars, 2,522 shot, and 38,835 pounds of gunpowder.[227]

The militia reinforcements continued to arrive at Fort Edward in the days following the surrender at Lake George, cresting at 4,239 on August 12.[228] However, some estimates of total troop strength at Fort Edward ran as high as 6,000-7000 men.[229] (Sixteen-year-old Benedict Arnold and 19-year-old Ethan Allen marched with their separate Connecticut militia companies to relieve Fort William Henry, serving a total of 14 days each.) Regardless of the number of reinforcements, Major General Webb felt justified in his decision not to aid the troops at Lake George. In a letter to Lord Loudoun on August 11, he maintained that information from a Canadian prisoner that the French force "consisted of Eleven or Twelve thousand Men…put it out of my power to be of any Service to the besieged" at Fort William Henry.[230] After the surrender at Lake George, fear of a French attack on Fort Edward spread throughout the army. During the evening of August 9 "a heavy firing of Musquetry…[from] the Bulk of the Militia" camped on the banks of the Hudson River alarmed the garrison inside the fort.[231] The edgy militia reinforcements had fired in unison after sentries discharged their muskets at what they thought were Indians.

Montcalm never planned a full-scale attack on Fort Edward; the last contingent of the French army withdrew from the smoldering ruins of Fort William Henry on August 16 and Montcalm left Carillon on August 29. By August 17, 1,308 provincial militiamen had departed from Fort Edward. A short time later, a scouting party led by Captain Israel Putnam observed "one of our Sloops lies out in the Lake…in order to give the earliest Intelligence," but in early September French deserters revealed that the two captured sloops had been "dismasted…and sunk" at the north end of the lake.[232] On September 17 Private Rufus Putnam (second cousin of Israel) accompanied a scouting party to Lake George and "discovered nothing but the Ruins of the famous Fort and the Bodies of those men that the Enemy so barbarously mur[d]ered."[233] Laden with fresh turnips from the fort's garden, the men returned to Fort Edward.

On November 1, after a two-hour interview with Lord Loudoun in Albany, Lieutenant Colonel George Monro collapsed and plunged down a set of stairs and "Fell into a Fitt."[234] He recovered briefly but died two days later of apoplexy (stroke). No doubt, his death on November 3, 1757, was related to the burning rage that he harbored toward Daniel Webb for not sharing intelligence on the movement of the French army on Lake George and his failure to send reinforcements to Fort William Henry. Webb was subsequently ordered back to England and in less than four years was promoted to the rank of Lieutenant General.

The story of the siege and "massacre" at Fort William Henry was not forgotten by the populace of early America, especially after the publication in 1826 of James Fenimore Cooper's romanticized classic, *The Last of the Mohicans*. By that time Cooper was generally recognized as America's leading novelist. In 1824, prior to writing *The Last of the Mohicans*, he visited the region, viewing the cave at Glens Falls (present-day Cooper's Cave), where he commented that "I must place one of my old Indians here," and traveled the length of Lake George aboard the steamboat *Mountaineer*.[235] The book became a staple in schools and the story was made into nine feature films (1911-1992), two animated movies, and three television series.*

Lake George remained relatively tranquil for the rest of 1757, but during the following year a new campaign would engulf the region once again in bloody conflict.

---

*One of the two films made in 1911 of *The Last of the Mohicans* was actually shot on location at Lake George; another film based on the novel was produced in 1914. A 1920 version featured Wallace Berry as Magua and was filmed at Big Bear Lake and Yosemite Valley. A 12-episode movie serial produced in 1932, starring Harry Carey as Hawkeye, was the first talkie version. The success of the 1936 *Last of the Mohicans*, filmed in Sherwood Forest and Cedar Lake, California, helped advance the career of Randolph Scott. Local Boy Scouts were hired during the filming to teach Indian actors to "whoop…in an acceptable Cooper manner."[236] The 1947 movie *Last of the Redman*, featured Buster Crabbe as Magua. Three years later, the *Iroquois Trail*, loosely based on Cooper's *The Last of the Mohicans*, starred George Montgomery as Hawkeye. Michael Mann's 1992 version, featuring Daniel Day-Lewis, Madeline Stowe, Russell Means, Eric Schweig, and Wes Studi, was filmed in the mountains of North Carolina. Mann purchased the rights to the 1936 script and produced the most authentic depiction of hostilities during the French and Indian War of all the versions of *The Last of the Mohicans*, insisting on the use of flintlocks, black powder, and realistic Native American dress and weapons. The 1956 syndicated television series, *Hawkeye and the Last of the Mohicans*, with Lon Chaney as Chingachgook, was shot in Canada and shown in 39 episodes. A 1971 BBC television series was filmed in Scotland and an NBC TV series with Steve Forest as Hawkeye aired in 1977. Two animated versions of Cooper's novel were produced in 1975 and 1987.[237]

7. Battle of Carillon 1758

FOLLOWING THE DESTRUCTION OF FORT WILLIAM HENRY, British officials soon began preparations for a new campaign to capture Forts Carillon and St. Frédéric before pushing into Canada. The 1758 British expedition to Carillon, involving more than 15,000 troops, was the largest and bloodiest campaign of the French and Indian War. The lengthy mobilization and optimism for conquest that preceded the expedition were not sufficient to insure triumph on the battlefield. With only a quarter of the troops compared to the British, Major General Louis-Joseph de Montcalm was able to withstand the onslaught of a numerically-superior enemy. His victory at Carillon in 1758, however, would be the last great success of the French empire in North America.

During the fall of 1757, British scouting parties were dispatched to the area surrounding Carillon to gather intelligence on the French position. On September 21, 1757, Major Robert Rogers* returned to Fort Edward following the unsuccessful Louisbourg expedition. Rogers arrived with approximately 450 men, including 56 ranger cadets. (Fifty were volunteers from British regiments.) His instructions to the cadets on wilderness warfare were in substance the first ranger school. Major General Daniel Webb immediately began sending the ranger leader on scouting expeditions to Ticonderoga. On one of these forays during October, Rogers wrote that "Lord Howe did us the honour to accompany us…to learn our method of marching, ambushing, retreating, & c."[2] Ranger Captain John Stark, a member of the scouting party with Howe, later suggested that Howe had treated him with "great kindness and respect."[3] At the time, 33-year-old George Augustus Howe, son of Lord Viscount Howe, was a colonel in the 55th Regiment (brigadier general in America after December 29, 1757). Howe benefited from his association with the rangers, adopting many of their tactics and ordering alterations to his men's standard British uniform to better accommodate wilderness warfare.

John Campbell, the Earl of Loudoun and British commander in chief in America, sent orders to Rogers to record the methods employed by the rangers on their scouting forays. Accordingly, Rogers created the first manual of war tactics written in America. Rogers'

*At the time Robert Rogers' rank of major was considered a local rank in America. The *Boston Weekly News-Letter* of September 2, 1756, noted that Rogers had a "Brevet for Major" (limited exercise of rank), while commanding in the field. He was referred to as a major in most provincial diaries and newspapers, but as a captain by British officials. On April 6, 1758, Major General James Abercromby promoted Rogers to "Major of the Rangers" and a year later Major General Jeffery Amherst declared "in public orders" that Rogers had the "rank of Major in the army" from the date of his commission as "Major of the Rangers."[1]

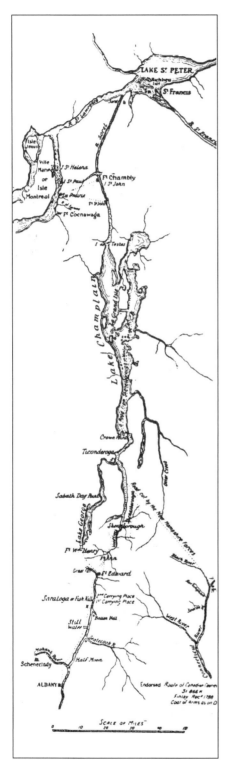

rules of ranging stood the test of time, being reissued to the rangers in World War II and to the Special Forces during the Vietnam War. Completed on October 25, 1757, at Fort Edward, the 28 rules included instructions for marching through the wilderness, reconnoitering, handling prisoners, crossing rivers, protecting flanks, gaining the high ground, circling behind a pursuing enemy, retreating, changing routes during scouting missions, etc.[4]

On November 8 Lord Loudoun met with Rogers and Lieutenant Colonel William Haviland of the 27th Regiment at Fort Edward. (Haviland had replaced Webb at the fort.) Loudoun ordered Rogers on another reconnaissance of Fort Carillon to be accompanied by Captain James Abercrombie of the 42nd Regiment, along with two engineering officers. Due to a bout of scurvy, Rogers was replaced by Captain John Stark, who led the party to the top of Rattlesnake Hill (present-day Mount Defiance). Abercrombie and engineers Matthew Clerk and Samuel Holland made drawings and notes of Carillon. After a failed attempt to seize a French prisoner, the English scouting detachment came under fire from the cannons of the fort and made a hasty retreat. Abercrombie, noted for his prickly personality, subsequently complained to Loudoun about the performance of the rangers during the reconnaissance foray.[5]

Under orders from Haviland, Rogers and 150 men left Fort Edward on December 17, 1757, to "Distress the Enemy at Carillon & if possible to take a prisoner."[6] Four days later, 27 sick rangers were sent back and Rogers and his remaining men camped "by the Great Brook" (present-day Hague Brook).[7] On December 24 Rogers and his detachment arrived within 600 yards of Fort Carillon. The rangers captured a "Sergeant of the Marine," who divulged that the garrison at the fort "consisted of three hundred & fifty Regulars and about fifty Workmen" and that another 150

Eighteenth-century route from Albany to Canada. From *An Historical Journal of the Campaigns in North America* by Captain John Knox (1769).

soldiers and 14 Indians were stationed at Crown Point.[8] While the cannons from the fort fired ineffectively, Rogers killed Carillon's 17 head of cattle and set fire to the fort's stockpile of firewood. With a touch of humor, Rogers left a note on the horns of one of the animals for the commandant of the fort, thanking him for "the fresh meat."[9] French officials regarded the note as "an ill-timed and very low piece of braggadocio."[10] Rogers returned to Fort Edward on December 27. Ironically, while he was trying to create havoc for the French at Carillon, the officers' barracks at Fort Edward accidently burned to the ground on Christmas night after the "R[e]gulars Had a Gen[er]al Frolick" in celebration of the holiday."[11]

The reconnoitering of Carillon that Loudoun had ordered during the fall of 1757 was a necessary prerequisite for his projected winter expedition to Forts Carillon and St. Frédéric. In an October 17 letter to William Augustus, the Duke of Cumberland (son of King George II), Loudoun outlined a strategy of using 3,000 regulars and 1,000 rangers to attack the French forts. Loudoun suggested that the expedition would be "much easier in the Winter" and planned to personally command the army in the field.[12] The scheme involved the use of horse-drawn sleighs on the ice of Lake George, taking along mortars, a few light cannons, and scaling ladders. The deputy-quartermaster general, Lieutenant Colonel John St. Clair, had reservations about the ambitious plan, questioning whether the engineers could "carry on their approaches in the frost and Snow."[13]

Meeting with Lord Loudoun at his Fort George headquarters in New York City on January 9, 1758, Rogers listened to an admonition regarding disciplinary problems associated with an earlier mutiny of rangers at Fort Edward over a flogging incident. Rather than reducing the size of the ranger force that Lieutenant Colonel Haviland had recommended, Loudoun approved five more ranger companies, including one Indian company. On January 13 Rogers took the opportunity to present his own plan to Loudoun "to take Crown Point with four hundred men" by capturing sleighs traveling from St. Jean to Fort St. Frédéric, putting the clothes from the French prisoners onto his men, and gaining entry to the fort by deception.[14] However, by January 28, preparations for Loudoun's winter expedition became apparent to the men at Fort Edward as "a Great Number of Slays came Here Lo[a]ded with provisions & a Great Number of Shells," wrote 20-year-old Sergeant Jabez Fitch from Norwich, Connecticut.[15] On February 10, sleighs loaded with provisions "Constantly Kept Coming" all day long; over the next five days more sleighs arrived, including many with "artillery & a Number of Scaling Ladders."[16]

At the beginning of February Loudoun turned over field command of the winter expedition to Lord Howe. On February 11 Lieutenant Mathew Leslie, an engineer in the 48th Regiment, departed from Fort Edward for Lake George with a number of horse-drawn sleighs and 42 rangers under Captain John Stark. The detachment was to test winter conditions for the impending expedition. Leslie returned to Fort Edward two days later and reported to Howe in Albany the next day about the difficulty in traveling through more than four feet of snow that covered the road to the lake. The severe winter environment would require more snowshoes to be used by rangers to tramp down the snow ahead of a column of regulars. Howe recommended a deferment of the expedition.[17] It was not until February 27, however, that the garrison at Fort Edward learned that the expedition had been "La[i]d Aside & all ye Stor[e]s" were to be sent back to Albany.[18] Although the chief problem lay with the difficult winter conditions, part of the blame for

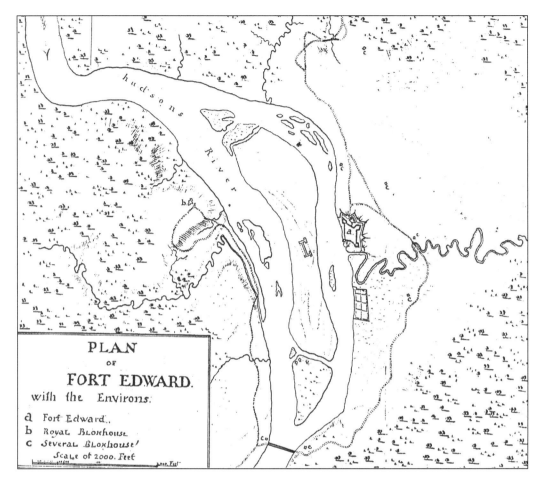

"Plan of Fort Edward with the Environs," 1758.
(Crown Collection, New York State Library)

the cancellation was ascribed to Rogers for not making arrangements for his men to make enough snowshoes.

Meanwhile, irregular warfare continued to intensify around Fort Edward. In retaliation for Rogers' bold Christmas Eve raid on Fort Carillon, Jean-Baptiste Levrault de Langis Montegron (Langy), an ensign in the Troupes de la Marine, led "a detachment of 50" Canadians and Indians on a raid near Fort Edward.[19] On the morning of February 8, a party of men from the fort, accompanied by a guard of 18 regulars and a sergeant, were sent into the forest to cut firewood. Within sight of the fort, the French and Indian detachment attacked, driving the English party "into ye Woods Like so many Sheep or Cattle where they Tomahawk[ed]...a Ser[geant] & 11 men of ye R[e]gulars...Kil[le]d & Scalp[e]d, [and] 4 Wounded & 6 Mis[s]ing."[20] Rogers and his men attempted to pursue Langy's detachment, but the French raiders had disappeared into the forest.

After learning of plans from Langy's captives for a winter expedition against the French forts, a detachment of 16 French troops under a Canadian officer appeared at Fort

Edward on February 17 under a flag of truce. The French party arrived with the excuse of retrieving French prisoners, but the real reason was to judge preparations for the British expedition. Rogers facetiously inquired about "the fresh meat" that he had left at Carillon (ie., the cattle killed on Christmas Eve), but the French officer somberly replied that Rogers should "be careful" when he came again to Carillon.[21]

The day after the news of the cancellation of Howe's winter expedition (February 28), Haviland ordered a scouting party under Captain Israel Putnam from Pomfret, Connecticut, to take a prisoner at Carillon. Inauspiciously, Haviland announced that Rogers would lead an expedition of 400 rangers against the French forts, following the return of Putnam's detachment. This revelation disturbed Rogers, who feared that the French could take prisoners or capture deserters from Putnam's party who could divulge Rogers' forthcoming expedition. The incident highlighted the ongoing hostility between Rogers and Haviland. Haviland was particularly unhappy over the failure to subject rangers, who had been involved in the December 1757 mutiny, to British discipline. He was also upset with the rangers for the violation of his instructions not to fire their muskets near the fort. About one in the afternoon of February 28, Putnam's 115-man detachment headed north. The next day was "V[e]ry P[l]eas[a]nt," according to Jabez Fitch, and Haviland and a number of his officers "Made themselv[e]s Much Sport in Sliding Down ye Bank on a Slay & in Dancing on ye Ice" at Fort Edward.[22] Putnam and his men did not have fun, however, on their week-long scouting mission, returning to Fort Edward on March 6. As Rogers feared, one man had disappeared. In addition, a driver of a sleigh returning provisions to Albany was captured by Ottawa Indians during an ambush on March 6. Now two men could disclose Rogers' plans.

BATTLE ON SNOWSHOES

Under orders from Haviland, Rogers departed from Fort Edward on March 10, but with only 183 men instead of the 400 originally planned. On the second night Rogers and his detachment camped on the east side of Lake George; the next day they stopped briefly at Sabbath Day Point and spent the night at Friends Point in present-day Hague.[23] At three o'clock in the afternoon the following day (March 13), the rangers were traveling on snowshoes through four-foot-deep snow between Bald Mountain and Trout Brook (Bernetz Brook) when Rogers' advance guard apprised him of an enemy party of 96 Indians and some Canadians marching south on the frozen brook. The rangers immediately laid down their packs, lined the east bank of Trout Brook, and prepared to attack the enemy party.

Earlier two Abenaki scouts had discovered "fresh tracks" of an enemy party, so the commander at Fort Carillon, Captain Louis-Philippe Le Dossu d'Hébécourt, dispatched more scouts to verify the presence of an English detachment.[24] On March 12, 200 Indians had reached Carillon from Montreal in preparation for a raid on Fort Edward. One of the Indians, identified as "an old sorcerer," was said to have gone into "a trance" after drinking brandy at the Indian encampment at Ticonderoga and revealed that "the English had sent out a raiding party destined for Carillon."[25] The following day a large number of French and Indians set out for Lake George, and shortly thereafter five or six scouts returned to the main body, reporting "fresh tracks of 200 men."[26] With that news, the French and Indian party marched west to attack the English raiders.

A collision course between the French and Indians and Rogers' detachment was now certain. When the advance party of 96 Indians, led by Ensign de la Durantaye, was "nearly opposite to our left wing," Rogers "fired a gun, as a signal for a general discharge upon them."[27] The fusillade instantly killed a substantial number of Indians, compelling the remaining party to flee. Rogers ordered Ensign Gregory McDonald and his men to pursue the retreating Indians, but he "soon found that the Party we had engaged w[as] only the Advance Guards of the Enemy" and McDonald quickly retreated.[28] During the interim, some of Rogers' men scalped the Indians who had been killed in the initial fire.[29] The main French and Indian detachment, consisting of another 205 men under Ensign Langy, now reversed the course of the engagement, surprising and pursuing the rangers. Taking control of the tumultuous situation, Rogers shouted orders to his men to retreat and reorganize higher on the bank where they had dropped their packs earlier. About 50 of his men did not make it back; the rest "rallied, and drew up in pretty good order, where they fought with such intrepidity and bravery" that the enemy retreated, Rogers later wrote.[30] The rangers again began to scalp the fallen enemy, Lieutenant Edward Crofton recalled, "but [we] were soon prevented by the Enemys making a third attack."[31] After "three quarters of an Hour" of the renewed onslaught, Second Lieutenant William Phillips reported to Rogers that "about 200 Indians were going up the Hill on our Right to take possession of the rising Ground upon our Backs."[32] Rogers ordered Phillips to take the hillside before the enemy could and sent Lieutenant Edward Crofton to take possession of the left flank of the hill. With "more than 100...men killed" and the barrage of fire unrelenting, the rangers' center broke; Rogers and "twenty men ran up the hill to Phil[l]ips and Crofton, where we stopped and fired on the Indians."[33] (The site of this final engagement is believed to be near the present clubhouse of the Ticonderoga Country Club on Route 9N.) Phillips was forced to surrender and, with darkness closing in, Rogers decided to retreat to Lake George with his few surviving rangers. Phillips and his men were tied to trees and many were hacked to pieces. (Phillips lived through the ordeal and escaped captivity in 1758.) Rogers and his remaining rangers used the ranger rule on retreat (dispersing in many directions) and reassembled at Lake George later that evening.

The route of retreat used by Rogers remains a mystery. The tale that has given "Rogers Rock" its name suggests that Rogers was chased by the Indians to the edge of the 700-foot, granite precipice of Bald Mountain overlooking Lake George, where he tossed his pack over the cliff, reversed his snowshoes and backtracked to an easier decent to the icy lake below. When the Indians observed Rogers walking on the frozen surface of the lake, they believed that he had been endowed with the "Great Spirit" and ended their pursuit. Rogers did not mention the incident in his journal, but he sometimes omitted details of his exploits. Although most of the tale is seemingly implausible, Rogers did somehow escape from his Indian pursuers by climbing down the mountainside to the lake surface. The story was repeated shortly thereafter and did not originate in the tourist literature of the nineteenth century. On October 23, 1760, Christopher French, a British captain in the 22nd Regiment, noted in his diary "a place called Rogers' Leap from his having jumped

Facing page: **"Ambush on Ice." Rangers scalping the dead after their attack on the advance French and Indian party on present-day Trout Brook. This was the initial skirmish of the March 13, 1758, Battle on Snowshoes. (Drawing by Gary S. Zaboly)**

down it to escape from Indians."[34] Four land petitions in 1766 called the cliff either "Rogers' Leap" or "Rogers's Rock," and Lieutenant James Hadden, with the British army at Lake George in 1777, referred to the landmark as "Rogers's Rock famous for his descending a part of it."[35]

In his official report Rogers wrote that he had reached the lake "in the Evening about 8 o'Clock, and found there several wounded Men, which I took with me to the place [Friends Point] where we left the [hand] Sleighs."[36] Rogers immediately dispatched a messenger to Fort Edward for help. That night Rogers and the surviving rangers remained at their encampment. Rogers, along with the other rangers, had no coats that night because they had thrown them down during the battle in an effort to reduce their visibility to the enemy (green jackets against the white snow). After the Indians discovered a coat with Rogers' commission papers in the pocket, the French assumed that they had killed the famous scout. The following morning the remnants of Rogers' detachment, including several more men who managed to reach the rendezvous point in the morning, trudged southward, pulling their wounded comrades on the hand sleighs. Late in the day Rogers met the relief party from Fort Edward under Captain John Stark at Sloop Island (Diamond Island), where they camped for the night.

Rogers Rock. (Photo by the author)

At Fort Edward Sergeant Jabez Fitch noted the arrival of the decimated ranger detachment on March 15: "About 3 o Clock ye Party Began to Com[e] in in Small Numbers—about 5 o Clock I Se[e] ye Majr Com[e] in Him Self Being in ye Rear of ye Whol[e]—This was a Vast Cold & Tedious Day, Esp[e]cially for ye Wounded Men…The Whol[e] Scout consisted of 180 & About 40 Return[e]d 5 of which were wounded."[37] The ranger loss, by any measure, was very high. About 104 men were killed during the engagement, four later died of their wounds at Fort Edward, and 16 privates were captured, and nearly all were killed.[38] Two volunteers from the British 27th Regiment, Captain-Lieutenant Henry Pringle and Lieutenant Boyle Roche, were lost in the wilderness for a week after the battle and surrendered at Fort Carillon. The two officers were exchanged in 1760.

The casualty rate of Rogers' detachment was the highest of any major battle in the northern theater. The French reported that the Indians had taken between 114 and 146 scalps at the battle scene, but they would often cut a large scalp into two pieces to increase bounty payments.[39] Rogers exaggerated the estimate of the Indians killed in the battle (150) and most French authorities underestimated their losses; but the commander at Carillon, Captain d' Hébécourt, revealed that "we had a wonderful result but it cost us dearly through the loss which we suffered."[40]

EXPEDITION TO CARILLON

News of a change in command of the British forces in North America finally reached the colonies in March 1758. William Pitt, the secretary of state for Great Britain, had recalled Lord Loudoun on December 30, 1757, but the letter to colonial governors did not arrive in North America until early March. Political struggles in Britain, as well as the failure of the expedition to Louisbourg and the destruction of Fort William Henry, weighed heavily on the decision. In 1758 Pitt prepared plans for a three-theater military offensive against French positions at Louisbourg, Fort Carillon, and Fort Duquesne and recommended Major General James Abercromby for the appointment of commander in chief of British forces in North America. The appointment of Abercromby by King George II included instructions to "cultivate the best Harmony, and Friendship possible with the several Governors of Our Colonies."[41] Pitt wrote to the governors that the position of commander in chief would henceforth be limited to a military role, thus ending interference with colonial governors and assemblies. Legislatures would have more independence and direct financial aid from Britain, which in turn assured support from colonial legislatures for the forthcoming military campaigns. Pitt assumed greater control over North American military operations, however. Although Abercromby had the official title of commander in chief, essentially his authority centered on the expedition to capture the French forts on Lake Champlain as a prelude to an invasion of Canada. Colonel Jeffery Amherst, aide-de-camp to General John Ligonier during the War of Austrian Succession, was recommended to Pitt by Ligonier (then commander in chief of all British forces) to head the Louisbourg expedition with the rank of major general. Brigadier General John Forbes, who had served on Lord Loudoun's senior staff, was given the task of capturing Fort Duquesne.

Major General Abercromby had a long but relatively undistinguished military career. In 1736, after 19 years of service, Abercromby was still a captain, but his election to Parliament two years earlier would eventually serve to advance his prospects. In 1746, during the War of Austrian Succession, Abercromby was promoted to colonel and served as a deputy quartermaster general in France, suffering a wound while serving in the Netherlands the next year. He retired after the war but returned to the army in 1756 to serve as

**James Abercromby. Painting by
Allan Ramsay (1760).
(Fort Ticonderoga Museum)**

a deputy to Lord Loudoun with the rank of major general in North America (colonel of the 44th Regiment). In 1756 Loudoun wrote that Abercromby "is a good Officer, and a very good Second Man anywhere."[42] Although Abercromby had been ill over the winter, he was reported to be "in perfect health" prior to the expedition.[43] Upon his appointment, Abercromby wasted little time in preparing for the northern campaign. On March 15, 1758, he sent a circular letter to the colonial governors, informing them of his appointment and requesting that "a Body of Twenty Thousand Men" be raised.[44] He cited "abuses" whereby good men were excused from serving "for some Pecuniary Consideration," and therefore recommended that men be "fairly drafted out of your best Militia" and urged the rejection of those "unfit for the Service."[45] He also requested that the men report with their "own Arms…Powder Horn, shot Bag…and also with a good Blanket."[46]

The appointment of 33-year-old George Augustus Howe as second in command and field commander of the expedition was expected to provide the energetic leadership needed for the campaign. Howe, a member of Parliament since 1747, succeeded to his father's title, becoming the Third Viscount Howe in 1735. Arriving in America in 1757 as a colonel of the 60th Regiment, Lord Howe was appointed colonel of the 55th in late September and elevated to brigadier general in America on December 29, 1757. Howe added vigor and spirit to the army, discarding tradition to meet the requirements for fighting in the wilds of America. He was exceedingly popular with the troops and on close terms with provincial officers and men. Contemporaries called him "sober, temperate, modest and active," an officer who "exercised his Regulars in Bush-Fighting; accustomed himself to long Marches; [and] carry'd his own Provisions."[47] Howe persuaded Abercromby to order changes in the uniforms and baggage for the expedition: troops were instructed to cut the brims of their hats and no one could carry "more than one Blanket and a Bearskin, no Sash nor Sword, nor even Lace…The Regulars as well as Provincials…cut their Coats so as scarcely to reach their Waist…No Women to follow the Camp, to wash our Linen; Lord Howe who is second in Command, has already sh[o]wed an Example, by going himself to the Brook, and washing his own Linen."[48]

The northern campaign was beset with enormous logistical difficulties. The attempt to raise 20,000 provincial troops, provide equipment, provisions, and bateaux created prolonged delays, compromising swift action. A shortage of skilled labor delayed the building of bateaux in Albany. The plan to have provincial troops supply their own muskets was less than successful, forcing the purchase of arms from merchants and the hiring of gunsmiths to repair old muskets. It was not until June 13 that British ships arrived in New York harbor with 10,000 arms (most were 46-inch "Brown Bess" muskets), 4,000 tents, and artillery for the campaign. Because of these delays, there was little training and most of the time was spent on the long trek to Lake George. The provincial troops had limited time available to master the intricate firing drills of eighteenth-century warfare, which involved shooting volleys in lines. As a consequence, men unfamiliar with handling arms were more prone to accidents.[49]

Amassing provincial and British troops at Fort Edward and then at Lake George required several months to accomplish. In early April Lieutenant Colonel Francis Grant of the 42nd Highland Regiment marched to Fort Edward with regulars from the 42nd and 55th Regiments. Grant, who replaced Haviland as commander of Fort Edward, ordered Rogers and his men on scouting forays "pretty constantly, in order to discover any parties of the enemy…and to reconnoitre" the French forts.[50] In early June Lord Howe reached Fort Edward and set up his living quarters in a tent. British regiments continued to pour into Fort Edward, and on June 9 Major General Abercromby arrived. Under the command of Howe, the 42nd, 44th, and 55th Regiments, along with the New Jersey regiment, rangers, and Stockbridge Indians, departed for Lake George on June 17, "escorting 173 Ox Teams with Provisions, 90 Wagons each carrying a Bateau, and 30 Whale Boats on Trucks/long Carriages with low Wheels, drawn by Men."[51] On the first day the 3,000-man column only reached the Halfway Brook Post, about seven miles north of Fort Edward. On the return trek from reconnoitering Ticonderoga, Robert Rogers stopped at the outpost and

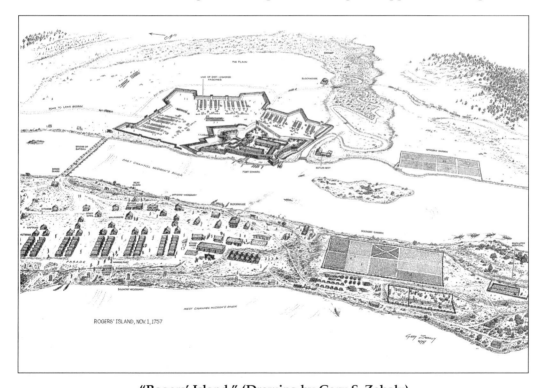

"Rogers' Island." (Drawing by Gary S. Zaboly)

provided Howe "with a plan of the landing-place, the fort at Carillon, and the situation of the lakes."[52] Rogers proceeded to Fort Edward to make his report to Abercromby and was subsequently ordered to join Howe on the march to Lake George. A short time later, Abercromby decided that the Halfway Brook Post needed strengthening for the protection of the convoys and ordered that a picketed fort be built there. On June 23 Private Amos Richardson from Massachusetts recorded "Cutt[i]n[g] Timber…to Bu[i]ld a p[ic]ket fort," and six days later Abel Spicer from Connecticut arrived at Halfway Brook, observing "a small picket fort which contains an acre and a half or two acres of ground."[53]

The progress of the expedition was impeded by the slow advance of the provincial troops to Fort Edward. Although a considerable number of provincial troops had reached Fort Edward before June 20, other regiments filtered into the fort from June 24 to June 30. Some of the men who had arrived earlier, like Ensign Thomas Alexander of Northfield, Massachusetts, were pressed into work details at Fort Edward, including building "a breast work" and a 464-foot "bridge of boats…laid over the river."[54] The pontoon bridge, located on the north side of the fort, connected the island to the east shore of the Hudson River. The 50-acre island, an integral part of the military complex at Fort Edward, was the site of the ranger camp, which encompassed log huts, barracks, a blockhouse, storehouse, smallpox hospital, sutler's cabin, large garden, and other structures.[55] Although the island was most often referred to simply as "the island" or "the Great Island," some published reports in 1758 used the name "Rogers's Island."*

On June 26 Major General Abercromby arrived at the Lake George encampment. Just before leaving Fort Edward, Abercromby declared that the capitulation agreement of 1757, which had prohibited troops who had surrendered at Fort William Henry from serving "in the same manner" for 18 months, was "null & void" and the men were "hereby empowered & commanded to serve" again.[57] Abercromby's justification was based on the violation of the capitulation agreement by the French "in a most notorious & flagrant manner, by Murdering, Pillaging and Captivating many of His Majesty's good Subjects."[58] The decree was presented to every British and provincial regiment in North America and notification of the change was sent to the governor-general of New France, Pierre de Rigaud de Vaudreuil de Cavagnial.

In late June caravans of men and supplies continued to make their way to Lake George. On June 27 Captain Asa Foster of Andover, Massachusetts, noted that "about a thousand oxen…had been employed in carrying provisions to supply the army" at the lake.[59] When provincial troops reached the lake, some were disheartened by the ruins of Fort William Henry, including Obadiah Harris of Wrentham, Massachusetts, who noted a "M[e]l[a]nc[h]oly Sight."[60] The site of the ruins, however, was quickly transformed into a new stockaded fort. Benjamin Glasier, a ship carpenter from Ipswich, Massachusetts, arrived at Lake George on June 22 with 150 carpenters and "beg[a]n to work to picket in a fort where the old on[e] stood," and Private Rufus Putnam from Brookfield, Massachusetts, wrote that he was "employed in building two Picket Forts, in building floating batteries, and in fixing boats."[61] On June 29 Abercromby confirmed that the men were "making a Stockaded Post, where the late Fort stood, & another Work of the same kind on the

*The name "Rogers's Island" appeared in the *New-York Mercury* on September 11, 1758, ("Extract of a Letter from Rogers's Island…August 23") and in the *Boston Evening-Post* on October 2, 1758 ("Extract of a Letter from Rogers's Island…Sept.11"). The name Rogers Island may also have been linked to the family of General Thomas Rogers, who owned the island during the late eighteenth and early nineteenth centuries.[56]

Rising Ground where the entrenched Camp was last Year."[62] Five days later Dr. Caleb Rea, a surgeon from Danvers, Massachusetts, mentioned the presence of the picketed forts and a "Hosp[i]t[a]l" at Lake George.[63]

By the beginning of July, Abercromby had amassed the largest army ever assembled in North America. While Abercromby may have lacked experience as a field commander, he demonstrated organizational skills in collecting men and supplies for the 1758 campaign. Virtually all the open land surrounding the southern end of the lake was covered with tents housing the huge army. British regiments included the 27th Foot, 42nd Foot (Highlanders), 44th Foot, 46th Foot, 55th Foot, 60th Foot (Royal Americans), 80th Foot (Gage's Light infantry) and two battalions of artillerymen. Fifteen provincial regiments were comprised of seven from Massachusetts,* four from Connecticut, and one each from New Hampshire, New Jersey, New York, and Rhode Island. In addition, Colonel John Bradstreet commanded about 1,600 bateaumen, Major Robert Rogers headed 800 rangers, and Sir William Johnson led 440 Mohawks. (Johnson arrived with them at Ticonderoga on July 7.) In all, the army numbered approximately 17,100 men.

Although impressive in number, provincial troops (accounting for about 3/5 of the total army) lacked the necessary training for a first-rate army. Most had only trained for a few days and several regiments did not receive their muskets until a short time before the expedition. As a consequence, accidents with firearms were common in the provincial ranks. Dr. Caleb Rea noted that one provincial soldier "had his leg shot to Pieces by another's carelessly discharging his Gun."[64] The wounded solder had his leg amputated but died the next morning. On June 28 Rea recorded that three shooting accidents occurred within the space of one or two days.

On the morning of July 3 the army was "paraded" before Abercromby and Howe, prior to being "exercise[d] [in]…Bush Fi[gh]ting" and other maneuvers.[65] In the days preceding the departure of the army, the men toiled at loading provisions and supplies into the flat-bottomed, double-ended bateaux. Abercromby anticipated that each bateau would "carry 22 Men with 30 Days Provisions," but provincial troops recorded varying quantities of provisions aboard their bateaux.[66] Young Abel Spicer reported only "three days provision," and other men noted provisions for 4 to 6 days.[67] (However, a number of provincial troops mentioned 30 days of provisions on board their vessels.)[68]

On July 5 "at Daybreak the General [drum] was Beat," Chaplain John Cleaveland from Massachusetts wrote, and "the Tents were immediately struck" and packed aboard the bateaux.[69] Captain Alexander Moneypenny, a brigade major in the regulars, noted the assembly of troops at five in the morning, but the departure time ranged from 6 a.m. to 9 a.m., according to the diaries of the men.[70] The difference in the departure times reflected the vast size of the armada, which took hours to organize and to depart. Seth Tinkham, a sergeant in a Massachusetts provincial regiment, remarked that "we Got into our whale boats before sunrise, and rowed off about a mile, and sta[ye]d until Col. Bradstreet gave his orders to go forward."[71] Writing to William Pitt, Abercromby described the expeditionary force as "6367 Regulars, Officers, Light-Infantry, & Rangers included, & 9024 Provincials including Officers and Batteau men [who] embarked in about 900 Batteaux &

*Only six Massachusetts regiments participated in the expedition to Ticonderoga. Colonel Ebenezer Nichols' Massachusetts regiment did not leave with the army for Carillon on July 5; troops from the regiment had accidentally killed a regular during target practice the day before and were ordered to remain at the Lake George camp.

135 Whaleboats, the Artillery, to cover our Landing, being mounted on Rafts."[72] To defend against any "batteries erected [by the French] to intercept our passage through the Narrows," surgeon James Searing noted that "three r[a]deau[x] or floating batteries were prepared, two upon batteaux and one made of timber; upon each of which were mounted two field pieces [four-pound cannons]."[73] The 48 pieces of artillery (cannons, mortars, and howitzers) with "200 Rounds for each" were transported over the lake on rafts, built by laying platforms over bateaux.[74] The armada was organized into "Four Columns"; the regulars were assigned to the bateaux in the two center columns; the provincials manned the two outside columns of bateaux; the rangers and light infantry aboard whaleboats headed the columns; the rafts with the artillery and horses and bateaux with provisions followed in the rear, accompanied by a rearguard of light infantry.[75] An eyewitness suggested that the fleet "covered the Lake from Side to Side, which…extended from Front to Rear [a] full seven Miles; and by the Time the Rear had left…there was not any of the Lake to be discern[e]d."[76] Samuel Thompson from Woburn, Massachusetts, was ordered to remain at the Lake George camp during the expedition; He observed that the troops "set off as fast as they could" beginning at daylight, but he could still see the huge flotilla "till noon" on the water.[77] The laborious rowing of the boats was aided by a day "not very hot" and an army "in good he[a]lth and h[igh] spir[i]t[s]."[78] The fleet "was very beautiful to See," Samuel Fisher wrote, and pleasing to hear with "fine Music," coming from French horns, bagpipes, drums, fifes, and trumpets.[79] Although acknowledging the "great Prospect" of the expedition, Lieutenant Colonel Melancthon Taylor Woolsey, muster master of the New York provincial regiment, recognized the gravity of the situation and wrote to his brother while on board a bateau that "our fates will Be unalterably fix[e]d. But I have a Strong Im[presssion] that I shall survive the Day of Battle and not because I Desire to Hide myself."[80] (Woolsey survived the battle but died of dysentery on September 28, 1758.)

"About sundown we got to the Sabbath Day Point and landed," Benjamin Jewett noted in his diary.[81] At Sabbath Day Point some of the troops viewed "several men's bones," remaining from the ambush of Colonel John Parker's detachment in 1757; others observed "the greatest number of rattle-snakes" ever seen.[82] The men were ordered to go through the motions of setting up a camp and making "a great Number of large Fires along the Shore" in an effort to mislead French scouting parties.[83] Between ten p.m. and one a.m. the British and provincial troops quietly renewed their voyage northward in shifts.[84] The subterfuge apparently had its desired effect, because French troops at their advance posts were apparently taken by surprise upon the arrival of the British forces early on the following morning. The extent of the surprise, however, is uncertain, since French scouts had "hoisted and lowered" a white flag as a signal of "bateaux on the lake" on the afternoon of July 5 and later that same day scouts returned to Montcalm's camp with a report of "a great" number of bateaux on Lake George.[85]

Meanwhile, the French army at Carillon began preparing for the impending onslaught of the British and provincial army. The French were aware of British plans well ahead of time from published recruiting notices, from information disclosed by English prisoners captured by their Indian allies, and through a visit to Fort Edward on June 19 by a French officer under a flag of truce, using the guise of an arrangement for a prisoner exchange. Major General Louis-Joseph de Montcalm had arrived at Carillon on June 30 and immediately heard reports of a British force of "20 and 25,000 men" assembling at

"Abercromby's Spearhead," depicting Major Robert Rogers and his rangers aboard whaleboats ahead of the columns of bateaux. (Drawing by Gary S. Zaboly)

Lake George.[86] Although Governor-General Pierre de Rigaud de Vaudreuil had planned to deploy 5,000 men at Carillon by the middle of June, a political and personal rivalry with Montcalm resulted in a postponement of reinforcements to the fort. In June Vaudreuil had dispatched a 1,600-man diversionary force, under Brigadier General François (François-Gaston) de Lévis, to the Mohawk Valley, despite an insufficient number of troops at Carillon. Montcalm was beset with a number of other problems, including less participation from France's Indian allies, particularly the western Indians who had contracted smallpox after the 1757 campaign against Fort William Henry and who were disgruntled over the issue of plunder following the surrender of the fort. Poor harvests in Canada resulted in a shortage of food, handicapping New France's ability to marshal adequate provisions for the army. Newspapers reported that the French population was "reduced to a quarter of a Pound of Horse Flesh a Day, and a pint of Bran [processed wheat] to make their Bread."[87] Because Fort Carillon could never hold all of the French troops during an attack, Montcalm surveyed the area surrounding the fort on July 1, with engineers Nicolas Sarrebource de Pontleroy and Jean-Nicolas Desandrouins and other officers, to select a site for a defensive position. The following day the initial dimensions for an entrenchment were marked out on the high ground about a half-mile west of the fort.

On July 6 Obadiah Harris wrote that "about…Sun Ris[e] we Came Within Sight of the

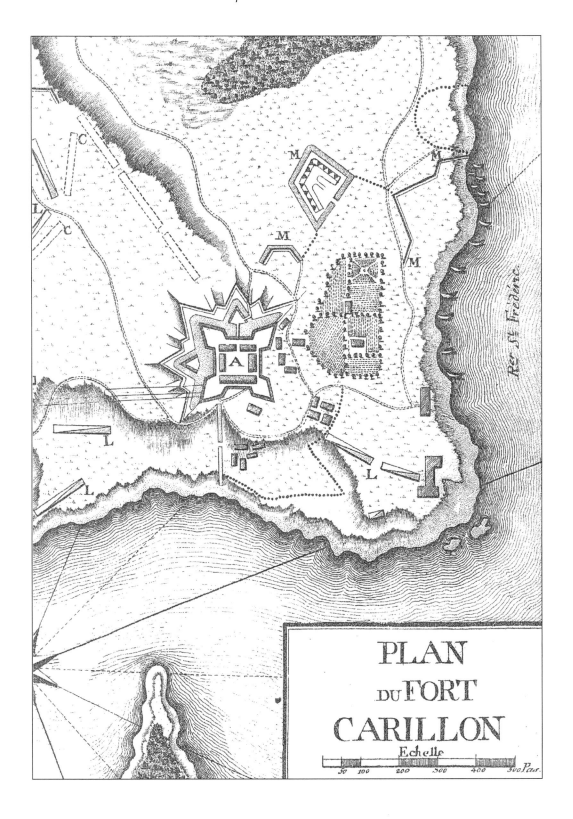

[French] Advance Guard at the northern end of Lake George."[88] At five o'clock in the morning, the vanguard of the British forces, composed of Bradstreet's bateaumen, Rogers' detachment of rangers, and Brigadier General Thomas Gage's light infantry, approached the outlet of the lake at present-day Ticonderoga. Before the landings, Howe, Bradstreet, and Rogers had rowed within a quarter-mile of the French camp "to observe the landing place."[89] (It was perhaps here that Brigadier General Howe made a fatal error. In June Howe had reviewed Rogers' scouting report and maps and could have recommended a landing site on the east side of the outlet of Lake George rather than the west bank, which required a long, difficult circuitous march to Carillon.)[90] After learning of the limited defenses of the French camp at the outlet, Abercromby gave orders for the army to land. Rogers and his 800 rangers were the first to disembark on the west shore (at present-day Baldwin), south of the main landing point. The light infantry then pushed ashore at the main landing zone (today's Howe's Cove), followed by the rest of the troops. Colonel Bradstreet and his bateaumen rowed north "a Mile further and Landed" near a blockhouse, which the French set on "fire at the first Sight of us," according to Captain David Waterbury of Connecticut.[91] Although the provincial troops were only a short distance from the landing site at daybreak, most recorded the time of their landing as either nine a.m. or ten a.m.[92] Landing with his Massachusetts regiment, Seth Tinkham and his comrades "ran up to an old breast work" and could "see the French striking their tents and running off."[93] The French troops fled, leaving "a great Quantity of Baggage; they destroyed their Ovens…But a great Number of Sheep, Poultry, and other Provisions fell into our Hands."[94] Captain François-Joseph, Chevalier de Germain of the La Reine Regiment had been dispatched with 150 men to support the troops at the portage; but upon viewing the size of the British army, Germain and his troops fired briefly and made a hasty retreat to Montcalm's camp. Volunteers under Captain Jean-Baptiste Duprat were also forced to fall back.

By early afternoon British troops were formed into four columns for the march to Ticonderoga following a trail along the west side of the outlet from Lake George (La Chute River). The route on the west bank would avoid two river crossings and circumvent French troops defending the sawmill and bridge at the lower (northernmost) falls. However, crossing the outlet did not prove to be that difficult. Although the French had burned the bridge of boats during their retreat from the portage camp, English provincial carpenters quickly began "Building a Bri[d]ge and then heaving up a Breast work" at the portage site (probably at the present-day natural stone dam). [95] About noon, Robert Rogers with a detachment of rangers was sent ahead to select and hold a crossing over the Bernetz Brook (present-day Trout Brook, which empties into the La Chute River on the west side). Under Lord Howe's leadership, four columns of nearly 7,000 men (two columns of regulars in the center and outside columns of provincials) marched north early in the afternoon. According to Lieutenant George Clerk of the 44th Regiment of Foot, the army marched "toward the fort [at] Ticonderoga in order to have invested it that afternoon"[96] One British participant wrote that "we continued our march through dark woods and swamps that were almost impassable."[97] Late in the afternoon "we w[e]re beset in ye rear of ye r[e]giment," Benjamin Jewett of Colonel Eleazer Fitch's Third Connecticut Reg-

Facing page: Detail of a "Plan of Fort Carillon" 1758 by Lieutenant Cöntgen Therbu, engineer. (National Archives of Canada)

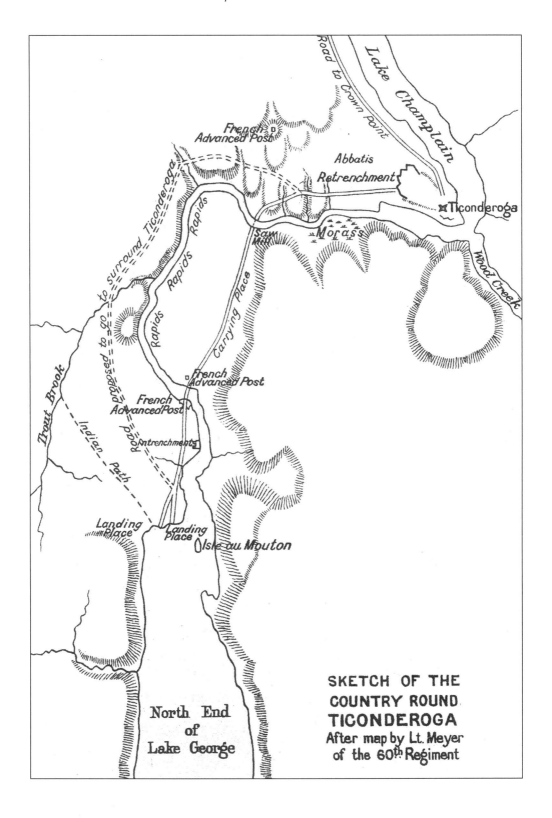

North End
of
Lake George

SKETCH OF THE
COUNTRY ROUND
TICONDEROGA
After map by Lt. Meyer
of the 60th Regiment

iment wrote, with an attack by the enemy and "as soon as ye fire began ev[e]ry r[e]giment made toward ye enemy as fast as they co[u]ld and soon drove them."[98] "Immediately on the Fire of the Enemy," Captain Hugh Arnot of the 80th Regiment noted, Lord Howe "advanc[e]d [to the left flank], and too boldly charging at the head of the L[igh]t Infantry received a Shot under the left Breast which went thro' his Lungs, his Heart, & Back bone, so that he died instantan[e]ously."[99] Captain Alexander Moneypenny was only six yards from Howe when the young noblemen "fell on his back and never moved only his hands quivered an instant."[100]

When the firing commenced, Colonels Phineas Lyman and Eleazer Fitch had already reached Bernetz (Trout) Brook with their regiments and were engaged in a conversation with Robert Rogers. Hearing the discharge of muskets, the three officers rushed to the scene of the engagement with their men. The skirmish involved a 350-man French scouting detachment under Captain de Trépezec and Ensign Jean-Baptiste Levrault de Langis Montegron (Langy), who had unwittingly stumbled upon the British and provincial columns in the thick forest. The French reconnaissance force had been dispatched the day before to a position between Mont Pélée (today's Rogers Rock) and the northern outlet of the lake and were subsequently cut off from their return route to Carillon by the advancing British and provincial army. Trépezec was mortally wounded, but before he died suggested that his detachment had become lost "through the fault of his guide"; Montcalm subsequently revealed that Trépezec had been "abandoned by a small number of his Indian…guides."[101] Hearing the battle, surgeon Caleb Rea wrote that it sounded like a "Thousand Guns fired, which made a terrible ro[a]ring in the woods," and Lieutenant Archelaus Fuller with a Massachusetts regiment remarked that the firing was "so smart" that the "earth trembled."[102] Although some eyewitnesses commented that the response of the army during the skirmish was well-disciplined and organized—"regulars formed & fired in heavy platoons"—others suggested that at the first fire "panic seized our soldiers."[103] While the "whistling of balls and roar of mus[k]etry terrified" one sixteen-year-old recruit from Massachusetts, the provincials and regulars held their ground and then vigorously pursued the fleeing remnants of the French detachment.[104]

After the engagement, Major William Eyre recounted that "we continued our March on toward the Fort," but as darkness approached an "Indian war cry" was heard, according to Captain Charles Lee, and "some Provincials & Rangers fir'd on each other & at length the fire became almost general…a very dismal tragedy."[105] Twenty-year-old Garrett Albertson of the Jersey Blues suggested that the accident occurred during the renewed march because the "army got bewildered or lost, and parted in two divisions" and "commenced firing on each other."[106] Albertson wrote that he couldn't remember feeling "greater distress of mind…I thought the hand of Providence was turned against us, in a lonely wilderness" and wished only that he could return home to his father and never participate in another military campaign.[107] The incidents of July 6 were a fatal setback for the expedition, and ended "in Confusion and disgraced the Army," Captain Joshua Loring concluded.[108] While the dispirited army roamed "through the woods, they acciden-

Facing page: **Map of the route from Lake George to Ticonderoga, redrawn from Lieutenant Elias Meyer's 1758 map. From** *The Passing of New France* **by William Wood.**

Empires in the Mountains

Louis-Joseph de Montcalm.
(National Archives of Canada)

George Augustus Howe.
(Fort Ticonderoga Museum)

tally" encountered Abercromby, according to 18-year-old Marinus Willett, serving with the New York provincials: "The poor old gentleman was standing under a huge tree, wrapped in a large cloak, with two regular regiments drawn around him to defend his person."[109] A large number of British and provincial troops remained in the forest overnight. The following morning the dispirited soldiers returned to the original landing site at Lake George.

The French detachment sustained substantial losses during the encounter, including 148 men captured. Many of the wounds suffered by the French soldiers were devastating; Private Garrett Albertson observed that "one poor fellow brought in [was] shot across his belly, with his hands holding up his entrails."[111] When the provincials marched back to the landing site on July 7, they discovered "Dead Bod[i]es...Strew[n] Quit[e] thick on the Ground...We Stumbled over them for awhile...[an] Awful Sight to Behold."[112] The French prisoners were temporarily held on Isle au Mouton (later renamed Prisoners Island) and transported to the southern end of Lake George on July 8.

The British and provincial losses were very small, but the death of Lord Howe would have a lasting impact. When Howe's body was carried back to the landing site at Lake George, "scarce an eye was free from tears," Captain Alexander Moneypenny noted, and Lieutenant Colonel Melancthon Taylor Woolsey lamented that Howe, "was the Soul of the Army."[113] Abercromby affirmed that Howe was "universally beloved and respected throughout the Army."[114] Surgeon Caleb Rea noted that the expedition became "a little Stagnant" following Howe's death, and Rogers recalled that it produced a "general consternation and languor through the whole" army.[115] Abercromby wrote to William Pitt that Howe's body had been "sent to Albany" where it was to be embalmed, but Dr. Rea disclosed that the body "was Brou[gh]t in and [e]mbalmed" at the northern Lake George camp, probably due to the hot weather.[116]

After the discovery of a skeleton and stone marker in Ticonderoga in 1889, many people were convinced that Howe had been buried there, but eyewitnesses in 1758 had viewed his body enroute to Albany. On July 8, 1758, Samuel Thompson, stationed at the recently-built stockade at the former site of Fort William Henry, noted "they brought Lord How[e] to ye Fort," and on the same day Amos Richardson, also at the southern end of Lake George, recorded that "th[e]y Brought in Lord How[e's] Corps[e] into our camp and th[e]y Car[ri]ed him to Albany."[117] Howe was buried at St. Peter's Church in Albany and reinterred twice at the church during the nineteenth century due to two rebuilding projects. His body was reinterred again in 1968 under the floor of a new vestibule.[118]

The loss of Howe and the breakdown of the march to Carillon brought the expedition to a standstill on July 7. Abercromby ordered the troops back to the original landing site at Lake George because of a lack of "Intelligence of the Troops that were missing," and because the men were "greatly fatigued" and "in Want of Provisions."[119] Early in the morning Lieutenant Colonel John Bradstreet, the energetic 43-year-old head of the "Battoe Service," "beg[g]ed" Abercromby "to give him the Command of Four or Five Thousand Men" to immediately take "Possession of the Saw Mill" on the La Chute River.[120]

Facing page: A South West View of the Lines and Fort of Tyconderoga **from Rattlesnake Hill (present-day Mount Defiance). Wash drawing by Thomas Davies. (National Archives of Canada) Although the scene shows the Ticonderoga peninsula in 1759, the view would be somewhat comparable to that of 1758.**

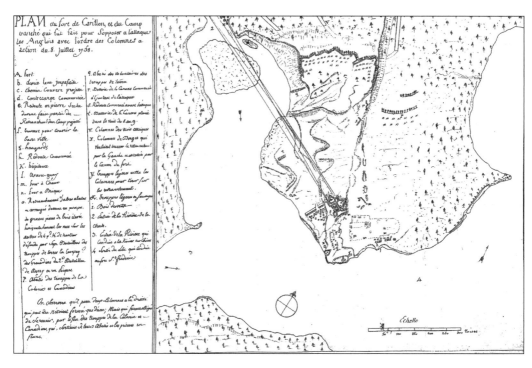

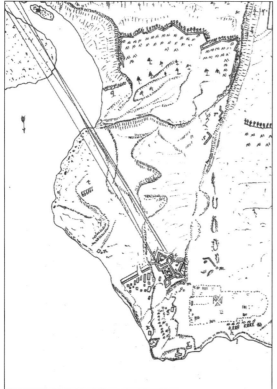

"Plan of Fort Carillon…8 July 1758," showing the English columns west of the French breastwork. Details left and below. (National Archives of Canada)

After an extended period of solicitation, Abercromby relented and gave Bradstreet permission to march forward. By mid-morning Bradstreet had departed with regulars of the 44th and 60th Regiments, rangers, and three provincial regiments.[121] Bradstreet and his troops took possession of the sawmill on the La Chute River, discovering that the French had "first destroy'd all they could, they burnt their wagons…partly cut down [burned] the mill…cut down their bridge."[122]

In the interim, the delay in the British advance provided Montcalm with crucial time to build a breastwork on a ridge ("Heights of Carillon") about a half-mile west of the fort. Meeting with his officers before sunrise on July 7, Montcalm rejected any suggestion to evacuate and ordered his army to construct the breastwork that engineers Pontleroy and Desandrous had marked out. At dawn nearly 3,000 soldiers and officers labored feverishly to build a one-third-mile-long entrenchment, which followed the sinuosity of the hillside. The wall was constructed of logs placed horizontally, and "in front" of the breastwork, French troops fashioned an abatis of "overturned trees whose cut and sharpened branches gave the effect of chevaux-de-frise [projecting spikes]."[123] Surgeon James Searing later described the breastwork as "logs, well fitted together, with slits…for loopholes—and made so high as to come above their heads" and Colonel Oliver Partridge of Hatfield, Massachusetts, suggested that the land in front of the entrenchment "resembled trees blown down by a hurricane, lying from the ground 10 feet high, so that there was no passing them without climbing or creeping."[124] Built in "24 hours," the breastwork was topped with sand bags and fitted with "plenty of wall-pieces" (small swivel cannons) that were loaded with deadly grapeshot (small iron balls). [125]

While the French were constructing their breastwork, Abercromby received word from Bradstreet that the French encampment on the La Chute River had been deserted and was now safely in British hands. At three o'clock in the afternoon on July 7, the rest of Abercromby's army began a march to the sawmill on the La Chute River by crossing a newly-constructed bridge over the northern outlet of Lake George and continuing along the portage road. By nightfall, provincial carpenters completed a second log bridge across the La Chute at the sawmill. Captain Samuel Cobb, commander of a company from a Massachusetts regiment and a well-known shipwright, noted that troops had "brought up 3 of our Brass Cannon and hove up a Breast work for our fortification" at the camp near the sawmill.[126] Late in the day on July 7 Abercromby sent his engineer, Lieutenant Matthew Clerk, along with Captains James Abercrombie and John Stark with 400 rangers, to observe the French position from Rattlesnake Hill (present-day Mount Defiance). The duties of senior engineer for the expedition fell to Clerk because Colonel James Montresor, the chief British engineer in North America, was very ill and Major William Eyre, a more experienced engineer, decided to command the 44th Regiment. (Abercromby pressured Eyre to choose between the 44th and the position of engineer, but Eyre may have resisted relinquishing the infantry command because he would qualify for a half-pay pension if wounded. Eyre would not receive a pension as an unauthorized engineer because he was not on the list of authorized engineers of the Ordnance Board.)[127] While Lieutenant Clerk was commissioned a "sub-engineer" and deemed "a stripling who had never seen the least service" by some, others, like Abercromby, had "a very good opinion" of the young Scottish engineer.[128] Clerk had reconnoitered Carillon in November 1757 and spent several months developing a plan to capture the French fort. William Grant, a lieutenant

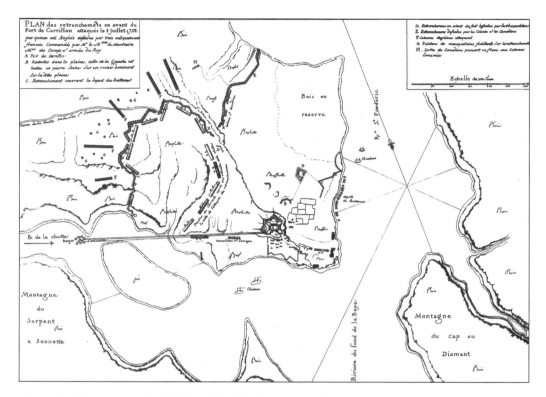

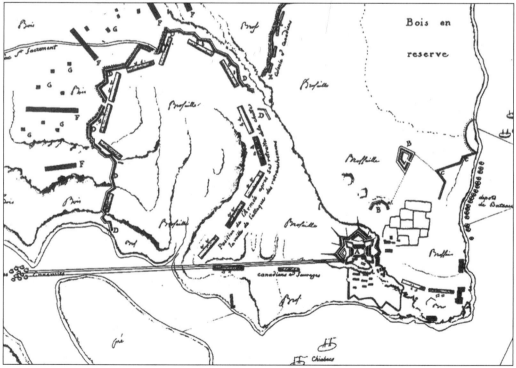

in the 42nd Regiment at the time of the battle, later wrote that after their reconnaissance to Rattlesnake Hill on July 7, the engineers reported to Abercromby that the French position "could be easily forced, even without cannon, if they were attacked with spirit."[129] However, Captain John Stark was said to have disagreed, maintaining that the French had made "formidable preparations."[130] At sunset William Johnson arrived with 440 Indians, who "formed a Circle, and their Chiefs made a fine harangue."[131] Before sunrise on July 8, Johnson and his Indian allies moved to Rattlesnake Hill, where they provided a diversion for another scouting party by firing at the fort, and by "hideous yelling," Seth Tinkham remarked.[132]

After dark on July 7, British and provincial troops, encamped at the sawmill, "heard the French all night chopping and felling timber to fortify their breastwork."[133] That evening 400 French troops, assigned to Brigadier General François de Lévis, reached Montcalm's camp; during the early hours of July 8, Lévis and Lieutenant Colonel Etienne-Guillaume de Senezergues de La Rodde arrived, along with 100 additional men, bringing the total French army at Carillon to 3,526 troops.[134] Montcalm deployed the Canadians and Troupes de la Marine just to the north of the breastwork and the battalions of the French regiments behind the breastwork: the La Reine at the northeast end, the Guyenne and Bearn on the north side, the Berry and Royal-Roussilion at the center, the Languedoc and La Sarre at the southwest end, and two volunteer companies of light infantry between the La Chute River and the southern end of the breastwork.

Early the next morning (July 8) Abercromby wanted the engineers to be "certain" of their assessment of the breastwork and "sent them out again to take as near a view of the lines as possible."[135] Although Abercromby wrote that he had "sent Mr. Clerk…to reconnoitre the Enemy's Entrenchment," other officers also mentioned that "Brad Street with an engineer" and "an engineer, who was a foreigner" (probably Lieutenant Charles Rivez, an engineering assistant) were dispatched to Rattlesnake Hill.[136] The report of the scouts left "no Doubt of the Practicability of carrying those works, if attacked before they were Completed," Abercromby later wrote.[137] According to Captain William Hervey, the engineers suggested that the breastwork could be "push[ed] down with our shoulders," but they may have had observed a simple log barrier "made of loose logs which served to cover the out parties" forward of the main entrenchment.[138] Upon confirmation of the intelligence report of July 7, it was "unanimously resolv'd by the General and Field Officers, to make the Attack immediately."[139] The rush to act was also related to information gathered from the French prisoners captured on July 6, who had revealed that 3,000 reinforcements were "hourly expected," causing Abercromby and his officers to decide "that we ought to lose no time on making the Attack."[140] This urgency, combined with the intelligence about the breastwork, resulted in a decision not to haul the artillery train from Lake George for the assault.

Lieutenant Clerk's reconnaissance of Rattlesnake Hill on the morning of July 8 largely centered on an attempt to find a location for a battery at the foot of the mountain to fire on the French entrenchment. Private Joseph Smith from Groton, Connecticut, recorded that at nine o'clock on the morning of July 8 a "Party of men" climbed Rattlesnake Hill to guard the engineer while he made "a Plan of the ground…to Place the art[il]lery."[141]In the

Facing page: **"Plan of the retrenchment…8 July 1758," indicating the line of French fire on the British artillery rafts and whaleboats and detail. (National Archives of Canada)**

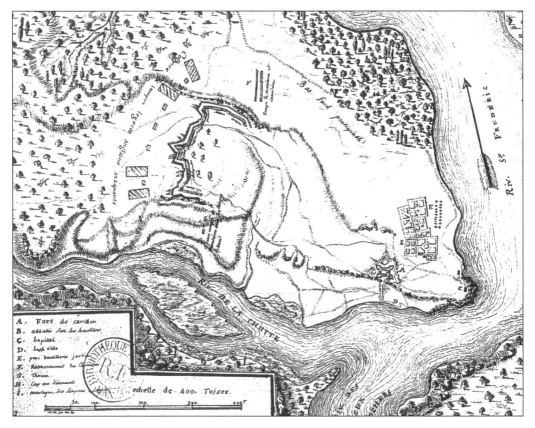

**Map of Montcalm's breastwork, the abatis, and other features of the fort,
including the layout of the garden. (National Archives of Canada)**

meantime, Benjamin Glasier was ordered to build two floating batteries to carry the cannons for the proposed battery. Dr. James Searing noted that at noon on July 8 "by the
directions of Mr. Clerk, engineer, in pursuance of his reconnoitre, r[a]deaus with two six
pounders each and one royal howitzer" were sent eastward on the La Chute River with
instructions for the crews to land at "an open place as described by the engineer and there
to enfilade [fire at] the enemy's works."[142] The hastily-made artillery rafts were towed by
ten whaleboats, but after reaching the open lake "shot and shells were fired at them from
the fort, they could find no such place as described [by Clerk]" and turned back. (The
French claimed to have sunk two of the vessels.) [143] William Johnson's Indian detachment
was to render a protective fire from Rattlesnake Hill to cover the landing of the artillery
rafts, but the effort ended prematurely.

On the morning of July 8, orders were issued to line up the troops for the march to
the French entrenchment. The first contingent of the army, consisting of rangers, light
infantry, and Bradstreet's "Battoemen"—more than 2,000 men in total—were to advance
ahead of the regulars and form a skirmish line. The rangers were assigned to the left
(north) side and "the Battoe-Men" to the center, and to "the Right the Light Infantry…In
their Rear, on the Left, the first Battalion of the New York Regiment; on their Right six

Boston Regiments…to support the Regulars, consisting of six Regiments (in case they should be forced to retire)…to be followed by the Connecticut and Jersey Troops, in the Rear of the Whole."[144] Overall, the instructions to the regulars were general. They were to form three columns and attack "all at once" and the "Pi[ck]ets were to begin the Attack sustained by the Grenadiers & they by the Battalions [of regulars]; The Whole were order'd to march up briskly, rush upon the Enemy's Fire, and not to give theirs until they were within the Enemies Breastwork."[145]

The evening before the battle, Montcalm had gathered his men and thoroughly explained his directions for the defense of the breastwork. After the drums beat to quarters at dawn, the French regulars waited apprehensively behind their entrenchment. There is some evidence, however, that Montcalm may still have been uncertain about making a stand at Carillon. Captain Pierre Pouchot of the Béarn Regiment wrote that "Montcalm was rather irresolute all that morning. He did not know whether to resist the enemy attack or to withdraw to St. Frédéric," but Pouchot assured him that the "trench works are immune from assault" and that he would have time to rethink his position since it would take several days for the British to "open up roads to bring in their artillery."[146] Three French deserters later revealed that "Montcalm was so certain of being defeated" if the British assaulted the breastworks a second time "that he ordered a Number of Battoes to be kept in Readiness…as they intended to abandon the Fort and Entrenchments, as soon" as the British "brought up their battering Cannon."[147] Nonetheless, on July 8 Montcalm appeared resolute to the majority of his men and in full command of the French position. Montcalm would personally command the troops at the center of the breastwork, Colonel François-Charles Bourlamaque directed the battalions on the southern end of the line, and Brigadier General Lévis was in charge of the northernmost section.

Before noon the British army "marched with great che[e]rfulness," Captain William Hervey noted, and John Noyes of Newbury, Massachusetts, recorded that the troops lined up "in a String [line] that was t[w]o mile[s] long."[148] At the very beginning of the engagement British plans for the assault ran into trouble. Rogers recounted that he was "within about three hundred yards of the breast-work when my advance guard was ambushed and fired upon by about 200 Frenchmen."[149] As a result of the skirmish, the planned position of the rangers had to be altered. The New York provincials, under Colonel Oliver DeLancey, were ordered "to Repair to Rogers Assistance," and some of William Johnson's Mohawks also joined Rogers.[150] When the New York regiment advanced, they were surprised by the enemy force still outside the entrenchment and a "smart fire" ensued, which eventually drove the surviving French troops behind their breastwork.[151] Hearing the "very heavy fire" and a "huz[z]a at the same time" from the New Yorkers and irregulars, Captain Hugh Arnot suggested that it "made our Gen'l believe & was so told (for He could not see what was a doing) that some part of the Army had enter'd their Lines."[152] Lieutenant Colonel William Haviland, commanding a brigade of the 27th Regiment seized the initiative to commence the attack, despite Abercromby's earlier order that the "Attack [was] not to begin till the whole Army was formed."[153] Led by Major Thomas Proby of the 55th Regiment, the pickets (light infantry) from the regulars (probably carrying more accurate muskets with "rifled [grooved] barrel[s]") along with the grenadiers, rushed forward but were stymied by enemy fire and the "almost inaccessible road to the Breast work & ye height of the same."[154] Abercromby subsequently noted that troops

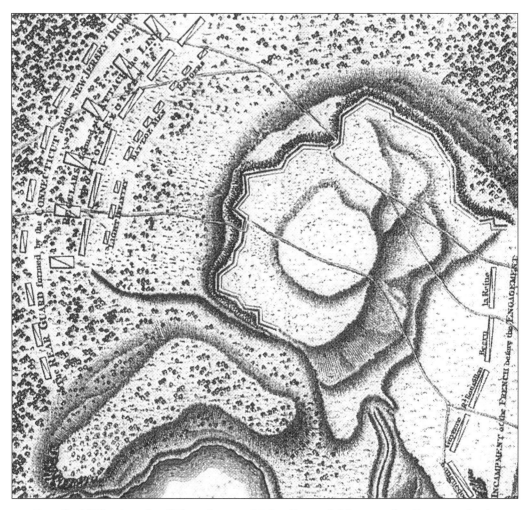

Detail of "The Attack of Ticonderoga; Major General Abercromby Commander in Chief." From *The History of the Late War in North-America* by Thomas Mante (1772).

"found the ground Cover'd with felled Trees, the Branches sharpened & pointed outwards, and a vast number of Pointed Stakes drove into the Ground, which rendered the road to the Enemies works...almost impassable."[155] Captain James Abercrombie, aide-de-camp to the general, indicated that Abercromby believed that the initial fighting only involved the irregulars, and "to his great surprise, when he came up with the Highlanders [42nd Regiment], he found all the rest of the Regulars attacking the Intrenchment," an action that violated the initial orders because the regiments had "joined piecemeal in the attack," rather than attacking with a unified force of six regular regiments.[156]

The attempt by the British regulars to cross the abatis of felled trees "proved a prodigious Difficulty, as they were continually falling down"; an eyewitness suggested that the regulars "marched on with great intrepidity...but were knocked down so fast, that it was very difficult for those behind to get over the dead and wounded."[157] The perilous struggle to traverse the abatis "gave the enemy [an] abundance of time to mow us down like a field of corn, with their wall-pieces and small arms," one regular officer remarked.[158] Major William Eyre noted that "we march'd a Battalion in Front three Deep; I was of [the] opinion we should attack it in Column" to minimize the width of the enemy's target, "but it was said this would cause confusion; in short, it was said [earlier] we must attack Any Way, and not be losing time in talking or consulting how."[159] Others, seeing the carnage, also questioned the strategy. Chaplain John Cleveland from a Massachusetts regiment found the "conduct…to be marvelous strange to order the entrenchment to be forced with Small Arms, when they had cannon not far off," and Abner Barrows from Middleboro, Massachusetts, suggested that it was "a great over Sight that We had Not our Cannon—-two of our Cannon Got almost to us."[160] Both Benjamin Jewett and Lemuel Lyon in Colonel Eleazer Fitch's Third Connecticut Regiment recorded bringing artillery forward on July 8. They worked all morning "[u]nloading the Battoes [at Lake George] and at noon we set out down to the [saw] Mil[l]s with the Artill[e]r[y] & [when] we got near the Mil[l]s and we had orders to leave the Artill[e]r[y] ther[e]."[161] (A day earlier some of the light field cannons, to be used for the battery on Rattlesnake Hill, had been brought forward by provincial troops.)[162] The heavier siege artillery was left at Lake George because Abercromby believed that it would require the "Work of several Days" to transport it forward—too long, in his judgment, given the expected French reinforcements.[163] However, Abercromby's aide-de-camp favored "bringing up our artillery [the] next day."[164]

The charge of the French breastwork by the Scottish Highland Regiment (42nd Black Watch). Painting by Robert L. Dowling. (Fort Ticonderoga Museum)

The provincial troops viewed the carnage with disbelief: "It was Surpri[s]ing," Joseph Nichols remarked, that the regulars would rush the "Breast work for Such Slaughter."[165] Abel Spicer observed "the regulars push on as fast as possible and marched up to the breast works ten deep and fired volleys…and they fell like pigeons," and Benjamin Jewett noted that the "French cut them down amazin."[166] The tenacity of the Highlander Regiment (42nd Scottish Black Watch), who fought their way into the French entrenchment, was recognized by friend and foe alike. Private Spicer observed that the Highlanders rushed "upon the breast works with their swords and bayonets," but a blast of grapeshot "killed almost all that had got into the trenches."[167] Another participant suggested that some of the Highlanders "got upon the top of the French Lines every time an attack was made," but "not being properly supported," the men were cut off.[168] Montcalm reported that the British grenadiers and Highlanders charged "for 3 hours without retreating or breaking," and his aide, Captain Bougainville, added that the Highlanders "returned unceasingly to attack, without becoming discouraged."[169] The high casualties resulted from a lethal rate of fire from the best marksmen of each French company at the loopholes in the breastwork, aided by fellow soldiers who handed them loaded muskets.[170] Witnesses suggested that a French soldier "might easily fire 10 Rounds before" British troops could reach the entrenchment, and Captain Desandrouins later estimated that each French soldier had "fired 70 to 80 shots" during the battle.[171] The use of grapeshot in the French wallpieces (swivel guns) also had devastating consequences. A Massachusetts soldier noted that one wallpiece had "killed 18 Grenadiers dead upon the spot" and a New Jersey provincial recalled that grapeshot had been "fired through our army," causing "sulphur, smoke and fire through the day."[172] Given the hopelessness of the attack, why did the British troops continue their offensive? Surely the strict training and discipline of the British military combined with maintaining regimental tradition played a role. But, as is the case even today, soldiers fight to sustain their comrades so as not to let them down. Lieutenant William Grant of the 42nd Regiment later noted the "determined bravery" of the men in his regiment, who "did not mind their fellow-soldiers tumbling down about them, but still went on undauntedly. Even those that were mortally wounded cried aloud to their companions, not to mind or lose a thought upon them, but to follow their officers, and charge the enemy, and to mind the honour of their king and country."[173]

Just after three o'clock in the afternoon, as the regulars were about to fall back, Captain Jean d'Anglars de Bassignac in the Royal Roussillon Regiment placed a red handkerchief at the end of his musket as a signal, but the British misinterpreted the gesture as a surrender, reporting that the French "clubbed their arms, showed themselves on their breastwork, and beckoned to us to come up."[174] British troops ran to the breastwork to accept the surrender, but French troops "fired upon us and Killed our men in Great Numbers."[175] French troops had an entirely different perception of the incident. Observing the British troops marching forward, the French soldiers believed that the British were surrendering until Captain Pierre Pouchot realized the mistake and shouted to his men to fire, "shooting down two or three hundred of them."[176] British and provincial soldiers also mentioned "another Deceit" whereby French troops "raised their hats above the Trenches which our People fired at…we did little other Damage than cutting some of the Hats to Pieces."[177]

Additional provincial regiments, held heretofore in reserve, were called into the battle about mid-afternoon. The New Jersey and New York regiments had been previously engaged, but now troops from Rhode Island and Connecticut were ordered into the fray.[178] However, Colonel Oliver Partridge reported that colonels from the regulars approached officers of the Massachusetts regiments with instructions "that the provincials should make an assault, the regulars being broken and defeated," but "most of our colonels knowing there were no such orders, and that the attempt would be [in] vain and only prove the death of their men, refus'd to stir."[179] Nevertheless, some of the captains of Massachusetts companies took their units into the fighting. Sixteen-year-old David Perry from Massachusetts and his fellow soldiers ran forward, and "got behind trees, logs, and stumps…The ground was strewed with the dead and dying…I could hear the men screaming and see them dying all around me."[180] Perry and his comrades could not stand erect because of the intensity of the fire, so they hid behind a large pine log, but one of the men "raised his head a little above the log and a ball struck him in the centre of the forehead, and tore his scalp clear back to the crown."[181] Many of the provincials were terrified by the ferocity of the French fire. As "the bullets began to whistle round us I felt a tremor or panic of fear," Private Garrett Albertson recalled; "I really thought my hat was rising off my head" and prayed for help, after which "my panic left me—my hat settled on my head, and I felt calm and composed."[182] Other provincials, like Lieutenant Archelaus Fuller from Massachusetts, were horrified by the scene of carnage: "a soreful Si[gh]t to behold the De[a]d men and wounded" with broken limbs and mortal wounds and to hear their cries.[183]

One of the fundamental problems with the British attack involved the lack of communication by the commander with individual units. Captain Charles Lee of the 44th Regiment later asserted "that no General was heard of, no Aid[e] de Camps seen, no instruction receiv'd."[184] Colonel Oliver Partridge also raised the issue of Abercromby's direction of the battle: "If you ask, where the Gen'l was? Somewhere behind, I can't tell where…Did the Gen'l consult nobody? Nobody can tell."[185] Abercromby, however, was present at the battle, contrary to earlier historical accounts.[186] Abercromby's aide-de-camp later revealed that the general "came up with the Highlanders" early in the battle and a French map showed that Abercromby would have had a partial view of the battle from his position on a rock outcropping on the La Chute River to the right of the provincial rear guard.[187] Private Peter Pond in the Fourth Company of Colonel Nathan Whiting's Second Connecticut Regiment recounted that at the end of the battle Abercromby "came from left to Ri[gh]t in the rear of the troops…and Ordered a Retreat Beat."[188] Captain Joshua Loring, on the other hand, wrote that no orders for the retreat were given and the men "Left without any Orders…and made a Slow Orderly retreat to the Saw Mill."[189] Abercromby did have runners and three aides to deliver his messages, but some orders were disregarded or misunderstood or never reached their destination due to the turmoil of the battle.[190] In contrast, Montcalm, wearing only his waistcoat and brandishing a sword, was at the breastwork and gave orders directly to his officers and troops.

"Around six o'clock," Captain Bougainville noted that British troops made "another attempt at the center against [the] Roussilion and Berry [regiments]," and the engagement "continued till sunset" according to Captain Salah Barnard from Deerfield, Massachusetts.[191] Although two regular officers suggested that the retreat had begun "about 5 o'clock," most provincial participants wrote that the drum beat for retreat occurred at sun-

Detail of "The Marquis de Montcalm Congratulating his troops after the Battle of Carillon, 8 July 1758." Watercolor by Harry A. Ogden. (Fort Ticonderoga Museum)

set.[192] The rangers, light infantry, and some provincials continued a cover fire during the retreat of the rest of the army, preventing the French from scaling their breastworks and pursuing the British troops. Apparently, not every unit received word of the retreat. "We lay there till near sunset," Private Perry recalled, "and not receiving orders from any officer, the men crept off leaving all the dead and most of the wounded," and Abner Barrows, also with a Massachusetts regiment, remarked that he "fear[ed] a great many Wounded men fell into the hands of our Enemy & the Slain all Lay on the spot."[193] The men made their way to the breastwork in the rear that had been built earlier by Massachusetts troops. Abel Spicer recalled that during the retreat so many dead and wounded men lay in the road "that a man could hardly walk without treading on them."[194] Garrett Albertson later recounted that the French "were out plundering our dead and wounded, with candles and lanterns."[195]

The next day Captain Bougainville recorded that French troops began "burying our dead and those the enemy had left" and additional burials occurred on July 10, when Montcalm "had the English buried who were beginning to infect the outside of the abati[s]"; two weeks later Bougainville revealed that "a great number of [British] corpses on litters" were discovered.[196] Montcalm later wrote that the battlefield was not reconnoitered "until the next day, and the delay of a night has been fatal to the wounded who remained there"; of the 70 British wounded that were removed, "the majority of them…died" and 34 were sent to Montreal as prisoners.[197] However, Lieutenant John Small of the 42nd Regiment, who carried a letter from Abercromby to Montcalm regarding the exchange of prisoners a few weeks later, revealed that the French had killed all of the severely wounded British soldiers, whom they could not care for.[198] (While encamped at Ticonderoga 18 years later during the American Revolution, Colonel Anthony Wayne referred to the former site of the battle as a "place of Skulls—they are so plenty here that our people for want of Other Vessels drink out of them whilst the soldiers make tent pins of the shin and thigh bones of Abercr[o]mb[y]'s men.")[199]

In contrast to the disarray and confusion that enveloped the British forces following the battle, Montcalm "had wine and beer conveyed to the field of battle, to refresh the troops," and along with Brigadier General François de Lévis "passed in front of all the battalions and expressed how pleased they felt at their conduct."[200] Fully expecting a renewed British onslaught the next day, Captain Bougainville noted that "we worked all night to secure defilade [breastworks] against the neighboring heights by traverses, to perfect the abatis of the Canadians and to finish the batteries on the right and left [which were] commenced in the morning."[201]

On the evening after the conclusion of the battle, British and provincial troops were encamped behind the breastworks near the sawmill until "about midnight [when] we were all mustered," Rufus Putnam noted, and Garrett Albertson recounted that "word came that the French were going down the lake, to cut off our retreat and take our bateaux."[202] Faced with a weakened army and expecting 3,000 French reinforcements, Abercromby decided that "we sustained so considerable a Loss, without any Prospect of better Success, that it was no longer prudent to remain before it, and it was therefore judged necessary for the Preservation of the Remainder of so many brave Men" to retreat to avoid the risk of a French advance southward "if a Total Defeat had ensued."[203] Apparently, Abercromby relied on the advice of his closest aide, Captain James Cunningham, to abandon the expedition. William Johnson attempted to dissuade Abercromby from retreating, but was unsuccessful in changing his mind.[204] The apprehension felt by Cunningham and Abercromby was so great that orders were sent to the commander at the Lake George camp to "forward all the heavy artillery back to New York" and "soon expect a large body of the enemy down at your Post."[205] However, Captain Joshua Loring reported that "everybody was Eager for renewing the Attack the Next morning," so when orders to march to the bateaux at Lake George were received at "Nine in the Evening," the troops were taken by surprise.[206] The wounded men were the first to be taken back to the bateaux; other regiments received orders piecemeal or not at all. Private David Perry's unit "started back to our boats without any orders and pushed out on the Lake for the night," while Lieutenant Archelaus Fuller fell asleep near the camp at the sawmill and awoke to discover "that the army was ch[i]efly gon[e]."[207] In the darkness most of the men marched hurriedly back to the Lake George landing site on a muddy path, arriving at daybreak. Captain Charles Lee concluded that Abercromby had "shamefully abandon'd these advantageous posts and retreat'd to his battoes with so much hurry, precipitation and confusion as to give it entirely the air of a flight."[208] During the night provincial troops were employed "getting the stores [including cannons] on board" the vessels at Lake George, but "150 barr[e]ls of flo[u]r" and the whaleboats portaged to the La Chute River were destroyed.[209]

The following morning an overwhelming sense of panic unnerved the retreating troops as they scrambled to the bateaux. While the men waited for their bateaux, they were mistakenly "alarmed by the rangers," causing "a Great fluster thinking they were Our Enemy, the Cry was push off push off."[210] "The Cry of Enemy made our People Cry out," Joseph Nichols wrote, as the troops worked feverishly to extricate the bateaux "15 deep" on the shore.[211] The army turned into a "confused rabble," according to Colonel Henry Babcock, crowding "30 Men into Each Battoe," noted Samuel Fisher.[212] The distress was compounded by the lack of "much food for three days" and little sleep.[213] Captain Charles Lee denounced Abercromby for his hasty departure: "He threw himself into one of the first boats, [and] row'd off."[214] Most of the British army embarked after nine o'clock on the morning of July 9.

The confusion of the departure left some of the units without orders. On the evening of July 8, Captain David Waterbury and 500 Connecticut troops were ordered to a point of land on the Lake George shore to thwart a possible French attack on the departing British bateaux. Most of his men deserted their posts during the night, and the next morning Waterbury sent a messenger to discover why they had not been relieved and to request further orders. When the first messenger failed to return, Waterbury dispatched another to the British encampment at the sawmill where he found not "One Man Left" and the sawmill ablaze, the bridge destroyed, and barrels of flour broken open.[215] Waterbury and his remaining men ran to the landing site and found that most of the army had left, but managed to find a few bateaux and pushed off in pursuit of the rest of the army.

"Having a fine Northerly Bre[e]ze," Abercromby's broken army "made Sails of Blankets and Tents" but still "rowed all day without any thing to eat," arriving "about sunset" on July 9 at the southern end of Lake George.[216] The men were "all dejected" and felt "melancholy and still as from a funeral"—a far cry from the optimism of their departure four days earlier.[217]

Late in the day on July 9, French volunteers reconnoitered as far as the sawmill on the La Chute River, finding the area abandoned and the mill burned. At daybreak on July 10 Montcalm detached Brigadier General Lévis with eight grenadier companies, some Canadian militia, and volunteers to check on the position of the British army. The French troops discovered "wounded, provisions and baggage abandoned; remains of burnt barges [bateaux or whaleboats] and pontoons [artillery rafts]" and "more than 500 pairs of shoes complete with buckles" in the muddy road.[218] On July 11 François-Pierre de Vaudreuil, brother of the governor-general of New France, arrived at Montcalm's camp with 3,143 reinforcements, consisting chiefly of Canadian militia and Indians. On July 12, with his army formed into a square at the French lines, Montcalm reviewed his triumphant soldiers, thanking them in the name of the king and calling on a priest to celebrate mass. He subsequently dedicated a huge wooden cross at the French lines.

British losses were staggering by any account. Abercromby's official report on July 12 disclosed 1,944 killed or wounded—"1610 Regulars and 334 Provincials."[219] However, additional men succumbed to their wounds in the days that followed. Lieutenant Matthew Clerk, whose flawed assessment of the breastwork doomed so many to their deaths, died on July 18 from wounds suffered during the battle. The French listed 377 casualties from the battle on July 8 and a total of 527, which included the losses from the July 6 engagement.[220] How did such a monumental British failure occur, given the obvious advantage of its forces, numbering more than four times the men of Montcalm's army? From the beginning of the offensive on July 6, poor decisions were made, including moving the army along the west side of the La Chute River, Lord Howe's judgment in leading columns through an uncharted wilderness, and the failure to use rangers as scouts ahead of the columns of soldiers. The engagement on July 6 had caused a collapse of British momentum and allowed the French valuable time to construct their breastwork. Considered by some officers as "the brains of the English army," Howe left a vacuum upon his death and the field strategy in the hands of Abercromby.[221] Abercromby's fear that Montcalm's troops would be "strengthening their works" and his expectation of French reinforcements led to the decision to rush the entrenchment without taking the time to transport the siege artillery to the front.[222] Although Abercromby had the advantage in troop strength, he placed little faith in the effectiveness of his 9,000 provincials, suggesting that "no real dependence is to be had upon the Bulk of the Provincials"; their officers were "worse than their Men," and some "have actually deserted and shamm'd

Sickness."[223] The negative attitude toward provincials stemmed partly from the environment of political independence and flexibility in military service in the provincial army. Provincial soldiers were clearly unwilling to accept the blind allegiance and discipline required of professional soldiers in the British army.

The explanation for the defeat clearly rests with the British strategy based on faulty intelligence and a failure to consider rational options. In the wake of Howe's death, Brigadier General Thomas Gage did not step forward to manage the field strategy during the battle on July 8, and so many British officers were lost during the initial assaults that few were left to take leadership roles in subsequent attacks. The haste to assail the French position may have been unnecessary; Abercromby could have deprived Montcalm's troops of supplies, forcing a retreat from Ticonderoga. Captain Bougainville later observed that if "the enemy took measures to cut us off…it would be necessary to abandon Carillon" because Montcalm had "only five days supplies."[224] Abercromby's faulty judgment might also be related to his health and state of mind. In a letter to John Apply (former secretary to Lord Loudoun) written from Ticonderoga, Abercromby lamented the tragic loss of Howe on July 6 and revealed his own physical condition. Apply disclosed the contents of the letter to Governor Pownall of Massachusetts, noting that the army had "scarcely any Sleep" for two nights, and that Abercromby "having Marched on Foot every Step…was so fatigued when he came to his Ground that afternoon [July 7] that he was scarce able to stand."[225] In August Abercromby wrote that "the great Fatigue of my Body could be surpassed by nothing but the extensive Anxiety of my Mind."[226] Later, young soldiers, like 17-year-old William Parkman from Massachusetts, spoke disparagingly of Abercromby—"an aged gentleman, and infirm in body and mind."[227]

Provincial troops lost faith in Abercromby's leadership and the capability of the British army. Rufus Putnam, who later served as an officer during the American Revolution, concluded that the expedition to Ticonderoga had been "the most injudicious and wanton sacrifice of men that ever came within my knowledge or reading."[228] The experience of provincial troops serving with British regulars during the French and Indian War made them less intimidated in the face of British ultimatums during the 1770s and more secure in their political ideals and military ability.

Many of the provincial troops at the Lake George camp were immediately assigned to a number of work projects in the days following their return from Ticonderoga. The first task was to unload the bateaux and turn in any equipment, arms, packs, and kettles not belonging to them. However, Captain David Waterbury disclosed that some of the provisions in the bateaux were in "a bad condition."[229] Although hungry troops drew an allowance of pork, flour, rice, and butter on July 10, a shortage of provisions thereafter reduced daily rations and led to dissension among the troops. In addition, the men were plagued by an outbreak of "Diarrhea and Dysentery" in the camp, and several men were also "Taken with the small pox" and sent to the hospital at Fort Edward.[230] Efforts were implemented to stem the tide of disease in the camp by having dirt "Thrown into the Necessary Houses Every Morning," removing "Everything that Will Promote infection," and having the cooking take place "without the Lines."[231] On July 13 Benjamin Glasier noted going "to work on the [h]ospit[a]l" and nine days later "making Cab[i]ns for the wounded men."[232] However, most of the wounded men from the battle at Ticonderoga had been transported to Fort Edward.

Several other major projects occupied the time of provincial soldiers after the Ticonderoga campaign. On July 13 Lieutenant Archelaus Fuller "was ordered to work upon the hill in order to build a Fort," and Private Abel Spicer noted that troops from Colonel Nathan Whiting's Second Connecticut Regiment were engaged in "clearing a place to build a breast work on a small hill which lieth about 100 rods south from the southwest corner" of the picketed camp at the remains of Fort William Henry. [233] The fort was subsequently named Fort Gage. (A Ramada Inn was built on the site of Fort Gage in the late 1970s.) Provincial troops were also ordered to construct "a bre[a]st work al[l] round our campments" at the lake in an effort to defend against a possible French attack.[234] They also worked removing pine tree stumps using block and tackle, leveling "the rocky hill," and building large storehouses, a sawmill, wharf, and various houses.[235] Captain Henry Champion in Colonel Nathan Whiting's regiment was ordered to the "first Island in ye lake" with 100 men "to build a breastwork at ye North End of this Island" to serve as an early warning outpost, and he was given instructions to use "rockets for signals to ye camp if ye enemy approached by night or otherwise."[236] Champion subsequently identified the island as "Diamond Island," and Amos Richardson noted in his diary that he suffered from a bad sunburn on his back while "Looking [for] Dimons in the Lake" while stationed on the island.[237] (The island was famous for large diamond-like crystals found in the shallow water during the late eighteenth and early nineteenth centuries.)

As Abercromby's army began to settle into a routine at Lake George, a new expedition was approved to destroy Fort Frontenac on Lake Ontario, the supply depot for New France's western forts and outposts. Lieutenant Colonel John Bradstreet, head of the bateau service, had earlier been granted permission for the campaign by Lord Loudoun, but Abercromby had set aside the venture in order to devote more resources to the Ticonderoga operation. Despite the fear of a French attack, Abercromby was persuaded by Bradstreet on July 13 to detach troops for the campaign, which, if successful, might salvage some honor for his 1758 army. Under the command of Brigadier General John Stanwix of the 62nd Regiment, Bradstreet and his men proceeded to the "Great Carrying Place" in western New York, arriving on August 10. Before the arrival of Stanwix and Bradstreet, New York troops had begun construction of a fort, consisting of earthworks and palisades located just northwest of the Mohawk River (present-day Rome, N.Y.). Fort Stanwix would replace three smaller forts—Fort Craven, Fort Williams, and Fort Newport, that had guarded the portage between the Mohawk River and Wood Creek.

Bradstreet's expedition to Fort Frontenac involved 3,092 men—2,517 provincial troops, 60 rangers, 270 "Battoe Men," 155 regulars, 20 artillery men, and 70 Indians.[238] On August 12 the bateaux and whaleboats for the expedition were transported to Wood Creek, and four days later Bradstreet and his army departed. Late on August 25 Bradstreet landed without opposition within a mile of Fort Frontenac (present-day Kingston, Ontario). By August 27 Bradstreet had placed his cannons only a few hundred yards from the fort. With most French troops assigned to the protection of Fort Carillon, Fort Frontenac had a meager garrison of only 110 soldiers and a number of women and children. Eight French sloops and one schooner moored near the fort were undermanned and no threat to the raiders. After a brief cannonade from Bradstreet's guns early on the morning of August 27, the commander of the fort surrendered. After destroying the fort, burning thousands of barrels of provisions, disabling 60 cannons, and sinking seven of the vessels,

Bradstreet's army departed on August 28 for Oswego, taking the two largest sloops loaded with prisoners and captured booty. Three days later, the British raiders reached Oswego and burned the two sloops after transferring the captured goods to bateaux. The raid was a logistical triumph and a blow to New France's ability to supply its western outposts.[239]

Following the victory at Ticonderoga, Governor-General Pierre de Rigaud de Vaudreuil chastised Montcalm for not pursuing Abercromby's army and ordered him to embark on a new offensive against the British. For the most part, Montcalm simply ignored Vaudreuil's instructions, as he had in 1757 when the Canadian governor pressured him to attack Fort Edward after the destruction of Fort William Henry. Given the inadequacy of provisions at Carillon to support a major campaign and the limited British military targets at Lake George, Montcalm felt justified in resisting Vaudreuil's directives. Vaudreuil proposed attacking British wagon convoys that supplied the Lake George camp. These raids, Vaudreuil suggested, would result in a precipitous British retreat from the lake, leaving provisions, artillery, bateaux, and other supplies sorely needed by New France. But Montcalm felt that the British wagon convoys primarily transported sutlers' goods and were not important enough to warrant large-scale military operations.

While Montcalm had praised the Canadian troops in his letter of July 9 to Governor Vaudreuil, he omitted the favorable remarks in his official report of July 25. This omission outraged Vaudreuil, who criticized Montcalm in a letter to the minister of the marine for his handling of the defense of Carillon and his poor treatment of the Canadians and Indians. Vaudreuil asked the minister "to demand of his Majesty the recall of the Marquis de Montcalm."[240] Montcalm had sent letters to the same minister, complaining about repeated directives from Vaudreuil, and suggested that the Canadians had been sent to Carillon too late to be of any use and, like the Indians, were only fit for raiding parties.[241]

The controversy between Montcalm and Vaudreuil was also reflected in the criticisms of Fort Carillon by associates of Montcalm. Andre (Jean-Baptiste) Doreuil, financial commissary of wars in Canada and a friend of Montcalm, wrote a letter to the minister of war in late July 1758, suggesting that "Fort Carillon is worth nothing…An ignoramus constructed it—a relative [cousin] of M. de Vaudreuil," and Captain Bougainville referred to Michel Chartier de Lotbinière, the engineer who supervised construction of the fort, as "no more than an astronomer among engineers," who was only concerned "in putting his cash box in order" during the battle on July 8.[242] The negative comments about Fort Carillon by Montcalm's engineers, Nicolas Sarrebource de Pontleroy and Jean-Nicolas Desandrouins, largely centered on the small size of the fort and its location, requiring the addition of redoubts and storehouses outside the fort. However, after the British captured the fort in 1759, many observers were impressed by the quality of the buildings, despite its size.

A number of construction projects were undertaken at Fort Carillon during 1758, including several before the July 8 battle. Work progressed on the moat, demilunes, and glacis (sloping earth bank before the fort). Pontleroy and Desandrouins supervised the building of the "outer works" at Carillon after the July battle, and the breastworks were rebuilt by laying logs horizontally—"five trees for a base, four above, three, two, and one" at the top.[242] A French deserter subsequently informed British officers at the Lake George camp that the breastwork had been reconstructed "in a much stronger Posture of Defense than before," and Robert Holmes, a lieutenant in the rangers, reported "that the Enemy have erected some Block-Houses at the Breast-Work."[244]

AMBUSH AND PURSUIT

Luc de La Corne (La Corne Saint-Luc) emerged as a leader of New France's Indian allies during King George's War and was fluent in four or five Indian languages. Appointed a captain in 1755, he led a division of Indians during the siege of Fort William Henry in 1757. (National Archives of Canada)

The temporary lull in hostilities ended on July 20 when ten British soldiers were ambushed near the Halfway Brook Post, a stockade manned by Colonel Ebenezer Nichols' Massachusetts regiment. Jacques-François Legardeur de Croisille de Courtemanche, a captain in the Troupes de la Marine, had been sent earlier from Fort Carillon with 600 Indians and Canadians "to annoy and intercept the English [wagon] trains."[245] Upon hearing the firing, English officers and soldiers rushed out of the Halfway Brook Post to aid the victims of the assault, but they were attacked by the same Canadian and Indian raiding party. Captain Asa Foster of Andover, Massachusetts, who was sent out soon after the ambush to retrieve the dead, discovered bodies "mangled in a dreadful manner"—most had been scalped.[246] "A terrible day as ever I saw," Joseph Holt of Wilton, New Hampshire, noted in his journal and listed the names of 26 soldiers who had been killed, wounded, or were missing in the attack.[247]

Only eight days later, a second ambush occurred on the road to Lake George. After a delay due to lacrosse games at Carillon between the Canadian Iroquois and Abenaki Indians, Captain Luc de La Corne (also known as La Corne Saint-Luc) departed from Carillon on July 24 with a detachment of nearly 400 Indians and 200 Canadians. A convoy of 38-40 provision wagons and carts left Fort Edward on July 28 with an insufficient complement of guards, numbering only 45-50 men. The wagon train traveled "about five miles" north of Fort Edward when hundreds of Indian yells and musket blasts enveloped the convoy; some of "the Provincials took to their heels," and 30-40 individuals were killed, including a number of women.[248] Henry Champion noted "38 teams and wagons destroyed" that had been loaded with "letters, stores, officers' baggage and money to pay ye Regulars" and also recounted a dramatic escape: "one woman sprang out of ye wagon and ran back and escaped, one little child, a girl, ran back in the path like a quail, a wagoner who cut his horses' ropes and cleared him from ye wagon rode back [on] ye path, took her by ye hand, catched her up before him and saved her."[249] Each wagon had a team of four or more oxen and provincial diarists reported a large number of oxen were killed (between 126-187); the French recorded that they had killed "230 oxen and took 80 scalps and 64 prisoners—men, women, and children."[250]

Upon hearing the commotion and firing, troops at the Halfway Brook Post dashed to the ambush site and "fell in with the Rear of the Enemy, who having made free with the Liquor, were so drunk that it would have been an easy Matter to have cut them off, but Col. [John] Hart of the New Hampshire Regiment…refus[ed] to come up [with 300 troops from Fort Edward], [and] the Enemy got off unhurt."[251] Hart was placed "in Confinement…to be tried by a Court-Martial," but later was "acquitted with…honor."[252] At the scene of the attack, witnesses were taken aback by the devastation, with "Provisions scatter'd in the Road," including boxes of melted chocolates that had dissolved and mixed with rivulets of blood to form "a sickening and revolting specta[c]le."[253] Joseph Jones in Major Israel Putnam's company of the Third Connecticut Regiment followed an adjacent trail and discovered "the corpse of a woman, which had been exposed to the most barbarous indignities and mutilations," and James Henderson noted that three or four women had been "Killed in a barbarous manner strip[p]ing them naked and cutting them after a cruel manner."[254] On July 29 Captain John Wrightson reported to Abercromby that he had sent "260 Men to Assist in Burying the Cattle" and to retrieve provisions; on the following morning Wrightson ordered "150 men" to continue burying the oxen.[255]

In response to the attack, Abercromby ordered Majors Robert Rogers and Israel Putnam to pursue the raiders with "a Detachment of 700 Men…[composed of] Light Infantry, Rangers & Provincials."[256] Abercromby personally "saw them all off [in bateaux] by two o'clock in the Morning" on July 29; some of the men had been "drafted out" of several regiments and departed "in less than one hour" from the time they had been notified.[257] Rogers and Putnam planned to leave their bateaux on the east shore of the Narrows, cross the mountains, and intercept the French raiding party at South Bay. About two hours after sunrise on July 29, the English detachment landed on the east side of the lake and immediately traversed the mountains to South Bay, leaving 60 men to guard the bateaux and provisions. In the evening, the men who had been left to guard the bateaux rowed south to inform Captain Henry Champion, commanding the advance post on Diamond Island, that they had observed "at least 20 or 30 of the enemy's bateaux come round Sabbath Day Point."[258] Champion quickly placed his 100 men on alert on the north end of the island. After hearing the news of the sighting of the French bateaux, Abercromby ordered a second detachment, consisting of approximately 1,000 men under the command of Lieutenant Colonel William Haviland, along with Colonel Phineas Lyman, to "protect Major Rogers' battoes" on the east shore of Lake George.[259] Leaving at two in the morning on July 30, the second detachment "landed on the island where the battoes were, 2 miles from Sabbat[h] [Day] Point, [near the] east shore," and found "no signs of an enemy," and concluded that the sighting was a false alarm "occasioned by fear."[260] Nine provincial soldiers, who had probably observed an English scouting party, were subsequently court-martialed for rendering a false report and deserting their post. They were found guilty and sentenced to 40 lashes, but eight soldiers were pardoned and one officer reprimanded.

Rogers and Putnam returned to Lake George late at night on July 30. Rogers had reached Lake Champlain too late to intercept the French and Indians, but he did catch a glimpse of the French bateaux and canoes leaving South Bay. He reportedly had observed "three women [captives] alive in one bateau, but our men were about half an hour too late to give them fire."[261] Rogers discovered a regular from the 55th Regiment in such a weakened condition as a result of being lost in the wilderness for weeks that he had to be carried on a stretcher 11 miles over the mountain to Lake George. Although the exhausted soldier claimed to have been captured by three Indians at "Bloody Pond" and later to have escaped, he actually had deserted from his regiment before the expedition to Ticonderoga.[262] The troops under Rogers and Putnam, along with Haviland's reinforcements, spent a stormy night on an island a short distance from the eastern shore. The men remained on the island until the evening of July 31, when they began their voyage south, only to be hailed by Captain Champion's men at the advance post on Diamond Island. Champion had received a letter from Abercromby with orders for Rogers and Putnam to return to South Bay and march to Fort Edward in an effort to intercept another enemy party that had "fired on some of our men" between the Lake George camp and Fort Edward.[263] Rogers' men spent an uncomfortable night on Diamond Island, bivouacking on the crowded isle and sleeping in their bateaux. In the morning the detachment rowed about ten miles further north, landing on two adjacent islands on the east side of the lake.

**Lieutenant Joseph Marin de La Malgue (second from the left) landing at
Wood Creek with his party of Canadian militiamen and Indians in August 1758.
(Drawing by Gary S. Zaboly)**

The next day Rogers and Putnam awaited additional provisions before departing for South Bay on the following morning (August 2) with nearly 800 rangers, light infantry, provincial troops, and volunteers from the regulars. On August 3 the men camped at South Bay and the next day they separated, and "Rogers with the Remainder of the Party lay in Ambush a little above where Wood Creek discharges itself into South Bay."[264] About five o'clock on the afternoon of August 6, Putnam and his men rejoined Rogers at Wood Creek after their position was exposed when two Indians spotted one of Putnam's men fishing. Rogers' position had also been uncovered when a regular with his detachment yelled "Pray what Boat may You be?" to six Indians in a canoe, who immediately "made off as fast as they could."[265] After more than 100 sick men were sent to Fort Edward on August 7, Rogers and Putnam marched south with the remaining troops and camped at the ruins of Fort Anne at Wood Creek, originally built under Francis Nicholson during Queen Anne's War. With no sign of the enemy, Rogers and Putnam became overconfident and relaxed normal safeguards. On the morning of August 8 "Rogers and another officer [Ensign William Irwin of the light infantry] shot at a mark for a wager."[266] After the shooting match, the detachment marched single file on a trail through the dense foliage with Putnam and his Connecticut provincials in the lead, followed by regulars under Captain James Dalyell, and Rogers in the rear with his rangers.

Meanwhile, Lieutenant Joseph Marin de La Malgue, who had left Carillon on August 4 with 225 Canadian militia and 219 Indians, had heard the firing from the shooting match and sent scouts to investigate. With a report of an enemy party marching south, Marin quickly deployed his men "in a half moon" along the trail and surprised the English troops with "two volleys" of fire about a mile south of their campsite at Fort Anne.[267] Putnam was captured by the Indians, but Captain John Durkee from Norwich, Connecticut, "kept in the action," despite two wounds, "encouraging his men with great earnestness and resolution," Rogers reported.[268] A very hot fire then struck Dalyell's regulars at the center of the column. Hearing the firing, Rogers and his men pushed forward, flanking to the right to form "a half circle and then we began to drive them," Abel Spicer recounted.[269] Rogers sent 100 men to a small hill that overlooked the French position and then yelled to the officer on the hill, asking if he wanted more men, assuring him that he could "have 500, which was [meant]…to frighten the French."[270] Believing that the English detachment was "receiving a reinforcement" and facing the desertion of 60 Canadians, Marin yielded to the urgent demands from his Indians to retreat, "who feared that they would not be able to carry off some wounded."[271] The engagement lasted two hours, leaving 40-54 English dead or missing and 40-50 wounded; the French reported losses of only 13 dead and ten wounded, but Rogers returned to Fort Edward with 54-56 scalps and two prisoners.[272] On August 19 Abercromby wrote to William Pitt that "I must not omit, doing Rogers the Justice to say, that he merits much to be commended…[he] acted the whole Time with great Calmness" during the battle on August 8.[273]

The ordeal of the captivity of Israel Putnam, however, was not over. During the battle, Putnam was brought to the rear and lashed firmly to a tree. A young Indian thereafter made a sport of throwing his tomahawk as close to Putnam's head as possible without hitting him. A French officer then shoved the barrel of his musket against Putnam's body and pressed the trigger. The weapon either misfired or was not loaded, and the officer quickly smashed him in the face with its butt. As the French and Indians were driven back, Putnam found himself in the crossfire of the combatants with musket balls tearing into the tree and through his clothes. When the French retreat began, he was untied from the tree, stripped of his shoes and nearly all his clothes, and forced to carry many of the French packs belonging to the wounded men. At the encampment that night, Putnam was again

***Rescue of Major Israel Putnam* from torture at the hands of Indians
by Joseph Marin de La Malgue. Oil painting by J. L. G. Ferris.
From the 1906 Glens Falls Insurance Company calendar. (Author's collection)**

tied to a tree, and the Indians heaped brush around him and set it on fire. A sudden down-pour extinguished the flames and a second attempt to burn Putnam was made, but Marin, hearing the howling of the Indians, pushed through them, kicked the flaming brush away, and untied the captive. Putnam was brought to Fort Carillon and then sent to Montreal. He was among the 114 prisoners exchanged by the French on November 10, 1758.*

SHIPBUILDING AT LAKE GEORGE

During the months after the battle at Carillon, the British and provincial forces at Lake George embarked on a major shipbuilding effort under the direction of Royal Navy Captain Joshua Loring. Born in Boston, Massachusetts, in 1716, Loring commanded a privateer during King George's War and later became a lieutenant in the Royal Navy through the influence of Governor William Shirley. Prior to the Abercromby expedition, Loring attained the rank of post captain in command of naval construction and activity on the lakes. His first undertaking at Lake George following the Ticonderoga campaign was "to build a Sloop not only for the Protection and Security" of the Lake George camp, according to Abercromby, "but also by Cruising to and fro, up the Lake to watch and discover

*Major Israel Putnam continued his service until the end of the Seven Years' War. He narrowly escaped death again as one of the few survivors of a shipwreck off the coast of Cuba during the 1762 expedition to Havana. As a militia brigadier general in June 1775, 57-year-old Putnam commanded the Connecticut troops at the Battle of Bunker Hill and two years later was commissioned a major general in the Continental Army. Suffering a stroke in December 1779, Putnam retired from the army and died on May 29, 1790, in Brooklyn, Connecticut.

the Motions of the Enemy."[274] On July 19 Captain Samuel Cobb, a 39-year-old shipwright from present-day Maine, recorded that he "Began to Work on a Sloop to Draft and Mould her," and the next day the carpenters, including Benjamin Glasier, "Began to cut Timber for the Sloop."[275] To facilitate work on the sloop, the troops at Lake George began "building a shipyard at ye southeast corner of ye Lake, building a breastwork round it, building [a] saw-pit in it."[276] By July 28 considerable progress had been made on the sloop; according to Massachusetts shipwright William Sweat, "we got the floor timber in & Stages [probably frames/futtocks] all up, set for the wales [hull planking/strakes]."[277] On August 6 Cobb promised Loring that he would launch the sloop "as Soon as possible," but the next day he had difficulty working, complaining that he had "not one Day of perfect health Since I came to the lake which I take to be the cause of the Un[w]holesomeness of the air, the place seems to be full of Uncleanness."[278]

Detail of "A Map of the retrenched Camp at Lake George in 1758," showing a dock and defensive post at the southeast corner of the lake, a "Stockaded post & Hospital" in the center, and another defensive post built at the ruins of Fort William Henry. (Fort Ticonderoga Museum)

On the morning of August 9 the shipwrights "finished Graving" (cleaning and tarring the bottom) and "tried to La[u]nch" the sloop, but the vessel only moved ten feet on the ways before becoming stuck.[279] The next day the men raised the upper section of the ways and successfully launched the new sloop. An eyewitness referred to the vessel as "A Flat Bottom'd Sloop…50 Feet Keel" and newspapers soon reported that the sloop, named the

Earl of Halifax, was "51 Feet Keel, about 100 Tons…to carry 18 six and four Pounders, 20 Swivels, 50 Sailors, and a Company of Marines on board."[280] However, the exact armament varies in the original accounts. Abercromby wrote that the vessel had "14 Six & four Pounders," but Loring noted "Sixteen Guns four pounders," and Abel Spicer observed "ten four pounders" aboard and "two more…to be carried and twelve swivels."[281] On August 25 the sloop sailed to the Narrows, returning the following day. After a second cruise on September 2, the *New-York Gazette* described the sloop as "a pretty Vessel, and sails well."[282] The *Halifax* made four more cruises on the lake during 1758 (September 12, 23, and October 4, 11).

The *Halifax* took part in the August 28 celebration of Major General Jeffery Amherst's victory at Louisbourg. (Rumors of the success at Louisbourg had filtered through the army for more than a month, but Abercromby did not receive official confirmation from Amherst until August 28.) The troops were ordered to assemble at five o'clock in the afternoon for a ceremony that began with chaplains offering a "thanksgiving to Almighty God" for the victory; each regiment formed a line along the breastwork "for a rejoicing fire, which was begun

Sloop *Earl of Halifax*. Detail of the drawing "A Perspective View of Lake George [and] Plan of Ticonderoga" by Captain-Lieutenant Henry Skinner, published in the November 1759 issue of *The Universal Magazine*. (Library of Congress)

by the Can[n]on from ye Sloop, then followed by 21 can[n]on at ye Lower Side [of] ye Breastwork near ye Lake, then ye small Arms."[283] After a total of 63 cannon blasts and three successive rounds of musket fire, 7,000 troops "finished with three Huzzas."[284] The evening concluded with a great bonfire on the parade ground and rejoicing with rum and beer. (A similar celebration would occur at Lake George on September 11, with the news of Bradstreet's success at Fort Frontenac.)

The capture of Louisbourg, the most substantial French fortification in North America, was a significant step toward the ultimate defeat of New France. Amherst's troops had landed at Gabarus Bay on June 8, 1758, and proceeded with a formal siege of Louisbourg. After an unrelenting bombardment of the French stronghold, Chevalier Augustin de Drucour, the governor of Louisbourg, signed a capitulation agreement on July 27, 1758, without the provision of "honors of war." As a consequence of the carnage at Fort William Henry in 1757, Amherst would not offer the "honors of war" to the French garrison. Several hundred cannons, 5,637 prisoners of war, and a large number of civilians were taken by Amherst upon the surrender. On August 12 Amherst received a letter from Abercromby (written on July 18), requesting reinforcements in order "to make a second…more successful Attempt" on Carillon in the fall.[285] Five battalions of Amherst's troops departed aboard transports for Boston on August 27 and 28 on the first leg of the long journey to Lake George. The victorious troops were greeted in Boston with booming cannons "and the Bells of the Town were rung; in the Evening there w[ere] Bonfires, and a great variety of Fire works."[286] Thousands of local citizens came to see the troops camped on the Boston Common, bringing a plentiful supply of liquor for them.

Meanwhile, on August 23 Captain Cobb and ten carpenters, including Benjamin Glasier, again trudged into the forest, accompanied by a guard of 30 regulars, to cut "timber for a Row Gall[e]y of 40 feet long 15 feet wide 5 feet deep to Carry 12 pounders in the Stern and Swivels on a Side to go with 24 Oars."[287] On September 9 Colonel Phineas Lyman wrote that the men were "building Two Row Galleys, w[hi]c[h] will carry each a Twelve pound[e]r besides some smaller pieces"; five days later surgeon Caleb Rea noted that the "Row Gall[e]ys…fir[ed] their Cannon."[288] Apparently a few "Bay Boats" were also built at Lake George during the fall of 1758. On September 20 shipwright William Sweat recorded the launching of a "Larg[e] Bay Boat" and eight days later disclosed that "2 more Bay Boats [were] finished."[289] A week and a half earlier Captain Samuel Cobb had reported the launching of an unidentified "boat 36 feet long 9 feet Wide 3 feet 3 inches deep."[290]

To provincials like Christopher Comstock there was little distinction between the row galleys, radeaux, and bay boats. In October Comstock noted that "there has been 4 Row gal[l]eys built and there is one a building."[291] The last vessel mentioned by Comstock was actually the larger of two radeaux under construction at the lake. He noted that "the top [of the radeau] Tumbl[es] in Something Like a gambrel Roof house" with three-inch-thick planks.[292] On September 18 Captain Cobb and his carpenters had begun work on a 52-foot-long radeau, under the direction of Captain Thomas Ord of the Royal Artillery. Designed as a floating fort, the seven-sided radeau (French for raft) had a flat bottom and lower sides that inclined slightly outward while the upper sides angled inward at a steep angle to protect the crew. The radeau was propelled by a large number of oars ("sweeps") and square sails rigged on one or two masts. Influenced by the ideas of a British merchantman captain, ship chandler John Dies had recommended in 1755 that William Johnson build a flat-bottomed "float" with sides "high Enough for a Breast work to Cover the Men, with portholes cut…also holes to Run oars out…[and] Mount Some of your Field Pieces…[which] might be of Servi[ce] to Cover the army when Landing."[293] A year later William Shirley suggested that Abercromby use a "floating Battery" to attack Forts Carillon or St. Frédéric from Lake Champlain in conjunction with a land assault.[294]

Viewing the new vessel at Lake George, many provincials had some difficulty describing the unique shape of the radeau. In early October Chaplain John Cleaveland walked to the lakeside building site "to see the famous R[a]deau to carry Cannon on ye Water, some call it Ord's Ark, it is planked up higher than a man's Head Shelving in or arching inwards to defend men's Bodys & Heads with Port-Holes for ye Cannon."[295] Dr. Rea also visited the site and sketched the outline of a "very odd" vessel in his journal with the description that it was "seven squared sided like this figure, besides she Tumbles in & makes seven squares more, so that she is truly fourteen square besides her bottom & top."[296] Captain Henry Champion called it "a large floaty thing…51 feet in length" with a "flaring waist about 5 feet high, then turns with an elbow or timber and covers over ye top" and he drew an outline of the radeau with the notation: "The name of this creature is Tail and End, or Land Tortoise."[297] By then the radeau was "in a very good way," according to shipwright William Sweat.[298]

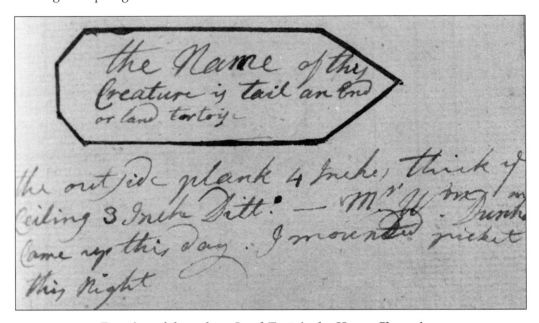

Drawing of the radeau *Land Tortoise* by Henry Champion.
(Connecticut State Archives)

While the boat building progressed, troops were beset with rumors of a renewed effort to capture Fort Carillon. On September 23 surgeon Rea reported that "the Camp [was] strongly alarm[e]d again with ye notion of going to Ticonderog[a] and 600 Regulars [Amherst's reinforcements] about to jo[i]n us for that purpose."[299] Five days later the same rumor spread throughout the Lake George camp. During the same period three wagons "loaded with swivels" (small cannons) arrived at the lake for use on the new boats, which led the men to believe an offensive was still possible.[300] Brigadier General James Prevost had urged Abercromby to embark on a second attempt on Carillon, but the effort was largely an empty proposal to bolster his own importance. On the other hand, Prevost's August 20 letter to Abercromby suggesting the expedition may have prompted the commander into action, including reviewing intelligence on the French forts with his chief engineer, Colonel James Montresor, and ordering a report on the artillery required for a siege of Fort Carillon from his chief artillery officer, Captain Thomas Ord.[301] However, before reaching Albany with his five battalions, Amherst received a letter from Abercromby on October 2, instructing him to leave his troops and proceed to Lake George. Two days later Abercromby ordered the "Troops to halt at Albany 'till further orders."[302] Late in the day on October 5, Amherst arrived at Lake George and met with Abercromby and his officers the following morning. They concluded to "lay aside" an attempt on Carillon "for the Present" due to the "Strength of the Enemy at Ticonderoga…and the Season advancing past wherein the Troops cannot hold the field in this back Country."[303] The meeting was followed by a formal inspection of the army by Abercromby and Amherst.

Nine days later, the troops at Lake George began preparations to safeguard their vessels from French raiding parties during the winter because all British and provincial troops were to evacuate the camp at the lake. On October 15 the men began to pull the bateaux out of the lake, and the next day William Sweat recorded "two of our Large Boats [probably bay boats] w[ere] sunk this night."[304] To prevent the vessels from being taken by the French or destroyed, they were deliberately sunk with the intention of retrieving them the following year. By mid-September Abercromby had a recommendation from Brigadier General Thomas Gage to prepare for the winter by sinking the sloop and other vessels in "the Night at the Lake by Capt Loring & a few Trusty Men."[305] On October 18, 150 wagons arrived to carry bateaux to Fort Edward and the sloop *Halifax* returned from her sixth cruise. Two days later, amid snow squalls, the sloop was "ha[u]led into the new wharf & strip[p]ed [of] guns & Rigging."[306] On October 20, after a month of labor, Captain Cobb recorded the launch of two radeaux, the largest, the *Land Tortoise*, measured "50 foot Long [and] 19 Wide."[307] The next day William Sweat disclosed that "we tried our Radow to se[e] how fast she would Row," and Cobb noted that the radeau "Rowed well...with 26 Oars."[308] On October 22 Captain Champion noted "a large number of bateaux sunk" and "cribs made of planks fastened on ye sides of ye sloop and to ye Land

Port side of the bow of the radeau *Land Tortoise*, lying at a depth of 107 feet in Lake George. (Photo by the author)

Turtle or Tail and End, and filled with stone to sink, & C."[309] Sweat's diary entry for October 22 reflected the difficulty in sinking the unconventional *Land Tortoise*,* "which we got Ready at Sun set, & we Sunk her once; But one side Rise again, so that we were forced to work the chief of the night, Before we could keep her Down."[311] The sloop *Halifax* was sunk the same night or the following night.[312] Early in October Private Abel Spicer had observed "one of the row galle[y]s out of the lake and loaded...on a pair of wheels," but five days later the vessel was back in the lake, and on October 24 he noted that the row galleys were sunk.[313] Over 200 bateaux were sunk along the southeast shore of the lake, and the whaleboats were taken "as far as the island [Diamond Island] to Be Sunk."[314] Other whaleboats were brought "up ye creek opposite ye Long Island, [and] concealed... in a cranberry swamp"; the men returned to the Lake George camp "by land."[315] In his report to Abercromby, Captain Joshua Loring provided an account of the "stores" buried at the camp and vessels "Sunk in Different Parts of the Lake as Mark[ed] in the Plan."[316]

As the wagons hauled supplies and bateaux to Fort Edward, the troops at Lake George "knocked down the barracks within the new Picket Fort, and they bur[ied] the guns belonging to the Sloop, and the boards of the barracks, and the Sloop irons"; the "guard house and ye Stone House, Hospital and a vast number of huts and rubbish destroyed and burnt; ye great lake-house burnt."[317] Most of the ordnance and other naval stores were transported to Fort Edward, but 14 cannons and carriages, 28 swivel guns, some of the sloop's rigging, and hundreds of oars and paddles were buried at the Lake George camp.[318]

On October 25 and 26 the army finally marched for home. Private John Noyes departed on the first day "and Lodged in the Woods and it snowed all Night and all the Next Day" as the men trudged to Fort Edward.[319] After a deserter arrived at Fort Carillon and informed the French of "buried artillery, shells and shot" at the British camp at Lake George and the deliberate sinking of bateaux and "a sloop of twelve guns," Montcalm sent a detachment to "obtain any portion possible of those articles."[320] The French party found some of the stores, "the location of the bark [sloop], fifty sunken barges [bateaux]," and retrieved "Some Guns that were buried and Burnt the Carriages."[321] While the French detachment discovered the location of the sloop, there is no documented evidence to date that the French raiders attempted to raise it or any other large vessel.

Within a few weeks of the departure of the British army from Lake George, William Pitt's letter of September 18, recalling Abercromby and appointing Jeffery Amherst as the British commander in chief, reached North America. After visiting with the governor of Massachusetts in Boston on October 24, Amherst returned to Halifax, Nova Scotia, on November 9, where a copy of Pitt's dispatches awaited him. Amherst sailed back to Boston and then traveled overland to New York City, where he received a letter from Brigadier General John Forbes "with the news that the enemy had on the 24th of November blown up Fort Duquesne and that he had taken possession of it the same evening."[322] Forbes' troops had reached Fort Duquesne by cutting a road through a primeval forest, establishing supply depots along the way. In failing health, Forbes was carried back to

---

*Using side-scan sonar in June 1990, an archaeological team led by Joseph W. Zarzynski discovered the 52-foot-long radeau *Land Tortoise* at a depth of 107 feet in Lake George. Over the next two years, the oldest intact warship in North America underwent a complete archaeological survey under the direction of Dr. D. K. Abbass. In 1994 the *Land Tortoise* became one of New York's "Submerged Heritage Preserves" and four years later was designated a National Historic Landmark.[310]

Philadelphia, where he died in March 1759. James Abercromby returned to England and was promoted to the rank of lieutenant general in March 1759, but he never saw active duty again. Pitt now counted on Amherst to defeat French forces in North America.

The deliberate sinking of the radeau *Land Tortoise* on October 22, 1758, by provincial troops. Shipwright William Sweat related the difficulty in sinking the vessel: "we got Ready at Sun set, & we Sunk her once; But one side Rise again, so that we were forced to work the chief of the night, Before we could keep her Down." Painting by Tim Cordell. (Lake George Historical Association)

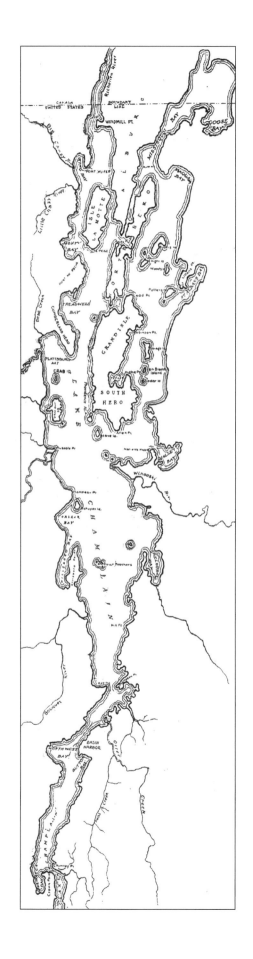

8. British Advance to Lake Champlain 1759

THE AMBITIOUS PLANS FOR 1759 by the British secretary of state, William Pitt, included an invasion of New France after the capture of Forts Carillon and St. Frédéric, the seizure of Fort Niagara on Lake Ontario, and a campaign to take Quebec City. Major General Jeffery Amherst, the 42-year-old British commander in chief, surmounted significant funding delays from England and from the financially-strapped colonies and succeeded impressively in organizing the logistical support for the expeditions to Lake Champlain and Lake Ontario. Convinced that British authorities were finally treating the colonies as equal partners in the effort to defeat the French, colonial legislatures were more inclined to provide solid support for the 1759 campaign, despite debts from prior mobilizations. Amherst's appeal to the New York Assembly for a large loan, secured by eventual reimbursement from the British treasury, was unprecedented, but surprisingly, won approval.[1]

From his headquarters in New York City, Amherst solicited colonial governments for provincial recruits. In January he promised commissions to men who raised a specified number of troops and suggested that "every Man is to be well cloath'd, and be furnish'd with a good Firelock, Powder Horn, Shot Bag…and a good Blanket."[2] Amherst required that the recruits be in Albany by March 20 "without fail," and only "young, strong, active Men, accustomed to Hardships, and the Use of a Gun," would be accepted.[3] Drained of men by previous campaigns, northern colonial officials eventually had to raise enlistment bounties to achieve needed troop levels. In the end, approximately 17,000 provincial troops were recruited for the campaign.

In preparation for the invasion of Canada, accurate intelligence on Fort Carillon was needed to plan the expedition. Late on March 3, Robert Rogers departed from Fort Edward with 90 rangers, 217 regulars, and 52 Indians led by Captain John Lottridge.[4] Arriving at the northern end of Lake George at eight on the morning of March 7, Rogers sent two rangers and two Indians forward to reconnoiter the area. Before noon Rogers and an engineer, Lieutenant Diedrick Brehm of the 60th Regiment (Royal Americans), accompanied by 49 rangers and 45 Indians, climbed Rattlesnake Hill (present-day Mount Defi-

Facing page: **Map of Lake Champlain from Crown Point to the Richelieu River. (Author's collection)**

181

ance). Brehm observed the French lines and later made a definitive examination of the breastwork by moonlight. Accompanied by ten rangers and Lieutenant James Tute, Brehm entered the French breastwork through a sally port (narrow passageway), noting that the entrenchment consisted of "large d[o]uble logs fix[ed] with cros[s] pieces of wood…about 14 or 15 feet thi[c]k, and about 7 feet high…the Logs are very thick and several of them ex[c]eed two feet."[5] He also observed two batteries and the infamous abatis of felled trees with sharpened branches. His closer assessment of the breastwork was quite different from the one based on the view from Rattlesnake Hill. "From the Top of this mountain," Brehm recounted, the breastwork looked "like a Fence of Rails about a Field and Logs very small."[6] Because they were suffering from the bitter cold, Rogers sent the regulars, along with Tute and 30 rangers, back to an earlier campsite at Sabbath Day Point. Taking the Indians and the rest of the ranger detachment, Rogers crossed Lake Champlain eight miles south of Carillon to attack a French work detail cutting timber on the east side of the lake. Rogers and his detachment trudged northward and attacked the French party, working at a site opposite the fort. After the deadly strike on the French woodcutters, Rogers and his men fled with "seven Prisoners," but "eighty Indians and Canadians rushed out of the Fort, and pursued our Men closely, being back[ed] by about 150 French regulars."[7] As the Indians and Canadians began overtaking the English party, Rogers and his men made a successful stand on "a rising Ground" about a mile south of the original engagement, forcing the enemy to retreat.[8] A short time later, Rogers' detachment withstood another attack before marching to Sabbath Day Point, arriving at midnight. Two-thirds of his men suffered from frostbitten feet. The next day the entire British party marched to Long Island on Lake George, and on the following morning a detachment from Fort Edward with horse-drawn sleighs for the disabled men met Rogers on the ice of Lake George.

The expedition provided clear information on Carillon's defenses, including a description of the fort itself taken from French prisoners. Brehm reported a 16-foot-thick "Parapet of Earth" around the fort, an 8-foot-wide main gate constructed of oak planks, "40 Can[n]ons in the Fort, the largest 12 p[oun]ders," two unfinished stone ravelins, the absence of a well inside the fort, and houses in the "lower Town [south side of the fort], consisting of a large Store house, Brewery and Sutlers" houses, and surrounded by a wooden palisade.[9]

Intent on beginning the northern campaign as early as possible, Amherst departed from New York City on April 29 aboard a sloop, disembarking at Albany on May 3 amid a 17-gun salute. On May 13, as British troops poured into Albany, Amherst wrote to Captain Joshua Loring that he would need "two Brigs for the Navigation of Lake Champlain" and instructed him to make arrangements for the purchase of rigging for the vessels; eight days later he again wrote to Loring, adding "Two Snows [similar to a brig but rigged with a trysail mast] capable of Mounting Eighteen Six Pounders" and ordered him to engage 70 "good" ship carpenters.[10] Amherst also advertised in newspapers for sutlers to "Convey to the Lake, Live Cattle, Sheep, Fowls, Eggs, Butter and Cheese," where "a Market shall be established."[11] However, the sutlers "must not…employ Waggons or Carts drawn by Horses," but instead use "Ox Teams or Ox Carts."(This stipulation was rescinded in July.) [12]

Most of the British regular regiments reached Albany during the first weeks of May, but the provincial regiments arrived in Albany piecemeal between May 20 and the first two weeks of June. (However, troops from the Rhode Island and New York regiments had arrived between May 6 and May 18.) By May 30 only 2,550 provincial troops, about half the total number expected, were present in Albany. In late May British regulars began their trek to Fort Edward, and at the beginning of June additional men from the 42nd Regiment (Royal Highland Regiment) and troops from Massachusetts were dispatched to Fort Edward. On a "Severely Rainy" June 1, William Henshaw, a second lieutenant in a Massachusetts company, noted that he had struck his tent at five in the morning for the first leg of the journey to Fort Edward aboard bateaux, each loaded with "32 Barrels" of provisions, and complained that rowing against a strong current in the Hudson River was "Very Fatiguing."[13] On June 3 Amherst left Albany with the 77th Foot, arriving at Fort Edward on the afternoon of June 6.

Major General Jeffery Amherst. Painting by Joseph Blackburn (1758). (Mead Art Museum, Amherst College)

While awaiting the arrival of troops and supplies at Fort Edward, Amherst assigned 600 men to make repairs to the military road to Lake George and ordered the construction of a series of outposts and stockaded forts along the route as way stations for transporting supplies and as protection against French and Indian attacks, which had plagued the corridor during 1758. The Four-Mile Post, closest to Fort Edward, was described as "a small rectangular stockade with two bastions and a ditch"; Fort Amherst, on the south side of Halfway Brook, consisted of "a rectangular stockade," mounting "three four-pounders"; the Halfway Brook Post, situated just north of Halfway Brook, had been built as a "Pi[ck]et Fort" (stockade) in 1758 and rebuilt by Amherst's troops in 1759; Fort Williams, approximately three miles south of Lake George (sometimes called the Three Mile Post), was also described by eyewitnesses as a "stockaded fort"; and Fort Gage, located on a hill one mile southwest of Lake George, was a redoubt (small stockaded fort) that had been built in 1758 and reconstructed in 1759.[14]

By mid-June the process of moving supplies to Lake George was well underway. On June 15 Robert Webster of the Fourth Connecticut Regiment recorded that "two or three hundred wagons went from Fort Edward to the Half Way Brook [Post] loaded with shells, balls and bateaux."[15] On the evening of June 17, after a day of heavy rain, a Canadian major, a drummer, and four soldiers from Fort Carillon reached Fort Edward under a flag of truce with letters from Major General Louis-Joseph de Montcalm and Brigadier General François-Charles de Bourlamaque regarding a prisoner exchange. The actual reason for the visit, one that Amherst had expected, was to scrutinize British preparations for the forthcoming expedition. With barely 3,000 troops at Fort Carillon, Bourlamaque was

understandably anxious after hearing exaggerated reports that the British force numbered 25,000 men.

Before dawn on June 21 the drums beat the "general" at Fort Edward and the men
struck their tents for the march to Lake George. Two days earlier Amherst listed 6,537 regulars and 4,839 provincial troops in the "Army for Lake George," and on June 21 "about
7000" men made the formal march in two columns to the lake, along with 500 wagons and
carts carrying bateaux, whaleboats, and provisions. (Between June 25 and July 6, 1,527
barrels of pork, 1,262 barrels of flour, and 45 barrels of butter were transported to Lake
George.)[16] Unfortunately, Amherst had chosen a scorching hot day to leave Fort Edward.
With heavy packs, the men trudged more than ten miles before resting at the unfinished
Fort Williams. Private Webster noted that "two men died on the march with the heat,"
and Samuel Warner in Colonel Timothy Ruggles' Massachusetts regiment complained
that the officers did not carry packs and "the general and other big officers had hors[e]s"
and had no "Compass[i]on upon poor Sold[i]ers."[17] The main body of troops arrived at
Lake George before dusk and quickly pitched its tents, but the rear guard did not reach
the lake until sometime after nine at night.

The next morning Amherst accompanied the chief engineer, Colonel James Montresor, to select "ground for building a fort" and ordered two bridges repaired that spanned
brooks at the south end of the lake, as well as the wharfs restored that the "enemy had
broke[n] up."[18] Over the next few days Montresor had William Brasier survey the ground
and, after consulting with Lieutenant Colonel William Eyre, altered his plan for the fort.
Montresor presented the final plan to Amherst on June 30, and two days later the "foun-
da[t]ion of Fort G[e]org[e] [was] Laid"; Captain-Lieutenant Henry Skinner in the Royal
Artillery Regiment, noted that the army was "employed in erecting an irregular fort on a
rock, which is to be built of stone, casem[a]ted, and large enough to contain a garrison of
600 men…They have very good stone for lime and clay for bricks on the spot."[19] By July
6, 1,500 men were engaged in building the fort. Writing to his wife on July 12, Henry True,
a chaplain in the New Hampshire regiment, related that the fort was being constructed of
"stone and lime, where ye old breastworks was, encompassing about 2 or 3 acres of foundation…by ye water a new Redoubt built to command ye lake."[20] A few weeks later Lieutenant William Henshaw suggested that the stone walls of the new fort were "about 14
Feet thick."[21] In reality, two forts were under construction at Lake George—a four-bas-
tioned stone fort, set back from the lake, and a wood stockaded fort with three bastions
and barracks positioned on an elevation closer to the lake. On July 7 Samuel Warner
described the stockaded fort on the "North End" of "Element Hill" as "14 squares or
turns…made with wood and stone and a Hosp[i]tal of Stone" 132 feet by 18 feet; two days
later he observed the buildings in the stockaded fort again and revised his description:
"inste[a]d of one Hospit[a]l there is three more all in a few Rods of one an[o]ther one
ston[e] two wood House[s]."[22]

The troops at Lake George were also faced with another laborious task—digging up
all the cannons, ammunition, and equipment buried there late in 1758. On July 4 a provincial soldier noted that "24 more [cannons] Dug up in one hole, and the next day a British
officer remarked that "the guns belonging to the sloop were dug up to-day; they were
buried between [soldiers'] graves"[23] In addition to unearthing weapons, Robert Webster
disclosed that the "regulars and a part of our Regiment [Fourth Connecticut] dug up three

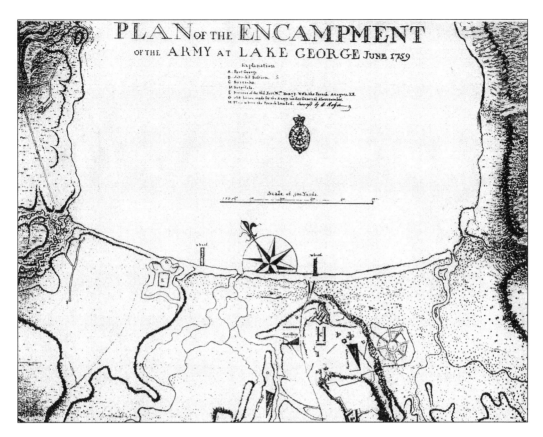

"Plan of the Encampment of the Army at Lake George June 1759," showing Fort George as a stockaded post near the lake (A), a completed bastion of the stone fort (B), barracks (C), hospitals (D), and the octagon-shaped garden. (National Archives of Canada)

or four acres for a garden," located on the east side of Fort George and laid out in an octagonal shape.[24]

To proceed to Ticonderoga, Amherst first needed to retrieve the vessels that Abercromby's men had deliberately sunk in the lake in 1758 as a means of protection from French raiding parties. On July 4, after ten days of backbreaking work, the sloop *Earl of Halifax* was "Drag[ge]d" to the wharf for refitting.[25] A new mast was subsequently cut for the sloop, cannons mounted, and 70 tons of shot and shells loaded aboard the vessel. Two 40-foot row galleys were also raised from Lake George. One was recovered prior to July 12 and the second was raised from a depth of "40 feet" and brought to the shore on July 16.[26] Two new vessels were hurriedly built at the lake in preparation for the expedition to Fort Carillon. On July 5 Salah Barnard, an officer from Deerfield, Massachusetts, noted that a vessel called the "Snowshoe [was] launched today."[27] The *Snow Shoe*, a large, elliptically-shaped sailing scow, subsequently hauled "cattle and horses," as well as provisions, to Ticonderoga.[28] Because the radeau *Land Tortoise* could not be relocated in Lake George, construction of a new radeau, under the direction of Major Thomas Ord, began

Detail of a *View of the Lines at Lake George, 1759*, showing the radeau *Invincible* and sloop *Halifax*. Painting by Thomas Davies, first lieutenant in the Royal Artillery during the 1759 campaign. The painting was signed "T. D. 1774," when Davies had the rank of captain. (Fort Ticonderoga Museum)

during the first week of July. With the help of 100 workmen, the radeau *Invincible* was completed in record time and launched on July 16. Although the hasty construction resulted in "a little mistake in the height of the Port Holes," Amherst concluded that "she will do," and on July 20 the crew successfully "Fired every gun out of her."[29] Captain-Lieutenant Henry Skinner noted that the new radeau "carried four 24 pounders and four 12 pounders" and transported the heavy field artillery needed for the siege of Fort Carillon.[30] Provincial soldiers, including James Henderson from Rutland, Massachusetts, had difficulty describing the unusual-looking vessel: "They call it an Ark of Redoubt."[31] In addition, thirteen rafts, slated to carry the artillery on field carriages, were "made by building a stage on three battoes"; two additional rafts, each constructed by placing a platform on two bateaux were designated to transport some of the horses.[32] A 36-foot row galley, hauled to the lake from the Hudson River, was described by Amherst as "the English flat-bottomed boat with a three-Pounder in her [bow] mounted as a Swivel" that carried 50 men.[33] Hundreds of bateaux and scores of whaleboats were also employed, but many were so leaky that they sank during loading, requiring temporary submersion to swell the boards and the use of fascines (bundles of sticks) on the floors of the vessels to keep the cargo dry.

Gen. Jeffery Amherst's Encampment (Fort George) Summer 1759. **Painting by Ernest Haas, showing the stockaded fort, barracks, the stone bastion, the garden, the radeau** *Invincible,* **the sloop** *Halifax,* **and two 40-foot row galleys. (Lake George Battlefield [Fort George] Alliance)**

While British and provincial troops worked to prepare for the expedition, a number of ambushes and skirmishes occurred. While fishing near an island in late June, four regulars and a ranger officer were nearly captured by Indians from Fort Carillon. The English party frantically rowed to shore and ran four miles before the Indians ended their pursuit. The five men returned safely to the Lake George camp, "but without...Coat, Breeches, shoes or Hose."[34] On July 2, 16 men from the Jersey Blues were ambushed about a mile from the Lake George camp while gathering combustible materials for Amherst's baker. Only four of the New Jersey provincials escaped and six men were "butchered...in a most shocking manner."[35] Returning from a scout to Ticonderoga in three whaleboats on July 6, Captain Jacob Naunauphtaunk and a party of 30 Stockbridge Indian rangers and several other rangers were ambushed in the Narrows. French-allied Indians, aboard seven war canoes, intercepted the detachment, forcing them to the shore where some of the men escaped into the mountains. A number of the English party were captured, including Naunauphtaunk.[36] With reports of the presence of French and Indians in the Narrows, Amherst sent a detachment into the islands "to entice out any party of the enemy" and engage them.[37] At daybreak on July 12 Major Robert Rogers and 100 rangers and Indians departed in whaleboats, followed by Major John Campbell with 300-400 regulars in bateaux and one of the 40-foot row galleys, mounting an 18-pound cannon. "Two [whale] Boats of Rangers were sent forward," Captain Salah Barnard reported, and "were fir[e]d on by the Enemy" from an island, killing a sergeant and wounding a Stockbridge Indian ranger.[38] Rogers and his men attacked the French and Indians, who immediately fled in 20 canoes. The crew of the row galley fired their cannon prematurely and the cannonball fell short; the men rowed forward and a subsequent shot "s[a]nk one of their canoes."[39] Rogers and his men landed on the island and found a breastwork, "which our people set fire to & burned…down."[40]

In contrast to earlier campaigns, the troops at Lake George remained in good health and high spirits. Amherst's logistical preparations were successful in assuring an abundant supply of fresh food. To prevent scurvy, Amherst provided an ample amount of spruce beer, made by boiling the cuttings from the tops of spruce trees in water and molasses. (Amherst recorded the specific recipe for spruce beer in his journal.)[41] The mood of the army remained positive in spite of harsh British military discipline. On July 13 Lemuel Wood from Boxford, Massachusetts, observed the execution of a deserter from the 27th Regiment at the Lake George camp. The prisoner knelt down and clenched his hands as a platoon composed of six regulars fired "through ye Body" and immediately a second platoon "fir[e]d [at] him through ye head and Blowed his head all to P[i]eces."[42] In contrast, a Connecticut soldier sentenced to death for desertion was brought before a firing squad and "at the Last Minut[e]. . .Repr[i]ev[e]d," and a Rhode Island soldier received 1,000 lashes at Fort Edward rather than a death sentence for desertion;* "The Poor Man Cried out very much," according to James Henderson.[44] Sometimes sentences were reduced; on July 20 two regulars in the 80th Regiment were sentenced to be whipped 750 lashes each for stealing goods from a sutler, but one received 400 lashes and the other 300.[45]

On July 20, troops worked loading provisions, ammunition, gunpowder, and 51 pieces of artillery aboard the boats. Some of the vessels sank with the weight, including "one raft, with two 10 inch mortars," which was left behind.[46] Amherst issued orders for the troops "to strike their tents at 2 oclock tomorrow morning."[47] At two a.m. on July 21 the drum beat ("general") sounded and between three and four in the morning the men struck their tents. By six the first vessels began to depart; by nine the last vessels left the wharfs. Amherst's army of 5,854 regulars and 5,279 provincial troops consisted of seven regular regiments (1st Foot, 17th Foot, 27th Foot, 42nd Foot, 55th Foot, 77th Foot, and the 80th Foot), nine provincial regiments (two from Massachusetts, four from Connecticut, and one each from New Hampshire, New Jersey, and Rhode Island), along with rangers, grenadiers, and two battalions of Royal Artillery. The armada of vessels was organized into four long double columns headed by the English flat-bottomed boat and an advance

---

*Most provincial soldiers are generally assumed to have been young. However, an advertisement in the June 25, 1759, *New-York Gazette*, offering a reward for the capture of deserters from the New York regiment, listed six of nine deserters over the age of 25; three were over 40 years old.[43]

Facing page: "**Line of Vessels on Lake George under General Amherst, 1759,**" **delineating the four double columns of bateaux, the English flat-bottomed boat in the lead, the radeau** *Invincible*, **the artillery rafts, the row galleys, the provision boat** *Snow Shoe*, **and the sloop** *Halifax* **in the rear. (Public Record Office, London)**

Flat bottom boat.

Gage's Light Infantry.

Radeau

Lyman.

Worster.

Fitch.

Babcock.

Lawarell.

Rugg[l]s 1st Batt[n]. and Schuyler w[th]. Artillery Stores.

2d Masters.
Engineers.
Gen[ls]. Light baggage.

Hospital

Commissaries

Sutlers.

Provision boat.

Batt[n]. w[th]. Horses.

Whiting

Rangers.

Light Infantry.

Grenadiers.

Willard.

2d Batt[n]. Ruggls.

Fryer.

Montgomery.

R. Highlanders.

Smithelling.

Ardeene.

Royals.

Halifax Sloop.

Radeau *Invincible* leading the column of artillery rafts on Lake George on July 21, 1759. (Drawing by Gary S. Zaboly)

guard of the light infantry in 43 whaleboats. The left column consisted of two rows of bateaux manned by provincial troops and accompanied by a row galley armed with an 18-pound cannon; the second column from the left was led by the radeau *Invincible*, followed by 13 rafts loaded with artillery mounted on carriages, two provincial units rowing bateaux side by side carrying the artillery stores; and a double line of bateaux followed with the engineers, luggage, tools, hospital, carpenters, sutlers, and the provision boat *Snow Shoe* and two rafts transporting the horses; the third column from the left was comprised of bateaux rowed two abreast by the regulars and Highlanders; the fourth double column of bateaux on the far right consisted of the rangers, light infantry, grenadiers, and two provincial regiments, and was escorted by a row galley, mounting a 12-pound cannon. A formation of 21 bateaux (two deep) spanned the width of the four columns at the rear, followed by the sloop *Halifax*.[48] Flag signals were made by the *Invincible* and *Halifax*. Amherst's flotilla departed on a "Cloudy but Pleasant morning" with troops displaying "great Che[e]rfulness, and were in Health and high Spirits."[49] The men were ordered to row "gently" and "in turns" and to sleep when not rowing in order to "be [a]lert & fit for service" upon landing.[50] As the wind increased, the troops used blankets for sails on their bateaux. During the afternoon, "it began to Rain," which "made it impossible to keep the Columns…together."[51] Buffeted by strong winds, the fleet came to anchor at "8 o'clock" in the evening near present-day Hague, out of sight "from the Enemys Post" and within view of "ye great smooth rock" (Rogers Rock).[52] The stiff wind continued, so the rafts were tied to the radeau *Invincible*. The men spent the night in their boats "Tossing to & fro" and "were Continual[l]y Forced to Row back in order to Keep in their places Which Kept them awake all Night."[53]

"At day break" Amherst's fleet proceeded north again and the first contingent of the right column, composed of rangers, light infantry, and grenadiers, landed "at six o'Clock" on the east side of the lake at present-day Weeds Bay (just south of Black Point in Ticonderoga), "within about two miles of the enemy's advanced guard."[54] "At 8 o'Clock" two Massachusetts regiments under Colonels Timothy Ruggles and Abijah Willard "landed at the same Place."[55] Meanwhile, the rangers, light infantry, and grenadiers were ordered to march to the sawmill to cut off the enemy and secure the area before the main army landed. The "rest of the Army did not land till three hours after…at the [abandoned French] advanced guard [farther north] on the east side."[56]

Although there were nearly as many French troops at Fort Carillon as in 1758, the circumstances were very different in 1759. Supplies and reinforcements from France were minimal in 1759 because the French council of ministers resolved to focus its resources on the European theater of the Seven Years' War. In addition, the food harvest of 1758 in New

France declined significantly and the colony had endured a brutally-cold winter. Rations were in short supply and disease was prevalent at Fort Carillon in 1759. Brigadier General François-Charles de Bourlamaque, third in command of French forces in North America and a participant in the 1758 defense of Fort Carillon, was now in command of the fort. Bourlamaque was dispatched to Carillon with "a force of three thousand men, consisting of the battalion of La Reine, the two of Berry, the Colonial Troops and Canadians." (Bourlamaque later suggested that he had only "a total of two thousand three hundred men," not counting several hundred Indians.)[57] Bourlamaque had orders from the governor of New France, Pierre de Rigaud de Vaudreuil de Cavagnial, "not to think of defending Forts Carillon and St. Frédéric, but to abandon them one after the other, as soon as the English army made its approach, and fall back" to Isle aux Noix in the Richelieu River.[58]

Fort Ticonderoga. Photo by John Tichy. (Fort Ticonderoga Museum)

On the morning of July 22, the British advance guard of rangers, light infantry, and grenadiers proceeded to the sawmill on the La Chute River. Rogers and his rangers easily outpaced the regulars, arriving at the sawmill first. He found the bridge across the river intact and "immediately crossed it with my Rangers, and took possession of the rising ground on the other side, and beat from thence a party of the enemy, and took several prisoners, killed others, and put the remainder to flight."[59] Bourlamaque personally led "three hundred…Indians and the grenadiers and volunteers" against the ranger contingent, but he found it "impossible…to induce the Indians" to fight; however, he did manage to have "the other light troops" fire before retreating to the fort.[60]

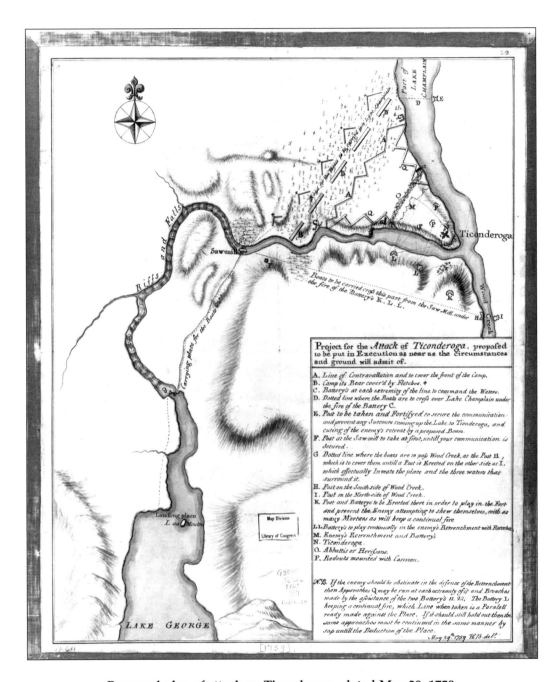

Proposed plan of attack on Ticonderoga, dated May 29, 1759.
Pen and ink and watercolor by William Brasier.
(William Faden Collection, Library of Congress)

The portage road, which connected the French advance post on Lake George to the sawmill, was obstructed with trees that had been deliberately cut down onto the road by French soldiers. The New Jersey regiment and a battalion from a Massachusetts regiment cleared the trees within two hours.[61] Amherst immediately had the bridge over the La Chute River repaired, ordered four cannons forward, and had several breastworks built. Chaplain Eli Forbush, a minister of the Second Church of Brookfield, Massachusetts, noted that the army's march forward occurred with "a noble Calmness and intrepid Resolution, ye whole Army seemed to pertake of ye very Soul of ye Commander"; earlier, Colonel Nathan Whiting suggested that Amherst appeared "cool & very clever."[62] Timothy Ruggles' and Abijah Willard's Massachusetts regiments were sent east along the La Chute River, establishing a post "with[i]n about half a mile of ye fort" at the base of Rattlesnake Hill, where a breastwork was constructed.[63] Late in the day on July 22, the Massachusetts troops assigned to the post on Rattlesnake Hill reported "that the enemy were seen loading batteaus, and some making off toward Lake Champlain."[64]

Early on the morning of July 23, just as the British and provincial army began their march toward the French breastwork, "intelligence came in from Colonel Ruggles' post that the enemy had abandoned the lines."[65] Lemuel Wood in Colonel Willard's Massachusetts regiment noted that the French had "set the[i]r huts on fire and houses near the fort," and shortly thereafter British troops reached the abandoned French breastwork.[66] James Henderson, also in a Massachusetts regiment, described the breastwork as "a very strong thing being cannon proof" that extended "across the Ismus or Neck of Land where Lake George Em[p]ties itself into Lake Champlain" and Jesse Parsons in Colonel David Wooster's Third Connecticut Regiment noted that the huge breastwork "looks like the Work of Ages...so that 3 Thousand men...Would Keep of[f] 20000" besiegers.[67] As the British troops entrenched behind the French breastwork, "the Enemy fired about 500 Cannon Shot and about 60 Shells" from Fort Carillon.[68]

On the morning of July 23 Amherst received reports that all the tents of the French troops had been "struck and that the whole was gone off in the Sloops and batteaus"; Brigadier General Bourlamaque had evacuated the majority of his army, about 2,600 men, and "encamped...two leagues and a half [about eight miles] from Carillon" before moving to Fort St. Frédéric on July 28.[69] He left Captain Louis-Philippe Le Dossu d'Hébécourt of the La Reine Regiment to delay the British advance and "blow up the fort and to retire as soon as the enemy would have erected their first batteries."[70] In addition to bombarding the British troops, the French employed their Indian allies in hit-and-run attacks on British positions. On the night of July 23/24 the Indians attacked the British light infantry and "by an unhappy Mistake two Parties of ours [British] fired upon each other," leaving one officer dead and 12 men wounded.[71]

Meanwhile, other British and provincial troops had been busy bringing the artillery forward from Lake George. Late on July 22 Captain-Lieutenant Skinner noted that the poor condition of the road to the French lines resulted in placing several field pieces "upon rafts a little below the falls [on the La Chute River] and land[ing]" them "within a quarter mile" of the French breastwork; the next day troops brought "planks...[to build] floats for the 24 pounders."[72] On July 24 more of the British siege artillery was brought to the front lines "as fast as possible," while the men "proceeded in entrenching within a little way of ye fort," despite the "enemy fir[ing] 500 balls and bombs."[73]

On the following day Private Robert Webster recorded that "we got the General's boat [the "English flat-bottomed boat"] over in to Lake Champlain" and Henry Skinner noted that the vessel "was carried on a carriage."[74] On July 26 the two 40-foot row galleys were transported from Lake George to Lake Champlain and on the same day a "Large gun[d]ol[a] or two mast[ed] Bo[a]t [the *Invincible* or *Snow Shoe*]" arrived at Ticonderoga from Fort George with "90 or...100" horses, which allowed the "Artillery and stores...[to be] forwarded with great dispatch" to the siege lines being prepared.[75]

The French bombardment of the British lines continued at a frenzied pace on July 25 and 26. Colonel Roger Townshend, Amherst's deputy adjutant-general, was killed on July 25 by a cannonball, "which carried away his Right Arm and Breast," while he was attempting to "Get on the Top of the Entrenchment to take a View" of the French position.[76] The exact circumstances of Townshend's death, however, vary in individual accounts.* His death was "lamented" by provincial officers and the words "worthy," "brave," "humane," and "generous" were used to describe him.[78] His death was the result of French gunners correctly calculating the distance to the British trenches and camp.** On July 25 Lemuel Wood recorded that six men were "Kil[l]ed in ye trench with a bomb" and Jesse Parsons related that during the night "one of their Shells burst in A tent and Kill'd Every Man in it."[81] A newspaper suggested that no one "could get a Wink of Sleep for Shot and Shells falling," and Sergeant Daniel Sizer in the First Connecticut Regiment reported on July 26 that the French "fired as often as once a minut[e]."[82]

By late in the day on July 26, Amherst's batteries, deployed on planked artillery platforms behind eleven embrasures, were ready to open fire. Two batteries, one consisting of six 24-pounders and the other of two 12-pounders, were "about 400 yards from the Fort" on the right and "about 450" on the left; a third battery of three mortars was even closer to the fort.[83] On the evening of July 26 Amherst dispatched Rogers with 60 rangers in the English flat-bottomed boat and two whaleboats to cut the log boom, which the French had "laid across the lake opposite the fort."[84] About ten o'clock at night several French deserters appeared at the British camp with news that the troops at the fort "were then embarking in their bateaux...leaving a match to the magazine, which would blow up the whole Fort."[85] Amherst "offered a hundred guineas" to the deserters to return to the fort and cut the fuses, but the men insisted that they didn't know where the fuses were located.[86] "About 11 o'Clock at night," Lemuel Wood related, the fort's magazine exploded with a "very Lo[u]d and Shaking" thunderous boom, which could be heard at the northern landing on Lake George.[87] Private John Hurlbut in the First Connecticut Regiment remarked that the explosion "killed about Fifty" horses from "a fine stable...over the magazine."[88] Just before the blast, Amherst had sent a message to Rogers to attack the French evacuees who were fleeing the fort. When the fort exploded, Rogers' detachment had not yet sawed through the log boom. His men quickly cut the boom and pushed northward, forcing the

*Lemuel Wood in Colonel Abijah Willard's Massachusetts regiment recorded that Colonel Townshend was "Cut of[f] in two Parts with a Can[n]on Ball as he was Riding at ye generals Side near ye Trenches," but Lieutenant John Grant in the 42nd Regiment wrote that Townsend had forgotten his spyglass while forward of the British lines and was struck by a cannonball as he returned to retrieve it.[77]

**Despite the bombardment, Samuel Merriman from Northfield, Massachusetts, reported that some troops had risked death and injury on July 25 by penetrating the French garden located on the east side of the fort and "fetch[ing] a[n] armful of cabbage" and delivering it to Amherst, who "ga[v]e them two dol[l]ars."[79] Rewards were also offered for cannonballs and shells "left by the enem[y] during the campaigns."[80]

crews of ten French bateaux onto the eastern shore; the rangers seized more than 50 barrels of gunpowder, a large quantity of ammunition, and 16 prisoners. (Some of the prisoners included men from a French scouting detachment returning to Carillon.)

The fort continued burning the rest of the night and at six in the morning a sergeant of the light infantry cut down the French flag inside the fort and presented it to Amherst. The men were ordered to take all the camp kettles and form a bucket brigade from the lake in an effort to douse the fire in the fort. (It would take until July 30 before the fire was completely extinguished.) Amherst also "ordered all the French boats… fished up" and the construction of boats for use on Lake Champlain "for carrying 24-Pounders that I may be superior to the Enemy's Sloops."[89] It was not until September 13, however, that provincial troops were able to retrieve "two Large Flat bottomed Boats" that had been taken by the French from Fort William Henry in August 1757 and sunk at the northern Lake George landing.[90]

With the evacuation of French troops from Carillon, British and provincial troops moved their camp "within the Lines, and began to level the [newly-constructed] Trenches and batteries."[91] The mere threat of Amherst's batteries was enough to cause the French to evacuate, leaving 30 pieces of artillery in the fort.[92] Careful planning and the methodical deployment of the British batteries resulted in a minimum of casualties—"16 men killed, 51 wounded" and one missing, according to Amherst.[93] Amherst's success at Ticonderoga was celebrated at Fort Edward by ordering "All [British] Prisoners Pardoned," according to Lieutenant William Henshaw.[94]

Most of the men were impressed by Fort Carillon, although a few, like Sergeant Daniel Sizer, who had entered the fort on July 27 "to Look for plunder," were disappointed that the French had "Car[r]ied away all their Valuable treasure."[95] Colonial newspapers reported that the engineers suggested that Carillon was the "best and strongest Fortification…in America" with "fine Barracks of Stone and Mortar," missing "only their Roofs," which had been torn off by the garrison to prevent fires from spreading during the anticipated siege.[96] Lemuel Wood wrote that "North Am[er]ica has not a Stronger one of ye Bigness—ye walls are Ch[i]efly Stone and Lime about 24 feet high…under ye walls of ye fort there [are] Large Rooms for Sold[i]ers to live in and Dark Prisons arched all Ro[u]nd with stone and Lime…in ye north East Corner of ye fort there is a Large Room under ye walls arched very Neatly with brick. At one End of it there [are] 2 Very Large Ovens and Conveniences for Baking."[97] Jesse Parsons reflected on the "Strength and beauty" of the fort, concluding that "Such a place of Strength" was not "Equall'd in America."[98] He also observed the huge cross "about 20 or 25 Feet high" that had been erected by Montcalm in 1758 at the French breastwork to commemorate his army's victory.[99]

In a letter to Secretary of State William Pitt, Amherst wrote that he had ordered "the fort at Ticonderoga to be repaired on the same plan" as the French configuration, which would "save great time and expenses"; Amherst noted that the counterscarps (retaining walls) of the glacis and ditch were of masonry construction, as well as "Two ravelins," and the "four bastions [were] built with logs on the rocks, which are covered with some masonry to level the foundation."[100] He reported that only "a small part" of the fort was "ruined"; "one bastion, and part of two curt[a]in [walls], demolished…The casemates are good; the Walls of the Burnt Barracks are not Damaged."[101] During the last days of July, provincial troops cleaned debris from the site of the explosion and laid "New Foundations

Where it Was Shaken to pieces," discovering huge logs two and a half to three feet in diameter from the magazine that had been "Flung Thirty Rods...and pitch'd Endways into the Ground 3 and 4 Feet" deep and splintered as if struck by lightning.[102]

On July 28 Amherst received an account of the accidental death of Brigadier General John Prideaux at Fort Niagara, who had walked in front of a mortar at his own siege lines at dusk on July 20. At the end of May, Prideaux and his troops had departed from Schenectady with orders to rebuild the British base at Oswego and proceed westward to capture Fort Niagara, the vital French fortress that supplied their western posts. Prideaux and his troops arrived at Oswego on June 27, where they rendezvoused with Sir William Johnson and 600 warriors from the Iroquois Six Nations. (By the end of the campaign the Iroquois numbered more than 900.) The Iroquois had decided to aid the British and expel the French in order to maintain their influence over other Indians in the Ohio territory. Prideaux left about 1,300 men at Oswego under Lieutenant Colonel Frederick Haldimand to initiate construction of a new fort (Fort Ontario). Prideaux and Johnson departed for Niagara on July 1 with nearly 3,000 troops and Iroquois warriors aboard bateaux and whaleboats, arriving four miles east of the fort on July 6. Under the command of Captain Pierre Pouchot, a competent regular officer, the garrison at Fort Niagara numbered only 486 troops and nine officers because a large contingent of men had been sent westward to augment French forces at Fort Machault.

A week after their arrival, British artillerymen opened fire with mortars on Fort Niagara, and on July 17 they commenced a barrage with their siege guns. Johnson assumed command following the death of Prideaux on July 20. On July 24 a 1,600-man French relief force was decisively defeated (Battle of La Belle Famille) by a detachment of British regulars, New York provincials, and Iroquois deployed behind a hastily-constructed breastwork and abatis located southeast of the fort. The next day Pouchot surrendered his outnumbered army to Johnson. Upon receiving the news of the death of Prideaux on July 28, Amherst dispatched Brigadier General Thomas Gage to Oswego to assume command of the western army. A week later Amherst finally received a report that Niagara had surrendered on July 25.[103]

Amherst planned to advance quickly to Fort St. Frédéric, but the presence of a French squadron on the lake impeded the move. On July 29 scouts disclosed that the French had "two Sloops and a Schooner" at Crown Point, and Amherst asserted that he "shall be ready sooner" with his fleet on Lake Champlain than the French expect.[104] The French schooner *La Vigilante*, under the command of Joseph Payant St. Onge, had been built by Nicholas-René Levasseur at St. Jean, Quebec, in 1757. Three French sloops or "xebecs," *La Musquelongy* (The Muskellunge), *La Brochette* (The Pike), and *L'Esturgeon* (The Sturgeon), had been constructed by Levasseur and his son Pierre, along with assistant shipbuilder Louis-Pierre Poulin de Courval Cressé, at St. Jean during the fall of 1758 and the spring of 1759. Jean d'Olabaratz, a 31-year-old naval officer, commanded the French fleet on Lake Champlain in 1759.[105]

Even before the French evacuation of Fort Carillon, Amherst had ordered the construction of new vessels for Lake Champlain, and on July 26 carpenters "beg[a]n to cut Timber for a Brig of 20 Guns."[106] Reverend Eli Forbush described the boats that were slated to escort Amherst's army to Crown Point—"two [new] rydaus [radeaux]...four ro[w] galleys yt [that] carry one 18 [pounder] in each of [their] bows, one flat boat and one six

Fort Niagara. (Photo by the author) *Below:* Amherst's sketch of Fort Carillon 1759. From *The Journal of Jeffery Amherst,* edited by J. Clarence Webster.

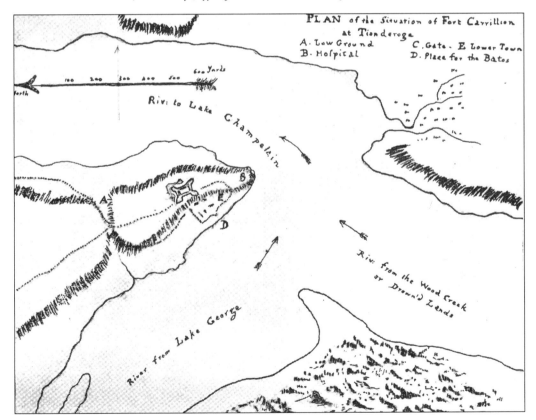

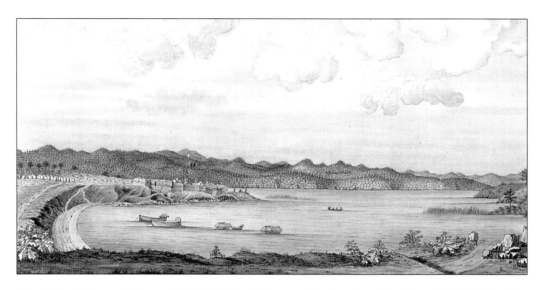

South East View of Crown Point 1759 by Thomas Davies, showing Fort St. Frédéric after the four-story stone citadel had been demolished, the two row galleys that had been moved from Lake George, and the two small radeaux built at Ticonderoga. (National Archives of Canada)

pounder and four bayboats with swivels."[107] On August 1 Amherst received an account from a ranger officer, Lieutenant John Fletcher, that the French had blown up the four-story citadel at Fort St. Frédéric. Fletcher reported that the French had "burnt and destroy'd everything" and could be seen retreating "15 miles down the Lake" in sloops and bateaux.[108] Because the halyard for the flag had been destroyed, preventing Fletcher from raising the British flag, he carved his name on the flagstaff. The French had also destroyed much of their garden, but the rangers returned to Amherst's camp with "some c[ucu]mbers & ap[p]les."[109]

The "general" drum beat for assembly was sounded at two o'clock in the morning on August 4 for the voyage from Ticonderoga to Crown Point. The army was again formed into columns of bateaux and whaleboats, accompanied by the new small radeaux and the row galleys transferred from Lake George. Because of a stiff north wind, the troops did not reach Crown Point until the evening. Many of the provincials were unimpressed with the famous French fortress. Colonel Nathan Whiting, commander of the Second Connecticut Regiment, concluded that the "old Fort is very trifling for one that made so much noise in the World."[110] James Henderson from Massachusetts noted that the stone walls were only "Two feet thick" and could have been easily breached by a six-pound cannon; the octagonal citadel was reduced to "a very Large heap of Stones."[111] "The remainder of the Fort is pretty [e]ntire," the *New-York Gazette* reported; "It is a regular square Stone Building, with four Bastions, but only defensible against small Arms; no Ramparts for Cannon," and the *New-York Mercury* mentioned that "not more than four or five Pieces of Cannon could be found."[112]

On August 6, only two days after arriving, Amherst ordered Lieutenant Colonel William Eyre "to trace out the ground for a fort."[113] (Eyre had also been directed to supervise the rebuilding of the fort at Ticonderoga.) Within days, hundreds of troops were assigned to work on the new fort at Crown Point. By August 13 Amherst had 1,500 work-men there; two days later the foundation of the fort was laid. On August 20 an officer wrote of the "great Progress" that had been made on the fort, which measured "900 Yards in Circumference" and included plans for trenches "14 Feet deep…two Thirds of the Way in solid Rock."[114] A few days later James Henderson disclosed that the walls were "23 feet Thick being made with very large Timbers" and predicted the huge five-bastioned fort would be "invincible" when completed.[115]

In addition to building the fort, Amherst assigned troops to a variety of projects. He ordered 100 rangers to cut a road from Crown Point to Ticonderoga, 200 rangers to open another road to Fort Number Four on the Connecticut River, a number of reconnoitering parties to scout farther north, several redoubts to be constructed, and the French garden at Crown Point to be expanded. On August 16 Amherst gained information from a desert-er regarding the armaments on the four French warships (the ten-gun schooner *Vigilante* and eight-gun sloops, *Musquelongy*, *Brochette*, and *Esturgeon*). All the vessels were said to carry a combination of four- and six-pound cannons, except the sloop *Musquelongy*, which mounted "2 brass 12-Pounders and 6 Iron six-Pounders."[116] Upon learning of more spe-cific details, Amherst sent for Captain Joshua Loring to reevaluate plans for the British fleet. Loring concluded that the brig under construction would not be sufficient to assure naval superiority and, after conferring with Major Thomas Ord, decided that a radeau mounting six 24-pound cannons would be the most expedient way of enlarging the fleet. Ord, the commander of the artillery, had supervised the construction of the radeaux *Land Tortoise* and *Invincible* at Lake George. Returning from a scouting expedition on Septem-ber 1, Joseph Hopkins, a sergeant-major in the rangers, arrived at Crown Point with three prisoners taken near Isle aux Noix and reported that the French had built a new sloop (later named the *Waggon*). [117] Amherst immediately embarked on two courses of action.

A South View of Crown Point **1759. Watercolor by Thomas Davies.
(National Archives of Canada)**

He ordered Major Thomas Ord to "prepare some fire darts [incendiary devices]" for Hopkins to use to burn the French vessel and met with Joshua Loring to make arrangements "to build a Sloop of 16 Guns."[118] Sergeant Hopkins and ten men were sent to Isle aux Noix with fire darts, hand grenades, and combustibles, but they were discovered on September 11 by French guards. The French crew "fired with Some Swivels from the Vessel" and the saboteurs barely escaped "leaving the Combustibles at her bow."[119] Hopkins reported to Amherst that "the Enemy does not intend to rig her as She is laid across the Channel wt [with] Six Guns run out on one Side, two Portholes Shut up, [and] pickets Drove in the Channel from the Island & opposite Shore."[120] Amherst complained that Hopkins and his men had not followed his orders and attempted to set fire to the vessel "at ten at Night instead of two in the morning."[121]

On September 10 Amherst received news that a small detachment sent on August 8 under a flag of truce to the Abenaki village of St. Francis (St. Francois-de-Sales or Odanak) had been taken prisoner. The village, located on the St. Francis River approximately 50 miles northeast of Montreal, was infamous for its warriors, who had ruthlessly attacked English settlements—killing the inhabitants or taking them captive. The flag of truce of the British party was actually a ruse; the real intention was to deliver a message to Major General James Wolfe, who was besieging Quebec City, and to obtain information on the progress of his campaign. (A day before sending the party to Wolfe via St. Francis, Amherst had dispatched a volunteer from a ranger company with the same message, but on a more circuitous route.) Two regular officers, Captain Quinton Kennedy and Lieutenant Archibald Hamilton, were disguised as Indians and accompanied by Captain Jacob Cheeksaunkun and five Stockbridge Indians when they were captured by Abenakis from St. Francis. Amherst was angered by the incident, especially because of reports of the "inhumane treatment" received by the captives, which turned out to be false.[122] Rogers resurrected his proposal for an attack on St. Francis, which Amherst quickly embraced. Amherst instructed Rogers to "Remember the barbarities that have been committed by the enemy's Indian scoundrels…Take your revenge…[but] it is my orders that no women or children are [to be] killed or hurt."[123] Amherst also authorized Rogers' offensive in order to forestall a French reinforcement of La Galette, which he had ordered taken by Brigadier General Thomas Gage.[124] (However, on September 18 Amherst received a letter from Gage that he had decided against an attack on La Galette, a direct violation of his orders.)

ST. FRANCIS EXPEDITION

On the evening of September 13, 1759, Rogers and approximately 200 men, consisting of 110 rangers, 24 Indians, 45 provincial troops, and 21 volunteers from the regulars, departed from Crown Point in 17 whaleboats.[125] The nature of the expedition was kept as secret as possible. The destination of the expedition was not revealed to the troops stationed at Crown Point and Rogers' detachment traveled only at night to avoid detection by the French and their Indian allies. Faced with stormy conditions and a cold pelting rain, Rogers and his men did not arrive at their destination of Missisquoi Bay (near present-day Philipsburg, Quebec) until September 23, ten days after leaving Crown Point. After hiding their whaleboats and provisions for the return voyage, the men began a 12-day journey inland on September 24 and shortly thereafter entered a vast swamp; "the water most of the way was near a foot deep."[126] By then Rogers had already sent slightly more than a fifth of his men back to Crown Point due to illness and accidents. He had also left two Stockbridge Indians to watch the whaleboats. Within two days the Indian guards caught up to Rogers with the discouraging report that the vessels had been discovered and destroyed by the French and Indians. (Some of the whaleboats were taken to Isle aux Noix.) Brigadier General François-Charles de Bourlamaque, commanding the French fortification at Isle aux Noix, had dispatched a total of 350 men to Missisquoi Bay; two hundred of the troops began a pursuit of Rogers; the rest, composed "of Canadians and Indians," were posted at the site of the burned whaleboats in case Rogers and his party returned.[127] With the discovery of his whaleboats, Rogers realized that he could not return to Lake Champlain and decided upon an earlier plan to retire via Lake Memphremagog and the Connecticut River. Rogers sent ranger Lieutenant Andrew McMullen, who had become lame in the trek crossing the bog, and six injured and sick men back to Crown Point with a request to send provisions to the junction of the Connecticut and Ammonoosuc Rivers (opposite the Wells River).

"Hauling the Whaleboats Ashore at Missisquoi Bay," shows Robert Rogers and his rangers landing during a rainstorm on September 23, 1759, in preparation for their march to the village of St. Francis. (Drawing by Gary S. Zaboly)

After nine days of "excessive fatigue," Rogers and his 142 remaining men emerged from the Missisquoi swamp.[128] The French detachment that pursued Rogers' raiding party found it impossible to follow tracks in the swamp and returned to Isle aux Noix. On

October 5 Rogers reached the proximity of St. Francis and that night he and two officers, disguised as Indians, "went through the Town" undiscovered, observing "the Indians in a great Frolick, singing and having the War Dance"; a half-hour before sunrise Rogers and his men, divided into three divisions, burst into the settlement and "broke open their Houses, shot some as they lay in Bed, while others attempting to flee…were tomahawked or run thro with Bayonets."[129] Rogers' men observed "6 or 700 English Scalps waving in the Wind, upon the Tops of Poles."[130] When the killing ended, the houses in the village were torched and at about seven o'clock in the morning the entire affair was over. Private Robert Kirkwood, a volunteer from the 77th Regiment, called the attack "the bloodiest scene in all America, our revenge being completed."[131] Although Rogers suggested that "we had kill[ed] at least two hundred Indians," the French reported that St. Francis was "entirely denuded of its warriors" and only 30 Indians were killed, two-thirds being women and children.[132]

With no time to waste because Indian parties would soon be in pursuit of the raiders, Rogers and his troops quickly divided the Indian corn found in the village storehouses, which they hoped would sustain them on their arduous journey home. Some of the men, however, wasted valuable space in their knapsacks for plunder, including Wampum necklaces, candlesticks, gold coins, scalps, and silver chalices from the church at St. Francis. Taking along six prisoners and five liberated English captives, Rogers' detachment marched southeast following the St. Francis River, then south toward Lake Memphremagog. After a council of war, Rogers and his men agreed to separate into small parties and rendezvous at the junction of the Connecticut and Ammonoosuc Rivers. However, the men fell prey to piecemeal attacks by their Indian pursuers. One party of approximately 20 men led by Lieutenants James W. Dunbar and George Turner were decimated by the Indians—only eight survived.

The retreating English parties were now faced with starvation. After four days without any food, a party led by Lieutenant George Campbell ate their leather cartridge boxes and stumbled upon "some human bodies not only scalped but horribly mangled, which they supposed to be those of some of their own party [Dunbar and Turner detachment]…they fell like Cannibals, and devoured part of them raw."[133] Sergeant David Evans later recounted eating broiled powder horns and musket ball pouches, as well as seeing "three human heads" in a comrade's knapsack, from which "he cut a piece…and ate it."[134] Other survivors later reported that they lived "on Roots and Bark, Toad-stools, some old Beaver skins, and Scalps, as there was but little Game to be had."[135]

After receiving Rogers' message from Lieutenant Andrew McMullen, Amherst dispatched ranger Lieutenant Samuel Stevens to Fort Number Four to gather provisions and transport them to the rendezvous point at the junction of the Connecticut, Ammonoosuc, and Wells Rivers. However, due to the raging river swollen by recent runoff, Stevens and several men made camp three miles downstream and traveled overland each day to the Wells River site, periodically firing muskets as a signal to Rogers' detachment. Concluding that Rogers would never reach Wells River, Stevens departed from the rendezvous site on October 20, only two hours before Rogers and his starving men arrived. Finding Stevens' campfire still burning, they fired their guns as a signal, but Stevens mistook the musketry for the enemy and decided not to return. (Stevens was later court-martialed and dismissed from the service.) Rogers lingered at the site for six days, constructing a raft of pine logs and fashioning small trees into paddles. Leaving most of his emaciated detachment at the Wells River camp, he paddled south on the Connecticut River with three others as far as White River Falls (Junction). Rogers and his comrades built another raft below the falls, which eventually carried them to Fort Number Four, arriving on October 31. He immediately sent provisions upstream to the survivors at the Wells River campsite. After leaving the village of St. Francis, Rogers calculated that he had lost three officers and 46 men, but the total loss was probably 55 men.[136] Many men in Rogers' party were discharged at Fort Number Four; Rogers and 21 men finally returned to Crown Point on December 1, 1759. The fame of Robert Rogers was probably at its peak after the St. Francis raid because the story appeared in provincial newspapers throughout the colonies.*

EXPEDITION TO CANADA

Meanwhile at Crown Point, work continued on the new fort. Fort Crown Point would become the largest fortress built by the British in North America during the eighteenth century. Designed for 4,000 troops, the main pentagon-shaped fortification encompassed six acres of parade ground. Three Georgian-style stone barracks, an armory, a guard house, a hospital, storehouses, and a ten-acre garden would eventually be located on the grounds. Newspapers reported that the fort was "a regular Pentagon, with Out-Works, sufficient to contain 1000 Men in Winter" and would require "2 or 3 Years" to complete.[137] The three "Out-Works" were redoubts or small forts—Gage's Redoubt, the Light Infantry Redoubt, and the Grenadier Redoubt—built "upon Hills that partly command[ed] the large Fort."[138] Amherst also ordered the construction of several blockhouses, including the "Windsor, Richmond & Riverhead, running South South East from the head of…[Bulwagga] Bay to the Lake."[139] By late August, 1,600 men were working daily on the fort. However, many of the men who were assigned to construction duties would show up for breakfast, but fail to appear at the fort to work. As a consequence, men were ordered to "take their breakfast with them" to the construction area.[140]

While troops were working on the fort at Crown Point, others were rebuilding the fort at Ticonderoga. Ensign Ebenezer Dibble of the Third Connecticut Regiment recorded measurements of the structures at the fort during the early fall of 1759. He noted a stone barracks 98 feet long by 60 feet wide, a framed barracks 173 feet by 46 feet, another stone barracks 190 feet by 50 feet, a magazine 209 feet by 30 feet, divided into "small Ro[o]ms and Cas[e]m[a]tes from End to End…a Larg[e] Bak[e] hous[e] and 2 ovens" 32 feet by 26 feet, and mentioned being ordered to "Raise a Store Hous[e]" 92 feet by 39 feet.[141] Earlier, Lemuel Wood had described the Lotbinière Redoubt located at the end of the Ticonderoga peninsula, which was connected to the fort by a covered way ("road picketed all the way on both sides"): "there is a Small fort very Strong, form[e]d Partly by Nature, ye walls not very high but Ro[u]nd, next [to] ye water it is at Least 60 foot from ye top of ye walls to ye water…and Down at ye Bottom of which by ye water Sid[e] there is a battery with some Can[n]on…with a winding way up ye Rocks to ye fort."[142]

Work also continued on Fort George, but the British occupancy of Ticonderoga and

*The story received renewed public interest with the publication of Kenneth Roberts' best-selling novel *Northwest Passage* in 1937 and the 1940 MGM movie version of the book starring Spencer Tracy and Robert Young. The outdoor scenes were filmed in the Idaho wilderness around Lake Payette, where replicas of Crown Point and the village of St. Francis were constructed.

Detail of *A South View of the New Fortress at Crown Point,* showing "the New Fort" (A), the "Ruins of the Old Fort [St. Frédéric]" (B), the "Light Infantry [Redoubt]" (C), and the radeau *Ligonier* (upper right corner). Watercolor by Thomas Davies. (Winterthur Museum) *Below:* Plan of the three redoubts at Crown Point. From *A Set of Plans and Forts in America* (1763).

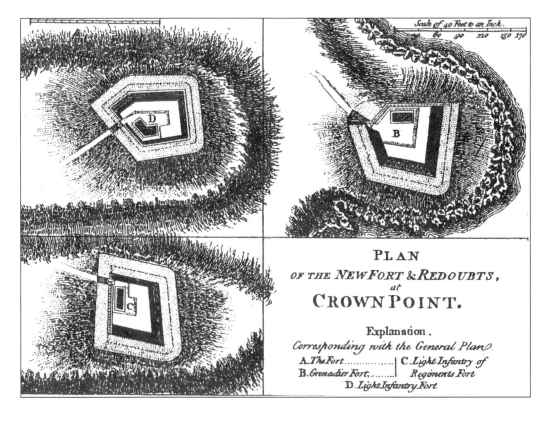

Crown Point lessened the need for a strong fortification at Lake George. On August 3, tools and nails were ordered to Ticonderoga from Fort George. On September 8 Amherst wrote to Colonel James Montresor at Fort George, ordering him to "finish the Citadel Bastion, retrench it at the Gorge [space between two curtain angles of a bastion], that it may form a small Fort of itself...[for] 150 Men...The Hospital may be given up...[a] great Number are not wanted at Fort George, a small Garrison in the [stockaded] Fort by the Lake with Barracks within it, added to the...Citadel Bastion will do for the present."[143] Amherst ordered 30 masons at Fort George to be sent to Crown Point, instructing Montresor to "cease Your Works according to the foregoing plan."[144] Two and a half months later Montresor "walked with the General to the Bastion & round the works & Barracks & [he] seemed well pleased."[145]

Amherst's most formidable task before the launch of his Canadian offensive involved completing the small squadron of vessels to challenge the French fleet on the lake. Numerous breakdowns at the Ticonderoga sawmill and competition for workmen and materials for the construction of Crown Point delayed the completion of the three vessels. Amherst lamented the rivalry between officers, particularly Loring and Ord, and tried "to convince them their duty is to forward everything for the good of the Service and to assist one another."[146]

The French continued to have naval superiority on the lake. On August 11 Amherst sent two bateaux, each armed with a three-pound cannon, along with "the Radeau with a 12 Pounder" to patrol the eastern shoreline of the lake as far as Otter Creek, about 18 miles north of Crown Point.[147] Subsequent intelligence on the French fleet placed "four Vessels [of] the Enemy...below les Isles au Quarte Vents [Four Brothers Islands]" on August 14, and a month later Robert Rogers, while on his journey to St. Francis, observed "two French Sloops & a Schooner...laying off the Otter [Creek]."[148] Amherst was also concerned about the lack of intelligence regarding the number of French troops that he would face in Canada. He had no news of Major General James Wolfe's expedition against Quebec. If Wolfe failed, Montcalm could move troops to Isle aux Noix and stop Amherst's advance.

The 90-foot brig *Duke of Cumberland* was launched at six o'clock on the evening of August 30 at Ticonderoga, only 20 days after the vessel was begun. Because of low water levels in the lake, Captain Loring "launched her Before the Quarter Deck was laid to keep her as high" as possible.[149] Although Amherst anticipated that the brig would "Mount Twenty Guns," he later noted an armament of "six 6 pounders, twelve 4 pound[e]rs & twenty Swivels" with a complement of "70 Seamen & 60 Marines."[150]

On August 22 Loring had written to Amherst that he had begun "to cut the plank" for Major Thomas Ord's radeau, and five days later Ord requested four-inch-thick planks in lengths of 60 feet.[151] Ord complained that the planks sent by Loring "will not do for building the Radeau," but Loring insisted that the sawmill could not cut them to that length, which would require that the planks be "cut by hand."[152] On the afternoon of September 29 Ord launched the radeau at Crown Point. Ord "christened his Radeau the Ligonier"; "She is 84 feet long & 20 feet broad on the Platform [bottom], where the Guns run out she is 23 feet & to carry six 24-Pounders."[153] Newspapers called the *Ligonier* "a Floating Castle...contriv'd so that 'tis impossible for the Enemy to board her. She rows with 40 Oars on each Side, and has two large Masts with square Sails and running rigging."[154] When

Ord tried the *Ligonier* "against the wind, she would not do very well," Amherst recorded.[155]

On September 14 Loring informed Amherst that he had "finished hauling the timber for the Sloop" and would "Lay the Keel on Sunday."[156] The next day Amherst responded to Loring, suggesting that perhaps the British could be "Masters of the Lake" with the "Brig [and] Radeaux boats without waiting for the Sloop," but nevertheless, he urged Loring to build the sloop "as fast as possible."[157] At long last the 115-ton sloop *Boscawen* was launched on October 7 at Ticonderoga and given a 10-gun salute from the brig *Duke of Cumberland*.[158] Built of oak, the 80-foot *Boscawen* with a crew of "60 sea-

Detail of *A North View of Crown Point*, by Thomas Davies, showing the 84-foot radeau *Ligonier*. (Library of Congress)

men and 50 marines" would mount "four 6 pounders, twelve 4 pounders, and 22 swivels."[159] Outfitting the vessels at Lake Champlain required searching the other military posts for six- and four-pound cannons and building gun carriages. At the beginning of October Amherst was still looking for additional crewmen for the new vessels. Colonel Montresor received a letter at Fort George from Amherst on October 2, requesting that he "send all the sailors from the Post to Crown Point."[160]

Detail of *A South View of the New Fortress at Crown Point* that shows the sloop *Boscawen* and the brig *Duke of Cumberland* at anchor. Watercolor by Thomas Davies. (Winterthur Museum)

On October 10 Loring arrived at Crown Point with the brig *Duke of Cumberland*. The sloop *Boscawen*, under the command of a former Royal Navy midshipman, Lieutenant Alexander Grant of the 77th Regiment, reached Crown Point the next day. At the last minute crewmen for the vessels were still being recruited. On the evening of October 10 an additional "52 seamen," detached from provincial regiments, were given assignments on the brig and sloop.[161] Losing no time, Amherst began forming his columns of boats on the lake "at two o'clock" on the afternoon of October 11, defying Brigadier General Bourlamaque's earlier expectation "that Mr. Amherst has no intention to come here [Isle aux Noix] this year."[162] Just before departure, many British soldiers were apprehensive of a voyage on Lake Champlain. One regular wrote that "our Battoes are all newly clean'd, and fitted with Masts and Sails; which, I am afraid will cause some of 'em to go to the Bottom: especially as this Lake is not like Lake George, for the Waves in it rise sometimes as high almost as in the Main Ocean; and it is so wide for 80 Miles that you cannot discern the opposite Shore from either Side."[163] The expeditionary force, numbering more than 5,000 men, consisted of regulars with a contingent of rangers. William Gavit, a lieutenant in Colonel Henry Babcock's Rhode Island regiment, grumbled that "We Poor Provincials Must Stay to finish it [Fort Crown Point] While General Amherst With the Regulars [ha]s Gone to…[be] masters…of the Lake."[164]

The British force was organized into four columns with "two boats abreast" in each column; the 80th Foot (Gage's Light Infantry) served as the advance guard and the "Rangers & Indians form[ed] the Rear Guard."[165] The columns were escorted by five artillery boats, consisting of three row galleys and two small radeaux.* According to Amherst, the radeau *Ligonier* was deployed "in the Center," forward of the columns; an artillery boat with a 12-pound cannon led the first column on the right; an artillery boat with a howitzer was at the head of the second column; and another boat with a howitzer led the third column; the fourth column was headed by a boat mounting a 12-pounder, and another boat with a 12-pounder was positioned "in the Center of the rear of the whole, following the Rangers."[171]

Captain Loring and Lieutenant Grant departed with the brig *Duke of Cumberland* and sloop *Boscawen* on a fair wind at four o'clock in the afternoon of October 11. As the vessels sailed northward on the blue waters of the lake on a crisp autumn day, the men gazed

---

*The type and size of the artillery on the five boats is subject to some differences in the original sources. Jeffery Amherst specified a howitzer on two of the vessels and a 12-pound cannon on each of the other three. However, on October 11 Samuel Merriman in a Massachusetts regiment observed "two ark [radeaux] which mounted 1-24 pounder each & some mort[a]rs & se[v]er[a]l bo[a]ts & three Row gal[l]eys which mounted on[e] 18 pounder each & some mort[a]rs besides some 6 & 8 pounders & pret[t]y many swi[v]els."[166] Merriman, who helped load the vessels, may have included some artillery being transported for the planned siege of Isle aux Noix. An "extract" from a letter written at Crown Point on October 7 disclosed that the two small radeaux carried "two 6 pounders and two 13 inch Mortars each, and four Row Gallies, carr[ied] each one 24-pounder and a Hoet [mortar or howitzer]."[167] On August 11 Amherst had ordered one of the small radeaux out on a patrol on Lake Champlain, but the vessel carried only a single "12 Pounder" at the time.[168] A letter written at Crown Point on September 20 described "5 Row Gallies which mount 18 Pounders, each of them one; the Gun is placed fore and aft and fires out of the Head; they row with 14 Oars on each Side, carry 30 Men, and can fight and go well," as evidenced by the July 12, 1759, skirmish on Lake George, which involved one of the row galleys.[169] (In July one of the row galleys mounted a 12-pounder and the other an 18-pounder.) Another eyewitness to the departure of Amherst's flotilla on October 11 noted "the flat bottomed English Boat on the Right, and the other boat with the 3 pounder on the left."[170]

**View of Lake Champlain north of present-day Westport. Some of the regulars were apprehensive of waves on the broad lake, "sometimes as high" as the ocean.
(Photo by the author)**

upon the high mountain peaks of the Adirondacks to the west and the more distant Green Mountains to the east. Amherst instructed Loring to attempt to "get pas[t] the Enemies Sloops if possible unperceived," cutting them off from "their Post at Isle Aux Noi[x]" and to "take or Destroy" them.[172] Loring was directed "not [to] wait for the Army, which the Artillery in boats will cover."[173]

On October 11 Amherst's troops rowed the flotilla of bateaux, whaleboats, and artillery boats into the night, heeding instructions that the "Men row in turns, and that those that do not, go to sleep, that the Army may be able to proceed Night and Day."[174] In a letter to the acting governor of New York, Amherst reported that the brig and sloop succeeded in "getting beyond three of the Enemy's Vessels [near Four Brothers Islands] before Day Break."[175] However, during the night Major John Reid of the Royal Highlanders Regiment, who led the second column of bateaux, mistook "the light in the Brig for the one in the Radeau [*Ligonier*]" and at the break of day found himself "amongst the enemy's sloops" at Four Brothers Islands.[176] The French sloops (*Musquelongy, Brochette,* and *Esturgeon*) opened fire on the British bateaux. Reid and almost all of the Highlanders managed to escape, but one bateau was captured with Lieutenant Alexander Mackay and 20 men.[177] Amherst heard the "Enemy firing" at dawn on October 12 and "made all the sail with the Radeau [*Ligonier*]" to come to the aid of the retreating Highlanders.[178] Observing the French sloops in the distance, Amherst ordered the crews of his flotilla of bateaux and whaleboats to form a single, immense column and row close to the western shore with the artillery boats alongside. The French sloops did not attack Amherst's armada and the column continued north for the rest of the day. With the "men being fatigued" from rowing more than 24 hours against a wind blowing "very hard," Amherst accepted the advice of New Jersey's Colonel Peter Schuyler and "got into a bay…covered from the wind" before nightfall.[179] The army landed at "Ligonier Bay" (south of present-day Ligonier Point on Willsboro Point) and the rangers were ordered "on an island" (identified a few days later as "Schuyler Island").[180]

Meanwhile at daybreak on October 12, Loring had sailed "45 miles" north with the brig and sloop and observed the schooner *Vigilante* "with two topsails…coming toward him and he immediately gave chase."[181] The French commander of the schooner, Joseph Payant St. Onge, sailed through the shallow water between two islands (probably present-day Bixby Island and Young Island on the west side of South Hero Island). The veteran Lake Champlain captain had lured Loring's vessels into a trap. Just as Loring reached firing range of the *Vigilante*, both British warships ran aground. The sloop *Boscawen* was freed from the bottom with little difficulty, but the crew of the brig *Duke of Cumberland* was "forced to take out 8 Guns & all the Troops" to free the vessel from a shoal.[182]

During "this Delay," Loring caught "Sight of the Enemys Sloops" fleeing from Amherst's armada; the French crews had mistaken "the Radeau and one of the Boats" for the British brig and sloop.[183] Jean d'Olabaratz, commanding the three French sloops, had been attempting to reach Isle aux Noix, but powerful north winds hampered his progress. Loring "gave chase…& drove them into a bay & anchored at the mouth [of Cumberland Bay] in order to prevent" the French vessels from escaping.[184] D'Olabaratz anchored adjacent to the western shore near present-day Cliff Haven, west of Crab Island. Meeting on the *Musquelongy*, d'Olabaratz and his officers resolved to scuttle their vessels during the night. The French decision to abandon their vessels was believed to have been influenced by Lieutenant Alexander Mackay, who had been captured by d'Olabaratz the night before, and had "greatly magnif[ied] our naval strength" to his captors.[185] During the night, two ranger scouting parties, led by Sergeants Nathaniel Burbank and John Rossier, heard "a great hammering & noise" coming from the French crews scuttling their sloops, two of which were sunk in relatively shallow water ("five fathom") so "they might easily get them off or up again."[186] Most of d'Olabaratz's crews walked through the forest for nine days before reaching Montreal, but some of his men, aboard two small boats, managed to elude Loring and reported the British advance to Bourlamaque at Isle aux Noix. On the morning of October 13 Loring was astonished to find that one of the French sloops (*Musquelongy*) had been run on shore and the other two sunk. On the same day Loring dispatched a letter to Amherst reporting that he had ordered Lieutenant Alexander Grant and the crew of the *Boscawen* to retrieve the *Musquelongy* and to "Save the Stores, Guns, [and] Rigging" of the other two French sloops, while he attempted to "cut off the Schooner [*Vigilante*]" from reaching Isle aux Noix.[187] Amherst immediately sent a return message to Loring, but the crews of two whaleboats were forced to return on October 17 because of "a Constant Violent Contrary Wind" which produced waves comparable to those "seen at Sea."[188]

On the morning of October 18 Amherst finally received the news that Quebec City had been taken by Major General James Wolfe's army on September 13 and that Wolfe had been killed. Amherst concluded that the British victory at Quebec would bring "the whole [French] Army to Montreal so that I shall decline my intended operations & get back to Crown Point."[189] A larger French force at Montreal could now reinforce Bourlamaque at Isle aux Noix and repel Amherst's 5,000-man expeditionary force.

The Quebec campaign had been a protracted enterprise. In late June, Wolfe had landed 8,500 troops on Isle d'Orléans, north of Quebec in the St. Lawrence River. Wolfe's forces soon became stalemated following an ineffectual shelling of the French position and the failure of several British attacks, including a loss at the Battle of Montmorency Falls on July 31. The French sent nine fireships loaded with munitions against the British fleet anchored in the river, but the attempt failed to damage the besieger's vessels. At a loss for a new strategy, Wolfe embarked on a scorched-earth policy, destroying 1,400 farms.[190] Consumed by illness, Wolfe did not settle on a new offensive plan until September.

During the early morning hours of September 13, Wolfe set in motion a heretofore secret plan to send troops up the 175-foot-high cliffs at Anse au Foulon to reach the Plains of Abraham on the west side of Quebec City. Wolfe's successful operation was aided by subterfuge: crews from the British fleet had rowed small boats back and forth east of the city, convincing Major General Louis-Joseph de Montcalm that the attack would occur there. By the time Montcalm had accurate intelligence and rushed with his men to the Plains of Abraham, Wolfe had more than 4,000 troops spread across a half-mile-long line. Montcalm was aghast upon viewing the size of the British force and decided upon an immediate attack on Wolfe's army before the Redcoats could entrench on the field. Although Colonel Louis Antoine de Bougainville had several thousand troops eight miles to the west at Cap Rouge, it would require a march of a few hours to reach Quebec, and Montcalm was uncertain when these reinforcements would arrive. Mounting his horse and brandishing a sword, Montcalm ordered the assault on the line of Redcoats at about ten in the morning. His army was about equal in number to that of the British, but his force included a considerable number of Canadian militiamen. The French battalions fired first at a distance, then reloaded and advanced in an uneven line. The British regulars waited until the French ranks were 40 to 60 yards away before blasting them with a double-shotted volley from two ranks. The French battalions broke and the men fled with the British regulars in pursuit. French casualties, numbering over 600, occurred mainly during the initial action, whereas British losses, similar in number to the French, largely occurred when the British regulars chased the French troops and were hit by fire from the Canadian militia and Indians posted on the flanks of the battlefield. Montcalm and Wolfe were both mortally wounded during the battle. Bougainville and the reinforcements from Cap Rouge arrived shortly after the defeat of the French army and pulled back before engaging the Redcoats.

Brigadier General George Townshend reestablished control of the British army on the battlefield and during the afternoon ordered the men to entrench in preparation for the siege of Quebec. After convening a council of war at a French encampment northeast of Quebec, the governor of New France ordered the French troops to retreat to a camp at Jacques-Cartier, 28 miles to the west on the St. Lawrence River. Before the French army could be reorganized under Major General François (François-Gaston) de Lévis, Quebec surrendered; generous terms, which included the honors of war, were signed on September 18 by Jean-Baptiste Nicholas-Roch de Ramezay.[191]

On October 18, the day that Amherst received the news about Quebec and decided to abandon his campaign, the stormy weather on Lake Champlain finally abated. After six days at Ligonier Bay, Amherst ventured north with some of his army to the site of the salvage operation of the French sloops, landing his troops on present-day Crab Island. (The rest of the British troops remained at the camp at Ligonier Bay.) By then the *Musquelongy*

"The Death of General Wolfe." Engraving from a painting by Alonzo Chappel.
(Library of Congress)

had been repaired and Loring set off again with the *Duke of Cumberland*, the *Boscawen*, and the newly-acquired French sloop, along with 200 rangers and the light infantry aboard whaleboats, to locate the elusive French schooner. The *Vigilante*, however, had already returned to Isle aux Noix. Loring sailed to the northern end of the lake; Captain James Dalyell with the light infantry reconnoitered so close to Isle aux Noix that the garrison was able to fire "one shot at them from the Island."[192]

In the meantime, on October 19 Amherst recorded "an appearance of winter" and resolved to return immediately to Crown Point, ordering his troops to leave Crab Island and row south.[193] By nightfall Amherst and his men had reached the rest of the army at Ligonier Bay. On the afternoon of October 21 Amherst disembarked at Crown Point and promptly ordered 900 regulars to work on the fort for the rest of the day.

On October 26 Loring arrived at Crown Point after his unsuccessful attempt to capture the French schooner. He reported that it was feasible to recover the two sunken French sloops. Later the same day, Amherst ordered Lieutenant Alexander Grant to take the "Boscawen and the Amherst [*Musquelongy* renamed and commanded by Lieutenant Charles Robertson], together with the two Small Radeaus" and a party of 200 men with equipment to raise the two French sloops and "Save every part of their Stores, Guns & rigging."[194] Grant departed with the vessels on October 27 while Loring proceeded to Ticonderoga with the *Duke of Cumberland* to begin preparations for docking and securing the fleet over the winter. On November 1 Grant notified Amherst that he had "raised the Stern of one of the Vessels above water after great Labour, being assisted by the other Sloop and have now three Cables under the Said Wreck."[195] On November 16 Amherst wrote to Loring at Ticonderoga that Grant had arrived at Crown Point with the "two French Sloops which he Weighed up" and noted that the "Enemy had thrown over board two brass Guns* from each Sloop…as Lieut. [Alexander] Mackay Informs me," which was confirmed "by the [empty] Carriages left in the Sloops."[197] On the following day all the sloops sailed to their winter quarters at Ticonderoga. Major Thomas Ord's "Return of Guns…Found on board the Three French Sloops" listed eight iron 4-pound cannons and five swivel guns on the *Musquelongy*, six iron 4-pounders and two swivels on the *Brochette*, and six iron 4-pounders and four swivels on the *Esturgeon*.[198]

On October 31 Amherst noted a "Very hard frost," which inhibited the mortar from setting at the fort under construction at Crown Point.[199] The next day Ebenezer Dibble in Connecticut's Third Regiment described "a Great stir…for hom[e]" among some of the Massachusetts and New Jersey troops posted at Ticonderoga.[200] With the expiration of their enlistments, about 200 of the men at Ticonderoga marched off, but they were forced to return by soldiers sent by Amherst with orders to bring them back; however, John Woods, who was among the departing Massachusetts troops, wrote that the men with him "refused to go Back" and continued their march home.[201] On November 5 Amherst received news that "100 of [Timothy] Ruggles' Deserters" had been taken "on the Road to [Fort] No.4."[202] The next day the deserters arrived at Crown Point and were pardoned by Amherst.

After three o'clock on the afternoon of November 10, the garrisons at the British forts had a respite from their work schedule to celebrate the king's birthday. According to Amherst, "the three Forts [redoubts at Crown Point] fired seven Guns each fol[l]owed by a Volley from each Corps…The Fortress [at Crown Point] then fired 21 Guns…The Park of artillery then fired 21 Guns" and the men were lined up for "a running [sequential musket] fire from right to left," ending with "a General Volley" and "three Huzzas."[203] The garrison at Fort Ticonderoga also celebrated the occasion with a 24-cannon salute. Rum and beer were provided to all the troops, enlivening the celebration. The very next day Amherst lamented that the "Provincials have got home in their heads & will now do very little good. I hear they are deserting from every Post," even though they had "a good deal of money due to them."[204] Amherst finally relented, allowing some of the provincial regiments to begin their march home on November 12. More than half departed by November 17, leaving only one Massachusetts and two Connecticut regiments until November 24 and 25.

On the evening of November 14 Major James Grant of the 77th Foot arrived at Crown Point with word that an escort of two officers and 40 Canadians under a flag of truce were

---

*Two elegantly-engraved 12-pound brass cannons, a swivel gun, and other artifacts were raised from Lake Champlain in 1968 near Cliff Haven.[196] One cannon is presently on display at Clinton Community College and the other at the Crown Point State Historic Site Visitor Center. The two cannons had been taken from Fort William Henry by Montcalm's army after the surrender of the fort in 1757. Upon the French evacuation of Fort Carillon in 1759, the two cannons were mounted on the sloop *Musquelongy* and then thrown overboard when the vessel was scuttled in October 1759.

near Otter Creek with British and provincial prisoners. A newspaper later reported that "242 English Prisoners" were "to be exchang'd for as many French Prisoners who were at Albany on their Way up from New York."[205] Reaching Crown Point the next morning, the English captives included Captain Quinton Kennedy and Lieutenant Archibald Hamilton, whose capture had prompted the St. Francis raid, and Lieutenant Alexander Mackay, taken by d'Olabaratz on the lake on October 12.

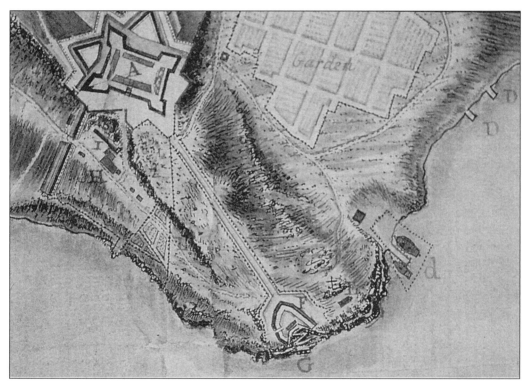

Detail of a "Survey of the Fort at Ticonderoga and its Environs. . .and part of Lake Champlain" November 1759, showing the location of the British wharf (d). Ink and watercolor by William Brasier. (Crown Collection, British Museum)

Safeguarding the British naval fleet at Ticonderoga over the winter was a major priority. Amherst instructed the winter garrison to have no "less than four [s]entries on board" the vessels at night.[206] After considering the construction of a blockhouse to protect the vessels, Amherst and his officers instead decided on "surrounding them with Palisades and having two Guns out…the[i]r Sterns and also two in their Bows with a G[u]ard on Board and four Sentries."[207] The radeau *Ligonier* continued to transport supplies from Ticonderoga to Crown Point until late in the season, carrying 1,600 barrels of provisions on one trip alone. In early December the troops tried to sink the *Ligonier* in Lake Champlain as a means of protection from French raiding parties during the winter, but the men "could not by any means get the Rad[e]au Sunk" and suffered frostbite in the process.[208]

During November the three large vessels on Lake George were still in service, carrying supplies from Fort George to Ticonderoga. (However, the radeau *Invincible* had to undergo repairs and the transport *Snow Shoe* had to be caulked because of numerous leaks.)[209] A November 1 report by Loring on the vessels at the Lake George landing at Ticonderoga listed the carrying capacity of each vessel for transporting troops on their way home or to winter quarters. Each of the 95 bateaux that were "fit for Service" could carry 25 men.[210] Six whaleboats were to carry 13 men each, the sloop *Halifax* could take 200 passengers, the *Snow Shoe* 100, and two "Small Lighters not Repaired" were able to handle another 100.[211] The Lake George squadron was not sunk for winter protection as had been the case in 1758; instead the vessels were guarded by the garrison at Fort George. In addition to the three larger vessels, 120 bateaux and 41 whaleboats were "left at Fort George," according to the December 1, 1759, "Return" of vessels.[212]

After leaving orders for the officers of the winter garrison (27th Foot) at Crown Point, Amherst departed for Ticonderoga with the rest of the regulars and 100 rangers, aboard bateaux organized into one column with "four boats abreast."[213] Amherst also left 200 rangers at Crown Point as part of the winter contingent. At Ticonderoga Amherst noted that the barracks had been completed. (The barracks at Crown Point had been finished ten days earlier.) During a blinding snowstorm on November 26, Amherst and the regulars hurriedly set off in bateaux from Ticonderoga for Fort George. The regulars landed late in the day at Sabbath Day Point, but Amherst pressed on to Fort George.[214] The regulars disembarked at Fort George on the afternoon of November 27 and "Encamped in the woods as far as Bloody pond."[215]

Amherst walked with Colonel James Montresor "to the Bastion [at Fort George] & round the works & Barracks" and ordered Montresor to build a "casemate under the Rampart of the East Flank of the Bastion."[216] Amherst also asked him to remain at Fort George long enough to "receive the French Prisoners, sh[o]wing them civility."[217] French prisoners were being returned to Canada in exchange for the English captives who had reached Crown Point on November 15. Captain Pierre Pouchot, taken prisoner upon the surrender of Fort Niagara, was among the French parolees, staying at Fort George on the night of December 1, 1759. Pouchot described Fort George as a "square fort measuring about 80 toises [511 feet] on each exterior side. The lower part of the rampart is more than 18 feet thick and made of masonry. The parapet is of timbers placed one on top of the other, all well cut to size and banked up with earth twelve feet thick…a bastion completed, entirely casemated like a redoubt."[218] Pouchot also provided a brief description of the stockaded fort located nearer to the lake: "There is another, and much smaller, square fort…constructed of horizontal timbers. On the upper part there is a fraise" (palisade of pointed stakes fastened together with a strip of wood).[219]

Amherst marched with his troops to Albany where they boarded sloops on the Hudson River. However, as a result of adverse winds and ice, the vessels could not leave and the troops were forced to march southward. Amherst spent the next six days walking in the bitter weather to New York City. Although Amherst's army failed to invade Canada, it succeeded in taking both French forts on Lake Champlain, as well as achieving naval control, and building stronger British bases at the lakes. The British victories at Fort Niagara and Quebec City set the stage for a final campaign to conquer New France in 1760.

9. *Expedition to Canada 1760*

IN 1760 British forces were poised for the last great campaign of the war in North America. France, on the other hand, was nearly bankrupt from the escalating cost of the European theater of the Seven Years' War and was forced to suspend payment on its financial commitments in Canada. Desperately-needed supplies, along with only 400 regulars, were sent from France in the spring of 1760 aboard five transport vessels, escorted by a single 30-gun frigate. Three of the provision ships were intercepted by the Royal Navy shortly after leaving France and the remaining three vessels were eventually trapped by British warships in a bay south of the mouth of the St. Lawrence River.

New France would be forced to stand alone in the face of a British and provincial juggernaut. Major General Jeffery Amherst's ambitious plan involved an attack on the French army in Canada by "three Avenues...that I may force them to Divide their Troops, which will Weaken them in Every part."[1] British forces were slated to converge on Montreal from three different directions, completely encircling the French troops. Leading the main army of nearly 11,000 men on the most difficult route, Amherst planned to move east on the St. Lawrence River from Lake Ontario, while Lieutenant Colonel William Haviland (brigadier general in America) pushed north on Lake Champlain with 3,500 troops, capturing Isle aux Noix and the other forts on the Richelieu River before advancing to Montreal. Brigadier General James Murray would proceed west from Quebec on the St. Lawrence River with troops from his garrison and reinforcements from Louisbourg. The simplest and easiest route to Montreal for Amherst's entire army would have been along the Lake Champlain-Richelieu River corridor; but his planned pincer attack from the west and east via the St. Lawrence River would block the French from slipping away and thus end the war in North America.

The task of organizing a large army in North America was the responsibility of Amherst as commander in chief. William Pitt, the British secretary of state, wrote to Amherst in January, informing him that the king had sent circular letters to the colonial governors ordering "the same, or a greater number, if possible, of Men" to ensure "the success of the ensuing decisive and (it is greatly hoped) last Campaign in North America."[2] Pitt urged Amherst to expedite the recruitment of provincial troops so that the campaign could begin by May 1. Although past mobilizations had seemingly exhausted the number of available recruits, colonial legislatures voted to raise a total of 21,180 men; 15,942 troops were eventually mustered, the largest number (4,964) being enlisted from Massachusetts.[3] The recruitment of provincial troops, however, did require the authoriza-

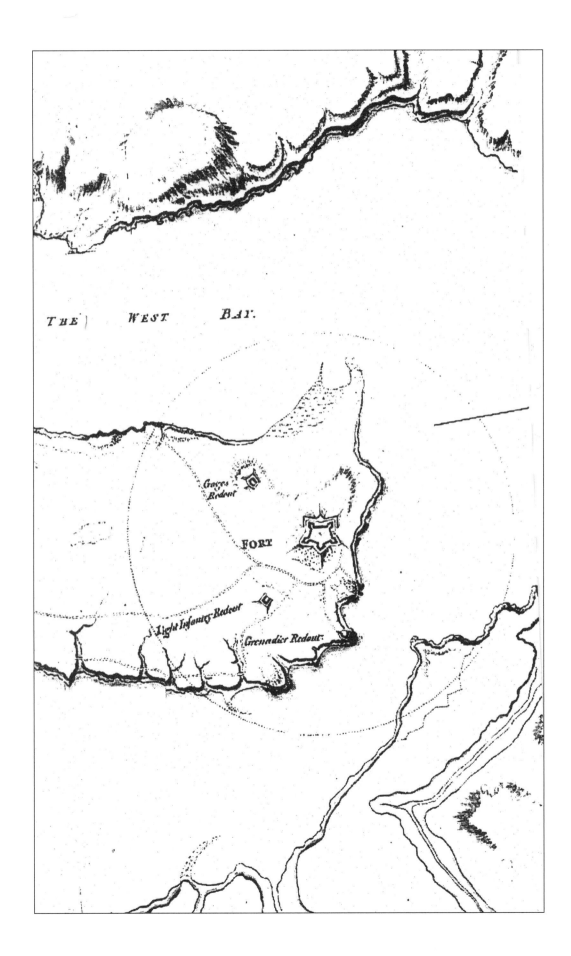

THE   WEST   BAY.

Gages
Redout

FORT

Light Infantry Redout

Grenadier Redout

tion of bounty payments to enlistees by colonial legislatures. The expectation of a successful, final campaign encouraged the colonies to cooperate with the Crown's requests, but the mounting cost of the war created a financial dependence on Great Britain for reimbursements.* However, the expansion of private-sector businesses and other employment related to supplying and transporting provisions to the army accelerated economic growth in the colonies and led to increased specialization and commercialization of agriculture.[5] Because sailing vessels could be built 30 to 50 percent cheaper in the colonies than in Britain, shipbuilding became a major industry in New England. Likewise, provincial workers were employed in building "Batteaus and whale boats…at Schenectady," under the supervision of Colonel John Bradstreet.[6]

During the early months of 1760, the garrisons at the forts at Lake George and Lake Champlain had to endure harsh winter conditions, including episodes of scurvy and frostbitten limbs. Despite the evacuation of the French forts at Lake Champlain in 1759, French and Indian war parties still roamed the lake valley. On February 12 Major Robert Rogers with 16 unarmed ranger recruits caught up to an English column of 14 sutlers' sleighs on the ice in transit to Crown Point from Ticonderoga. Soon after Rogers reached the caravan, the sleighs came under attack "five miles from Ti[c]onderoga by about 70 Indians or French dressed like Indians."[7] Ironically, the attack occurred in the vicinity of the ambush of French sleighs by Rogers in 1757 (see chapter 6). The sutlers frantically turned their sleighs around and fled to the safety of Fort Ticonderoga, but Rogers pushed on to Crown Point, arriving as darkness set in. Rogers appealed to Haviland for his consent to take the rangers stationed at the fort on an immediate pursuit of the attackers, but the fort's commander was unwilling to risk the small detachment of rangers on an uncertain nighttime operation. The losses in the attack included "Two Indians and a Squaw" killed and "four Rangers and a Slayman" captured.[8] The French party also captured a ranger sleigh carrying 1,196 pound sterling—£800 for the ranger payroll at Crown Point and £396 that belonged to Rogers. The next morning Rogers and his rangers returned to the scene of the ambush, discovering four dead horses and the bodies of his Indian allies. In addition, Rogers found "Bundles of Sticks Covered with Combustibles," apparently intended to be used to burn the British fleet at Ticonderoga.[9] The French and Indian attacks continued the next month. With the permission of Haviland, ranger Captain James Tute crossed the lake on March 31 to fish with three fellow rangers and five regulars, but the fishing party was captured by a French and Indian detachment.[10] (Tute had been captured the previous September and exchanged on November 15, 1759.)

By late March Haviland began delineating construction plans for Crown Point in letters to Amherst. He reported that sections of the lake were free of ice, including the area from the "Old Fort to the Point where the Chimney stands on the other side of the Lake."[11] He informed Amherst that the "Garden Seeds [had] not yet Arrived" and that he had built a "three Wheel," one-horse cart to "bring Earth to the Fort" and wished for "one hundred

---

*Wartime expenditures by the colonies amounted to 2.5 million pound sterling, of which 1.1 million or approximately 42 percent was reimbursed by Parliament. The reimbursement, however, varied considerably among colonies. Massachusetts spent £818,000 and was reimbursed 43 percent, whereas Connecticut's expenditures of £259,875 were reimbursed at 89.2 percent.[4]

Facing page: Detail of a "Plan of [the] Southern Part of Lake Champlain," showing the British fort and redoubts at Crown Point. (National Archives of Canada)

of them."[12] His summer plans included a road from the "Garden to the large Old Lime Kiln, where most of [the] Timbers may be landed."[13] Late the following month, Haviland reported that the well was "about 20 feet deep," the lime kilns were under repair, and excavation of clay for brick making had begun.[14] More extensive construction at Crown Point would await the arrival of the provincial regiments.

Amherst was also committed to the reconstruction of Fort Ticonderoga, including repairing the barracks that had been partially destroyed by a fire. On May 27 Lieutenant Diedrick Brehm, an engineer from the 60th Regiment, provided a list of recommended construction projects at Ticonderoga. Brehm suggested that the "officers Barracks" be rebuilt "with Brick partitions between each Room," adding brick partitions in the "Soldiers Barracks," erecting another barracks, building a hospital, "a Smit[h]s Shop, a Brewhouse [and]…a Communication under ground to convey the Privy into the Lake."[15] He also suggested repairing chimneys, laying platforms and floors, raising the sides of the covered way, and adding palisades between the redoubt and the fort. Amherst also hoped to complete the abridged fortifications at Lake George, ordering "Capt Lt Williams Engineer to Fort George to finish the works there."[16] Amherst directed that a "Boundary be marked at fifteen hundred yards Distance from…the Bastions" of Fort George, whereby no structure was to be erected.[17]

Before the expedition to Isle aux Noix began, the British fleets on the lakes had to be readied for service. From his New York City headquarters on April 13, Amherst ordered three of the vessels at Ticonderoga (the brig *Duke of Cumberland* and sloops *Musquelongy* and *Brochette*) into operation to protect the British forts at Lake Champlain "against any Sudden Attack of the Enemy" and to "Annoy the Enemy if they should" venture onto the lake.[18] He assigned 90 seamen to the three vessels—"Fifty for the Brig and 20 each" for the sloops.[19] In 1760 Amherst appointed Lieutenant Alexander Grant of the 77th Regiment to command the Lake Champlain fleet, instructing him to mount the "English & French Guns that were on board…last Year, without taking any Guns from Crown Point."[20] He also directed Grant to "pursue and Fight" enemy parties on the lake and take prisoners by deploying "Rangers and Troops You will have on board," and "take a View" of Isle aux Noix."[21]

During the second week of May, Grant sailed north with the brig *Duke of Cumberland* and one sloop, carrying Robert Rogers and a detachment of 60 rangers and 30 light infantry, along with their whaleboats stacked on the decks. Rogers was sent "to reconnoitre Nut Island, and the garrison there, the landing place &c."[22] (Isle aux Noix was called Nut Island for its Walnut trees.) On the first leg of the voyage, Grant reached Cumberland Bay at one o'clock in the morning and remained there for four or five hours before setting sail again; at noontime he anchored "within Eight Miles of the Fort [at Isle aux Noix]," observing a French "Row Gall[e]y with forty Oars."[23] The next night Rogers rowed ashore with three rangers to make his observations of the French post. On May 12 Grant "observed a Scout of Indians in 4 Canoes" trying to reach the island, and so he directed his gunners to ready the cannons and ordered rangers in two whaleboats, armed with "a Supply of hand Gr[e]nades," to pursue the Indians after the guns from the brig had fired.[24] The rangers rushed ashore before the cannons were fired and the Indians fled. However, "four or five [Indians were] killed and Wounded" and "all their Canoes and Some Blankets" taken.[25] On May 13 Rogers returned to the *Duke of Cumberland*, informing

Grant that the French were "busy night and day Picketing [driving wooden stakes into] the West Channel and Getting out Some Large Boats."[26] With an outbreak of smallpox on the brig, Grant decided to head back to Crown Point.

On May 18 Amherst issued orders to the acting commander at Fort George, Captain Edward Forster of the 17th Regiment, to have the "Sloop [*Halifax*]…baled out by a Sergeant of the Royals & ten Seamen of the Provincials" and be made ready for service.[27] On the same day, Amherst also wrote to Lieutenant Colonel John Darby (17th Regiment) at Ticonderoga, informing him that the detachment of ten provincial seamen was to "bale out the French Sloop" and refit the vessel after finishing with the *Halifax*, and then crew the *Snow Shoe*.[28] Although the *Snow Shoe* had been built in 1759, Darby wrote to Forster on May 20 that he hoped "the new Snow Shoe will be ready to transport" provisions to the Ticonderoga landing at the northern end of Lake George.[29] Three days later Forster informed Amherst that Darby had departed from Fort George with the *Snow Shoe* early in the morning, carrying a load of biscuits and "16 Barrels of Flo[u]r, 20 Barrels of Beef, [and] 229 Barrels of Pork."[30] In early June Amherst ordered that "all the Sutlers" arriving at Fort George use the *Snow Shoe*, rather than bateaux when moving their goods north.[31] The radeau *Invincible*, also suitable for carrying military provisions, was mired "in Mud" at the northern Lake George landing, but two large scows docked at Fort George were each assigned a crew of "a Sergeant and Nine Men" and pressed into service.[32] (The two scows, which had been taken from Fort William Henry and later sunk by Montcalm's soldiers in 1757, were raised by Amherst's troops at the northern end of Lake George in 1759.)

After returning to Crown Point from his scouting mission to Isle aux Noix, Rogers was summoned to Amherst's headquarters in Albany, meeting with him during the last week of May. Having received a report that the French were attempting to recapture Quebec City from Brigadier General James Murray's forces, Amherst ordered Rogers on an offensive to "alarm the Enemy & force some of their troops away from Quebec."[33] Commanding 300 men, consisting of 275 rangers and 25 soldiers from the light infantry, Rogers was ordered to proceed to St. Jean on the Richelieu River "to surprize the fort, and destroy the vessels, boats, provisions, or whatever else may be there for the use of the troops at Isle au[x] Noix…[then] March to Fort Chamblé, where you will do the same."[34] Amherst also directed Rogers to send a detachment of 50 men to destroy Wigwam Martinique, an Indian village on the Yamaska River located to the west of the St. Francis River.

Rogers' diversionary expedition, however, would actually take place after the French siege of Murray's forces at Quebec had ended. (The news of the French withdrawal would not reach Amherst until June 11.) Hauling a dozen cannons, Major General François (François-Gaston) de Lévis and a 7,000-man army had reached the outskirts of Quebec on April 27. After receiving reports of a French advance, Murray marched troops to Sainte-Foy, about six miles west of Quebec, to cover the retreat of 800 light infantry, who had been assigned to advance posts. Murray retired to the city on the evening of April 27 and held a council of war. The next day Murray resolved to make a stand on the Plains of Abraham, the site of the British victory in 1759, and deployed 22 cannons and over 3,000 men there. After a fierce three-hour battle on April 28, Murray's army was forced into a disorderly retreat to Quebec's protective walls, leaving all their cannons behind (most had been spiked). The British and French casualties from the battle, numbering 1,104 and 833 respectively, exceeded those of the 1759 battle. Lévis then began preparations for a siege of Quebec City, while awaiting the arrival of the French fleet. On May 11, after nearly two weeks of careful preparation, Lévis opened his inadequate batteries on the garrison inside Quebec. But with the arrival of British warships, Lévis was forced to abandon the siege on May 13 and retreat westward.[35]

ROGERS' EXPEDITION: POINT AU FER AND ST.THERESE

On June 1 Rogers embarked from Crown Point with 250 men aboard the brig *Duke of Cumberland* and sloops *Boscawen, Musquelongy,* and *Brochette,* which carried bateaux and whaleboats on their decks.[36] The vessels, under the command of Lieutenant Alexander Grant, first sailed into Missisquoi Bay, where ranger Lieutenant Robert Holmes and 50 men were set ashore on June 3 with instructions to annihilate Wigwam Martinique. Rogers sent a second party of four men to Murray at Quebec with a letter from Amherst. Grant next sailed the fleet into the main lake near Isle La Motte, and Rogers and about 200 men boarded their whaleboats and bateaux on the evening of June 4, landing on the shore of present-day Kings Bay (adjacent to Point au Fer). Two of the sloops followed closely, but Rogers ordered the commander of the vessels to cruise farther north near Windmill Point in order to draw French attention away from Rogers' landing site. Due to heavy rain on June 5, Rogers and his men were unable to march north. During the afternoon Rogers observed several French boats patrolling the lake, and after dark he rowed out to the British sloops and ordered them to return to Grant's position at Isle La Motte. On the morning of June 6, Rogers' reconnoitering parties informed him that 350 of the enemy from Isle aux Noix had landed north of his position and were marching to attack his detachment. With the early warning, Rogers was able to deploy his men to their best advantage. About eleven in the morning, the French and Indians engaged Rogers on the Point au Fer peninsula. One ranger officer later wrote that the attack began on Rogers' left wing "with [the] usual intrepidity and yelling," as the rangers fired back briskly; the Indians came so close that "we exchanged shots across the boats, and when the Indians found that they could not load fast enough" to match the fire of the rangers, "who had cartridges," they "threw stones at us."[37] With a log for protection on the right flank, Rogers ordered Lieutenant Jacob Farrington and 70 rangers to the rear of the French position. As Farrington initiated his attack, Rogers "pushed" the French and Indian detachment "in front, which broke them immediately," and he chased them "about a mile, where they retired to a thick cedar swamp, and divided into small parties."[38] By then it began to rain hard again and the pursuit ended. During the three-hour clash the rangers used most of their 60 rounds of ammunition. The battle was the largest engagement in the lake valley since 1758 and one of Rogers' most successful, despite being outnumbered by the French and Indian force. Rogers noted that 16 rangers and an ensign in the 17th Regiment had been killed and eight rangers, two light infantrymen, and a ranger captain wounded. The latter officer died before reaching Crown Point; the French had 32 killed and 19 wounded.[39] Rogers rowed to Isle La Motte, "where we landed, buried our dead, and sent the wounded to Crown Point."[40]

Reinforcements, consisting of a detachment of 25 Stockbridge Indians and 30 light infantry troops under Lieutenant Caesar McCormick, reached Rogers on June 9 at Isle La

Motte.[41] At the same time, Rogers was finalizing plans for his second offensive. "With two Hundred Twenty men," Rogers wrote in a letter to Amherst a few days later, "Landed the 10th about Midnight on the west Shore Opposite to Isle [L]a Mot[t]e from thence Marchd as fast as Possible to St. Johns [St. Jean]," arriving "the Evening of the Fifteenth at 11 oClock."[42] Rogers hoped to employ a subterfuge by having McCormick, who spoke fluent French, lead the light infantry into the fort "with their coats turned" inside out, showing their white linings to resemble French uniforms.[43] However, Rogers discovered that Fort St. Jean had more regular troops, including 17 sentries, than he had anticipated, and so at two in the morning he began marching his troops to the stockaded fort at St. Therese, about nine miles farther north on the Richelieu River. At eight in the morning, Rogers reconnoitered the small picketed fort; two hours later, as the French garrison opened the gate for a hay cart, Rogers and his men dashed into the fort "without Firing a Single Gun," capturing the post, along with 15 houses and 78 prisoners.[44] Rogers freed the women, children, and other civilians, and departed with 26 prisoners, after burning the fort, village, hay, and provisions and killing the horses and cattle. Rogers' men found 14 bateaux and six canoes at the fort, which they destroyed, sparing eight bateaux that were used by the raiders to cross to the east side of the Richelieu River.

Soon 600 French and Indians arrived at St. Therese, "where they had the mortification to see us opposite to them staving their boats, and marching off, without having it in their power to pursue us for want of boats."[45] A second detachment of 800 French troops from Isle aux Noix pursued Rogers and his men along the eastern shoreline. Although the advance guard of the French flying column engaged some of the rangers, the main French force was not able to overtake Rogers. On June 19 Lieutenant Alexander Grant wrote to Amherst describing the extraction of Rogers' party: "Major Rogers and all his party with 26 French prisoners came on shore [at Windmill Point]…made a smok[e] and fired some Guns."[46] Grant dispatched boats to the shore, and within a half-hour all of Rogers' detachment were safely aboard. Just after Rogers boarded the brig *Duke of Cumberland*, "The enemy soon after appeared on the shore where we embarked."[47]

The prisoners taken by Rogers provided a wealth of intelligence for the British, divulging that Fort Chambly was manned by 150 men and Fort St. Jean by 300. While Fort St. Jean was protected by only 12 cannons mounted on ramparts, the fortifications on Isle aux Noix were secured by about 100 cannons and "a sloop [*Waggon*], a schooner [*Vigilante*], and a row gall[e]y [*Petit Diable*]," which had two "24 pounders about 24 Swivels and rows [with] 24" oars.[48] The prisoners also revealed that at St. Jean "there is a Row Gall[e]y there Almost Finished Calld the Old Devil [*Grand Diable*] which Mounts four Twenty-four Pounders [and has] 60 Oars and 60 Swivels."[49] After the interrogation, the prisoners were sent to Crown Point aboard one of the sloops, while Rogers waited for Lieutenant Robert Holmes and his party to return. On June 21 the sloop *Brochette*, commanded by James Riddle, rejoined Grant's fleet after picking up Holmes and his men at Missisquoi Bay. Holmes and his detachment had lost their way and never reached Wigwam Martinique, but the third party of four men successfully delivered Amherst's letter to Murray in Quebec. Grant departed for Crown Point shortly thereafter, because the brig *Duke of Cumberland* was so leaky that had her guns been fired, the vessel would have been "ready to Sink as she has not been Ca[u]lk'd Since she was built."[50]

PREPARATIONS FOR THE CANADIAN INVASION

Amherst's final campaign of 1760, which was to have begun on May 1, suffered a number of delays. On May 9 Amherst complained that "Not a Provincial yet come" and wrote to several colonial governors the next day "to press the march of Troops to Albany."[51] In a letter to Secretary of State Pitt on June 21, he again blamed the lack of provincial troops for the slow start of the campaign: "The Sloth of the Colonies in raising their troops, and sending them to their Rendez-vous, made it impracticable for me to move the Troops on."[52] In reality, the enormous task of transporting military stores and provisions from Albany to Oswego and to Crown Point had as much to do with the slow progress of the campaign as recruitment delays.

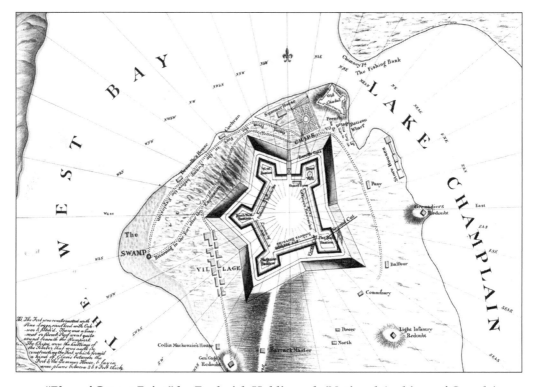

"Plan of Crown Point" by Frederick Haldimand. (National Archives of Canada)

On June 12 Amherst formally notified Lieutenant Colonel William Haviland (brigadier general in America) that he would command the "Troops that are to Assemble at Crown Point...The attack on the Isle au[x] Noix will be Your Care."[53] Meanwhile, Amherst ordered Haviland to "make all the Use You can of the Intermediate Space in finishing the Works at Crown Point, Rebuilding the Barracks at Ticonderoga [damaged by a fire], & Completing the Works at Fort George."[54] He also urged Haviland to use troops "for pressing and Annoying the Enemy" and to employ the vessels in such a manner as to "keep the Enemy in a Continual Alarm."[55]

Most of the provincial regiments arrived at Crown Point during the last two weeks of June. Along the way to Lake Champlain, many of the men wrote of their impressions of the forts. In June Chaplain Samuel MacClintock from Greenland, New Hampshire, described Fort Number Four (Charlestown, New Hampshire) as "a square [ha]ving 3 curtains [walls], one side only piqueted [picketed] with 4 bastions & a 12 pounder in each bastion."[56] Captain Samuel Jenks of Chelsea, Massachusetts, suggested that Fort Edward was "well built, but not well situated…to stand a siege" and Lieutenant Thomas Moody from York, Maine (part of Massachusetts at the time), visited the infamous breastworks and fort at Ticonderoga, "which are prodigious strong [and] a Very strong Fort Built with Stone & Lime."[57] At Crown Point, Moody wrote that the fort "Far surpasses the Idea that I conceived of it," and Chaplain MacClintock suggested that Crown Point was "a very grand plan & w[he]n finished will be perhaps the strongest fortress in the King's domin-[io]ns."[58] A letter published in the *New Hampshire Gazette* noted that Crown Point's western defenses consisted of "a Line of Block Houses and a Breast Work" and described the main fort as "an irregular Pentagon with five Bastions…on about seven Acres of Land; the Wall at the Platform is 40 Feet thick, made of Timber and Earth; a Casem[a]te round the Wall in the inside 20 Foot deep; the Trench round the Wall, which is ma[de] out of a solid Rock is…near 14 Feet deep and of the same width; and the Glacis…made with Stone and Lime, the Foot of it to extend to the Redoubts" and the "old French Fort here, part of which is still standing, was weak and inconsiderable."[59]

During the long wait before the embarkation of the army, provincial troops labored on numerous construction projects. "A 1000 men [were] employed daily at the works on the new Fort," Chaplain MacClintock recorded.[60] Captain Jenks supervised 100 men working in the "King's Garden, which is the finest garden I ever saw in my life, having at least 10 acres [e]nclosed."[61] Detachments of hundreds of men were sent northward along the lake to cut timber and raft the logs to Crown Point. Haviland complained to Amherst that "great delays for want of proper Timber" had slowed the progress on the casemates, but by early August "a good Supply" of timber provided some optimism for the completion of the casemates and bastions—named the "Prince of Wales Bastion," "Princess of Wales Bastion," "Princess Emelia Bastion," "Prince Edward Bastion," and the "Kings Bastion."[62] (Subsequently, four of the five bastions were renamed the West Bastion, Southwest Bastion, Magazine Bastion, and Flag Staff Bastion.)[63] Other troops had the back-breaking task of moving supplies to Crown Point. Lieutenant John Bradbury from present-day York, Maine, was sent to Ticonderoga with 300 troops to load bateaux "with 20 Barrels of provision[s] [each]," for a total of "1800 barrels."[64] The weather during July was far from ideal for heavy labor; the men complained of days that were "very sultry, hot…much hotter" than in New England.[65] In addition, smallpox, the scourge of eighteenth-century armies, spread among the troops, requiring several smallpox hospitals to be built.[66]

As in some of the previous campaigns, most of the women were sent back before the beginning of military operations. At Ticonderoga on June 14 Captain Jenks observed "great numbers of the camp ladys came down from Crown Point on their way to Albany; s[o]m[e] of them interceding to be taken back."[67] A month later Jenks described an altercation between a sutler and his "very fine mistress," traveling in a bateau, in which the merchant "struck her" and "held her under water" after she jumped overboard; Jenks remarked "that I wish it were the fate of all these sort of ladys that follow the army."[68]

Detail of *A North View of Crown Point* by Thomas Davies. The remains of Fort St. Frédéric can be seen in the left foreground and the new fort in the center. (Library of Congress)

While awaiting the launch of the expedition to Canada, officers tried to maintain strict discipline among the troops. Infractions of rules, disparaging language, defiant behavior, and desertion were often handled harshly. On June 12 Amherst instructed Haviland that it "may be absolutely necessary that Examples" be made in cases of desertion and that "the sentence may be immediately Executed."[69] Eight days later, seven soldiers (six regulars) were sentenced to 500 to 1,500 lashes for desertion, but Haviland pardoned them with the caveat that "this is ye last time."[70] Other infractions were dealt with more firmly. Four days after the pardons for the deserters, a provincial soldier was "whipt a 100 lashes at post for disobeying orders & insolent language" and in July another provincial received 50 lashes for telling his sergeant, "dam[m] ye to hell & wishing him there."[71] Provincial diarists noted more than a half-dozen incidents of "insolent language," "mutinous talk," and "Swearing," resulting in punishments ranging from 50 to 900 lashes on the "naked Back with a Cat of Nine tails."[72] Enforcement, however, did not always go smoothly. When a regular was confined by a provincial officer "for abusive language," a riot ensued whereby a mob of regulars "with clubs" freed the prisoner by knocking down the sentries at the guard house.[73] Two or three muskets were fired and a regular was wounded in the melee. Troops from the Rhode Island regiment later recaptured the prisoner. Despite the risk of brutal punishment, transgressions continued. Three men from Captain Jenks' Massachusetts company were found guilty of "writing…orders to the Sutlers" and forging Jenks' name; Jenks ordered the company to witness the punishments of 50 to 250 lashes "to deter any from such vile practises."[74] On August 1 David Holden, the First Sergeant in Captain Leonard Whiting's Massachusetts company, noted that "a follower of the army [sutler] Rec[eive]d 1000 Lashes for Stealing & was Drum[me]d out of

Camp with a Halter about his Neck" with a note pinned on his shirt describing "his Crime."[75] Punishment by lashes was the sentence for cases involving neglect of duty, striking others, and desertion; one Massachusetts provincial soldier received 500 lashes for "[e]nlisting twice & d[e]serting afterwards."[76]

The troops at the Crown Point camp spent their spare time in a variety of ways. Captain Jenks frequently noted the "old custom" of consuming liquor in the evening: "At night we concluded by drinking to wives & sweethearts, which is as constantly observ[e]d as any duty we have in camp."[77] There were restrictions on the availability of liquor, however. On July 22, orders were issued that "No liquor of any sort to be sold to soldiers by sutlers or people after gun firing" and "any soldier found in the [sutlers'] market after that hour will be sent to prison."[78] The very next day a sutler disobeyed orders by selling "his liquors to the soldiers & several of the regulars got drunk"; one of the regulars caused some damage and "was whipt one thousand lashes."[79] Two sutlers had their casks "stove to pieces" and were banished from Crown Point and "if…found" at any post between Albany and Crown Point, "they will be whipped and drummed out."[80]

Other diversions at the Crown Point camp included "swimming," especially during the "Extrem[ely] hot weather" in July, and a whaleboat race between provincial and regular crews.[81] The amount of time devoted to prayer services was reduced compared to earlier campaigns. Because of "very hot" weather on July 6, "the priest chose…to drink wine under a shed" and cancelled his sermon, according to Lieutenant Bradbury.[82] On another Sunday, Captain Jenks "heard a band of music at the commanding officers tent while they were dining," which he described as "very delightful" but inappropriate "on such days of sacred appointment."[83] Sergeant Holden recorded a prayer service held on the parade ground by a provincial chaplain on the evening of July 18, which was "ye first Pra[ye]rs We had had since we Came in Camp" on June 16.[84] The prayer service had followed a duel between two regular officers. Luckily, the men were poor shots: "They made 2 Tr[i]als, but did not wound either."[85]

Despite some distractions, preparations for the 1760 campaign proceeded in an orderly manner. On July 9 Amherst reached Fort Ontario at Oswego, the launching point for his expedition to Montreal. Two weeks later, Sir William Johnson arrived at Oswego with his Indian allies, numbering 1,330 men, women, and children, including 706 warriors who would accompany Amherst's army.[86] "To please the Indians," Amherst allowed them to name the two large warships—the *Onondaga* and *Mohawk*—that were slated to escort the expedition.[87] On the 29th of July, Amherst wrote to Haviland, directing him to embark with his army for Isle aux Noix on August 10. The date would coincide with Amherst's departure from Oswego and was intended to allow a coordinated pincer attack on Montreal—an ambitious plan given the state of communications and logistics during the eighteenth century. Despite the challenges, there was reason for optimism. In June French deserters revealed that troops in Canada were "in utmost Distress for Provisions of all Kinds."[88] By July provincial troops were "all in high Spirits" because they were "certain the Enemy have had no Reinforcement, either Men, Provisions or Ammunition…and have no Way to flee."[89] An Indian, who had been captured near St. Francis with Captain Jacob Cheeksaunkun in 1759 (Captain Quinton Kennedy's party), managed to escape from his captors and made his way to a British post at Oneida Lake on July 21. He reported that French troops at Montreal were "thoroughly convinced of their Inability" to withstand a siege and that Governor Vaudreuil was "determined to make the best Terms in his Power, on the first Approach of our Army."[90]

In the meantime, preparations for the expedition to Isle aux Noix continued at Crown Point. Lieutenant Colonel Thomas Ord of the Royal Artillery reported that 37 cannons, mortars, and howitzers were available for the expedition.[91] In addition, a "Return of Small arms" at Fort Ticonderoga in early June listed 4,000 serviceable "muskets of different Patterns" and 21,000 bayonets.[92] Given the extended period in the camp at Crown Point, extra time was available for target practice, but restrictions were placed on the amount of ammunition and powder expended. In late June Major John Hawks recorded that recruits of "ye regulars to practice with powder and ball at a mark...between the hours of 5 and 8 in the morning," but they were not to exceed "12 rounds per month."[93] On July 6 a provincial officer noted that "the Regulars exercised at Firing of Platoons," and another provincial officer subsequently indicated that his troops had "drawn 6 rounds p[e]r man in order to fire at a mark."[94] On multiple occasions Captain Jenks observed artillerymen "practise Throwing...shells," making "several very good shots."[95] Even with all the firing at Crown Point, Indian raiding parties continued their hit-and-run attacks. About six o'clock in the morning of July 8, a party of Indians attacked the rangers "just by their encampment on the other [east] side of the lake," killing one ranger and wounding six, "4 of them mortally."[96] The rangers "were making a Raft" when the attack occurred and "returned the fire,"

The 80-foot sloop *Boscawen* 1760. (Painting by Ernest Haas)

pursuing their assailants for "Eight Miles."[97] On August 6, Indians captured a regular at the blockhouse located near Bulwagga Bay. He was strip[ped] of his Clothes," but managed to escape and ran back to the blockhouse.[98]

Preparations for the Lake Champlain expedition also involved readying the British fleet. On June 23 Haviland informed Amherst that "the two Small Raddoes and the three prows [row galleys] are fitting to Carry the Artillery Stores, as they are Stronger and better than Batteaus for that Service."[99] A new mast was ordered for the radeau *Ligonier* by Lieutenant Colonel Ord on July 10, and he apprised Haviland that "Eight French Batteaus" would be used in addition to the other vessels to carry artillery stores.[100] Ord also requested 97 bateaux, but many needed substantial repairs, so Haviland ordered "the English Sloop [*Boscawen*] to be Rigged, as she was in pretty good repair, which Col. Ord thinks will Carry all the Powder and. . .Ammunition without taking the Ninety Seven Batteaus."[101] The 90-foot brig *Duke of Cumberland* had already been in service for nearly two months when Captain Jenks observed the brig return from a cruise on July 1: "She is a fine looking vessel & it seem[s] much as if I were at home [in present-day Maine] seeing a brig come in & come to anchor."[102] On July 2 the *Duke of Cumberland* and the recently-rigged *Boscawen* sailed from Ticonderoga to Crown Point, arriving late in the afternoon; but "Just against our Point the Sloop R[a]n aground and about 9 [o] Clock [in the evening] they got her off," wrote Private Lemuel Wood of Boxford, Massachusetts.[103] Two days later the brig began "firing 2 rounds to clear her guns" and subsequently received a complement of "1 Capt., 3 Subs, 5 Serg[ean]ts & 111 Seaman" from the Massachusetts and Rhode Island regiments.[104] While the two larger warships were undergoing their final preparations, the former French sloops served as "advance Guard" boats "stationed down the lake."[105] On August 2 "the brig & sloops. . .sail[e]d on a cruise…to take [a] post at an island 7 miles this side [of] Isle aux Noix."[106]

Prior to the departure of the army, Massachusetts troops temporarily sank their leaky bateaux "to keep them tight" and then "Put masts" into the vessels.[107] On August "8th, 9th, 10th, the army [was] employed chiefly in loading the Beddous [bateaux], sloops & boats," according to Chaplain MacClintoch.[108] "We are all in the greatest hurry and Confusion," Lieutenant Moody wrote on August 9, while "getting in readiness to Embark."[109] Haviland had planned on leaving with his army on August 10, the same day that Amherst had scheduled his departure from Oswego, but delays necessitated a one-day postponement of the embarkation of the Lake Champlain expedition. On the evening of August 10, the troops at Crown Point listened to a sermon by Reverend William Crawford and a speech by Brigadier General Timothy Ruggles of Massachusetts, who commanded the provincial regiments and served as second in command of the expedition. Ruggles admonished his men to do their duty: "We are going against a murderous, cruel, Bloodthirsty Enemy; who ha[s] upwards of a Hundred Years been. . .driving our Neighbors, our Relations, and our Families, from their Possessions. . .with the greatest Barbarities. . . Remember [Fort] WILLIAM HENRY. What Massacres were made there, after a Capitulation, by these inhuman Wretches!"[110] With his comments on Fort William Henry, Ruggles was overcome with emotion and turned to his officers, exhorting them to exert themselves "to the utmost" to "put an End to a long, and Tedious War."[111] Lieutenant Moody remarked that it was "a very Glorious Speech which seem'd to animate us."[112]

ISLE AUX NOIX EXPEDITION

On the morning of August 11, "upon ye S[i]gnal of a Gun from the artillery Park, the General [Drum] Beat" and the men "Struck their Tents" between nine and ten o'clock; following a second discharge of the gun, the troops marched to the boats, carrying their tents.[113] At "half an hour After twelve" Haviland's army departed from Crown Point, but "the wind was very strong against us."[114] Haviland's 3,400-man army* consisted of about 1,600 British regulars (17th Foot, 27th Foot, four companies from the 1st Foot or Royal Regiment, and a detachment of Royal artillerymen) and 1,800 provincial troops (Massachusetts, New Hampshire, and Rhode Island regiments, and six companies of rangers, including one company of Indians).[116] The total number "voted" to be recruited for the Isle aux Noix campaign by colonial legislatures included 5,000 from Massachusetts, 1,000 from Rhode Island, and 800 from New Hampshire.[117]

The army "Embarked in three [double] columns"—one column of regulars, another of Rhode Island and New Hampshire troops, and a third of Massachusetts men—with "the Rangers [in]…front of ye whole," according to Captain Jacob Bayley from a New Hampshire regiment, who also noted that "a large brig and 2 sloops were at Windmill Point at this time."[118] The radeau *Ligonier* was to provide signals to a fleet of "380" boats "of all sizes," and a detachment of the Royal Artillery troops, under Lieutenant Colonel Ord, "followed the columns" in the artillery boats at the rear.[119] The list of vessels that departed on August 11, however, is subject to some inconsistencies in the original diaries of the participants.** About sunset, after a journey of only six to eight miles, a signal was made for the fleet to land on the west shore. Lieutenant Bradbury described the landing site as "a Sandy point," where the army "Lodged on Board ye Battoes," and Lieutenant Moody wrote that the troops "encamp'd by the side of a rocky Precipice where the Rattle Snakes were plenty."[124] The next morning the army departed at sunrise, but due to adverse winds, Haviland reported that "the Raddoes [and the] Sloop w[i]th ammunition [probably the *Boscawen*]…were left behind."[125] After battling the strong winds for hours, the army "Landed at Butt[o]nmold Bay [present-day Vergennes, Vermont] at 3 oclock" in the afternoon and "encamp[ed] on ye Shore."[126] On the following day (August 13), Haviland's fleet of bateaux embarked between eight and nine in the morning, leaving the "Raddoes & Sloops…behind."[127] The men rowed about three miles into a stiff gale before

*The figure of 3,300 troops plus a detachment of Royal artillerymen was used in Thomas Mante's authoritative *The History of the Late War in North-America*, published in 1772. Eyewitnesses apparently overestimated the size of the army. Lieutenant Bradbury recorded 5,433 men and Chaplain MacClintock 5,400 troops in the expeditionary force on August 11, and colonial newspapers reported 5,000-5,600 troops. British records listed a total of 6,212 provincial troops raised for Crown Point and the other northern forts.[115]

**Sergeant David Holden wrote that "the Army S[e]t Sail…[with]One Brig [*Duke of Cumberland*], 4 Sloops [*Boscawen, Musquelongy, Brochette,* and *Esturgeon*], 3 R[a]deau[x] [*Ligonier* and the two smaller radeaux], 3 Prows [row galleys], 2 Large Boats [bay boats], 263 Bateau[x] Large and Small, 41 Whale Boats, [and] 12 Canoes," and Lieutenant Thomas Moody recorded virtually the same diary entry.[120] In his journal written several years later, Major Robert Rogers noted that the fleet embarked with "one brig, three sloops, and four r[a]deau[x]."[121] However, Captain Samuel Jenks, Lieutenant John Bradbury, and Captain Jacob Bayley wrote that the brig and at least two sloops had sailed earlier to take a post at the northern end of the lake, and several additional journal keepers disclosed that Haviland's fleet met the brig and sloops near Isle La Motte on August 15. In addition, on August 13 Haviland "received An Express" from Lieutenant Alexander Grant, reporting "an Engagement" with French vessels in which the "brig & sloops…dro[v]e them back to the island [Isle aux Noix.]."[123]

the crews of six bateaux were ordered to the rear "to help tow" the *Ligonier*, and they "Kept her in tow till 10 o'clock at night," when the bateau crews cast off and rejoined the rest of the army, "Encamp[ed] Near L[i]g[o]nier Bay Harbour on the west Side of the Lake."[128] Just before daybreak, "the Raddoes & Sloops" finally reached the campsite at Ligonier Point.[129] About sunrise the fleet set out once again, but "a prodig[i]ous sea & hard wind [with fierce rain] obliged us to make a harbour on ye north side of…Sc[h]uylers Island," Captain Jenks wrote, but "We have lost 7 rangers by the canoe split[t]ing & 2 of the recruits fell over…[and] several battoes missing."[130] On August 15 "a good gale" propelled Haviland's army to Isle La Motte where the men "encamped" and were ordered "to Clean their Arms & replace the damaged Ammunition."[131] Chaplain MacClintock remarked that at Isle La Motte "we joined our brig & sloop[s] which had been sent down some time before to reconnoitre."[132] On the sixth day of the difficult voyage from Crown Point, the British flotilla departed from Isle La Motte on a note of "pleasant" weather, forming a line "4 miles [long] & [which] made a very beautiful appearance."[133] As the fleet neared Isle aux Noix early on the afternoon of August 16, "the enemy's schooner [*Vigilante*] & reddow [row galley *Grand Diable*] came out to meet us," but after "fir[ing] Several Shots," they were driven back by the British vessels.[134] The radeau *Ligonier*, the two smaller radeaux, and the row galleys were anchored "opposite the Island" and ordered to fire a gun "every five or ten Minutes," while the grenadiers, light infantry, and rangers reconnoitered the east shore in preparation for the army's landing.[135] "With all our battoes abre[a]st," the British and provincial task force "row[e]d right to shore" on the east side of the Richelieu River about a mile and a half south of the fort, disembarking in the afternoon, while "the Ligonier r[a]d[eau] & prows [row galleys] kept a fire on the enemys fort & vessels to favor our landing."[136] The vessels "continued [firing] till night," as the men "threw up breast works."[137]

The fortifications on Isle aux Noix were begun in May 1759 as a defensive outpost in the event of the evacuation of Forts Carillon and St. Frédéric. The small island (four-fifths of a mile long) was heavily fortified to block the passage of British forces and was originally intended as an "essential defensive point" that would be held "to the last," according to Governor Vaudreuil.[138] Intelligence gathered in 1759 by a British scouting party and from three French prisoners revealed that Isle aux Noix was defended by "Fascine Batteries and 70 Pieces of Cannon" and would be difficult to capture because "the Channel on each side is very narrow [about 1,000 feet on the west side and 750 feet on the east side] and both Shores…[were] quite a Swamp."[139] The 1759 fortifications, built under engineer François Fournier, consisted of a mile and a quarter of zigzag entrenchments with three redans (defensive projections from the line) and encompassed nearly two-thirds of the island. Circumstances had changed by 1760, so Vaudreuil instructed the next engineer, Michel Chartier de Lotbinière, who had supervised the construction of Fort Carillon, to complete the fortifications on the island as a post that would only serve to delay a British advance. In 1760 Lotbinière built a second defensive line, about a quarter mile in length, within the first entrenchment on the southern section of the island. He also directed construction of two redoubts (St. Louis and St. Antoine) and a blockhouse, and an abatis on the northern end of the island.[140]

In addition to the entrenchments, the main fort on the southern end of the island contained barracks, storehouses, a chapel, and the commander's house. Sergeant Holden

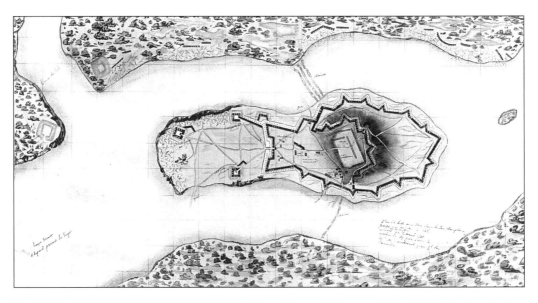

Plan of Isle aux Noix (1760) by Louis Antoine de Bougainville, showing the fortifications on the island and chains stretching across the east and west channels of the river. (National Archives of Canada)

Left: Colonel Louis Antoine de Bougainville, commander of the French fortifications at Isle aux Noix in 1760. (National Archives)

described the works on the island as "a very Strong Fortress," which was "Strongly Pi[ck]eted in all Round," and later Lieutenant Moody noted that the "outside Wall [wa]s built of Timbers and Joists" with 47 embrasures (openings for cannons), while the inside wall was partly constructed of "Timber and Dirt" and "Fascines and Dirt" with 50 embrasures.[141] Although Moody mentioned only 44 cannons at Isle aux Noix, Captain Jenks reported that more than 60 pieces of artillery were found there, and an inventory of the artillery after the surrender of the island listed 77 pieces, including 14 iron swivel guns.[142] While Colonel Louis Antoine de Bougainville, in command at Isle aux Noix in 1760, had sufficient cannons for the defense of the island, he complained that there was "no gunner here who knows how to aim."[143] The 1760 garrison was only about one-half the number of men present a year earlier. According to French authorities, the garrison at Isle aux Noix consisted of "1,650 men including the navy," and French prisoners indicated that "1000 Canadians and nearly 600 Regular Troops" were on the island before the siege began.[144] Although Bougainville had a small naval fleet, the vessels were not considered a match for the British flotilla, so the captains of the vessels were under orders to retreat in the face of the British warships to avoid being cut off from the island. Instead of using their vessels to prevent the passage of the British vessels, the French relied on a defensive boom to block the channels on each side of Isle aux Noix. Captain Jacob Bayley described the boom as "very strong," being constructed by "fasten[ing] 5 logs abreast with iron staples & [chain] links 1 1/2 inches in diameter, the whole anchored every 10 ft" to the bottom of the river with stone slabs; and the "upper side" of the island was "picketed 2 rods into the water & a vast deal of boards thrown" into the channel.[145] (A 1759 French plan to dam the river and flood the shoreline below the fort in order to prevent the erection of British batteries was not successful.)

On August 17, the day following the arrival of the invading task force, the defenses of the fort were tested by the British vessels, resulting in a deadly incident. After receiving a report that the French garrison "had Abandon'd the Island, as they had ceas'd firing," Haviland ordered one of the small radeaux and three row galleys to probe the fort.[146] "About 8 oClock" on the morning of August 17, a radeau was ordered to "Bore Toward the fort" until "fir'd upon," but when the vessel maneuvered "very near the fort" and "tack'd about" to retire, a cannon shot tore "through ye fas[ci]nes [protective barrier of sticks]" on the boat.[147] The cannonball struck "the Men Sitting on the Quart[er] Deck," severing "8 legs from 6 men."[148] A captain of the Royal Artillery Regiment lost both legs and died later that day; amputations were performed on the wounded men, but two more soldiers died shortly thereafter and the survivors were transported to a small island lying three miles to the south of Isle aux Noix. Earlier, Haviland had ordered provincials with the "General Hospital to be landed on an Island two miles in the rear of the Army," which has since been known as Hospital Island.[149]

On August 18, British and provincial troops engaged in several construction projects in preparation for the siege. Lieutenant Bradbury noted that troops "Cleard a Ro[a]d & Built a Bridg[e] almost opposite ye fort"; other provincial troops reported the completion of the first breastwork, gathering 3,500 fascines, and "erecting batter[ie]s" on a "point…opposite the island."[150] Despite persistent rain and an outbreak of "Bloody Flux" (dysentery) in the camp, the men pressed forward.[151] However, by the evening of August 18 "it rained so hard the workmen were Oblidged to quit"; the rain did not stop the French row galley *Grand Diable* from approaching the British position, but the vessel was quickly "beat[en] back by a Raddoe & prow."[152] Grapeshot fired from a French battery killed one ranger and wounded two provincial soldiers in a boat, who had been sounding the east channel near the boom. Late in the morning of August 19, provincial troops struck their tents and marched north along the eastern shoreline "through a Low Sunken Swamp" and "encamped opposite" the fort at "the Point."[153]

The men hurriedly "built a fine breastwork in front & beg[a]n one in the rear," while

French gunners "kept firing cannon," but inaccurate aiming only "Cut of[f] the tops of ye trees."[154] The rain continued on the following day (August 20), as the men labored to construct the breastworks. "About 3 o'clock in the Afternoon," Lieutenant Moody recorded, "the French opened a Battery of four Pieces of Cannon" and "Fir'd about 30 rounds."[155] The firing did little damage, but the next day a cannonball wounded five provincial troops; "2 had each a leg & thigh cut off, 2 each an arm & one his private parts"; another ball "struck a tree," causing a splinter to tear "away a part of a regulars buttocks."[156] Despite the "constant fire" of French "12,9, & six pound shot & langr[a]ge [assorted nails etc. enclosed in a case]" on August 21, Captain Jenks concluded that it was "very remarkable that the enemy have not killd great[er] numbers, when we are so much exposed."[157] During the day, "Our redows [radeaux] fired several shot on them," Jenks noted, but the shelling from the British vessels failed to interrupt the French batteries.[158] Through the exertion of officers and soldiers, the rear breastwork was completed "before sunset" on August 21.[159] Later that night, the first of two false alarms caused a turmoil among British and provincial troops. The men had been ordered on alert for an enemy raid after the sighting of a number of French boats landing on the east side of the river north of the British camp. About midnight the first alarm was sounded and "every Man was Ordered" to the breastwork after a warning emanated from "the 17th Regim[en]t on our left," Chaplain MacClintock noted, whereupon "above 500 guns were precipit[ous]ly fired at & over the breast work by Brigadier Ruggles's first Battalion—none killed or wounded" in the reckless nighttime action, although several shots penetrated the breastwork between the men who "stood three deep."[160] After the second false alarm before daybreak, Lieutenant Bradbury concluded that "through the goodness of god no Damage Done Neither from ye enemy nor from us."[161] The morning of August 22 began on an inauspicious note when "a great number of small arms were fired in Ruggles's Reg't at a stump, thinking it was an Indian."[162] During the remainder of the day, the troops continued building batteries "as fast as possible" and "all hands" were employed bringing the "cannon on the shore."[163]

    The troops at the breastworks worked feverishly on August 23 to complete the batteries, which were "within musket Shot [of the French entrenchment] where I could see ye French walk on ye walls," Lieutenant Bradbury reported.[164] In preparation for the opening of the British batteries, the brig *Duke of Cumberland* was sent "on shore to g[e]t fas[c]ines to hang over her sides, so as to att[a]ck the fort at the same time" as the shore batteries commenced firing.[165] "At 3 o'clock [on August 23] a gun was fired from the Prow [British row galley]," MacClintock recounted, and "Immediately all the drums in the line began to beat a point of war, while the music played for…10 minutes, then another gun fired from one of the Prows—Immediately the batteries opened."[166] (Following the beating of drums and "a band of music," the provincials were to end the ceremony by "singing psalms," according to Captain Jenks.[167]) The three British batteries consisted of "about 30" pieces of artillery, including "4 large Mortars, 2 of 13 and 2 of 10 inches Diameter…a Battery of six Twenty-four Pounders, another of 3 long Twelves, and 3 Royal H[o]witzers, and a…Battery of 7 Royals."[168] The barrage from the British batteries had a devastating effect on the French fort, "which soon made the houses fly to p[i]e[c]es," as well as damaging the magazine, and "cut[ting] away" a mast on a French row galley.[169] The British gunners continued their fire into the night and at midnight a party of provincial soldiers, enticed by a reward offered by Haviland, made their first attempt to sever the French boom, spanning the eastern channel of the island. Captain Jenks complained that he "had no sleep" because of the firing from both the French and British entrenchments during the unsuccessful operation to cut the boom: "the enemy would fire volleys of small arms…then our battery would return it with grape shot & mort[a]rs," leaving the nighttime air filled with "all fire & smok[e]."[170]

During a cold rain on the following day, British artillerymen continued their cannonade, as provincial troops erected another battery farther north. While working on the new battery during the evening, the crew suffered "15 Kill'd and Wounded," including a Massachusetts sergeant, who died after "one hand [was] Shot off and his other Arm Mangled."[171] By this time, the men were "exceedingly Fatigued" and their diary entries reflected the strain; Lieutenant John Frost remarked that it was "the Lord's Day, a most Ter-[ri]bl[e] Day it is. Instead of going to Church, nothing but the Roaring of Cannons and mort[a]rs; the alarms of war and a Cr[y] for human Blood."[172]

On August 24 Haviland ordered Lieutenant Colonel John Darby with a detachment of grenadiers, light infantry, and rangers to haul "A Mortar, two twelve pounders, a Six pounder & two Royals" to a post opposite the northeastern end of Isle aux Noix, in order to destroy the French fleet and "Cut off their Communication" with St. Jean.[173] The deployment of Darby's party was postponed until the next morning due to heavy rain. Darby's men began their mile-long trek along the heavily-wooded eastern shore "at five in the Morning" on August 25 and opened their battery at "about ten" a.m.[174] According to Robert Rogers, who had joined Darby's two regular companies with his five ranger companies (one of Stockbridge Indians), the detachment had drawn only "two light ho[w]itzers and one six-pounder" through the woods.[175] Just as the firing commenced, the captain of the *Grand Diable* "Cut his Cable in Order to get" away, but a west wind "blew

"The Siege of Isle aux Noix in 1760." Redrawn from a map by Chevalier de Johnstone, noting the location of the British batteries on the east shore of the river (b, c) and the path of retreat of the French garrison (g). (National Archives of Canada)

her to the east shore."[176] (Although Haviland and others, including a French official, wrote that the captain of the *Grand Diable* had cut his cable, Rogers and several partici-pants recounted that "the first shot from the six-pounder cut the cable.")[177] A French crew ventured out "in a Row Galley to tow her back," Chaplain MacClintock recalled, but they "were obliged to retreat with considerable loss" because of British fire.[178] The barrage from the light infantry and rangers devastated the *Grand Diable*, shooting "the Captain's head off, and the others [on board] were glad to surrender on any terms."[179]

The other French vessels "weighed anchor" in a frantic attempt to escape, but they ran aground "in turning a point" on the north side of Rivière du Sud.[180] Under orders from Darby, Rogers and his rangers dashed along the eastern shoreline and forded the river before firing on the stranded vessels. The rangers swam to the schooner *Vigilante*, wield-ing "their tomahawks," and captured the vessel.[181] When the action was over, the rangers and light infantry had succeeded in taking the entire French fleet: the schooner *Vigilante*, sloop *Waggon*, row galleys *Grand Diable* and *Petit Diable* (also called tartans), and four small gunboats or jacaubites (named for Louis-Thomas Jacau de Fiedmont), each "carrying an 8-pounder" in the bow.[182] Although no casualties occurred among the rangers or the regulars during the seizure of the French vessels, two privates from provincial regiments were killed, and several were wounded while attempting to complete a battery.[183]

On August 26 Lieutenant Moody complained of another "Rainy Day," which made it "very uncomfortable for our Poor Soldiers," who were engaged in "ha[u]ling Cannon to arm the French Vessels."[184] Haviland ordered the men to place the cannons on the cap-tured French prizes and dispatched crews from the ranks of the provincials to man the vessels. The captured French vessels were then moved near the west shore to prevent French reinforcements from St. Jean from reaching the island. The firing from the French batteries was relatively light on August 26, but the British batteries "fired Very warmly," including shelling from a new battery positioned farther north, which had opened "Just at night."[185]

At "6 o'clock" on the morning of August 27, the French opened their first battery, and soon afterwards all their batteries began firing "briskly," which was quickly matched by the British artillery.[186] Sergeant Holden observed that the "thick foggy morning" was made worse by the "Smoke of the Cannon & b[o]mbs," which "Played very Smartly on Both Sides."[187] The French fire (the "hottest...yet"), combined with a barrage from the British entrenchments, sounded as if "the Heavens & Earth w[ere] Coming together."[188] About two o'clock in the afternoon, a shell from a French battery penetrated an embra-sure in the British entrenchment, detonating an explosion of two barrels of powder and 20 to 30 shells. The "unlucky shot from the enemy," Lieutenant Bradbury wrote, "set our magazine on fire which blew one provincial 40 feet in the air."[189] The French gunners "kept a very smart fire all day" on the British lines until sunset, but the British artillery-men maintained a "Very hard" fire on the French fort into the night.[190] After dark, Havi-land directed Darby's detachment to move their artillery across "to the west Shore to Cut off the Enemy's retreat," but the order came too late.[191]

While on guard duty at "two o'clock" in the morning of August 28, Lieutenant Brad-bury discovered a French deserter, who "gave an account that the French had left the island; at four o'clock [in the morning]...15 or 20 more" deserters arrived at the British camp with "the same account."[192] Major Rogers and Lieutenant Moody both recorded that the French garrison had abandoned Isle aux Noix "about midnight" on August 28, but a French official suggested that Bougainville and his troops had evacuated the fort "on the 27th at 10 o'clock at night."[193] Just before sunrise "the signal of surrender was hoisted by the French" and "Immediately the gr[e]nadiers & light infantry" took possession of the fort.[194] Lieutenant Moody wrote that a French "Capt. And 30 Privates," along with "a great many" sick and wounded were found inside the fort.[195] In addition, "about 60 pieces of cannon & s[o]m[e] mort[a]rs, a great number of shot & shells & 500 barrels of powder & 100 barrels of pork & 200 of flo[u]r & 30 head of cattle" were discovered in the fort.[196] Captain Jenks grumbled that provincial officers and troops were prevented from entering the fort by the regulars: "we have done most…of the fatigue during the siege…[and were] more exposed" to enemy fire, yet "den[ie]d the liberty to go & se[e] what [we] have fought for."[197] The provincials were instead ordered to draw the field pieces from the shore batteries and to load them on the vessels in preparation for the attack on Fort St. Jean. On August 28, the brig *Duke of Cumberland* and sloop *Boscawen* finally "passed by the island, having cut away the French boom."[198]

Aerial view of Isle aux Noix. The island was occupied by troops during the American Revolution and the War of 1812. Fort Lennox was constructed between 1819 and 1829 on the original ruins of the 1759/ 1760 French fort. (Parks Canada)

On the night of August 28/29, Haviland ordered Rogers and a large detachment of rangers to board whaleboats and bateaux and pursue Bougainville's army to Fort St. Jean, about 12 miles to the north. Bougainville's troops had been delayed in reaching the fort after becoming lost in the woods on the western shore the night before. At the break of day on August 29, Rogers and his men "camp[ed] in si[gh]t" of Fort St. Jean, according to Sergeant Samuel Merriman, a Massachusetts soldier who accompanied Rogers' party.[199]

At daylight, Rogers discovered that the fort had "just [been] set on fire," but he succeeded in taking two French prisoners, who revealed that Bougainville had departed from
Fort St. Jean for Montreal "about nine o'clock the night before."[200] The men with Rogers
"cook[ed] some Vittles" and "fortif[ied] the loghouses" near the river in order to protect
their boats.[201] Leaving 200 rangers at Fort St. Jean, Rogers departed with about 400 men,
including two companies of Indians, in an attempt to overtake Bougainville's army.
According to Rogers, he "pursued with such haste" that he caught up to the French rear
guard and "immediately attacked" them, causing the French party to flee to
Bougainville's main army.[202] Rogers chased the French detachment all the way to
Bougainville's encampment. The French party scurried across a river, dismantled the
bridge after them, and stood ready behind "a good breast-work."[203] Two men with Rogers
were killed and one lieutenant wounded in the action, but the rangers "Brought in 17 Prisoners."[204] Recognizing that the "enemy [was] to[o] num[e]rous," Rogers returned with his
men to Fort St. Jean to rejoin Haviland's army.[205]

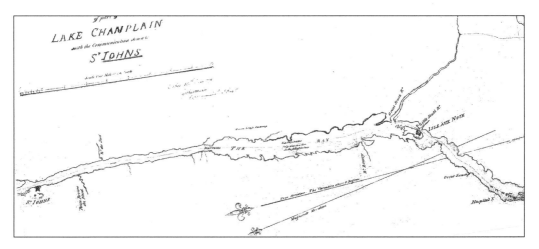

**"Plan of part of Lake Champlain [Richelieu River]," showing the location of Hospital
Island, Isle aux Noix, and "St. Johns" (St. Jean). (National Archives of Canada)**

In the interim, the troops on the eastern shoreline, opposite Isle aux Noix, were packing and loading artillery in the boats during the day of August 29. The next day the men
arose at daybreak, struck their tents a half hour after reveille, and "set of[f] at 10 oclock
a.m." in bateaux, accompanied by the French "Grand Dia[b]l[e] & row galley, & our small
reddows & prows."[206] As Haviland's flotilla approached Fort St. Jean, the men observed
"a great smok[e]" from the fire set by the French and landed at "5 o'clock" in the afternoon, finding Rogers waiting.[207] On August 31 the men carried out orders to build breastworks around their encampment, but later the orders were rescinded to allow time to prepare for a move north against St. Therese. Late in the day Captain Jenks observed that
"one of our sloops" arrived at St. Jean, along with a captured "row galley" and "several
other boats," and he recorded that most of the artillery had been unloaded.[208] That afternoon Lieutenant Bradbury had time to walk around the ruins of Fort St. Jean, noting "10

or 12 chimneys standing," two houses "4 stories high," a "vessel on ye stocks and one burned," ten acres cleared around the fort, and he concluded that the fort was "not very strongly fortified."[209]

On September 1 Haviland's troops struck their tents once again and packed the bateaux for the voyage to Fort St. Therese, about nine miles farther north on the Richelieu River. Lieutenant Holden disclosed that the troops had orders that "none of the Inhabitan[ts] [were to be] Plunder[e]d or Ill Us[e]d, under the penalty of hanging."[210] Holden suggested that the policy was to deter French Canadians from joining the French army. The British troops did not leave St. Jean until about three in the afternoon, arriving at St. Therese at six o'clock in the evening. Some of the provincials at the rear of the flotilla stopped for the night and slept in

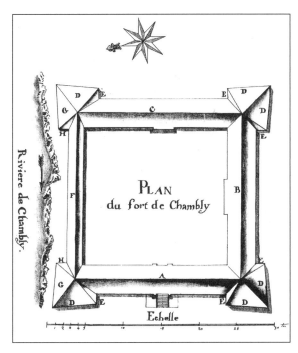

"Plan of Fort Chambly."
(National Archives of Canada)

their bateaux, preferring to navigate the shoals and rapids of the Richelieu River in daylight the next morning. In the meanwhile, Rogers and his rangers had been sent forward to secure oaths of allegiance to the British Crown from the local inhabitants. The British invaders found the fort at St. Therese burned (see page 221)and deserted, but "the Stockad[e] & Pi[c]kets [still] Standing."[211] Lieutenant Bradbury observed a "considerable number of houses standing" and "a very fine field of wheat, peas, oats, and other fruit," but the troops were "not allowed to take anything on pain of death."[212] But the next day several French families traded "Green Peas & other Com[m]odities" for salt pork and sold horses, and also provided "assistance in Drawing our Artillery."[213]

On September 3 some of the provincial troops completed new breastworks at St. Therese, while others began preparations for the siege of Fort Chambly, several miles farther north. Originally constructed of wood in 1665, the fort was rebuilt as a stone fortification between 1709 and 1711. New intelligence on Fort Chambly suggested that the siege would be a short affair. On September 2, ten rangers had pursued 100 French soldiers near the fort, capturing "5 prisoners & kill[ing] one."[214] The prisoners revealed that the garrison "would not surrender the fort without [the British] firing two cannon at them."[215] On the morning of September 4 a detachment under Lieutenant Colonel John Darby, "consisting of about 1,000 men," was ordered by Haviland to capture Fort Chambly.[216] The main detachment hauled "two twelve pounders, one Six & three Royal Mortars" along the west shore, while a second party of 200 men with "one Six pounder [and] one Royal Mortar" proceeded to a position on the east shore.[217] Just before the siege commenced on September 4, Rogers and his rangers joined Darby's forces. After a "Discharge of 2 Cannon & 2 Shells," the 60-man French garrison surrendered.[218]

While Haviland's army pushed north into Canada, the forces under Jeffery Amherst and James Murray advanced on Montreal from the west and east. During the siege of Isle aux Noix, Haviland and his officers received information from French prisoners on the progress of the British forces on the St. Lawrence River. Direct messages also arrived "by express" from Murray on August 26 and September 5.[219] By then, some of Haviland's officers reported "hear[ing] a constant firing of cannon" in the distance.[220]

AMHERST'S CAMPAIGN ON THE ST. LAWRENCE

On August 10 Amherst had departed from Oswego with the largest of the three British armies, consisting of 10,142 regular and provincial troops, accompanied by 706 Indians, the latter force led by Sir William Johnson.[221] After several days of a difficult voyage on the rough waters of Lake Ontario, Amherst's army entered the St. Lawrence River and on August 15 passed Captain Joshua Loring, who had taken the wrong channel with the warships *Onondaga* and *Mohawk*. Later, on the same day, Amherst reached Lieutenant Colonel Frederick Haldimand's advance corps, which had left Oswego four days before the main army. Late on the day of August 16, Amherst's men observed the 10-gun French brig *Outaouaise* on patrol. At "8 in the Morning of the 17th," Colonel George Williamson, the chief artillery officer on the expedition, attacked the French warship with five row galleys, firing 118 rounds into the vessel before the captain surrendered.[222] Amherst immediately renamed the captured vessel the *Williamson*.

Amherst was now about to approach the first substantial obstacle on his journey to Montreal—Fort Lévis. The fort, located on Isle Royale/Isle Orakointon (present-day Chimney Island), was about three miles south of La Présentation (today's Ogdensburg, New York). Fort Lévis was garrisoned by only 300 French troops under Captain Pierre Pouchot, who had been exchanged late in 1759 and assumed command of the fort in March 1760. In the months before the British invasion, Pouchot and his men significantly strengthened the defenses of the fort by enlarging the parapets, fashioning embrasures for the cannons, and constructing a gallery (covered passageway), glacis, ditches, and an abatis.[223] On August 18 Amherst advanced with his army in two columns: one rowed along the south shore under Lieutenant Colonel Haldimand and landed near a point suitable for the erection of a battery, and the second column under Amherst followed the north shore with the largest part of the army, comprised of regulars, provincials, and Sir William Johnson's Indian allies. One of the row galleys with Amherst's troops was sunk by fire from the fort, but Amherst succeeded in establishing a foothold near the fort to erect batteries. The brig *Williamson* (formerly *Outaouaise*), under the command of Lieutenant Patrick Sinclair, anchored within firing range of Fort Lévis. Amherst now had use of two islands north of the fort, Isle à la Cuisse (Spencer Island) and Isle de la Magdelaine (Drummond Island), to establish batteries. On the following day, he viewed the islands with Colonel Williamson and Lieutenant Colonel William Eyre to select locations for the batteries on each island. On the afternoon of August 19, Loring finally arrived with the *Onondaga* and *Mohawk*.

All of the British batteries, including one located at Pointe de Ganataragoin on the

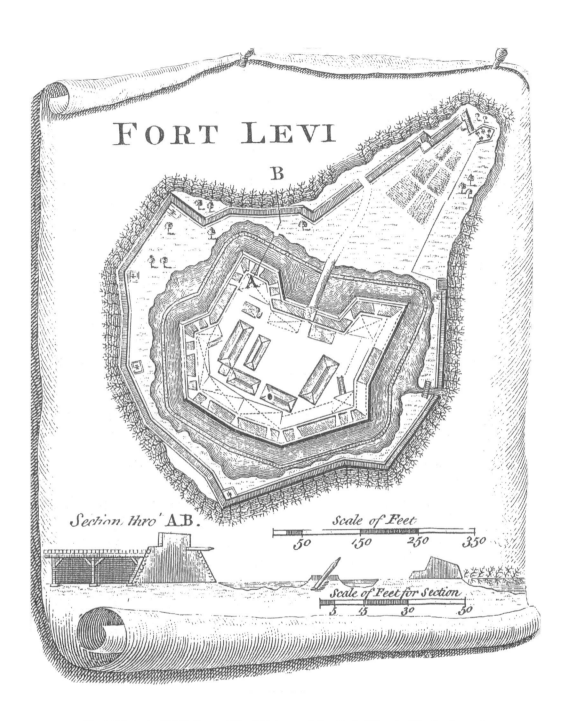

Fort Lévis in 1760. From *The History of the Late War in North-America* by Thomas Mante (1772).

south shore of the river (Chimney Point, New York), opened fire on the fort on August 23. At the same time, Amherst ordered Loring to sail the three warships into firing position of the fort, while the grenadiers and light infantry prepared to make an amphibious assault on the island stronghold. The *Mohawk* arrived near the fort first, but a cannonball from the fort damaged the vessel, requiring the commander, Lieutenant David Phipps, to cut the anchor line, and the vessel drifted downstream. Sinclair's vessel, the *Williamson*, also drifted away after a cannonball severed the anchor cable. The *Onondaga* subsequently ran aground and struck her colors late in the afternoon; the incident immediately fell under a cloud of controversy.*

The British bombardment of the island continued during the night of August 23/24, preventing the French garrison from making repairs. All the British "Mortars continued playing very smart" on the French island during the day of August 24, but return fire from the fort dwindled to "v[e]ry Little."[232] Captain Pouchot later revealed that the French garrison "fired very little in order to conserve the small quantities of powder & shot…left."[233] By then, the British cannonade had "put out of action all the cannon of the bastion facing the island" and "the powder magazine…[lay] extremely exposed."[234] The British continued their barrage all night and increased the shelling the following day. By the afternoon of August 25, Fort Lévis was "nothing more than a shambles of lumber & fascines," according to Pouchot, who complained of "red-hot shot" being fired by British batteries.[235] "About 5 o'clock" on the afternoon of August 25, "the English flag was lifted" on one corner of the fort and "the Drums Beat for a parley."[236] Pouchot dispatched a letter to Amherst, suggesting that "if necessity placed me in the position of surrendering the fort I hope to deserve favorable treatment."[237] Amherst ignored the "if" and sent back his terms of capitulation, demanding a reply in ten minutes. With little choice, Pouchot accepted the terms, and at seven o'clock in the evening the British grenadiers took possession of the fort. During the siege, the British had "21 men killed & 23 wounded," while the French suffered "12 killed…& 35 wounded."[238]

On the day of the surrender Amherst prohibited Johnson's Indian allies from entering the fort, and two weeks later he wrote a letter to Secretary of State Pitt, reporting that "Sir William Johnson has taken unwearied Pains in keeping the Indians in humane

*Amherst suggested that the *Onondaga* "very unwisely tr[i]ed to get farther off & the stream drove her on nearer & aground," allowing heavy fire from the fort to batter the vessel.[224] The damage to the vessel caused it to list "over in the direction of the fort," so that "its gun decks were touching the water."[225] After the *Onondaga* had "struck her colours," a boat was observed "about five o'clock" rowing from the *Onondaga* to the fort; Colonel Williamson's battery "took it to be Capt Loring or Capt [Thomas] Thornton" and "fired at it," but missed.[226] Amherst blamed Loring for the surrender, but Colonel Nathan Whiting wrote that the vessel had struck its "Colours without orders from Commodore Loring & that the Master [Thornton] & two men got into the boat contrary to his orders" and surrendered at the fort.[227] Whiting also noted that Loring had "the calf of the Leg Shot away" during the action.[228] Three days after the incident, Loring wrote a letter to the Admiralty to explain his behavior. He maintained that the crew had lowered the British flag against his wishes and that he had threatened them with a musket if they rowed to the island to surrender. But he relented after a few moments and allowed Thornton and the two sailors to row to Fort Lévis in order to stall the French until help from Amherst could arrive.[229] At six o'clock in the evening a detachment of grenadiers in two whaleboats passed through "Grape Shot and small Arms, as thick as Hail" to reach the *Onondaga* "and hoisted the English Colours."[230] After suffering heavy casualties, the grenadiers were forced below deck and they abandoned the vessel during the night. The next night Amherst sent men in two whaleboats to guard the *Onondaga*. They "found two New Yorkers on board…left drunk tho' one was wounded."[231]

bounds…not a peasant, woman or child has been hurt by them, or a house burnt" since entering Canada.[239] (However, Amherst did note in his journal that the "Indians scratched up the dead bodys and scalped them.")[240] Although Amherst delivered goods from the fort (shirts, combs, knives, deer skins, pieces of canvas, etc.) to the Indians, the majority of Johnson's allies were "exceedingly disappointed at not being permitted to butcher and scalp" the fort's garrison, and they departed for their villages taking 20 British whale-boats.[241] In a letter to Pitt, Johnson admitted that "many of our Indians, thro[ugh] disgust left us, but there still remained a sufficient number" to provide intelligence.[242] The incident underestimates the important role that the Indians played in the ultimate success of Amherst's 1760 campaign. The large number of Iroquois warriors that accompanied Amherst's expedition provided tangible proof of a workable alliance between the British and the Indians, allowing Johnson and the Iroquois emissaries to better make the case for peace with the British army at the Indian villages along the way to Montreal. Before the surrender of Fort Lévis, Johnson had met with delegates from the Canadian "Seven Nations," who "ratified a Treaty with us, whereby they agreed to remain neutr[al] on condition that we…treated them as friends" in the future.[243] By the time Major General Lévis met with the chiefs of the local Indian villages in early September in Montreal to seek their help, news had arrived that an Indian settlement on the St. Lawrence River had made peace with the British, and the chiefs left the conference.[244]

In the five days following the surrender of Fort Lévis, Amherst's troops leveled their batteries, began rebuilding the French fort (renamed Fort William Augustus after the son of King George II), refitted their vessels, raised the scuttled 10-gun French schooner *Iro-*

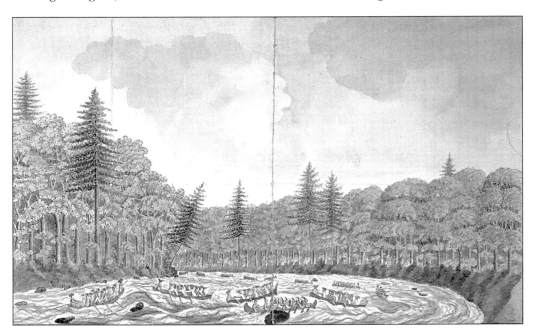

A View of Passage of the Army…down the Rapids of [the] *St. Lawrence River* **1760.**
Watercolor by Thomas Davies. (National Archives of Canada)

quoise (renamed *Anson*), and made final preparations for the voyage to Montreal. On August 31 Amherst and his army embarked for Montreal, traveling 24 miles on the first day, safely passing through the rapids of Long Sault. Over the next two days Amherst covered a total of 38 miles, but on September 3 heavy rain and wind delayed the army for a full day. On September 4 British and provincial troops faced the most treacherous part of the voyage—Cedar Rapids. Amherst had earlier selected 19 French and Canadian crewmen from the French brig *Outaouaise* as pilots for the journey on the river, and ten Canadian Akweasnes also accompanied his bateaux as river guides.[245] The pilots told Amherst that "it was very unusual to find so much water in the River" at that time of year; the British bateaux fleet, organized into a single column, "found it very bad & difficult to pass" the rapids on September 4, despite lightening the vessels "by putting most of the men on Shore" to hike around "the cascades."[246] Private Robert Kirkwood of the 77th Regiment of Foot claimed that his bateau covered "15 miles in 15 minutes" and suggested that if a vessel missed the main channel it would be "dash'd to pieces."[247] Amherst recorded that he lost 84 men, 37 bateaux, 17 whaleboats, one row galley, as well as artillery stores and muskets in passing the rapids.[248] More men were lost passing the rapids than during the siege of Fort Lévis.

On September 5 Amherst's troops were engaged in repairing their boats and remained at their encampment at Isle Perrot. The "Inhabitants of the Island," Amherst wrote, had "abandoned their houses" and "r[a]n into the woods," but the "Oath of Allegiance [was] tendered to them," and they returned to their houses, "as much surprized with their treatment as they were happy."[249] Colonel Nathan Whiting commented that the "General...forbid all plundering," and concluded that "never an Army...did Less damage in m[ar]ching through a Country...though I don't think as a people they deserve it from us, considering the many barbarous inhumanit[ie]s they have committed on our people."[250]

SURRENDER OF NEW FRANCE

On the morning of September 6, Amherst's army "rowed in four Columns" a short distance and landed at "Eleven o'Clock" on the southern side of Montreal at Lachine "without Opposition," except for "some flying Part[ies] [that] r[a]n into Montreal, after a few Shots."[251] The British troops quickly organized their equipment and "marched directly for the Town," arriving about "4 o'Clock...before the Walls" of Montreal.[252] During the night, Amherst's men hauled 14 pieces of artillery to their forward encampment. "About 8 o'Clock" the next morning, Colonel Louis Antoine de Bougainville and an aide rode to one of Amherst's advance posts under a flag of truce with a letter from Governor-General Vaudreuil, proposing "a Suspension of Arms till they should hear from France"; in response, Amherst allowed Vaudreuil only "till Twelve o'Clock" to submit terms of capitulation.[253] (Three years earlier Bougainville had carried a letter to the commander at Fort William Henry from Montcalm, suggesting the surrender of the garrison.) At noon Amherst received a copy of the proposed articles of capitulation from Vaudreuil. Amherst and his officers pored over the proposal, rejecting and altering some of the provisions before returning the document to Vaudreuil. Although the "honors of war" were seemingly granted in article two (and again in five) of the capitulation, Amherst inserted new language in article one, requiring that French troops "lay down their arms, and shall not serve during the present war."[254] Major General François de Lévis dispatched Jean-Guil-laume Plantavit de Lapause de Margon (adjutant general in the Guyenne Regiment) with a letter to Amherst protesting the treatment of French troops. Amherst responded by insisting that he could not "alter...the conditions" of the surrender and informed Lapause that he would not change the provisions because of the "infamous part the troops of France had acted in exciting the savages to perpetrate the most horrid...barbarities."[255] Lévis' objection to the surrender terms not only involved the absence of "honors of war" for the French troops, but the stipulation in the capitulation prohibiting officers from serv-ing again during the war meant that their pay would be cut in half for the remaining years of the war. Lévis appealed to Vaudreuil to allow French troops to retire to nearby Isle Sainte-Hélène and make a final stand for the honor of France, but the governor-general refused the request. In protest, Lévis burned the French regimental flags, rather than turn them over to Amherst.

"An East View of Montreal, in Canada." Drawing by Thomas Patten, engraving by Pierre Charles Canot, 1762. (National Archives of Canada)

In the intervening time, the armies of Murray and Haviland had converged on Mon-treal. After waiting several days in the vicinity of Montreal for Amherst to arrive, Brigadier General James Murray landed with his men "below the town" of Montreal on September 7 on "the eastern extremity of the island."[256] Haviland's army marched as quickly as possible to Montreal after the surrender of Fort Chambly. Even before news of the capitulation reached Haviland's men, their opinion of the inhabitants began to mod-erate. At St. Therese Captain Jenks observed "very pret[t]y children as ever I saw any-where in my life. I can not find in my heart that I could kill such innocents, although they have done it many a time on our frontiers."[257]

The main contingent of troops left St. Therese at noon on September 7, reaching Chambly by four o'clock. On the first leg of the journey to Montreal, "about a hundred"

French wagons were employed to carry "baggage & provisions," prompting Jenks to suggest that it "look[ed] quite strange to see these Can[a]dians helping our army along to destroy the only place of refuge the miserable creatures have left in their country."[258] The British and provincial troops rested at Chambly and then marched toward Montreal "till 12 o'clock at night," camping during an intense rain with "nothing to cover us except the clothes we had on."[259] The men marched again at daybreak, "so much fatigued," Lieutenant Bradbury wrote, that he was "scarce[ly] able to stand."[260] Finally on September 8, the Lake Champlain army "Arrived at Longue[u]il about 12" noon, Brigadier General Haviland recorded.[261]

On the evening of September 7 Amherst's troops were still uncertain about the outcome of the surrender negotiations, so "we Lay on our Arms at Night Expecting the Enemy to Sally out on us."[262] But at daybreak on September 8, Amherst received a letter from Vaudreuil that he had resolved to sign the 55 articles of capitulation as amended. The French governor-general had little choice, given the inadequate resources available to defend Montreal—few cannons and insufficient ammunition, the vulnerability of wooden structures in the city to incendiary shells, the absence of Indian allies, the desertion of the Canadian militia, and a mere 2,132 troops* left to defend the city. The capitulation document was copied and signed by Amherst on the afternoon of September 8, and shortly thereafter Haldimand and his troops marched into Montreal to take possession of the city. Pleased with the result of the campaign, Amherst noted in his journal that "never [have] three Armys setting out from different & very distant Parts from each other jo[i]ned in the Center, as was intended, better than we did."[265] Celebrations were held throughout the colonies upon hearing the news of the conquest of New France. The "whole Town" of Boston "was illuminated" by "two large Bonfires erected with scaffolding 5 stories high" on hills, accompanied by a "great Variety of Fireworks."[266] October 9 was designated by the governor of Massachusetts as a "Day of public and solemn Thanksgiving…on account of the glorious Reduction of all Canada."[267]

Although French officers objected to some of the articles of capitulation, the terms were, in fact, magnanimous in a number of ways. French troops were to be transported back to France, rather than being held as prisoners of war. Amherst was very generous in his treatment of the inhabitants of Canada. On the day following the capitulation, Amherst ordered his troops "not [to] disgrace themselves by the least appearance of inhumanity, or by any unsoldierlike behavior of seeking…plunder: but that, as the Canadians are now…British subjects, they may feel the good effect of his Majesty's protection."[268] Amherst allowed the free exercise of the Catholic religion, recognized the laws and customs of Canada, and ended the feudal-like judicial authority of manorial lords, but allowed land owners in Canada to retain their holdings. His benevolent handling of the Canadians would later be the basis for the liberal Quebec Act of 1774, which would preempt Canadian support for the American Revolution.

---

*Major General Lévis' "return of the troops of the line at Montreal on September 9" listed 2,132 men, but a British return noted 2,413 men (omitting women, children, and servants), which coincided with the number of soldiers later transported to France.[263] Amherst's higher total of 3,508 included Troupes de la Marine.[264]

RETURN TO LAKE CHAMPLAIN

Despite the end of hostilities, Amherst still intended to complete construction of the forts in New York. On September 9 Amherst ordered the provincial regiments under Brigadier General Timothy Ruggles to march the next day to Chambly and then to "proceed to Crown Point to go on with the works."[269] By noon on September 10 the Lake Champlain army departed, bivouacking without tents in the rain at the site of Bougainville's last encampment. The provincial troops arrived at Chambly the following day and marched to St. Therese two days later, where they boarded bateaux for the voyage to Crown Point, stopping first at Isle aux Noix to pick up troops that had been left there two weeks earlier. Four hundred troops, including the sick and wounded, had remained at Isle aux Noix under Colonel John Thomas, who had commanded a Massachusetts regiment during the siege of the island.[270] Lieutenant Moody, who had stayed on the island for the two weeks, was glad to leave "this Terrible Isle," unable to imagine "a Place more Stinking & lo[a]thsome where our Poor Men l[i]e groaning and gasping" for life, afflicted with smallpox and other illnesses.[271] The troops departed from the island on the morning of September 15, rowing in wind and rain, but the next day a favorable wind allowed the men to deploy the sails on the fleet of bateaux, organized in "3 colum[n]s, 2 battoes abreast."[272]

On September 17 the provincial troops returned to Crown Point and resumed working on the fort. Captain George Garth, who had remained at Crown Point in charge of the construction after Haviland's departure on the expedition to Canada, wrote to Amherst in August that "very little Work [had been] done" due to the availability of only 200 men for duty each day, but he pledged to "proceed as soon as possible [on] the Barracks for the Officers & Soldiers."[273] Amherst wrote to Garth from the St. Lawrence River on August 26, approving Garth's decision to make one of the barracks a "Slight framed work" because of the inability to bring "Masons from New York" in time.[274] Amherst suggested that the return of the troops from Montreal would hasten the construction at Crown Point. However, sickness among the returning soldiers compromised the work on the fort. On September 21 Lieutenant Moody reported that it was a "Sickly Time [for] our poor Men," suffering from "Fevers & Fluxes [dysentery]," outbreaks of "spot[t]ed Fever," and smallpox.[275] On September 26 Captain Jenks remarked that the men "die very fast" and "about 1,200" provincials were "unfit for duty & [a] great many more taken sick almost every day," leaving only about one third of the provincials "fit for duty."[276]

The provincial regiments faced a number of problems during the autumn of 1760. An early onset of cold weather made life miserable at the Crown Point camp. Captain Jenks and his fellow officers sat in their cabin most of the day on October 1 with "our feet wrap[ped] in our blankets to keep them warm," and Lieutenant Moody complained of the "extreme cold" on November 9, made worse by "lying in open Tents."[277] On a number of days, Jenks grumbled about the odors emanating from the encampment at Crown Point: "Today [September 23] I walked about 5 or 6 miles, in order to keep out of the smell of ye camp."[278] He also complained of the dearth of sermons performed by the chaplains, who were paid a monthly stipend by the colonial governments. Jenks concluded that it was "a very ill use of that money," especially because the payment came from a "1/8 cut out of every doll[a]r paid to the soldiers."[279] When one of the chaplains from Massachusetts finally preached his next sermon two weeks later, Jenks took out his watch and recorded a sermon of only eight minutes.

Discipline problems again plagued the Crown Point camp, as they had prior to the expedition to Canada. Sergeant Holden recorded numerous cases of disciplinary action involving provincial soldiers, including punishments of "100 Lashes" for deserting from a work party, "100 Lashes for Insolent Language" to an officer, and "500 Lashes for Mutiny & Disobedience of orders."[280] In the latter case, William Matthews from the New Hampshire regiment was to receive a total of 500 lashes, 100 at a time, before five different regular and provincial regiments. Following the lashes, Matthews was to be "Drum[me]d out of the army with a Halter about his neck," but after receiving only "20

A View of the Church of Notre-Dame-de-la Victoire, Quebec City, showing the destruction of Quebec's Lower Town as a result of the British bombardment of 1759. Painting by Dominic Serres 1760. (National Archives of Canada)

odd Lashes," he "was taken with fits" and "Drop[p]ed for Dead," so the punishment was suspended.[281]

There were also some altercations in the camp among the British regular regiments. According to Sergeant Holden, on the night of October 4 "a mighty Discord" erupted when the regulars "Disput[ed] who had the best Right to a woman…till it came to Blo[w]s & their Hubbub Raised…the whole Camp."[282] A month later Captain Jenks jokingly observed that "the camp ladys now, like the swallows, are seeking a more convenient climate to winter in, for they are packing off."[283] Other diversions, such as drinking, proved less contentious. Jenks and his comrades resumed the "custom of drinking to wives & sweethearts" in the evenings.[284] Jenks and others also had time to take notice of the wildlife in the area, including "vast numbers of pigeons flying & geese" and "wol[v]es on the other side [of] the lake."[285]

In the meantime, Amherst had issued a flurry of orders to resolve the unfinished business of the 1760 campaign. On September 12 Amherst ordered Rogers to the west with 200 rangers, where he presided over the surrender of all French posts, including Detroit on December 1. Amherst sent the New York and New Jersey troops to complete repairs on Fort William Augustus (Fort Lévis) before their return to Oswego. On September 22 he provided "our Indians" with a reward of "necessarys and trinkets" and "ordered them home."[286] On October 3 Amherst arrived at Quebec and walked through the city, which he described as "a heap of ruins."[287] A week later he reached Chambly and on October 12 landed at Isle aux Noix. After examining the island's batteries, Amherst concurred with Brigadier Haviland's assessment that it would not be worth manning as a post, so he decided to raze all the works. Amherst ordered that Isle aux Noix "be entirely destroyed" and that all the cannons be collected, as well as the "Shot, Shells, Utensils, Tools…Iron of all kinds, Planks" and anything "that could be used at Crown Point."[288] He directed Colonel Thomas and 200 provincial soldiers to begin the destruction of Isle aux Noix, "immediately," leaving only "two or three of the best Houses, one of which is to be picketed round" for use by "a few Rangers" over the winter.[289] He ordered Lieutenant Pullen, commanding the sloop *Boscawen*, to stop at Isle aux Noix after leaving St. Jean and "be loaded with Artillery, Ammunition, and Stores" before sailing to Crown Point.[290] Amherst also ordered vessels from Crown Point to Isle aux Noix to take the rest of the cargo. The destruction of the fortifications on the island was met with approval by the provincials. Captain Jenks hoped that the "infernal island" would never be inhabited again and "be blot[t]ed out of memory to all ages."[291]

Amherst arrived at Crown Point at daylight on October 15 and immediately "walked around the works," remarking that he "thought more had been done."[292] The next day he ordered "all the men to work [so] that no time may be lost before the winter comes on."[293] Despite his duties managing the army, Amherst had time to examine a beaver dam located on a creek about eight miles to the north, disassembling the structure to "see the contexture of it."[294] On October 23 he sent home 500 provincial troops who were too sick to work. Before leaving Crown Point on October 27, Amherst issued orders to keep the men "constantly Employed till the 20th of November," weather permitting.[295] He departed for Ticonderoga aboard the captured French row galley *Grand Diable*, commenting that it was "not near so good as our Row Galleys."[296] After inspecting Fort Ticonderoga, he boarded a bateau at nine the next morning for the voyage to Fort George, arriving at eleven o'clock at night after battling stiff winds on Lake George. On October 29, Amherst suggested that the enclosed bastion at Fort George, mounting only 15 cannons, was "very small and a bad defense, but [i]t was the shortest, cheapest & best method of finishing" the fort.[297]

Although Fort George continued as a military post, the forts between Fort Edward and Lake George were rapidly decommissioned.* Amherst reached Albany on November 1 and eight days later signed "a Deed of Gift of the Post at Halfwaybrook" to "Mr. Cooper," instructing the "present Garrison to March out," taking the "Ammunition, Artillery & Tools."[303] The initial arrangement to transfer the forts had actually begun with a land grant on February 22, 1760, of "the Small pic[k]eted Post, commonly known by the name Three Mile Post [Fort Williams]" to "James Bradshaw and others" and a second "Small pic[k]eted Post…[called] Forster's Post" to Daniel Prindle, where "One or More Public Houses" were planned.[304]

With the departure of Amherst from Crown Point, Brigadier Haviland supervised construction activity at the fort. Upon his return from Canada in early October, Haviland expressed disappointment in the progress of construction at Crown Point.[305] The animosity toward Haviland by some provincials reappeared upon Amherst's departure in late October. On the day that Amherst left, Captain Jenks remarked that he was apprehensive that Haviland would keep the provincial regiments working until the end of November because "he delights to fatigue ye provincials."[306] Several weeks later Jenks heard that Haviland had fallen "down & broke[n] his leg. Poor man! I am sorry it was his leg."[307]

Despite dwindling manpower due to illnesses and the increasing desertion of the provincial troops, the men "Finished Raising the New Wooden Barra[c]k[s]…120 feet in Length" on the first of November; ten days later Haviland reported that the wooden barracks had been "covered on every side and Roof."[308] On November 10 the garrison at Crown Point took a brief respite from their work and "Fired 21 Cannon in Honour of…King Georges Birthday."[309] (News of the death of King George II on October 25, 1760, did not reach Amherst in New York City until December 31.) The effort to complete the stone barracks at Crown Point was not without risk. On a cold November 15, after a six-inch snowfall the day before, the carpenters were "Shingling the Stone Barra[c]k[s]" when "one of the Stages Broke & three men fell from the Roof."[310] Two days later, Haviland sent a letter to Amherst, suggesting that little had been done at the fort since November 11 due to "Violent rain" followed by "a great fall of Snow with [a] hard frost."[311] On November

*Three weeks before Amherst's inspection of Fort George, Colonel George Williamson described the military posts from Fort George to Fort Edward on his journey to Albany. Williamson suggested that Fort George had only "11 embrasures" (openings for cannons) in the stone bastion, had "several small habitations" outside the fort, and "a stoc[k]ade square enclosing two [?]…barracks."[298] He commented that the road to Fort Edward was "made by laying stems of small trees across & very close to one another…about the thickness of one's thigh…12 or 14 inches" in diameter.[299] The first fort on the military road, about "3 3/4 miles" south of Lake George, was a square stockade (called Fort Williams/Three Mile Post) that could "contain about 30 men"; the Halfway Brook Post, "7 1/2 miles" farther was described as a much larger irregular-shaped stockade with wooden buildings and "Guns & a small Artillery Magazine," built to easily accommodate "100 Men"; the third post (perhaps the Four-Mile Post) was a square-shaped stockade "3 3/4 miles farther," similar in construction to the Three-Mile Post.[300] (Another post, probably Fort Amherst, was only observed by Williamson from a distance.) At Fort Edward, Williamson commented that the land was "well clear'd all round, has [a] Good Garden…but it is com[m]anded from land across the river," where the Royal Blockhouse stood.[301] The island (present-day Rogers Island) encompassed "Storehouses & [a] hospital," and the bridge over the Hudson River consisted of "22 boats serving as Pontoons kept together by a stout Cable."[302]

24 Haviland wrote that the "Stone Barracks" had been finished, but the wooden barracks had no chimneys, so "the Officers must remain in Huts outside of the Fort."[312]

With the weather deteriorating, Massachusetts and Rhode Island troops at Crown Point received orders on November 17 to strike their tents at daybreak on the following morning and march to Fort Ticonderoga. (The New Hampshire regiment was ordered to depart on November 20.) Drawing provisions for eight days, the troops marched to Fort Ticonderoga on November 18 and spent the night and part of the next morning at the fort, "waiting for our bread to be baked" because the oven at Crown Point had collapsed.[313] The majority of provincial troops followed the road to Fort Number Four on their trek home, but others, including Lieutenant Bradbury's unit, boarded bateaux at the Lake George landing on the evening of November 18 and "rowed till 3 o'clock at night."[314] Bradbury and his regiment encamped near Sabbath Day Point, arriving at Fort George late the next morning. The journey home took them nine to fifteen days, because they had to contend with cold, blustery weather for most of the way, as well as periods of snow and rain.

With the end of the 1760 campaign, the remaining troops at Lake Champlain were occupied preparing the vessels for winter quarters. Before leaving Crown Point in October, Amherst informed Lieutenant Alexander Grant that Haviland would order the fleet "Laid up at Ticonderoga" at the end of the navigation season and recommended "Sergeant [William] Friend* of the Royal [Regiment]…to be Aiding and Assisting in any Service" with the vessels over the winter, along with "three or four Seamen" from the fleet.[316] On November 17 Haviland notified Amherst that ice on the lake compelled him "to hurry our Vessels [to] Ticonderoga to Lay them up."[317] Five days later Haviland recorded that the lake was "frozen up" and the brig *Duke of Cumberland*, the schooner *Vigilante*, and the sloops *Musquelongy*, *Boscawen*, and *Esturgeon*, were "put up" at Ticonderoga, but two sloops (*Waggon* and *Brochette*) were "Down the lake yet."[318] On November 24 Haviland confirmed that the "great Radeau [*Ligonier*] and the two Di[ab]les were Caught by the Ice near the sawmills."[319]

Amherst reached New York City on November 26 and received a hero's welcome with cannon salutes and fireworks illuminating the night sky. On December 17 Secretary of State Pitt commissioned Amherst the "Commander in Chief in North America," creating the position of a defacto governor-general of the continent with broad powers.[320] Early in 1761 Pitt shifted his focus to the Caribbean, requiring Amherst to organize expeditions against French possessions.

CONSTRUCTION 1761-1763

The tasks assigned to the 4,000 provincial troops at the Lake George and Lake Champlain forts in 1761 involved a continuation of the construction projects first begun in 1759, as well as hauling artillery and stores from Canada. A prerequisite for the deployment of troops to the forts entailed the preparation of the vessels at the two lakes. Lieutenant

*Sergeant William Friend of the Royal Regiment (1st Foot) was honorably discharged from the army in 1765 and the following year petitioned for a land grant of 200 acres on the west shore of Lake George, encompassing present-day Friends Point in Hague. A fictitious story about Friends Point, involving the near skirmish between two English scouting parties, was first popularized in Henry Marvin's 1853 book, *A Complete History of Lake George*.[315]

Alexander Grant, the commander of the Lake Champlain fleet, wrote to Amherst on April 13 that he was about to "Hove Down" the three small French sloops to "Clean their Bottoms" and would later repair their rigging.[321] Because of a shortage of carpenters and sailors, Grant recommended sinking "the vessels that are not [to be] put in use this season to preserve their Bottoms Except the Brig [*Duke of Cumberland*]...as it's not safe to Sink her," but Amherst replied that it was "better not to Sink any of the vessels" because all the boats would be used.[322] By mid-June the five sloops, the row galley *Petit Diable*, and the radeau *Ligonier* were at Crown Point and the schooner *Vigilante* and row galley *Grand Diable* were "ready at Ticonderoga," but were unable to "move for want of hands."[323] In July the four French sloops, the sloop *Boscawen*, and the two French row galleys were fully employed, carrying thousands of pounds of provisions (flour, beef, pork, peas, oatmeal, etc.) from St. Jean to Crown Point.[324] The *Duke of Cumberland* was not placed in service because Grant planned to "heave [her] down...to caulk her."[325]

The provision boat *Snow Shoe* was in use on Lake George in the late spring of 1761, but the sloop *Halifax* was never placed in service after 1760. (The *Halifax* was listed under the notation "Lost [or] broken Up 1760" on an inventory of lake vessels and as "Lay'd up and Decay'd" on a subsequent "Return" of vessels.)[326] In July "all the Stores...in the Storehouse at Fort George belonging to...the Earl of Halifax" were sent onboard the *Snow Shoe* to Ticonderoga.[327] Captain John Wrightson, the commander at Fort Ticonderoga, wrote to Amherst on June 23 that the radeau *Invincible*, which had been "lying at the landing" for nearly two years "buried in Mud," was "forced out of her bed and carr[i]ed Almost to the Little falls" by a "Strong squal[l]."[328] Wrightson recommended repairing the radeau and "a large French Boat at the Landing"; Amherst agreed, suggesting that the vessels "both [would] be Useful in taking the Artillery & Stores over the Lake."[329] Twelve days later Wrightson reported that the radeau was repaired and in very good condition, but the timber of the French vessel was too rotten to bother repairing. (The "large French Boat" may have been one of the two sloops taken from Fort William Henry by Montcalm's men in August 1757.) In late July the "Artillery and Stores" from St. Jean were placed on the *Invincible* at the northern Lake George landing because Wrightson considered the *Snow Shoe* "more convenient for carrying the troops" on a voyage to the southern end of the lake.[330]

On January 7, 1761, Amherst had written to Pitt that he "thought it would be proper" to finish the forts, "and that the Provincials should furnish men for the Service."[331] In 1761 Amherst raised 2,000 troops from Connecticut, 1,637 from Massachusetts, and 438 from New Hampshire for the work at the forts in the Champlain Valley.[332] Even though the campaign against New France had ended, the provincial troops recruited in 1761 represented about two-thirds of the number that had been present a year earlier at Lake Champlain. The majority of construction in 1761 occurred at Crown Point, Amherst's most important project. The men struggled to haul timber and stones for the ongoing work on the bastions, barracks, redoubts, and firing platforms. They also worked to mount the artillery, ranging from 6-pound to 18-pound iron cannons. Although less construction had been scheduled for Fort Ticonderoga, a number of projects were undertaken: walls were rebuilt, "the Barracks in the Redoubt [was] Lin[e]d with Bricks," the foundations repaired, "a Sink [built] that completely conv[e]ys the Water from the interior Parts of the Fort," "a brew House & Smith Forge" were finished, and "3874 Boards and 473 Rafters" were cut at the sawmill and sent to Crown Point.[333] In a letter to Amherst, Wrightson maintained that everything would have been completed at Ticonderoga "had not Col. Haviland Call[ed] all the Masons and Provincials to Crown Point."[334] Fort Ticonderoga also received a number of cannons (four 6-pounders, four 9-pounders, four 12-pounders, and two 18-pounders) "with their standing Iron Trunk Carriages."[335] Similarly, the garrison at Fort George was ordered "to Mount on the Platforms" 6-, 9-, and 12-pound iron cannons.[336]

Near the close of the 1761 season, the row galley *Grand Diable*, fully loaded with 150 barrels of flour, sank at Crown Point. During the evening of October 22, the vessel was "dr[iv]en from her anchor" by high winds and enormous waves, which resulted in "water Dashing in at the row Ports [which] fill'd [the vessel] in [a] few minutes & Sunk" it.[337] "The Master [Mr. Ward]" of the *Grand Diable* later told Lieutenant Alexander Grant that the accident occurred as a result of the boat "being so Deeply Loaded" with cargo; although the barrels of flour were salvaged, Grant reported that he could not raise the vessel* itself because it was "so Badly put together" that it would fall apart, so he decided to "Save as much of her planks and timbers" as possible.[340] With the sinking of the *Grand Diable*, the *Petit Diable* was employed in transporting provisions to Crown Point from Ticonderoga.

Amherst's main energies in 1761 and 1762 were devoted to the management of expeditions to the Caribbean and elsewhere. Dominica was taken in 1761 and the uprising of the Cherokees in the Carolinas quelled. In 1762 British forces succeeded in capturing Martinique, St. Lucia, Grenada, the Grenadines, and St. Vincent. Following a Franco-Spanish alliance, Britain declared war on Spain on January 4, 1762, and British and provincial troops captured Havana in August, after a long, deadly siege. In June 1762 French troops landed and occupied St. John's, Newfoundland, requiring Amherst to dispatch his brother William with 1,500 troops to retake the island. On September 18, only five days after the British had landed, the French surrendered to Lieutenant Colonel William Amherst.

In 1762 Jeffery Amherst continued building the massive fort at Crown Point, raising 3,559 provincial troops from Massachusetts, Connecticut, and New Hampshire for the task. After an eleven-day march, Ebenezer Dibble, an ensign in Colonel Nathan Whiting's Second Connecticut Regiment, arrived at Lake George on June 7 and six days later reached Crown Point. His diary reflects the routine work that had occupied provincial soldier-laborers over the previous three years at Crown Point, including lugging stones and working with "329 men…in the Kings" and "Prin[c]es" bastions.[341] Chaplain Henry True from Hampstead, New Hampshire, reached Crown Point on July 10 and, on the following afternoon, preached before a gathering of "between 2 and 3 thousand," who "looked

---

*In 1909 Fred Nadeau raised the wreckage of a 72-foot-long vessel near the Crown Point ferry slip. The wreck, probably the row galley *Grand Diable*, was subsequently moved to the parade ground inside the fortress and accidently burned in a grass fire in 1926.[338] The abandoned radeau *Ligonier* may have been confused with the wreckage of the *Grand Diable*. On April 15, 1771, Captain Gavin Cochrane sent a letter to Lieutenant General Thomas Gage, the commander in chief in North America, that "the great floating Battery [*Ligonier*], built by [Major Thomas] Ord, which besides cannon used to carry 2000 Barrels of provisions, & for near…ten years has la[i]n near the Gr[e]nadier Redoubt full of Water & deep sunk in the mud (it is called the Grand Diable) [sic] has of late taken several trips [on its own], full of Water as it is; first over to Chimney Point, and from thence two or three Miles to the Northward…the next intelligence I had of it was that it had come back & gone up the bay at the back of this Fort & was lying at the head of it."[339] If the vessel could be moved, Cochrane suggested that he could use it as a breakwater to protect the boats at the fort from north winds.

Aerial view of the British fort at the Crown Point State Historic Site.
(Photo by the author)

very solemn."[342] Reverend True remained at Crown Point until October 4, occupying his time praying with the men and visiting the sick in the hospitals. Although True implied that illness was prevalent at Crown Point, Colonel Nathan Whiting wrote to his wife on September 4 that "we are very healthy; I have not Lost any of my Company & two only of the Regiment," adding that he had "a Little Garden" and chickens and a cow.[343]

The garrison at Crown Point was once again supplied by the fleet of vessels commanded by Lieutenant Grant. The sloops *Boscawen*, *Brochette*, *Esturgeon*, *Musquelongy*, and *Waggon* and schooner *Vigilante* had their cannons removed and were listed as "fitted for Carrying Provisions" on the British roster for 1762; the brig *Duke of Cumberland* was recorded as "heave[d] down her Bottom overhauled."[344]

In September Colonel William Eyre was sent by Amherst to assess the progress of the work around Crown Point. On September 29 he wrote to Amherst that the parapets at Crown Point would be completed in approximately ten days, the glacis and scarp were "very forward," the three redoubts were nearly finished, and he concluded that the majority of work was excellent.[345] Eyre suggested that "Masons can be employ'd" most of the winter laying a floor of flat stones and masonry in the casemates.[346] In his letter to Amherst, Eyre pleaded for "leave to go home to Settle my private Affairs that are going to ruin."[347] However, he did not obtain a leave until 1764. Ironically, after surviving the Battle of Lake George in 1755, the first French assault on Fort William Henry in March

1757, the 1758 Battle of Carillon, and the campaigns of 1759 and 1760, Eyre died as a result of an accident. On his voyage home in 1765, Eyre drowned when his ship sank just before reaching the English coastline.

On November 15, 1762, Ensign Dibble and most of the provincial soldiers began their long trip home. However, several hundred provincial troops remained at the forts over the winter. On November 26, 1762, a cessation of arms was ordered by King George III, after an agreement on the preliminary articles of peace had been signed by representatives of Britain, France, and Spain. The King's proclamation ordering the cessation of arms did not arrive in New York City until January 1763. The formal treaty (Treaty of Paris) was signed in Paris on February 10, 1763, ending the Seven Years' War.

Even though the war was over, six provincial companies from Massachusetts, Connecticut, and New Hampshire were stationed at Crown Point during the summer of 1763.[348] Amherst wrote to Lieutenant Alexander Grant on April 24, approving his plan to have the vessels on Lake Champlain "in Readiness by the time the Lake becomes passable."[349] On August 6 Grant informed Amherst that he could not "muster one [s]entry over the four vessels...dock'd" at Ticonderoga, as a result of "the Great Desertion" of provincials and the inability of Captain John Ormsby at Ticonderoga or Lieutenant Colonel Robert Elliot at Crown Point to "spare a man."[350] Grant suggested that he had taken "all the precautions in my power by S[i]nking the vessels as far as Consisting [possible]," leaving the decks above water "and mounting some Guns & Swivels on them."[351]

CONSEQUENCES OF PEACE

With the end of the war, Amherst was anxious to return home. But hostilities in May 1763 with Native Americans ("Pontiac's War") on the western frontier delayed his departure. The Indians were disgruntled over the failure of Great Britain to honor commitments and treaties, the Crown's unwillingness to restrict English colonists from lands assigned to them, the lack of compensation for Indian lands used for military purposes, and the reduction in trade goods (particularly ammunition and rum). [352] Sir William Johnson argued for the continuation of generous gifts to the Indians, but Amherst reduced the outlays, largely based on budgetary constraints and his own lingering animosity toward Indians. Johnson rightly concluded that providing gifts to the Indians was much cheaper than maintaining large detachments of regular troops on the frontier. British troops were successful in putting down the uprising and strengthening their grip over the western territories. The final peace treaties with the Indians were signed in September and November 1764. On November 17, 1763, before the end of the hostilities with the Indians, Amherst departed for England aboard the sloop-of-war *Weasel*, with "no thought of returning to America."[353] During the American Revolution, Amherst twice refused a request of King George III to return to America and take charge of the British army.

The end of the war left Great Britain with all of Canada and France's territories east of the Mississippi River, but the consequences of peace would sow the seeds of discontent with the English colonists. The British Proclamation of 1763, meant to alleviate friction with the Indians, prevented colonial governors from making land grants beyond the sources of rivers flowing into the Atlantic Ocean, thus prohibiting English settlements west of the Appalachian Mountains. But the colonists, who had fought side-by-side with the British, were understandably irritated by a policy that would shut them out of the western territories. The attempt by British authorities to placate the Indians backfired by creating conditions that led to the revolt of the colonists, which would eventually diminish the power of Native Americans. The alliance of some Indian nations with Great Britain during the American Revolution sealed their fate. After the war, Americans quickly pushed westward with little regard for the native population.

The doubling of Great Britain's national debt, largely the consequence of the Seven Years' War, along with the cost of supporting thousands of British troops in America, resulted in proposals in England to raise taxes in the colonies. But the call for revenue came at a time when Americans no longer needed the British army for protection from France. In addition, the French and Indian War helped nurture an American identity and provided young men with the military experience and confidence that could be tapped for a corps of officers during the American Revolution. Americans would be less intimidated by the British army after observing the incompetence of many officers, particularly during the 1758 campaign against Fort Carillon. The contemptuousness with which provincials were treated by regular officers during the war bred a disaffection with Britain. In short, the war created the circumstances that directly led to the independence of the 13 colonies.

With the end of the French and Indian War, peace had finally arrived in the Champlain Valley, after more than a century of raids and battles. But in a few short years, the lakes would again be engulfed in war.

10. Epilogue: Forts Revisited

A S A CONSEQUENCE OF THE FRENCH AND INDIAN WAR, the forts and battle-fields of Lake George and Lake Champlain became places of considerable interest to both American and British travelers. Following the American Revolution, the ruins of the forts often evoked powerful feelings in visitors to the lakes. Nineteenth-century travel guides chronicled the fierce battles at the lakes and described the remains of the forts and sites connected to the wars. With the publication of James Fenimore Cooper's *The Last of the Mohicans* in 1826, public attention was drawn to the French and Indian War. Fifty-eight years later, Francis Parkman's *Montcalm and Wolfe* revived interest in the war between Britain and France in North America.

Some of the earliest descriptions of the forts were written shortly after the war had ended. In 1765 Lord Adam Gordon, a colonel in the 66th Regiment and a member of Parliament, made a grand tour of the northern sites of the French and Indian War, providing detailed descriptions of the fortifications. He characterized Fort Frederick in Albany as "an old Stone Fort…and a Stockade, also a large Hospital, Barracks and Store houses…but being built of Wood, and in a hurry, they are like every public Work in America—going fast to ruin."[1] Gordon visited Fort Stanwix, suggesting that the log work was "going to ruin so fast" that it would be "all down" in three years.[2] He found Fort Niagara's stock-ade "totally gone" and the rest of the works in need of constant repair; Gordon described Fort William Augustus (formerly Fort Lévis) as "Mouldering" and not worth repairing.[3]

After stays at Quebec City and Montreal, Gordon entered the Richelieu River, noting that the works at Isle aux Noix were crumbling and that the island had been rented to a farmer. At Crown Point he suggested that the English fort was "built in a most masterly manner. It has five Bastions, Mounts 105 Guns, and has Casemates for 4000 Men," but the "Wood Work is beginning to give" and "Scarce any Guns…[were actually] Mounted"; the ditch and glacis were unfinished, "nor any out Work of any Sort [finished], except three fortified redoubts with Cannon."[4] Gordon also noted fine stone barracks for both soldiers and officers, but they were incomplete.

Lord Gordon next examined Fort Ticonderoga, concluding that the works were "ruin-ous," but Montcalm's "famous Lines…were immensely strong, having three or four Bat-teries, all five Logs high."[5] He also observed the redoubt (Lotbinière) overlooking the wharf, a blockhouse near the sawmills on the La Chute River, and another blockhouse at the northern Lake George landing.

At Fort George, Gordon described two forts: "a Small Stockade Fort, tumbling down and not ten[a]ble" near the lake and a "little above this (and now Called Fort George) we have a Complet[e] Bastion built of Stone, the Casemates of Wood; It mounts ten Guns."[6] About 14 miles farther south he described Fort Edward as a "Log Work, all in ruin, there are about 24 Guns, most of which are falling into the Casemates."[7] A blockhouse (Royal Blockhouse) commanded the fort and Rogers Island was still clear of trees.

Two years after Gordon's trek, Francis Grant, son of Sir Francis Grant (Lord Cullen), made the identical journey to the northern fortifications and other prominent sites of the French and Indian War. Stopping at St. Jean on the Richelieu River, Grant noted that the fort was "abandoned and burned," but "a few houses and new Settlements" were present.[8] Reaching Crown Point on July 17, 1767, Grant wrote a description similar to that of Gordon in 1765. Grant added that the English fortress was "now going fast to decay" and "no part of [Fort St. Frédéric]…remains standing."[9] He observed several houses at Crown Point that were inhabited by sutlers and traders. The next day Grant inspected Fort Ticonderoga, which he characterized as "a square, defended by two ravelins" with "a strong redoubt [Lotbinière] for the defense of the shipping, which are laid up here, consisting of a large Brigantine which mounted 20 guns, two Schooners, two Sloops, and some small craft; also a Sloop constantly employed in the summer season between this place and St. John's [St. Jean]."[10] The brig was the *Duke of Cumberland*; one of the vessels identified as a schooner was the *Vigilante*; one sloop was the *Boscawen,* and the other, either the *Brochette*, *Esturgeon*, or *Waggon*. The sloop still in service in 1767 was the *Musquelongy*, which had carried William Gilliland's goods* from Ticonderoga to Crown Point a year earlier.[12] Grant also provided one of the most detailed accounts of the 1758 French breastwork at this time: "These lines still remain entire, and are very strong. They extend all the way from the river [La Chute River] to…Lake [Champlain], about 2 miles in length…built of large round logs of wood, and are about 8 feet thick at [the] bottom, narrowing to the breadth of one log at the top. These logs are very large, and at angles morticed into one another; the lines are about [a] man['s] height."[13]

At the northern landing on Lake George, Grant observed "a Block House in which Lieut. Stoughton,** who has a grant of land round it, now lives."[15] At five in the morning Grant embarked for Fort George aboard a bateau, stopping at Samuel Adams' tavern at Sabbath Day Point before arriving at the southern landing on Lake George late in the day. The stockaded fort near the lake had apparently deteriorated to the point that Grant remarked that "there is no fortification except a redoubt mounting 12 guns, about 200 yards from the shore, and some barracks."[16] By 1767 the garrison at Fort George had been reduced to a half company of soldiers.[17] The next day Grant rode on horseback to Fort Edward, observing Bloody Pond along the way. At Fort Edward, Grant noted "the Hospital, the buildings of which still remain" on the "opposite shore to the Fort," apparently referring to Rogers Island.[18] Fort Edward had been abandoned by the British a year earlier and the stores transferred to Crown Point.[19]

*William Gilliland began a settlement (present-day Willsboro, New York) along the Boquet River in 1765. Gilliland's cattle had been carried from Fort George to the northern Lake George landing aboard the *Snow Shoe*, the only war-era vessel still in service on Lake George during this period.[11]

**John Stoughton, a former provincial officer from East Windsor, Connecticut, had served for three years under Phineas Lyman. Stoughton and his two brothers later formed a partnership with Samuel Deall to develop a lumber and trade business in Ticonderoga. The business alliance ended with the drowning of John Stoughton in Lake George when his schooner sank on November 25, 1767. "Three wagon loads of goods" were lost in the disaster, but "one horse, six cows and five sheep were saved."[14]

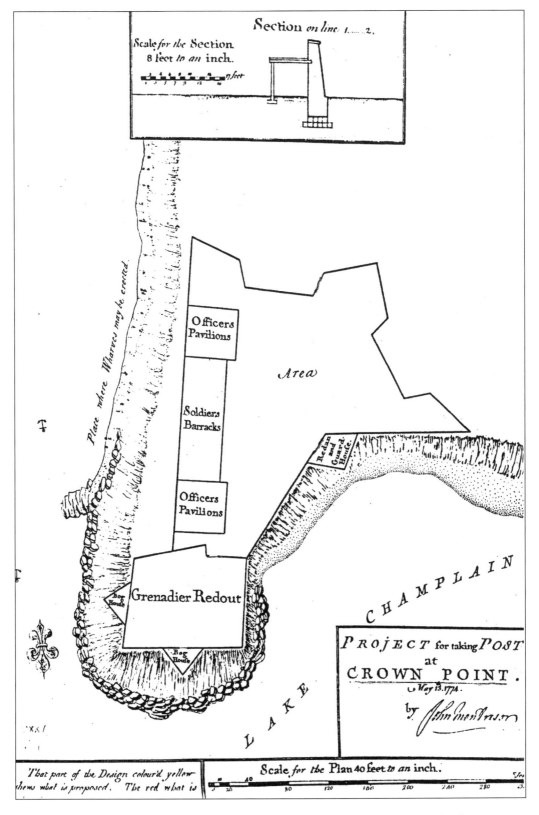

Section on line 1...2.

Scale for the Section
8 feet to an inch.

Place where Wharves may be erected

Officers Pavilions

Soldiers Barracks

Officers Pavilions

Redan and Guard House

Grenadier Redout

Area

LAKE CHAMPLAIN

PROJECT for taking POST at CROWN POINT.
May 13. 1774.

by John Montresor

That part of the Design colour'd yellow shews what is proposed. The red what is

Scale for the Plan 40 feet to an inch.

Plans for an enlargement of the Grenadier Redoubt at Crown Point by
Captain-Lieutenant John Montresor. (Crown Collection, New York State Library)

A massive fire at Crown Point, accidently started in the Soldiers' Barracks by "two... Soldiers Wives boiling soap" on April 21, 1773, led to an explosion of 100 barrels of powder in the adjacent Magazine Bastion which substantially destroyed the fort.[20] On October 6, 1773, Major General Frederick Haldimand, acting commander in chief of British forces in America, wrote to William Legge, the secretary for the American colonies, that Crown Point had been abandoned and that Fort Ticonderoga would be reinforced, but Haldimand warned that Ticonderoga was "in a most ruinous condition," requiring "considerable repairs."[21] The following spring Haldimand dispatched Captain-Lieutenant John Montresor, an engineer with considerable experience during the French and Indian War and the son of Colonel James Montresor, to inspect the forts at Ticonderoga and Crown Point and to make recommendations. On May 13, 1774, Montresor reported that Fort Ticonderoga was in a "ruinous" condition and Crown Point was "an amazing useless Mass of Earth."[22] Montresor proposed an enlargement of the Grenadier Redoubt at the latter fort (present site of the Champlain monument) to serve as the main fortification at Crown Point. Following Haldimand's recommendation of Montresor's plan to Legge, Lieutenant General Thomas Gage, the British commander in chief in North America, endorsed the project in a letter to Legge but added repairs at Ticonderoga to the plan. On November 2, 1774, Legge approved the revival of the posts at Crown Point and Ticonderoga, but it was too late in the season to initiate any construction. In early May 1775, Gage ordered the 7th Regiment of Foot to Crown Point, but before British troops could reach Lake Champlain, the forts were taken by the Americans.

THE FORTS DURING THE AMERICAN REVOLUTION

By 1775 a collision between Great Britain and her American colonies seemed inevitable. On March 29, 1775, John Brown of Pittsfield, Massachusetts, advised the Boston Committee of Correspondence to seize Fort Ticonderoga "should hostilities be committed by the King's Troops."[23] Three weeks after the first shots were fired at Lexington, the Americans captured the fort. During the early morning hours of May 10, 1775, Colonel Ethan Allen, along with Captain Benedict Arnold, crossed Lake Champlain from Hands Cove (present-day Shoreham, Vermont) with 83 men and seized Fort Ticonderoga. Late the following day the insurgents took control of Fort George from a 65-year-old retired British captain living on half-pay in a nearby cottage. On May 12 Colonel Seth Warner captured Crown Point with a detachment of Green Mountain Boys. The fort was occupied at the time by only nine men and ten women and children. The raids yielded 86 cannons at Fort Ticonderoga and 111 at Crown Point, although many of the pieces were unusable.[24] In December 1775 Colonel Henry Knox began his herculean trek from Ticonderoga to Boston, hauling 59 cannons, mortars, and howitzers.

During the Revolutionary War the forts witnessed renewed activity. Many soldiers recorded descriptions of the forts in their journals, but oftentimes they varied considerably. In September 1775 Captain Henry Livingston of the Third New York Regiment wrote that Fort George was "much out of repair altho still defensible, being built mostly of stone" with "a few wretched Hovels that were formerly used as Barracks"; but two months later Aaron Barlow, a sergeant in the Fifth Connecticut Regiment, noted that he had "lodged this night in the Barracks" at Fort George.[25] The following spring Charles

Carroll of Maryland, one of the emissaries dispatched to Canada with 70-year-old Benjamin Franklin, stayed at Abraham Wing's inn at Queensbury. Carroll mentioned that "the ruins only of Fort Edward remain."[26] On the afternoon of April 18, 1776, Carroll reached Lake George, finding Fort George "in as ruinous condition as Fort Edward, it is a small bastion, faced with stone" with "one barrack, which occupied almost the whole space between the walls."[27] Eleven days earlier, Chaplain Ammi R. Robbins had described Fort George as a "small stone fort with convenient brick barracks in the midst, containing six rooms" which could accommodate "several regiments"; on a subsequent evening Robbins "prayed and sung at night in the large new barrack; great numbers attended."[28]

After a two-day voyage through the ice-choked waters of Lake George aboard an open bateau, Carroll and his party arrived at the northern landing on the lake on April 20, 1776. Carroll had the same opinion of Fort Ticonderoga as of Fort George—"in a ruinous condition" and only "a few pieces of cannon mounted on one bastion," but mentioned that the ramparts were "faced with stone."[29] At the old French lines he found that the "trunks of the trees remain to this day piled up, but they were fast going to decay."[30] Chaplain Robbins also viewed the French lines in 1776, observing "many holes where the dead were flung in, and numbers of human bones—thigh, arms, etc.—above ground. Oh, the horrors of war."[31] Although Carroll and others found Ticonderoga in a ruinous condition, others, such as Sergeant Aaron Barlow, referred to the fortification as "a very strong beautiful fort," and Reverend William Emerson wrote that it had "a Number of very fine Barracks…of Stone, that makes as good an Appearance at a Distance, as Harvard College."[32]

After a few days at Ticonderoga, Carroll and his party rowed northward to Crown Point, arriving on the afternoon of April 24, 1776. Carroll described the devastation caused by the fire and explosion of 1773, which "thr[e]w down the barracks—at least the upper stories" and shook the earth "as if there had been an earthquake."[33] Carroll commented that the "wood-work of the barracks wa[s] consumed by fire, the stone work of the first stories might be easily repaired."[34] Despite the fire damage, Sergeant Barlow thought that the barracks were "very beautiful, three in number, three stories high," but the "wooden work is consumed by fire. The stone work is all good and strong"; however, Barnabas Deane, another eyewitness, called Crown Point "one heap of rubbish."[35]

Following the American retreat from Canada in June 1776, the posts on Lake Champlain were strengthened in anticipation of a British invasion. Initially, an attempt was made to patch up Crown Point, including procuring "timber to repair the Stone Barracks," and the chief engineer, Colonel Jeduthan Baldwin, "Laid out Som[e] works on Chimn[e]y point."[36] However, a council of officers, meeting in early July 1776, resolved to abandon Crown Point because the fort was beyond repair. Major General Horatio Gates, the field commander of the Northern Army, wrote that the "ramparts are tumbled down, the casemates are fallen in, the barracks burnt and the whole a perfect ruin, that it would take fives times the men of our army, for several summers, to put it in defensible repair."[37] Despite opposition to the withdrawal by 21 field officers, Crown Point was evacuated in July, except for one Pennsylvania regiment left to man a redoubt on the shore of the lake. When British warships arrived at Crown Point on October 13, 1776, the Americans "set the place in flame[s]" and retreated to Ticonderoga.[38]

The most substantial commitment of manpower by the Americans at Lake Champlain in 1776 was devoted to a new fort on the eastern shore opposite Fort Ticonderoga, named Mount Independence on July 28, 1776. Under the direction of Jeduthan Baldwin, the four-and-a-half acre site would eventually encompass a star-shaped stockaded fort, redoubts, several batteries, and storehouses. New batteries and redoubts were also constructed at Fort Ticonderoga. In late August Baldwin "laid out a Redoubt on the N.W. side...at the old French lines."[39] Fourteen cannons were deployed at the lines and a total of 24 pieces of artillery were mounted at five redoubts (Jersey, Sandy, Oblong, Circular, and Stone Redoubts), but only a few 12-pounders and 9-pounders were mounted inside the fort.[40]

Not only did Fort George serve as a way station during the 1776 campaign, but also as a hospital for the American soldiers infected with smallpox and other diseases after the tumultuous retreat from Canada. Major General Gates wrote to George Washington on July 29, 1776, informing him that the Northern Army was "infected with pestilence: the clothes, the blankets, the air, and the ground they walk upon. To put this evil from us, a General Hospital is established at Fort George...where every infected person is immediately sent."[41] The official "Return of the Sick of the General Hospital at Fort George" between July 12-26, 1776, listed 1,497 patients.[42] The hospital at Fort George was not a single structure, however. Chaplain Ammi Robbins visited the "west hospital" on July 21, 1776, commenting that "never was such a portrait of human misery as in these hospitals"; the next day he paid a visit to the "long hospital."[43] In August, Robbins traveled to the Ticonderoga camp where he visited sick troops, living under "miserable" conditions in tents before being transported to the hospitals at Fort George. He encountered a "very sick youth" from Massachusetts, who begged Robbins to pray for him and to send for his mother to nurse him, adding that "she was opposed to my enlisting; I am now very sorry; do let her know I am sorry."[44]

Faced with an overwhelming British force in July 1777, the Americans withdrew from Ticonderoga, Mount Independence, Fort George, Fort Edward, and Fort Anne (a small stockaded fort about 11 miles south of present-day Whitehall). Fort Ticonderoga and Mount Independence were evacuated in the early morning hours of July 6. After spirited fighting with British troops at Fort Anne, the Americans set fire to the outpost on July 8 and fled to Fort Edward. Fort George, however, was not abandoned until July 16, after the fort had been set ablaze along with five vessels (two on the stocks). Prior to the abandonment of the fort, wagon loads of provisions, guns, stores, and bateaux were hauled to Fort Edward. Subsequently, Major General Philip Schuyler, commander of the Northern Department, defended his orders to evacuate Fort George in a letter to George Washington by disparaging the value of the fortification, describing it as "an unfinished bastion...In it was a barrack capable of containing between thirty and fifty men."[45] When the British advanced closer to Fort Edward at the end of July, Schuyler ordered the garrison to retreat. Justifying his decision, Schuyler suggested to Washington that Fort Edward was "nothing but...ruins" and "so utterly defenseless that I frequently galloped my horse in one side and out the other."[46]

As the British proceeded south on Lake Champlain in early July, a number of officers noted that additional defensive works had been constructed by the Americans at the old forts. The works included a redoubt at Coffin Point, just south of Crown Point on the west shore. (A year earlier, Lieutenant James Hadden also observed "a work" on Chimney Point.)[47] At Ticonderoga Lieutenant William Digby wrote that the "Americans strengthened these lines [old French lines] with additional works and a block house" and mentioned several other "new block houses."[48] At Fort George Lieutenant Hadden described "Barracks for about a hundred Men" inside "a small square Fort faced with Masonry," but the Americans had blown up "the Magazine on the side next [to] the water, which demolish'd that Face."[49] Hadden also noted that the troops were "employed in clearing a post on Gage's Hill [formerly Fort Gage] which commands the Fort."[50] Three weeks after the surrender of Lieutenant General John Burgoyne's army at Saratoga (October 17, 1777), British troops burned or damaged most of the fortifications at Lake George and Lake Champlain and evacuated to Canada. Early on the morning of November 8, 1777, "all the newly built blockhouses, huts, barracks, magazines, etc. were set afire" by British and German soldiers at Mount Independence and Ticonderoga; fifty powder barrels exploded at Fort Ticonderoga, causing large pieces of the old fort to fly "high into the air."[51] The breastworks at the old French lines were demolished and Fort George and the breastworks on Diamond Island were burned. Despite the destruction, the southernmost forts in the region, including Forts Anne, Edward and George, were subsequently reoccupied by American forces.

The lake valleys did not return to the peaceful solitude that had existed during the period between the French and Indian War and the American Revolution. A series of well-planned British raids devastated communities in both Vermont and New York from 1778 to 1780. On May 3, 1779, William Collins, an American deserter, reported to British authorities that the Americans had repaired Fort George "and have built some barracks near the water side."[52] Two months later a detachment from the Fort George garrison, along with several family members, was attacked by 25 Mohawks, accompanied by three British soldiers, while "gathering Huckleberries on Fourteen-Mile Island."[53] Nine Americans, including two women, were killed and eight taken prisoner. The largest British raiding party, involving a force of 1,000 regulars, Loyalists, and Indians, penetrated deep into New York during the fall of 1780. After forcing the surrender of the American garrison at Fort Anne, the raiders compelled the capitulation of the small garrison at Fort George. Once again Fort George was set afire, and the British detachment departed in two divisions—one party aboard bateaux and the second on foot. On October 15 the second party climbed "over a Mountain known commonly by the Name Rogers' Rock, from the top of which we had a most beautyfull prospect of Lake George."[54] While British troops enjoyed the view, American militiamen reached Fort George and discovered "twenty-two slaughtered and mangled men."[55]

The British returned briefly to the Champlain Valley in 1781 with a force of 1,000 regulars and Loyalists under Colonel Barry St. Leger to establish a presence in the region while secret negotiations took place with a group of Vermonters to make Vermont a Royal Province. In a letter to George Washington, Philip Schuyler disclosed the contents of an October 26th scouting report, which suggested that British troops were "refortifying Tyconderoga" and "drawing materials for the repair of the Fort."[56] The British presence at Ticonderoga, however, was short-lived. Following the disclosure of the contents of a suspicious letter written by St. Leger to the governor of Vermont, a furor arose among the citizens. Shortly thereafter, St. Leger received the news that Lord Cornwallis had surrendered his army at Yorktown. St. Leger returned to Canada, ending the last military occupation of Fort Ticonderoga.

However, the forts were not forgotten. Prior to the signing of the Treaty of Paris on September 3, 1783, George Washington made his headquarters at Newburgh on the Hudson River, and in late July 1783 embarked on an inspection tour of the fortifications in northern New York. Washington and his party boarded three bateaux at Fort George and proceeded to the northern landing on Lake George. The bateaux were transferred to Lake Champlain, and after viewing Fort Ticonderoga, the party traveled on to Crown Point. On August 6, 1783, Washington wrote to the superintendent of finance seeking funds to support plans to have the quartermaster general "prepare Batteaux and other means of Transportation to the upper Posts, [for the delivery] of the Cannon, Stores and Provisions which will be absolutely necessary for possessing and maintaining" the forts.[57] With the end of the war, the notion of maintaining the forts ended. Settlements in the lake valleys quickly expanded, and the forts became convenient sources of building materials. Fort Ticonderoga was stripped of flooring, doors, windows, iron objects, and a substantial amount of stone.

THE TOURIST ERA BEGINS

During the late eighteenth and early nineteenth centuries, a number of travelers recorded their impressions of the historic ruins in the lake valleys. In 1784 Peter Sailly traveled to the region from France to find a place to settle with his family. Accompanied by William Gilliland, who had founded Willsboro in 1765, Sailly visited Fort Edward on July 16, noting that the "ruins of the rampart and ditch only remain," but the next day he suggested that Fort George was "yet in good repair."[58] On July 18 he viewed the site of Fort William Henry, observing the "remains of the old ramparts of earth...covered with wild cherry trees," and "a little above the fort...the remains of an entrenched camp" with a graveyard in the center "covered with strawberries and wild roses."[59] A few days later Sailly scrutinized "very high and strong walls of stone" at Fort Ticonderoga, as well as the "ruins of several batteries" and the "ruins of the houses of the French inhabitants."[60] At Crown Point he described ramparts "of earth and wood" and remarked that the fort was obviously "not in repair."[61]

In 1791 two future presidents, Thomas Jefferson and James Madison, visited Lake George and Lake Champlain. Jefferson wrote that he had viewed "Forts William Henry and George, Ticonderoga, Crown Point & c. which have been scenes from a very early part of our history" and recounted the story of Rogers Rock.[62] Madison noted the presence of "a few families" at Fort George, who were employed "in the litter trade & ferriage thro the Lake"; at Fort Edward he observed a half dozen houses and commented that the fort "could only be defensible agst. small arms."[63] Five years later, Isaac Weld, a well-to-do 21-year-old British traveler, visited Fort Ticonderoga and Crown Point. Weld lodged at the same tavern on the shoreline at Fort Ticonderoga where Jefferson and Madison had stayed in 1791. The tavern, operated by Charles Hay and his wife Mary, was described by Weld as "a large house built of stone," located in the "Old King's Store" near the old military wharf.[64] Weld concluded that Fort Ticonderoga was "not likely" to be rebuilt, and the following day he referred to Crown Point as "a heap of ruins."[65]

In 1800, 24-year-old Abigail May visited Ticonderoga and wrote one of the first detailed tourist descriptions of the fort. She had traveled from Boston to the therapeutic

Ruins of Fort Ticonderoga by William R. Miller. (Print, author's collection)

springs of Ballston Spa for relief from "spasms" and an apparent nerve disorder in her hand. May journeyed to Lake George with a group of boarders from the Aldridge House at Ballston Spa, spending the night at "the only house that could accommodate us" on the southern shore of Lake George, which had "the appearance of a Goal [gaol or jail]."[66] The next day the group was rowed to Ticonderoga, staying overnight at a tavern on the east side of the outlet (Alexandria). The following morning the party was transported by wagon to the ruins of the fort. May "paced over the stones awe struck," noting that the "chimne[y]s are [e]ntire, the walls of the houses, and peaks of the roof—the window and door frames—the ramparts, fortifications…yet remain—but over grown with nettles and weeds, such a scene of desolation I never beheld."[67] She remarked that "the stone alone remain[ed]"; the wood and glass had been carried away by early settlers.[68] The group was shown "the sally ports—the Guard room—the bakers room—and descended into some subterraneous cells"; May wrote that "every thing makes this spot teem with melancholy reflections—I knew not how to leave it, and ascended the wagon with regret."[69] May and her fellow excursionists proceeded to the tavern of widow Hay (mother of the wagon driver/guide), where Jefferson and Madison had lodged nine years earlier. After "a fine dinner, of Chickens, Ham, green Peas, Cucumbers, Custards & c," the touring party returned to Lake George for the return voyage.[70] (Five years after May's visit, Elkanah Watson described the tavern as an "old one story…stone house kept by Mother Hay, a squat old Englishwoman.")[71]

OWNERSHIP OF THE GARRISON GROUNDS

Just after the turn of the nineteenth century, the garrison grounds at Fort George, Fort Ticonderoga, and Crown Point were officially deeded by New York State to Columbia and Union Colleges. Following the American Revolution, the three forts had reverted to state ownership. In an effort to "promote science and literature," the New York State legislature enacted provisions on March 31, 1790, to aid Columbia College and other "academies,"

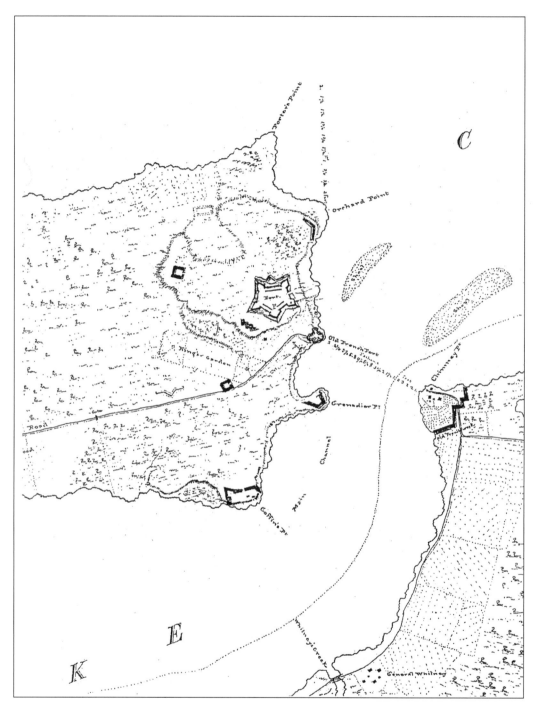

**Detail from a "Sketch of Crown Point" (November 1815)
by U.S. topographical engineers. (National Archives)**

which were suffering from "a deficiency of…funds," by providing grants of the garrison grounds of the three forts.[72] The colleges could thereafter collect rents from leases or sell the property.

A grant of the garrison grounds at Crown Point to Columbia and Union Colleges was not completed until 1801, formalizing an earlier agreement (1796) to transfer the parcel to the colleges. Eleven years later Union College conveyed its deed to Columbia College, and in 1828 Columbia College sold the parcel to Sylvester Churchill. When Churchill sold the land to James and Samuel Murdock in 1839, he inserted the stipulation that future owners would be prohibited from "tearing down any of the ramparts or walls or carrying away any of the material."[73]

The garrison grounds of Fort Ticonderoga were deeded to Columbia and Union Colleges by the state of New York in 1804. William Ferris Pell had first viewed the ruins of Fort Ticonderoga in 1789 at the age of ten from the deck of a sailing vessel, while traveling to New York City with his family. Years later, after his business of importing mahogany and marble prospered in New York City, Pell fulfilled his plan to acquire the property. Pell first leased the parcel in 1816 and in 1820 purchased the 546-acre garrison grounds from Columbia and Union Colleges. He immediately attempted to end the dismantling of the fort by settlers. After his first house (Beaumont) burned on the shore of Lake Champlain in 1825, Pell built a larger house, called The Pavilion, the following year.

Much more development occurred in the vicinity of Fort George at the southern end of Lake George than in the areas surrounding Fort Ticonderoga and Crown Point. Immediately after the Revolutionary War, petitions for the land at Fort George flooded the

"View of Lake George" 1813, showing Fort George in the foreground. This image was probably based on the "Perspective Painting of Lake George" by Ezra Ames (1812). (Print, author's collection)

offices of state officials. On July 26, 1783, four settlers leased "the Tract of Land commonly called Fort George" for one year, with the stipulation that no "Bricks, Timber or
Stones...be removed" or fortifications be "taken down."[75] James Caldwell, an Albany
merchant and mill owner, had the greatest success in obtaining land at the southern end
of Lake George during the late eighteenth and early nineteenth centuries. In June 1785
Caldwell and Udney Hay, the former quartermaster general at Fort Ticonderoga (1777),
acquired a total of 2,200 acres at Lake George, and in January 1787 Hay sold his half to
Caldwell.[76] In 1802 the state deeded the garrison grounds at Fort George to Columbia and
Union Colleges. Nine years later (June 1, 1811), the colleges sold 1,724 acres, including
Fort George, to James Caldwell for $5,000, but the deed was not recorded until 1818.[77]
Some of the parcel was subsequently divided into lots and sold. (On May 17, 1823, "lot
number seven of a tract commonly called the Garrison Ground...containing 50 acres" was
slated to be sold at public auction at the "Lake George Coffee-House" in the village of
Caldwell.)[78]

   Despite the legal transfer to private ownership, the garrison grounds at Lake George
served as a setting for military activity once again during the War of 1812. Major General James Wilkinson, a veteran of the American Revolution and commander of the northeastern division of the army in 1813 and early 1814, was scheduled to appear at a court-
martial at the southern end of Lake George on April 25, 1814, on charges of "Neglect of
duty," "unofficer-like conduct," and "Intoxication."[79] As a result of Wilkinson's challenge
to the authority of the court, Major General George Izard dismissed the panel of officers
slated to hear the case and followed instructions from the secretary of war to "post-
pone...assembling the court until the end of the campaign."[80] Wilkinson was exonerated
in 1815 and honorably discharged from the army. In early September 1814, 4,000 troops
under Izard's command bivouacked on the garrison grounds at Fort George before their
march westward to Sackets Harbor on Lake Ontario.[81]

AGE OF TOURISM

By the time that Yale Professor Benjamin Silliman arrived at Lake George in late September 1819, the population of the village of Caldwell had grown to "five or six hundred
inhabitants."[82] Silliman, the most prominent American professor of science during the
early nineteenth century, was a protégé of the late Timothy Dwight, the former president
of Yale College and the author of *Travels in New-England and New-York*. Dwight's book,
based on his travels in 1802 and 1811, initiated a style that combined history with descriptions of the scenery, which was soon imitated by subsequent travel writers during the
nineteenth century. Silliman's own book, *Remarks Made on a Short Tour between Hartford and Quebec in the Autumn of 1819*, adopted Dwight's approach. Nearly four
decades after the last occupation of Fort Edward, Silliman observed "walls...in some
places still twenty feet high, notwithstanding what time and the plough have done to
reduce them; for the interior of the Fort, and in some places, the parapet are now planted
with potatoes."[83] In comparison to the garrison grounds of the forts at Lake George and
Lake Champlain, Fort Edward quickly passed into private ownership, but its ruins
remained visible for many decades.

   At Lake George, Silliman described the "circular mossy walls of stone" at Fort George that were "still twenty feet high and in pretty good preservation," and suggested that a tavern located on the shore was once "one of the old barracks, formerly belonging to the fort."[84] He also examined "Bloody Pond," which was "shaped exactly like a bowl; it may be two hundred feet in diameter…and covered with pond lilly."[85] Two years later, Silliman visited the region again, making a more thorough examination of the ruins of Fort Ticonderoga. He found the French lines "still in fine preservation, running quite across the peninsula…The ditch is even now very deep…the parapet was higher than the top of my head."[87] (The French lines had been strengthened by French troops following their victory over James Abercromby's army in 1758 and again by American troops during the Revolution.) Silliman concluded that Fort Ticonderoga was "one of the finest ruins in America"; "The walls, the barracks, the subterraneous magazines, the kitchens [bakery] and store rooms, the covered ways and advanced works of Ticonderoga are of solid masonry."[88] Although the roofs and "a part of the walls of the barracks" had been destroyed, Silliman still found the ruins quite remarkable; "The half burnt timbers still remain in the walls, and the subterraneous structures as well as the proper walls of the fort have escaped with little injury."[89] Silliman was pleased that "the garrison ground…has fallen into the hands of a gentleman [William Ferris Pell], whose good sense and just taste will not permit a stone to be removed."[90] Other visitors had similar comments regarding Pell's ownership. In 1825 Alexander Bliss suggested that Pell "will neither sell nor lease, nor even suffer a public house to be erected anywhere on his ground," and a few years later James Stuart wrote that Pell "prevents any f[u]rther dilapidation of the works, and has put the whole in good order—especially the gardens, formerly called the King's garden, to which he has been at pains to bring varieties of trees, shrubs, and fruits."[91]

Following the practice of combining history with descriptions of scenery developed by Timothy Dwight and Benjamin Silliman, Theodore Dwight, Jr., authored six editions of *The Northern Traveller* (1825-1841). Theodore Dwight, Jr., who had studied under his uncle Timothy Dwight at Yale College, devoted considerable space to the Lake George-Lake Champlain region in his travel guide. He noted that the remains of Montcalm's 1757 trenches, located in the village of Caldwell, "may still be traced."[92] In contrast to William Ferris Pell's attempt to preserve the integrity of the ruins of Fort Ticonderoga, James Caldwell, according to Dwight, had granted permission to a local resident "to dig in the ruins of the fort," allowing the digger to keep "a quantity of interesting antiquities for sale."[93]

Dwight provided very detailed descriptions of Fort Ticonderoga and Crown Point. He indicated that the "remains of the breast work can yet be seen" at the "Old French Lines," constructed in a "zig-zag" manner, but that young trees now "interrupt the sight."[94] "Bodies of men have been dug up hereabouts within a few years" at the lines, according to Dwight.[95] Upon approaching the fort itself, Dwight observed the "remains of several distinct lines of small redoubts"; on reaching the fort, he found the ditch "still eight feet deep in some places" and "8 or 9 yards" wide, and the walls of the fortress "20 or 25 feet high" in places.[96] He also reported that the walls of the barracks "remain on the north, south, and west sides."[97] Dwight described the French bakery under the northeast bastion as a room "arched, measur[ing] about 35 feet in length," with a fireplace and "two arched ovens"; "The cellars south of this, which belonged to the demolished building are almost filled up, have a room or two with fire places still distinguishable."[98] Dwight then walked eastward to the "Grenadiers Battery" (Lotbinière Redoubt) perched on the rock ledge overlooking Lake Champlain, finding traces of the covered way "distinctly visible" and the walls of the battery "faced with stone, with five sides, one of which measures about 180 feet," but the wall on the lakeside had "slipped down the bank...The remaining parts are nearly entire, and about 10 feet high."[99]

Moving north, Dwight next covered the ruins of Crown Point, mentioning the Grenadier Redoubt (present site of the Champlain monument) and the ruins of Fort St. Frédéric. Amherst's main fort still had walls "about 20 or 25 feet high" and "a convenient path running entirely round upon the top, interrupted only by the gates at the north and south sides."[100] Near the north gate, he discovered "the remains of a covered or subterraneous way to the lake shore."[101] Inside the fortress, Dwight observed "long ruinous buildings of stone, two stories high...the first 220 feet long."[102] "The timbers in the south barracks are burnt black," Dwight noted, but "a portion of the shingled roof...serves to cover a little hay mow and the nests of robins; while some of the [fort] entrances and other parts are fenced up for a sheep fold."[103]

During the summer of 1830, Jared Sparks, a prolific writer and editor of documents pertaining to American history (later a professor of history and president of Harvard), embarked on a long journey to visit the sites of the French and Indian War and the American Revolution. He kept meticulous notes on the sites, including measurements of the remains of fortifications, and sketched "plans" of each fort. He also maintained a journal ("Tour for Historical Research") while on the trip and later carefully edited and rewrote all the entries.

After traveling to Portland, Maine, by steamboat, Sparks journeyed overland to Quebec, then proceeded to Montreal. On August 13 he left Montreal for St. Jean and from there traveled by carriage to Fort Chambly. Sparks described the fort as "a square structure, measuring 210 feet on each side; with towers at each corner...The [stone] walls are irregularly pierced for cannon and Musquetry."[104] Sparks noted that the fort was "still standing in perfect repair," largely because it continued to be garrisoned by the British army (until 1870).[105] On August 14 he viewed the works at St. Jean, finding extensive breastworks—often 20 feet high from the bottom of the surrounding ditch. The fortifications at St. Jean had been extensively rebuilt after the French and Indian War. Sparks boarded a southbound steamboat (probably the *Franklin*) at St. Jean, stopping briefly at Isle aux Noix. Fort Lennox, built between 1819 and 1829 to guard the frontier against the Americans, was constructed on the original ruins of the 1759 French fort on Isle aux Noix. Sparks was unimpressed with the island—"a mere swamp at times" and "more fit for crocodiles."[106]

He passed by "the old, decaying, octagonal fortification at Rouses Point," built to guard the American frontier, but abandoned after a land survey under the Treaty of Ghent revealed that the fort lay on Canadian soil.[107] (The fort had also been plagued by foundation problems.) On the evening of August 14 the steamboat docked briefly at Burlington, and Sparks was treated to a magnificent sunset over "the distant mountains [of the Adirondacks]...uplifting their lofty heads to the heavens, and marking an irregular but bold outline on the sky, now purpled with the rays of the setting sun; this scene, with all its accompaniments of grandeur and beauty, was one of the finest that I have ever witnessed."[108] Sparks retired to his berth but was awakened at one a.m. to disembark at Chimney Point, where he was rowed to shore and walked to a tavern.

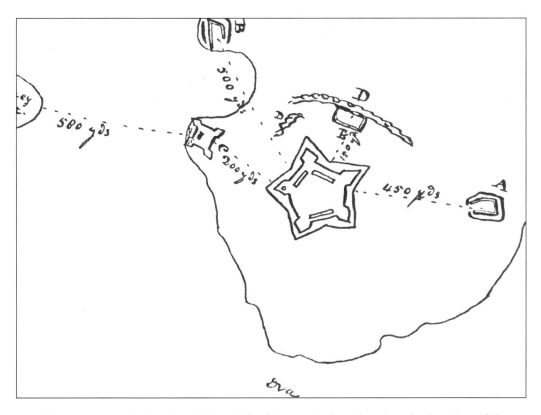

Jared Sparks' second drawing ("Plan II") of Crown Point, showing the location of Gages Redoubt (A), the Grenadier Redoubt (B), natural rock formations (D), and a "small rectangular breastwork" (E). (Houghton Library, Harvard University)

The next morning he was transported across the lake in a log canoe and spent the day examining Crown Point. Sparks wrote that "a house now in ruin" lay inside Fort St. Frédéric, and that the nearby British fortress had "a tenement, which a family has contrived to form out of the ruined barracks."[109] His inspection of Crown Point involved the measurement of various features of the fortifications. The curtain wall on the northeast side of the British fort was "20 to 30 feet high from the bottom of the ditch" and extended "75 yards" between the bastions.[110] Three stone barracks* were each "225 feet long, two storied & containing 32 large rooms, making the whole 96 rooms," but Sparks suggested that only the "walls of two of them are still sound."[112] In his "Plan" of Fort St. Frédéric, Sparks noted "walls of...solid masonry...10 or 12 feet in perpendicular height" and found evidence of "a covered way to the river [Lake Champlain] for water."[113] "An immense mass of stone" remained at the former site of the citadel.[114] Sparks discovered the ruins of only two of the three British redoubts: Gages Redoubt ("redoubt A") had a U-shaped breastwork (30 yards on one side) surrounded by "a ditch with a perpendicular wall of mason-

---

*An archeological study of the Soldiers' Barracks during the 1970s revealed that the structure was actually four Georgian-style houses joined together to form a 218-foot-long building.[111]

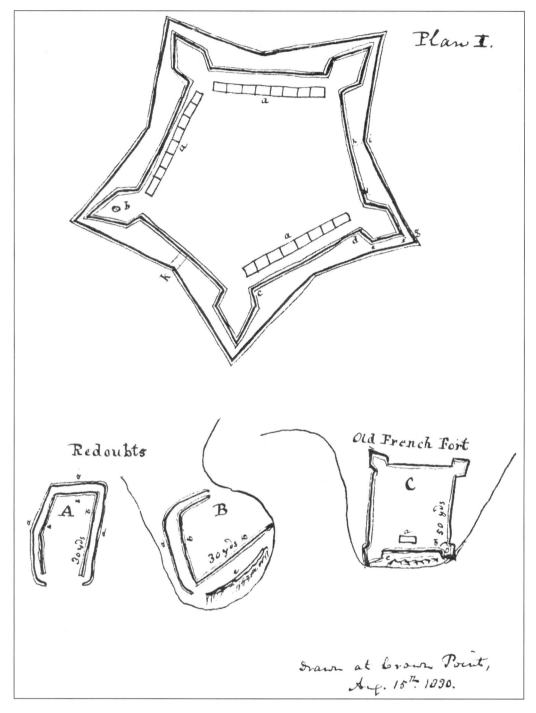

Jared Sparks' drawing of August 15, 1830, shows the British fort at Crown Point, two redoubts, and Fort St. Frédéric. (Houghton Library, Harvard University)

ry," and the Grenadier Redoubt ("redoubt B") was somewhat similar in design with an outer masonry wall and an inner breastwork "more than 30 feet high" from the edge of the lake.[115] Along the ridge that extended from the British fort to Gage's Redoubt (Bulwagga Bay side), Sparks found "innumerable little square structures of stone," some as large as 15 feet on each side with walls/foundations built of "well squared" stones "without mortar," some "still 3 or 4 feet high."[116] (These stone formations were the remains of provincial huts.)

On August 16 Sparks traveled by wagon to the tavern at the outlet of Lake George (Alexandria), where he rented a horse and rode to Fort Ticonderoga. He took measurements of its most prominent features and the following morning rode to the fort again. While he was taking measurements of the French lines, his horse ran away, and he futilely chased it before walking back to the hotel. Two days later the horse was found minus the saddle, and the owner demanded "eight dollars" from Sparks for the saddle—an amount Sparks considered "twice as much as it [wa]s worth."[117] (To make matters worse, Sparks had cut his foot on glass the same day while walking along the La Chute River.)

Sparks commented that the French lines were "yet in a good state of preservation, and perfectly distinct in every part," and extended "about 900 yards" in total length.[118] He noted the additions that had been made to the original lines after the famous 1758 battle, including a breastwork east of the main lines, double trenches in one of the sections, and an adjacent section pierced for cannons. He also observed several redoubts and a breastwork on the north side of the fort. He measured a "Redoubt" west of the fort near the La Chute River—"40 yds. square" in the vicinity of the 1758 French battery—but William Ferris Pell informed Sparks that it "was used as a cemet[e]ry."[119] Sparks described the Lotbinière Redoubt as "about 40 yards long" with "perpendicular stone walls, earthed within."[120]

At the fort itself, Sparks observed a "ditch encircling the whole fort" (except at the south curtain wall), ravelins on the north and west sides, a 150-yard-long covered way on the south side of the fort that extended to the lake, "subterranean rooms" in the west ravelin, and a "subterranean magazine [French bakery inside the northeast bastion] more than 30 feet long...arched over."[121] The barracks "walls on the south & west sides are still standing entire, and some remnants of those on the north," Sparks recorded.[122]

On August 19 Sparks boarded the steamboat *Mountaineer* at the northern Lake George landing for the voyage to the south end of the lake. Along the way, he gazed upon "the much admired scenery of Lake George," which "more than answered my expectations" based on "praises...lavished upon it from all quarters," and given the "charm" of the islands, the lake "surpasse[d] the Rhine" River in scenery.[123] Due to his injured foot, Sparks procured a wagon and driver to take him to Fort William Henry, Fort George, and Bloody Pond. He found the site of Fort William Henry so degraded that it was "not easy to ascertain its original dimensions," but he guessed that it was about "150 yards in diameter"; Sparks, however, clearly could see the "remains of an old wharf" underwater to the east of the fort.[124] He then walked to the site of Fort George, writing that it had "high walls of stone...clumsy and imperfect" about "15 to 20 feet" in height, and he characterized the structure as "very irregular, about 70 yds long & 50 wide."[125] The interior of the fort was "much taken up with subterranean apartments strongly walled and covered over," and the fort had evidence of a "covered way to the Lake."[126] Sparks also examined a founda-

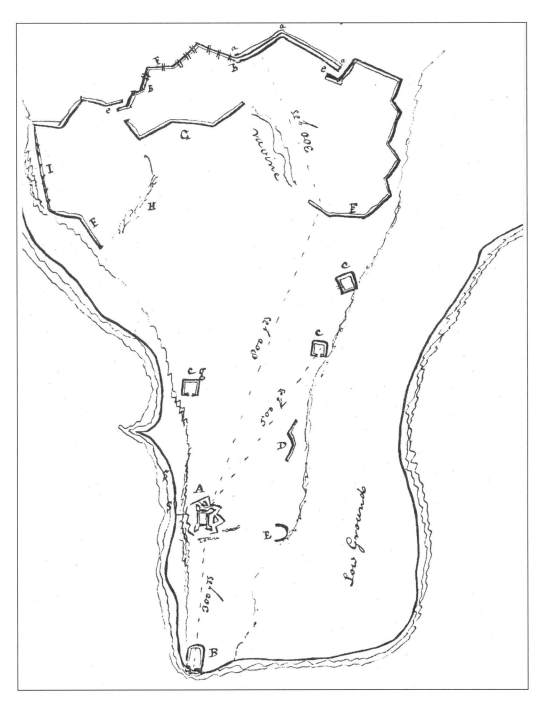

Jared Sparks' third drawing ("Plan III") of Fort Ticonderoga notes the location of the Lotbinière ("Grenadiers") Redoubt (B), several other redoubts (c, c, cg, E), the French lines (F, F, F) with openings for cannons (b, b), two separate breastworks (D, G), and a stone wall (I). (Houghton Library, Harvard University)

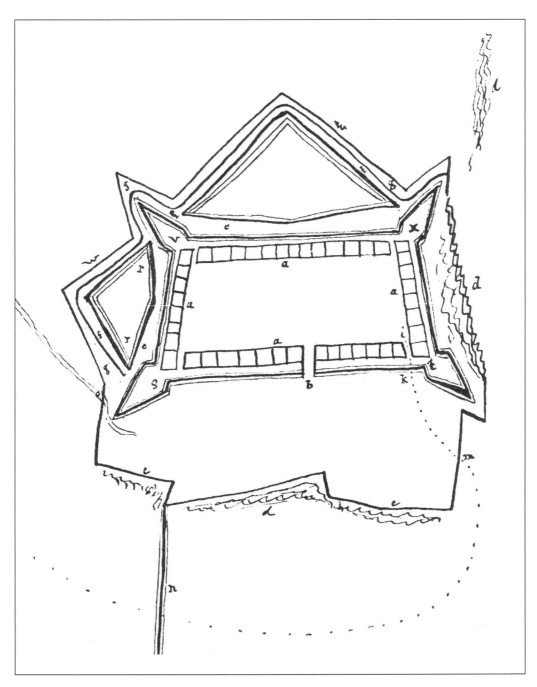

Jared Sparks' fourth drawing ("Plan IV") of Fort Ticonderoga in 1830 delineated four barracks (a, a, a, a), the fort's entrance (b), the South Battery Wall(c, c, m), "the passage through which Ethan Allen entered the fort" (i and k), the "Covered Way to the River" (n), and "subterranean rooms" in the West Demilune (ravelin) (r, r). (Houghton Library, Harvard University)

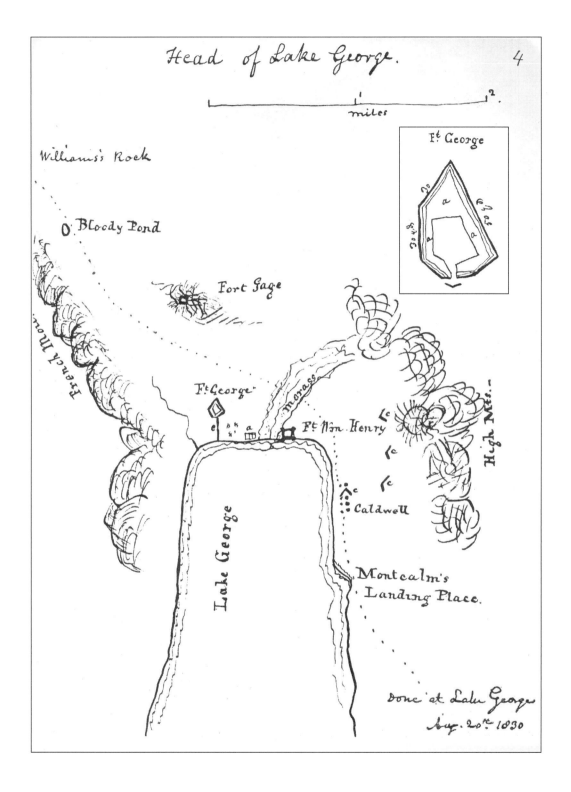

Head of Lake George.   4

Williams's Rock

Bloody Pond

Fort Gage

French Mtn.

Ft. George

morass

Ft. Wm. Henry

High Mts.

Caldwell

Lake George

Montcalm's Landing Place.

Ft. George

Done at Lake George
Aug. 20th 1830

tion on the lakeshore just east of West Brook, which he surmised was "a very large ware-house, doubtless used in the Revolution."[127] (This may have been the remains of a building that both Abigail May and Benjamin Silliman mentioned earlier as the structure that was being used as a tavern.)

Sparks then rode three miles to Bloody Pond, estimating its diameter as 200 feet. He later visited the site of Fort Edward, finding that it was "in the midst of the present village, and has been laid out into house lots, and more than half of the old Fort has been partially leveled and converted into gardens. The east and south sides of the Fort are in a partial state of preservation and the embankments fifteen or twenty feet high. But the owner is digging them down, and the whole structure will soon disappear."[128]

Other travelers to the region would provide less analytical observations of the fortifications at Lake George and Lake Champlain. Nathaniel Hawthorne first visited the ruins of Fort Ticonderoga in 1832, where he met a "young lieutenant of the engineers recently from West Point," but Hawthorne quickly tired of his "scientific guidance" and would "have been glad of a hoary veteran to totter by my side, and tell me, perhaps, of the French garrisons and their Indian allies."[129] On another visit Hawthorne had an opportunity to examine the ruins by himself. "After rambling all over the ramparts," he "sat down to rest…in one of the roofless barracks…overgrown with grass, nettles and thistles…The exterior walls were nearly entire, constructed of gray, flat, unpicked stones…The roof, floors, partitions, and the rest of the wood-work, had probably been burnt, except some bars of staunch old oak, which were blackened with fire, but still remained embedded into the window-sills and over the doors. There were a few particles of plaster near the chimney…I closed my eyes on Ticonderoga in ruins, and cast a dream-like glance over pictures of the past, and scenes of which this spot had been the theatre."[130]

In the summer of 1842, 18-year-old Francis Parkman, destined to become the most authoritative historian of the French and Indian War during the nineteenth century, traveled to Lake George and "visited and examined every spot where events" of the war had occurred.[131] During his sophomore year at Harvard College, the idea of writing about the French and Indian War materialized, and Parkman wrote to Professor Jared Sparks, seeking "details of military operations around Lake George."[132] Parkman enlisted a fellow student at Harvard, Henry Ore White, to accompany him on the trip, but White was not always agreeable to follow Parkman's lead. On July 16, 1842, Parkman climbed down the rocky ledges of the Hudson River at Glens Falls to view "Cooper's Cave," made famous by James Fennimore Cooper's novel *The Last of the Mohicans*. (Cooper visited the cave in 1824.) Parkman lamented that the "noble cataract" at the falls was nearly "concealed under a huge, awkward bridge" and surrounded by mills and a "dirty village."[133] Later

Facing page: **Jared Sparks' 1830 drawing "Head of Lake George" shows the probable location of Montcalm's batteries (c, c, c), Fort William Henry, Fort George and a "covered way to the Lake" (e), the "foundation…of a very large warehouse" (a) near the lake, Fort Gage, Bloody Pond, and Ephraim Williams' Rock. (Houghton Library, Harvard University)**

Insert: **In his drawing of Fort George, Jared Sparks described a "large space (a, a, a) between the exterior and interior walls…arched over & covered with earth, containing…rooms & vaults." (Houghton Library, Harvard University)**

**"Ruins of Fort Ticonderoga—Lake Champlain" by William R. Miller,
engraved by S. V. Hunt. (Print, author's collection)**

the same day Parkman rode by Williams' Rock and Bloody Pond—"a little dark, slimy sheet of stagnant water, covered with weeds and pond-lilies, and shadowed by the gloomy forest."[134] After spending the night at a tavern in Caldwell, Parkman walked the remains of Fort William Henry, which he suggested were "much larger" than he had imagined; "the earthen mounds cover many acres," but he complained that a road had been constructed "directly through the ruins" and the glacis had turned "into a flourishing cornfield, so that the spot so celebrated in our colonial history is now scarcely to be distinguished."[135] However, he did observe "untouched parts" of the fort, "especially on the embankment," bordering the lake, and he "could easily…trace" Montcalm's 1757 lines several hundred yards to the west.[136] Parkman also mentioned a nearby gravesite where "bones and skulls [had been] dug up in great numbers."[137] He found evidence of "recent digging in William Henry"; an old farmer hoeing in a cornfield suggested that it was the work of "some fools…with a wizard and a divining rod…dig[ging] for money in the ruins…[who] went at midnight for many successive nights and dug till daylight."[138] (Fictitious stories of treasure persisted well into the twentieth century.) Parkman also scrutinized the ruins of Fort George, which were "in much better preservation" than Fort William Henry and "under the special protection of Mr. [William] Caldwell, the owner of the village" (son of the late James Caldwell).[139] In addition to examining the ruins of the forts, Parkman observed "spikes and timbers of sunken vessels*…along the southern beach."[142] On July 18 Parkman and White departed from Caldwell in a rented rowboat and over the next week explored the lake, arriving on July 26 at the Homelands Dock (also called Cooks Landing) in Ticonderoga. The pair boarded a stagecoach at the landing and rode to the village of Ticonderoga, where Parkman asked directions to Fort Ticonderoga. "I've heerd of such a place seems to me," the fellow replied, "but I never seen it, and couldn't tell ye where it be."[143] Parkman was astounded by the answer but received similar responses from others in the village before finally finding a resident who knew the way to the fort. After walking two miles, Parkman approached "the remains of a high earthen parapet with a ditch running through…wood[s] for a great distance" and concluded that it was the remnants of the French lines.[144] As he hiked farther, he observed "breastworks and ditches in abundance, running in all directions" and "Still farther, were two or three square redoubts."[145] Finally, Parkman peered at "a cluster of gray, ruined walls, like an old Chateau, with mounds of earth and heaps of stones…I was astonished at the extent of the ruins…All around were ditches of such depth that it would be death to jump down, with walls of masonry sixty feet high."[146] He surveyed the Lotbinière Redoubt, noting the envelopment of the stone walls with weeds and vines. Parkman ended his journal entry for the day with another criticism: "The senseless blockheads in the neighborhood have stolen tons of the stones to build their walls and houses."[147] Parkman and Ore boarded a steamboat bound for Burlington on Lake Champlain and then traveled through the Green Mountains to southern Canada, returning to Boston on a route that passed by the White Mountains. In subsequent decades Parkman uncovered original documents in North America, England, and France that dealt with the French and Indian War and produced a distinguished series of books on the subject, including his acclaimed two-volume *Montcalm and Wolfe* (1884).

Six years later historian Benson J. Lossing, author of *The Pictorial Field-Book of the Revolution*, carefully scrutinized the ruins of Fort Ticonderoga, finding the "mounds and ditches" at the French lines "still very conspicuous," and he correctly identified "an under-ground arched room" under the northeast bastion as the bakery: "the entrance steps are very much broken, and the passage is so filled with rubbish that a descent into it is difficult. It is about twelve feet wide and thirty long. On the right is a window, and at the end were a fire-place and chimney, now in ruins. On either side of the fire-place are ovens, ten feet deep…This bakery and ovens are the best-preserved portions of the fortress."[148] Lossing lamented that "Year after year the ruins dwindle" and noted that years earlier his guide (Isaac Rice) had helped load a vessel with stones and bricks from the fort that were used to construct an earthen-ware factory at Missisquoi Bay.[149]

At Crown Point Lossing observed "four large buildings" within the English fort: "One of them has been entirely removed [the armory] and another, two hundred and eighty-seven feet long, is almost demolished [unfinished officers' barracks]…The walls of the other two [barracks]—one, one hundred ninety-two, and the other two hundred and sixteen feet long, and two stories high—are quite perfect, and one of them was roofed and

*Parkman may have seen unretrieved bateaux that Major General James Abercromby's troops had sunk in 1758 for winter storage. Some of these bateaux were still clearly visible during the late nineteenth century.[140] He may also have observed the 44-foot-long wreckage of a sloop-like vessel lying in 15 feet of water just east of the ruins of Fort William Henry. The vessel was probably a sloop burned by French besiegers during their March 1757 attack on Fort William Henry.[141]

Left: Engraving of the "Bakery" at Fort Ticonderoga (1848).

Below: Engraving of the Soldiers' Barracks and the remains of the unfinished officers' barracks (1848).

Both from *The Pictorial Field-Book of the Revolution*, Volume 1 (1851), by Benson J. Lossing.

inhabited until two or three years [ago]."[150] Lossing concluded that Crown Point was in a much better state of preservation than Fort Ticonderoga, remarking that the present owner will not allow stones to be removed.

Anniversaries of historic events in the lake valleys were often the subject of grand celebrations. Amelia M. Murray, an English traveler, was present at the hundredth anniversary observance of the 1755 Battle of Lake George. Following a church service, which included lectures on the details of the battle, cannons were fired and "a beautiful array" of 24 boats was "marshaled in [a] line upon the lake" as English and French flags fluttered in the wind and "the band played God save the Queen."[151] In the evening the sky was "illuminated by a liberal display of rockets and Roman candles."[152] At the time of the celebration, "a subscription was proposed for raising a monument on the old battle-field to the heroes who fell there, particularly the gallant Indian chief Hendrick."[153] A monument to William Johnson and King Hendrick was not erected until 1903.

Remains of South Barracks. Engraving by Harry Fenn in *Picturesque America*, edited by William Cullen Bryant. (Author's collection)

The ruins of Ticonderoga continued to captivate visitors during the late nineteenth century. After "two or three hours" sketching and examining the ruins of Fort Ticonderoga, Amelia M. Murray suggested that it was "the only interesting ruin I have seen in America."[154] In 1858 Flavius Cook also maintained that the fort was "one of the best preserved ruins...on the continent," writing that the West Barracks were "yet standing; those to the south, partially ruined; those to the east and north, entirely destroyed, except for the foundations and cellar walls...Roofless, doorless, windowless, the old barracks have a ghastly appearance."[155] In 1866 a newspaper reported that the present state of preservation of Ticonderoga was more the result of the "extent of the fortifications than the watchful care of the inhabitants" and deplored "the shocking vandalism of the farmers" who were pulling down walls and carrying away stones for fences.[156]

In 1873 Seneca Ray Stoddard, owner of a fledgling photography business in Glens Falls, published his first guidebook, *Lake George; (Illustrated.) A Book of To-Day*, and in the same year produced a similar-sized guide, *Ticonderoga: Past and Present*, which covered the history and the state of the ruins of the fort. His Fort Ticonderoga guide was only published once, while the Lake George guidebook would be republished in annual editions through 1915 (with the addition of Lake Champlain beginning in 1889). Stoddard's Ticon-

"The Barracks." From *Ticonderoga: Past and Present* (1873) by Seneca Ray Stoddard.

deroga guidebook delineated features sometimes overlooked by other writers. He reported that "a great pile of stones" marked the former "entrance to the covered way"; the
stone walls of the covered way were "thirty-three inches apart" and could "be easily
traced to where they seem to enter the fort at the south-east corner of the parade-
ground."[157] Stoddard also mentioned that the West Barracks was "still standing," but that
the South Barracks was "nearly gone" and only the foundation remained "where the east
line stood."[158] On the north side "the foundation can be traced along the front and across
the ends…the remains of four heavy piers or columns of mason work" were still present
facing the parade ground.[159] The Lotbinière Redoubt had "seven angles, the side fronting
the water curved inward," according to Stoddard, and "on the north and west" of the
main fort were "two high bastions" (actually demilunes/ravelins) with a ditch and an
outer wall "now almost level with the plain."[160] In the northeast corner he described the
bakery and suggested, as Lossing had 25 years earlier, that it was the best preserved part
of the ruins.

Fort Ticonderoga continued to hold the public's interest throughout the nineteenth
century. On May 10, 1875, an estimated crowd of 6,000 people gathered inside the ruins
of the fort to commemorate the centennial of its capture by Ethan Allen. Despite a fire that
had destroyed much of the business district in Ticonderoga 40 days earlier, a local "Centennial Committee," working with Grand Army of the Republic posts in the Champlain
Valley, coordinated the appearance of bands and drum corps from the lake valley, as well
as the Vermont National Guard. The celebration included a line of march along Ethan
Allen's 1775 route to the fort, where an audience listened to patriotic speeches.[161]

Interest in the two forts at the southern end of Lake George also continued during this
period. Seneca Ray Stoddard described the remains of Fort William Henry in his first Lake
George guidebook, published in 1873. The ruins of the fort were adjacent to the Fort William Henry Hotel, which had been built in 1855 and expanded in 1866 by lengthening the
facade to a width of 337 feet and extending a wing in the rear to 250 feet. Fortunately, the

expansion of the hotel left the grounds of the fort untouched. Stoddard reported that the ruins were "under the pines" and the "outline well preserved…nearly square, flanked on the west, south and a part of the east side, by a ditch."[162] Stoddard mentioned a fence on the east side of the ruins and a sunken dock with "the charred remains of an old hulk…about 40 feet in length," which he suggested had been burned by French raiders in March 1757; "Shell[s] and cannon balls" had been raised from the wreck, according to Stoddard, as well as "two small cannon" in 1820.[163] In the same guidebook he wrote that the ruins of Fort George were "but a great heap of earth sloping off from the edge to the center and north, and held in place by the walls, which are quite well preserved on the east side. A great share of the stone work ha[d] been removed and burned for lime."[164] (Stoddard repeated virtually the same descriptions of the Lake George forts in his guidebooks for the next 42 years.)

Ruins of Fort Ticonderoga. (New York State Historical Association)

In 1879 Samuel Greene Wheeler Benjamin, a prolific travel writer, authored a story on Lake George for *Harper's New Monthly Magazine*. Benjamin suggested that the outline of Fort William Henry was "still more or less discernible," and he also observed the "fragments of the wharf" underwater.[165] He found Fort George still "picturesque" with "velvety moss cushioning the moldering ramparts" and noted that "a few years ago the lake could be distinctly seen from the fort, but the pines have since grown up, and form a massive screen."[166]

Crown Point was also included in the descriptions of travel writers during the late nineteenth century. In his 1874 guide to the Adirondacks, Stoddard reported that "the remains of lines of cellars, flagged walks, etc." of a village were present near Fort St. Frédéric.[167] William H. H. Murray ("Adirondack Murray"), who wrote *Lake Champlain and Its Shores* in 1890, described the remnants of the English village on the Bulwagga Bay side

The remains of the "old hulk" mentioned in Seneca Ray Stoddard's 1873 Lake George guidebook. Raised by William S. Tuttle on July 2, 1903, the 44-foot sloop wreck yielded numerous eighteenth-century military artifacts. The vessel was subsequently dismantled for souvenirs. (Lake George Historical Association)

of the English fort. Murray mentioned that "signs of ancient fences and enclosures of gardens and door yards may still be seen," as well as "an old street...ancient cellars" and "two large graveyards."[168]

In his 1889 Lake George/Lake Champlain travel guide, Stoddard noted that the "grounds [at Crown Point] have been fitted up by the Champlain Transportation Company for the accommodation of picnic parties that are brought here by their steamboats, with a dancing pavilion, refreshment rooms, platforms and open spaces for games, swings and other" activities.[169] (As early as 1821, the Lake Champlain Steam-boat company offered "popular excursions" for tourists "who may wish to view the remains of those ancient fortresses, Ticonderoga and Crown Point.")[170] Charles Possons' 1891 guidebook also reported that Fort St. Frédéric was "a popular excursion point" and "a regular landing" for the Champlain Transportation Company, where "walks lead from the dock to the ruins, and a fine pavilion has been erected for dancing or assemblies."[171] Possons disclosed that only "two of the barracks remain in partial preservation"; the third barracks (unfinished officers' barracks), which Benson Lossing found nearly demolished four decades earlier, had been further dismantled in the early 1870s by the Crown Point Iron Company to provide stones for their nearby railroad wharf.[172] The company's rail line extended from the lake to their mines at Hammondville.

Above: "Lake George, from the top of Fort George, Caldwell Village." Woodcut by William R. Miller. (Print, author's collection) *Right:* Fort George. From *Lake George; (Illustrated.) A Book of To-Day* (1873) by Seneca Ray Stoddard. *Below:* The Barracks at Crown Point. (Postcard, author's collection)

RESTORATION OF FORT TICONDEROGA

At the end of the nineteenth century, proposals surfaced to protect the ruins of Fort Ticonderoga. A bill before Congress in 1889 would have authorized the purchase of the fort by the federal government and the placement of a monument on the property. At the same time, ideas for the commercial development of the property were reported in newspapers.[173] The legislation was not approved, and in October 1897 the Ticonderoga Historical Society was organized "with the primary purpose of finding a means of preservation of Old Fort Ticonderoga," which led to the resurrection of the idea of a federal purchase.[174] The Ticonderoga Historical Society enlisted the support of patriotic societies throughout the United States, which resulted in the introduction of another bill in Congress in February 1898 to purchase the property. However, the outbreak of the Spanish-American War eclipsed the legislative effort. A new bill, which would have appropriated $40,000 for the purchase of both Fort Ticonderoga and Crown Point by the federal government, was introduced in Congress on January 6, 1902. The legislation was intended to empower the Secretary of War "to take measures for…[the] protection and preservation" of the two forts and would have provided "suitable buildings on the grounds for…visitors."[175] Once again, the bill failed to pass. At the August 1904 meeting of the New York State Historical Association, Mrs. Elizabeth Watrous, a summer resident of nearby Hague, rendered a fervent appeal for a renewed attempt to preserve Fort Ticonderoga as a national park. Watrous succeeded in bringing yet another preservation bill before Congress in early 1906. Although she enlisted the support of several notable political figures, including President Theodore Roosevelt, the bill failed to win approval.[176]

On July 23, 1908, the *Ticonderoga Sentinel* reported that the Ticonderoga Pulp and Paper Company "eagerly sought" the purchase of the fort lands, but the Ticonderoga Historical Society had an ally in Howland Pell, the family manager of the property, who pledged his support of a plan to have the federal government acquire the property.[177] With the approach of the three hundredth anniversary of Samuel de Champlain's voyage, the Ticonderoga Historical Society planned "a fresh attempt" to have a bill before Congress to procure the property, and so the society scheduled a clambake in September to highlight the historic importance of the fort.[178]

At the September 2, 1908, clambake, held on the fort grounds adjacent to The Pavilion, a letter from President Theodore Roosevelt was read, endorsing the plans of the society to have the fort purchased by the federal government.[179] In his speech at the picnic, the state historian supported "nationalization" of the fort grounds, but a former editor of the *Ticonderoga Sentinel* called for the "town of Ticonderoga [to] purchase the property for a town park" and later seek Congressional appropriations for the "restoration of the fort" and the "old French lines."[180] Stephen H. P. Pell, great grandson of William Ferris Pell, was among the 150 people in attendance who listened intently to the passionate oratory to save the fort. Alfred C. Bossom, a young English architect, displayed his highly-detailed drawings for a restoration of the fort. Bossom's elaborate plans, coupled with the enthusiastic speeches, coalesced Pell's earlier sentiment for preserving the fort. Soon after, Pell brought his wife, Sarah Gibbs Thompson Pell, to the fort and seriously discussed the idea of a restoration with her. Shortly thereafter, they solicited Sarah's father, Robert M. Thompson, who had founded the International Nickel Company in 1902, for financial

**Remains of the West Barracks and the wall on the west end of the
South Barracks at Fort Ticonderoga. (Postcard, author's collection)**

support. His aid enabled the Pells to purchase the other shares of the property "from the different members of the family, who were most gracious about the transfer."[181] By the middle of November 1908, Stephen and Sarah Pell had acquired ownership of the fort property and hired Bossom to oversee the restoration of the fort and The Pavilion. The news of the purchase, however, was not initially greeted with enthusiasm locally. The *Ticonderoga Sentinel* reported that "the fond dream of the Ticonderoga Historical Society...to have the historic old ruins pass into government ownership [was] knocked in the head," and instead the ruins passed "into the hands of a millionaire."[182] But the diligent effort by the Pells to restore the fort soon eclipsed any criticism.

One of Stephen Pell's first actions involved raising the wreckage of a warship (Jeffery Amherst's brig *Duke of Cumberland*) from the shallow water alongside the old military dock (north of the Lotbinière Redoubt).* During the winter of 1909, workmen cut through the ice and dragged the 90-foot-long vessel to the shore with the use of horses and two windlasses. They discovered a number of relics in the hull, including a 1756 button, dirks, bayonets, tomahawks, and cannonballs.[183] Unfortunately, the brig was erroneously displayed as Benedict Arnold's schooner *Revenge* for nearly four decades before the roof of a shed collapsed on the vessel, and the wreckage slowly deteriorated.[184]

---

*During the early 1980s, two other large vessels from the French and Indian War, the sloop *Boscawen* and one of the captured French sloops, were discovered underwater buried in mud near the old military dock at Ticonderoga. Over two summers (1984 and 1985), the Champlain Maritime Society (forerunner of the Lake Champlain Maritime Museum) conducted an underwater archaeological study of the *Boscawen*, under the direction of Arthur B. Cohn with Kevin J. Crisman as the project archaeologist. Hundreds of colonial-era artifacts were recovered and preserved using state-of-the-art techniques. The artifacts were subsequently turned over to the Fort Ticonderoga Museum.

Top: Remains of the brig *Duke of Cumberland* raised at Ticonderoga in early 1909. *Middle:* The restored West Barracks at Fort Ticonderoga, ca. 1912. *Bottom:* Aerial view of Fort Ticonderoga (ca. early 1920s), showing the partially restored South Barracks and the unrestored North and West Demilunes. (Postcards, author's collection)

During the last week of March 1909, preliminary work began at the ruins of Fort Ticonderoga. Documents from British, French, and Canadian archives aided in the restoration of the fort and its outer defenses. By the first week of April, the excavation of the West Barracks had "been carried to the lower floor, revealing a well preserved fireplace in one corner," and on April 13 "workmen uncovered 153 cannon balls," 600-700 "small shot," "17 bar shot," and tools.[185] Following Bossom's instructions, crewmen made extraordinary progress on the West Barracks. The exterior walls of the barracks, as well as a temporary roof, were completed in time for the visit by President William Howard Taft and other dignitaries on July 6, 1909, during the Champlain Tercentenary celebration. The Flag Bastion on the South Battery Wall was also rebuilt in time for the occasion.

The restoration of the rest of the fort continued for decades. Workers had to excavate deep piles of rubble to find the original floors and the bottoms of the ditches. As a consequence, great quantities of artifacts were uncovered, including more cannonballs, grapeshot, gunlocks and barrels, tomahawks, buttons, glassware, shovels, axes, hinges, etc. Despite the earlier removal of stones by farmers and others, workers often discovered that "at least ninety per cent" of the original stones from the walls were present in the adjacent ditches.[186] Work on the South Barracks, which had begun in 1914, was suspended in 1915 after the walls had reached a height of only six feet. The reconstruction of the barracks did not resume until 1930, and the completed structure was opened to the public the following year. The restoration of the South Battery Wall was completed in 1923, the West Demilune (also called a ravelin) in 1928, the North Demilune in 1930, and the north and east terrepleins and adjacent curtain walls during the 1930s and 1940s.[187]

In 1931 Stephen and Sarah Pell conveyed the entire property, including a sizeable portion of Mount Independence, to the Fort Ticonderoga Association, a non-profit educational institution pledged "to preserve, maintain and develop the Fort and its museum and the surrounding grounds for the benefit of the public."[188] Over the years Stephen Pell acquired nearly 200 pieces of period artillery and one of the finest collections of eighteenth-century military artifacts. In 1977 the Fort Ticonderoga Association purchased the land holdings of the Mount Defiance Corporation, adding 480 acres to the institution's properties. Today the FTA owns more than 2,000 acres, thus maintaining the historic vistas of the eighteenth century.

The last major structure to be rebuilt inside the fort occurred nearly 100 years after the restoration of the West Barracks. Under the leadership of Executive Director Nicholas Westbrook, the exterior of the "magasin du Roi," the large French military storehouse on the east side of the fort, was reconstructed between 2005 and 2008. The interior of the structure was finished as the Mars Education Center, and the original French bakery under the northeast section of the fort was saved and presently awaits structural reinforcement before being opened once again to the public.

PRESERVATION OF CROWN POINT

During the first phase of the Fort Ticonderoga restoration, the Crown Point forts reverted to state ownership. The garrison grounds of the French and English forts at Crown Point had passed through the hands of several private owners during the nineteenth century. In 1895 Colonel LeGrand B. Cannon, president of the Champlain Transportation Company

from 1864 to 1895, purchased the grounds, encompassing "The Forts," from the heirs of James and Samuel Murdock.[189] On July 6, 1903, Cannon sold more than 300 acres, including a parcel with the "Garrison Grounds," to John F. Nadeau of Crown Point.[190] Nadeau suggested that measures would be taken to secure the ruins from "vandals," including "many tourists, thousands of whom visit the ruins annually taking...stones broken from the fortifications or barracks."[191] During the winter of 1909, Nadeau raised the wreckage of a 70-foot-long vessel near the ferry slip at Crown Point. The wreck may have been the remains of the captured French row galley *Grand Diable* that had sunk at Crown Point in 1761. The vessel was exhibited near the shore of the lake during the Tercentenary celebration and was subsequently hauled to the parade ground of the English fort for display, where it was later consumed by a grass fire.[192]

The Champlain Tercentenary events began in Vergennes on July 3, 1909, and then moved to Crown Point on July 5, where speeches, Indian pageants, a parade, and fireworks entertained the public. The Indian pageants, performed by 168 Iroquois aboard a 300-foot-long platform of barges, dramatized "Hiawatha," Champlain's voyage on the lake, and his 1609 battle.[193] The final Tercentenary activity occurred at Crown Point in 1912 when the Champlain Memorial Lighthouse, exhibiting a large bronze statuary of Samuel de Champlain flanked by a French voyageur and a Huron guide, was dedicated. (On September 19, 2009, the memorial was rededicated for the 400th anniversary of Champlain's exploration of the lake.)

On March 21, 1910, Nadeau and his wife sold a 25-acre parcel of land, "being a part of the Garrison Grounds," to Witherbee, Sherman and Company for $100.[194] Four days later, the president of the company, Frank S. Witherbee, wrote to the governor of New York, Charles E. Hughes, that the corporation had "secured possession of these ruins and desire to present them...to the state of New York for the purpose of creating a state park

Above: **The Officers' and Soldiers' Barracks at Crown Point (ca. late 1920s). (Delaware and Hudson Railroad Collection, New York State Library)** *Facing page, top:* **Officers' Barracks at Crown Point, 1907. (Postcard, author's collection)** *Middle:* **The wreck of the French row galley *Grand Diable* displayed on the parade ground at Crown Point. (Collection of Hudson Hagglund)** *Bottom:* **Champlain Tercentenary celebration at Crown Point on July 5, 1909. (Collection of Cheryl Lamb)**

to preserve them for all time."[195] Witherbee noted that the "barracks and earthworks [were] still standing in excellent condition" and that the property had visible "evidence" of "streets and many houses" from the eighteenth-century villages adjacent to the forts.[196] The offer of the land was quickly accepted by the state.

In the decade following the gift of the Crown Point forts, the state implemented measures to preserve the site. In 1915 the New York State legislature approved funds for the excavation of Fort St. Frédéric. During the following year, the remains of the limestone walls of the French fort were uncovered and in subsequent years were partially rebuilt. Steel cables and turnbuckles were installed (ca. 1914-1916) in sections of the English barracks to hold the walls in place. Gunite (a cement-like material) was sprayed inside the Officers' and Soldiers' Barracks in 1912 and again in 1934 in an attempt to stabilize the walls, but the application created long-term problems of moisture retention, resulting in the fracturing of the limestone during frost cycles. By 1928 the state had acquired 86 more acres at Crown Point, and in later years the state purchased several more parcels, including 275 acres in 1962. The additional land allowed a wider range of archaeological work in subsequent years. In 1968 the stone walls of the Light Infantry Redoubt were excavated and left uncovered. Fort St. Frédéric was excavated again at this time, but the employment of a backhoe to unearth artifacts and the failure to maintain adequate records of the specific locations of the retrieved objects compromised the integrity of the project.[197]

In 1975 the garrison grounds at Crown Point were transferred from the New York State Department of Environmental Conservation to the Office of Parks and Recreation (now Parks, Recreation and Historic Preservation); the following summer a new visitor center/museum was opened at the site (remodeled in 2009). Many artifacts from previous archaeological excavations at Crown Point were displayed in the museum, and a considerable number of them were placed on exhibit at the Adirondack History Center Museum in Elizabethtown.

In order to maintain the soundness of the barracks walls, the mortar was replaced during the 1977 season. An archaeological study of the Soldiers' Barracks was also concluded in the same year, revealing original construction details of the barracks and new information on the nature of eighteenth-century cultural materials.[198] Archaeologists from the Bureau of Historic Sites conducted an archaeological study from 1985 to 1988 at a site west of the English fort, where a proposed maintenance building was to be located. The excavation uncovered features of provincial officers' huts that were first mentioned by Jared Sparks in 1830. The investigators discovered evidence that contradicted an earlier "conclusion that Provincial encampments were disorderly," finding instead that the camps were "regularly spaced."[199] Stabilization maintenance continues at Crown Point, as well as archaeological excavations, including an investigation of eighteenth-century village sites by Dr. Paul R. Huey in 2008 and 2009.

LAKE GEORGE BATTLEFIELD PARK

Because of the prodding by the newly-organized Society of Colonial Wars, the state of New York at the end of the nineteenth century began the acquisition of lands encompassing the remains of Fort George and the 1755 battlefield. On February 24, 1898, New York State purchased a portion of lot 26, "called the Garrison Lands or Grounds," from Harriet C. Parmelee Nivert for $1,000, and five days later the state bought eight and three-quarters acres, "being a part of [lot 26]…of the Garrison Ground," from the family of John W. Dowling for $4,000.[200] New legislation in 1900 made provision for the purchase of additional acreage for the battlefield park: seventeen and a half acres, consisting of "a part" of lot 27, the "Garrison Ground…commonly known as the Fort George lot," for $7,500, and an adjoining parcel of seven acres, also "being a portion" of lot 27, for $5,000.[201] The Lake George Battlefield Park now consisted of a total of 33 1/4 acres and was placed under the custodianship of the New York State Historical Association. On April 24, 1899, the Regents of the University of New York had granted a charter to the New York State Historical Association, headquartered in Caldwell, "to promote historical research, to disseminate knowledge of the history of the State…to establish a library and museum at Caldwell, to mark places of historic interest, and to acquire custody or control of historic places."[202]

A monument, consisting of bronze figures of William Johnson and King Hendrick, was dedicated at the Lake George Battlefield Park on September 8, 1903. The two-ton statuary, designed by sculptor Albert W. Einert, stands nine-feet above its granite pedestal. The monument, first proposed in 1855, was erected by the Society of Colonial Wars to commemorate the 1755 victory of provincial troops and their Mohawk allies at Lake George. The ceremonies began on September 7, 1903, with an "eighteen-gun salute" by the First Battery of the New York National Guard as several governors of the northeastern states arrived at the train station at Lake George.[203] The celebration included military maneuvers by troops of the U.S. Cavalry and National Guard, parades, speeches, and a dance at the Fort William Henry Hotel. On the afternoon of September 8, the governors of New York, Vermont, and Connecticut, and the lieutenant governor of Massachusetts were "stationed at the four corners of the battle monument" and pulled the cords unveiling the statues before a huge crowd.[204] (Two additional statues were later erected in the battlefield park: a bronze sculpture of a Native American in 1921 and a large bronze statue of Father Isaac Jogues in 1939.)

Interest in the French and Indian War sites in the Lake George region continued in subsequent years. In 1908 the New-York Historical Society purchased Bloody Pond for $200. Although Bloody Pond is identified by a historic marker on the east side of route 9N, some modern researchers suggest that the location of the pond may actually have been farther east.[205] (Surprisingly, none of the travel writers or historians who visited the region ever raised a question about its identification or location.) Inspired by the reconstruction of Fort Ticonderoga, a "systematic excavation" of Fort George, financed by a donation to the New York State Historical Association, began in 1921 under the direction of Assemblyman Stewart MacFarland, the superintendent of the battlefield park.[206] Newspapers reported that the "east wall ha[d] been entirely refaced" and "with the exception of the upper parts, the stone walls of the various [interior] walls are in an excellent state of preservation."[207] The fort, however, was only partially rebuilt. Encouraged by the "80,000" tourists who visited "the reconstructed ruins of Fort Ticonderoga," the *Lake George Mirror* in 1930 urged the New York State Historical Association and the state of New York to rebuild the fort, suggesting that the "walls of Fort George, the old trenches and underground passage to the lake, the first village, the burying ground, the site of General Amherst's Camp, all could be brought back again."[208] Newspapers also suggested that "hundreds of relics…scattered about" the battlefield park could be placed in a muse-

um on the grounds.[209] A 1924 dig by the Field Exploration Committee of the New-York Historical Society, sanctioned by the custodians of the grounds (New York State Historical Association), had unearthed French buttons and other relics on the site.[210] The battlefield park, however, remained relatively unchanged for the next half-century. As the twentieth century drew to a close, it was apparent that new signage at the park was overdue. In 1998 the Department of Environmental Conservation, the state agency in charge of both the battlefield park and the adjacent campground, commissioned Bateaux Below, Inc., to prepare the historical text for ten interpretive signs that were later erected by the DEC.

The first professional archaeological excavation at Fort George was authorized by the DEC in 2000. The six-week-long dig, sponsored by the Archaeology Field School at Adirondack Community College, was led by Dr. David Starbuck, who had supervised numerous archaeological excavations in the Champlain and Hudson River Valleys. The crews discovered two limestone foundations, believed to be remnants of barracks, under two feet of soil at the site of the 1759 stockaded fort. Large quantities of broken wall plaster were found inside the most northerly foundation, which measured 17 feet wide by 67 feet long. The plaster may indicate that the structure had been used as an officers' barracks. The archaeological team also recovered an extraordinarily large number of artifacts, including thousands of pottery fragments, musket balls, pieces of clay tobacco pipes, nails, buttons, belt buckles, cuff links, wine and medicine bottles, a knife, a spade, a key,

Above: **Fort George after the reconstruction of the east wall in 1921. From a J. S. Wooley postcard mailed in 1928. (Author's collection)** *Facing page, top:* **Bronze statues of William Johnson and King Hendrick at the Lake George Battlefield Park, dedicated on September 8, 1903. (Postcard, author's collection)** *Middle:* **A 1903 photograph of Bloody Pond by Seneca Ray Stoddard. (Postcard, author's collection)** *Bottom:* **Ruins of Fort George in 1920. (New York State Museum)**

a cannonball, and animal and fish bones. The 2001 field school discovered more artifacts and the remains of foundations from at least eight additional structures, including hut sites.[211] As a result of the abundance of artifacts, DEC officials disclosed that the department would be "working closely with the Adirondack Regional Chamber of Commerce to develop an interpretive center near Fort George," a proposal long advocated by history-minded citizens.[212] The renewed interest in Fort George led to the formation of the Lake George Battlefield (Fort George) Alliance, dedicated to preserving the site and educating the public about the historical significance of the battlefield park. The group financed the preservation of the artifacts found during the 2000-2001 digs. All of the artifacts were preserved at the Lake Champlain Maritime Museum's Conservation Laboratory and were subsequently turned over to the New York State Museum by the Alliance.[213]

RECONSTRUCTION OF FORT WILLIAM HENRY

The ruins of Fort William Henry languished for 195 years before any archaeological work occurred at the site. Despite the years, the outline of the fort, including four mounds of earth covering the four bastions, was still discernible. Luckily, the site had not been commercially developed and the land served as a park for the guests of the first Fort William Henry Hotel (1855-1909), and for the second one from 1911 until the reconstruction of the fort during the early 1950s. The grounds, sheltered by tall pine trees, were accessible to hotel patrons by pathways marked with signage of the fort's features. Only the end of an outdoor bowling alley from the hotel intruded on the site of the fort.[214] Financially compromised by the Great Depression, the Delaware and Hudson Company sold the hotel and 20 acres of land to Guy Davenport in 1939, who sold the property in 1952 to the Fort William Henry Corporation, a firm organized by a group of regional businessmen headed by Harold Veeder, an Albany real estate broker.[215] The corporation leased the hotel and immediately made arrangements for an archaeological excavation of the site of Fort William Henry in preparation for the construction of a full-size replica of the fort.

A few test pits were dug in the ruins in late 1952, and the next year the corporation hired Stanley Gifford, an archaeologist and former museum administrator, to direct a full excavation of the site. Using copies of the original 1755 construction plans, Gifford and his team discovered brick- and stone-lined rooms under the East and West Barracks and hundreds of artifacts. The corporate investors, who had hoped to raise public interest in the fort, were encouraged by the 60,000 visitors who observed the excavation during the first year of operation.[216] Gifford and his team were under pressure to complete their work ahead of the construction crew. Digging at the site of the northwest bastion, Gifford discovered a large cache of cannonballs, mortar shells, and musket balls.[217] He also excavated the parade ground, some of the moat, and a portion of the cemetery adjacent to the west side of the fort. His crews uncovered 12 skeletons in the cemetery, as well as other human remains in various parts of the fort itself. The owners of the fort resolved to make the cemetery a permanent part of the museum and erected a log building over the site. The reconstructed fort opened to the public in 1955, but excavations continued at the fort. In 1957 a group of five skeletons was discovered under the brick floor of the East Barracks. One skull was missing and another skeleton had eight musket balls lodged in its bones.[218]

As a result of the adoption of more restrictive policies regarding the display of human

"View from the [Fort William Henry] Hotel Lawn," showing a sign for the fort's "Magazine." Stereoscopic view published by E. & H. Anthony & Co. (Author's collection) *Below:* Volunteer archaeologist John P. N. Wappett excavating skeletons in the military cemetery at Fort William Henry, 1954. (Fort William Henry Museum)

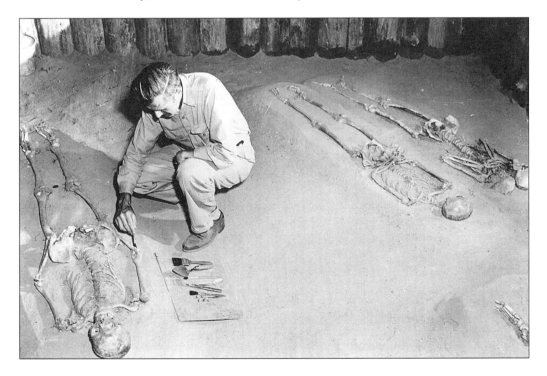

remains by museums nationwide, the Fort William Henry Corporation decided to stop exhibiting the skeletons after nearly 40 years of public viewing. In 1993, prior to their reinternment, forensic anthropologists Dr. Maria A. Liston of Adirondack Community College and Dr. Brenda J. Baker of the New York State Museum analyzed the skeletons. Their examination indicated that the skeletons probably belonged to the victims of the 1757 massacre of the garrison's sick and wounded by Montcalm's Indian allies. The pathological findings also revealed a multitude of physical problems, including herniated discs, torn muscles, amputations, fractured bones, systemic infections, tubercular lesions, and evidence that one victim had been beheaded.[219]

Beginning in 1997, the site of Fort William Henry was the subject of a four-summer excavation by the Archaeology Field School of Adirondack Community College, under the direction of Dr. David Starbuck. The objectives of the dig included a recovery of additional artifacts, a task made more difficult because Gifford's final excavation report was missing, and his field records were lost in a fire at the fort that destroyed the West Barracks in 1967. Archaeologists were also interested in determining the accuracy of the location of the 1950s reconstruction.

The 1990s digs confirmed that the 1755 fort had been constructed on top of a prehistoric Native American campsite, validating Stanley Gifford's earlier discovery of thousands of prehistoric pottery shards, javelin points, flint scrapers, ground-stone axes, and other projectile points. In the late 1990s, crews found similar artifacts—hundreds of prehistoric arrowheads, tools, pottery shards, etc.[220] The 1990s excavation, involving multiple

Fort William Henry after reconstruction (ca. early 1960s). (Postcard, author's collection)

sites inside and outside the fort, uncovered thousands of eighteenth-century artifacts, including ceramic shards, wine and medicine bottle fragments, musket balls, gunflints, mortar shell fragments, grapeshot, cutlery, buckles, buttons, and nearly 30,000 animal bone and tooth fragments.[221] Starbuck and his crew were able to excavate inside the original foundations of the West Barracks, finding numerous artifacts, burned timbers, fireplace bricks, and the massive base of a nine-foot stone fireplace. Because a section of the stone fireplace base had been dismantled during the reconstruction of the West Barracks during the 1950s, the archaeological team surmised that the Fort William Henry Corporation "chose not to build" on the original footprint of the West Barracks and instead built the replica barracks 15 feet west of the original site.[222] The entire west curtain wall was also reconstructed eight to ten feet from the original footprint.[223]

THE FATE OF FORT GAGE

Unfortunately, some of the French and Indian War fort sites did not survive. Fort Gage, consisting of a 1758 stockaded fort labeled on a contemporary map as the "Provincial light Infantry" redoubt and a nearby smaller "Advanced Guard," was located on a hill 200 feet above the lake, one mile south of the site of Fort William Henry.[224] The ruins of the fort survived undisturbed until the construction of an electric trolley line in 1901 by the Warren County Railroad, which cut through the remains of the fort. The trolley company was consolidated into the Hudson Valley Railroad on August 14, 1901, and the Fort Gage site became a station stop on the new trolley line.[225] Thereafter, Seneca Ray Stoddard's guidebooks mentioned that "the trolley cuts through the big hill" at the site of the ruins of Fort Gage but suggested that the "lines of earthworks may still be traced through the pines that now cover them."[226] The trolley line crossed the eastern edge of the fort, leveling the north wall and damaging sections of the south wall.[227] The construction of the Northway (Interstate 87) during the early 1960s destroyed the tip of the northwest bastion; the combination of the trolley and the highway projects compromised "perhaps 40% of the visible earthworks" of Fort Gage, according to state archaeologists.[228] Despite the damage to the site, officials from the Bureau of Historic Sites (New York State Office of Parks and Recreation) reported that "well preserved earthworks and a bastion" were present in 1972.[229] Three years later, prior to the construction of a large motel on the site, a Glens Falls developer bulldozed the remains of the fort without seeking a permit from the Adirondack Park Agency. Before the APA could ascertain the legality of the developer's action, the site was bulldozed again and the owners scaled down the size of the project to a 99-room motel, thus avoiding APA review.

Fortunately, however, the owner of the property granted permission to authorities to conduct an archaeological survey of the site. State archaeologists, working with local members of the New York State Archaeological Association and the Lake George Institute of History, Art and Science, excavated 28 ten-foot-square plots over an eight-week period during the spring of 1975. The archaeological team, led by Lois M. Feister and Paul R. Huey of the Division of Historic Preservation, discovered a number of features of the fort, including six hearths, the south moat, the northwest bastion, a breastwork, foundation stones, and lime kilns. The crew recovered unused musket balls, clay tobacco pipe fragments, hand-made nails, buttons, gunflints, a mouth harp, a pewter spoon, a knee buckle, a rare canteen fragment, a tin dish, and hundreds of identifiable animal bones. The bone findings suggest that the diet of the troops consisted primarily of domestic animals—47% pig, 43% cow or ox, 5% sheep, and 5% deer—but no fish or birds.[230] The artifacts were conserved at the state's Peebles Island archaeological laboratory and later returned to the owner. Although the salvage excavation yielded vital information about Fort Gage and held the promise of additional discoveries, the site was ultimately destroyed to make way for a Ramada Inn (presently the Lake View Hotel). All of the archaeological resources of Fort Gage may not have been lost in the 1975 motel construction. In 1994 archaeologist Scott Padeni identified the 1758 advance post of Fort Gage on a nearby undeveloped hillside. He also found evidence of significant "pot-hunting."[231]

EXCAVATION OF ROGERS ISLAND

 Rogers Island has perhaps had the most archaeological investigation of any historic location in the region. Earl E. Stott, a lifelong history buff and teenage excavator during the Fort Ticonderoga restoration, purchased 40 acres of Rogers Island in 1960 (nearly 60 percent of the island) in order to preclude development of the site and to search for artifacts. For the next quarter century he sponsored archaeological digs, involving hundreds of volunteers. Over the years, Stott uncovered two rows of hut sites, more than a dozen fireplaces, and numerous building sites, and recovered musket balls, ice creepers, utensils, glass fragments, plates, cups, buttons, buckles, coins, gunflints, cannonballs, hinges, bayonets, clay pipe fragments, etc.[232] Unfortunately, inadequate excavation records were kept and the artifacts, which were turned over to Stott, were not properly conserved or curated.[233]

In 1988 Stott sold the island, and the new owners, who planned to build a marina at the southern end of the island, engaged Dr. David Starbuck to oversee a phase one survey of the area, as required by New York State law if construction might impact sensitive archaeological sites. Although there was no legal requirement to archaeologically survey more of the island, the new owners endorsed Starbuck's proposal for annual summer field excavations. Beginning in the summer of 1991, Starbuck supervised six archaeological field schools through Adirondack Community College at Rogers Island. The crews documented the remains of a 90-foot-long by 13-foot-wide storehouse, a large barracks with two massive double-sided fireplaces, several 11-foot-square hut sites, a 16-foot-square foundation of a structure believed to have been used by officers, and multiple well-preserved brick fireplaces. In 1994 the persistence of field supervisor Matthew Rozell resulted in the discovery of the smallpox hospital, a site that had eluded earlier diggers for years.[234]

The island was sold once again in the mid-1990s, and the new landowner, Frank Nastasi, invited Starbuck's archaeological crews back to the island for digs in 1997 and 1998. During the 1997 season, Nastasi employed power equipment to remove hundreds of tons of dredged material from the barracks site. (In 1964 Earl Stott had removed about 10,000 cubic yards of sediment, which had covered the barracks area with ten feet of overburden. The state of New York had deposited the material there during the dredging of the river from 1909 to 1918.) The elimination of the dredge overlay in 1997 allowed the diggers to reach the original soil level. New pits were opened and two more hut sites were discovered, as well as the foundation of a large building that had been occupied by officers. The six field schools during the 1990s yielded an extraordinary number of artifacts, including prehistoric projective points, pottery and ceramic shards, coins, window glass fragments, musket balls, gunflints, buttons, buckles, clay tobacco pipe fragments, wine bottles, tools, hinge fragments, horseshoes, pieces of canteens, muskets, bayonets, tableware, animal bones (mostly from cows and pigs), and even amputated human finger bones.[235] The artifacts were conserved at an on-site archaeological laboratory in a former Mobil Oil terminal building. The structure has since been transformed into the Rogers Island Visitors Center, which opened in 2001. The center displays hundreds of artifacts from the island, as well as professionally-designed exhibits, covering the earlier presence of Native Americans in the region, the French and Indian War, and the archaeological study of the island. After receiving additional grants, the Rogers Island Visitors Center was slated to expand its exhibits in 2010. At the time of this writing, the sale of Rogers Island to New York State was still pending, as well as the sale of the adjacent site of the Royal Blockhouse (on the west bank of the Hudson River) to the Archaeological Conservancy.

EXCAVATION OF FORT EDWARD

The nearby site of Fort Edward was not protected from development, and a large number of houses now occupy the original footprint of the fort. A visitor to the site in 1856 noted that the property was in the process of being "cut up into lots for small dwellings," yet the "remains of the fort" were "still visible," and the ruins of the barracks and "three sides [of the fort could be] easily traced."[236] By the late nineteenth century private owners of the site had excavated to a "depth of several feet" and recovered a "large collection of relics," which were later sold.[237]

Although the site of Fort Edward is located under a residential neighborhood, Dr. David R. Starbuck found the property owners "wonderfully receptive" to an excavation of their yards by his Adirondack Community College field school.[238] The 1995 excavation revealed the remains of the East Casemate room (located under the original ramparts on the east side of the fort), the fort's moat, and sufficient sections of charred timbers to establish the eastern and western boundaries of the fort. The archaeologists discovered intact wood beams stretching more than 125 feet along the western side of the fort parallel to the Hudson River and three destroyed fireplaces in a row. The fireplaces, each separated by 34 feet, may be evidence that this site was the center of the West Barracks. Sections of a casemate room, located at the southeast corner of the fort, were excavated in 1996; some of the beams were found at a depth of six feet in the cellar of one of the houses.[239]

Beginning in 2001, a series of summer field schools concentrated in the area of a storehouse/sutler's house located just south of the site of Fort Edward. The site had been previously dug by illegal "pot hunters." The archaeologists discovered one of the best-preserved structures in the Fort Edward area. The building, measuring 45 feet long and 12 feet wide, may have been one of the earliest storehouses erected at the site.[240] Excavation of the building uncovered a multitude of important artifacts: tableware, barrel hoops, buttons, strap hinges, window glass, shards of stoneware, nails, musket balls, gunflints, fragments of wine bottles, coins, a mouth harp, a bayonet, and a large supply of unused tobacco pipes.[241]

ROLE OF HISTORIC PRESERVATION

By revealing tangible historic items, archaeologists have generated renewed interest in the history of eighteenth-century America. Archaeology has played a key role in explaining military activity at the fortifications in the Hudson River-Lake George-Lake Champlain corridor. It not only provides answers to research questions concerning eighteenth-century military sites, but also lends an air of excitement to the process of unearthing long-entombed artifacts. The thrill experienced by an archaeological digger on the discovery of an artifact last held by an eighteenth-century soldier is palpable. As an underwater photographer on the radeau *Land Tortoise* archaeological study, I can attest to the exhilaration of first viewing an intact French and Indian War vessel, last seen by British and provincial troops on October 22, 1758.

The memory of the hardships and sacrifices endured by eighteenth-century troops has been sustained through museum exhibits at the Rogers Island Visitor Center, Fort William Henry, Fort Ticonderoga, and Crown Point. The portrayal of eighteenth-century soldiers, rangers, and Native Americans by re-enactors has rekindled interest in the long-forgotten struggle for North America by opposing English and French armies. The forts today offer a variety of experiences—from the impressive restoration of Fort Ticonderoga to the eerie solitude of the empty, roofless barracks at Crown Point, surrounded by the windswept, grass-covered earthen remains of bastions and curtain walls. Once, the fate of a continent was settled with the blood and courage of troops at these wilderness outposts. Theodore Roosevelt would be satisfied with the recognition that the battlefields and forts in the Champlain Valley have received. In 1903, in support of the monument commemorating the Battle of Lake George, President Roosevelt stressed the importance of "keeping alive a sense of continuity with the historic past" at "these two lakes which formed a highway of warfare."[242]

**Remains of the French lines at Fort Ticonderoga (Carillon), where the British and provincial army suffered more than 1,900 men killed or wounded in 1758.
(Photo by the author)**

APPENDIX
French and Indian War Forts and Exhibits in the Lake Champlain, Lake George, and Hudson River Corridor

Rogers Island Visitor Center
11 Rogers Island Drive
Fort Edward, NY 12828
Phone (518) 747-3693
www.rogersisland.org

Lake George Battlefield Park/ Fort George
Beach Road
Lake George, NY 12845
Phone (518) 668-3352
www.lakegeorgehistorical.org/fort-george.htm

Fort William Henry Museum
Canada Street
Lake George, NY 12845
Phone (518) 668-5471
www.fwhmuseum.com

Lake George Historical Association
Old Warren County Court House
290 Canada Street
Lake George, NY 12845
Phone (518) 668-5044
www.lakegeorgehistorical.org

Land Tortoise National Historic Landmark, New York State Submerged Heritage Preserve
Department of Environmental Conservation
Lake George, NY 12845
Phone (518) 668-3352
www.dec.ny.gov

Fort Ticonderoga National Historic Landmark
100 Fort Road, PO Box 390
Ticonderoga, NY 12883
Phone (518) 585-2821
www.fort-ticonderoga.org

Crown Point State Historic Site
21 Grandview Drive
Crown Point, NY 12928-2852
Phone (518) 597-4666
www.lakechamplainregion.com/cphistoricsite

Lake Champlain Maritime Museum
4472 Basin Harbor Road
Vergennes, VT 05491
Phone (802) 475-2022
www.lcmm.org

Clinton County Historical Museum
98 Ohio Avenue
Plattsburgh, NY 12903
Phone (518) 561-0340
www.clintoncountyhistorical.org

Fort Lennox National Historic Site of Canada
1 61st Avenue
Saint-Paul-de-L'Île-aux-Noix
Quebec JOJ IGO
Phone (450) 291-5700
www.pc.gc.ca/eng/lhn-nhs/qc/lennox

Fort Chambly National Historic Site of Canada
2 Rue De Richelieu Street
Chambly, Quebec J3L 2B9
Phone (450) 658-1585
www.pc.gc.ca/eng/lhn-nhs/qc/fortchambly

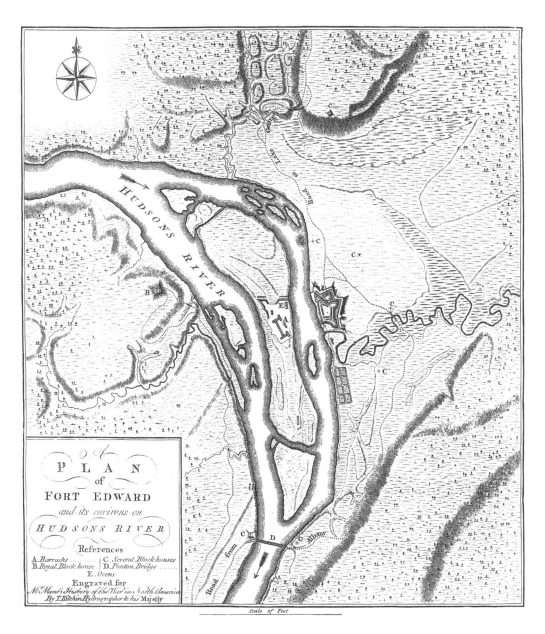

Plan of Fort Edward and Rogers Island, engraved by T. Kitchin.
From *The History of the Late War in North-America* by Thomas Mante (1772).

Notes

ABBREVIATIONS

AAS   American Antiquarian Society, Worcester, Massachusetts

AB   Abercromby Papers, Huntington Library, San Marino, California

BFTM   *The Bulletin of the Fort Ticonderoga Museum*

Coll. Conn. HS   *Collections of the Connecticut Historical Society*

Coll. NYHS   *Collections of the New-York Historical Society*

CSL   Connecticut State Library, Archives Division, Hartford, Connecticut

EIHC   *The Essex Institute Historical Collections*

JP   James Sullivan and others, eds., *The Papers of William Johnson*, 14 vols. (Albany: The University of the State of New York, 1923-1965)

LO   Loudoun Papers, Huntington Library, San Marino, California

MASS HS   Massachusetts Historical Society, Boston

NAC   National Archives of Canada, Ottawa

NEHGR   *New-England Historical and Genealogical Register*

NYSL   New York State Library, Albany, New York

NYCD   E. B. O'Callaghan, ed., *Documents Relative to the Colonial History of the State of New York*, 10 vols. (Albany: Weed, Parsons and Company, 1853-1858)

NYD   E. B. O'Callaghan, ed., *The Documentary History of the State of New York*, 4 vols. (Albany: Weed, Parsons & Co.: Charles Van Benthuysen, Public Printers, 1849-1851)

PRO   Public Record Office, London
      CO   Colonial Office Papers
      WO   War Office Papers

INTRODUCTION

1. John F. Kennedy, foreword to *Naval Documents of the American Revolution*, ed. by William Bell Clark (Washington, D.C.: Naval History Division, Department of the Navy, 1964), Volume 1, ix.

1. CONTEST FOR A CONTINENT 1609-1713

1. H. P. Biggar, ed., *The Works of Samuel De Champlain* (Toronto: The Champlain Society, 1925), Volume 2, 96; Champlain was told by his Indian allies that they had to "pass a rapid" (falls on the La Chute River) and "enter another lake" (Lake George) to reach their "enemies." After the engagement with the Mohawks, Champlain observed the "rapid," which points to Ticonderoga as the probable site of the battle. Ibid., 93.
2. Ibid., 99.

3. Ibid., 100.
4. Francis Jennings, *The Ambiguous Iroquois Empire* (New York: W. W. Norton & Company, 1984), 80; *NYCD*, 1:182.
5. *NYCD*, 1:180.
6. Jennings, *Ambiguous Iroquois*, 87, 89, 95, 100; Dean R. Snow, *The Iroquois* (Cambridge, MA: Blackwell Publishers, Inc., 1994), 109-11, 114-15.
7. Reuben Gold Thwaites, ed., *Travels and Explorations of the Society of Jesus Missionaries in New France* (Cleveland: The Burrows Brothers Company, 1898), Volume 22, 277; The fort was subsequently burned by the Iroquois. *NYCD*, 9:20; Guy Omeron Coolidge, *The French Occupation of the Champlain Valley from 1609 to 1759* (1938; reprint ed., Fleischmanns, NY: Purple Mountain Press, 1999), 22.
8. Thwaites, *Travels and Explorations*, 27: 267; Allan Greer, ed., *The Jesuit Relations: Natives and Missionaries in Seventeenth-Century North America* (Boston: Bedford/St. Martin's, 2000), 104; William Smith, Jr., *The History of the Province of New-York From the First Discoveries to the Year 1732*, ed. Michael Kammen (Cambridge, MA: The Belknap Press of Harvard University Press, 1972), Volume 1, 194.
9. John Gilmary Shea, trans., "Of the Captivity of Father Isaac Jogues, of the Society of Jesus, Among the Mohawks in 1642 and 1643," *Coll. NYHS* 3 (2nd Series) (1857): 175-76.
10. Ibid., 181-82.
11. Thwaites, *Travels and Explorations*, 29: 48-49; See also Floyd G. Lounsbury, *Iroquois Place-Names in the Champlain Valley* (Albany: The University of the State of New York, 1965), 41-46.
12. Ibid., 55-57.
13. *NYCD*, 2: 248.
14. Ibid., 248-49, see also 250-53.
15. Ibid., 611-12.
16. *NYCD*, 9: 20.
17. Ibid., 25-27.
18. A small wooden fort, built by the French during the fall of 1666 at Ticonderoga, was "close to the falls which separate the two bodies of water." See Roger R. P. Dechame, "The First Fort at Fort Ticonderoga," *BFTM* 15 (Winter 1988): 11.
19. *NYCD*, 1: 70; See also Coolidge, *French Occupation*, 36; *NYD*, 1: 69-70.
20. *NYCD*, 9: 271.
21. Ibid., 338.
22. Ibid.
23. Ibid.
24. *NYCD*, 9: 400.
25. *NYD*, 1: 286.
26. *NYCD*, 9: 423.
27. Ibid., 435.
28. *NYD*, 1: 301.
29. Coolidge, *French Occupation*, 59.
30. *NYCD*, 4: 193-94.
31. Ibid., 196.
32. *NYD*, 2: 285.
33. Ibid., 287.
34. Ibid., 290-91; *Encyclopedia of New York State*, s.v. "Leisler Jacob."
35. *NYCD*, 9: 457.
36. Samuel A. Green, ed., *Two Narratives of the Expedition Against Quebec, A.D. 1690* (Cambridge, MA: John Wilson and Son, 1902), 38; French sources claimed that 2,000 English troops landed. *NYCD*, 9: 457.
37. Green, *Two Narratives*, 39; For additional information on the problems with the English attack, see Emerson W. Baker and John G. Reid, *The New England Knight: Sir William Phips 1651-1695* (Toronto: University of Toronto Press, 1998), 98-99.
38. *NYCD*, 3: 800, 805; See also Theodore C. Corbett, *A Clash of Cultures of the Warpath of Nations* (Fleischmanns, NY: Purple Mountain Press, 2002), 41; Allen W. Trelease, *Indian Affairs in Colonial New York: The Seventeenth Century* (Lincoln: University of Nebraska Press, 1997), 305-6.
39. *NYCD*, 3: 800-801.
40. Ibid., 802; In the same journal Peter Schuyler mentioned that 266 men were on the expedition. Ibid., 805.
41. Ibid., 802.
42. *NYCD*, 9: 550.
43. *NYCD*, 4: 19. There are some inconsistencies in the dates in the English version and French account of the engagements and retreat. *NYCD*, 9: 550-61; *NYCD*, 4: 6-7, 14-19; See also Corbett, *Clash of Cultures*, 43-47; Coolidge, *French Occupation*, 64-66.

44. *NYCD*, 9: 837-39; Coolidge, *French Occupation,* 77.
45. *NYCD*, 9: 830-31.
46. *NYCD*, 5: 254. This number includes 800 Native Americans; other documents list 661 and 682. Ibid., 270, 272.
47. Rev. Thomas Buckingham, "A Diary of the Land Expedition Against Crown Point in the Year 1711," in *Roll and Journal of Connecticut Service in Queen Anne's War* (Hartford, CT: Acorn Club, 1916), 36.
48. Ibid., 40; *NYCD*, 5: 277.
49. Samuel Niles, "Niles History of the Indian and French Wars," *Collections of the Massachusetts Historical Society* 5 (Fourth Series) (1861): 329-30.
50. *NYCD*, 5: 277; The French observed "about 1,500 to 1,600 dead bodies, of which about a score were women, part of whom had infants in arms," and they also saw "horses, sheep, dogs, and poultry" on the shore. Edward P. Hamilton, *The French and Indian Wars* (Garden City, NY: Doubleday & Company, Inc.,1962), 55.
51. *NYCD*, 5: 277.
52. Buckingham, "A Diary," 43.
53. John Wolfe Lydekker, *The Faithful Mohawks* (New York: The Macmillan Company, 1938), 33.

2. FORT ST. FRÉDÉRIC

1. *NYCD*, 9: 1021.
2. Ibid., 1023.
3. Ibid., 1022-23.
4. Ibid., 1025.
5. Guy Omeron Coolidge, *The French Occupation of the Champlain Valley from 1609 to 1759* (1938; reprint ed., Fleischmanns, NY: Purple Mountain Press, 1999), 99; Peter S. Palmer, *History of Lake Champlain*, 4th ed. (1886; reprint ed., Fleischmanns, NY: Purple Mountain Press, 1992), 5.
6. *The American Weekly Mercury*, 7 October to 14 October 1731.
7. *NYCD*, 9: 1034.
8. William Smith, Jr., *The History of the Province of New-York*, ed. by Michael Kammen (Cambridge, MA: The Belknap Press of Harvard University Press, 1972), Volume 1, 194.
9. Ibid., 1037.
10. Ibid., 1038.
11. Ibid., 1038, 1045.
12. René Chartrand, *French Fortresses in North America 1535-1763: Québec, Montréal, Louisbourg and New Orleans* (New York: Osprey Publishing, 2005), 10.
13. [Emmanuel] Crespel, *Travels in North America with a Narrative of His Shipwreck* (London, Sampson Low, 1797), 41-42; See also Henry Wayland Hill, *The Champlain Tercentenary*, First Report, 2nd ed. (Albany: J.B. Lyon Company, State Printers, 1913), 394-95.
14. Ibid., 44-45.
15. Ibid., 44.
16. Coolidge, *French Occupation*, 122-23.
17. Ibid.
18. *NYCD*, 9: 1095.
19. Coolidge, *French Occupation*, 124.
20. Samuel G. Drake, *A Particular History of the Five Years French and Indian War* (1870; reprint ed., Bowie, MD: Heritage Books, Inc., 1995), 268; Arthur Latham Perry, *Origins in Williamstown*, 3rd ed. (Williamstown, MA: Arthur Latham Perry, 1900), 169-70.
21. Theodore C. Corbett, *A Clash of Cultures of the Warpath of Nations* (Fleischmanns, NY: Purple Mountain Press, 2002), 177.
22. Adolph B. Benson, ed., *Peter Kalm's Travels in North America* (New York: Wilson-Erickson, Inc., 1937), Volume 2, 382; See also Russell Bellico, *Chronicles of Lake Champlain: Journeys in War and Peace* (Fleischmanns, NY: Purple Mountain Press, 1999), 59; For a fresh look at Kalm's travels see Paula Ivaska Robbins, *The Travels of Peter Kalm, Finnish-Swedish Naturalist, in North America, 1748-1752* (Fleischmanns, NY: Purple Mountain Press, 2007).
23. Benson, *Kalm's Travels*, 1: 379-80.
24. Corbett, *Clash of Cultures*, 178-79, 185, 190; Coolidge, *French Occupation*, 124-25.
25. *NYCD*, 9: 1050.
26. *NYCD*, 6: 582. In 1755 William Johnson also mentioned that the French "have a vessel which sails and brings all sorts of supplys from Crown Point." *JP*, 2:75.
27. *NYCD*, 10: 36.
28. Seth Pomeroy, *The Journals and Papers of Seth Pomeroy*, ed. by Louis Effingham De Forest (New York: Society of Colonial Wars in the State of New York, 1926), 21.

29. Ibid., 28.
30. Ibid., 35.
31. *NYCD*, 10: 38, 76; See also *Boston Evening-Post*, 2 December 1745.
32. *NYCD*, 10: 38; *Boston Evening-Post*, 2 December 1745; *NYCD*, 6: 288; See also Drake, *A Particular History*, 86-87.
33. Coolidge, *French Occupation*, 126.
34. *NYCD*, 10: 76; See also Corbett, *Clash of Cultures*, 135.
35. *Boston Evening-Post*, 2 December 1745.
36. *NYCD*, 6: 286; Governor Clinton reiterated the request shortly thereafter in a letter to the Lords of the Trade. *NYCD*, 6: 288.
37. Perry, *Origins in Williamstown*, 163.
38. *NYCD*, 10: 34.
39. *NYCD*, 6: 310.
40. *Boston Evening-Post*, 8 September 1746; See also *Boston Weekly News-Letter*, 28 August 1746.
41. *NYCD*, 6: 314; Corbett, *Clash of Cultures*, 144-46.
42. *NYCD*, 10: 89; See also Drake, *A Particular History*, 135.
43. *NYCD*, 10: 42.
44. Ibid., 52.
45. Ibid.
46. *NYCD*, 10: 77.
47. Ibid., 35, see also 34.
48. Drake, *A Particular History*, 254; For an "extract" of John Norton's letter regarding the attack on Fort Massachusetts see *Boston Evening-Post*, 15 September 1746; See also George Sheldon, *History of Deerfield, Massachusetts* (Deerfield, MA: Pocumtuck Valley Memorial Assoc., 1895), Volume 1, 543-45.
49. Drake, *A Particular History*, 256.
50. Ibid., 257.
51. Ibid., 260.
52. *NYCD*, 10: 35.
53. Most of those taken at Fort Massachusetts were held in captivity for a year. For a list of captives and the dates that they were returned, see Perry, *Origins in Williamstown*, 187. For a list of other captives who died in Quebec see "Norton's Redeemed Captive" in Drake, *A Particular History*, 278-294.
54. *Boston Weekly News-Letter*, 28 August 1746; Drake, *A Particular History*, 125; *Boston Evening-Post*, 1 September 1746.
55. *Boston Evening-Post*, 22 September 1746; *Boston Weekly News-Letter*, 25 September 1746.
56. Perry, *Origins in Williamstown*, 193.
57. Ibid., 198; See also Wyllis E. Wright, *Colonel Ephraim Williams: A Documentary Life* (Pittsfield, MA: Berkshire County Historical Society, 1970), 24.
58. *Boston Weekly News-Letter*, 30 April 1747; For the French version of the four-day siege, see *NYCD*, 10: 97.
59. *Boston Weekly News-Letter*, 30 April 1747.
60. Ibid.
69. Ibid.
62. *Boston Weekly News-Letter*, 2 April 1747.
63. *Boston Weekly News-Letter*, 23 April 1747.
64. *Boston Gazette*, 7 July 1747; *Boston Evening-Post*, 6 July 1747; Luc de La Corne later reported that 45 prisoners and 28 scalps were taken. Perry, *Origins in Williamstown*, 163.
65. *Boston Gazette*, 14 July 1747; *NYCD*, 10: 102, 108, 110; *NYCD*, 6: 387.
66. *Boston Evening-Post*, 20 July 1747; See also *NYCD*, 6: 383.
67. *Boston Gazette*, 15 September 1747; *Boston Weekly News-Letter*, 10 September 1747.
68. Ibid.
69. *NYCD*, 6: 384.
70. *Boston Weekly News-Letter*, 10 September 1747; *NYCD*, 6: 389.
71. *NYCD*, 6: 389.
72. *Boston Gazette*, 15 September 1747; *Boston Weekly News-Letter*, 17 September 1747; *NYCD*, 6: 390.
73. *Boston Gazette*, 25 August 1747; *Boston Weekly News-Letter*, 27 August 1747.
74. *NYCD*, 6: 406.
75. Corbett, *Clash of Cultures*, 154; Coolidge, *French Occupation*, 145; See also *NYCD*, 6: 618-19; On February 12, 1748, Governor George Clinton again requested funds from the New York Assembly, including money for repairs to the fort at Albany and "for removing the cannon from Saratoga to Albany." *Boston Gazette*, 1 March 1748.
76. *NYCD*, 10: 148.
77. *Boston Gazette*, 10 November 1747; See also *Boston Weekly News-Letter*, 12 November 1747; *Boston Evening-Post*, 2 November 1747; Drake, *A Particular History*, 153.

78. Eleazer Melven, "Journal of Capt. Eleazer Melven," *Collections of the New-Hampshire Historical Society* 5 (1837): 209.
79. Ibid., 211.
80. Drake, *A Particular History*, 160-61, 163, 168-71; Coolidge, *French Occupation*, 147; Samuel Niles, "Niles History of the Indian and French Wars," *Collections of the Massachusetts Historical Society* 5 (Fourth Series) (1861): 378-80.
81. Timothy J. Shannon, *Indians and Colonists at the Crossroads of Empire: The Albany Congress of 1754* (Ithaca, NY: Cornell University Press, 2000), 124; Benson, *Kalm's Travels*, 1: 342.
82. *NYCD*, 6: 442.
83. Ibid., 446.
84. *NYCD*, 6: 439.
85. Ibid.
86. Ibid., 440.
87. Ibid.
88. Benson, *Kalm's Travels*, 2: 391.
89. Ibid., 392.
90. Ibid., 397.
91. Phineas Stevens, "Journal of Capt. Phineas Stevens to and from Canada—1749," *Collections of the New-Hampshire Historical Society* 5 (1837): 201.
92. Ibid., 203-4.
93. Ibid., 204.
94. Ibid., 205.
95. *NYCD*, 10: 210, 214-15; Drake, *A Particular History*, 179.
96. *NYCD*, 6: 580-81.
97. Ibid., 582; This account was later published in the *Boston Evening-Post*, 26 May 1755.

3. EXPEDITION TO FORT ST FRÉDÉRIC

1. *NYCD*, 6: 993; *NYCD*, 10: 275.
2. Theodore C. Corbett, *A Clash of Cultures of the Warpath of Nations*, (Fleischmanns, NY: Purple Mountain Press, 2002), 155-56.
3. D. Peter MacLeod, *The Canadian Iroquois and the Seven Years' War* (Toronto: Dundurn Press, 1996), 49-50.
4. *NYCD*, 6: 782.
5. Ibid.
6. *NYCD*, 6: 801.
7. Ibid., 802.
8. Ibid., 870.
9. Timothy J. Shannon, *Indians and Colonists at the Crossroads of Empire: The Albany Congress of 1754* (Ithaca, NY: Cornell University Press, 2000), *159*.
10. Ibid., 83.
11. Ibid.
12. "Journal of the Proceedings of the Congress Held at Albany, in 1754" *Collections of the Massachusetts Historical Society* 5 (3rd Series) (1836): 70.
13. Ibid., 72.
14. *NYCD*, 6: 936.
15. Ibid., 921.
16. Ibid., 925.
17. Ibid., 943; On February 13, 1755, Governor William Shirley of Massachusetts had requested that the legislature support construction of a fort "upon the rocky Eminence" overlooking Fort St. Frédéric. Charles Henry Lincoln, ed., *Correspondence of William Shirley* (New York: The Macmillan Company, 1912), Volume 2, 128.
18. *NYCD*, 6: 961.
19. *NYD*, 2: 651, 653; Another set of instructions from William Shirley stated that "one or more Batterys [were] to be Erected upon the Rocky Eminence" near Fort St. Frédéric. If any resistance were to occur, "You are to attack" and dislodge the French. *JP*, 1: 473.
20. *NYD*, 2: 652.
21. Walter Kendall Watkins, "Lake George Expedition 1755," *The Society of Colonial Wars of the Commonwealth of Massachusetts* (1906): 153-54.
22. William M. Fowler, Jr., *Empires at War: The French and Indian War and the Struggle for North America 1754-1763* (New York: Walker & Co., 2005), 69.
23. John Grenier, *The First Way of War: American War Making on the Frontiers* (New York: Cambridge Univer-

sity Press, 2005), 113; See also Stephen Brumwell, *Redcoats: The British Soldier and War in the Americ-as 1755-1763* (Cambridge, U.K.: Cambridge University Press, 2002), 199.

24. Cadwallader Colden, *History of the Five Indian Nations of Canada* (New York: A.S. Barnes and Company, 1904), Volume 2, 218; See also Fintan O'Toole, *White Savage: William Johnson and the Invention of America* (New York: Farrar Straus, and Giroux, 2005), 77; In 1755 Thomas Williams had heard that William Johnson "has the war dance, when the Indians painted up the General" during the conference at Fort Johnson. Thomas Williams, "Correspondence of Doctor Thomas Williams of Deerfield, Mass., A Surgeon in the Army," *The Historical Magazine* 7 (April 1870): 209.

25. *JP*, 2: 570-77; O'Toole, *White Savage*, 115.

26. *NYCD*, 6: 972.

27. Ibid., 978.

28. Ibid., 979.

29. Ibid., 980.

30. Ibid., 983.

31. Barbara J. Sivertsen, *Turtles, Wolves, and Bears: A Mohawk Family History* (Bowie, MD: Heritage Books, 1996), 23, 32-33, 62, 64, 66, 136; *Encyclopedia of New York State*, s.v. "King Hendrick"; Edward Dodge, "King Hendrick," *Fort George Advice* (Spring 2004): 3-4.

32. *JP*, 9: 203.

33. *NYCD*, 6: 984.

34. *JP*, 1: 733.

35. *NYCD*, 6: 986.

36. *JP*, 1: 841.

37. Seth Pomeroy, *The Journals and Papers of Seth Pomeroy*, ed. by Louis Effingham De Forest (New York: Society of Colonial Wars in the State of New York, 1926), 102.

38. *JP*, 2: 7, 10.

39. Watkins, "Lake George Expedition 1755," 154; See also Theodore Burnham Lewis, Jr., "The Crown Point Campaign 1755," *BFTM* 12 (October 1970): 417.

40. James Hill, "The Diary of a Private on the First Expedition to Crown Point," ed. by Edna V. Moffett, *The New England Quarterly* 5 (1932): 605.

41. *JP*, 1: 730-31.

42. Elisha Hawley, "Capt. Hawley's Journal," in *History of Northampton*, Volume 2, by James R. Trumbull (Northampton, MA: Press of Gazette Printing Co., 1902), 256.

43. John Burk, "John Burk's Diary," in *History of the Town of Bernardston*, by Lucy Cutler Kellogg (Greenfield, MA: Press of E. A. Hall & Co., 1902), 42; See also Pomeroy, *Journals and Papers*, 105.

44. Burk, "John Burk's Diary," 42; The same day Captain Richard Godfrey noted that "we had to draw up every Battoe over a ladder" at the falls. Richard Godfrey, "A Journal of the March of Captain Richard Godfrey's Company, 1755," in *History of Taunton, Mass.*, by Samuel H. Emery (Syracuse, NY: D. Mason, 1893), 421; Colonel Joseph Blanchard wrote that bateaux were "the most stupid invention for ye use that ever was." Nathanial Bouton, ed., *Provincial Papers: Documents and Records Relating to the Province of New-Hampshire* (Manchester, NH: James M. Campbell, State Printer, 1872), Volume 6, 431.

45. *Boston Gazette*, 4 August 1755.

46. Hawley, "Capt. Hawley's Journal," 256.

47. Burk, "John Burk's Diary," 43.

48. Godfrey, "Journal of the March," 421-22.

49. Pomeroy, *Journals and Papers*, 107-8; Christopher Champline wrote that "Gen. Lyman has finished a block fort of near 70 feet square and had almost picketed it in." Christopher Champline, August 14, 1755, unpublished letter (M-202B), Fort Ticonderoga Thompson-Pell Research Center; See also *NYCD*, 10: 332.

50. James Gilbert, "A Journal Kept by James Gilbert," *Magazine of New England History* 3 (1893): 190; See also Pomeroy, *Journals and Papers*, 107.

51. Burk, "John Burk's Diary," 43; *NYD*, 2: 679; Champline, letter; See also *JP*, 9: 209.

52. Nathan Whiting, "Letters of Col. Nathan Whiting," *Papers of the New Haven Historical Society* 6 (1900): 137.

53. Gilbert, "Journal," 191; At Fort Johnson a month earlier, Lieutenant Colonel Nathan Whiting remarked that the Indians with William Johnson were "of all Sex and Sizes who by their od[d] shapes and painting Look[e]d more Like so many Devils than human Creatures." Whiting, "Letters," 136; Captain William Hervey described Mohawks as having "rings...in their noses and ears...their heads were painted all over with vermillion." William Hervey, *Journals of Hon. William Hervey* (Bury St. Edmund's: Paul & Matthew, Butter Market, 1906), 3.

54. *JP*, 1: 818.

55. Ibid., 732.

56. Delphina L. H. Clark, *Phineas Lyman—Connecticut's General* (Springfield, MA: Connecticut Valley Historical Museum, 1964), 16.
57. *JP*, 9: 210.
58. *JP*, 1: 783.
59. Ibid.
60. Ibid., 861.
61. Burk, "John Burk's Diary," 44; See also Hawley, "Capt. Hawley's Journal," 257.
62. *NYCD*, 6: 1000; Gilbert, "Journal," 192; *Boston Weekly News-Letter*, 4 September 1755.
63. *JP*, 1: 860; Pomeroy, *Journals and Papers*, 110.
64. *NYCD*, 6: 1001-2; On August 15 a council of officers had endorsed an offer of reinforcements from Connecticut and New York. *NYD*, 2: 681.
65. *NYD*, 2: 682.
66. *JP*, 1: 777.
67. *JP*, 1: 861, 883.
68. Hill, "Diary," 607; Burk, "John Burk's Diary," 44.
69. *JP*, 2: 31.
70. *JP*, 2: 66, 84.
71. Pomeroy, *Journals and Papers*, 110.
72. Hawley, "Capt. Hawley's Journal," 257.
73. Pomeroy, *Journals and Papers*, 110. The following day Pomeroy reported that Johnson and his officers had a "good din[n]er of cold, bo[i]l[e]d & roast venison dr[a]nk good fresh lemon punch & wine." Ibid., 111. The Mohawks had killed three deer the day before.

4. BATTLE OF LAKE GEORGE 1755

1. John Burk, "John Burk's Diary," in *History of the Town of Bernardston,* by Lucy Cutler Kellogg (Greenfield, MA: Press of E. A. Hall & Co., 1902), 44.
2. James Gilbert, "A Journal Kept by James Gilbert," *Magazine of New England History* 3 (1893): 193.
3. *NYCD*, 6: 999.
4. Elisha Hawley, "Capt. Hawley's Journal," in *History of Northampton*, Volume 2, by James R. Trumbull (Northampton, MA: Press of Gazette Printing Co., 1902), 257; See also Seth Pomeroy, *The Journals and Papers of Seth Pomeroy*, ed. by Louis Effingham De Forest (New York: Society of Colonial Wars in the State of New York, 1926), 112; Gilbert, "Journal," 193-94.
5. *JP*, 1: 869.
6. *JP*, 2: 13.
7. Ibid., 10.
8. Christopher Champline, August 14, 1755, unpublished letter (M-202B), Fort Ticonderoga Thompson-Pell Research Center.
9. Burk, "John Burk's Diary," 44.
10. Ibid., 45.
11. *NYD*, 2: 689.
12. Ibid.
13. Gilbert, "Journal," 194; James Hill, "The Diary of a Private on the First Expedition to Crown Point," ed. by Edna V. Moffett, *The New England Quarterly* 5 (1932): 608; John Burk had a slightly different entry on September 4, 1755: "Began to build a fort." Burk, "John Burk's Diary," 45; On September 3 Nathan Whiting wrote that "our people [are] building a fort & Stone House" at Lake George. Nathan Whiting, "Letters of Col. Nathan Whiting," *Papers of the New Haven Historical Society* 6 (1900): 138.
14. Hill, "Diary," 608.
15. *JP*, 1: 883; This information, similarly worded, appeared in a Boston newspaper. *Boston Gazette*, 1 September 1755.
16. Theodore Burnham Lewis, Jr., "The Crown Point Campaign 1755," *BFTM* 13 (December 1970): 26.
17. *NYCD*, 10: 316. Dieskau suggested that his troops arrived on "August 16 and 17." Ibid.
18. *JP*, 2: 18-19; See also the total number of troops listed in the papers found on Major General Dieskau. PRO, CO 5/46, University Publications of America, microfilm reel 1, frame 236.
19. *NYCD*, 10: 319.
20. Ibid., 313.
21. Ibid., 316.
22. Ibid.
23. Roger R. P. Dechame, "Why Carillon?" *BFTM* 13 (Fall 1980): 432-46; PRO, CO 5/46, UP microfilm reel 1, frame 638; Carrion's name is listed as Philippe Dufresnoy Carion in Jack Verney, *The Good Regiment: The Carignan-Salières 1665-1668* (Montreal & Kingston: McGill-Queen's University Press, 1991), 167.

24. Lewis, "Campaign," 43.
25. *NYCD*, 10: 338; Later Governor Vaudreuil wrote that "M. de Dieskau persuaded himself that the main body had retired." Ibid., 319.
26. Ibid., 338.
27. Ibid., 316, see also 335.
28. Ibid., 335; These figures were from a report by Lieutenant Colonel Pierre-André Gohin, Comte de Montreuil, second in command of the expedition. The numbers, however, vary in other reports. *JP*, 2: 26-27, 58, 72; *New-York Mercury*, 22 September 1755.
29. *NYCD*, 10: 320, see also 41; Thomas Mante, *The History of the Late War in North-America* (1772; reprint ed., New York: Research Reprints, Inc., n.d.), 30.
30. Ibid., 328.
31. Pierre Pouchot, *Memoir Upon the Late War in North America Between the French and English*, trans. Michael Cardy and ed. Brian Leigh Dunnigan (Youngstown, NY: Old Fort Niagara Association, Inc., 1994), 87; See also *NYCD*, 10: 344.
32. *NYCD*, 10: 320, 335, 339. Although Governor Vaudreuil wrote that Dieskau "sent back 200 men from Carillon" to guard the canoes and bateaux at South Bay, Lieutenant Colonel Pierre-André Gohin, Comte de Montreuil, reported that Dieskau "left all his bateaux under a guard of 120 men," who had originally accompanied the expedition. *NYCD*, 10: 320, 335.
33. Ibid., 320; Dieskau may have camped near Cold Brook on September 6. John W. Krueger, *A Most Memorable Day: The Battle of Lake George, September 8, 1755* (Saranac Lake, NY: North Country Community College Press, 1980), 24.
34. *JP*, 2: 16.
35. Ibid., 53.
36. Ibid., 17; See also Daniel Claus, *Daniel Claus' Narrative of His Relations with Sir William Johnson and Experiences in the Lake George Fight* (New York: Society of Colonial Wars in the State of New York, 1904), 12; Godfrey, "Journal of the March," 422-23; Burk, "John Burk's Diary," 45.
37. Claus, *Narrative*, 12.
38. Ibid.; Johnson's message, discovered by the French on the body of Jacob Adams, directed Blanchard "to withdraw all the troops there within the Works thrown up." *JP*, 9: 228.
39. *JP*, 9: 229.
40. Ibid.; See also Hawley, "Capt. Hawley's Journal," 259; *NYCD*, 10: 320, 339, 367; *NYD*, 2: 691.
41. D. Peter MacLeod, *The Canadian Iroquois and the Seven Years' War* (Toronto: Dundurn Press, 1996), 69.
42. Daniel Emerson, "A Journal of My Procedure with the Army to Crown Point—Begun July Ye 8, 1755," in *Ipswich Emersons*, by Benjamin Kendall Emerson (Boston: Press of David Clapp & Son, 1900), 90; Nathaniel Folsom, "Captain Folsom's Fight," *Proceeding of the Massachusetts Historical Society*, 18 (2nd Series) (1903/1904): 318. Folsom "found Adams & found also eleven wagons almost consumed." Ibid.
43. *NYCD*, 10: 317.
44. *NYCD*, 6: 1014.
45. *NYCD*, 10: 342; Claus, *Narrative*, 13; See also *The London Magazine* (October 1759): 534.
46. *NYCD*, 10: 342.
47. Ibid.
48. *NYD*, 2: 691; *Boston Gazette*, 22 September 1755; *New-York Mercury*, 29 September 1755.
49. Hawley, "Capt. Hawley's Journal," 259; See also Claus, *Narrative*, 13.
50. Claus, *Narrative*, 13.
51. Timothy Dwight, *Travels in New-England and New-York* (New Haven, CT: S. Converse, 1822), Volume 3, 363; For more details of Dwight's trips to Lake George see Russell P. Bellico, *Chronicles of Lake George: Journeys in War and Peace* (Fleischmanns, NY: Purple Mountain Press, 1995), 205-25.
52. Dwight, *Travels*, 374.
53. Gilbert, "Journal," 195; *JP*, 9: 229.
54. Gilbert, "Journal," 195; See also *NYCD*, 6: 1013.
55. Gilbert, "Journal," 195.
56. E. Hoyt, *Antiquarian Researches: Comprising a History of the Indian Wars* (Greenfield, MA: Ansel Phelps, 1824), 273. The eyewitness also mentioned seeing a herd of deer "rushed down the valley and passed between the men, indicating great fright." Ibid.
57. Stanley Pargellis, ed., *Military Affairs in North America 1748-1765* (1936; reprint ed., New York: Archon Books, 1969), 139; Arthur Latham Perry, *Origins in Williamstown* (New York: Charles Scribner's Sons, 1894), 370.
58. Dwight, *Travels*, 348.
59. *Research and Mapping of Colonial Road Between Fort Edward and Fort William Henry* (Glens Falls, NY: Warren County Historical Society, 2005), 30.

60. Samuel Blodget, *A Prospective–Plan of the Battle near Lake George on the Eighth Day of September, 1755 with an Explanation thereof* (Boston: n.p., 1756), 1.

61. Claus, *Narrative*, 13.

62. Ibid., 13-14; Years later John Norton essentially repeated the same version of the story. Carl F. Klinck and James J. Talman, eds., *The Journal of Major John Norton 1816* (Toronto: The Champlain Society, 1970), 266; Later versions of the incident had different wording, including that Hendrick had informed Ephraim Williams that he had "scented Indians." Hoyt, *Antiquarian Researches*, 273-74.

63. Claus, *Narrative*, 14; Another contemporary source, based on direct testimony, supported this statement. Charles Chauncy, *A Second Letter to a Friend; Giving a more particular Narrative of the Defeat of the French Army at Lake-George* (Boston: Edes and Gill, 1755), 4.

64. *NYCD*, 6: 1008.

65. *NYCD*, 10: 342; Governor Vaudreuil reported that "two of our Indians…fired" first. Ibid., 321; See also Daniel Dulany, "Newsletter of 9 December 1755," *The Pennsylvania Magazine of History and Biography* 3 (1879): 29.

66. *NYCD*, 6: 1013.

67. Phineas Lyman, "Second Letter of General Lyman to His Wife," *History of Durham, Connecticut*, by William Chauncey Fowler (Hartford: Press of Wiley, Waterman & Eaton, 1866), 136; Pomeroy, *Journals and Papers*, 137. Thomas Williams noted that the fighting had ended about ten-thirty. Thomas Williams, "Correspondence of Doctor Thomas Williams of Deerfield, Mass., A Surgeon in the Army," *The Historical Magazine 7 (April 1870)*: 212.

68. Chauncy, *Second Letter*, 5; Johnson's letter to the colonial governors on September 9 stated that "about ten o'clock" some of the retreating troops and Mohawks reached the Lake George camp. *NYD*, 2: 692.

69. Wyllis E. Wright, *Colonel Ephraim Williams: A Documentary Life* (Pittsfield, MA: Berkshire County Historical Society, 1970), 157.

70. "Historical Sketch of the Life and Character of Colonel Ephraim Williams, and Williams College, Founded in 1793, in Consequence of His Liberal Bequest," *Collections of the Massachusetts Historical Society* 7 (First Series) (1801): 50; Arthur Latham Perry, *Origins in Williamstown*, 3rd ed. (Williamstown, MA: A. L. Perry, 1900), 355; See also James Austin Holden, "Colonel Ephraim Williams," *New York State Historical Association Proceedings*, Volume 1 (1901): 48; Edward J. Dodge, "Ephraim Williams," *Fort George Advice*, Fall 2004, 4-5, 8.

71. Pomeroy, *Journals and Papers*, 114.

72. *NYCD*, 6: 1008.

73. Claus, *Narrative*, 14.

74. Emerson, "Journal," 91.

75. *NYD*, 2: 692.

76. Pargellis, *Military Affairs*, 139.

77. Pomeroy, *Journals and Papers*, 114.

78. Chauncy, *Second Letter*, 6; Perry, *Origins in Williamstown* (1894), 370.

79. Claus, *Narrative*, 15; Later in his description, Claus mentioned "the Line of Wagons." Ibid., 17; Chauncy wrote that a participant reported that the breastwork consisted of "bodies of trees laid singly upon the ground, round the Camp, and in many places so as not to touch one another." Chauncy, *Second Letter*, 8; Blodget recalled that the breastwork "was nothing more than Bodies of Trees laid singly on the Ground. They were hastily fell'd while our Men were retreating" from the first engagement. Blodget, *Prospective-Plan*, 2.

80. *NYCD*, 10: 367, 322, 335.

81. *NYD*, 2: 692; One of the early written accounts of the battle by E. Hoyt, who interviewed some of the participants, noted that "old Fort George, now in ruins, occupies the eminence a little in the rear of the ground on which Johnson's line was formed." Hoyt, *Antiquarian Researches*, 275.

82. Blodget, *Prospective-Plan*, 2-3.

83. Pargellis, *Military Affairs*, 139.

84. Lyman, "Second Letter," 136; See also *Boston Gazette*, Supplement, 29 September 1755.

85. Lyman, "Second Letter," 136; Perez Marsh reported that the "fright [of the retreating detachment] was so great they disheartened many soldiers in ye camp." Perry, *Origins in Williamstown* (1894), 370.

86. Lyman, "Second Letter," 137; Delphina L. H. Clark, *Phineas Lyman—Connecticut's General* (Springfield, MA: Connecticut Valley Historical Museum, 1964), 19.

87. Pargellis, *Military Affairs*, 139; Perry, *Origins in Williamstown* (1894), 370.

88. Pargellis, *Military Affairs*, 139.

89. Ibid.

90. *NYCD*, 10: 342-43.

91. Claus, *Narrative*, 14.

92. *NYD*, 2: 692; See also Pomeroy, *Journals and Papers*, 114.

93.   Thomas Fitch, "Colony of Connecticut to Thomas Robinson," *Collections of the Connecticut Historical Society* 17 (1918): 158.

94.   *NYCD*, 6: 1005; Krueger, *Most Memorable Day*, 37. The letter from the gunner also mentioned that "Our Blacks behaved better than the Whites," but he may have been referring to Indians. Ibid; Historian Harold E. Selesky found that about one percent of soldiers serving in Connecticut regiments during the French and Indian War were Black. Harold E. Selesky, *War and Society in Colonial Connecticut* (New Haven: Yale University Press, 1990), 174; For a detailed discussion of Black soldiers in the French and Indian War see Scott A. Padeni, "The Role of Blacks in New York's Northern Campaigns of the Seven Years' War," *BFTM* 16 (1999): 152-69.

95.   *NYCD*, 10: 339; Godfrey, "Journal of the March," 423.

96.   Emerson, "Journal," 91.

97.   Lyman, "Second Letter," 137; Pomeroy, *Journals and Papers*, 114; On October 30, 1755, Governor Thomas Fitch of Connecticut wrote that "the engagement was doubtless the hottest that Ever happened in this Country." Thomas Fitch, "The Fitch Papers: Correspondence and Documents During Thomas Fitch's Governorship…1754-1766," *Coll. Conn. HS* 17 (1918): 159.

98.   Williams, "Correspondence," 212.

99.   Ibid.

100. Lyman, "Second Letter," 137.

101. Blodget, "Prospective-Plan," 3.

102. Charles Henry Lincoln, ed., *Correspondence of William Shirley* (New York: The Macmillan Company, 1912), Volume 2, 260; See also *JP*, 2: 32.

103. Lyman, "Second Letter," 138; Joseph Burt, an eyewitness, later told Timothy Dwight that "Gen. Johnson, at the commencement of the battle, received a flesh wound in his thigh…He bled freely, but was able to walk away from the army to his tent." Dwight, *Travels*, 366.

104. Edward Cole, "A Letter to a Gentleman in New-York," October 22, 1755, in *Early American Imprints*, ed. by Clifford K. Shipton (Series 1: Evans Reader Digital Collections), 7392; *New-York Mercury*, 17 November 1755.

105. *NYCD*, 6: 1003; *New-York Mercury*, 18 September 1755; See also Milton W. Hamilton, *Sir William Johnson* (Port Washington, NY: Kennikat Press, 1976), 165, 173-74, 357 (note 54).

106. Claus, *Narrative*, 17.

107. *JP*, 13: 197.

108. William Johnson would later try the therapeutic springs at Lebannon Springs and Ballston Spa for relief from the lingering wound that he received during the Battle of Lake George. *JP*, 2: 631; *JP*, 12: 515; *JP*, 8: 258.

109. *JP*, 9: 230.

110. *NYCD*, 6: 1005.

111. Blodget, *Prospective-Plan*, 3.

112. *NYCD*, 10: 335, see also 322.

113. Ibid., 335.

114. Ibid., 336.

115. *NYCD*, 10: 343.

116. Claus, *Narrative*, 15; See also Dulany, "Newsletter," 31.

117. *NYCD*, 10: 343.

118. Pomeroy, *Journal and Papers*, 138.

119. *NYCD*, 10: 336.

120. Ibid., 323.

121. Godfrey, "Journal of the March," 423; Hill, "Diary," 608; Williams, "Correspondence," 212.

122. *NYD*, 2: 693; Lyman, "Second Letter," 137; Seth Pomeroy also wrote that the fighting lasted "till about 5…[o'] Clock aft[e]rno[o]n." Pomeroy, *Journals and Papers*, 138; Thomas Fitch mentioned that provincial troops pursued the French and returned with "Prisoners, Arms & c." Fitch, "Fitch Papers," 159.

123. Pargellis, *Military Affairs*, 139; Daniel Claus deviated from other accounts by suggesting that the troops had orders not to pursue the French: "Nothwithstanding the Orders against a pursuit, some New Eng. Men for the sake of Plunder went to the field of action." Claus, *Narrative*, 15; Later published accounts criticized Johnson for not pursuing the French: "Why the enemy was not pursued, when their retreat became general, no tolerable reason has ever yet been assigned; and Mr. Johnson, in his letter, seems very artfully to evade it." [William Livingston], "A Review of Military Operations in North America," *Collections of the Massachusetts Historical Society* 7 (1st Series) (1800): 108.

124. Folsom, "Captain Nathaniel Folsom's Fight," 319.

125. Ibid.

126. *NYCD*, 6: 1008.

127. *NYD*, 2: 694; Burk, "John Burk's Diary," 46.

128. Folsom, "Captain Nathaniel Folsom's Fight," 320.
129. Ibid.
130. *NYCD*, 10: 323.
131. Folsom, "Captain Nathaniel Folsom's Fight," 320.
132. Ibid., 320-21.
133. Ibid., 322.
134. *NYD*, 2: 694; Gilbert, "Journal," 195.
135. *NYD*, 2: 694; Burk, "John Burk's Diary," 46; Blodget, *Prospective-Plan*, 3-4; Joseph Blanchard, "A Letter from Col. Blanchard to the commanding Officer at Albany," *Minutes of the Provincial Council of Pennsylvania* 6 (1851): 624; Blanchard gained the information from "two of our party run off" and returned to Fort Lyman. Ibid.; See also Emerson, "Journal," 91.
136. Folsom, "Captain Nathaniel Folsom's Fight," 321.
137. Godfrey, "Journal of the March," 423; Gilbert, "Journal," 195; Others also recorded the information about the third engagement on September 8 rather than the following day. Burk, "John Burk's Diary," 46.
138. Folsom, "Captain Nathaniel Folsom's Fight," 321.
139. Pomeroy, *Journals and Papers*, 115.
140. Ibid.; Burk, "John Burk's Diary," 46; James Hill reported that, in addition to Ephraim Williams, "139 more on the spot and on the Retreat" were killed. Hill, "Diary," 608; Perez Marsh recorded 216 dead and 96 wounded. Perry, *Origins in Williamstown* (1894), 370.
141. *NYCD*, 6: 1007.
142. Alan J. Clark, "Casualties of the Battle of Lake George," (unpublished paper, 1997), 3-5, 7, 9.
143. *NYCD*, 6: 1005.
144. Oscar Reiss, *Medicine and the American Revolution: How Diseases and Their Treatments Affected the Colonial Army* (Jefferson, NC: McFarland & Company, 1998), 29, 32, 35.
145. Pomeroy, *Journals and Papers*, 143.
146. Samuel Chandler, "Extracts from the Diary of Rev. Samuel Chandler," *NEHGR* 17 (October 1863): 350; Williams, "Correspondence," 213.
147. Lewis, "Campaign," 66.
148. Claus, *Narrative*, 17.
149. *New-York Mercury*, 22 September 1755; Claus, *Narrative*, 17.
150. *NYCD*, 10: 360-61, see also 324, 356.
151. *JP*, 2: 40.
152. *NYCD*, 10: 343; Daniel Claus noted that the Mohawks demanded Dieskau's "Watch, Buckles & c. as Trophies." Claus, *Narrative*, 16.
153. *JP*, 2: 45-46; On September 16 Seth Pomeroy reported that "ye French General [was] Carr[ie]d On a horse Litter." Pomeroy, *Journals and Papers*, 117; For news of Dieskau's arrival in Albany, see *Boston Gazette*, 3 November 1755.
154. *JP*, 2: 184-85; See also Fintan O'Toole, *White Savage: William Johnson and the Invention of America* (New York: Farrar Straus, and Giroux, 2005), 143.
155. Folsom, "Captain Nathaniel Folsom's Fight," 321.
156. Hill, "Diary," 609.
157. Burk, "John Burk's Diary," 46; Pomeroy, *Journals and Papers*, 115.
158. Trumbull, *History of Northampton*, 2: 279-80.
159. *JP*, 2: 196.
160. Ibid., 199.
161. *New-York Mercury*, 6 October 1755.
162. James Henderson, "James Henderson's Journal," in the *The First Century of the Colonial Wars in the Commonwealth of Massachusetts* (Boston: Society of Colonial Wars, Mass., 1944), 200.
163. New York State Archives, Land Survey Field Books, A 4019-77, H U I, Reel 14, Volume 40, 278; *From Cambridge to Champlain* (Middleboro, MA: Lawrence B. Romaine, 1957), 28.
164. Jared Sparks, "Plans & Descriptions of Gates's Camp, Ticonderoga, Crown Point, St. John's and Other Places," 1830, MS, 3a, 4, Houghton Library, Harvard University, Cambridge, MA.
165. Francis Parkman, "Parkman at Lake George," *Scribner's Magazine*, July 1901, 24; Bellico, *Chronicles of Lake George*, 288.
166. *Colonial Road*, item 2, 33.
167. *NYCD*, 6: 1010, see also 1014.
198. *NYCD*, 6: 1012.
169. Pomeroy, *Journals and Papers*, 118.
170. *Boston Gazette*, 29 September 1755.
171. *JP*, 9: 357; See also O'Toole, *White Savage*, 145.

5. STALEMATE AND NEW FORTS

1. *JP*, 2:74.
2. *NYCD*, 6: 1004.
3. Ibid., 1015; James Hill, "The Diary of a Private on the First Expedition to Crown Point," ed. by Edna V. Moffett, *The New England Quarterly* 5 (1932): 612; *NYD*, 4: 270.
4. Hill, "Diary of a Private," 609, 615; Nathaniel Dwight, "The Journal of Capt. Nathaniel Dwight of Belchertown, Mass., During the Crown Point Expedition, 1755," *The New York Geneological and Biographical Record* 33 (April 1902): 67; Samuel Chandler also reported an alarm on November 5. Samuel Chandler, "Extracts from the Diary of Rev. Samuel Chandler," *NEHGR* 17 (October 1863): 350.
5. *JP*, 2: 49; Thomas Williams, "Correspondence of Doctor Thomas Williams of Deerfield, Mass., A Surgeon in the Army," *The Historical Magazine* 7 (April 1870): 213.
6. Williams, "Correspondence," 214-15.
7. Seth Pomeroy, *The Journals and Papers of Seth Pomeroy*, ed. by Louis Effingham De Forest (New York: Society of Colonial Wars in the State of New York, 1926), 121.
8. *JP*, 2: 166; See also Milton W. Hamilton, *Sir William Johnson* (Port Washington, NY: Kennikat Press, 1976), 174.
9. *NYCD*, 6: 1014.
10. *JP*, 2: 178.
11. Chandler, "Diary," 352.
12. Hill, "Diary of a Private," 616; Pomeroy, *Journals and Papers*, 124, see also 120.
13. Nathaniel Dwight, "The Journal of Capt. Nathaniel Dwight of Belchertown, Mass., During the Crown Point Expedition, 1755," *The New York Geneological and Biographical Record* 33 (January 1902): 6.
14. *JP*, 2: 145.
15. *New-York Mercury*, 3 November 1755. The article also mentioned the gift of cattle and oxen.
16. Phineas Lyman, "Second Letter of General Lyman to His Wife," in *History of Durham, Connecticut*, by William Chauncey Fowler (Hartford: Press of Wiley, Waterman & Eaton, 1866), 138; Milton Hamilton, "Battle Report: General William Johnson's Letter to the Governors, Lake George, September 9-10, 1755," *Proceedings of the American Antiquarian Society* 74 (Part 1, 1964): 28-29; See also *Boston Gazette*, Supplement, 29 September 1755.
17. *JP*, 2: 108.
18. Ibid., 129.
19. *New-York Mercury*, 17 November 1755; Edward Cole "A Letter to a Gentleman in New-York," October 22, 1755, in *Early American Imprints*, ed. by Clifford K. Shipton (Series 1: Evans Readex Digital Collections), 7392.
20. Ibid.; See also Daniel Dulany, "Newsletter of 9 December 1755," *The Pennsylvania Magazine of History and Biography* 3 (1879): 30.
21. Delphina L. H. Clark, *Phineas Lyman—Connecticut's General* (Springfield, MA: Connecticut Valley Historical Museum, 1964), 23.
22. [William Livingston], "A Review of Military Operations in North America," *Collections of the Massachusetts Historical Society* 7 (1st Series) (1800): 110; Clark, *Phineas Lyman*, 23-24.
23. *JP*, 2: 152, see also 63, 117.
24. Ibid., 143-44.
25. Ibid., 120.
26. Pomeroy, *Journals and Papers*, 120; *NYD*, 4: 260-61.
27. *JP*, 2: 158.
28. Ibid., 160; See also Pomeroy, *Journals and Papers*, 123.
29. JP, 2: 178-79.
30. Ibid., 213-14.
31. *New-York Mercury*, 20 October 1755.
32. Chandler, "Diary," 350.
33. *JP*, 2: 16; *NYD*, 2: 695.
34. Pomeroy, *Journals and Papers*, 115.
35. *JP*, 2: 39-40.
36. *NYCD*, 6: 1015.
37. *JP*, 2: 77, see also 53.
38. Charles Henry Lincoln, ed., *Correspondence of William Shirley* (New York: The Macmillan Company, 1912), Volume 2, 282.
39. *JP*, 2: 99.
40. Ibid., 117.
41. Ibid.

42. Ibid., 118.
43. *JP*, 1: 847; For a succinct discussion of French fort design see David R. Starbuck, *Massacre at Fort William Henry* (Hanover, NH: University Press of New England, 2002), 7.
44. Hill, "Diary of a Private," 611; Seth Pomeroy recorded October 1 as the beginning of construction: "Begun this Day to build a fort for Cannon & one quarter of our Army wa[s] appointed to work at it." Pomeroy, *Journals and Papers*, 121.
45. Stanley Pargellis, ed., *Military Affairs in North America 1748-1765* (1936; reprint ed., New Haven: Archon Books, 1969), 178; *JP*, 2: 219.
46. Dwight, "Journal" (January 1902): 8.
47. *JP*, 2: 223.
48. Hill, "Diary of a Private," 613.
49. *JP*, 2: 130.
50. *JP*, 9: 267-68.
51. Ibid., 307.
52. In the spring of 1756 engineer Harry Gordon depicted only one completed barracks, which faced the east side. Harry Gordon, "Plan of Fort Edward," Crown Collection, NYSL; See also Samuel Blodget, *A Prospective-Plan of the Battle near Lake George on the Eighth Day of September 1755 with an Explanation thereof* (Boston: n.p., 1756), 5.
53. Hill, "Diary of a Private," 614-15.
54. *JP*, 2: 279; Dwight, "Journal" (April 1902): 67; Chandler, "Diary," 351.
55. Chandler, "Diary," 351.
56. Blodget, *Prospective-Plan*, 5.
57. Dwight, "Journal" (April 1902): 66.
58. William Eyre, "Plan of Fort William-Henry," NAC.
59. Dwight, "Journal" (April 1902): 66.
60. *NYD*, 4: 260-61; In early November James Connor reported "between 150 or 160 men" at the French camp. *NYD*, 4: 276.
61. Ibid., 261.
62. Ibid.; *Boston Gazette*, 20 October 1755; Gary Stephen Zaboly, *A True Ranger: The Life and Many Wars of Major Robert Rogers* (Garden City Park, NY: Royal Blockhouse, llc, 2004), 107-8; Timothy J. Todish, *The Annotated and Illustrated Journals of Major Robert Rogers* (Fleischmanns, NY: Purple Mountain Press, 2002), 34; Hill, "Diary of a Private," 611; Pomeroy, *Journals and Papers*, 120.
63. *NYD*, 4: 270; See also Hill, "Diary of a Private," 612.
64. *JP*, 9: 288.
65. Dwight, "Journal" (January 1902): 9; Hill, "Diary of a Private," 613.
66. *NYD*, 4: 272; Zaboly, *A True Ranger*, 114.
67. *NYD*, 4: 273; Zaboly, *A True Ranger*, 114-15.
68. *Boston Gazette*, 24 November 1755; James Hill reported that the bateaux were fitted with "Wal[l] p[i]e[c]es and Bl[u]nder B[u]s[s]es." Hill, "Diary of a Private," 614.
69. *NYD*, 4: 273; Scott Padeni, "Skirmish at the Isle of Mutton," *The Lake George Nautical Newsletter* 3 (1994), 1, 8; See also Todish, *Journals of Rogers*, 40; Pomeroy, *Journals and Papers*, 120-21.
70. *NYD*, 4: 273.
71. *JP*, 2: 290.
72. Dwight, "Journal" (April 1902): 67; Chandler, "Diary," 351; See also Hill, "Diary of a Private," 615.
73. *JP*, 2: 303.
74. Ibid., 306-7.
75. Fred Anderson, *A People's Army* (Chapel Hill: The University of North Carolina Press, 1984), 126.
76. Chandler, "Diary," 351; See also Dwight, "Journal" (April 1902): 68; Hill, "Diary of a Private," 616-17.
77. The earthquake may have measured 6.0 on a Richter scale. Jourdan Houston, "The Great Earthquake of 1755," *American Heritage*, August/September 1980, 107; Epaphras Hoyt wrote that 100 chimneys were leveled and hundreds more shattered. E. Hoyt, *Antiquarian Researches: Comprising a History of the Indian Wars* (Greenfield, MA: Ansel Phelps, 1824), 282.
78. Dwight, "Journal" (April 1902): 68.
79. Ibid.
80. *JP*, 2: 228.
81. Ibid., 305.
82. Ibid., 319.
83. Ibid., 320-22.
84. Daniel Claus, *Daniel Claus' Narrative of His Relations with Sir William Johnson and Experiences in the Lake George Fight* (New York: Society of Colonial Wars in the State of New York, 1904), 18.
85. "The Marquis De Vaudreuil to the Sieur De Lotbiniere," *BFTM* 1 (January 1928): 2.

86. Ibid.
87. Thomas B. Furcron and Elizabeth Ann Boyle, "The Building of Fort Carillon, 1755-1758," in *Fort Ticonderoga* (Ticonderoga: Fort Ticonderoga Museum, 1955), 21-22; *Boston Gazette*, 20 October 1755; Pomeroy, *Journals and Papers*, 119 ; Todish, *Journals of Rogers*, 34-35; Zaboly, *A True Ranger*, 108.
88. "The Building of the Fort," *BFTM* 2 (January 1931): 92-93; In July 1756 Louis-Joseph de Montcalm noted that the "fort consists of pieces of timber and layers bound together with traverses [horizontal cross beams], the interstices [spaces] filled in with earth." *NYCD*, 10: 433.
89. *NYCD*, 10: 368.
90. "The Building of the Fort," 93.
91. Zaboly, *A True Ranger*, 118-19; Although Robert Rogers noted on November 14, 1755, that he had seen "three new barracks" in the fort, this entry was written ten years later for publication in the *Journals of Major Robert Rogers* (1765). His memory of the number of barracks and the exact date may have been muddled by the ten-year time interval. Todish, *Journals of Rogers*, 40.
92. Dwight, "Journal" (April 1902): 70.
93. Ibid.
94. Chandler, "Diary," 352; See also Dwight, "Journal" (April 1902): 70.
95. *JP*, 2: 336; Earlier at a meeting in Albany, William Shirley and other officials agreed to a garrison of 600 at the forts. *JP*, 13: 70-71.
96. *JP*, 2: 330-31.
97. Ibid., 331.
98. Ibid., 332.
99. Jeduthan Baldwin, "Journal Kept by Capt. Jeduthan Baldwin While on the Expedition Against Crown Point, 1755-56," *Journal of the Military Service Institute* 39 (July-August 1906): 124-26; Baldwin noted "Thanksgiving day" on December 4, 1755. Ibid., 124.
100. *JP*, 2: 358.
101. *JP*, 2: 282-83.
102. Ibid., 363.
103. *JP*, 9: 355; Hamilton, *Sir William Johnson*, 190, 193.
104. Fintan O'Toole, *White Savage: William Johnson and the Invention of America* (New York: Farrar Straus, and Giroux, 2005), 149-50, 154; Stanley McCrory Pargellis, *Lord Loudoun in North America* (Hamden, CT: Archon Books, 1968), 76-77.
105. *New-York Mercury*, 5 January 1756.
106. *JP*, 2: 343-44; Hamilton, *Sir William Johnson*, 195.
107. [William Livingston], "A Review of Military Operations in North America," *Collections of the Massachusetts Historical Society* 7 (1st Series) (1800): 108, 110, 112.
108. *The London Magazine* (October 1759): 535.
109. John Entick, *The General History of the Late War: Containing It's Rise, Progress, and Event* (London: Edward Dilly and John Millan, 1763), Volume 1, 162.
110. Ibid.; A second book, published in London in 1772, also supported Johnson. "The success of General Johnson gave security to the northern provinces." Thomas Mante, *The History of the Late War in North-America* (1772; reprint ed., New York: Research Reprints, Inc., n.d.), 41.
111. Entick, *General History*, 162-63.
112. Ammi Ruhamah Cutter, "Dr. A. R. Cutter's Journal of his Military Experience, 1756-1758," in *A History of the Cutter Family of New England*, by William Richard Cutter (Boston: David Clapp & Son, 1871), 61.
113. Ibid., 62.
114. Pargellis, *Lord Loudoun*, 91; See also Pomeroy, *Journals and Papers*, 152-53.
115. Pargellis, *Military Affairs*, 178.
116. Ibid.
117. Ibid., 179.
118. PRO, CO 5/47, UP microfilm reel 2, frame 22.
119. Ibid.
120. Ibid., frames 14-16.
121. Ibid., frames 17-21.
122. Ibid., frames 24-25.
123. Ibid., frame 26.
124. Ibid., frame 31-32.
125. Ibid., frame 32.
126. Cutter, "Journal," 64-65.
127. Ibid., 64.
128. *Boston Gazette*, 13 September 1756; On October 16, 1756, Dr. Ammi Cutter recorded that the fleet included "1 Sloop about 40 tons, 2 smaller about 20 Tons each, another Sloop on ye Ways" as large as the first one. Cutter, "Journal," 66; See also L0 1752.

129. L0 1437.
130. L0 1710; In August Lieutenant Colonel Ralph Burton recorded "two small Sloops of about twenty Tons each, have four Swivels mounted on each, One Sloop of 30 Tons launched" on August 23 and another sloop on the stocks and "Two large Scows." PRO, CO 5/47, UP microfilm reel 2, frame 23; Captain Jeduthan Baldwin also mentioned a sailing barge. Baldwin, "Journal," 129.
131. L0 1710; See also *Boston Weekly News-Letter*, 23 September 1756.
132. Gaspard-Joseph Chaussegros de Lery, "Diary kept at the Fort," *BFTM* 6 (July 1942): 136; See also Baldwin, "Journal," 129.
133. PRO 281/2, WO 34/46B, fol.1; Lincoln, *Correspondence of William Shirley*, 471.
134. L0 1219; See also *Boston Weekly News-Letter*, 1 July 1756. The same newspaper article noted that Major General Winslow had about 6,600 men and was "determin[e]d to March in about a Fortnight" against the French. Ibid.
135. *NYD*, 4: 285; *Boston Weekly News-Letter*, 2 September 1756.
136. Zaboly, *A True Ranger*, 135 (note 34).
137. L0 1219.
138. Zaboly, *A True Ranger*, 133; Todish, *Journals of Rogers*, 47; *NYD*, 4: 286.
139. *NYD*, 4: 286; See also *Boston Weekly News-Letter*, 2 September 1756.
140. De Lery, "Diary," 136.
141. Ibid., 132, 138.
142. Ibid., 139.
143. Ibid., 132, 136-37; See also Michel Chartier de Lotbinière's letter of October 31, 1756, in "The Building of the Fort," *BFTM* 2 (January 1931): 93.
144. Furcron and Boyle, "Building of Fort Carillon," 32.
145. Ibid.; De Lery, "Diary," 138.
146. Furcron and Boyle, "Building of Fort Carillon," 31.
147. Louis Antoine de Bougainville, *Adventure in the Wilderness: The American Journals of Louis Antoine de Bougainville 1756-1760*, trans. and ed. Edward P. Hamilton (Norman, OK: University of Oklahoma Press, 1964), 33; Lotbinière's letter in "The Building of the Fort," 93.
148. Furcron and Boyle, "Building of Fort Carillon," 53-55, 62-64.
149. John Graham, "The Journal of Rev. John Graham," *Magazine of American History* 8, Part 1 (1882): 211; See also Zaboly, *A True Ranger*, 138; Todish, *Journals of Rogers*, 46.
150. Bougainville, *Journals*, 29.
151. Ibid., 33.
152. Ibid.
153. Ibid., 51.
154. Ibid.
155. L0 1776.
156. Bougainville, *Journals*, 38; [Carte des environs du lac George ou St.-Sacrement, pour servir a l'intelligence des operations militaires dans la région, 1755-1756], Ministere de la France d'Outre-mer Atlas Colonies, Volume 3, No. 71, 901/1755, NAC.
157. Bougainville, *Journals*, 40; Zaboly, *A True Ranger,* 143, 145 (note 66); *New-York Mercury*, 11 October 1756; Cutter, "Journal," 65.
158. French and Indian War Collection 1754-1774, "A Soldier at Fort William Henry, 1756," Octavo Volume 2, American Antiquarian Society, Worcester, Massachusetts; *New-Hampshire Gazette*, 7 October 1756; *Boston Weekly News-Letter*, 7 October 1756; *New-York Mercury*, 11 October 1756.
159. Bougainville, *Journals*, 41.
160. De Lery, "Diary," 134.
161. Graham, "Journal," 212.
162. Cutter, "Journal," 65.
163. Ibid.
164. Pargellis, *Lord Loudoun*, 178-80.
165. Cutter, "Journal," 65.
166. Ibid., 66; In contrast, William Shirley had promised full pardons for deserters from the regulars, if they returned before July 20, 1756. *New-York Mercury*, 14 June 1756.
167. French and Indian War Collection, "A Soldier at Fort William Henry."
168. Cutter, "Journal," 66.
169. French and Indian War Collection, "A Soldier at Fort William Henry."
170. Todish, *Journals of Rogers*, 56; During July of 1756, a French deserter revealed that the French had "3500" men at Carillon, "400 of which at the advanc'd Guard, and about 200 up the Lake [George] about a League f[a]rther for a Look-out." *Boston Weekly News-Letter*, 5 August 1756; *New-York Mercury*, 23 August 1756.

171. French and Indian War Collection, "A Soldier at Fort William Henry."
172. Ibid.
173. Zaboly, *A True Ranger*, 150.

6. FORT WILLIAM HENRY UNDER SIEGE 1757

1. L0 2704; See also Robert Rogers, *Journals of Major Robert Rogers* (1765; reprint ed., Ann Arbor, MI: University Microfilms, Inc., 1966), 40.
2. L0 2704.
3. Rogers, *Journals,* 61.
4. *Boston Weekly News-Letter*, 10 February 1757; See also Rogers, *Journals,* 41; L0 2704.
5. *New-York Mercury*, 7 February 1757.
6. Thomas Brown, *A Plain Narrativ[e] of the Uncommon Sufferings and Remarkable Deliverance of Thomas Brown* (Boston: Fowle and Draper, 1760), 6; For Thomas Brown's journal see Russell P. Bellico, *Chronicles of Lake George: Journeys in War and Peace* (Fleischmanns, NY: Purple Mountain Press, 1995), 48-58.
7. L0 2704; See also *Boston Weekly News-Letter*, 10 February 1757.
8. L0 2704.
9. Burt G. Loescher, *The History of Rogers Rangers* (San Francisco: Burt G. Loescher, 1946), Volume 1, 137, 348; *New-Hampshire Gazette,* 29 April 1757; See also *NYCD*, 10: 570.
10. *New-York Gazette*, 7 February 1757; See also Gary Stephen Zaboly, *A True Ranger: The Life and Many Wars of Major Robert Rogers* (Garden City Park, NY: Royal Blockhouse, IIc, 2004), 160.
11. *NYCD*, 10: 551.
12. Ibid., 570.
13. PRO, CO 5/48, UP microfilm reel 2, frames 372-73; See also *New-Hampshire Gazette*, 22 April 1757; *Boston News-Letter*, 28 April 1757.
14. Louis Antoine de Bougainville, *Adventures in the Wilderness: The American Journals of Louis Antoine de Bougainville 1757-1760,* trans. and ed. Edward P. Hamilton (Norman, OK: University of Oklahoma Press, 1964), 95.
15. PRO, CO 5/48, UP microfilm reel 2, frame 374.
16. *NYCD*, 10: 571.
17. PRO, CO 5/48, UP microfilm reel 2, frame 366; Bougainville, *Journals*, 96.
18. PRO, CO 5/48, UP microfilm reel 2, frame 366.
19. Caleb Stark, *Memoir and Official Correspondence of Gen. John Stark* (1860; reprint ed., Boston: Gregg Press, 1972), 20; See also Luther Roby, *Reminiscences of the French War; Rogers' Expeditions and Maj. Gen. John Stark* (Concord, NH: Luther Roby, 1831), 43.
20. PRO, CO 5/48, UP microfilm reel 2, frame 350. In a letter on March 25, Eyre wrote that the noise was heard at one o'clock in the morning of March 19. Ibid., frame 357; See also Stark, *Memoir*, 21; *NYCD*, 10: 571.
21. Bougainville, *Journals*, 96.
22. PRO, CO 5/48, UP microfilm reel 2, frame 367.
23. Ibid., frame 351.
24. Ibid., frame 358; See also *Boston Weekly News-Letter*, 14 April 1757; *New-Hampshire Gazette*, 15 April 1757.
25. Bougainville, *Journals*, 96.
26. PRO, CO 5/48, UP microfilm reel 2, frames 346-47.
27. Ibid., frame 347; See also *New-Hampshire Gazette*, 15 April 1757.
28. PRO, CO 5/48, UP microfilm reel 2, frame 347.
29. Ibid., frame 348.
30. Ibid., frame 359, see also frame 353.
31. Ibid., frame 371.
32. Ibid., frame 360; *NYCD*, 10: 572.
33. Bougainville, *Journals*, 97; *NYCD*, 10: 572; Arthur G. Doughty, ed., *Report of the Public Archives for the Year 1929* (Ottawa: F. A. Acland, 1930), 52; See also *New-Hampshire Gazette*, 15 April 1757; PRO, CO 5/48, UP microfilm reel 2, frame 361.
34. PRO, CO 5/48, UP microfilm reel 2, frame 364; A newspaper reported that "several of their Dead have been hooked out of a Hole in the Ice." *New-Hampshire Gazette*, 29 April 1757.
35. Bougainville, *Journals*, 97; *NYCD*, 10: 572.
36. PRO, CO 5/48, UP microfilm reel 2, frame 362.
37. Stanley McCrory Pargellis, *Lord Loudoun in North America* (Hamden, CT: Archon Books, 1968), 235.
38. Stanley Pargellis, *Military Affairs in North America 1748-1765* (Hamden, CT: Archon Books, 1969), 371; PRO, CO 5/48, UP microfilm reel 2, frame 546; L0 4020A.
39. Pargellis, *Lord Loudoun,* 232.

40. Thomas Mante, *The History of the Late War in North-America* (1772; reprint ed., New York: Research Reprints, Inc., n.d.), 87; Dr. Cutter recorded the embarkation of the transports from New York City on May 24-26, 1757. Ammi Ruhamah Cutter, "Dr. A. R. Cutter's Journal of his Military Experience, 1756-1758," in *A History of the Cutter Family of New England*, by William Richard Cutter (Boston: David Clapp & Son, 1871), 67.

41. Cutter, "Journal," 68; See also Mante, *Late War*, 88.

42. Cutter, "Journal," 68.

43. *NYCD*, 10: 509.

44. Bougainville, *Journals*, 117.

45. Ibid., 112, 102; Bougainville remarked that the "spirit of greed, of gain, of commerce, will always destroy the spirit of honor, glory, and military spirit." Ibid., 102.

46. Thomas B. Furcron and Elizabeth Ann Boyle, "The Building of Fort Carillon, 1755-1758," in *Fort Ticonderoga* (Ticonderoga: Fort Ticonderoga Museum, 1955), 38-39; James Montresor, "Journals of Col. James Montresor," *Coll. NYHS* 14 (1881): 19.

47. Jabez Fitch, Jr., *The Diary of Jabez Fitch, Jr., in the French and Indian War 1757*, 3rd ed. (Fort Edward, NY: Rogers Island Historical Association, 1986), 3.

48. Ibid., 4.

49. Phineas Lyman, *General Orders of 1757* (1899; reprint ed., Freeport, NY: Books for Libraries Press, 1970), 34.

50. Bougainville, *Journals*, 102, 109-11; Fitch, *Diary*, 1-2.

51. Bougainville, *Journals*, 110.

52. Ibid., 119.

53. Zaboly, *A True Ranger*, 172; Bougainville, *Journals*, 113; Loescher, *Rogers Rangers*, 1: 174-75; *NYCD*, 10: 568.

54. Fitch, *Diary*, 4.

55. Ibid., 5; See also Benjamin Hayward, "Diary of Ensign Hayward," in *The Fort Edward Book*, by Robert D. Bascom (Fort Edward, NY: James D. Keating, 1903), 94; Bougainville, *Journals*, 116.

56. Seth Metcalf, *Diary and Journal of Seth Metcalf* (Boston: The Historical Records Survey, 1939), 6.

57. *Boston Weekly News-Letter*, 4 August 1757; See also Fitch, *Diary*, 8; Metcalf, *Diary and Journal*, 7; Bougainville, *Journals*, 121-22.

58. Metcalf, *Diary and Journal*, 7; Montresor, "Journals," 19; See also L0 4020A.

59. *Boston Weekly News-Letter*, 4 August 1757; Montresor noted that the Mohawks reported that Montcalm was advancing with "6 Battalions…with 300 vessels & all the Cannon taken at Ohio and Oswego." Montresor, "Journals," 20.

60. James Montresor reported that the "loss of several of the Party with one Lieut killed," but Seth Metcalf noted that the Indians "kil[le]d and took ne[a]r twenty men." Montresor, "Journals," 20; Metcalf, *Diary and Journal*, 7.

61. *New-York Gazette*, 22 August 1757; Montresor, "Journals," 22; Bougainville, *Journals*, 141-42; Bougainville noted that the Indians returned with 32 scalps, but "they know how to make two or even three out of one." Ibid., 142; See also Fitch, *Diary*, 14; *NYCD*, 10: 593; *Boston Weekly News-Letter*, 4 August 1757; Luke Gridley, *Luke Gridley's Diary of 1757* (Hartford, CT: Acorn Club, 1906), 43-44.

62. François de Lévis, *Journal Des Champagnes Du Chevalier De Lévis En Canada De 1756 à 1760* (Montréal: C. O. Beauchemin & Fils, 1889), 85; Bougainville, *Journals*, 113,131-32.

63. [Carte des environs du lac George ou St-Sacrement, pour servir a l'intelligence des operations militaires dans la région, 1755-1756], Ministere de la France d'Outre-Mer Atlas Colonies, Volume 3, No. 71, 901/1755, NAC.

64. Bougainville, *Journals*, 132; *NYCD*, 10: 594; Adam Williamson noted that McGinnis "fired on a boat of the Enemy with 14 or 16" men, many of whom were killed and "fell down in the Bottom of the boat." Adam Williamson, "Notebook of French Siege of Fort Wm Henry," Williamson Family Papers, July 21, 1757, microfilm A-573, NAC; At Fort Edward on July 21 Colonel James Montresor recorded "an account from Fort Wm Henry that 2 of Capt. McGinnis party were brought in wounded by a ser[g]eant. That he had killed four of the Enemy." Montresor, "Journals," 21; See also Rueben Gold Thwaites, ed., *Travels and Explorations of the Jesuit Missionaries in New France* (Cleveland: The Burrows Brothers Company, 1900), Volume 70, 105, 107.

65. Bougainville, *Journals*, 138.

66. *New-York Mercury*, 1 August 1757; *Boston Weekly News-Letter*, 18 August 1757; *New-Hampshire Gazette*, 19 August 1757; *The London Magazine* (September 1757): p.n.a. Although this letter gave the date of July 21 for Parker's departure, Major General Daniel Webb's letter to Lord Loudoun used the date of July 23, as did Jabez Fitch, Jr. PRO, CO 5/48, UP microfilm reel 2, frame 545; Fitch, *Diary*, 15; Captives from the Parker's detachment also gave the date of departure as July 23. Bougainville, *Journals*, 142; Adam Williamson wrote that Parker had departed with "300 men" on "22/23." Williamson, "Siege," July 22/23, 1757; *The Universal Magazine* later reported that Parker had left with

three of his New Jersey companies and "two companies of the New York regiment." *The Universal Magazine* (October 1757): 182.

67. *NYCD*, 10: 599.

68. PRO, CO 5/48, UP microfilm reel 2, frame 541; L0 4020A.

69. Bougainville, *Journals*, 140.

70. *NYCD*, 10: 647; Adam Williamson wrote that Parker had 26 vessels. Williamson, "Siege," July 24, 1757.

71. *New-York Mercury*, 1 August 1757; Bougainville, *Journals*, 142; Thomas Mante's suggestion of a decoy was probably based on the same letter published in newspapers and *The London Magazine*. Mante, *Late War*, 85; For a scenario of the ruse perpetrated by the French and Indians at Sabbath Day Point see Bob Bearor, *Leading By Example: Partisan Fighters & Leaders of New France 1660-1760* (Bowie, MD: Heritage Books, Inc., 2002), Volume 1, 71-72.

72. Williamson, "Siege," July 24, 1757; *NYCD*, 10: 599.

73. Bougainville, *Journals*, 142; Williamson, "Siege," July 24, 1757.

74. PRO, CO 5/48, UP microfilm reel 2, frame 546; Williamson, "Siege," July 24, 1757.

75. Thwaites, *Travels and Explorations*, 70: 125.

76. Bougainville, *Journals*, 142-43.

77. Thwaites, *Travels and Explorations*, 70: 125.

78. PRO, CO 5/48, UP microfilm reel 2, frame 545; L0 4020A.

79. Thwaites, *Travels and Explorations*, 70: 139, 141.

80. Seth Tinkham, "Diary of Seth Tinkham," in *History of Plymouth County, Massachusetts*, comp. by D. Hamilton Hurd (Philadelphia: J. W. Lewis & Co., 1884), 996; See also *NYCD*, 10: 734.

81. PRO, CO 5/48, UP microfilm reel 2, frame 546.

82. Montresor, "Journals," 23.

83. James Furnis, "An Eyewitness Account by James Furnis of the Surrender of Fort William Henry, August 1757," ed. by William S. Ewing, *New York History* 42 (1961): 311; Engineer Adam Williamson recorded work on the breastworks from July 29 to 31. Williamson, "Siege," July 29, 30/31, 1757.

84. L0 4479; Father Roubaud described the entrenched camp as "a fortified rock faced with palisades [logs] secured by heaps of stones." Thwaites, *Travels and Explorations*, 70: 155.

85. Montresor, "Journals," 24.

86. L0 4479.

87. Montresor, *Journals*, 24.

88. PRO, CO 5/48, UP microfilm reel 2, frame 548; L0 4020A; James Furnis noted that the "two Row Galleys…were ready to launch," when they were burned by the French. Furnis, "Eyewitness Account," 314.

89. Gridley, *Diary*, 46; See also Montresor, "Journals," 25.

90. Pargellis, *Lord Loudoun*, 235, 245-46; "The Colden Papers-1755-1760," *Coll. NYHS* 5 (1921): 156.

91. L0 4479; PRO, CO 5/48, UP microfilm reel 2, frame 548; L0 4020A.

92. *NYCD*, 10: 606-7. Bougainville's figures in his journal differ from his official report because in the official document the Troupes de la Marine were included with the regulars, but in his journal the troops of the Marine were added to the militia totals. Bougainville, *Journals*, 152-53; See also D. Peter MacLeod, *The Canadian Iroquois and the Seven Years' War* (Toronto: Dundurn Press, 1996), 100, 212 (note 18).

93. Bougainville, *Journals*, 146.

94. Ibid., 147.

95. Ibid., 331.

96. Ibid., 154; Brigadier Lévis noted 2,970 men, including 800 Indians in his division. Lévis, *Journal Des Champagnes*, 88.

97. Bougainville, *Journals*, 156; One English officer, who later viewed the artillery rafts, described them as "a good invention." L0 4385; See also L0 4020A.

98. Bougainville, *Journals*, 156; *NYCD*, 10: 601.

99. *NYCD*, 10: 601; Bougainville's journal is a little confusing regarding the bay where the artillery was landed, implying that two bays were involved—one for the artillery and one for the camp. Bougainville, *Journals*, 157-58; Ian K. Steele, *Betrayals: Fort William Henry and the "Massacre"* (New York: Oxford University Press, 1990), 94; Apparently, the artillery rafts were moored in a bay to the north overnight and unloaded at "artillery cove" at the main camp the next day. A contemporary map of the siege shows that the landing site for the artillery and the base camp were the same. H3/1250, Fort William Henry [1757], NMC0007807, NAC.

100. Thwaites, *Travels and Explorations*, 70: 145.

101. L0 6660; Furnis, "Eyewitness Account," 311.

102. Bougainville, *Journals*, 158; Father Rouband described the funeral of a Nippissing warrior who had been killed during the engagement. The dead warrior was adorned with "porcelain necklaces, silver bracelets, ear and nose rings [and] magnificent garments"; his face and body were painted in "brilliant colors" and his weapons placed with his body. Thwaites, *Travels and Explorations*, 70:149.

103. James L. Kochan, ed., "Joseph Frye's Journal and Map of the Siege of Fort William Henry, 1757," *BFTM* 15 (1993): 346; See also Joseph Frye, "A Journal of the Attack of Fort William Henry," Parkman Papers 42: 137, MASS HS; There are some discrepancies in numbers. The detailed tally of troops after the surrender included 122 Royal Americans and only 57 men from the New York regiment. *NYCD*, 10: 624.

104. *NYCD*, 10: 621-25; See also *The Universal Magazine* (October 1757): 182; Frye estimated that 2,200 troops were fit for duty. Kochan, "Frye's Journal," 347.

105. L0 4479; L0 6660.

106. Furnis, "Eyewitness Account," 311.

107. L0 6660; "A Journal Kept During the Siege of Fort William Henry, August 1757," *Proceedings of the American Philosophical Society* 37 (1898): 146; *New-York Gazette*, 29 August 1757; *Boston Gazette*, 5 September 1757; *New-Hampshire Gazette*, 9 September 1757.

108. "Journal Kept During the Siege," 146; Bougainville, *Journals*, 159; *NYCD*, 10: 601; See also L0 5309.

109. PRO, CO 5/48, UP microfilm reel 2, frame 556.

110. Kochan, "Frye's Journal," 348.

111. L0 5309.

112. Kochan, "Frye's Journal," 348; *New-York Gazette*, 29 August 1757; *New-Hampshire Gazette*, 5 September 1757.

113. PRO, CO 5/48, UP microfilm reel 2, frame 557.

114. Ibid.

115. George Bartman, "The Siege of Fort William Henry, Letters of George Bartman," *Huntington Library Quarterly* 12 (August 1949): 419.

116. Fitch, *Diary*, 17; According to James Montresor, the prisoner disclosed that the French army consisted of "4000 Indians, 3000 Regulars, 4000 Canadians & Militia." Montressor, "Journals," 38; See also Gridley, *Diary*, 46-47.

117. Bartman, "Letters," 420-21.

118. Lyman, *General Orders, 63.*

119. Thwaites, *Travels and Explorations*, 70: 163.

120. *New-York Gazette*, 29 August 1757; *NYCD*, 10: 602; Williamson, "Siege," August 3, 1757.

121. Bougainville, *Journals*, 161.

122. PRO, CO 5/48, UP microfilm reel 2, frame 558.

123. Kochan, "Frye's Journal," 349.

124. Ibid., 350.

125. "Journal Kept During the Siege," 147. (This journal was written later and some dates are incorrect and some entries are a re-creation of events that occurred over more than one day.); Williamson, "Siege," August 6, 1757.

126. Montresor, "Journals," 39.

127. Ibid.

128. PRO, CO 5/48, UP microfilm reel 2, frame 554.

129. Montresor, "Journals," 26-27.

130. Timothy Dwight, *Travels in New-England and New-York* (New-Haven: S. Converse Printer, 1822), Volume 3, 381. Johnson was said to have marched three miles before being recalled by Webb. In this version, Johnson "attempted to run him [Webb] through with his sword," according to the recollection of Jedediah Strickney. M.A. Stickney, "Massacre at Fort William Henry, 1757," *EIHC* 3 (1861): 81; Louis Antoine de Bougainville related a secondhand story in a letter to is mother in 1758. Bougainville suggested that Johnson was so infuriated by Webb's inaction that he threw his belongings at the general's feet in disgust. Bougainville, *Journals*, 333; See also Steele, *Betrayals*, 168-69, 173; Fintan O'Toole, *White Savage: William Johnson and the Invention of America* (New York: Farrar, Straus and Giroux, 2005), 189-90; Edward P. Hamilton, *The French and Indian Wars* (Garden City, NY: Doubleday & Company, Inc., 1962), 201-2.

131. William H. Hill, *Old Fort Edward Before 1800* (1929; reprint ed., Mililani, HI: The Sleeper Co., 1994), 135.

132. Bartman, "Letters," 422; Webb may have also been encouraged by the arrival of George Augustus Howe on August 6.

133. L0 4041; For a reprint of the Webb-Monro correspondence see Edward J. Dodge, *Relief is Greatly Wanted* (Bowie, MD: Heritage Books, Inc., 1998), 66-72.

134. Bougainville, *Journals*, 166; Williamson, "Siege," August 7, 1757; Steele, *Betrayals*, 105.
135. L0 6660.
136. Ibid.
137. *NYCD*, 10: 603; Some of the Indians "aspired to become gunners and one" pointed and fired a cannon accurately. Thwaites, *Travels and Explorations*, 70: 165, 167.
138. Stickney, "Massacre," 80.
139. Williamson, "Siege," August 7, 1757.
140. L0 4394.
141. L0 4479.
142. L0 5309.
143. "Journal Kept During the Siege," 148; See also Bellico, *Chronicles of Lake George*, 72.
144. Kochan, "Frye's Journal," 351; *NCYD*, 10: 603; Bougainville, *Journals*, 167; Another French report stated that the skirmish occurred at midnight. Arthur G. Doughty, ed., *Report of the Public Archives for the Year 1929* (Ottawa: F. A. Acland, 1930), 100.
145. Bougainville, *Journals*, 167; *NYCD*, 10: 603; Doughty, *Report*, 100; Kochan, "Frye's Journal," 351.
146. Bougainville, *Journals*, 168.
147. Bartman, "Letters," 423.
148. L0 4041.
149. "Journal Kept During the Siege," 149.
150. Ibid.; Kochan, "Frye's Journal," 352.
151. H3/1250, NMC0007807, NAC; Crown Collection, 2: 1:29 [1757], NYSL; H2/1250, NMC0007805, NAC.
152. [John Rocque], *A Set of Plans and Forts in America: Reduced from Actual Surveys* (London: Mary Ann Rocque, 1765); David R. Starbuck, *Massacre at Fort William Henry* (Hanover, NH: University Press of New England, 2002), frontispiece.
153. Furnis, "Eyewitness Account," 312.
154. L0 4394.
155. L0 6660; L0 4394.
156. L0 6660.
157. L0 5309.
158. L0 4158.
159. Kochan, "Frye's Journal," 352; L0 4394; See also "Journal Kept During the Siege," 149; *Boston Gazette*, 29 August 1757.
160. Bougainville, *Journals*, 169; *NYCD*, 10: 604; James DeLancey suggested that the white flag was raised at six o'clock in the morning. Steele, *Betrayals*, 109; James Furnis noted that the council of officers occurred at five in the morning. Furnis, "Eyewitness Account," 312.
161. Kochan, "Frye's Journal," 353-55; *New-York Gazette*, 29 August 1757; *New-Hampshire Gazette*, 9 September 1757; Mante, *Late War*, 93-94; *NYCD*, 10: 617-18; L0 6660.
162. Bougainville, *Journals*, 170; *NYCD*, 10: 650.
163. Fred Anderson, *Crucible of War: The Seven Years' War and the Fate of Empire in British North America* (New York: Alfred A. Knopf, 2000), 196; Steele, *Betrayals*, 110-16; MacLeod, *The Canadian Iroquois*, 106.
164. Furnis, "Eyewitness Account," 313.
165. Thwaites, *Travels and Explorations*, 70: 177; Another participant wrote that the "Savages Scaled the Walls and came in" the fort on August 9. L0 6660.
166. Thwaites, *Travels and Explorations*, 70: 179.
167. L0 4660; See also affidavit of Joseph Ingersoll. L0 4654.
168. Rogers, *Journals*, 55.
169. Jonathan Carver, *Travels Through the Interior Parts of North America in the Years 1766, 1767, and 1768* (1778; reprint ed., Minneapolis: Ross and Haines, Inc., 1956), 325-26.
170. *NYCD*, 10: 632.
171. Kochan, "Frye's Journal," 355.
172. Steele, *Betrayals*, 152; Two months after the incident, Governor Vaudreuil suggested that English officers "had made several of them [Indians] drunk with rum" and another French source asserted that English soldiers, "in spite of all advice…had given the Indians rum to drink." *NYCD*, 10: 633; Doughty, *Report*, 96; See also Bougainville, *Journals*, 173; Jean-Nicolas Desandrouins, *Le Maréchal De Camp Desandrouins 1729-1792*, ed. L'Abbé Gabriel (Verdun: Imprimerie Renvé-Lallemant, 1887), 107.
173. L0 4345.
174. Doughty, *Report*, 95.
175. *New-York Gazette*, 29 August 1757; *The Universal Magazine* (October 1757): 183.
176. Furnis, "Eyewitness Account," 313; Kochan, "Frye's Journal," 356.
177. Furnis, "Eyewitness Account," 313.
178. L0 6660.

179. Ibid.
180. Ibid.
181. Kochan, "Frye's Journal," 356.
182. Furnis, "Eyewitness Account," 313; L0 6660.
183. Kochan, "Frye's Journal," 356.
184. "Affidavit of Miles Whitworth" in Francis Parkman, *Montcalm and Wolfe* (Boston: Little, Brown, and Company, 1905), Volume 2, 447; Lord Loudoun's diary included a report that Saint-Luc de La Corne had attempted to recover the belongings of the English from the Indians, but after ten minutes, he ceased his efforts, "saying it was impossible to save them." Zaboly, *A True Ranger*, 180-81.
185. Furnis, "Eyewitness Account," 313. Furnis also wrote that the Indians "took my Horses," which were to pull the single cannon stipulated in the articles of capitulation. Ibid.
186. "Journal Kept During the Siege," 150 (commas were added for clarity); See also Kochan, "Frye's Journal," 356.
187. Carver, *Travels*, 317-18. There is a possibility that the exchange could have been subject to language misinterpretation.
188. Metcalf, *Diary and Journal*, 10; See also *New-York Gazette*, 22 August 1757; *Boston Gazette*, 29 August 1757; Samuel Angell to Governor William Greene, August 14, 1757, *The Historical Magazine* 8 (November 1870): 259; LO 6660; Desandrouins, *Le Maréchal*, 106, 109; "Journal Kept During the Siege," 150.
189. "The Colden Papers—1755-1760," *Coll. NYHS* 5 (1921): 168; *Boston Gazette*, 29 August 1757; *New-York Gazette*, 22 August 1757; An original document noted that the troops discarded "Arms, Am[m]unition and everything." L0 6660.
190. Carver, *Travels*, 316; See also Stickney, "Massacre," 82.
191. Kochan, "Frye's Journal," 356.
192. Ibid.
193. "Journal Kept During the Siege," 150.
194. Furnis, "Eyewitness Account," 314.
195. C. E. Potter, *The History of Manchester* (Manchester, NH: C. E. Potter, Publisher, 1856), 314-15; Desandrouins, *Le Maréchal*, 106; Private Jonathan Carver also heard the "war-hoop" at this time. Carver, *Travels*, 319.
196. Kochan, "Frye's Journal," 356; Carver, *Travels*, 319; Another participant referred to the scene as a "Shocking Spectacle." L0 6660.
197. L0 6660.
198. "Journal Kept During the Siege," 150.
199. Kochan, "Frye's Journal," 356.
200. PRO, CO 5/48, UP microfilm reel 2, frame 566-67; Desandrouins, *Le Maréchal*, 109-10.
201. Angell to Greene, 259.
202. Metcalf, *Diary and Journal*, 10; Fitch, *Diary*, 19.
203. *New-York Gazette*, 22 August 1757; *Boston Gazette*, 29 August 1757; The same story was published in England a short time later. *The London Chronicle*, 11-13 October 1757; *The London Magazine* (October 1757): 494-95.
204. Thwaites, *Travels and Explorations*, 179, 181, 185.
205. Kochan, "Frye's Journal," 356; Samuel Angell noted that the men "all scattered in the woods," Angell to Greene, 259.
206. Carvel, *Travels*, 319; PRO, CO 5/48, UP microfilm reel 2, frame 566.
207. *NYCD*, 10: 616; See also Bougainville, *Journals*, 172; Captain Pierre Pouchot suggested that the "French interpreters" had encouraged the Indians "to steal the baggage." Pierre Pouchot, *Memoir Upon the Late War in North America Between the French and English*, trans. Michael Cardy and ed. Brian Leigh Dunnigan (Youngstown, NY: Old Fort Niagara Association, Inc., 1994), 120.
208. *NYCD*, 10: 633; Desandrouins, *Le Maréchal*, 107; L0 6660.
209. Fitch, *Diary*, 19; In a letter written on August 11, 1757, Major General Daniel Webb wrote that some of the escapees arrived at Fort Edward "about two o'clock yesterday morning in a most distressing Situation, and have continued dropping in ever since." PRO, CO 5/48, UP microfilm reel 2, frame 567.
210. Carver, *Travels*, 322-24.
211. Potter, *History of Manchester*, 315.
212. Ibid., 316; See also William Howard Brown, *Colonel John Goffe: Eighteenth Century New Hampshire* (Manchester, NH: Lew A. Cummings Co., 1950), 147.
213. Potter, *History of Manchester*, 315-16; Brown, *Colonel John Goffe*, 146-47.
214. Furnis, "Eyewitness Account," 314.
215. Desandrouins, *Le Maréchal*, 109-10.
216. *NYCD*, 10: 616, see also 633.
217. MacLeod, *Canadian Iroquois*, 112.

218. John Entick, *The General History of the Late War: Containing It's Rise, Progress, and Event* (London: Edward Dilly and John Millan, 1763), 2: 401.
219. Thwaites, *Travels and Explorations*, 70: 183.
220. Montresor, "Journals," 29; *NYCD*, 10: 634; Bougainville, *Journals*, 174; Gridley, *Diary*, 49.
221. L0 4309; Steele, *Betrayals*, 133-35, 138; See also a "Return of the State of the following Corps that were at Fort William Henry." L0 4309; At the end of November 1757, 250 men were still missing. L0 6660.
222. Bougainville, *Journals*, 177-78; See also *NYCD*, 10: 625, 629; Father Roubaud noted 21 dead, "three of whom were Savages," and about 25 wounded. Thwaites, *Travels and Explorations*, 70: 199.
223. Scott A. Padeni, "The Role of Blacks in New York's Northern Campaigns of the Seven Years' War," *BFTM* 16 (1999): 161-63.
224. Thwaites, *Travels and Explorations*, 70: 199.
225. L0 6660.
226. Fitch, *Diary*, 20.
227. Bougainville, *Journals*, 177; According to British documents, the French seized 1,800 barrels of pork, 1,400 barrels of flour, one 12-pound cannon, two 9-pounders, four 4-pounders, and one 7-inch howitzer. L0 6660.
228. *JP*, 2: 730.
229. Samuel Angell noted that "We have about four thousand militia here and two thousand troops." Angell to Greene, 259; In a letter to George Washington, Joseph Chew suggested that 7,000 troops were at Fort Edward. Stanislaus Murray Hamilton, ed., *Letters to Washington and Accompanying Papers* (Boston: Society of Colonial Dames of America, 1899), Volume 2, p.n.a.
230. PRO, CO 5/48, UP microfilm reel 2, frame 565.
231. *New-Hampshire Gazette*, 2 September 1757.
232. *Boston Evening-Post*, 12 September 1757; L0 4407.
233. E. C. Dawes, ed., *Journal of Gen. Rufus Putnam* (Albany: Joel Munsell's Sons, 1886), 46.
234. Zaboly, *A True Ranger*, 190.
235. Edward E. Stanley, *Journal of a Tour in America 1824-1825* (London: R&R Clark, Ltd, 1930), 34; See also Bellico, *Chronicles of Lake George*, 249-50.
236. Bertil O. Osterberg, *Colonial America on Film and Television* (Jefferson, NC: McFarlan & Company, 2001), 172.
237. Ibid., 14-15, 125-30, 132, 141, 157-58, 161, 166-67, 169, 171-72, 175-76, 178-80.

7. BATTLE OF CARILLON 1758

1. *Boston Weekly News-Letter*, 2 September 1756; Burt G. Loescher, *The History of Rogers Rangers* (San Francisco: Burt G. Loescher, 1946), Volume 1, 437; Gary Stephen Zaboly, *A True Ranger: The Life and Many Wars of Major Robert Rogers* (Garden City Park, NY: Royal Blockhouse, IIc, 2004), 143, 260; Timothy J. Todish, *The Annotated and Illustrated Journals of Major Robert Rogers* (Fleishmanns, NY: Purple Mountain Press, 2002), 161.
2. Todish, *Journals of Rogers*, 70.
3. Caleb Stark, *Memoir and Official Correspondence of Gen. John Stark, With Notices of Several Other Officers of the Revolution* (1860; reprint ed., Boston: Gregg Press, 1972), 24.
4. Robert Rogers, *Journals of Major Robert Rogers* (1765; reprint ed., Ann Arbor, MI: University Microfilms, Inc., 1966), 60-70; See also LO 4701; John Campbell, the Earl of Loudoun, was familiar with many tactics of irregular warfare from his experience a decade earlier in Europe. See Peter E. Russell, "Redcoats in the Wilderness: British Officers and Irregular Warfare in Europe and America, 1740 to 1760," *The William and Mary Quarterly* 35 (October 1978): 638, 645.
5. Zaboly, *A True Ranger*, 190-91.
6. LO 5314.
7. Ibid.
8. Ibid. Rogers' report also noted that he "found where the French had hid the Boats taken at Fort William Henry [in 1757] with a great number of Cannon Balls, but as the Boats were under water [at the northern end of Lake George] I could not burn them." Ibid.
9. *NYCD*, 10: 837.
10. Ibid., 703.
11. Jabez Fitch, Jr., *The Diary of Jabez Fitch, Jr., in the French and Indian War 1757* (Fort Edward: Earl and Jean Stott, 1986), 39.
12. Stanley Pargellis, ed., *Military Affairs in North America 1748-1765* (1936; reprint ed., New York: Archon Books, 1969), 400.
13. LO 4391.
14. LO 5398.

15. Fitch, *Diary*, 45.
16. Ibid., 47-48.
17. Zaboly, *A True Ranger*, 203.
18. Fitch, *Diary*, 50.
19. *NYCD*, 10: 697; See also *JP*, 2: 787.
20. Fitch, *Diary*, 46-47.
21. *NYCD*, 10: 837.
22. Fitch, *Diary*, 51.
23. In 1802 Timothy Dwight's guide identified Friends Point as the site of Rogers' camp on March 13, based on the account of an eyewitness. Timothy Dwight, *Travels in New England and New York*, ed. Barbara Miller Solomon (Cambridge, MA: The Belnap Press of Harvard University Press, 1969), 250; See also Russell P. Bellico, *Chronicles of Lake George: Journeys in War and Peace* (Fleischmanns, NY: Purple Mountain Press, 1995), 221. Friends Point was named for William Friend, who received a land grant for the parcel in 1771.
24. Louis Antoine de Bougainville, *Adventures in the Wilderness: The American Journal of Louis Antoine de Bougainville 1756-1760*, trans. and ed. Edward P. Hamilton (Norman, OK: University of Oklahoma Press, 1964), 198.
25. *NYCD*, 10: 837; Pierre Pouchot, *Memoir Upon the Late War in North America Between the French and English*, trans. Michael Cardy and ed. Brian Leigh Dunnigan (Youngstown, NY: Old Fort Niagara Association, Inc., 1994), 130.
26. *NYCD*, 10: 838; Pouchot, *Memoir*, 130.
27. Rogers, *Journals*, 85.
28. *New-Hampshire Gazette*, 7 April 1758.
29. Ibid. Rogers reported that the rangers had "scalped about Forty Indians," Ibid.
30. Rogers, *Journals*, 85.
31. Zaboly, *A True Ranger*, 211.
32. *New-Hampshire Gazette*, 7 April 1758.
33. Rogers, *Journals*, 87.
34. Zaboly, *A True Ranger*, 213; Todish, *Journals of Rogers*, 100; See also John F. Ross, *War on the Run: The Epic Story of Robert Rogers and the Conquest of America's First Frontier* (New York: Bantam Books, 2009), 180-82.
35. "Petition of James Scott," September 1, 1766, "Petition of George Robertson," September 21, 1766, "Petition of Hugh Jackson," September 22, 1766, "Petition of William Friend," September 16, 1766, *New York Colonial Manuscripts, Indorsed Land Papers*, Volume 21, 134, 151-52, 149 (a), NYSL; Horatio Rogers, ed., *Hadden's Journal and Orderly Books: A Journal Kept in Canada and Upon Burgoyne's Campaign in 1776 and 1777* (1884; reprint ed., Boston: Gregg Press, 1972), 104; See also Jeduthan Baldwin, *The Revolutionary Journal of Col. Jeduthan Baldwin 1775-1778*, ed. Thomas Williams Baldwin (Bangor, ME: De Burians, 1906), 100; Bellico, *Chronicles of Lake George*, 184, 221-22.
36. *New-Hampshire Gazette*, 7 April 1758.
37. Fitch, *Diary*, 53.
38. Loescher, *Rogers Rangers*, 1: 370; Although the April 29, 1758, issue of the *Boston Gazette* reported that "20 men" thought to be killed or captured had "since got safe in," a later edition of the *Boston Evening-Post* disclosed that 30 of the captives had been "kill'd and cut to Pieces after they had capitulated." *Boston Gazette*, 29 April 1758; *Boston Evening-Post*, 29 May 1758.
39. *NYCD*, 10: 838; Bougainville, *Journals*, 198; *NYCD*, 10: 693.
40. Loescher, *Rogers Rangers*, 1: 387.
41. AB 7.
42. Robert Kirk, *Through So Many Dangers: The Memoirs and Adventures of Robert Kirk, Late of the Royal Highland Regiment*, eds. Ian McCulloch and Timothy J. Todish (Fleischmanns, NY: Purple Mountain Press, 2004), 129; Pargellis, *Military Affairs*, 235.
43. AB 431.
44. AB 44(a).
45. Ibid.
46. Ibid. If the musket should "be lost" or "no longer fit," during the campaign, Abercromby promised a monetary reimbursement. Ibid.
47. *New-Hampshire Gazette*, 28 July 1758; Serious questions have been raised concerning the effectiveness of Howe's reforms in dealing with "bush-fighting." See Stephen Brumwell, *Redcoats: The British Soldiers and War in the Americas, 1755-1763* (Cambridge, U.K.: Cambridge University Press, 2002), 218.
48. *Boston Evening-Post*, 3 July 1758; See also Alexander Monypenny, "The Monypenny Orderly Book," *BFTM* 12 (December 1969): 336-37; AB 407; Lord Howe was said to "always lay in his tent with the regiment," even when better quarters were available. He had the barrels of his troops' muskets "all blackened," their hair cut short, and ordered that nothing be carried unless "absolutely necessary." [Ann

Grant], *Memories of an American Lady* (1808; reprint ed., New York: Research Reprints, Inc., 1970), Volume 2, 67-68.

49. M. John Cardwell, "The British Expedition Against Fort Ticonderoga in 1758," (M.A. thesis, The University of New Brunswick, 1990), 20-32, 143; M. John Cardwell, "Mismanagement: The 1758 British Expedition Against Carillon," *BFTM* 15 (1992): 240, 261-65, 268-70.

50. Rogers, *Journals*, 105-6.

51. AB 397; Captain William Hervey wrote that more than "300 carriages" were used. William Hervey, *Journals of Hon. William Hervey* (Bury St. Edmund's: Paul & Mathew, Butter Market, 1906), 48.

52. Rogers, *Journals*, 110.

53. Anderson, 76; Amos Richardson, "Amos Richardson's Journal, 1758," *BFTM* 12 (September 1968): 272; Abel Spicer, "Diary of Abel Spicer from June 5th Until September 29th, 1758," in *History of the Descendants of Peter Spicer*, comp. by Susan Spicer Meech and Susan Billings Meech (Boston: F. H. Gilson, 1911), 394; Bellico, *Chronicles of Lake George*, 99.

54. Thomas Alexander, "Ens. Alexander's Diary," in *History of Northfield, Massachusetts*, by J. H. Temple and George Sheldon (Albany: Joel Munsell, 1875), 303; James Henderson suggested that the bridge was supported by 22 boats. James Henderson, "James Henderson's Journal," in *The First Century of Colonial Wars in the Commonwealth of Massachusetts* (Boston: Massachusetts Society of Colonial Wars, 1944), 196.

55. Gary S. Zaboly, "Rogers' Island," in Todish, *Journals of Rogers*, 80-83; David R. Starbuck, *Rangers and Redcoats on the Hudson* (Lebanon, NH: University Press of New England, 2004), 47-77.

56. *New-York Mercury*, 11 September 1758; *Boston Evening-Post*, 2 October 1758; William H. Hill, *Old Fort Edward Before 1800* (Fort Edward: William H. Hill, 1929), 266-68; See also *New-York Gazette*, 11 September 1758; *New-Hampshire Gazette*, 6 October 1758; Todish, *Journals of Rogers*, 79, 83.

57. PRO, CO 5/50, UP microfilm reel 3, frame 4.

58. Ibid.

59. Asa Foster, "Diary of Capt. Asa Foster of Andover, Mass.," *NEHGR* 54 (January 1900): 183; Newspapers reported "Above 1000 Wagons in the Service." *Boston Evening-Post*, 10 July 1758.

60. Obadiah Harris, "Journal of Obadiah Harris 1758," HM 591, 5, Huntington Library, San Marino, California.

61. Benjamin Glasier, "French and Indian War Diary of Benjamin Glasier of Ipswich, 1758-1760," *EIHC* 86 (1950): 74-75; E.C. Dawes, ed., *Journals of Gen. Rufus Putnam 1757-1760* (Albany: Joel Munsell's Sons, 1886), 63.

62. AB 397; "A Map of the retrenched Camp at Lake George in 1758" showed several stockaded forts, including one partially covering the site of Fort William Henry, another at the southeast corner of the lake, and one on the future site of Fort George. Fort Ticonderoga Thompson-Pell Research Center.

63. Caleb Rea, "The Journal of Dr. Caleb Rea, Written During the Expedition Against Ticonderoga in 1758," *EIHC* 18 (1881): 102; On June 29 Joseph Holt wrote that he "Moved into the stockade," and the next day Abel Spicer mentioned constructing "a small breast work...to pitch our tents within." Joseph Holt, "Journals of Joseph Holt, of Wilton, N.H.," *NEHGR* 10 (January 1856): 307; Spicer, "Diary," 393; Bellico, *Chronicles of Lake George*, 99.

64. Rea, "Journal," 98; On July 4, 1758, Amos Richardson noted "a fine firing," but "some of our men Did sh[oo]t one of the Reg[u]l[a]rs Throu the Head, which killed h[i]m D[e]ad." Richardson, "Journal," 274; Other soldiers also reported accidents with firearms. See Spicer, "Diary," 393; Lemuel Lyon, "Military Journal for 1758," in *The Military Journals of Two Private Soldiers, 1758-1775*, by Abraham Tomlinson (1854; reprint ed., New York: Books for Libraries Press, 1970), 17-18.

65. Samuel Fisher, "Diary of Operations Around Lake George 1758," MS, Library of Congress, 3; Rea "Journal," 101.

66. AB 397.

67. Lyon, "Military Journal," 20; Spicer, "Diary," 393; Alexander, "Diary," 304; Seth Tinkham, "The Diary of Seth Tinkham," in *History of Plymouth County, Massachusetts*, by D. Hamilton Hurd (Philadelphia: J. W. Lewis. & Co., 1884), 996.

68. Foster, "Diary," 184; Henry Babcock, Letter, "Lake George 10th July 1758," in *A List of Rhode Island Soldiers & Sailors in the Old French & Indian War, 1755-1762*, by Howard M. Chapin (Providence: Rhode Island Historical Society, 1918), 12; See also *New-York Gazette*, 24 July 1758.

69. John Cleaveland, "Journal of Rev. John Cleaveland Kept While Chaplain in the French and Indian War 1758-1759," *BFTM* 10 (no. 3, 1959): 197; John Cleaveland, "The Journal of the Rev. John Cleaveland," *EIHC* 12 (July 1874): 181.

70. Alexander Moneypenny, "The Moneypenny Orderly Book," *BFTM* 12 (October 1970): 439; Archelaus Fuller wrote that the "[w]hol[e] army pushed of[f] the boats about six [o']clock." Archelaus Fuller, "Journal of Col. Archelaus of Middleton, Mass., in the Expedition Against Ticonderoga in 1758," *EIHC* 46 (1910): 213; Rufus Putnam, Caleb Rea, and Benjamin Jewett recorded seven a.m. Dawes, *Journal of Rufus Putnam*, 67; Rea, "Journal," 102; Benjamin Jewett, "The Diary of Benjamin Jewett—1758," *Nation-*

al Magazine 17 (1892-93): 62; Abel Spicer, however, wrote "about 9 o'clock." Spicer, "Diary," 394; Bellico, *Chronicles of Lake George*, 100.

71. Tinkham, "Diary," 996.

72. AB 436; On August 19, 1758, Captain Joshua Loring wrote that the expedition consisted "of About Sixteen Thousand Eight Hundred Men, on Board about Eight hundred Bateaux, and One hundred and Sixty five Whale Boats." Joshua Loring, Chatham Papers, PRO 30/8/96, fol. 97.

73. Dr. James Searing, "The Battle of Ticonderoga, 1758," *Proceedings of the New York Historical Society* 5 (1847): 113; Newspapers reported "two floating Castles with two Pieces of Cannon, four-pounders, mounted on each." *Boston Evening-Post*, 17 July 1758; See also *New-York Mercury*, 24 July 1758.

74. Hugh Arnot, "Journal or Proceed-ings of the Army…" in Nicholas Westbrook, comp. and ed., " 'Like roaring lions breaking from their chains' : The Highland Regiment at Ticonderoga," *BFTM* 16 (1998): 33-34; Newspapers listed 40 artillery pieces. *Boston Evening-Post*, 7 August 1758; *New-York Gazette*, 14 August 1758; See also Searing, "Battle of Ticonderoga, 1758," 113.

75. AB 407; Nathan Whiting, *Orderly Book of Colonel Nathan Whiting: Second Connecticut Regiment at Lake George 1758* (Hartford: CSL, 1940), 34; See also PRO 291/2, WO 34/76, fol. 148; *Boston Evening-Post*, 17 July 1758.

76. *Boston Evening-Post*, 17 July 1758; *Boston Gazette*, 17 July 1758.

77. Samuel Thompson, *Diary of a Lieut. Samuel Thompson*, ed. by William R. Cutter (Boston: Press of David Clapp & Son, 1896), 9.

78. Fuller, "Journal," 213; Charles Lee also suggested that the men were "in perfect health & spirits." Charles Lee, "Narrative—Enclosed in Letter of September 16th 1758," *Coll. NYHS* (1871): 9 (See Lee's original letter in the Fort Ticonderoga Thompson-Pell Research Center); James Searing mentioned "the great spirit of the troops." Searing, "Battle of Ticonderoga, 1758," 113.

79. Fisher, "Diary of Operations," 5.

80. Melancthon Taylor Woolsey, *Letters of Melancthon Taylor Woolsey* (Champlain, NY: Moorsfield Press, 1927), 12-13.

81. Jewett, "Diary," 62; Rufus Putnam also recorded "about dark." Dawes, *Journal of Rufus Putnam*, 67; Captain William Hervey of the 44th Regiment noted landing "at 7 evening." Hervey, *Journals*, 49. (Sunset on July 5, 1758, would have been at 7:38 p.m., according to the US Naval Observatory, Astronomical Applications Department.) James Abercromby, however, wrote that he landed at 5 o'clock. AB 436.

82. Tinkham, "Diary," 996; Garrett Albertson, "A Short Account of the Life and Travels and Adventures of Garrett Albertson, Sr.," *BFTM* 4 (July 1936): 44; See also *NYCD*, 10: 734; Captain James Murray described rattlesnakes at Lake George as "about four feet long and as thick as the small of one's leg." Frederick B. Richards, *The Black Watch* (Ticonderoga, NY: Fort Ticonderoga Museum, 1926), 23.

83. *New-York Mercury*, 24 July 1758; See also Ian Macpherson McCulloch, *Sons of the Mountains: The Highland Regiments in the French & Indian War, 1756-1767*, Volume 1 (Fleischmanns, NY: Purple Mountain Press, 2006), 88.

84. The troops departed at intervals. Benjamin Jewett and William Sweat reported their departure as ten p.m., William Hervey recorded 11 p.m., Caleb Rea 12 a.m. or one a.m., and Samuel Cobb noted one a.m. Jewett, "Diary," 62; William Sweat, "Captain William Sweat's Personal Diary of the Expedition Against Ticonderoga," *EIHC* 93 (1957): 43; Hervey, *Journals*, 49; Rea, "Journal," 102; Samuel Cobb, "The Journal of Captain Samuel Cobb," *BFTM* 14 (Summer 1981): 18; Cobb's journal was first published in 1871 with a notation that the author was unknown, "Journal of a Provincial Officer, in the Campaign, in Northern New York, in 1758," *The Historical Magazine* 10 (July 1871): 113-22.

85. *NYCD*, 10: 722; Bougainville, *Journals*, 226.

86. *NYCD*, 10: 737; Bougainville, *Journals*, 228.

87. *Boston Evening-Post*, 10 July 1758; For a discussion of the poor harvests in Canada, see William M. Fowler, Jr., *Empires at War: The French and Indian War and the Struggle for North America 1754-1763* (New York: Walker & Company, 2005), 136-37; After observing French provisions at the outlet of Lake George, Captain Hugh Arnot disputed claims of the "starving condition" of the French army. Arnot, "Journal," 35-36.

88. Harris, "Journal," 8; See also Loring, Chatham Papers, fol. 96.

89. Rogers, *Journals*, 112.

90. Cardwell, "British Expedition," 149; Abercromby had also examined Rogers' June 1758 scouting report. AB 397.

91. David Waterbury, "Personal Roster and Diary of Captain David Waterbury in the Lake George Campaign," typed transcript, 7-8, Fort Ticonderoga Thompson-Pell Research Center.

92. Fuller, Rea, and Sweat mentioned landing at nine a.m., while Champion, Smith, Spicer, and Waterbury recorded ten a.m. Hervey landed with the regulars at eight a.m. Fuller, "Journal," 213; Rea, "Journal," 102; Sweat, "Expedition," 43; Henry Champion, "The Journal of Colonel Henry Champion," in *Champion Genealogy*, by Francis Bacon Trowbridge (New Haven, CT: F. B. Trowbridge, 1891), 419; See original

"Accounts & Journals of Captain Henry Champion of Colchester, Campaign of 1758," CSL; Joseph Smith, "Journal of Joseph Smith, of Groton," *Connecticut Society of Colonial Wars Proceedings* 1 (1896): 306; Spicer, "Diary," 394; Waterbury, "Personal Roster and Diary," 7; Hervey, *Journals*, 49.

93. Tinkham, "Diary," 996; See also Harris, "Journal," 8.
94. *New-York Mercury*, 24 July 1758; See also *Boston Evening-Post*, 24 July 1758; Glasier, "Diary," 76.
95. Cleaveland, "Journal," *BFTM*: 196; Glasier, "Diary," 76.
96. George Clerk, Letter, 16 July 1758, in Westbrook, "Like Roaring Lions," 90.
97. Captain John Knox, *An Historical Journal of the Campaigns in North America*, Volume 1, (1769; edited by Arthur G. Doughty, 1914-1916; reprint ed., Freeport, NY: Books for Libraries Press, 1970), 190.
98. Jewett, "Diary," 63; Rogers later recalled that the "fire began in the rear of Col [Phineas] Lyman's regiment." Rogers, *Journals*, 113.
99. Arnot, "Journal," 38; See also Peter Pond, "Experiences in Early Wars in America," *The Journal of American History* 1 (1907): 91; Lord Howe was either 33- or 34-years-old at the time of his death. Both *The Dictionary of the National Biography* and *American National Biography* fail to report the month and day of his birth in 1724. The DNB suggests that Howe's mother was the illegitimate daughter of King George I. Leslie Stephen and Sidney Lee, eds., *The Dictionary of National Biography* (London: Oxford University Press, 1917), Volume 22, Supplement, 875; John A. Garraty and Mark C. Carnes, *American National Biography* (New York: Oxford University Press, 1999), Volume 11, 324-25.
100. S. H. P. Pell, *Fort Ticonderoga, A Short History* (Ticonderoga, NY: Fort Ticonderoga Museum, 1978), 29; A Connecticut provincial soldier wrote that "Lord How[e]...imprudently March'd Without his Arms at the Head of the Regulars." Jesse Parsons, "Journal for 1758," transcript. Fort Ticonderoga Thompson-Pell Research Center (original in a private collection), July 6, 1759.
101. *NYCD*, 10: 722, 738; See also Bougainville, *Journals*, 228.
102. Rea, "Journal," 103; Fuller, "Journal," 213.
103. Albertson, "A Short Account," 44; *NYCD*, 10: 735; Major William Eyre suggested that the "firing threw our Regulars in to some kind of a Consternation." William Eyre to Robert Napier, July 10, 1758, in Pargellis, *Military Affairs*, 418.
104. David Perry, "Recollections of an Old Soldier," *BFTM* 14 (Summer 1981): 5.
105. Pargellis, *Military Affairs*, 419; Lee, "Narrative," 10.
106. Albertson, "A Short Account," 44-45; See also Parsons, "Journal," July 6, 1758.
107. Albertson, "A Short Account," 45.
108. Loring, Chatham Papers, fol. 97.
109. William W. Willett, *A Narrative of the Military Actions of Colonel Marinus Willett* (1831; reprint ed., New York: The New York Times &Arno Press, 1969), 14.
110. AB 445; *NYCD*, 10: 726; *The Scots Magazine* (August 1758): 437; Captain Hugh Arnot noted 150 prisoners. Arnot, "Journal," 38; The *New-York Mercury* reported 152 prisoners. *New-York Mercury*, 24 July 1758; Montcalm mentioned 156 taken and Captain David Waterbury listed 172 captives. *NYCD*, 10: 738; Waterbury, "Personal Roster and Diary," 8.
111. Albertson, "A Short Account," 44.
112. Pond, "Experiences," 91; Joseph Nichols, "Joseph Nichols Military Journal 1758-59," Henry E. Huntington Library, HM 89, 20.
113. Pell, *Fort Ticonderoga*, 29; Woolsey, *Letters*, 15.
114. AB 445; Rogers later echoed the same words: "This noble and brave officer being universally beloved by both officers and soldiers." Rogers, *Journals*, 114; Newspapers reported that Howe's death was "universally lamented" by the army. *Boston Gazette*, 17 July 1758; *Boston Evening-Post*, 17 July 1758.
115. Rea, "Journal," 103; Rogers, *Journals*, 114.
116. AB 436; Rea, "Journal," 103.
117. *New York Times*, 11 October 1889; Thompson, *Diary*, 9; Richardson, "Journal," 275; See also *Boston Evening-Post*, 17 July 1758; *Boston Gazette*, 17 July 1758; *New-Hampshire Gazette*, 21 July 1758.
118. *Lake George Mirror*, 15 July 1911; Ian McCulloch, "Stream of Consciousness," *Adirondack Life*, May/June 2002, 25.
119. AB 436.
120. Loring, Chatham Papers, fols. 96-97.
121. Ibid.; The *Boston-Evening Post* noted that John Bradstreet moved forward with "1200 Regulars, and a Body of Provincials and Rangers." *Boston Evening-Post*, 24 July 1758; See also *New-York Gazette*, 24 July 1758 and 31 July 1758; *New-Hampshire Gazette*, 28 July 1758; Captain James Abercrombie wrote that the 44th Regiment, the first battalion of the Royal Americans (60th Foot), and "two Reg[imen]ts of Provincials & 1000 Battoe Men" were sent to the sawmill. Westbrook, "Like Roaring Lions," 68.
122. Samuel Hopkins, "Selections from the Correspondence and Papers," *Proceedings of the New Jersey Historical Society* 7 (1854): 127; Although most accounts suggest that the French encampment at the sawmill was deserted, Benjamin Glasier wrote that Bradstreet's men "Drove them off...and took twenty

one more prisoners." Glasier, "Diary," 76.

123. Bougainville, *Journals*, 230; *NYCD*, 10: 739, 743; Montcalm's report noted that "all the sections [of the entrenchment] flanked each other reciprocally." *NYCD*, 10: 739.

124. Searing, "Battle of Ticonderoga, 1758," 116; Hopkins, "Correspondence," 127; Joseph Nichols wrote that the French breastwork was "Built So High that Our Enemy Could Stand Behind & Receive our Fire without Danger." Nichols, "Journal," 22; Charles Lee suggested that the height of the breastwork "was at least eight feet." Lee, "Narrative," 12; Peter Pond recounted that the abatis consisted of "Lim[b]s of the Trees and Sharpen[ed]...at Both Ends." Pond, "Experiences," 92; See also *New-York Mercury*, 24 July 1758; *Boston Evening-Post*, 24 July 1758; *New-Hampshire Gazette*, 28 July 1758.

125. *NYCD*, 10: 753; Westbrook, "Like Roaring Lions," 57; Rea, "Journal," 105; Alexander Colden, "Eye-Witnesses' Accounts of the British Repulse at Ticonderoga," *The Canadian Historical Review* 2 (December 1921): 362.

126. Cobb, "Journal," 19; On July 7 Abel Spicer wrote that "we took two brass cannon with us." Spicer, "Diary," 394.

127. Ian M. McCulloch, " 'Like roaring lions breaking from their chains': The Battle of Ticonderoga 8 July 1758," in *Fighting for Canada: Seven Battles, 1758-1945* (Toronto: Robin Brass Studio, 2000), 399 (note 12).

128. Westbrook, "Like Roaring Lions," 81-82; Lee, "Narrative," 12.

129. *The Scots Magazine*, Volume 20 (1758): Appendix, 698; Westbrook, "Like Roaring Lions," 53-54, 56; See also Searing, "Battle of Ticonderoga, 1758," 115; Rogers, *Journals*, 114.

130. Stark, *Memoir*, 26; See also Harris, "Journal," 9.

131. Rea, "Journal," 104; William Johnson passed "the French prisoners on the lake" being transported south. Searing, "Battle of Ticonderoga, 1758," 115.

132. Tinkham, "Diary," 996; See also Westbrook, "Like Roaring Lions," 40.

133. Albertson, "A Short Account," 45.

134. *NYCD*, 10: 723, 733, 739, 743; Bougainville, *Journals*, 230-31; Arthur G. Doughty, ed., *Report of the Public Archives for the Year 1929* (Ottawa: F. A. Acland, 1930), 104; Montcalm recorded 3,506 men in his army before the battle. Louis-Joseph de Montcalm, *Journal Du Marquis De Montcalm Durant Ses Campagnes En Canada De 1756 à 1759*, ed. H.-R. Casgrain (Quebec: Imprimerie De L.-J. Demers & Frère, 1895), 398.

135. *The Scots Magazine*, Volume 20 (1758): Appendix, 698.

136. AB 436; Colden, "Eye-Witnesses' Accounts," 361; Hervey, *Journals*, 50; Westbrook, "Like Roaring Lions," 56; See also McCulloch, "Battle of Ticonderoga," 52, 402 (note 58).

137. AB 445.

138. Hervey, *Journals*, 50; Searing, "Battle of Ticonderoga, 1758," 116; See also McCulloch, *Seven Battles*, 52-53; René Chartrand, *Ticonderoga 1758: Montcalm's Victory Against All Odds* (Oxford, U.K.: Osprey Publishing, 2000), 60.

139. *Boston Evening-Post*, 24 July 1758; *Boston Gazette*, 24 July 1758; *New-York Gazette*, 31 July 1758; See also *The Scots Magazine*, Volume 20 (1758): Appendix, 698.

140. AB 445.

141. Smith, "Journal," 306; Abel Spicer had nearly the identical entry, except that the engineer had returned at eight o'clock in the morning. Spicer, "Diary," 394; A friend of Matthew Clerk's family later suggested that Clerk "had intended to have erected a Battery up that Hill [Rattlesnake Hill]." Westbrook, "Like Roaring Lions," 85.

142. Glasier, "Diary," 76; Searing, "Battle of Ticonderoga, 1758," 116; See also Spicer, "Diary," 394; *NYCD*, 10: 735; Dawes, *Journal of Rufus Putnam*, 69.

143. Searing, "Battle of Ticonderoga, 1758," 116-17; *NYCD*, 10: 723, 749, 816, 846; See also Dawes, *Journal of Rufus Putnam*, 71; Glasier, "Diary," 76; *New-Hampshire Gazette*, 28 July 1758; *New-York Gazette*, 31 July 1758.

144. *New-York Mercury*, 24 July 1758; *Pennsylvania Journal*, 27 July 1758.

145. AB 436; AB 445; *NYCD*, 10: 736; Regulars were ordered not to fire until "within the Breast-Works" on "Pain of Death." *Pennsylvania Journal*, 27 July 1758.

146. Pouchot, *Memoir*, 145.

147. *New-York Mercury*, 24 July 1758; *Pennsylvania Journal*, 27 July 1758; *Boston Evening-Post*, 31 July 1758; *The Scots Magazine*, Volume 20 (August 1758): 439; Jean-Nicolas Desandouins, *Le Maréchal De Camp Desandrouins 1729-1792*, ed. L'Abbé Gabriel (Verdun: Imprimerie Renvé-Lallemant, 1887), 171; Cardwell, "British Expedition," 101; See also Cleaveland, "Journal," *EIHC* 12: 189.

148. Hervey, *Journals*, 50; William Parkman, "Journal of William Parkman," *Proceedings of the Massachusetts Historical Society* 7 (1879-80): 244; John Noyes, "Journal of John Noyes of Newbury in the Expedition Against Ticonderoga, 1758," *EIHC* 45 (1909): 74; Captain David Waterbury wrote that the regulars marched "in the front four in Rank and Fifteen Hundred in Files and the Proven[c]ials March[ed] in the Rear." Waterbury, "Personal Roster," 8-9.

149. Rogers, *Journals*, 114-15.

150. Nichols, "Journal," 22; Rogers, *Journals*, 114-15; The ranger detachment included Stockbridge Indian rangers. Zaboly, *A True Ranger*, 232; The Stockbridge Indian rangers were led by a father and son: Captains Jacob Cheeksauken and Jacob Naunauphtaunk. This may have been the basis for James Fenimore Cooper's Chingachook and Uncas in *The Last of the Mohicans*. McCulloch, "Battle of Ticonderoga," 399 (note 8).
151. Rogers, *Journals*, 115; Zaboly, *A True Ranger*, 230; McCulloch, *Sons of the Mountains*, 1: 95; Bougainville, *Journals*, 238.
152. Westbrook, "Like Roaring Lions," 41.
153. Ibid., 68.
154. Ibid., 40-41.
155. AB 445.
156. Westbrook, "Like Roaring Lions," 69; See also Pargellis, *Military Affairs*, 421. No definitive family relationship has been established at this time between Major General James Abercromby and his aide Captain James Abercrombie.
157. *New-York Mercury*, 24 July 1758; Babcock, Letter, 12-13; See also *Boston Evening-Post*, 24 July 1758; *New-Hampshire Gazette*, 28 July 1758.
158. *The Scots Magazine*, Volume 20 (1758): Appendix, 699.
159. Pargellis, *Military Affairs*, 420.
160. Cleaveland, "Journal," *BFTM*: 198; Abner Barrows, "Diary of Abner Barrows," in *History of the Town of Middleboro*, by Thomas Weston (New York: Houghton Mifflin, 1906), 97; Captain Hugh Arnot made a similar remark earlier: "It is said the attack would have stop'd there until our Cannon came up," but the precipitous attack disrupted any reconsideration of the strategy. Westbrook, "Like Roaring Lions," 41; Lieutenant Colonel Melancthon Woolsey felt that it was "a Great Error" not to use cannon. Woolsey, *Letters*, 15; See also Daniel Shute, "A Journal of the Rev. Daniel Shute, D.D., Chaplain in the Expedition to Canada in 1758," *EIHC* 12 (April 1874): 137.
161. Lyon, "Military Journal," 22; Jewett, "Diary," 63; See also Rea, "Journal," 104.
162. Champion, "Journal," 419; Cobb, "Journal," 19; Abel Spicer wrote that "two brass cannon" were brought to the sawmill on July 7 and the next day "a number of men [were] sent after some more of the cannon and the whale boats and artillery stores." Spicer, "Diary," 394.
163. Westbrook, "Like Roaring Lions," 74; However, Abel Spicer wrote that at "the height of action the rest of the artillery stores was brought up to the place where we encamped and there was a guard set over it." Spicer, "Diary," 407.
164. Westbrook, "Like Roaring Lions," 69.
165. Nichols, "Journal," 22.
166. Spicer, "Diary," 395; Jewett, "Diary," 63; Archelaus Fuller wrote that the regulars dropped their packs, fixed their bayonets, and fought "very co[u]rage[ous]ly." Fuller, "Journal," 214.
167. Spicer, "Diary," 395.
168. Colden, "Eye-Witnesses' Accounts," 361-62.
169. *NYCD*, 10: 740; Bougainville, *Journals*, 233.
170. McCulloch, *Sons of the Mountains*, 97.
171. Colden, "Eye-Witnesses' Accounts," 362; Desandrouins, *Le Maréchal*, 186; Participants said that "the oldest soldiers present never saw so furious and so incessant a fire." *The Scots Magazine*, Volume 20 (1758): Appendix, 698.
172. Tinkham, "Diary," 997; Albertson, "A Short Account," 46; See also Rea, "Journal," 105; Spicer, "Diary," 395.
173. *The Scots Magazine*, Volume 20 (1758): Appendix, 699.
174. *The Scots Magazine*, Volume 20 (August 1758): 439; Pouchot, *Memoir*, 147; Spicer, "Diary," 395; Rea, "Journal," 105; *New-York Mercury*, 24 July 1758; *Boston Evening-Post*, 24 July 1758; *The Pennsylvania Journal*, 27 July 1758.
175. Harris, "Journal," 10; See also Nichols, "Journal," 22.
176. Pouchot, *Memoir*, 148.
177. *New-York Gazette*, 31 July 1758; See also *Boston Evening-Post*, 24 July 1758; Spicer, "Diary," 395.
178. Zaboly, *A True Ranger*, 232; Dawes, *Journal of Rufus Putnam*, 70; Babcock, Letter, 13; Pargellis, *Military Affairs*, 421; Fuller, "Journal," 214.
179. Hopkins, "Correspondence," 127.
180. Perry, "Recollections," 6; Benjamin Jewett also wrote that the "New [E]ngland men kept behind tre[e]s and logs as much they co[u]ld." Jewett, "Diary," 63.

181. Perry, "Recollections," 6.
182. Albertson, "A Short Account," 45-46.
183. Fuller, "Journal," 214.
184. Lee, "Narrative," 12.
185. Hopkins, "Correspondence," 128.
186. The first published history of the Seven Years' War suggested that Abercromby had not advanced "the whole time farther than the [saw] mills." John Entick, *The General History of the Late War: Containing It's Rise, Progress, and Event* (London: Edward Dilly and John Millan, 1763), Volume 3, 258. Thomas Mante's definitive history of the war suggested that Abercromby "remained during the greatest part of the attack, at the Saw-mills"; subsequent historians followed this account until fresh documents were released by the Fort Ticonderoga Museum. Thomas Mante, *The History of the Late War in North-America* (1772; reprint ed., New York: Research Reprints, n.d.), 151.
187. Westbrook, "Like Roaring Lions," 69, 65-67; "Plan du Fort de Carillon" shows Abercromby's position. Cartographic and Architectural Division, NAC (c13277).
188. Pond, "Experiences," 92.
189. Loring, Chatham Papers, fol. 98.
190. McCulloch, *Sons of the Mountains*, 1: 99.
191. Bougainville, *Journals*, 234; *NYCD*, 10: 724, 846; Salah Barnard, "Journal of Major Salah Barnard," MS, Fort Ticonderoga Thompson-Pell Research Center.
192. Hervey, *Journals*, 50; *The Scots Magazine*, Volume 20 (August 1758): 439; Benjamin Glasier noted that the "army fought them till dark," and Joseph Smith wrote that the "[e]ngagement [lasted] till night"; Henry Champion stated that the retreat began "A little before sunset" and Archelaus Fuller noted that it occurred "before dark." Glasier, "Diary," 76; Smith, "Journal," 307; Champion, "Journal," 419; Fuller, "Journal," *EIHC*: 214; See also Westbrook, "Like Roaring Lions," 90; Waterbury, "Personal Roster," 9; A letter published in the *New-York Mercury* reported that "the whole were ordered to retreat; about 5 o'Clock we retired." *New-York Mercury*, 24 July 1758.
193. Perry, "Recollections," 6; Abner Barrows, "Diary of Abner Barrows," in *History of the Town of Middleboro*, by Thomas Weston (New York: Houghton Mifflin, 1906), 97.
194. Spicer, "Diary," 407; Rufus Putnam also mentioned that "the path all the way was full of wounded men." Dawes, *Journal of Rufus Putnam*, 71.
195. Albertson, "A Short Account," 47; Marinus Willett recalled the story of a wounded British lieutenant colonel who was scalped and killed by Montcalm's Indians. Willett, *A Narrative*, 18-19; *NYCD*, 10: 847.
196. Bougainville, *Journals*, 234, 250-51; *NYCD*, 10: 848; Another French document noted that "nearly 500 dead bodies" were found on July 10, 1758. *NYCD*, 10: 746.
197. *NYCD*, 10: 775, see also 847.
198. McCulloch, *Sons of the Mountains*, 1: 110 (note 84).
199. Charles J. Stille, *Major-General Anthony Wayne and the Pennsylvania Line in the Continental Army* (Philadelphia: J. B. Lippincott Company, 1893), 37.
200. *NYCD*, 10: 724.
201. Bougainville, *Journals*, 234.
202. Dawes, *Journal of Rufus Putnam*, 71; Albertson, "A Short Account," 47; See also Spicer, "Diary," 395; John Noyes wrote that his unit "was Ral[l]ied about midnight and we Stay[e]d while all the wounded w[e]re carried by us." Noyes, "Journal," 74.
203. AB 436; See also AB 445.
204. McCulloch, *Sons of the Mountains*, 1: 233; Shute, "Journal," 138.
205. John Cleaveland, "The Journal of Rev. John Cleaveland," *EIHC* 13 (January 1875): 63.
206. Loring, Chatham Papers, fol. 99; Babcock, Letter, 13.
207. Perry, "Recollections," 7; Fuller, "Journal," 214.
208. Lee, "Narrative," 14.
209. Searing, "Battle of Ticonderoga, 1758," 117; Smith, "Journal," 307; Rea, "Journal," 105-6; Some newspapers reported that British troops left "300 Barrels of Pork and Flour." *Boston Evening-Post*, 24 July 1758; *New-York Gazette*, 31 July 1758.
210. Spicer, "Diary," 395; Fisher, "Diary of Operations," 11.
211. Nichols, "Journal," 24; See also Lyon, "Military Journal," 23.
212. Babcock, Letter, 13; Fisher, "Diary of Operations," 10.
213. Cleaveland, "Journal," *EIHC* 12: 185; Tinkham, "Diary," 997.
214. Lee, "Narrative," 14.

215. Waterbury, "Personal Roster," 9.
216. Rea, "Journal," 106; Fisher, "Diary of Operations," 11; Tinkham, "Diary," 997.
217. Cleaveland, "Journal," *EIHC* 12: 185; Perry, "Recollections," 7.
218. *NYCD*, 10: 741; Pouchot, *Memoir*, 150; See also *NYCD*, 10: 746, 749, 753, 797; Bougainville, *Journals*, 235; Russell P. Bellico, *Chronicles of Lake Champlain: Journeys in War and Peace* (Fleischmanns, NY: Purple Mountain Press, 1999), 94-95.
219. AB 436; See also PRO 272, WO 34/30, fol. 23; AB 425; AB 445; Gertrude Selwyn Kimball, ed., *Correspondence of William Pitt* (New York: The Macmillan Company, 1906), Volume 1, 300; Newspapers reported nearly the same number. *Boston Evening-Post*, 24 July 1758; *New-Hampshire Gazette*, 28 July 1758; *Boston Gazette*, 24 July 1758; Several newspapers listed the names of casualties. *New-York Mercury*, 24 July 1758; *Pennsylvania Gazette*, 27 July 1758; *New-York Gazette*, 31 July 1758; See also AB 425 for a list of officers killed and wounded.
220. *NYCD*, 10: 744, 751; See also Bougainville, *Journals*, 236; Jean-Nicolas Desandrouins' list of casualties on July 8 included 33 officers and 340 soldiers. Desandrouins, *Le Maréchal*, 185-86.
221. Babcock, Letter, 13.
222. Westbrook, "Like Roaring Lions," 74-75.
223. Ibid., 76.
224. Bougainville, *Journals*, 237.
225. AB 431.
226. Westbrook, "Like Roaring Lions," 77.
227. Parkman, "Journal," 243; Rufus Putnam wrote that Abercromby was "frequently called granny." Dawes, *Journal of Rufus Putnam*, 66; Provincial soldiers also called him "Mrs. Nabbycrombie." Francis Parkman, *Montcalm and Wolfe* (Boston: Little, Brown, and Company, 1884), 120.
228. Dawes, *Journal of Rufus Putnam*, 72.
229. Waterbury, "Personal Roster," 11, see also 19.
230. Rea, "Journal," 109, 107; Spicer, "Diary," 396; Seth Tinkham noted that "Our company most all sick by reason of the late fight [at Ticonderoga]." Tinkham, "Diary," 997.
231. Waterbury, "Personal Roster," 25.
232. Glasier, "Diary," 77-78; Archelaus Fuller and Lemuel Lyon both recorded working on the hospital in July. Fuller, "Journal," 216; Lyon, "Military Journal," 24; Glasier also mentioned building "a home" for the "head" engineer on July 11 and the death of an engineer on July 15 (probably Matthew Clerk). Glasier, "Diary," 77.
233. Fuller, "Journal," 215; Spicer, "Diary," 398; On August 24 Chaplain John Cleaveland mentioned a "Provincial Redoubt…on a very high Narrow Ridge of Ground about a quarter of a Mile from the South-West Corner of our Breast Work." Cleaveland, "Journal," *BFTM*: 214.
234. Fuller, "Journal," 215; Noyes, "Journal," 74; Glasier, "Diary," 77; Sweat, "Expedition," 44.
235. Champion, "Journal," 420; Sweat, "Expedition," 44, 50; Glasier, "Diary," 83-84; Fisher, "Diary of Operations," July 12, 1758.
236. Champion, "Journal," 420.
237. Champion, "Journal," 426; Richardson, "Journal," 284; Benjamin Silliman mentioned the crystals in 1819. Bellico, *Chronicles of Lake George*, 237.
238. Shute, "Journal," 143; Thomas Mante listed 2,952 men on the expedition. Mante, *Late War*, 152; Another participant in the campaign noted 3,332 troops. Richard Atkins, "Diary 1758," transcript, Lake Champlain Maritime Museum.
239. For additional information see the *Boston Gazette*, 28 August 1758; *New-York Gazette*, 11 September 1758; *Boston Gazette*, 25 September 1758; *Boston Evening-Post*, 25 September 1758; Fowler, *Empires at War*, 152-55; Fred Anderson, *Crucible of War: The Seven Years' War and the Fate of Empire in British North America, 1754-1766* (New York: Alfred A. Knopf, 2000), 260-65; See also Cleaveland, "Journal," *BFTM*: 225, 227.
240. *NYCD*, 10: 783, see also 737-41, 756-61, 777-86.
241. Ibid., 756, 761.
242. Ibid., 769; Bougainville, *Journals*, 245, 239.
243. Bougainville, *Journals*, 244, 268. Bougainville also suggested building a "dug-in" battery on Mutton Island (Prisoners Island). Ibid., 268.
244. *New-York Gazette*, 25 September 1758; *Boston Evening-Post*, 2 October 1758; On August 30 Captain John Cleaveland wrote that a French deserter revealed that the breastwork stretched "from Lake to Lake…and mounted Cannon." Cleaveland, "Journal," *BFTM*: 216.
245. *NYCD*, 10: 848. This source suggested that the raiding party consisted of "300 Indians and 200 Canadians," and Bougainville noted that the detachment was nearly 600 men, "more than four hundred of them Iroquois, Abnaki, and Ottawa Indians." Bougainville, *Journals*, 245.
246. Foster, "Diary," 185; See also Lyon, "Military Journal," 25; Fuller, "Journal," 216; Sweat, "Expedition," 45; Glasier, "Diary," 77-78; Spicer, "Diary," 397; Henderson, "Journal," 197-98; Smith, "Journal," 307;

Boston Evening-Post, 7 August 1758; *New-York Gazette*, 14 August 1758; *Boston Gazette*, 14 August 1758.

247. Holt, "Journals," 308; See also Thompson, *Diary*, 11-12.

248. Sweat, "Expedition," 45; Cleaveland, "Journal," *EIHC* 12: 194; A very wide range (20-40) of deaths due to the ambush were noted in provincial diaries and journals. Fuller, "Journal," 216; Spicer, "Diary," 398; Henderson, "Journal," 199; Smith, "Journal," 308; Foster, "Diary," 185; Holt, "Journals," 308; Champion, "Journal," 422; Rea, "Journal," 117; Richardson, "Journal," 280; See also *New-York Mercury*, 7 August 1758; *New-York Gazette*, 14 August 1758.

249. Champion, "Journal," 422.

250. Rea, "Journal," 117; Fuller, "Journal," 216; Holt, "Journals," 308; Foster, "Diary," 185; Smith, "Journal," 308; Henderson, "Journal," 198; *NYCD*, 10: 817; See also Pouchot, *Memoir*, 152.

251. AB 495; See also *New-York Gazette*, 21 August 1758.

252. *New-York Gazette*, 21 August 1758; Cleaveland, "Journal," *EIHC* 12: 194, see also 13:53.

253. AB 495; A. W. Holden, *A History of the Town of Queensbury* (Albany: Joel Munsell, 1874), 323-24.

254. Holden, *History*, 324; Henderson, "Journal," 199; Jesse Parsons reported that a woman "Great With Child" was cut open and a four-year-old boy was "Cut and mangled in A most inhuman manner and his head placed on A pole." Parsons, "Journal," July 28, 1758.

255. AB 489.

256. PRO, CO 5/50, UP microfilm reel 3, frame 35.

257. Ibid., Spicer, "Diary," 398; See also Bellico, *Chronicles of Lake George*, 105-9; Glasier, "Diary," 78,

258. Champion, "Journal," 422; Jesse Parsons mentioned only "Six Battoes Coming Toward them." Parsons, "Journal," July 29, 1758.

259. Hervey, *Journals*, 51; PRO, CO 5/50, UP microfilm reel 3, frame 35; Champion, "Journal," 422; Glasier, "Diary," 78, Cleaveland, "Journal," *EIHC* 12: 195-96.

260. Hervey, *Journal*, 51.

261. Champion, "Journal," 423; See also Fuller, "Journal," 217.

262. Spicer, "Diary," 399; Glasier, "Diary," 79; See also Fuller, "Journal," 217.

263. Champion, "Journal," 423; See also Spicer, "Diary," 399.

264. AB 522.

265. Ibid.; Spicer, "Diary," 400; See also Leonard Spaulding, "French and Indian War Record," in *The Vermont Historical Gazette*, Volume 5, ed. by Abby Maria Hemenway (Brandon, VT: Carrie E. H. Page, 1891), 29.

266. Smith, "Journal," 308; See also Champion, "Journal," 424; Cleaveland, "Journal," *EIHC* 13: 57; Spicer, "Diary," 400; Spaulding, "French and Indian War Record," 29; Zaboly, *A True Ranger*, 240.

267. Champion, "Journal," 424; *NYCD*, 10: 818. André (Jean-Baptiste) Doreil, financial commissary of wars, wrote that Marin's force consisted of "50 Regulars, 100 Canadians and 150 Indians," but Bougainville noted a French party of "219 Indians and 225 Canadians." Ibid.; Bougainville, *Journals*, 258.

268. Rogers, *Journals*, 118. Rogers referred to Durkee as a lieutenant, but he was listed on the Connecticut rolls as a captain in the Third Connecticut Regiment. *Rolls of Connecticut Men in the French and Indian War 1755-1762* (Hartford: Connecticut Historical Society, 1905), Volume 2, 65-66.

269. Spicer, "Diary," 400.

270. Ibid., 401.

271. *NYCD*, 10: 818.

272. Cleaveland, "Journal," *EIHC* 13: 59; Rea, "Journal," 180; Alexander, "Diary," 304; Spaulding, "French and Indian War Record," 29; Henderson, "Journal," 199; Noyes, "Journal," 75; Rogers, *Journals*, 119; Glasier, "Diary," 80; PRO, CO 5/50, UP microfilm reel 3, frame 39; AB 522; *Boston Gazette*, 21 August 1758; Bougainville, *Journals*, 261; See also *NYCD*, 10: 819; For a full account of the battle see Todish, *Journals of Rogers*, 130-46.

273. PRO, CO 5/50, UP microfilm reel 3, frame 40.

274. Abercromby to Pitt, 19 August 1758, MASS HS, Parkman Papers, 42: 253; PRO, CO 5/50, UP microfilm reel 3, frame 28.

275. Cobb, "Journal," 20; Glasier, "Diary," 77.

276. Champion, "Journal," 420; On September 3 Chaplain John Cleaveland noted that the troops were ordered to build "a Stockade to hold about 200 men where the ship or vessel was built." Cleaveland, "Journal," *BFTM*: 217.

277. Sweat, "Expedition," 45.

278. Cobb, "Journal," 22.

279. Glasier, "Diary," 80; See also Sweat, "Expedition," 46.

280. Parsons, "Journal," August 11, 1758; *New-York Gazette*, 11 September 1758; *Boston Gazette*, 28 August 1758.

281. PRO, CO 5/50, UP microfilm reel 3, frame 29; Loring, Chatham Papers, fol. 100; Delphina L. H. Clark, *Phineas Lyman—Connecticut's General* (Springfield, MA: Connecticut Valley Historical Museum, 1964), 42; Spicer, "Diary," 402; See also "Anonymous Journal," *BFTM* 12 (September 1968): 294; French scouts

reported that the sloop mounted 12 four-pound cannons. Bougainville, *Journals*, 279; Jesse Parsons also reported "12 Guns" on the *Halifax*. Parsons, "Journal," August 11, 1758.

282. *New-York Gazette*, 25 September 1758.
283. Rea, "Journal," 185; Chaplain John Cleaveland wrote that the troops assembled at six o'clock in the evening and "had Time only for Singing" before the firing began. Cleaveland, "Journal," *BFTM*: 215.
284. Rea, "Journal," 186; See also Spicer, "Diary," 403; Lyon, "Military Journal," 32; Glasier, "Diary," 81; Champion, "Journal," 426.
285. AB 450.
286. *Boston Evening-Post*, 18 September 1758.
287. Cobb, "Journal," 24; See also Glasier, "Diary," 81.
288. Clark, *Phineas Lyman*, 42; Rea, "Journal," 191.
289. Sweat, "Expedition," 52; On October 6, 1758, Benjamin Glasier recorded "Corking the Bay Boats and at Night we La[u]nched one of them." Glasier, "Diary," 85.
290. Cobb, "Journal," 26.
291. Christopher Comstock, "Diary of Christopher Comstock 1758-59," October 9, 1758, Connecticut Historical Society.
292. Ibid.
293. *JP*, 1: 863, see also 875; The recommendation for floating batteries by John Dies reflected the ideas of John (or Jens) Mörke, a Danish-born, British merchantman captain. Thomas M. Barker and Paul R. Huey, *The 1776-1777 Northern Campaigns of the American War for Independence and Their Sequel: Contemporary Maps of Mainly German Origin* (Fleischmanns, NY: Purple Mountain Press, 2010), 91.
294. PRO, 281/2, WO 34/46B, fol.1.
295. Cleaveland, "Journal," *BFTM*: 229; Caleb Rea and John Noyes also called the radeau an "ark." Rea, "Journal," 203; Noyes, "Journal," 76; Chaplain Cleaveland described two 35-foot-long birch bark canoes, constructed "with Cedar Clap-Boards thin as brown paper and laid lengthways of ye Canoe upon which crossways of ye Canoe is another laying of Cedar bent to the Shape of ye Canoe." Each canoe could "carry 20 men," yet were "so light" that four men could carry it. Cleaveland, "Journal," *BFTM: 227*.
296. Rea, "Journal," 199; Joseph Holt called the radeau "the most odd vessel." Holt, "Journals," 310; The exact location where the radeau *Land Tortoise* was actually built is somewhat uncertain. On October 13, 1758, Chaplain Cleaveland walked to "ye Ground of ye Old Fort, French entrenchments, Battoes" and observed the "R[a]deaux upon the Stocks." Cleaveland, "Journal," *BFTM*: 230.
297. Champion, "Journal," 431.
298. Sweat, "Expedition," 53.
299. Rea, "Journal," 193, 197.
300. Champion, "Journal," 429; See also Rea, "Journal," 190.
301. Ian McCulloch, trans. and ed., " 'Believe Us, Sir, This Will Impress Few People!' Spin-Doctoring—18th Century Style," *BFTM* 16 (1998): 96-97; See also Pargellis, *Military Affairs*, 425-27; AB 557.
302. PRO, CO 5/50, UP microfilm reel 3, frame 270.
303. PRO 272, WO 34/30, fol. 36; See also *Boston Gazette*, 16 October 1758; *Boston Evening-Post*, 16 October 1758; The *New-York Gazette* reported that the French had "very greatly added to the Strength of the Fort." *New-York Gazette*, 30 October 1758.
304. Sweat, "Expedition," 54.
305. Thomas Gage, The Gage Papers, American Series I, 1755-February 1759, September 10, 1758, William L. Clements Library, University of Michigan, Ann Arbor, Michigan.
306. Sweat, "Expedition," 54; Rea, "Journal," 203; See also Spaulding, "French and Indian War Record," 30; "Anonymous Journal," *BFTM* 12 (September 1968): 296; Comstock, "Diary," October 20, 1758.
307. Cobb, "Journal," 30. On September 15 Abel Spicer wrote that the vessel was to be "50 foot long and 20 foot wide." Spicer, "Diary," 404.
308. Sweat, "Expedition," 54; Cobb, "Journal," 30.
309. Champion, "Journal," 433.
310. The 1990 archaeological team included Joseph W. Zarzynski, Russell P. Bellico, Robert R. Benway, Vincent J. Capone, James T. Crandall, John P. Farrell, and David Van Aken. See the DVD documentary "The Last Radeau: North America's Oldest Intact Warship"; Russell P. Bellico, *Sails and Steam in the Mountains: A Maritime and Military History of Lake George and Lake Champlain*, rev. ed. (Fleischmanns, NY: Purple Mountain Press, 2001), 82-83.
311. Sweat, "Expedition," 54; See also Cobb, "Journal," 30.
312. Caleb Rea and John Noyes recorded that the sloop and radeau were sunk on October 23 (perhaps during the night of the 22nd/23rd). Abel Spicer noted the sinking of the sloop and a row galley on October 24. Rea, "Journal," 204; Noyes, "Journal," 76; Spicer, "Diary," 406; See also Joseph Nichols, "Journal," 86.
313. Spicer, "Diary," 405-6; Henry Champion also mentioned "sinking all ye watercraft" on October 24. Champion, "Journal," 433.

314. Sweat, "Expedition," 54; AB 802; John Bradstreet's "State of the Battoes" listed 260 bateaux sunk in Lake George. PRO 160/1, 34/57, fol. 17.

315. Champion, "Journal," 432; Spicer, "Diary," 406; Henry Champion also mentioned placing "boats in ye swamps ye north side of ye creek opposite ye others" in "ye bay opposite Diamond Island," and in other areas. Champion, "Journal," 433.

316. AB 802; While Joshua Loring's account survived, the "Plan" is absent from the Abercromby Papers.

317. Thompson, *Diary*, 19; Champion, "Journal," 433; See also Spicer, "Diary," 406; Noyes, "Journal," 76.

318. "Return of Ordnance and Stores left at Fort Edward…24th December 1758" and "Return of His Majesty's Naval Stores at Fort Edward 29 December 1758," Gage Papers, American Series I; AB 802.

319. Noyes, "Journal," 76; See also Rea, "Journal," 204.

320. *NYCD*, 10: 889.

321. Bougainville, *Journals*, 292; Parsons, "Journal," June 21-29, 1758.

322. J. Clarence Webster, ed., *The Journal of Jeffery Amherst* (Toronto: The Ryerson Press, 1931), 105.

8. BRITISH ADVANCE TO LAKE CHAMPLAIN 1759

1. Fred Anderson, *Crucible of War: The Seven Years' War and the Fate of Empire in British North America, 1754-1766* (New York: Alfred A. Knopf, 2000), 321-22.

2. *New-York Gazette*, 12 March 1759.

3. Ibid.

4. Timothy J. Todish, *The Annotated and Illustrated Journals of Major Robert Rogers* (Fleischmanns, NY: Purple Mountain Press, 2002), 154-55; Gary Steven Zaboly, *A True Ranger: The Life and Many Wars of Major Robert Rogers* (Garden City Park, NY: Royal Blockhouse, IIc, 2004), 252; The list of participants on the expedition numbered 362 men in addition to Rogers, although the "whole" was reported as 358. See *New-York Gazette*, 20 March 1759; *Boston Gazette*, 9 April 1759.

5. "Lieutenant Brehm's Report," *BFTM* 11 (December 1962): 38-39.

6. Ibid., 41.

7. *New-York Gazette*, 20 March 1759; *Boston Gazette*, 9 April 1759; See also Robert Rogers, *Journals of Robert Rogers* (1765; reprint ed., Ann Arbor, MI: University Microfilms, Inc., 1966), 131.

8. Ibid.

9. "Lieutenant Brehm's Report," 40.

10. PRO 285/1, WO 34/64, fols., 196, 198.

11. *New-York Gazette*, 21 May 1759; *Boston Evening-Post*, 21 May 1759; *New-York Mercury*, 21 May 1759.

12. *New-York Gazette*, 4 June 1759; On July 6 Amherst rescinded this order, suggesting that sutlers could "make use of what carriages they shall think most convenient." *New-York Gazette*, 16 July 1759.

13. William Henshaw, "William Henshaw's Journal," *Proceedings of the Worcester Society of Antiquity* 25 (1909): 49; Rufus Putnam noted "20 barrels" in each bateau and Daniel Sizer wrote that each bateau was loaded with "20 Barrels of pork or 25 Barrels of Flo[u]r." E. C. Dawes, ed., *Journal of Gen. Rufus Putnam 1757-1760* (Albany: Joel Munsell's Sons, 1886), 84; Daniel Sizer, "Journal of the Campaign of 1759," MS, Connecticut Historical Society, June 2, 1759, (transcript, Fort Ticonderoga Thompson-Pell Research Center).

14. Gary Zaboly, "A Royal Artillery Officer with Amherst: The Journal of Captain-Lieutenant Henry Skinner, 1 May—28 July 1759," *BFTM* 15 (1993): 367-68; For the original account see Henry Skinner, "Proceedings of the Army Under the Command of General Amherst, for the Year 1759," *The Universal Magazine* (November 1759): 265-69, (December 1759): 284-88; James Henderson, "James Henderson's Journal," in *The First Century of the Colonial Wars in the Commonwealth of Massachusetts* (Boston: Society of Colonial Wars, Mass., 1944), 203.

15. Robert Webster, "Robert Webster's Journal," *BFTM* 2 (July 1931): 124; See also Dawes, *Journal of R. Putnam*, 86.

16. PRO, CO 5/55, UP microfilm reel 4, frame 419; R. Webster, "Robert Webster's Journal," 125; Amherst wrote that he had arrived at Lake George with "6,236" men. J. Clarence Webster, ed., *The Journal of Jeffery Amherst* (Toronto: The Ryerson Press, 1931), 25; Sizer, "Journal," June 21-July 6, 1759.

17. R. Webster, "Robert Webster's Journal," 128; Samuel Warner, "Extracts from Samuel Warner's Journal," in *An Historical Address—Town of Wilbraham*, by Rufus P. Stebbins (Boston: George C. Rand & Avery, 1864), 209.

18. J. C. Webster, *Journal of Jeffery Amherst*, 125.

19. Ebenezer Dibble, "Diary of Ebenezer Dibble," *Society of Colonial Wars in the State of Connecticut Proceedings* 1 (1903): 314; Zaboly, "Journal of Skinner," 372.

20. Henry True, *Journal and Letters of Rev. Henry True* (Marion, OH: Starr Press, 1900), 18.

21. Henshaw, "William Henshaw's Journal," 56.

22. Warner, "Journal," 210; William Amherst wrote that a "General Hospital is built beside some Regimen-

tal hospitals." John Clarence Webster, ed., *Journal of William Amherst in America* (London: Butler & Tannes, Ltd., 1927), 44.

23. Warner, "Journal," 210; Zaboly, "Journal of Skinner," 373; See also True, *Journals and Letters,* 18.

24. R. Webster, "Robert Webster's Journal," 131; William Amherst recorded that "near three acres of ground are cleared and laid out for greens." J. C. Webster, *Journal of William Amherst,* 44.

25. Salah Barnard, "Journal of Major Salah Barnard," July 4, 1759, MS, Fort Ticonderoga Thompson-Pell Research Center; J. C. Webster, *Journal of Jeffery Amherst,* 131; See also *New-York Gazette,* 23 July 1759.

26. Zaboly, "Journal of Skinner," 379; Lemuel Wood, "Diaries Kept by Lemuel Wood of Boxford," *EIHC* 19 (1882): 143; See also Russell P. Bellico, *Chronicles of Lake George: Journeys in War and Peace* (Fleischmanns, NY: Purple Mountain Press, 1995), 132; This is probably the same vessel that Captain Philip Skene discovered in the lake: "We have weighed a large boat that was sunk at the close of the campaign in forty fathom water." (The depth was actually 40 feet.) Captain John Knox, *An Historical Journal of the Campaigns in North America*, Volume 1, (1769; edited by Arthur G. Doughty, 1914-1916; reprint ed., Freeport NY: Books for Libraries Press, 1970), 492.

27. Barnard, "Journal," July 5, 1759.

28. John Woods, "John Woods His Book," September 12, 1759, French and Indian War Collections, Octavo, 1, AAS; On July 25 Colonel James Montresor noted that "the great boat with 70 horses" was sent to Ticonderoga with provincial soldiers and wagoneers. James Montresor, "Journals of Col. James Montresor," *Coll. NYHS* 14 (1881): 83.

29. J. C. Webster, *Journal of Jeffery Amherst,* 141.

30. Zaboly, "Journal of Skinner," 381; Without the new radeau, Amherst suggested that he would have "to leave the heavy guns behind." J. C. Webster, *Journal of Jeffery Amherst,* 131, see also 132.

31. Henderson, "Journal," 204.

32. Zaboly, "Journal of Skinner," 381; PRO, CO 5/56, UP microfilm reel 4, frame 502; See also PRO, CO 5/56, fol. 89.

33. J. C. Webster, *Journal of Jeffery Amherst,* 138; Zaboly, "Journal of Skinner," 378.

34. *New-York Gazette,* 16 July 1759; Henry Skinner wrote that the British party had been fishing "near Diamond Island." Zaboly, "Journal of Skinner," 370.

35. *New York Gazette,* 16 July 1759; See also Henderson, "Journal," 204; Henshaw, "William Henshaw's Journal," 51.

36. *New-York Gazette,* 16 July 1759; *Boston Evening-Post,* 23 July 1759; Zaboly, *A True Ranger,* 261; J. C. Webster, *Journal of Jeffery Amherst,* 133.

37. PRO, CO 5/56, UP microfilm reel 4, frame 501.

38. Barnard, "Journal," July 12, 1759; See also J. C. Webster, *Journal of William Amherst,* 42-43.

39. Zaboly, "Diary of Skinner," 375; A subsequent newspaper report suggested that the French and Indians had "lost 3 of their Battoes, and all the Hands kill'd or drowned." *Boston Gazette,* 8 October 1759; See also *Boston Evening-Post,* 30 July 1759; Robert Webster also recorded that "our men sank three of their bateaux." R. Webster, "Robert Webster's Journal," 131.

40. Barnard, "Journal," July 12, 1759.

41. J. C. Webster, *Journal of Jeffery Amherst,* 152.

42. Wood, "Diaries," 19: 74.

43. *New-York Gazette,* 25 June 1759; See also "Muster Rolls of New York Provincial Troops 1755-1764," *Coll. NYHS* 24 (1891): 60-496.

44. Sizer, "Journal," June 14-15, 1759; R. F. H. Wallace, ed., "Regimental Routine and Army Administration in North America in 1759," *Journal of the Society for Army Historical Research* 30 (Spring 1952): 17; Henderson, "Journal," 203.

45. Henshaw, "William Henshaw's Journal," 53.

46. Zaboly, "Journal of Skinner," 381; Montresor, "Journals," 82; On July 21 Jeffery Amherst noted that "Two ten Inch Mortars s[a]nk last night and the wharf gave way." J. C. Webster, *Journal of Jeffery Amherst,* 141; For a list of the artillery see Knox, *Historical Journal,* 1: 501.

47. J. C. Webster, *Journal of William Amherst,* 141; True, *Journals and Letters,* 10; Montresor, "Journals," 82; A few participants suggested that the "general beat" at three o'clock in the morning. Zaboly, "Journal of Skinner," 381; See also Warner, "Journal," 211; According to a newspaper report, "the Time was kept a secret" until orders to leave were issued. *New-York Gazette,* 30 July 1759.

48. Commissary Wilson, *Commissary Wilson's Orderly Book, 1759,* (Albany: J. Munsell, 1857), 88; See also Knox, *Historical Journal,* 1: 501-2; Thomas Mante, *The History of the Late War War in North-America* (1772; reprint ed., New York: Research Reprints Inc., n.d.), 210; John Hawks, *Orderly Book and Journal of Major John Hawks 1759-1760* (n.a., NY: Society of Colonial Wars, 1911), 42; J. C. Webster, *Journal of William Amherst,* 45; PRO, CO 5/56, UP microfilm reel 4, frames 505-6; PRO, CO 5/56, fol. 89; *New-Hampshire Gazette,* 8 August 1759; Richard Huck wrote that the sloop *Halifax* carried "70 Ton[s] of Artillery Stores & 600 Barrels of Powder." LO 6130.

49. Woods, "His Book," July 21, 1759; *New-Hampshire Gazette*, 3 August 1759.

50. Hawks, *Orderly Book*, 44.

51. Wood, "Diaries," 19: 144; J. C. Webster, *Journal of Jeffery Amherst*, 142.

52. Zaboly, "Journal of Skinner," 381; J. C. Webster, *Journal of Jeffery Amherst*, 142; Samuel Merriman, "Journal of Samuel Merriman," in *A History of Deerfield*, by George Sheldon (1895-1896; reprint ed., Somersworth, NH: New Hampshire Publishing Company, 1972), 664; See also True, *Journals and Letters*, 10; An account by Reverend Eli Forbush incorrectly labeled the mooring site on the evening of July 21 as Sabbath Day Point. Eli Forbush to Steven Williams, August 4, 1759, MS, Fort Ticonderoga Thompson-Pell Research Center.

53. Woods, "His Book," July 21, 1759; Jesse Parsons, "Journal for 1759," transcript, Fort Ticonderoga Thompson-Pell Research Center (original private collection), July 21-22, 1759; See also Barnard, "Journal," July 21, 1759; The artillery rafts "had very near been dr[i]ve[n] on shore" by the wind. *Boston Evening-Post*, 6 August 1759.

54. PRO, CO 5/56, UP microfilm reel 4, frame 506; *Boston Gazette*, 6 August 1759.

55. *Boston Gazette*, 6 August 1759.

56. PRO, CO 5/56, UP microfilm reel 4, frame 506; J. C. Webster, *Journal of William Amherst*, 45; The *Boston Gazette* reported that Gage's regiment landed on the "East-Side, above Mu[t]ton Island and Lyman's on the West.—all the rest of the Army went in their Boats as far as the Ovens [French advance post]." *Boston Gazette*, 6 August 1759.

57. *NYCD*, 10: 970, 1054.

58. Ibid., 1055.

59. Rogers, *Journals*, 139; Todish, *Journals of Rogers*, 166; See also Wood, "Diaries," 19: 145; *New-York Mercury*, 30 July 1759; Forbush to Williams, August 4, 1759.

60. *NYCD*, 10: 1055.

61. Dawes, *Journal of R. Putnam*, 89; Henderson, "Journal," 205.

62. Forbush to Williams, August 4, 1759; Arthur Chase, *History of Ware, Massachusetts* (Cambridge, MA: The University Press, 1911), 84; Lemuel Aiken Welles, ed., "Letters of Col. Nathan Whiting Written from Camp during the French and Indian War," *Papers of the New Haven Colony Historical Society* 6 (1900): 142.

63. Wood, "Diaries," 19: 145; See also Constantine Hardy, "Extracts from the Journal of Constantine Hardy," *NEHGR* 60 (1906): 238.

64. PRO, CO 5/56, UP microfilm reel 4, frame 508; See also Wood, "Diaries," 19: 146; J. C. Webster, *Journals of William Amherst*, 46; See also *New-Hampshire Gazette*, 3 August 1759, for an earlier report of the French leaving Fort Carillon.

65. PRO, CO 5/56, UP microfilm reel 4, frame 508; J. C. Webster, *Journal of William Amherst*, 46.

66. Wood, "Diaries," 19: 146; Newspapers reported a later time for the British arrival at the French breastwork. *Boston Gazette*, 6 August 1759.

67. Henderson, "Journal," 205; Parsons, "Journal," July 23, 1759.

68. *Boston Gazette*, 6 August 1759; See also *New-York Mercury*, 30 July 1759; Robert Webster noted that the "Enemy fired four hundred shot and shells at us." R. Webster, "Robert Webster's Journal," 133.

69. J. C. Webster, *Journal of Jeffery Amherst*, 143; See also Wood, "Diaries," 146; *Boston Gazette*, 6 August 1759; Bourlamaque later wrote that he departed "on the following night," but the date was not given. *NYCD*, 10: 1055; Captain-Lieutenant Henry Skinner reported that the French army had "gone up the Lake eight miles, and intrenched themselves at the Narrows." Zaboly, "Journal of Skinner," 386.

70. *NYCD*, 10: 1055.

71. *Boston Gazette*, 6 August 1759; J. C. Webster, *Journal of Jeffery Amherst*, 145; J. C. Webster, *Journal of William Amherst*, 48; True, *Journals and Letters*, 10; Dawes, *Journal of R. Putnam*, 9.

72. Zaboly, "Journal of Skinner," 282-83; Knox, *Historical Journal*, 1: 504-5; See also J. C. Webster, *Journal of Jeffery Amherst*, 144; Christopher D. Fox, " 'Without a single shot': The 1759 'Siege' of Fort Ticonderoga," Fort Ticonderoga Thompson-Pell Research Center, 15-16.

73. J. C. Webster, *Journal of Jeffery Amherst*, 144; True, *Journals and Letters*, 10.

74. R. Webster, "Robert Webster's Journal," 133; Webster used the date of July 25 for the transfer of the English flat-bottomed boat to Lake Champlain, but Henry Skinner and Lemuel Wood recorded July 24. Zaboly, "Journal of Skinner," 383; Wood, "Diary," 149; See also PRO, CO 5/56, UP microfilm reel 4, frame 511; Knox, *Historical Journal*, 1: 505.

75. Warner, "Journal," 211; Dawes, *Journal of R. Putnam*, 91 (Putnam's date of July 25 should be July 26); See also Wood, "Diaries," 19: 149.

76. *New-Hampshire Gazette*, 8 August 1759; Parsons, "Journal," July 25, 1759.

77. Wood, "Diaries," 19: 148; Ian Macpherson McCulloch, *Sons of the Mountains: The Highland Regiments in the French & Indian War, 1756-1767*, Volume I (Fleischmanns, NY: Purple Mountain Press, 2006), 158.

78. *New-Hampshire Gazette*, 8 August 1759.

79. Samuel Merriman, "Journal of Samuel Merriman," in *A History of Deerfield*, by George Sheldon (1895-1896; reprint ed., Somersworth, NH: New Hampshire Publishing Company, 1972), 665.
80. Hawks, *Orderly Book*, 34; Josiah Goodrich, "The Josiah Goodrich Orderbook," *BFTM* 14 (Summer 1981): 50.
81. Parsons, "Journal," July 25, 1759; Wood, "Diaries," 19: 148; See also Zaboly, "Journal of Skinner," 384.
82. *Boston Evening-Post*, 6 August 1759; Sizer, "Journal," July 26, 1759.
83. J. C. Webster, *Journal of Jeffery Amherst*, 146; J. C. Webster, *Journal of William Amherst*, 48; PRO, CO 5/56, UP microfilm reel 4, frame 511; Fox, "1759 'Siege,' " 20.
84. Rogers, *Journals*, 141; See also Zaboly, *A True Ranger*, 264; On the night of July 26, Jeffery Amherst ordered the placement of three tents and a campfire on the eastern shore, "which had a good effect for the Enemy kept firing at it." J. C. Webster, *Journal of Jeffery Amherst*, 146; See also *New-Hampshire Gazette*, 8 August 1759; *Boston Gazette*, 13 August 1759.
85. J. C. Webster, *Journal of William Amherst*, 50; J. C. Webster, *Journal of Jeffery Amherst*, 146.
86. J. C. Webster, *Journal of William Amherst*, 50.
87. Wood, "Diaries," 19:149; See also J. C. Webster, *Journal of William Amherst*, 50; Parsons, "Journal," July 26, 1759.
88. John Hurlbut, "The Journal of Colonial Soldier," *The Magazine of American History* 39 (1893): 396.
89. J. C. Webster, *Journal of Jeffery Amherst*, 147; *Boston Evening-Post*, 19 November 1759; *Boston Gazette*, 19 November 1759; *New-York Gazette*, 3 December 1759; PRO, CO 5/56, UP microfilm reel 4, frames 515-16.
90. Wood, "Diaries," 20:156; See also PRO 293/3, WO 34/81, fol. 37; On July 23 Henry Skinner noted that the troops "discovered in the Lake a sloop [sunk] with eight guns." Neither of the British sloops that had been captured by Montcalm in 1757 and later sunk in the lake were ever raised by Amherst's troops. Zaboly, "Journal of Skinner," 383; See also PRO 283/1, WO 30/50, fol. 58.
91. *Boston Evening-Post*, 19 November 1759; J. C. Webster, *Journal of Jeffery Amherst*, 146.
92. J. C. Webster, *Journal of Jeffery Amherst*, 147; See also Hurlbut, "Journal," 396; Forbush to Williams, August 4, 1759.
93. J. C. Webster, *Journal of Jeffery Amherst*, 146; PRO, CO 5/56, UP microfilm reel 4, frame 496; See also Parsons, "Journal," July 27, 1759; *New-York Gazette*, 6 August 1759; *Boston Gazette*, 6 August 1759.
94. Henshaw, "Journal," 55; The *New-York Gazette* reported that Amherst "ordered the 29th day of July to be observed as a day of thanksgiving in his camp." *New-York Gazette*, 20 August 1759.
95. Sizer, "Journal," July 27, 1759.
96. *Boston Evening-Post*, 6 August 1759; See also *Boston Gazette*, 6 August 1759; *New-Hampshire Gazette*, 8 August 1759; J. C. Webster, *Journal of William Amherst*, 52.
97. Wood, "Diaries," 19:185; See also *New-Hampshire Gazette*, 8 August 1759; *Boston Gazette*, 6 August 1759.
98. Parsons, "Journal," July 27, 1759.
99. Ibid.
100. *Boston Evening-Post*, 19 November 1759; *Boston Gazette*, 19 November 1759; *New-York Gazette*, 3 December 1759; *The Scots Magazine* (August 1759): 439; *The London Magazine* (September 1759): 499; *The Universal Magazine* (September 1759): 147.
101. *Boston Evening-Post*, 19 November 1759.
102. Parsons, "Journal," July 27-August 1, 1759.
103. For more details on the Niagara operation see Anderson, *Crucible of War*, 330-39; Pierre Pouchot, *Memoirs on the Late War in North America Between France and England*, trans. Michael Cardy and ed. Brian Leigh Dunnigan (Youngstown, NY: Old Fort Niagara Association, Inc., 1994), 190-235; Mante, *Late War*, 224-27; Brian Leigh Dunnigan, *Siege-1759: The Campaign Against Niagara* (Youngstown, NY: Old Fort Niagara Association, Inc., 1996), 21-108; J. C. Webster, *Journal of Jeffery Amherst*, 147, 151-52; *New-Hampshire Gazette*, 8 August 1759; *New-York Mercury*, 20 August 1759; *Boston Gazette*, 13 August 1759, 10 September 1759.
104. J. C. Webster, *Journal of Jeffery Amherst*, 148; For more details about the French fleet see *The London Magazine* (December 1759): 661; *New-York Mercury*, 24 September 1759, 8 October 1759.
105. Volume 4 of the *Dictionary of Canadian Biography* erroneously suggested that Jean D'Olabaratz's father, Joannis-Galand D'Olabaratz, had commanded the fleet on Lake Champlain in 1759, but Volume 5 corrected the error. *Dictionary of Canadian Biography Online* (accessed June 15, 2008). I wish to thank Nelson R. Disco for bringing this item to my attention.
106. PRO, CO 5/56, UP microfilm reel 4, frames 515-16; *New-Hampshire Gazette*, 8 August 1759.
107. Forbush to Williams, August 4, 1759. Although Eli Forbush mentioned that the radeaux built at Ticonderoga carried "Six 12 pounders in yr [their] sides and one 24 in ye bow," Amherst described "the Radeaus with a 12 Pounder." Ibid.; PRO 293/2, WO 34/80, fol. 124.
108. *Boston Gazette*, 13 August 1759; *New-Hampshire Gazette*, 17 August 1759; Amherst reportedly sent troops "to put out the Fire at Crown-Point." *New-York Gazette*, 6 August 1759.
109. Merriman, "Journal," 665.

110. Welles, "Letters of Whiting," 143.
111. Henderson, "Journal," 206.
112. *New-York Gazette*, 20 August 1759; *New-York Mercury*, 13 August 1759.
113. *The Universal Magazine* (September 1759): 147.
114. *Boston Evening-Post*, 3 September 1759.
115. Henderson, "Journal," 206.
116. J. C. Webster, *Journal of Jeffery Amherst*, 157; *The London Magazine* (December 1759): 661; Gertrude Selwyn Kimball, ed., *Correspondence of William Pitt* (New York: The Macmillan Company, 1906), Volume 2, 189.
117. Although Jeffery Amherst recorded that the sloop had been "pierced for 16 Guns," the sloop actually mounted only six to eight 4-pound cannons. J. C. Webster, *Journal of Jeffery Amherst*, 163; Haldimand Papers, "Misc. Papers Relating to the Provincial Navy 1775-1780," NAC, Microfilm H-1649, Volume 1, B144, fol. 99; "Endorsed List of the Vessels…1762," PRO, CO 5/62, UP microfilm reel 7, frame 446; Amherst suggested that the sloop had already been launched, but Salah Barnard wrote that the vessel was "on the stocks almost ready to launch." Barnard, "Journal," September 1, 1759.
118. J. C. Webster, *Journal of Jeffery Amherst*, 164.
119. PRO, 285/1, WO 34/64, fol. 212.
120. Ibid.; Although Amherst's letter referred to a sloop, French documents mentioned a barge moored in the channel. Ibid.; André Charbonneau, *The Fortifications of Île Aux Noix* (Ottawa: Minister of Supply and Services Canada, 1994), 57.
121. Ibid.; See also PRO 293/3, WO 34/81, fol. 2; Kimball, *Correspondence of William Pitt*, 2: 196.124.
122. Rogers, *Journals*, 144; Zaboly, *A True Ranger*, 270.
123. Rogers, *Journals*, 145.
124. Stephen Brumwell, *White Devil: A True Story of War, Savagery and Vengeance in Colonial America* (Cambridge, MA: Da Capo Press, 2005), 160.
125. Zaboly, *A True Ranger*, 270-71; *Boston Gazette*, 26 November 1759; Another newspaper account noted 230 men. *New-York Gazette*, 26 November 1759.
126. Rogers, *Journals*, 153.
127. Brumwell, *White Devil*, 181; *NYCD*, 10: 1042; Rogers noted 400 French and Indians. Rogers, *Journals*, 152.
128. Ian M. McCulloch and Timothy J. Todish, eds., *Through So Many Dangers: The Memoirs and Adventures of Robert Kirk Late of the Royal Highland Regiment* (Fleischmanns, NY: Purple Mountain Press, 2004), 65.
129. *Boston Gazette*, 26 November 1759; *New-York Gazette*, 26 November 1759.
130. *Boston Gazette*, 26 November 1759; See also Rogers, *Journals*, 154.
131. McCulloch and Todish, *Through So Many Dangers*, 66.
132. Rogers, *Journals*, 147; Todish, *Journals of Rogers*, 173; Pouchot, *Memoir*, 249; Brumwell, *White Devil*, 202; Zaboly, *A True Ranger*, 283; John F. Ross, *War on the Run: The Epic Story of Robert Rogers and the Conquest of America's First Frontier* (New York: Bantam Books, 2009), 251-52.
133. Mante, *Late War*, 223; Robert Kirkwood also wrote of cannibalism, involving the devouring of an Indian "squaw." McCulloch and Todish, *Through So Many Dangers*, 67.
134. Robert Rogers and John Stark, *Reminiscences of the French War; Containing Rogers' Expeditions—The Life and Military Services of Maj. Gen. John Stark* (Concord, NH: Luther Roby, 1831), 161.
135. *New-York Gazette*, 26 November 1759.
136. Rogers, *Journals*, 159; Zaboly, *A True Ranger*, 293; See also John R. Cuneo, *Robert Rogers of the Rangers* (1959; reprint ed., Ticonderoga: Fort Ticonderoga Museum, 1988), 114; Burt Garfield Loescher, *Genesis Rogers Rangers: The First Green Berets* (San Mateo: CA: Burt G. Loescher, 1969), Volume 2, 61, 223.
137. *Boston Evening-Post*, 17 September 1759; *Boston Gazette*, 17 September 1759.
138. *Boston Gazette*, 22 October 1759; See also "Crown Point Orderly Book," *The American Collector* (October 1926): 41; J. C. Webster, *Journal of Jeffery Amherst*, 162; Kimball, *Correspondence of William Pitt*, 2: 191.
139. PRO, CO 5/59, UP microfilm reel 6, frame 118; See also J. C. Webster, *Journal of Jeffery Amherst*, 176.
140. "Crown Point Orderly Book," 42.
141. Dibble, "Diary," 318.
142. Wood, "Diaries," 19: 185.
143. PRO 293/2, WO 34/80, fol. 114; See also J. C. Webster, *Journal of Jeffery Amherst*, 166.
144. PRO 293/2, WO 34/80, fol. 114; On September 10 Montresor noted that Amherst approved of his "proposal in finishing the Citadel Bastion, Powder Magazine & c Barracks for 150 men" at Fort George. Montresor, "Journals," 96.
145. Montresor, "Journals," 108.
146. J. C. Webster, *Journal of Jeffery Amherst*, 148.
147. PRO 293/2, WO 34/80, fol. 124; J. C. Webster, *Journal of Jeffery Amherst*, 154.
148. J. C. Webster, *Journal of Jeffery Amherst*, 156, 170.
149. PRO 285/1, WO 34/64, fol. 157.
150. Ibid., fol. 229; Kimball, *Correspondence of William Pitt*, 2: 199; See also Haldimand Papers, "Misc. Papers

Relating to the Provincial Navy 1775-1780," NAC Microfilm H-1649, Volume 1, B144, fol. 99; *The London Magazine* (December 1759): 662; PRO, CO 5/62, UP microfilm reel 7, frame 446; Some newspapers also reported that the brig would carry 20 cannons. *Boston Evening-Post*, 10 September 1759; *Boston Gazette*, 20 August 1759; Other newspapers noted 22 guns. *Boston Evening-Post*, 17 September 1759; *New-York Mercury*, 24 September 1759.

151. PRO 285/1, WO 34/64, fols. 152, 208.

152. Ibid., fols. 207, 155.

153. J. C. Webster, *Journal of Jeffery Amherst*, 174; PRO 285/1, WO 34/64, fol. 222; See also *New-York Mercury*, 17 September 1759.

154. *Boston Evening-Post*, 8 October 1759; *Boston Gazette*, 8 October 1759; *New-York Gazette*, 15 October 1759.

155. J. C. Webster, *Journal of Jeffery Amherst*, 178.

156. PRO 285/1, WO 34/64, fol. 159.

157. Ibid., fol. 213.

158. Hurlbut, "Journal," 396; Dibble, "Diary," 318; See also Sizer, "Journal," October 6, 1759.

159. *The London Magazine* (December 1759): 662; See also Hurlbut, "Journal," 396; Kimball, *Correspondence of William Pitt*, 2: 199.

160. Montresor, "Journals," 99; For additional information on the quest for men and cannons see PRO 285/1, WO 34/64, fols. 164-65, 216, 218-19.

161. "Crown Point Orderly Book," 42.

162. J. C. Webster, *Journal of Jeffery Amherst*, 179; Thomas M. Charland, "The Lake Champlain Army and the Fall of Montreal," *Vermont History* 28 (October 1960): 294.

163. *Boston Gazette*, 22 October 1759; *New-York Mercury*, 29 October 1759.

164. William Gavit, "The Gavit Letters, 1759," *BFTM* 14 (Fall 1983): 219; In a letter to his brother, Gavit provided a detailed description of his hut at Crown Point: "it is 9 feet Square 6 feet Hig[h]…it is stud[d]ed 3 feet Apart and Not Having Nails I Cut a G[r]o[o]ve in the Studs With a Chisel and So Put in My Cla[p]boards…About 10 inches broad." Ibid.

165. J. C. Webster, *Journal of Jeffery Amherst*, 179; PRO 293/3, WO 34/81, fol. 66.

166. Merriman, "Journal," 666.

167. *Boston Gazette*, 22 October 1759.

168. PRO, CO 5/56, fol. 70; PRO 293/2, WO 34/80, fol. 124.

169. *Boston Evening-Post*, 8 October 1759.

170. "Crown Point Orderly Book," 43.

171. PRO 293/3, WO 34/81, fol. 66; J. C. Webster, *Journal of Jeffery Amherst*, 179; See also Wilson, *Orderly Book*, 184.

172. PRO 285/1, WO 34/64, fol. 225.

173. PRO 293/3, WO 34/81, fol. 66.

174. Wilson, *Orderly Book*, 184.

175. PRO 272/1, WO 34/30, fol. 87.

176. Ibid.; *London Magazine* (December 1759): 662.

177. PRO 272/1, WO 34/30, fol. 87; See also McCulloch, *Sons of the Mountains*, 1: 167 (note 81).

178. PRO 272/1, WO 34/30, fol. 87; J. C. Webster, *Journal of Jeffery Amherst*, 180; Knox, *Historical Journal*, 2: 195.

179. J. C. Webster, *Journal of Jeffery Amherst*, 180.

180. Wilson, *Orderly Book*, 185, 187; *London Magazine* (December 1759): 662.

181. J. C. Webster, *Journal of Jeffery Amherst*, 180; See also PRO 272/1, WO 34/30, fol. 87.

182. J. C. Webster, *Journal of Jeffery Amherst*, 181; PRO 272/1, WO 34/30, fol. 87.

183. PRO 272/1, WO 34/30, fol. 87.

184. J. C. Webster, *Journal of Jeffery Amherst*, 181.

185. PRO 272/1, WO 34/30, fol. 88.

186. J. C. Webster, *Journal of Jeffery Amherst*, 183; *The London Magazine* (December 1759): 662; PRO 272/1, WO 34/30, fols. 87-88.

187. PRO 272/1, WO 34/30, fol. 88; See also *Boston Evening-Post*, 29 October 1759; *New-York Gazette*, 29 October 1759; *Boston Gazette*, 29 October 1759, 5 November 1759; Kimball, *Correspondence of William Pitt*, 2: 200.

188. PRO 272/1, WO 34/30, fol. 88; See also *New-York Mercury*, 29 October 1759.

189. J. C. Webster, *Journals of Jeffery Amherst*, 182.

190. Anderson, *Crucible of War*, 344.

191. For more details on the battle for Quebec see Anderson, *Crucible of War*, 344-68; William M. Fowler, Jr., *Empires at War: The French and Indian War and the Struggle for North America 1754-1763* (New York: Walker & Company, 2005), 203-14; Pouchot, *Memoirs*, 236-46; *Boston Evening-Post*, 22 October 1759.

192. J. C. Webster, *Journal of Jeffery Amherst*, 184; While returning to Crown Point, Captain Dalyell picked up

a crew member from the *Musquelongy*, who had become lost. The prisoner revealed that "the crews [of the sloops] were gone to Isle au[x] Noix." Ibid.

193. Ibid., 182-83.
194. PRO 293/3, WO 34/81, fol. 88; See also Christopher Comstock, "Diary of Christopher Comstock 1758-1759," Connecticut Historical Society, October 27, 1759; Dibble, "Diary," 319.
195. PRO 278/2, WO 34/42, fol. 26.
196. Frank Pabst, *Cannons & Anchors* (Plattsburgh: Studley Printing & Publishing, 2005), 5-10; James T. Hays, David E. Mize, and Richard W. Ward, "Guns Under Lake Champlain," *York State Tradition*, Winter 1969, 10.
197. PRO 285/1, WO 34/64, fol. 232; See also J. C. Webster, *Journal of Jeffery Amherst*, 191; *New-York Gazette*, 26 November 1759.
198. PRO, CO 5/57, UP microfilm reel 4, frames 901-2.
199. J. C. Webster, *Journal of Jeffery Amherst*, 185.
200. Dibble, "Diary," 319.
201. J. C. Webster, *Journal of Jeffery Amherst*, 186; Woods, "His Book," November 2, 1759; On November 11, 1759, Colonel James Montresor mentioned that "Lt. French & 42 Deserters were brought" to Fort George. Lieutenant French commanded the party that John Woods had marched away with. Montresor, "Journals," 106; See also Hurlbut, "Journal," 396; On November 1, 1759, William Henshaw reported that 12 Jersey Blues deserted and were forced by several officers to return to Fort Edward. Henshaw, "Journal," 63.
202. J. C. Webster, *Journal of Jeffery Amherst*, 187.
203. Ibid., 189-90; Dibble, "Diary," 321; See also Hurlbut, "Journal," 396.
204. J. C. Webster, *Journal of Jeffery Amherst*, 190.
205. *Boston Gazette*, 3 December 1759; Amherst expected 220 French prisoners to be transported to Canada. PRO 293/3, WO 34/81, fol. 132.
206. PRO 283/1, WO 34/50, fol. 160; See also PRO 285/1, WO 34/64, fol. 229.
207. PRO 283/1, WO 34/50, fol. 5.
208. Ibid., fol. 8.
209. PRO 285/1, WO 34/64, fol. 175.
210. Ibid., fol. 174.
211. Ibid. Although two lighters (generally described as small sailing vessels) were mentioned, this notation could refer to two scows that had been raised by provincial troops at the northern Lake George landing in September 1759. The scows had been taken by Montcalm's army in 1757 upon the surrender of Fort William Henry.
212. PRO 285/1, WO 34/64, fol. 179. The December 1, 1759, "Return" also had the notation "Besides 25 [bateaux] left for the French prisoners at Fort George." Ibid.
213. J. C. Webster, *Journal of Jeffery Amherst*, 193.
214. Ibid., 194; However, Colonel James Montresor noted that Amherst did not arrive until the night of November 27, 1759. Montresor, "Journals," 108.
215. Montresor, "Journals," 108.
216. Ibid., 108-9.
217. Ibid., 108.
218. Pouchot, *Memoirs*, 348.
219. Ibid., 349.

9. EXPEDITION TO CANADA 1760

1. PRO, CO 5/58, UP microfilm reel 5, frame 660.
2. Gertrude Selwyn Kimball, ed., *Correspondence of William Pitt* (New York: The Macmillan Company, 1906), Volume 2, 237.
3. J. Clarence Webster, *The Journal of Jeffery Amherst* (Toronto: The Ryerson Press, 1931), 328; See also Fred Anderson, *Crucible of War: The Seven Years' War and the Fate of Empire in British North America, 1754-1766* (New York: Alfred A. Knopf, 2000), 388, 794-95.
4. Elmus Wicker, "Colonial Monetary Standards Contrasted: Evidence from the Seven Years War," *Journal of Economic History* 45 (December 1985): 877; See also Peter Marshall and Glyn Williams, eds., *The British Atlantic Empire Before the American Revolution* (London, p.n.a., 1980), 98.
5. Anderson, *Crucible of War*, 389.
6. J. C. Webster, *Journal of Jeffery Amherst*, 199; See also PRO, CO 5/57, UP microfilm reel 5, frame 142.
7. PRO, CO 5/57, UP microfilm reel 5, frame n.a.; See also Gary Stephen Zaboly, *A True Ranger: The Life and Many Wars of Major Robert Rogers* (Garden City Park, NY: Royal Blockhouse, IIc, 2004), 294; Timothy J. Todish, ed., *The Annotated and Illustrated Journals of Major Robert Rogers* (Fleischmanns, NY: Purple Mountain Press, 2002), 195.

8. PRO, CO 5/57, UP microfilm reel 5, frame n.a.
9. PRO, 284/1, WO 34/51, fol. 13; Haviland described the combustible package as sticks "About a Foot or fifteen Inches long, tyed up in paper with pack thread, in Bundles about the thickness of a Mans wrist." Ibid.; See also Kimball, *Correspondence of William Pitt*, 2: 281.
10. Burt Garfield Loescher, *Genesis Rogers Rangers: The First Green Berets* (1969; reprint ed., Bowie, MD: Heritage Books, Inc., 2000), 84-85, 241-42.
11. PRO 284/1, WO 34/51, fol. 13; In a letter to William Pitt on April 28, 1760, Amherst reported that "an accidental fire...destroyed part of the barracks" at Ticonderoga. Kimball, *Correspondence of William Pitt*, 2: 280.
12. PRO 284/1, WO 34/51, fol. 13.
13. Ibid., fol. 14.
14. Ibid., fol. 18; Lieutenant Colonel Haviland noted that the "Brick yard is upon the left of where the Royal Highlanders Encamped." Ibid.
15. PRO 283/1, WO 34/50, fol. 23.
16. J. C. Webster, *Journal of Jeffery Amherst*, 201; See also PRO 283/1, WO 34/50, fol. 189.
17. PRO, CO 5/57, UP microfilm reel 4, frame 918.
18. PRO 284/2, WO 34/52, fol. 23.
19. Ibid.
20. PRO 285/2, WO 34/65, fol. 137. "Mr. Ward" would command the *Musquelongy* and "Mr. [James] Riddle" the *Brochette*. Ibid.
21. Ibid.
22. Todish, *Journals of Rogers*, 198.
23. PRO 284/1, WO 34/51, fol. 24.
24. Ibid.; A newspaper reported a slightly different version of the incident. The Indians were in "2 birch canoes [carrying]...70 men, but [when] the sloop fir[ed] on them, they immediately turn'd tail, and landed near where Rogers and his men lay and 'tis said he narrowly escaped." *Boston Evening-Post*, 9 June 1760.
25. PRO 284/1, WO 34/51, fol. 25.
26. Ibid.
27. PRO 159/1, WO 34/54, fol. 203; See also PRO 283/1, WO 34/50, fol. 179.
28. PRO 283/1, WO 34/50, fol. 179.
29. PRO 284/1, WO 34/51, fol. 27.
30. PRO 159/1, WO 34/54, fol. 183. Captain Edward Forster noted that the *Snow Shoe* departed on a fair wind and "is to Row," indicating that the vessel had both sails and oars. Ibid.
31. Ibid., fol. 213.
32. PRO 283/1, WO 34/50, fol. 59; PRO 159/1, WO 34/54, fol. 212.
33. J. C. Webster, *Journal of Jeffery Amherst*, 203; See also Robert Rogers, *Journals of Major Robert Rogers* (1765; reprint ed., Ann Arbor, MI: University Microfilms, Inc., 1966), 172.
34. Rogers, *Journals*, 173; See also J. C. Webster, *Journal of Jeffery Amherst*, 203-4.
35. For information on the fight at Quebec in 1760 see Ian Macpherson McCulloch, *Sons of the Mountains: The Highland Regiments in the French & Indian War, 1756-1767*, Volume 1 (Fleischmanns, NY: Purple Mountain Press, 2006), 217-38; Anderson, *Crucible of War*, 291-96; Pierre Pouchot, *Memoirs on the Late War in North America Between France and England*, trans. Michael Cardy and ed. Brian Leigh Dunnigan (Youngstown, NY: Old Fort Niagara Association, Inc., 1994), 253-57; *New-Hampshire Gazette*, 30 June 1760, 4 July 1760, 25 July 1760, 5 September 1760; *Boston Gazette*, 1 September 1760.
36. In his journal Rogers wrote that 250 men were on the expedition, but a newspaper reported "270 rangers and light infantry." Rogers, *Journals*, 175; *Boston Gazette*, 8 September 1760; See also *New-Hampshire Gazette*, 12 September 1760, *New-York Gazette*, 22 September 1760.
37. *Boston Gazette*, 8 September 1760.
38. Rogers, *Journals*, 180.
39. Ibid., 180-81; *Boston Gazette*, 8 September 1760; See also *Boston Evening-Post*, 23 June 1760; *New-Hampshire Gazette*, 27 June 1760, 18 July 1760; French deserters reported that "the Indians suffer'd greatly" and returned home "to bury their Dead." *New-York Gazette*, 30 June 1760.
40. *Boston Gazette*, 8 September 1760.
41. Zaboly, *A True Ranger*, 297; *Boston Gazette*, 8 September 1760.
42. PRO 284/1, WO 34/51, fol. 55; Five years later Rogers wrote that the date of the second landing was June 9 "about midnight" and a ranger officer suggested the "11th at night landed." Rogers, *Journals*, 183; *Boston Gazette*, 8 September 1760.
43. *Boston Gazette*, 8 September 1760.
44. PRO 284/1, WO 34/51, fol. 55.
45. *Boston Gazette*, 8 September 1760; One hundred twenty-three of the 600 men that the rangers observed

may have been English prisoners on their way to be exchanged. Loescher, *Genesis Rogers Rangers*, 102; J. C. Webster, *Journal of Jeffery Amherst*, 212.

46. PRO 284/1, WO 34/51, fol. 59; In his journal, written five years later, Rogers wrote that he reached Windmill Point on June 20. Rogers, *Journals,* 185.

47. Rogers, *Journals*, 185-86.

48. PRO 284/1, WO 34/51, fol. 57.

49. Ibid., fol. 58, see also fol. 57.

50. Ibid., fol. 59.

51. J. C. Webster, *Journal of Jeffery Amherst*, 198-99.

52. Kimball, *Correspondence of William Pitt*, 305.

53. PRO, CO 5/58, UP microfilm reel 5, frames 659-60.

54. Ibid., frame 662.

55. Ibid., frame 664.

56. Samuel MacClintock, *Rev. Samuel MacClintock's Journal 1760* (Crown Point, NY: Crown Point Road Association, Inc., 1972), 8.

57. Samuel Jenks, "Samuel Jenks, his Journal of the Campaign in 1760," *Proceedings of the Massachusetts Historical Society* 5 (2nd Series) (1889-90): 354; P. M. Woodwell, ed., *Diary of Thomas Moody* (South Berwick, ME: The Chronicle Print Shop, 1976), 17; Benjamin Glasier described Fort George as a "fine fort." Benjamin Glasier, "French and Indian War Diary of Benjamin Glasier of Ipswich, 1758-1760," *EIHC* 86 (1950): 91.

58. Woodwell, *Diary of Thomas Moody*, 18; MacClintock, *Journal*, 11.

59. *New-Hampshire Gazette*, 5 September 1760; The letter may have been written by Chaplain Samuel MacClintock. See MacClintock, *Journal,* 11.

60. MacClintock, *Journal*, 12.

61. Jenks, "Journal," 356.

62. PRO 284/1, WO 34/51, fol. 86.

63. "Plan of Crown Point," PRO, CO 5/91, fol. 215.

64. John Bradbury, "Diary of Old John Bradbury," in *Bradbury Memorial*, comp. by William Berry Lapham (Portland, ME: Brown Thurston & Company, 1890), 271; The supply lines from Albany involved the employment of 540 "Waggoners, Teamsters, Batteau & Scow Men." PRO 284/2, WO 34/52, fols. 57, 59.

65. Jenks, "Journal," 360, see also 359, 361; See also Woodwell, *Diary of Thomas Moody*, 19-21, 23.

66. Jenks, "Journal," 357, 359, 366; Bradbury, "Diary," 266-68, 272; Woodwell, *Diary of Thomas Moody*, 23; John Hawks, *Orderly Book and Journal of Major John Hawks 1759-1760* (NY: Society of Colonial Wars, 1911), 81.

67. Jenks, "Journal," 354.

68. Ibid., 364.

69. PRO, CO 5/58, UP microfilm reel 5, frame 665.

70. Hawks, *Orderly Book and Journal*, 74-75.

71. Jenks, "Journal," 356; David Holden, "Journal of Sergeant David Holden," *Proceedings of the Massachusetts Historical Society* 4 (2nd Series) (1887-1889): 394.

72. Jenks, "Journal," 356, 358, 360-61; Holden, "Journal," 393-94, 396; Bradbury, "Diary," 267-69, 274-75; Woodwell, *Diary of Thomas Moody*, 22-23; Lemuel Wood, "Diaries Kept by Lemuel Wood of Boxford," *EIHC* 20 (1883): 205, 290.

73. Jenks, "Journal," 361; Holden, "Journal," 394; Bradbury, "Diary," 268-69; John Frost, Jr., "Expedition Against Canada," *Old Eliot* 8 (1908): 113; William Haviland noted "disputes and Quar[r]els between the Regulars and Provincials." PRO 284/1, WO 34/51, fol. 76.

74. Bradbury, "Diary," 269; Jenks, "Journal," 361; See also Holden, "Journal," 394.

75. Holden, "Journal," 395; Two provincial soldiers wrote that the guilty party was a regular. Bradbury, "Diary," 273; Woodwell, *Diary of Thomas Moody*, 22.

76. Holden, "Journal," 394.

77. Jenks, "Journal," 362, see also 356-58, 360-61, 366.

78. Hawks, *Orderly Book and Journal*, 81; See also Holden, "Journal," 393.

79. Jenks, "Journal," 357; See also Hawks, *Orderly Book and Journal*, 81; Holden, "Journal," 393.

80. Jenks, "Journal," 358; Hawks, *Orderly Book and Journal*, 81; See also Holden, "Journal," 393-94.

81. Woodwell, *Diary of Thomas Moody*, 20-21; Bradbury, "Diary," 268.

82. Bradbury, "Diary," 267.

83. Jenks, "Journal," 356.

84. Holden, "Journal," 395; See also Jenks, "Journal," 362.

85. Jenks, "Journal," 362.

86. J. C. Webster, *Journal of Jeffery Amherst*, 221, 224-25.

87. Ibid., 223.

88. *New-York Gazette*, 30 June 1760.
89. *Boston Gazette*, 18 August 1760; *New-York Gazette*, 25 August 1760.
90. *New-York Mirror*, 18 August 1760; *Boston Gazette*, 25 August 1760.
91. PRO 284/2, WO 34/52, fol. 56.
92. Ibid., fol. 55.
93. Hawks, *Orderly Book and Journal*, 78; Hawks was promoted to lieutenant colonel between July 5 and August 12. Ibid., 85, 88-89.
94. Woodwell, *Diary of Thomas Moody*, 19; Jenks, "Journal," 362; Captain Jenks also observed rangers "practicing...shooting at marks." Ibid., 363.
95. Jenks, "Journal," 362, see also 366; See also Holden, "Journal," 395.
96. Jenks, "Journal," 359; See also Holden, "Journal," 394; Frost, "Expedition Against Canada," 112.
97. PRO 284/1, WO 34/51, fol. 67.
98. Wood, "Diaries," 20: 289.
99. PRO 284/1, WO 34/51, fol. 52.
100. Ibid., fol. 67.
101. Ibid.; The sloop *Boscawen* was commanded by "Lt. Pullen." PRO 278/2, WO 34/42, fol. 281.
102. Jenks, "Journal," 357.
103. Ibid., 363; Wood, "Diaries," 20: 208; See also Holden, "Journal," 395.
104. Jenks, "Journal," 363; Holden, "Journal," 395.
105. Holden, "Journal," 395; Jenks, "Journal," 365.
106. Jenks, "Journal," 365; Bradbury, "Diary," 273; Both Thomas Moody and Samuel MacClintock wrote that the vessels sailed north on August 3. Woodwell, *Diary of Thomas Moody*, 23; MacClintock, *Journal*, 11.
107. Jenks, "Journal," 365; Wood, "Diaries," 20: 290.
108. MacClintock, *Journal*, 12; On August 8 Lieutenant John Bradbury and 60 men "help[e]d to Lo[a]d ye Raddo with artillery." Bradbury, "Diary," 275.
109. Woodwell, *Diary of Thomas Moody*, 23.
110. *Boston Gazette*, 29 September 1760; *New-Hampshire Gazette*, 3 October 1760.
111. *Boston Gazette*, 29 September 1760.
112. Woodwell, *Diary of Thomas Moody*, 24.
113. Holden, "Journal," 396; Wood, "Diaries," 20: 290; Jenks, "Journal," 367.
114. PRO 292/1, WO 34/77, fol. 130; Wood, "Diaries," 20: 290; Haviland recorded the departure at 12:30 and Lemuel Wood wrote "about 12 o'clock." Ibid.; However, Lieutenants Thomas Moody and John Bradbury noted the time of departure as ten o'clock in the morning. Woodwell, "Diary of Thomas Moody," 24; Bradbury, "Diary," 275.
115. Thomas Mante, *The History of the Late War in North America* (1772; reprint ed., New York: Research Reprints, Inc., n.d.), 341; Bradbury, "Diary," 275; MacClintock, *Journal*, 13; *New-Hampshire Gazette*, 19 August 1760; *New-York Gazette*, 25 August 1760; J. C. Webster, *Journal of Jeffery Amherst*, 328.
116. Mante, *Late War*, 341; Captain John Knox, *An Historical Journal of the Campaigns in North America*, Volume 2, (1769; ed. by Arthur G. Doughty, Toronto: The Champlain Society, 1914), 525.
117. PRO 284/2, WO 34/52, fols. 57, 59-60, 53.
118. Jacob Bayley, "Capt. Jacob Bayley's Journal," in *History of Newbury, Vermont*, by Frederic P. Wells (St. Johnsbury, VT: The Caledonian Company, 1902), 379; See also Rogers, *Journals*, 188-89; Brigadier William Haviland indicated that the "Advanced guard" consisted of the grenadiers, light infantry, and rangers. PRO 292/1, WO 34/77, fol. 130.
119. Bartholomew Heath, "Letter of Bartholomew Heath of N.H., Aug. 28, 1760," in *Journal and Letters of Rev. Henry True* by Henry True (Marion, OH: Star Press, 1900), 29; Rogers, *Journals*, 189.
120. Holden, "Journal," 396; Woodwell, *Diary of Thomas Moody*, 24.
121. Rogers, *Journals*, 188; Thomas Mante's 1772 *History of the Late War in North America* listed the brig among the fleet that embarked on August 11, 1760. Mante, *Late War*, 341.
122. Jenks, "Journal," 365; Bradbury, "Diary," 273; Bayley, "Journal," 379; MacClintock, *Journal*, 14; Heath, "Letter," 29; Wood, "Diaries," 20: 291.
123. PRO 292/1, WO 34/77, fol. 130; Jenks, "Journal," 367.
124. Jenks, "Journal," 367; Bradbury, "Diary," 275; Woodwell, *Diary of Thomas Moody*, 24.
125. PRO 292/1, WO 34/77, fol. 130.
126. Bradbury, "Diary," 275; Bradbury suggested that they "Lodg[e]d very uncomf[or]table on ye oars." Ibid.; Holden, "Journal," 397.
127. PRO 292/1, WO 34/77, fol. 130.

128. Bradbury, "Diary," 275; Holden, "Journal," 397; William Haviland noted that "Several boats" reached the encampment at "five in the Even[in]g." PRO 292/1, WO 34/77, fol. 130.

129. PRO 292/1, WO 34/77, fol. 130; See also Jenks, "Journal," 367.

130. Jenks, "Journal," 367; See also Holden, "Journal," 397; Bradbury, "Diary," 276; Lieutenant Thomas Moody wrote that "1 Whale Boat is gon[e] with 7 Men…7 Battoes Missing." Woodwell, *Diary of Thomas Moody*, 25; Major Robert Rogers later recounted that "ten of my Rangers were thereby drowned." Rogers, *Journals*, 190.

131. Bayley, "Journal," 379; PRO 292/1, WO 34/77, fol. 130.

132. MacClintock, *Journal*, 14; On August 15 Ensign Bartholomew Heath suggested that the troops came "in sight of our 3 warlike vessels…One brig and 2 sloops." Heath, "Letter," 29; See also Wood, "Diaries," 291.

133. Jenks, "Journal," 368.

134. Ibid.; Holden, "Journal," 397; See also MacClintock, *Journal,* 14; PRO 292/1, WO 34/77, fol. 130.

135. PRO 292/1, WO 34/77, fol. 130.

136. Jenks, "Journal," 368; See also Heath, "Letter," 29.

137. Bradbury, "Diary," 276; Bayley, "Journal," 379; See also Wood, "Diaries," 20: 291; Holden, "Journal," 397; Woodwell, *Diary of Thomas Moody*, 26.

138. André Charbonneau, *The Fortifications of Île Aux Noix* (Ottawa: Minister of Supply and Services Canada, 1994), 19.

139. *New-York Mercury*, 24 September 1759.

140. Charbonneau, *Île Aux Noix*, 31-34, 39, 48.

141. Holden, "Journal," 399; Woodwell, *Diary of Thomas Moody*, 33.

142. Woodwell, *Diary of Thomas Moody*, 33; Jenks, "Journal," 374; Charbonneau, *Île Aux Noix*, 52; A newspaper reported "50 pieces of Cannon and one Mortar" on the island. *Boston Gazette*, 19 September 1760; In August 1759 Jeffery Amherst received intelligence that the French had "near 100 Cannon" at Isle Aux Noix. J. C. Webster, *Journal of Jeffery Amherst*, 157.

143. Charbonneau, *Île Aux Noix*, 52.

144. *NYCD*, 10: 1104; *New-York Mercury*, 8 September 1760; Other French sources noted 1,453 troops at Isle aux Noix and colonial newspapers reported 1,500 men. Charbonneau, *Île Aux Noix*, 51; *New-York Mercury*, 1 September 1760; *Boston Gazette*, 19 September 1760; On August 19 Lemuel Wood wrote that a French deserter divulged that "1500 men" were at the island. Wood, Diaries," 20: 292.

145. Bayley, "Journal," 379-80; See also Charbonneau, *Île Aux Noix*, 56; *New-York Mercury*, 8 September 1760.

146. PRO 292/1, WO 34/77, fol. 130; Lieutenant Thomas Moody wrote that the radeau was sent "to cover" the grenadiers who were landing on the "Point opposit[e]" the fort. Woodwell, *Diary of Thomas Moody*, 26.

147. Holden, "Journal," 397; Bradbury, "Diary," 276; Woodwell, *Diary of Thomas Moody*, 26; See also Jenks, "Journals," 368.

148. Woodwell, *Diary of Thomas Moody*, 26; Bayley, "Journal," 379; See also the *New-York Mercury*, 1 September 1760; *Boston Gazette*, 1 September 1760.

149. PRO 292/1, WO 34/77, fol. 130.

150. Bradbury, "Diary," 277; Woodwell, *Diary of Thomas Moody*, 26-27; Jenks, "Journal," 369.

151. Woodwell, *Diary of Thomas Moody*, 27; See also Bradbury, "Diary," 277.

152. PRO 292/1, WO 34/77, fol. 130.

153. Bradbury, "Diary," 277; Holden, "Journal," 398; Jenks, "Journal," 369.

154. Jenks, "Journal," 369; Wood, "Diaries," 2: 292; See also Frost, "Expedition Against Canada," 114.

155. Woodwell, *Diary of Thomas Moody*, 28.

156. MacClintock, *Journal*, 15; Heath, "Letter," 29.

157. Jenks, "Journal," 369.

158. Ibid.; Lieutenant John Frost, Jr., described the French barrage as "Very Hot," which "Wounded Six or Seven" men. Frost, "Expedition Against Canada," 114.

159. Wood, "Diaries," 20: 292; Lemuel Wood wrote that the night before "a Party of our men [were] sent to carr[y] fas[ci]nes" for the batteries. Ibid.

160. Woodwell, *Diary of Thomas Moody*, 29; MacClintock, *Journal*, 15.

161. Bradbury, "Diary," 278.

162. Heath, "Letter," 29.

163. Holden, "Journal," 398; Wood, "Diaries," 20: 292; See also Jenks, "Journal," 370.

164. Bradbury, "Diary," 278.

165. Jenks, "Journal," 370; Early in the morning of August 23 four Rhode Island men, aboard a British sloop anchored at Hospital Island, were sent ashore to cut wood and were attacked by Indians. MacClintock, *Journal*, 15; Heath, "Letter," 29.

166. MacClintock, *Journal*, 15; See also Holden, "Journal," 398; *New-York Mercury*, 15 September 1760.

167. Jenks, "Journal," 370.

168. Bayley, "Journal," 379; *New-York Mercury*, 15 September 1760; See also Wood, "Diaries," 20: 292.

169. Bradbury, "Diary," 279; MacClintock, *Journal*, 15-16.

170. Jenks, "Journal," 371; See also MacClintock, *Journal*, 16.

171. Woodwell, *Diary of Thomas Moody*, 30; See also Holden, "Journal," 398; Bradbury, "Diary," 279; Jenks, "Journal," 371; Frost, "Expedition Against Canada," 115.

172. Woodwell, *Diary of Thomas Moody*, 29-30; Frost, "Expedition Against Canada," 115.

173. PRO 292/1, WO 34/77, fol. 131; See also the *New-York Mercury*, 15 September 1760; Robert Rogers later wrote that the plan "was introduced by Col. Darby." Rogers, *Journals*, 190.

174. *New-York Mercury*, 15 September 1760; PRO 292/1, WO 34/77, fol. 131.

175. Rogers, *Journals*, 191; A newspaper report noted an artillery train of "two twelve Pounders and two Royal H[o]witzers." *New-York Mercury*, 15 September 1760.

176. PRO 292/1, WO 34/77, fol. 131; Rogers, *Journals*, 191.

177. PRO 292/1, WO 34/77, fol. 131; *New-York Mercury*, 15 September 1760; *NYCD*, 10:1104; Rogers, *Journals*, 191; Woodwell, *Diary of Thomas Moody*, 30; MacClintock, *Journal*, 16; *Boston Evening-Post*, 15 September 1760.

178. MacClintock, *Journal*, 16.

179. Bradbury, "Diary," 279; Sergeant Thomas Moody also noted that the captain of the *Grand Diable* "had his head Shot from his Body." Woodwell, *Diary of Thomas Moody*, 30; See also *New-York Mercury*, 15 September 1760.

180. Rogers, *Journals*, 191.

181. Ibid.

182. *NYCD*, 10:1104; MacClintock, *Journal*, 16; Holden, "Journal," 398; *New-York Mercury*, 8 September 1760; *Boston Gazette*, 19 September 1760; Haldimand Papers, "Misc. Papers Relating to the Provincial Navy 1775-1780," NAC, Microfilm H-1649, Volume 1, B144, fol. 99; "Endorsed List of Vessels," PRO, CO 5/62, UP microfilm reel 7, frame 446; "List of Vessels on the different Lakes," PRO 285/2, WO 34/65, fol. 109; Amherst Family Papers, U1350 014, fol. 139; Center for Kentish Studies, Kent, Great Britain.

183. Bradbury, "Diary," 280; See also MacClintock, *Journal*, 16.

184. Woodwell, *Diary of Thomas Moody*, 30.

185. Frost, "Expedition Against Canada," 115; Jenks, "Journal," 372; Lieutenant Bradbury noted firing "300 shells in the fort." Bradbury, "Diary," 280.

186. Bradbury, "Diary," 280.

187. Holden, "Journal," 399.

188. Heath, "Letter," 30; Holden, "Journal," 399.

189. Bradbury, "Diary," 280; Lieutenant John Frost, Jr., wrote that the explosion was the result of "the French firing hot shot." Frost, "Expedition Against Canada," 115.

190. Jenks, "Journal," 372; Frost, "Expedition Against Canada," 115; See also Holden, "Journal," 399.

191. PRO 292/1, WO 34/77, fol. 131. Perhaps William Haviland included this in his journal to blunt any criticism that he had failed to prevent the French retreat.

192. Bradbury, "Diary," 280; Sergeant David Holden mentioned that "20 French Regulars" surrendered at the British camp. Holden, "Journal," 399; See also Heath, "Letter," 30.

193. Rogers, *Journals*, 192; Woodwell, *Diary of Thomas Moody*, 31; *NYCD*, 10: 1104; Lieutenant John Frost, Jr., wrote that the French departed "Just before Day" and Chaplain Samuel MacClintock suggested that "the Enemy had evacuated the place early that morning." Frost, "Expedition Against Canada," 115; MacClintock, *Journal*, 16.

194. MacClintock, *Journal*, 16; Jenks, "Journal," 372.

195. Woodwell, *Diary of Thomas Moody*, 31; Chaplain Samuel MacClintock recorded that "40 or 50 effective" men and "the sick & wounded" were discovered at Isle aux Noix. MacClintock, *Journal*, 17; See also *Boston Gazette*, 19 September 1760.

196. Jenks, "Journal," 374. Captain Jenks wrote this journal entry on August 31, which he based on "the best information I can g[e]t." Ibid.; The *New-York Mercury* reported that the French left "50 Pieces of Cannon…1000 rounds Shot, 100 Shells, 100 Barrels of Powder, 50 Ditto Pork, 50 live Cattle; an Officer and 60 Men, as a Guard to the Sick and Wounded." *New-York Mercury*, 15 September 1760; See also the *Boston Evening-Post*, 15 September 1760; *Boston Gazette*, 19 September 1760.

197. Jenks, "Journal," 373; See also Wood, "Diaries," 20: 293.

198. Jenks, "Journal," 373.

199. Samuel Merriman, "Journal of Samuel Merriman," in *A History of Deerfield*, by George Sheldon (1895-1896; reprint ed., Somersworth, NH: New Hampshire Publishing Company, 1972), 667.
200. Rogers, *Journals*, 192.
201. Merriman, "Journal," 667; Rogers, *Journals*, 192.
202. Rogers, *Journals*, 193.
203. Ibid.; Merriman, "Journal," 667.
204. Holden, "Journal," 400; Jenks, "Journal," 374.
205. Merriman, "Journal," 667.
206. Jenks, "Journal," 373.
207. Ibid.; Bradbury, "Diary," 281; Rogers, *Journals*, 193-94; Sergeant David Holden wrote that the *Grand Diable* "had fir'd one or 2 Shots" on the approach to St. Jean, but he may have confused this with an action that occurred about "half way" to St. Jean when "our leading boats discovered s[o]m[e] enemy on the shore." Holden "Journal," 400; See also Jenks, "Journal," 373; Brigadier William Haviland noted that the army arrived at St. Jean at "half past two." PRO 292/1, WO 34/77, fol. 131.
208. Jenks, "Journal," 374; See also Wood, "Diaries," 20: 294.
209. Bradbury, "Diary," 281-82.
210. Holden, "Journal," 400.
211. Ibid.
212. Bradbury, "Diary," 282.
213. Holden, "Journal," 400.
214. Jenks, "Journal," 375.
215. Merriman, "Journal," 667.
216. Jenks, "Journal," 375.
217. PRO 292/1, WO 34/77, fol. 131.
218. Holden, "Journal," 401; See also Jenks, "Journals," 375; Merriman, "Journal," 668.
219. Jenks, "Journal," 372, 376; Holden, "Journal," 401; Wood, "Diaries," 2: 294.
220. Jenks, "Journal," 375.
221. J. C. Webster, *Journal of Jeffery Amherst*, 225; Mante, *Late War*, 301.
222. *New-York Mercury*, 22 September 1760; J. C. Webster, *Journal of Jeffery Amherst*, 231; See also the *New-York Gazette*, 8 September 1760; *New-York Mercury*, 8 September 1760; Lemuel Aiken Welles, ed., "Letters of Col. Nathan Whiting Written from Camp during the French and Indian War," *Papers of the New Haven Colony Historical Society* 6 (1900): 145; Whiting noted that each row galley had "a twelve pounder in [the] bow." Ibid.
223. Pouchot, *Memoirs*, 261.
224. J. C. Webster, *Journal of Jeffery Amherst*, 237.
225. Pouchot, *Memoirs*, 308.
226. J. C. Webster, *Journal of Jeffery Amherst*, 237; Mante, *Late War*, 305.
227. Welles, "Letters of Whiting," 146.
228. Ibid.
229. Pouchot, *Memoirs*, 308-10 (footnote).
230. *New-York Mercury*, 22 September 1760; See also the *New-Hampshire Gazette*, 3 October 1760.
231. J. C. Webster, *Journal of Jeffery Amherst*, 239.
232. *New-York Mercury*, 22 September 1760; Daniel Sizer, "Journal of the Campaign of 1760," MS, Connecticut Historical Society, August 24, 1760, (transcript, Fort Ticonderoga Thompson-Pell Research Center).
233. Pouchot, *Memoirs*, 312.
234. Ibid.
235. Ibid., 313.
236. Sizer, "Journal," August 25, 1760; Colonel Nathan Whiting also wrote that "about five oclock" the French raised the flag to parley, but other eyewitnesses suggested that this occurred at four o'clock. Welles, "Letters of Whiting," 146; *Boston Gazette*, 29 September 1760.
237. Pouchot, *Memoirs*, 502.
238. J. C. Webster, *Journal of Jeffery Amherst*, 240.
239. Ibid., 239; *New-Hampshire Gazette*, 12 December 1760.
240. J. C. Webster, *Journal of Jeffery Amherst*, 240.
241. *JP*, 10: 176; Mante, *Late War*, 306; Knox, *Historical Journal*, 2:555; J. C. Webster, *Journal of Jeffery Amherst*, 243.
242. *JP*, 3: 273
243. Ibid.
244. See Anderson, *Crucible of War*, 404-6, for details on the role of the Indians during Amherst's advance.
245. J. C. Webster, *Journal of Jeffery Amherst*, 235; D. Peter MacLeod, *The Canadian Iroquois and the Seven Years' War* (Toronto: Dundurn Press, 1996), 169; See also Pouchot, *Memoirs*, 316.

246. J. C. Webster, *Journal of Jeffery Amherst*, 244.
247. Ian M. McCulloch and Timothy J. Todish, *Through So Many Dangers: The Memoirs and Adventures of Robert Kirk, Late of the Royal Highland Regiment* (Fleischmanns, NY: Purple Mountain Press, 2004), 73.
248. J. C. Webster, *Journal of Jeffery Amherst*, 244; See also Sizer, "Journal," September 4, 1760; *New-Hampshire Gazette*, 3 October 1760, 12 December 1760.
249. Kimball, *Correspondence of William Pitt*, 2: 330.
250. Welles, "Letters of Whiting," 147-48.
251. Kimball, *Correspondence of William Pitt*, 2: 331; *New-Hampshire Gazette*, 3 October 1760.
252. *New-Hampshire Gazette*, 3 October 1760; See also *Boston Gazette*, 29 September 1760; *New-York Mercury*, 22 September 1760.
253. *New-Hampshire Gazette*, 3 October 1760.
254. *New-York Mercury*, 15 December 1760; See also Knox, *Historical Journal*, 2: 567; *NYCD*, 10: 1107-20; *New-York Gazette*, 15 December 1760; *New-Hampshire Gazette*, 12 December 1760.
255. Knox, *Historical Journal*, 2:561; *New-Hampshire Gazette*, 12 December 1760.
256. Kimball, *Correspondence of William Pitt*, 2:332; Knox, *Historical Journal*, 2:562; See also *Boston Gazette*, 29 September 1760; *New-Hampshire Gazette*, 3 October 1760.
257. Jenks, "Journal," 376.
258. Ibid., 377; See also Bradbury, "Diary," 283.
259. Bradbury, "Diary," 283.
260. Ibid.
261. PRO 292/1, WO 34/77, fol. 132.
262. Sizer, "Journal," September 7, 1760.
263. Knox, *Historical Journal*, 2: 589; PRO, CO 5/59, UP microfilm reel 6, frame 65; PRO 278/2, WO 34/42, fol. 270.
264. J. C. Webster, *Journal of Jeffery Amherst*, 249-50; See also Knox, *Historical Journal*, 2: 590.
265. J. C. Webster, *Journal of Jeffery Amherst*, 247.
266. *Boston Gazette*, 29 September 1760.
267. Ibid.
268. Knox, *Historical Journal*, 2: 566; *New-York Gazette*, 22 September 1760.
269. J. C. Webster, *Journal of Jeffery Amherst*, 247.
270. *Boston Evening-Post*, 15 September 1760; *Boston Gazette*, 19 September 1760; Woodwell, *Diary of Thomas Moody*, 31; Frost, "Expedition Against Canada," 115.
271. Woodwell, *Diary of Thomas Moody*, 34; Ironically, Dr. Lewis Beebe would make similar comments 16 years later in reference to Americans dying of smallpox on Isle aux Noix after their evacuation from Canada. Lewis Beebe, "Journal of a Physician on the Expedition Against Canada, 1776," *The Pennsylvania Magazine of History and Biography* 59 (October 1935): 336.
272. Jenks, "Journal," 380.
273. PRO 284/1, WO 34/51, fol. 90.
274. PRO 284/2, WO 34/52, fol. 79.
275. Woodwell, *Diary of Thomas Moody*, 35-38; See also Holden, "Journal," 403-4.
276. Jenks, "Journal," 382; On October 5 Brigadier General Haviland suggested that "one half of the Provincials are not fit for Service." PRO 284/1, WO 34/51, fol. 26.
277. Jenks, "Journal," 383; Woodwell, *Diary of Thomas Moody*, 39.
278. Jenks, "Journal," 381, see also 380.
279. Ibid., 381.
280. Holden, "Journal," 403-4; See also Bradbury, "Diary," 286, 288.
281. Holden, "Journal," 404.
282. Ibid.; See also Wood, "Diaries," 21: 64.
283. Jenks, "Journal," 388.
284. Ibid., 381, 384.
285. Ibid., 383-84; On October 12, 1760, Jenks observed "great numbers of brants [small dark-colored geese]…flying over camp." Ibid., 384; See also Woodwell, *Diary of Thomas Moody*, 36.
286. Kimball, *Correspondence of William Pitt*, 2: 338.
287. J. C. Webster, *Journal of Jeffery Amherst*, 257.
288. PRO 278/2, WO 34/42, fol. 280; See also PRO 284/2, WO 34/52, fol. 93; Amherst also ordered the destruction of Louisbourg. Kimball, *Correspondence of William Pitt*, 2: 361-62.
289. PRO 278/2, WO 34/42, fol. 280.
290. Ibid., fol. 281.
291. Jenks, "Journal," 387.
292. J. C. Webster, *Journal of Jeffery Amherst*, 260; After leaving Isle aux Noix, Amherst made his first stop "at

a very small island three miles from Isle au[x] Noix where Col. Haviland had established his Hospital." Ibid.

293. Ibid.
294. Ibid., 261.
295. PRO 284/2, WO 34/52, fol. 20; See also Kimball, *Correspondence of William Pitt*, 2: 356.
296. J. C. Webster, *Journal of Jeffery Amherst*, 261-62.
297. Ibid., 262.
298. George Williamson, "Description of Fort George, October 1760," Williamson Family Papers, NAC, Microfilm A 573.
299. Ibid.
300. Ibid.
301. Ibid.
302. Ibid.
303. PRO 159/1, WO 34/54, fol. 229.
304. Ibid., fol. 197.
305. Brigadier Haviland wrote that he "was in hopes of seeing the Works further Advanced than they are." PRO 284/1, WO 34/51, fol. 26.
306. Jenks, "Journal," 386.
307. Ibid., 389.
308. Holden, "Journal," 405; PRO 284/1, WO 34/51, fol. 99.
309. Holden, "Journal," 405; See also Frost, "Expedition Against Canada," 117.
310. Holden, "Journal," 405; See also Jenks, "Journal," 389.
311. PRO 284/1, WO 34/51, fol. 101.
312. Ibid., fol. 102; In the same letter Haviland reported that a regular had "Froze to Death" alongside a blockhouse, "occasioned by too much Rum." Ibid.
313. Jenks, "Journal," 390; See also PRO 284/1, 34/51, fol. 101.
314. Bradbury, "Diary," 289.
315. "Petition of William Friend," September 16, 1766, *New York Colonial Manuscripts, Indorsed Land Papers*, Volume 21, 149 (a) (b) (a copy of the petition courtesy of George Singer); Henry Marvin, *A Complete History of Lake George* (New York: Sibells & Maigne, Printers, 1853), 68.
316. PRO 278/2, WO 34/42, fol. 283; See also PRO 285/2, WO 34/65, fol. 162.
317. PRO 284/1, 34/51, fol. 101.
318. PRO 285/2, WO 34/65, fol. 40.
319. PRO 284/1, 34/51, fol. 102; One of the two sloops *(Brochette)* had returned from Canada. Ibid.
320. Kimball, *Correspondence of William Pitt*, 2: 372.
321. PRO 283/1, WO 34/50, fol. 50, see also fol. 54.
322. Ibid., fols. 54, 209.
323. PRO 284/1, WO 34/51, fol. 135.
324. PRO 287/1, WO 34/68, fol. 141.
325. PRO 283/1, WO 34/50, fol. 61; The wharf was lengthened by 100 feet at Ticonderoga. Ibid., fol. 216.
326. Amherst Family Papers, U1350 014, fol. 139, Centre for Kentish Studies, Kent, Great Britain; Haldimand Papers, "Misc. Papers Relating to the Provincial Navy 1775-1780," NAC, Microfilm H-1649, Volume 1, B144, fol. 99.
327. PRO 285/2, WO 34/65, fol. 60.
328. PRO 283/1, WO 34/50, fol. 59.
329. Ibid., fol. 214.
330. Ibid., fol. 65; See also PRO 284/1, WO 34/51, fols. 167, 178.
331. Kimball, *Correspondence of William Pitt*, 2: 382, see also 404.
332. J. C. Webster, *Journal of Jeffery Amherst*, 328.
333. PRO 283/1, WO 34/50, fol. 84.
334. Ibid.
335. George Williamson to Lieut. Brady, May 29, 1761, Williamson Family Papers, NAC, Microfilm A 573.
336. George Williamson to Sergeant Steward, May 29, 1761, Williamson Family Papers, NAC, Microfilm A 573.
337. PRO 283/1, WO 34/50, fol. 83; PRO 284/1, WO 34/51, fol. 209.
338. Peter Barranco, March 25, 2000, personal communication; contemporary photographs and postcards.
339. Gavin Cochrane to Thomas Gage, April 15, 1771, Gage Papers, Volume 102, Miscellaneous Papers Box. Courtesy of Gary S. Zaboly.
340. PRO 283/1, WO 34/50, fols. 86, 83.
341. Ebenezer Dibble, "Diary of Ebenezer Dibble," *Society of Colonial Wars in the State of Connecticut Proceedings* 1 (1903): 325-26.

342. Henry True, *Journal and Letters of Rev. Henry True* (Marion, OH: Star Press, 1900), 22.
343. Welles, "Letters of Whiting," 148-49.
344. PRO 285/2, WO 34/65, fol. 109.
345. PRO 287/2, WO 34/69, fol. 36.
346. Ibid., fol. 38.
347. Ibid., fol. 36.
348. PRO 284/1, WO 34/51, fol. 329.
349. PRO 284/2, WO 34/52, fol. 293.
350. PRO 283/1, WO 34/50, fol. 140.
351. Ibid.
352. For an excellent overview of the reasons for the Indian uprising see Timothy J. Todish and Todd E. Harburn, *A "Most Troublesome Situation":The British Military and the Pontiac Indian Uprising of 1763-1764* (Fleischmanns, NY: Purple Mountain Press, 2006), 33-49.
353. J. C. Long, *Lord Jeffery Amherst: A Soldier of the King* (New York: The Macmillan Company, 1933), 89.

10. EPILOGUE: FORTS REVISITED

1. Newton D. Mereness, *Travels in the American Colonies* (1916; reprint ed., New York: Antiquarian Press, Ltd., 1961), 416.
2. Ibid, 419.
3. Ibid., 424, 430.
4. Ibid., 443-44; Ralph Izard, who had met Lord Gordon in Quebec City, also visited Crown Point in August 1765, noting that the fort was "surprisingly decayed since last year." [Ralph Izard], *An Account of a Journey to Niagara, Montreal and Quebec in 1765* (New York: William Osborn, 1846), 28.
5. Mereness, *Travels*, 444.
6. Ibid., 445.
7. Ibid., 446.
8. Frances Grant, "Journal from New York to Canada, 1767," *Proceedings of the New York State Historical Association* 30 (1932): 318.
9. Ibid., 319.
10. Ibid., 320.
11. Winslow C. Watson, *Pioneer History of the Champlain Valley* (Albany: J. Munsell, 1863), 95.
12. Haldimand Papers, "Misc. Papers Relating to the Provincial Navy, 1775-1780," NAC, Microfilm H-1649, Volume 1, B144, fol. 99; PRO, CO 5/62, UP microfilm reel 7, frame 446; Watson, *Pioneer History*, 128.
13. Grant, "Journal," 320.
14. Jane M. Lape, ed., *Ticonderoga—Patches and Patterns from Its Past* (Ticonderoga, NY: The Ticonderoga Historical Society, 1969), 25.
15. Grant, "Journal," 320.
16. Ibid., 321.
17. Clarence Edwin Carter, comp. and ed., *The Correspondence of General Thomas Gage* (1933; reprint ed., Archon Books, 1969), Volume 2, 382, 410, see also 322.
18. Grant, "Journal," 321.
19. Carter, *Correspondence of Gage*, 2: 323; see also 1: 90.
20. PRO, CO 5/91, UP microfilm reel 1, frames 311, 314-16; Carter, *Correspondence of Gage*, 1: 351.
21. PRO, CO 5/90, UP microfilm reel 1, frames 254-55.
22. PRO, CO 5/91, UP microfilm reel 1, frames 563, 565.
23. Peter Force, ed., *American Archives*, Fourth Series, Volume 2 (Washington, D.C.: M. St. Clair Clarke and Peter Force, 1839), 244; For more details on the subsequent capture of Fort Ticonderoga see Russell P. Bellico, *Chronicles of Lake Champlain: Journeys in War and Peace* (Fleischmanns, NY: Purple Mountain Press, 1999), 187-203.
24. William Bell Clark, ed., *Naval Documents of the American Revolution* (Washington, D.C.: Naval History Division, Department of the Navy, 1964), Volume 1, 367; See also Peter Force, ed., *American Archives*, Fourth Series, Volume 5 (Washington, D.C.: M. St. Clair Clarke and Peter Force, 1844), 557.
25. Henry Livingston, "Journal of Major Henry Livingston, 1775," ed. by Gaillard Hunt, *The Pennsylvania Magazine of History and Biography 12* (1898): 12-13; Aaron Barlow, "The March to Montreal and Quebec, 1775," ed. by Charles Burr Todd, *American Historical Register* 2 (1895): 649.
26. Brantz Mayer, ed., *Journal of Charles Carroll of Carrollton, During His Visit to Canada in 1776* (Baltimore:

Maryland Historical Society, 1876), 60.

27. Ibid., 62-63.
28. Ammi R. Robbins, "Journal of the Rev. Ammi R. Robbins," in *History of Norfolk*, comp. by Theron Wilmot Crissey (Everett, MA: Massachusetts Publishing Company, 1900), 99.
29. Mayer, *Journal of Carroll*, 75.
30. Ibid., 74.
31. Robbins, "Journal," 101; Other participants in the 1776 campaign also mentioned the bones. Joseph Vose, "Journal of Lieutenant-Colonel Joseph Vose," *The Colonial Society of Massachusetts* 7 (Transactions 1900-1902): 250; *From Cambridge to Champlain* (Middleboro, MA: Lawrence B. Romaine, 1957), 29. The author of this journal had also viewed "Blood pond," where "many Bones are now to be seen in the Pond & about it." Ibid., 28.
32. Barlow, "March," 643; Lucinda A. Brockway, *A Favorite Place of Resort for Strangers: The King's Garden at Fort Ticonderoga* (Ticonderoga: Fort Ticonderoga, 2001), 18.
33. Mayer, *Journal of Carroll*, 79.
34. Ibid.
35. Barlow, "March," 644; B. F. DeCosta, *Notes on the History of Fort George* (New York: J. Sabin & Sons, 1871), 18; Chaplain Ammi Robbins described the fort and barracks as "amazing works." Robbins, "Journal," 102; Joseph Vose suggested that Crown Point must have been "the Grandest fort that ever was built in America," before the fire. Vose, "Journal," 251; A Massachusetts recruit wrote that the "Walls are from the Bottom of the Trench about 30 or 40 Feet High" and noted "Grand Stone Barracks." *From Cambridge to Champlain,* 29.
36. Jeduthan Baldwin, *The Revolutionary Journal of Col. Jeduthan Baldwin 1775-1778*, ed. by Thomas Williams Baldwin (Bangor, ME: De Burians, 1906), 58, see also 82; See also Horatio Rogers, ed., *Hadden's Journal and Orderly Books: A Journal Kept in Canada and Upon Burgoyne's Campaign in 1776 and 1777, by Lieut. James M. Hadden, Roy. Art.* (1884; reprint ed., Boston: Gregg Press, 1972), 33.
37. Peter Force, ed., *American Archives*, Fifth Series, Volume I (Washington, D.C.: M. St. Clair Clarke and Peter Force, 1848), 650.
38. Rufus Wheeler, "Journal of Lieut. Rufus Wheeler of Rowley," *EIHC* 68 (October 1932): 374; See also Jabesh Gould, "Jabesh Gould his Book," M-1956, Fort Ticonderoga Thompson-Pell Research Center.
39. Baldwin, *Journal*, 71; See also Donald Wickman, ed., "The Diary of Timothy Tuttle," *New Jersey History* 113 (Fall/Winter 1995): 73.
40. Ebenezer Elmer, "Journal of Lieutenant Ebenezer Elmer," *Proceedings of the New Jersey Historical Society* 3 (1848-1849): 44.
41. Force, Fifth Series, 1: 651.
42. Ibid., 857; Others also mentioned that the sick were sent to Fort George. Elisha Porter, "The Diary of Mr. Elisha Porter of Hadley," *The Magazine of American History* 29 (1893): 201.
43. Robbins, "Journal," 113.
44. Ibid.
45. Jared Sparks, *Writings of George Washington* (Boston: Russell, Odiorne, and Metcalf, 1834), Volume 4, 494.
46. William H. Hill, *Old Fort Edward Before 1800* (1929; reprint ed., Mililani, HI: The Sleeper Co., 1994), 324-25. On December 30, 1780, Major General François-Jean de Beauvoir Chastellux, third in command of the French expeditionary force in America, viewed Fort Edward, noting that the main fort was abandoned, but "a large redoubt with a simple parapet and a wretched palisade, is built on a more elevated spot; within are small barracks for about two hundred soldiers." However, there is no corroborating evidence to support this description. Robert B. Roberts, *New York's Forts in the Revolution* (Cranbury, NJ: Associated University Presses, Inc., 1980), 201-2.
47. Rogers, *Hadden's Journal*, 33; See also Gregory Furness and Timothy Titus, *Master Plan for Crown Point State Historic Site* (Waterford, NY: Office of Parks, Recreation and Historic Preservation, 1985), 31.
48. James Phinney Baxter, ed., *The British Invasion from the North, The Campaigns of Generals Carleton and Burgoyne from Canada, 1776-1777, With the Journal of Lieut. William Digby* (Albany, NY: Joel Munsell's Sons, 1887), 214; See also Thomas Anburey, *Travels Through the Interior Parts of America* (Boston: Houghton Mifflin Company, 1923), Volume 1, 186, 189.
49. Rogers, *Hadden's Journal*, 107; According to an April 1777 British intelligence report, a large barracks was located "on the North-East of the Citadel [Ford George], and about twenty yards from it."; the "General Hospital" was supposedly located "where Fort William Henry stood." DeCosta, *Fort George*, "Additions to Notes on the History of Fort George," 3.
50. Rogers, *Hadden's Journal*, 107. Hadden also mentioned "5 Farm Houses" near Fort George. Ibid.

51. Helga Doblin, trans. and Mary C. Lynn, *American Revolution, Garrison Life in French Canada and New York: Journal of an Officer in the Prinz Friedrich Regiment, 1776-1883* (Westport, CT: Greenwood Press, 1993), 86; Charlotte S. J. Epping, trans., *Journal of Du Roi the Elder* (Philadelphia: University of Pennsylvania, 1911), 110.

52. DeCosta, *Fort George*, "Additions," 3.

53. Ibid., 4-5.

54. Elizabeth Cometti, ed., *The American Journals of Lt. John Enys* (Syracuse, NY: The Syracuse University Press, 1976), 48; Enys was not the only soldier during the American Revolution to note Rogers' Rock. See Baldwin, *Journal*, 100; Rogers, *Hadden's Journal*, 104.

55. Winston Adler, ed., *Their Own Voices: Oral Accounts of Early Settlers in Washington County, New York* (Interlaken, NY: Heart of the Lakes Publishing, 1983), 101.

56. Philip Schuyler to George Washington, November 2, 1781, MS (1999.1134), Fort Ticonderoga Thompson-Pell Research Center.

57. John C. Fitzpatrick, ed., *The Writings of George Washington* (Washington, D.C.: United States Government Printing Office, 1938), 87.

58. Peter Sailly, "Diary of Peter Sailly on a Journey in America in the Year 1784," *New York State Library History Bulletin* 12 (February 1919): 63-64; When nine-year-old Samuel Cook moved to the village of Fort Edward with his family in 1788, he remembered that the fort was "quite perfect, though dilapidated" and three blockhouses were still present. Adler, *Their Own Voices*, 128.

59. Sailly, "Diary," 64.

60. Ibid., 64-65.

61. Ibid., 65.

62. J. Robert Maguire, ed., *The Tour to the Northern Lakes of James Madison & Thomas Jefferson May-June 1791* (Ticonderoga, NY: Fort Ticonderoga, 1995), 8, 29; For Jefferson's description of Lake George see Sarah N. Randolph, *The Domestic Life of Thomas Jefferson* (New York: Harper & Brothers Publishers, 1871), 201.

63. Maguire, *Tour*, 20, 22.

64. Isaac Weld, *Travels Through the States of North America* (1799; reprint ed., New York: Johnson Reprint Corporation, 1968), Volume 1, 292-93; Flavius J. Cook, *Home Sketches of Essex County: Ticonderoga* (Keeseville, NY: W. Lansing & Son, 1858), 29; Maguire, *Tour*, 8-9.

65. Weld, *Travels*, 294; For Weld's journal on Lake Champlain see Bellico, *Chronicles of Lake Champlain*, 273-93.

66. Abigail May, "The Journal of Abigail May," printed copy, New York State Historical Association, No. 1, 72 (see original in the Schlesinger Library of Radcliffe College of Harvard University); For more of Abigail May's journal at Lake George see Russell P. Bellico, *Chronicles of Lake George: Journeys in War and Peace* (Fleischmanns, NY: Purple Mountain Press, 1995), 191-203.

67. May, "Journal," No. 1, 76.

68. Ibid.

69. Ibid.

70. Ibid., No. 1, 77.

71. Maguire, *Tour*, 10; Watson commented that the ruins of Fort Ticonderoga had the "appearance of an ancient castle, enveloped in the mist of ages." Winslow C. Watson, ed., *Men and Times of the Revolution; or, Memoirs of Elkanah Watson* (New York: Dana and Company, Publishers, 1856), 353.

72. *Laws of the State of New-York* (Albany: Charles R. and George Webster, 1802), Volume 2, 242.

73. Timothy D. Titus, *Crown Point State Historic Site: An Historical Introduction* (Crown Point: New York Office of Parks, Recreation and Historic Preservation, n.d.), 14.

74. Brockway, *A Favorite Place*, 29.

75. *New York in the Revolution as Colony and State: A Compilation of Documents and Records from the Office of the State Comptroller* (Albany, 1901), 47-48; DeCosta, *Fort George*, 61-62; [E. B. O'Callaghan], comp., *Calendar of N.Y. Colonial Manuscripts: Indorsed Land Papers 1643-1863* (1864; reprint ed., Harrison, NY: Harbor Hill Books, 1987), 656.

76. Indenture, June 11, 1785, Caldwell Estate Records: Papers, Maps, Indentures; Indenture, January 13, 1787, Miscellaneous Record Book 3, 203, Warren County Records Storage Center, Lake George, N.Y.; In September 1787 James Caldwell acquired four additional parcels (2,000 acres in total) in present-day Hague. [E. B. O'Callaghan], *Indorsed Land Papers*, 767; See also H. P. Smith, ed., *History of Warren County* (1885; reprint ed., Interlaken, NY: Heart of the Lakes Publishing, 1981), 212.

77. Deed Record A-B Warren County, Book A, 434-36, Warren County Records Storage Center; See also James Caldwell Papers (1809-1830), Special Collections, Manuscript SC 20327, folder 2, 6, *NYSL*.

78. James Caldwell Papers, Manuscript SC 20327, folder 4.

79. James Wilkinson, *Memoirs of My Own Time* (Philadelphia: Abraham Small, 1816), Volume 3, 371-72, 381.

80. National Archives, Record Group 107, Microcopy 221, Roll 54, fol. n.a.; [George Izard], *Official Correspondence with the Department of War, Relative to the Military Operations of the American Army under the Command of Major General Izard on the Northern Frontier of the United States in the Years 1814 and 1815* (Philadelphia: Thomas Dobson, 1816), 1, 5.

81. [Izard], *Official Correspondence*, 75.

82. Benjamin Silliman, *Remarks, Made on a Short Tour, Between Hartford and Quebec in the Autumn of 1819* (New Haven, S. Converse, 1820), 154.

83. Ibid., 133.

84. Ibid., 144, 149; Silliman's conclusion that the tavern had once been a barracks was evidently based on a letter from Judge James Kent of Albany, who had "lodged at a dismal old house [in 1795] which had been a military barrack." George P. Fisher, *Life of Benjamin Silliman* (New York: Charles Scribner and Company, 1866), Volume 1, 293-94.

85. Silliman, *Remarks*, 160.

86. Ibid., 156.

87. Benjamin Silliman, *Remarks Made on a Short Tour Between Hartford and Quebec in the Autumn of 1819*, 2nd ed. (New Haven: S. Converse, 1824), 201; Timothy Dwight had written that the remains of the breastworks at the old French lines were "not more than four [feet high]" in 1802. Timothy Dwight, *Travels; in New-England and New-York* (New Haven, CT: S. Converse, 1822), Volume 3, 383.

88. Silliman, *Remarks*, (2nd ed.), 203-4.

89. Ibid., 204. Silliman also mentioned that the "old stone store-house" was then being "used as a tavern." Ibid.

90. Ibid., 203.

91. Alexander Bliss, "A Visit to Fort Ticonderoga in 1825 by Alex. Bliss," *BFTM* 8 (Summer 1949): 162; James Stuart, *Three Years in North America*, 3rd ed. (Edinburgh: Robert Cadell, 1833), Volume 1, 170.

92. [Theodore Dwight, Jr.], *The Northern Traveller*, 2nd ed. (New York: A.T. Goodrich, 1826), 165.

93. Ibid.

94. Ibid., 174.

95. Ibid.

96. Ibid., 175.

97. Ibid., 176.

98. Ibid., 177.

99. Ibid.

100. [Theodore Dwight, Jr.], *The Northern Traveller and Northern Tour* (New York: J. J. Harper, 1831), 187.

101. Ibid.

102. Ibid.

103. Ibid., 188.

104. Jared Sparks, "Tour for Historical Research," August 13, 1830, MS 141G, Volume 2, 47-48, Houghton Library, Harvard University, Cambridge, MA.

105. Ibid., 48.

106. Ibid., 49.

107. Ibid.

108. Ibid., 51.

109. Jared Sparks, "Plans & Descriptions of Gates's Camp, Ticonderoga, Crown Point, St. John's and Other Places," 1830, MS 128, 20, Houghton Library, Harvard University, Cambridge, MA; Sparks, "Tour," 52.

110. Sparks, "Plans & Descriptions," 20.

111. Lois M. Feister, *Archeological Excavations at the Crown Point Soldiers' Barracks 1976 & 1977* (Waterford, NY: New York State Office of Parks, Recreation and Historic Preservation, 1998), 127.

112. Sparks, "Plans & Descriptions," 20.

113. Ibid., 21.

114. Ibid.

115. Ibid., 20.

116. Ibid., 22; See also Charles L. Fisher, "The Archaeology of Provincial Officers' Huts at Crown Point Historic Site," *Northwest Historical Archaeology* 24 (1995): 84.

117. Sparks, "Tour," 53, 57.

118. Sparks, "Plans & Descriptions," 13.

119. Ibid.
120. Ibid.
121. Ibid., 15-16.
122. Ibid., 16.
123. Sparks, "Tour," 57.
124. Sparks, "Plans & Descriptions," 3.
125. Ibid., 3-4.
126. Ibid., 4.
127. Ibid.
128. Sparks, "Tour," 84.
129. Nathaniel Hawthorne, "A Visit to Ticonderoga 100 Years Ago," *BFTM* 4 (January 1936): 13; See also Alfred Weber, Beth L. Lueck, and Dennis Berthold, *Hawthorne's American Travel Sketches* (Hanover, NH: University Press of New England, 1989), 64-70.
130. Hawthorne, "Visit," 14-15.
131. Francis Parkman, *Montcalm and Wolfe* (1884; reprint ed., New York: Athenaeum, 1984), xxxii.
132. Howard Doughty, *Francis Parkman* (1962; reprint ed., Cambridge, MA: Harvard University Press, 1983), 29.
133. Francis Parkman, "Parkman at Lake George," *Scribner's Magazine*, July 1901, 23.
134. Ibid., 24; See also *Eastern Argus,* 8 November 1825.
135. Ibid.; An 1848 legal agreement regarding the construction of a proposed plank road at Lake George specified that the "said road was not [to be] built…through or over the ruins of Fort William Henry or Fort George." Deed Record Q-R Warren County, Book Q, 327-28, Warren County Records Storage Center, Lake George, N.Y.
136. Parkman, "Parkman at Lake George," 24.
137. Ibid.
138. Ibid.
139. Ibid. William Caldwell was the son of the original founder of the village, James Caldwell.
140. *Lake George Mirror*, 10 June 1793.
141. S. R. Stoddard, *Lake George (Illustrated) A Book of To-Day* (Glens Falls, NY: S. R. Stoddard, 1887), 56; See also Henry Marvin, *A Complete History of Lake George* (New York: Sibells & Maigne Printers, 1853), 48-49; B. F. DeCosta, *Lake George: Its Scenes and Characteristics* (New York: Anson D. F. Randolph & Co., 1869), 63; Ogden J. Ross, *The Steamboats of Lake George 1817 to 1932* (Albany: Press of the Delaware and Hudson Railroad, 1932), 33; *Lake George Mirror*, 11 July 1903.
142. Parkman, "Parkman at Lake George," 25.
143. Ibid., 30.
144. Ibid.
145. Ibid.
146. Ibid.
147. Ibid.
148. Benson J. Lossing, "A Visit to Ticonderoga 1848," *BFTM* 1 (January 1929): 24-25.
149. Ibid., 25.
150. Benson J. Lossing, *The Pictorial Field-Book of the Revolution* (New York: Harper & Brothers, Publishers, 1851), Volume I, 151.
151. Amelia M. Murray, *Letters from the United States, Cuba and Canada* (New York: G. P. Putnam & Company, 1856), 377; See also Cortlandt Van Rensslaer, *An Historical Discourse on the Occasion of the Centennial Celebration of the Battle of Lake George, 1755* (1856; reprint ed., Queensbury, NY: Warren County Historical Society, 2005), 33-35.
152. Murray, *Letters*, 377.
153. Ibid.
154. Ibid.
155. Flavius J. Cook, *Home Sketches of Essex County: Ticonderoga* (Keeseville, NY: W. Lansing & Son, 1858), 118.
156. "Visit to Fort Ticonderoga—Watering Place Letters, July 30, 1866," *BFTM* 9 (Summer 1954): 302-3.
157. S. R. Stoddard, *Ticonderoga: Past and Present* (Albany: Weed, Parsons and Company Printers, 1873), 53.
158. Ibid.
159. Ibid.
160. Ibid., 55, 58.
161. Lape, *Patches and Patterns*, 154-55.

162. S. R. Stoddard, *Lake George; (Illustrated.) A Book of To-Day* (Albany: Weed, Parsons and Company, Printers, 1873), 43.

163. Ibid., 44.

164. Ibid., 47.

165. S. G. W. Benjamin, "Lake George," *Harper's New Monthly Magazine*, August 1879, 325.

166. Ibid.

167. S. R. Stoddard, *The Adirondacks: Illustrated* (Albany: Weed, Parsons & Co., Printers, 1874), 19; See also Winslow C. Watson, *The Military and Civil History of the County of Essex, New York* (Albany: J. Munsell, 1869), 118.

168. W. H. H. Murray, *Lake Champlain and Its Shores* (Boston: De Wolfe, Fiske & Co., 1890), 90-91.

169. S. R. Stoddard, *Lake George (Illustrated,) and Lake Champlain. A Book of To-Day* (Glens Falls: S. R. Stoddard, 1889), 93; In his 1889 guide Stoddard also mentioned that the ruins of Fort St. Anne "may still be seen" on Isle La Motte. Ibid., 122.

170. Ogden Ross, *The Steamboats of Lake Champlain 1809 to 1930* (1930; reprint ed., Burlington: Vermont Heritage Press, 1997), 35.

171. Charles H. Possons, *Possons's Guide to Lake George; Lake Champlain and Adirondacks* (Glens Falls, NY: Chas. H. Possons, Publisher, 1891), 121; Possons also decried the presence of treasure hunters at Crown Point, who were still "Money digging." Ibid., 127.

172. Possons, *Possons's Guide*, 124; Lossing, *Pictorial Field-Book*, 151-52; *Historical Archeology at Crown Point* (Albany: New York State Parks & Recreation, 1976), [1].

173. Brockway, *A Favorite Place*, 61-62; [Christopher D. Fox], "The Community Says 'Save the Fort!'," [1], Fort Ticonderoga Thompson-Pell Research Center, n.d.

174. *Ticonderoga Sentinel*, 16 January 1902.

175. Ibid.

176. [Fox], "Community," [2].

177. *Ticonderoga Sentinel*, 23 July 1908.

178. Ibid., 2 July 1908, 20 August 1908.

179. Ibid., 3 September 1908.

180. Ibid., 10 September 1908.

181. Sarah G. T. Pell, "The Pavilion and the King's Garden," *BFTM* 7 (January 1947): 10; Brockway, *A Favorite Place*, 63-64; For additional information on Stephen and Sarah Pell and Robert Means Thompson see Carl R. Crego, *Fort Ticonderoga* (Charlestown, SC: Arcadia Publishing, 2004), 94-96.

182. *Ticonderoga Sentinel*, 29 October 1908.

183. Ibid., 4 March 1909, 1 April 1909; Work raising the vessel had begun in mid-December 1908 but had to be suspended because of thin ice. Ibid., 17 December 1908.

184. Russell P. Bellico, *Sails and Steam in the Mountains: A Maritime and Military History of Lake George and Lake Champlain*, rev. ed. (Fleischmanns, NY: Purple Mountain Press, 2001), 107.

185. *Ticonderoga Sentinel*, 1 April 1909, 8 April 1909, 15 April 1909.

186. "The Restoration of Fort Ticonderoga," *BFTM* 8 (1950): 255.

187. Crego, *Fort Ticonderoga*, 107, 111, 114-15, 121-22, 124, 126; In the late 1950s, after an archaeological team had begun excavating "20-odd foundations" at the site of the French village (near the South Battery Wall), John H. G. Pell considered restoring a few of the buildings. *Lake George Mirror*, 5 July 1957.

188. "The Restoration of Fort Ticonderoga," 257.

189. Book of Deeds, Volume 110, 416, Essex County Clerk's Office, Elizabethtown, N.Y.; *Warrensburg News*, 30 July 1903.

190. Book of Deeds, Volume 126, 228, see also 552, Essex County Clerk's Office.

191. *Warrensburg News*, 30 July 1903.

192. *Ticonderoga Sentinel*, 25 March 1909; Peter Barranco, March 25, 2000, personal communication; contemporary photographs and postcards.

193. Henry Wayland Hill, *The Champlain Tercentenary: First Report of the New York Lake Champlain Tercentenary Commission*, 2nd ed.(Albany: J. B. Lyon Company, State Printers, 1913), 86-88; *Ticonderoga Sentinel*, 15 April 1909.

194. Book of Deeds, Volume 146, 229-30, Essex County Clerk's Office.

195. *Ticonderoga Sentinel*, 7 April 1910, see also 5 May 1910.

196. Ibid., 7 April 1910.

197. Tom Anderson, "Crown Point," *Adirondack Life*, May/June 1981, 15; *Historical Archeology at Crown Point*, [1-2]; Furness and Titus, *Master Plan*, 19.

198. Feister, "Soldiers' Barracks," 46-69, 82-90, 93-105, 109-29.

199. Fisher, "Provincial Officers' Huts," 65, 69-84.

200. Deed Record 80, 229-30, 488-90, Warren County Clerk's Office, Lake George, N.Y.

201. Deed Record 87, 280-84, Warren County Clerk's Office; The 33-1/4-acre parcel was purchased from Harriet C. Parmelee Nivert and the seven-acre plot from Catherine T. R. Mathews and Anne S. Van Cortlandt. Ibid.; A newspaper article noted that a "substantial house" on the property that had been purchased earlier (1898) was "to be used as a museum." *New York Times*, 13 September 1900.

202. "Charter of the New York State Historical Association," *Proceedings of the New York State Historical Association* (1901): 7.

203. *New York Times*, 8 September 1903.

204. Ibid., 9 September 1903, see also 7 September 1903; *Ticonderoga Sentinel*, 30 July 1903.

205. *Ticonderoga Sentinel*, 30 July 1908; *Research and Mapping of the Colonial Road Between Fort Edward and Fort William Henry* (Glens Falls, NY: Warren County Historical Society, 2005), item 2, 33; See also David R. Starbuck, *The Great Warpath: British Military Sites from Albany to Crown Point* (Hanover, NH: University Press of New England, 1999), 112-13.

206. *Lake George Mirror*, 13 August 1921; The repair of the "east wall" of Fort George was made possible by a donation to the New York State Historical Association by George D. Pratt. "Battlefield Parks," *Proceedings of the New York State Historical Association* 20 (1922): 12.

207. *Lake George Mirror*, 13 August 1921.

208. Ibid., 5 July 1930.

209. Ibid.; In 1922 the New York State Historical Association had "hoped that one of the buildings [at Fort George] used as an officers quarters may in time be rebuilt and used as a museum." "Battlefield Parks," 13.

210. William Louis Calver and Reginald Pelham Bolton, *History Written with Pick and Shovel* (New York: The New-York Historical Society, 1950), 229-30; Newspaper stories also mentioned that artifacts had been found in the area of Fort George. *Lake George Mirror*, 30 July 1921; *Glens Falls Post-Star*, 3 July 1936.

211. David Starbuck, "Hallowed Ground: Exploring Lake George Battlefield Park," *Adirondack Life*, Annual Guide 2002, 19; For more information on the artifacts see *Fort George Advice: The Newsletter of the Lake George Battlefield Park (Fort George) Alliance*, Spring 2002, [3]; Spring 2003, [5]; Fall 2003, [7]; Spring 2004, 5; Fall 2004, 3; Spring 2005, 3; Fall 2005, 3; Fall 2006, 4; Fall 2007, 3-5, 7; Winter/Spring 2009, 3.

212. *Lake George Mirror*, 1 September 2000; See also *The Chronicle*, 27 November-4 December 1996; *Lake George Mirror*, 21 August 1988.

213. The artifacts were turned over to the New York State Museum in June 2003 and August 2008. *Fort George Advice*, Spring 2004, 1-3, Winter/Spring 2009.

214. *Ticonderoga Sentinel*, 12 August 1897; Gerald E. Bradfield, *Fort William Henry: Digging Up History* (Lake George, NY: French and Indian War Society, 2000), 123.

215. William Preston Gates, *History of the Fort William Henry Hotel* (Queensbury, NY: W. P. Gates Publishing Company, 2004), 21, 80.

216. Stanley M. Gifford, *Fort William Henry: A History* (Lake George, NY: Fort William Henry Museum, 1955), 57-59; David R. Starbuck, "A Retrospective on Archaeology at Fort William Henry, 1952-1993: Retelling the Tale of *The Last of the Mohicans*," *Northwest Historical Archaeology* 20 (1993): 8-26; David R. Starbuck, "Anatomy of a Massacre," *Archaeology*, November/December 1993, 43-46.

217. David R. Starbuck, *Massacre at Fort William Henry* (Hanover, NH: University Press of New England, 2002), 38, 36.

218. Ibid., 59-60; Bradfield, *Digging Up History*, 100; Gifford, *Fort William Henry*, 58.

219. Maria A. Liston and Brenda J. Baker, "Military Burials at Fort William Henry," in *Archaeology of the French & Indian War: Military Sites of the Hudson River, Lake George, and Lake Champlain Corridor*, ed. David R. Starbuck (Queensbury, NY: Adirondack Community College, 1994), 11-16; See also Starbuck, *Massacre at Fort William Henry*, 61-67.

220. Starbuck, *Massacre at Fort William Henry*, 86-92; Starbuck, "Retrospective," 14; David Starbuck, "The Big Dig," *Adirondack Life*, September/October 1998, 46-47; Gifford, *Fort William Henry*, 7-8.

221. Starbuck, *Massacre at Fort William Henry*, 119-23, 77.

222. Ibid., 49, 47, 115.

223. Bradfield, *Digging Up History*, 128.

224. "A Map of the retrenched Camp at Lake George in 1758" by Andrew Fraser, Fort Ticonderoga Thompson-Pell Research Center.

225. David F. Nestie, *A History of the Hudson Valley Railway* (Greenwich, NY: David F. Nestie, 1967), 10, 12.

226. S. R. Stoddard, *Lake George and Lake Champlain: A Book of To-Day* (Glens Falls, NY: S. R. Stoddard, 1914), 48.

227. Lois M. Feister and Paul R. Huey, "Archaeological Testing at Fort Gage, A Provincial Redoubt of 1758 at Lake George, New York," *The Bulletin and Journal of Archaeology for New York State* 90 (Spring 1985): 42.

228. Ibid.
229. Ibid., 40.
230. Ibid., 43-57; See also Starbuck, *Great Warpath*, 14-18.
231. Scott A. Padeni, "A Review of Potential Sites for the Archaeological Study of Military Life at Lake George's Southern End During the French and Indian War and American Revolution," 10, MS, 1994, Empire State College, Saratoga Springs, N.Y.; See also Starbuck, *Great Warpath*, 117-18.
232. [Earl E. Stott], *Exploring Rogers Island* (Fort Edward: The Rogers Island Historical Association, 1969), 24-29; See also the *Lake George Mirror*, 18 August 1961; Winston Adler, "An Island Dig," *Adirondack Life*, July/August 1986, 88, 91; David R. Starbuck, *Rangers and Redcoats on the Hudson: Exploring the Past on Rogers Island the Birthplace of the U.S. Army Rangers* (Hanover, NH: University Press of New England), 25-26, 28.
233. Starbuck, *Rangers and Redcoats*, 24, see also 27.
234. Ibid., 31-42, 69-76; Starbuck, *Great Warpath*, 59-72; Matthew A. Rozell, "Searching for Fort Edward's hospital of death," *The Post-Star*, 14 August 1995.
235. Starbuck, *Rangers and Redcoats*, 23-24, 34, 43, 46, 51, 79-93; [Stott], *Exploring Rogers Island*, 26; Starbuck, *Great Warpath*, 72-75.
236. Hill, *Old Fort Edward*, 238.
237. Ibid., 239.
238. Starbuck, *Great Warpath*, 78.
239. Ibid., 79-80; Starbuck, *Rangers and Redcoats*, 97-99.
240. Starbuck, *Rangers and Redcoats*, 101.
241. Ibid., 100-13.
242. *New York Times*, 9 September 1903.

Index

Abbass, D. K., 178
Abenakis, 23, 28, 31, 43, 45, 56, 58, 109, 111, 127, 135, 168, 200
Abercrombie, James, 132, 153, 158
Abercromby, James, 85, 89, 131, 139-41, 143, 147, 151, 153, 155, 157-59, 161, 163-66, 171, 174-79
Adams, Jacob, 57-58
Adirondack History Center Museum, 290
Adirondack Park Agency, 297
Albany Conference 1754, 43
Albany Indian Commissioners, 30
Albertson, Garrett, 149, 151, 161-63
Alexander, Thomas, 142
Algonquins, 11, 58, 104, 111
Allen, Ethan, 129, 258, 280
Amherst, Jeffery, 131, 139, 174, 176-78, 181-84, 186-88, 193-96, 198-200, 202, 205-15, 219, 222, 224, 238, 240-45, 247-53
Amherst, William, 251
Ammonoosuc River, 201-2
Angell, Samuel, 127
Anglars de Bassignac, Jean d', 160
Anse au Foulon, 210
Anthony's Nose, 112
Apply, John, 164
Arbuthnot, William, 120, 123
Arnold, Benedict, 129, 258
Arnot, Hugh, 149, 157
Augustus, William, 44, 110, 133

Babcock, Henry, 163, 207
Bagley, Jonathan, 82-83
Baker, Brenda J., 296
Bald Mountain, 135, 137
Baldwin, Jeduthan, 83, 259-60
Ballston Spa, 263
Barlow, Aaron, 258-59
Barnard, Salah, 161, 185, 188
Barron, Jonathan, 65
Barrows, Abner, 159, 162
Bartman, George, 115, 122
Bateaux, 48, 50, 57, 79-80, 112, 114, 140, 144, 178, 186, 190, 214, 227-28
Bateaux Below, Inc., 293
Battle of La Belle Famille, 196

Battle of Lake George, 58-70
Battle of Montmorency Falls, 210
Battle on Snowshoes, 135-39
Bayley, Jacob, 228, 231
Beauharnois de la Boische, Charles de, 23, 25, 28
Beauharnois, François, 27
Beaumont, 265
Benjamin, Samuel Greene Wheeler, 281
Bernetz Brook, 147, 149
Bernier, Benoit-François, 69
Bigot, François, 41
Bixby Island, 209
Black Point, 190
Blanchard, Joseph, 49, 57-58, 67
Bliss, Alexander, 267
Blodget, Samuel, 58, 60, 62-63, 78, 101, 127
Bloody Pond, 70, 170, 214, 256, 267, 271, 275-76, 291-92
Boscawen (sloop), 206-7, 209, 211, 220, 226-28, 235, 247, 249-50, 252, 256, 285
Boscawen, Edward, 55
Bossom, Alfred C., 284-85, 287
Bougainville, Louis Antoine de, 93-94, 104, 106, 108, 111-12, 117-18, 123-24, 160-62, 165, 167, 210, 230-31, 235-36, 242
Bourlamaque, François-Charles de, 100, 104, 106, 111, 114, 157, 183, 191, 193, 201, 207, 209
Boyle, Peter, 63, 65
Bradbury, John, 223, 225, 228, 231-32, 234, 236-37, 249
Braddock, Edward, 44-45, 117
Bradshaw, James, 248
Bradstreet, John, 143, 147, 151, 153, 155, 166, 217
Brasier, William, 184, 192, 213
Brehm, Diedrick, 181-82
British Proclamation of 1763, 253
Brochette, La (sloop), 196, 199, 208, 218, 220, 228, 249, 252, 256
Brown, John, 258
Brown, Thomas, 98
Buade de Frontenac, Louis de, 17-20
Buckingham, Thomas, 22
Bulwagga Bay, 203, 227, 271, 281
Burbank, Nathaniel, 209
Burk, John, 35, 49-52, 67-69
Burt, Joseph, 58

Burton, Ralph, 88
Bush, John, 129
Buttonmold Bay, 228

Caldwell, James, 266-67, 276
Caldwell, N.Y., 267, 276-77, 291
Caldwell, William, 276
Callières, Louis-Hector, 17
Campbell, George, 202
Campbell, John, 187
Campbell, John (Earl of Loudoun), 83, 85, 88-89, 93,
    95, 102-3, 106, 109-10, 117, 124, 126, 128-29, 131-
    33, 139-40, 166
Cannon, LeGrand B., 287, 289
Caribbean campaigns, 251
Carignan-Saliéres Regiment, 15
Carillon (name derivation), 56
Carrion du Fresnoy, Philippe de, 56
Carroll, Charles, 259
Carver, Jonathan, 124, 126-27
Castle Island, 11
Caughnawagas, 37, 47, 51, 58, 60, 104, 106, 115
Cayugas, 13
Cedar Rapids, 242
Champion, Henry, 166, 168-70, 175-77
Champlain Maritime Society, 285
Champlain Memorial Lighthouse, 27, 289
Champlain, Samuel de, 11
Champlain Tercentenary, 287, 289
Champlain Transportation Company, 282, 287
Champline, Christopher, 55
Chandler, Samuel, 68, 73, 76, 80, 82
Charles II, 13
Chartier de Lotbinière, Michel, 80, 82, 90, 94, 167, 229
Chaussegros de Léry, Gaspard, 25, 27
Chaussegros de Léry, Gaspard-Joseph, 90
Cheeksaunkun, Jacob, 200, 225
Chief Grey Lock, 23
Chimney Point, 20, 23, 217, 251, 259-60, 268
Christie, Gabriel, 115
Churchill, Sylvester, 265
Claus, Daniel, 46, 58, 60-62, 65-66
Cleaveland, John, 143, 159, 175
Clerk, George, 147
Clerk, Matthew, 132, 153, 155-56, 164
Cliff Haven, 209, 212
Clinton Community College, 212
Clinton, George, 29-30, 32-34, 37, 42, 49
Cobb, Samuel, 153, 173, 175, 177
Cochrane, Gavin, 251
Cockcraft, William, 69
Coffin Point, 260
Cohn, Arthur B., 285
Colden, Cadwallader, 30
Cole, Edward, 65, 73-74
Collins, Thomas, 115, 120
Collins, William, 261

Columbia College, 263, 265-66
Comstock, Christopher, 175
Cook, Flavius, 279
Cooks Landing, 277
Cooper, James Fenimore, 130, 255
Cooper's Cave, 130, 275
Corbière, Lieutenant, 108
Corlaer, Arendt Van, 13
Coulon de Villiers de Jumonville, Joseph, 42
Coulon de Villiers, Louis, 42
Courcelles, Daniel de, 15
Crab Island, 209-11
Crawford, William, 227
Crespel, Emmanuel, 25
Crisman, Kevin, Jr., 285
Crofton, Edward, 137
Crown Point, 20, 22-23, 25, 28, 32-33, 43-44, 55-56, 71,
    80, 133, 198-201, 203-7, 211-12, 214, 216-20, 222-
    28, 245-46 , 248-53, 255-60, 262-65, 268-70, 277-79,
    281, 283-84, 287, 289-90, 300
Crown Point Historic Site Visitor Center, 212
Crown Point Iron Company, 282
Cruikshanks, Charles, 113
Cumberland Bay, 218
Cunningham, James, 163
Cutter, Ammi Ruhamah, 85, 95

Dagneaux, Michel, 23
Dalyell, James, 171, 211
Darby, John, 219, 233, 237-38
D'Avaugour, Dubois, 14
Davenport, Guy, 294
Davies, Thomas, 186, 198-99, 204, 206, 224, 241
Deall, Samuel, 256
Deane, Barnabas, 259
DeLancey, James, 43-44, 48, 51, 60, 71
DeLancey, Oliver, 157
Delaware and Hudson Company, 294
De Muy, Jacques-Pierre Daneau, 31
Denonville, Jacques de Brisay, 16-17
Department of Environmental Conservation, 290,
    293-94
Desandrouins, Jean-Nicolas, 126-28, 145, 153, 160, 167
Diamond Island, 166, 169-70, 178, 261
Dibble, Ebenezer, 203, 212, 251, 253
Dies, John, 175
Dieskau, Jean-Armand, 55-58, 60, 62, 65-66, 68-70, 84
Digby, William, 260
Dinwiddie, Robert, 41
Dongan, Thomas, 16-17
Doreil, André (Jean-Baptiste), 167
Dowling, John W., 291
Dresden, N.Y., 57
Duke of Cumberland (brig), 205-7, 209, 211-12, 218,
    220-21, 227-28, 232, 235, 249-50, 252, 256, 285-86
Dunbar, James W., 202
Duprat, Jean-Baptiste, 147

Duquesne de Menneville, Ange, 41, 43
Durantaye, Sieur de la, 137
Durkee, John, 171
Dutch West India Company, 11
Dwight, Nathaniel, 73, 78, 80, 82
Dwight, Theodore, Jr., 267-68
Dwight, Timothy, 58, 60, 118, 266-67

Earl of Halifax (sloop), 173-74, 177-78, 185-90, 214, 219
Earl of Loudoun (sloop), 86, 89, 94-95
East Creek, 31
Einert, Albert W., 291
Elliot, Robert, 253
Emerson, Daniel, 61, 63
Emerson, William, 259
Entick, John, 84, 128
Evans, David, 202
Eyre, William, 49, 52, 62-63, 65, 73-78, 82-83, 96, 100-102, 149, 153, 159, 184, 198, 238, 252-53

Faesch, Rudolphus, 113, 123
Farrell, Catherine Johnson, 69
Farrell, Matthew, 69
Farrington, Jacob, 220
Feister, Lois M., 297
Fisher, Samuel, 144, 163
Fitch, Eleazer, 149
Fitch, Jabez, Jr., 104, 115, 127, 129, 133, 138
Fletcher, John, 198
Folsom, Nathaniel, 66-69
Forbes, John, 139, 178-79
Forbush, Eli, 191, 193, 196
Forster, Edward, 219
Fort Amherst, 183, 248
Fort Anne, 171, 260-61
Fort Beauséjour, 44
Fort Carillon, 81-82, 90, 93-94, 97-98, 100, 104, 107, 109, 111-12, 123, 129, 132, 134-35, 139, 142, 144-46, 151-53, 156, 166-68, 172, 176, 178, 181-83, 186-87, 190-91, 193, 195-97, 254
Fort Chambly, 20, 25, 221, 237, 243-45, 268
Fort Clinton, 29
Fort Cumberland, 44
Fort Dummer, 33-34
Fort Duquesne, 41, 44, 139, 178
Fort Edward, 21, 29, 49, 52, 74-75, 77-79, 82-83, 85, 87-89, 94-95, 97, 103-7, 109-10, 113-15, 117-18, 121-23, 125, 127-29, 131-35, 138-39, 141-42, 144, 165, 168, 170-71, 177-78, 181, 183-84, 188, 195, 248, 256, 259-62, 266, 275, 299
Fort Edward Creek, 78
Fort Frederick, 34, 36, 255
Fort Frontenac, 25, 56, 166, 174
Fort Gage, 166, 183, 261, 297-98
Fort George, 184-85, 187, 194, 203, 205-6, 214, 218-19, 222, 247-49, 256, 258-63, 265-66, 271, 274, 281, 283, 290-94

Fort Hinsdale, 34
Fort Hunter, 22
Fort Johnson, 45, 47, 70
Fort Le Boeuf, 41
Fort Lennox, 235, 268
Fort Lévis, 238-42, 255
Fort Lyman, 40, 50-52, 55-58, 61-63, 66-67, 70
Fort Machault, 41, 196
Fort Massachusetts, 31-32, 34, 100
Fort Nassau, 11-12
Fort Necessity, 42
Fort Niagara, 44, 56, 83, 181, 196-97, 255
Fort Nicholson, 21-22, 50
Fort Number Four, 29, 32, 35, 43, 199, 202-3, 223
Fort Ontario, 89, 196, 225
Fort Orange, 11-12, 14, 18
Fort Presque Isle, 41
Fort Richelieu, 13
Fort St. Anne, 15-16, 35
Fort St. Frédéric, 26-31, 33-35, 37-39, 43, 52, 56, 80, 90, 93, 96-97, 133, 181, 191, 193, 196, 198, 256, 268-70, 281, 290
Fort St. Jean, 28, 35, 93, 235-36
Fort Schuyler, 21
Fort Stanwix, 166, 255
Fort Ticonderoga, 203, 205, 212-14, 218, 223, 226-27, 247, 249-51, 253, 255-56, 258-63, 265, 271-73, 275, 277-80, 284-87, 291, 300
Fort Ticonderoga Association, 287
Fort Vaudreuil, 81, 90
Fort William Augustus, 241, 247, 255
Fort William Henry, 76-78, 82, 86, 88-89, 92, 94-98, 100, 102-4, 106-11, 113-18, 122-23, 128-30, 142, 145, 151, 173-74, 195, 212, 219, 227, 242, 250, 262, 271, 276-77, 280-81, 294, 296-97, 300
Fort William Henry Corporation, 294, 296-97
Fort William Henry Hotel, 280, 291, 294
Fort Williams, 183-84, 248
Foster, Asa, 142, 168
Four Brothers Island, 205, 207
Four-Mile Post, 183, 248
Fournier, François, 229
Fourteen-Mile Island, 261
Franklin, Benjamin, 43, 259
French, Christopher, 137
French Mountain, 57
Friend, William, 249
Friends Point, 135, 138
Frost, John, 233
Frye, Joseph, 113, 117, 121-22, 124-27
Fuller, Archelaus, 149, 161, 163, 166
Furnis, James, 110, 114, 123-24, 126, 128

Gage, Thomas, 45, 147, 165, 177, 196, 200, 258
Gage's Redoubt, 203-4, 268, 271
Garth, George, 245
Gates, Horatio, 259-60

Gavit, William, 207
George II (king), 28, 44, 52, 83, 110, 133, 139, 241, 248
George III (king), 253
Germain, François-Joseph, Chevalier de, 147
Gifford, Stanley, 294, 296
Gilbert, James, 50, 53, 55, 67-68
Gilliland, William, 256, 262
Gilman, Jeremiah, 58
Glasier, Benjamin, 142, 156, 165, 173, 175
Glen, Sander, 18
Godfrey, Richard, 50, 63, 68
Gohin, Pierre-André, Comte de Montreuil, 65-66
Gordon, Adam, 255
Gordon, Harry, 86, 88
Graham, John, 93-94
Grand Diable (row galley), 221, 229, 231, 233-34, 236, 247, 249-51, 289
Grant, Alexander, 207, 209, 211-12, 218, 220-21, 228, 249-51, 253
Grant, Francis, 141, 256
Grant, James, 212
Grant, John, 194
Grant, Noah, 79
Grant, William, 153, 160
Great Meadows, 42
Grenadier Redoubt (Crown Point), 203-4, 251, 257-58, 268-69, 271
Gridley, Richard, 77

Hadden, James, 260-61
Hague Brook, 132
Hague, N.Y., 135, 190, 284
Haldimand, Frederick, 196, 222, 238, 244, 258
Half Moon (ship), 11
Halfway Brook Post, 141-42, 168-69, 183, 248
Halifax (Nova Scotia), 103
Hamilton, Archibald, 200, 213
Hammondville, N.Y., 282
Hands Cove, 258
Hardy, Charles, 71, 73-74, 76-77
Harris, Obadiah, 142, 147
Hart, John, 169
Haviland, William, 131-32, 135, 157, 169, 215, 217, 222, 224, 227-28, 231-32, 234-35, 238, 243-44, 248
Hawks, John, 31, 226
Hawley, Elisha, 49-50, 52-53, 58, 68
Hawthorne, Nathaniel, 275
Hay, Charles, 262
Hay, Mary, 262-63
Hay, Udney, 266
Heights of Carillon, 153
Henderson, James, 70, 169, 186, 188, 193, 198-99
Hendrick, King (Theyanoguin), 32, 42-43, 47, 53, 58, 60-61, 70, 279, 291
Henshaw, William, 183-84, 195
Hertel de la Fresnière, Zacharie-François, 23
Hervey, William, 155, 157

Hill, Jack, 22
Hill, James, 49, 52, 55, 69, 76, 78
Hocquart, Gilles, 27
Holbourne, Francis, 103
Holden, David, 224-25, 228, 234, 237, 246-47
Holland, Samuel, 132
Holmes, Robert, 168, 220-21
Holt, Joseph, 168
Homelands Dock, 277
Hopkins, Joseph, 199-200
Hospital Island, 236
Howe, George Augustus, 131, 140-43, 147, 149, 151, 164
Howe's Cove, 147
Hudson, Henry, 11
Hudson Valley Railroad, 297
Huey, Paul R., 290, 297
Hughes, Charles E., 289
Huletts Landing, 90, 100
Hurlbut, John, 194
Hurons, 11, 13, 111, 127

Invincible (radeau), 186-88, 190, 194, 199, 214, 219, 250
Iroquois, 12, 14, 16-18, 21, 30, 34, 46, 48, 104, 111, 168, 196, 241, 289
Iroquoise (schooner renamed *Anson*), 242
Irwin, William, 171
Isle à la Cuisse, 238
Isle au Mouton, 79, 151
Isle aux Noix, 191, 200-201, 205, 209, 211, 217, 219-21, 226-27, 229-31, 233, 235-36, 245, 247, 255, 268
Isle de la Magdelaine, 238
Isle La Barque, 94, 107
Isle La Motte, 30, 35, 220, 229
Isle Orakointon, 238
Isle Perrot, 242
Isle Royale, 238
Isle Sainte-Hélène, 243
Izard, George, 266

James II (king), 17, 19
Jefferson, Thomas, 262
Jenks, Samuel, 223-26, 228-30, 232-33, 235-36, 243-45, 247-48
Jewett, Benjamin, 149, 159-60
Jogues, Isaac, 13, 291
Johnson, William, 30, 33, 40, 44-53, 55-58, 60-63, 65-67, 69-71, 73-74, 76, 78-80, 82-83, 110, 115, 117-18, 124, 143, 155, 163, 175, 196, 225, 238, 241, 253, 279, 291
Johnston, Thomas, 63, 92
Jones, Joseph, 169

Kaghswughtioni (Red Head), 46-47
Kalm, Peter, 27, 35
Kayaderosseras Patent, 46

Kennedy, Quinton, 200, 213, 225
King George's War, 28, 35
King William's War, 17, 20
Kings Bay, 220
King's Garden, 267
Kirkwood, Robert, 202, 242
Kisensik, 111
Knowlton, Thomas, 31
Knox, Henry, 258

La Chine, 17, 242
La Chute River, 56, 93, 104, 107-8, 147, 151, 153, 155-56, 161, 163-64, 191, 193, 255, 271
La Corne (Saint Luc), Luc de, 29, 32, 37, 124-25, 128, 168
La Famine, 17
La Galette, 200
La Prairie, 18-20
La Présentation, 238
Lake Andiatarocté, 13
Lake Champlain Maritime Museum, 285, 294
Lake George Battlefield (Fort George) Alliance, 294
Lake George Battlefield Park, 290-91
Lake Memphremagog, 201-2
Lake St. Sacrement, 13, 16, 20, 22, 33, 35, 44, 51-53, 55, 57
Lalemant, Jerome, 13
Land Tortoise (radeau), 8, 175-78, 185, 199, 300
Lapalme, Dominique-Jason, 25
Last of the Mohicans, The, 130, 255, 275
Le Dossu d'Hebecourt, Louis Phillipe, 135, 139, 193
L'Esturgeon (sloop), 196, 199, 208, 212
Le Febvre La Barre, Joseph-Antoine, 16
Le Mercier, François-Marc-Antoine, 57, 101
Le Prestre de Vauban, Sebastien, 25
Lee, Charles, 149, 161, 163
Legardeur de Croisille de Courtemanche, Jacques-François, 168
Legardeur de Saint-Pierre, Jacques, 32, 41, 58, 61
Legge, William, 257
Leisler, Jacob, 18-19
Leslie, Mathew, 133
Levasseur, Nicholas-René, 196
Lévis, François (François-Gaston) de, 93, 111-13, 145, 155, 162, 164, 210, 219, 241, 243-44
Levrault de Langis Montegron (Langy), Jean-Baptiste, 134, 137, 149
Light Infantry Redoubt, 203-4, 290
Ligonier (radeau), 204-8, 213, 227-29, 249-51
Ligonier Bay, 209-11, 229
Ligonier, John, 139
Ligonier Point, 209
Liston, Maria A., 296
Livingston, Henry, 258
Livingston, William, 74
Long Island (Lake George), 178, 181
Long Sault, 242

Loring, Joshua, 149, 161, 163, 172, 177-78, 181, 199-200, 205-7, 209, 211-12, 214, 238, 240
Lossing, Benson J., 277, 279, 282
Lotbinière Redoubt, 93-94, 203, 256, 267, 271-72, 277, 280, 285
Lottridge, John, 181
Louis IV (king), 17
Louis XV (king), 23, 25, 28, 55
Louisbourg, 28, 35, 44, 103, 139
Lusignan, Paul-Louis Dazemard de, 36, 98, 104
Lydius, John Henry, 29, 47, 52
Lyman, Phineas, 49-51, 60, 62, 64-65, 68, 73-74, 84, 88, 94, 107, 115, 149, 169, 175, 256
Lyon, Lemuel, 159

MacClintock, Samuel, 223, 227-29, 232, 234
MacFarland, Stewart, 291
Mackay, Alexander, 208-9, 212-13
Madison, James, 262
Mahicans, 12-13, 19
Marin de La Malgue, Joseph, 107, 124, 170-72
Marin de La Malgue, Paul, 29
Mars Education Center, 287
Marsh, Perez, 60-62
Masson, Jean, 85
Matthews, William, 246
May, Abigail, 262-63, 275
McCormick, Caesar, 220-21
McDonald, Gregory, 137
McGinnis, Robert, 107
McGinnis, William, 66, 68
McKeen, John, 127-28
McMullen, Andrew, 201-2
Melven, Eleazer, 34
Mercer, James F., 89
Merriman, Samuel, 194, 207, 235
Metcalf, Seth, 127
Micmacs, 111
Missisquoi Bay, 23, 200-201, 277
Mohawk (warship), 225, 238-40
Mohawks, 11-13, 15-16, 18-20, 30, 42-43, 46, 50-51, 53, 57-58, 60-61, 68-71, 79, 225, 261
Monckton, Robert, 44
Moneypenny, Alexander, 143, 149, 151
Monro, George, 102, 107, 110-11, 113-18, 120, 122-23, 128-29
Montagnais, 11
Montcalm, Louis-Joseph de, 84, 89, 93, 95-96, 98, 111-16, 118, 121, 123-24, 128-29, 131, 144, 149, 153, 157, 160-62, 164-66, 178, 183, 195, 205, 210
Montmagny, Charles-Jacques Hault, 13
Montresor, James, 110, 153, 184, 176, 205-6, 214
Montresor, John, 257-58
Moody, Thomas, 223, 227-28, 230, 232, 234-35, 245
Morse, John, 61
Motte, Captain de la (Pierre de Saint-Paul, Sieur de la Motte Lussière), 15

Mouet de Langlade, Charles-Michel, 107-8, 125
Mount Defiance, 82, 132, 153
Mount Defiance Corporation, 287
Mount Independence, 260-61, 287
Mountaineer (steamboat), 130, 271
Murdock, James, 265, 289
Murdock, Samuel, 265, 289
Murray, Amelia M., 279
Murray, James, 215, 219-20, 238, 243
Murray, William H. H., 281-82
Musquelongy, La (sloop), 196, 199, 208, 209-12, 218, 220, 228, 249, 252, 256

Nadeau, John F., 251, 289
Nastasi, Frank, 298
Naunauphtaunk, Jacob, 93, 187
New Amsterdam, 14
New-York Historical Society, 291, 293
New York State Archaeological Association, 297
New York State Historical Association, 284, 291, 293
New York State Museum, 294, 296
New York State Office of Parks, Recreation, and Historic Preservation, 290, 297
Nichols, Joseph, 160, 163
Nicholson, Francis, 21-22, 171
Nipissings, 58, 104, 111
Nivert, Harriet C. Parmelee, 291
Niverville, Joseph-Claude Boucher de, 32
Noble, Eli, 118
Noble, Esa, 53
Northwest Bay, 94, 100, 113
Northwest Passage, 203
Norton, John, 27, 31
Noyes, John, 157, 178

Odell Island, 78
Ogden, Jonathan, 106, 109
Ogdensburg, N.Y., 238
Ohio Company, 41
Olabaratz, Jean de, 196, 209, 213
Oneidas, 13
Onondaga (warship), 225, 238, 240
Onondagas, 13, 20, 225
Ord, Thomas, 110, 175-76, 185, 199-200, 205, 212, 226-28, 251
Ormsby, John, 113, 120, 253
Osborne, Danvers, 42-43
Oswego, 53, 89, 117, 123-24, 167, 196, 225, 227, 238
Ottawas, 104, 106, 109, 111, 126, 135
Otter Creek, 34, 90, 205, 213
Outaouaise, (brig), 238

Parker, John, 104, 108-9, 144
Parkman, Francis, 70, 255, 275-77
Parkman, William, 165
Parsons, Jesse, 193-95
Partridge, Oliver, 153, 161

Pavilion, The, 265, 284-85
Payson, Nathan, 51
Peace of Ryswick, 20
Péan, Michel-Jean-Hugues, 57
Pebbles Island, 297
Pécaudy de Contrecoeur, Claude-Pierre, 41, 94
Pell, Howland, 284
Pell, Sarah Gibbs Thompson, 284-85, 287
Pell, Stephen H. P., 284-85, 287
Pell, William Ferris, 265, 267, 271, 284
Pepperrell, William, 28
Perry, David, 161-62
Petit Diable (row galley), 221, 234, 249-51
Phélypeau, Jean-Frédéric, Comte de Maurepas, 25
Phillips, William, 137
Phipps, David, 240
Phips, William, 19
Pine Point, 114
Pitt, William, 103, 139, 143, 151, 171, 178-79, 181, 195, 215, 240-41, 250
Plains of Abraham, 210
Plantavit de Lapause de Margon, Jean-Guillaume, 243
Point au Fer, 220
Pointe a la Chevelure, 23-25
Pointe de Ganataragoin, 238
Pollard, John, 126
Pomeroy, Daniel, 68
Pomeroy, Seth, 28, 48, 50, 52, 58, 60, 64, 66, 68-71, 76, 82
Pond, Peter, 161
Pontiac's War, 253
Port Royal, Acadia, 22
Possons, Charles, 282
Potawatomis, 104, 106, 111
Pouchot, Pierre, 157, 160, 196, 214, 238, 240
Poulin de Courval Cressé, Louis-Pierre, 196
Pownall, Thomas, 52, 60, 67, 83, 165
Prevost, James, 176
Prideaux, John, 196
Pringle, Henry, 139
Prisoners Island, 79, 151
Proby, Thomas, 157
Pullen, Lieutenant, 247
Putnam, Israel, 79, 107, 110, 129, 135, 169-72
Putnam, Rufus, 129, 142, 163, 165

Quebec, 19, 21-22, 103, 181, 209-10, 219-20, 246-47
Quebec Act of 1774, 244
Queen Anne's War, 21-22

Ramezay, Claude de, 21
Ramezay, Jean-Baptiste Nicholas-Roch de, 210
Rattlesnake Hill, 82, 132, 153, 155-56, 159, 181-82, 193
Rea, Caleb, 143, 149, 151, 175-76
Reid, John, 208
Revenge (schooner), 285

Rice, Isaac, 277
Richardson, Amos, 142, 151, 166
Richelieu River, 13, 28, 35, 93, 191, 215, 219, 221, 237, 255
Richmond (blockhouse), 203
Riddle, James, 221
Rigaud de Vaudreuil de Cavagnial, Pierre de, 55-57, 67, 80, 100, 103, 106, 142, 145, 164, 167, 191, 226, 229, 242, 244
Rigaud de Vaudreuil, François-Pierre de, 30-32, 100, 102, 114, 164
Rigaud de Vaudreuil, Philippe, 21
River Indians, 19, 34
Riverhead (blockhouse), 203
Rivez, Charles, 155
Rivière du Sud, 234
Robbins, Ammi R., 259-60
Robertson, Charles, 211
Roche, Boyle, 139
Rocky Brook, 60
Rogers Island, 88, 96, 104, 141-42, 248, 256, 298-99
Rogers Island Visitors Center, 299-300
Rogers, Richard, 90, 106, 124
Rogers, Robert, 40, 55, 58, 71, 74, 78, 82, 89-90, 93-94, 96-98, 103, 106, 123, 129, 131-35, 137-39, 141, 143, 145, 147, 149, 157, 169-171, 181-82, 187-88, 191, 194, 200-203, 205, 217-21, 228, 233-38, 247
Rogers Rock, 138, 149, 190, 261-62
Rogers, Thomas, 142
Roosevelt, Theodore, 284, 300
Rossier, John, 209
Roubaud, Pierre, 109, 113, 116, 123, 127-29
Rouses Point, 35, 268
Royal Blockhouse, 256, 299
Rozell, Matthew, 298
Ruggles, Timothy, 77, 184, 190, 193, 227, 232, 245

Sabbath Day Point, 108-9, 135, 144, 169, 181, 214, 249, 256
Sailly, Peter, 262
St. Clair, John, 133
St. Francis, 200-203, 205, 213
St. Francis Expedition, 200-203
St. Frédéric (sailing vessel), 28
St. Jean, 55, 133, 196, 219, 221, 233, 250, 256, 268
St. Leger, Barry, 261
St. Martin, Sieur, 94
St. Onge, Joseph Payant, 28, 196, 209
Saint-Ours, François-Xavier de, 107-8
St. Thérèse, 221, 236-37, 243, 245
Saratoga fort, 29, 31-32, 49
Sarrebource de Pontleroy, Nicolas, 145, 153, 167
Schaghticokes, 19
Schenectady, N.Y., 15, 18, 34, 196, 217
Schuyler, Abram, 18
Schuyler Island, 209
Schuyler, John, 18-19, 21, 29

Schuyler, Peter, 19-21, 23
Schuyler, Peter (New Jersey regiment), 31, 33, 208
Schuyler, Philip, 29, 118
Schuyler, Philip (1733-1804), 79, 260-61
Searing, James, 144, 153, 156
Senecas, 13, 16-17
Senezergues de La Rodde, Etienne-Guillaume, 155
Shirley, William, 28-29, 32-35, 44, 47-49, 51, 53, 65, 76, 78-80, 83-85, 89, 172, 175
Silliman, Benjamin, 266-67, 275
Sinclair, Patrick, 238
Sizer, Daniel, 194-95
Skinner, Henry, 184, 186, 193-94
Sloop Island (Diamond Island), 138
Sloughter, Henry, 19
Small, John, 162
Smith, Joseph, 155
Snow Shoe (provision vessel), 185, 188, 190, 194, 214, 219, 250, 256
Society of Colonial Wars, 290-91
South Bay, 57, 169, 171
South Hero Island, 209
Sparks, Jared, 70, 268-73, 275, 290
Sparks, William, 96
Speakman, Thomas, 97
Spicer, Abel, 142-43, 160, 162, 166, 171, 174, 178
Spruce Beer, 188
Stanwix, John, 166
Starbuck, David, 293, 296-99
Stark, John, 97-98, 100, 131-33, 138, 153, 155
Stevens, Ezekiel, 128
Stevens, Phineas, 32, 35, 37
Stevens, Samuel, 202
Stoddard, Seneca Ray, 279-82, 297
Stoddert, Benjamin, 37
Stott, Earl E., 298
Stoughton, John, 256
Stuart, James, 267
Stuyvesant, Peter, 14
Sulte, Benjamin, 16
Sweat, William, 173, 176-77

Taffanel la Jonquiere, Jacques-Pierre, 35
Taft, William Howard, 287
Tanaghrisson (Half King), 42
Tejonihokarawa, Hendrick Peters, 47
Testard de Montigny, Jean-Baptiste, 31
Therbu, Cöntgen, 118
Thomas, John, 245, 247
Thompson, Robert M., 284
Thompson, Samuel, 144, 151
Thornton, Thomas, 240
Three Mile Post, 183, 248
Ticomb, Moses, 65
Ticonderoga Country Club, 137
Ticonderoga Historical Society, 284-85
Ticonderoga, N.Y., 18, 20, 55-56, 78-80, 89, 114, 143, 190, 195, 199, 217, 222, 256, 277, 284

Ticonderoga Pulp and Paper Company, 284
Tinkham, Seth, 109, 143, 147, 155
Townshend, George, 210
Townshend, Roger, 194
Tracy, Alexandre de Prouville, 14-16
Treaty of Aix-la-Chapelle, 35
Treaty of Paris, 253
Treaty of Utrecht, 22, 25
Treaty of Westminster, 14
Trépezec, Captain de, 149
Trout Brook, 135, 147
True, Henry, 184, 251
Turner, George, 202
Tute, James, 181, 217
Tuttle, William S., 282
Two Rocks, 57

Union College, 263, 265-66

Veeder, Harold, 294
Vergennes, VT., 228, 289
Vigilante, La (schooner), 196, 199, 209, 211, 221, 229, 234, 249-50, 252, 256
Vimont, Barthélémy, 13

Waggon (sloop), 199, 221, 234, 249, 252, 256
Walker, Hovendon, 22
War of Spanish Succession, 21
War of the Austrian Succession, 28
War of the League of Augsburg, 17, 20
Warm, Jacobus de, 18
Warner, Samuel, 184
Warner, Seth, 258
Warren County Railroad, 297
Washington, George, 41-42, 45, 260-62
Waterbury, David, 147, 163-65
Watrous, Elizabeth, 284
Watson, Elkanah, 263
Wayne, Anthony, 162
Weasel (sloop-of-war), 253
Webb, Daniel, 85, 89, 102, 109-11, 113-15, 117-18, 121-22, 126-31
Webster, Robert, 183-84, 194
Webster, Stephen, 74

Weeds Bay, 190
Weld, Isaac, 262
Wells River, 201-3
West Brook, 62, 65, 86, 275
Westbrook, Nicholas, 287
White, Henry Ore, 275, 277
Whiting, Nathan, 50, 60-61, 73, 82-83, 102, 193, 198, 240, 242, 252
Whitworth, Miles, 125
Wigwam Martinique, 219-221
Wilkinson, James, 266
Willard, Abijah, 190, 193
Willett, Marinus, 151
William III (king), 17
William's Rock, 276
Williams College, 61
Williams, Ephraim, 31-32, 34, 57, 60-61
Williams, Israel, 61
Williams, John, 86
Williams, Thomas, 31, 64, 68, 71
Williams, William, 32
Williams, William H., 61
Williamson (brig), 238
Williamson, Adam, 108, 118, 120
Williamson, George, 238, 248
Willsboro Point, 209
Windmill Point, 220-21
Windsor (blockhouse), 203
Winslow, John, 85, 89
Winthrop, Fitz-John, 18
Witherbee, Frank S., 289-90
Witherbee, Sherman and Company, 289
Wolfe, James, 200, 205, 209-11
Wood Creek, 19, 21-22, 30-31, 44, 51, 171
Wood, Lemuel, 188, 193-95, 203, 227
Woolsey, Melancthon Taylor, 144, 151
Wooster, David, 193
Wraxall, Peter, 48, 60, 62, 65-66, 68, 71
Wrightson, John, 169, 250-51

Young Island, 209
Young, John, 85, 110, 113, 122-23

Zarzynski, Joseph W., 8, 178

Edited by Russell P. Bellico

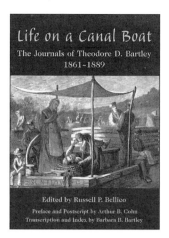

Life on a Canal Boat: The Journals of Theodore D. Bartley, 1861-1889

This 29-year record begins in 1861 with Bartley's purchase of a new sailing canal boat in Whitehall, NY, and traces his adventures with his wife and son aboard two additional canal boats on the canals and waterways of the Northeast. His daily entries and observations are one of the best records ever found of life onboard a canal boat.

Theodore Bartley lived during an era of extraordinary expansion of the American economy and rapid technological development. He operated his canal boats along the main commercial arteries linking resource supplies to the new industries of a growing nation.

Journal entries range from dramatic tales of near sinkings during gales on Lake Champlain to descriptions of the lives of ordinary people during the late 19th century. The journals of Captain Bartley provide an intimate portrait of the life of a canal boat family crisscrossing America during a period of extraordinary change.

Preface and postscript by Arthur B. Cohn; Transcription and index by Barbara B. Bartley

336 pages, illustrated, 7 x 10, 22.50, 978-1-930098-59-6

. . . .

Purple Mountain Press, established in 1973, publishes books of colonial history and books of New York State regional interest. It also publishes maritime books under its Harbor Hill imprint and imports the maritime books of Carmania Press (London).

For a free catalog, write Purple Mountain Press, PO Box 309, Fleischmanns, NY 12430-0309, or call 800-325-2665, or fax 845-254-4476, or email purple@catskill.net.

Visit the press on the web at www.catskill.net/purple.

Classic Champlain Valley Histories
by Russell P. Bellico

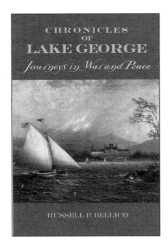 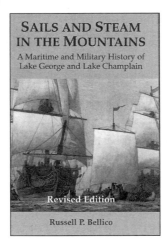 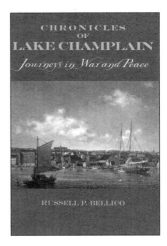

Chronicles of Lake George: Journeys in War and Peace

"In this anthology we hear firsthand reports of soldiers and travelers on Lake George during the past 250 years. Professor Bellico has scouted out vivid accounts from dozens of obscure sources. He introduces us to each of his travelers and carefully sets the stage for their journeys on this historic lake."

NICHOLAS WESTBROOK, DIRECTOR EMERITUS, FORT TICONDEROGA MUSEUM

415 pages, 200 illustrations, 7x10, 29.00, 978-0-935796-62-9

Sails and Steam in the Mountains:
A Maritime and Military History of Lake George and Lake Champlain

When it was published in 1992, this was the first new comprehensive history of the lakes in 30 years. The first printing received enthusiastic reviews, quickly sold out and the book was subsequently reprinted three times. Virtually the whole book has been rewritten for this revised edition, with additional materials from manuscript collections, underwater archaeology, and other sources.

Revised edition, 394 pages, 270 illustrations, 7x10, 29.00, 978-1-930098-17-6

Chronicles of Lake Champlain: Journeys in War and Peace.

"Russell Bellico has been a student of the Lake Champlain-Lake George corridor for more than three decades. He loves the region, recognizes its contributions to our present-day society, and is eager to share it with new generations. *Chronicles of Lake Champlain* combines the the best of historical source material to bring this special place to the reader."

ARTHUR B. COHN, DIRECTOR, LAKE CHAMPLAIN MARITIME MUSEUM

440 pages, 250 illustrations, 7x10, 29.00, 978-0-916346-70-6

Published by Purple Mountain Press, Ltd.

P.O. Box 309, Fleischmanns, NY 12430-0309, 800-325-2665, 845-254-4476 (fax)

purple@catskill.net www.catskill.net/purple   Free catalog